866112

An Introduction to
ACCOUNTING FOR
DECISION MAKING
AND CONTROL

THE WILLARD J. GRAHAM SERIES IN ACCOUNTING

Consulting Editor   ROBERT N. ANTHONY   *Harvard University*

An Introduction to
ACCOUNTING FOR DECISION MAKING AND CONTROL

EDWARD L. SUMMERS
Professor of Accounting
The University of Texas at Austin

1974

RICHARD D. IRWIN, INC. Homewood, Illinois 60430
Irwin-Dorsey International, London, England WC2H 9NJ
Irwin-Dorsey Limited, Georgetown, Ontario L7G 4B3

, 287045

658.4
S955i

© RICHARD D. IRWIN, INC., 1974

All rights reserved. No part of this publication may be reproduced, stored in a retrieval system, or transmitted, in any form or by any means, electronic, mechanical, photocopying, recording, or otherwise, without the prior written permission of the publisher.

First Printing, January 1974
Second Printing, July 1974

ISBN 0-256-01499-X
Library of Congress Catalog Card No. 73–85662
Printed in the United States of America

LEARNING SYSTEMS COMPANY—
a division of Richard D. Irwin, Inc.—has developed a PROGRAMMED LEARNING AID
to accompany texts in this subject area.
Copies can be purchased through your bookstore
or by writing PLAIDS,
1818 Ridge Road, Homewood, Illinois 60430.

RIDER COLLEGE LIBRARY

*I dedicate this book
to my beloved wife, Kathy,
and to our children,
Michael and Pamela*

Preface

THIS BOOK was written to help you learn how managers use accounting information for decision making and control in situations that require utilization of scarce resources.

There are never enough resources to go around in any society, regardless of that society's underlying principles of organization or values. In the United States, the majority of resources are still allocated through market processes—according to the demand for them for various uses by individuals.

Over the years, critics have identified shortcomings of this system of resource allocation. Yet most of us who have studied this system, and its shortcomings, are agreed that it is at least as efficient and equitable as any other in the world today, and that the major effort must be toward realizing the efficiencies possible with it, rather than replacing it with some other.

Accounting contributes information a market system must have to operate. Much of this information concerns the co-ordination and evaluation of activities of the large organizations dominating modern markets. Additional information consists of forecasts and other data required by specific decision-making situations. And still other information helps identify the public interests which responsible decision making must consider.

My plan for this book was to divide the material presented into four parts. The first part, consisting of two chapters, explains the logic and process of accounting. If you have had any previous course or courses in accounting, your instructor may choose to skip this. The second part gives the accounting knowledge which applies to co-ordination and evaluation of organization activities—profit analysis, budgeting, stardard costs, variance analysis, treatment of overhead, contribution analysis, and performance report preparation. The third part gives an introduction to the topic of information use in decisions. There, specific decision models are explained, their information requirements are detailed, and the extent to which accounting can satisfy these requirements is indicated. These chapters are not intended to make you familiar with the operation of the decision models—that properly comes in another course—but they will help you understand how decision makers rely on accounting information. The fourth part gives some idea of how accounting activities contribute to identifying the public interest for managers. Taxation, for example, is discussed only briefly from the point of view of computing tax liability, and more completely from the point of view of how tax policy affects resource allocation.

Your instructor knows best. He will select the parts of this book he considers best suited to your requirements. Follow the assignments faithfully and the knowledge written into this book will be yours.

ACKNOWLEDGMENTS

The first and most important acknowledgment must go to my wife Kathy and children Michael and Pamela, who have supported my commitment to writing this book and its accompanying instructor's guide since December, 1971.

Another important acknowledgment has been earned by almost 500 students who helped shape the narrative and problem materials through the undergraduate introductory managerial accounting course at The University of Texas. Teaching assistants Russell Tollefson and William Freund taught many of these students and pointed out ways to improve the materials. Sammy Smith of Texas Arts and Industry University taught a section using the preliminary materials; this project produced useful impressions of student response that were built in to the present manuscript.

My faculty colleagues at The University of Texas at Austin have been supportive. Jim Ashburne read and evaluated one early manuscript; others contributed suggestions based on partial readings. Glenn A. Welsch freely gave me the benefits of his textbook writing experiences; his advice has proven sound.

Among many sources of strength has been Robert Anthony, perhaps the first person outside The University of Texas to read my early materials. I am grateful to colleagues at other universities for dispassionately reviewing various drafts, and especially to Lester E. Heitger of Indiana University, Joel S. Demski of Stanford University, Russell Barefield of The University of Rochester, Bertrand Horowitz of The State University of New York at Binghampton, and Daniel Jensen of The University of Illinois at Champaign-Urbana. The literally hundreds of major and minor changes attributable to their comments have materially contributed to the effectiveness of this book.

December 1973   E. L. SUMMERS

Contents

PART I: What Is Accounting?

The purpose of this section is to describe the fundamental elements of accounting which are commonly useful in resource allocation decisions.

1. Accounting's Decision-Making Environment 3

    The major elements of decisions by individuals and organizations in an economic environment, the way information affects decisions, and the nature of the accounting function.

    Decisions and Accountants. Purposive Behavior and Satisfactions: *Goal Orientation.* Considering the Environment in Decision Making: *Potential Satisfaction of Decision Environment.* Information and Uncertainty of Environment. Economic Decisions: *Resource Control. Scarce Resources. How Resource Exchanges Happen. Resource Value. Resource Conversion. Substitution of Resources. Resource Distribution.* The Modern Economy: *The Private Sector. Management. Investors. The Public Sector. Overall.* The Accounting Profession. Decision Case 1–1: Forthright Fertilizer Company. Decision Case 1–2: Base Metal Mint.

2. The Accounting Description of Business Activity 32

    The foundations of accounting, the objectives of business activity measurement, and the types of accounting statements produced.

    Evolution of Accounting. Accounting for Business Activity. Typical Activities in a Business Entity: *The Activity Statement.* Simplifying Activity Reports and Business Profit Measurement. Stating All Account Balances in Historical Units: *How Profit and Activity Are Related.* A Variety of Accounting State-

xiii

ments: *Performance Report. Cash Basis Statement. Balance Sheet. Income Statement.* Decision Case 2–1: Ye Olde Estates.

PART II: Accounting in the Management Process

The purpose of this section is to show how accounting contributes to planning and control processes in an economic entity.

3. Activity Level Effect on Economic Performance 59

   How much activity should an economic entity carry on? What products or services should it offer? What prices should it charge?

   Cost and Revenue Classifications. Economic Theory and Cost-Volume Behavior: *Marginal Cost. Average Cost. The Accounting Approximation to Actual Costs. Revenue. Accounting Profit Estimation. Numerical Examples. Long- and Short-Run Decisions.* Applications of the Accounting Model: *Product Profitability. Profit Point. Cost and Price Changes. Two or More Products. Activity Analysis Using Percentages.* Maximizing Profit: *Condition for a Profit Maximum. Numerical Example. A Strange Fallacy.* Decision Case 3–1: William Wethers and Friends.

4. Accounting for Economic Activities 89

   The concepts of responsibility accounting, used to establish and report the results of organized economic activity, and to control it as necessary.

   Public Sector. Private Sector. The Factors of Production. Responsibility Centers: *Production Center. Service Center. Investment Center. Control at Responsibility Centers.* Cost and Revenue Classifications: *Controllable Cost. Relevant Costs and Revenues. Discretionary and Committed Costs. Direct Costs. Indirect Costs.* Valuation and Control Using Accumulated Costs: *Cost Allocation Basis. Detail at Production Center 2. Effect of Including Fixed Costs in Product Costs. Effect of Time Period on Cost Classification.* Typical Illustrations. Decision Case 4–1: Tornado Fence Company.

5. Fundamental Planning Using Accounting Information 116

   The basic business budget, the budgeting process, organizing to plan, installing a new budget, and examples of budget schedules and reports.

   Budget Process Organization: *Initial Budget Policies. The First Draft Budget.* Budget Components: *Period of Time. Function or Responsibility.* Preparation of an Operating Budget. Budget Installation: *Motivation. Systems Study.* Appendix 5A: An Example of Budget Forms and Process. Decision Case 5–1: Midtown Hotel.

6. Standard Costs and Control of Activities 159

   How control is accomplished using standard costs and variances, forecasting with standard costs, estimating standard costs, (Appendix) the learning effect.

Uses of Standard Costs: *Simplify Accounting Records. Increase Management Span of Control. Goals or Benchmarks. Rational Income and Asset Measurement. Standard Costs in Planning.* Control Using Variances from Standards: *Price Variance. Efficiency Variance. Standard to Actual Costs. Is a Variance Significant?* Establishing Standard Costs: *Simple Estimation Methods. Least Squares Regression Analysis. Comparison of Methods.* Maintenance of Standard Costs. Appendix 6A: The Learning Effect: *Learning Effect and Standard Costs. Classifying Activities. Computing Learning Effects.* Decision Case 6–1: Whoville Oil Company.

7. Treatment of Indirect Costs 194

Allocating costs to obtain information for control and planning when there are no direct associations between the activities controlled and the goods or services produced.

The Flow of Overhead. Illustrative Example. Performance Measurement at Service Centers: *Choice of Activity Base. Variable Overhead Rate. Allocable Overhead. Service Efficiency Variance.* Performance Measurement at Production Centers: *Standard Value of Activity Base. Variable Overhead Rate. Product-Allocated Overhead. Production Efficiency Variance. The Fixed Overhead Spending Variance. Performance Reporting.* Direct and Full Absorption Costing. Overhead Allocation and Decision Making. Decision Case 7–1: Valiant Company.

8. Accounting for Manufacturing Activity 220

The methods and significance of accounting used to plan and control manufacturing processes.

Job and Process Costing. Planning a Job. The Flow of Job Costs. Job Documentation: *Documentary Support.* Appraisal of Job Costing. Comparison of Job Costing with Process Costing: *Concept of Equivalent Units. Determination of Equivalent Units.* Decision Case 8–1: Boatsman Consulting Company.

9. Contribution Analysis of Planning Decisions 248

How to identify information that is relevant to a specific decision, then produce and use it in the decision.

What a Decision Model Is: *Decision Models Compared to Real Decision Processes. Significance to Accountants of Decision Model Analysis.* Accounting Information and Other Information Used in Economic Decisions. Contribution Analysis Illustrated: Make or Buy. Time Dimension of Contribution Analysis: Sunk Costs. Decisions Involving Joint Products: *Joint Products Illustrated. Costing Joint Products. Continuing a Joint Product.* Further Processing of Products. At What Level Should Joint Production Be Set?

xvi *Contents*

When Cost Allocation Can't Be Avoided. Decision Case 9–1: Welfare Administration Agency.

10. Preparing Information Reports for Management 280

    Using flexible budgets for control, preparing performance reports, effect of accounting information on individual behavior.

    Flexible Budgeting and Planning: *Questions to Ask*. Flexible Budgeting and Control: *Sales Variances. Recomputing an Expense Budget. Performance Analysis*. Presenting and Explaining Budget Variances. Planning Fixed Costs: *A Business Pitfall. Reduce Capacity, Increase Income*. Behavioral Dimension of Accounting Reports: *The Pressure Model. A General Model*. Decision Case 10–1: Trails Motor Coach Company.

PART III: Accounting Information in Specialized Decisions

Specific recognized and accepted models of common business decisions and how accounting information is significant in each of them.

11. Planning Capital Investments 315

    The net present value method of selecting capital investments and where accounting information makes this method work better.

    The Time Value of Money: *Determination of Investor's Target Rate of Return. Investor's Target Rate of Return Illustrated*. Information to Consider in Planning Capital Investment Decisions: *Net Cash Revenue or Cost Savings. Acquisition Lifetime. Depreciation and Tax Effects. Initial Cost of Acquisition. Risk of Acquisition. Mildew's Target Rate of Return*. Making the Decision. Other Factors in Investment Decisions. Decision Case 11–1: Campgo Company.

12. Inventory Management 345

    How to use EOQ inventory management models; some illustrative examples of the value of accounting information in setting order quantity and replenishment point.

    Inventory Management and Policy: *Inventory Models Lead to Inventory Policy*. Parameters Affecting Inventory Policy: *Typical Inventory Management Method*. Simple Economic Order Quantity Models: *Influence of Inventory Parameters on Inventory Management. Cost of Inventory Policy. Economic Order Quantity Models for Q* and S*. Applying the Models to Compute Inventory Policy. When the Shortage Cost Is Very High. Generality of Cost Formulas. Cost Savings. Delay in Restocking after Ordering. Safety Stock*. Sensitivity Analysis. Inventory Management Systems. Appendix 12A: *How the Optimal Economic Order Quantity Policy Was Computed When Controlled Shortages Are Permitted and 20 Percent of Deliveries Are a Day*

Late. Appendix 12B: Square Roots of Numbers 1–100. Decision Case 12–1: Candle Electric Company.

13. Cost Analysis for Project Planning and Control 372

    The "critical path" method of planning and how costs vary when a project is extended or expedited.

    Identifying Project Costs: *Step Costs. Project-Related Costs.* Estimating Step Costs: *Project Description. Step Completion Times. Step Completion Costs.* Planning Costs for Project as a Whole: *Stretching out Steps. Shortening the Critical Path.* Computer Applications. Control Using Critical Path Analysis Results. Decision Case 13–1: Electronic Digits, Inc.

14. Production Mix and Profit Maximization 402

    Linear programming is the decision model most suited to use of accounting information; this chapter shows why.

    Simplifying Assumptions—Linearity. Constraints and Capacities: *Illustrative Example. Constraints Arising from Productive Capacity. Constraints Describing Nonnegativity.* Objective Function. Graphical Solution. Additional Planning Information. Shadow Prices in Operations Control: *Shadow Prices in Companywide Control.* Appendix 14A: Where Do Shadow Prices Come From?: *Profit Balance.* Decision Case 14–1: Drane Company.

15. Decision Making and Information System Performance 435

    Review, analysis, and generalization from the preceding four chapters; the economic value of information in decisions and how to compute it.

    Some Basic Terminology. When Only One State Is Possible: *Expectations and Reality. Effect of Information System Error on Decisions. Cost of Information. Decision Models Sensitivity to Information.* When More Than One State Is Possible: *Decision Rules and Policies.* Decision Models for Uncertainty: *Capital Allocation. Inventory Management. Product Mix Analysis.* Some Problems in Providing Information for Decisions under Uncertainty: *When Information Isn't Information. Understanding Uncertainty.* Decision Case 15–1: Indios Handicraft Markets, Inc.

PART IV: Accounting in a Responsible Society

The quality of accounting analysis affects the quality of life. You read about two specific problems—inflation and taxes—and how accounting relates to them. The concluding chapter relates accounting to the more general problems of national goal setting, decision making, and social variable measurement.

16. Managerial Decisions and Price Changes 473

How inflation and deflation affect resource allocation; how accounting shows the effects of inflation on business entities.

The Money Supply. Specific and General Price Level Increases: *Specific Price Increases. General Price Increases.* Inflation and Business Planning: *Effect of Inflation on a Business. Maintaining Economic Power. Indices. Real Income. To Beat Inflation.* Accounting Statements and Price Changes: *Balance Sheet. The Income Statement. Monetary Gains and Losses.* Decision Case 16–1: Antenna Construction Company.

17. Taxes and Decision Making 501

The taxation of business: objectives, policies, and methods. How tax policies are determined. Why taxes are so complicated. Some current issues in taxation.

Tax Specialists, Processes, and Institutions. Tax Policies of Local Governments. Improving the Tax System: *Taxing Nonprofit Entities. Value-Added Tax. Federal-State Revenue Sharing. Negative Income Tax.* Accounting for Taxes. Accountants and Tax Policy. Appendix 17A: Computing the Corporate Income Tax: *Effect of Corporate Income Tax. Operating Income and Capital Gains. Capital Losses. Spreading Gains and Losses over Several Periods. Tax Deductions.* Decision Case 17–1: The Energy Shortage.

18. The Public Interest and Contemporary Accounting 528

Why accounting has opportunities to grow through helping define and pursue the public interest.

Factors Tending to Involve Accounting in Social Problems: *Accounting Is a Measurement Discipline. Accounting Is Entity Oriented. The Attest Function.* Accountants' Special Analytical Tools: *Performance Reports. Marginal Analysis. Forecasting. Data Banks. Systems Studies.* Accounting and Economic Policy: *Taxation. Subsidies.* Certification of Financial Statements. Accounting and Social Indicators.

Index 553

Part I

What Is Accounting?

1

Accounting's Decision-Making Environment

YOU ARE studying managerial accounting. A management accounting system exists in every organized economic entity, whether the entity is a business, cooperative, nonprofit institution, or government agency. Whereas financial accounting provides a clear historical record of economic activities and position to persons who are not active in the entity, management accounting must provide to decision makers—

a) Information that shows how well decision making is being done (performance evaluation), and
b) Information wanted for making decisions to be implemented in the future.

Because management accounting is so strongly oriented toward decision making, you should understand the decision-making environment and decision processes from an accounting point of view.

Decisions and Accountants

Accountants control and administer information systems, and make decisions about the allocation of resources to produce information economically. Accountants do not participate, however, in business operating decisions. They contribute important information for marketing, financing, forecasting, planning, and control decisions, but do not take part in these decisions. Accountants must be able to defend the integrity of the information they provide, since the decisions based on this information may have important consequences for an economic entity's welfare. There is an analogy between the role of accountants in business and physicists in science. Both measure complex phenomena. Neither is expected to use the data collected in an operational way (neither the physicist as engineer nor the accountant as decision maker).

A decision maker will, in any decision, have to choose one of several alternatives. The accountant avoids becoming personally identified with any of these alternatives, enabling the decision maker to accept accounting information as unaffected by the accountant's personal preferences. The accountant's objectivity is important to his function as an information system manager.

PURPOSIVE BEHAVIOR AND SATISFACTION

An observable characteristic of any individual or entity is purposive behavior—consistent patterns of activity with expectable outcomes. Among higher organisms, satisfaction may be derived from purposive behavior. Social workers derive satisfaction from actions which predictably reduce hunger, emotional distress, alcoholism, and other conditions of humanity. You may derive satisfaction from purposely watching or playing in a football game. A business entity's satisfaction may come from a higher market share, a nonpolluting factory, or a higher rate of return on capital.

A rational person or organization does not deliberately plan or execute activities expected to return dissatisfaction. Desire for satisfaction motivates behavior that is expected to result in satisfaction. This satisfaction may result from achieving goals.

Goal Orientation

One of the marks of a mentally vigorous person is ability to organize activities to achieve goals. This is goal orientation. Some goals are good grades, a salary increase, ownership of a car, or playing a complex role (on stage or in life) to an exacting standard. Each of us identifies goals expected to produce satisfaction, then sets out in pursuit of them. When someone asks what you are doing, you say, "I am tuning my engine to save $X."

Multiple Goals. One usually works toward more than one goal at a time. We may wish not to be hungry; we go to a restaurant. At the same time we wish to wear clothes which give others a desirable impression of ourselves; we select an appropriate wardrobe. Finally, while we eat we are trying to think of a way to acquire a new organ for our church.

Goal Conflict. Multiple goals conflict with one another. We may wish to own a custom sports car and at the same time continue working at our $500 per month job. These two goals are inconsistent; consequently, we settle for less ostentatious transportation or we take a more remunerative (and less satisfying) occupation.

Goal Priority. Most of us have goals that are more important than others. We know how important it is to find food as the time since our last meal increases. Observance of a personal taboo may be a surprisingly important goal—as may be abstinence from smoking or consumption of liquor. Avoidance of death becomes important very early in life.

Goal Metamorphosis. Goals change as time passes. If we do get the sports car, it becomes important to us to enter it in sports car races and win. We enter; we do not win. We decide that winning was not important after all and that we prefer driving in the country on sunny mornings. One may begin a college education with the goal of securing an engineering degree, then prefer a goal of securing an accounting degree.

Unfulfilled Goals. Not all goals are achievable. In fact, some goals are, by all evidence, not achievable at all. Yet "impossible dreams" are motivating forces in the lives of many of us, and we organize much of our behavior as if they were in fact reachable goals.

At any moment we have unfulfilled goals. *These unfulfilled goals lead us to seek alternative means of achieving them.* The study of decisions could begin in a number of places, but we choose to begin with an unmet goal. The decision comes about because there will be alternative ways this goal may be achieved—a number of courses of action which pursue the goal. We may choose only one.

CONSIDERING THE ENVIRONMENT IN DECISION MAKING

Our decision to pursue an unfulfilled goal depends on the sacrifice required compared with the amount and likelihood of satisfaction offered—which in turn depends on the "environment" in which we pursue the goal. Let us have the goal of crossing a busy intersection. The choices are to cross now, or in 30 seconds. For street crossing, a red light now is indicative of a different environment than a green light. A choice without looking at the light might be disastrous. In more complex situations the significance of the environment is the same. A decision maker must identify his choices, then anticipate all the possible environments, or *states,* which may exist when he puts his choice into effect.

Measuring Potential Satisfaction of Decision Environment

How does a decision maker look for the future environment that may prevail when he makes his decision? When we select among job offers, we define the environment in terms of such factors as advancement opportunity, compatibility with associates, salary, location, and so forth. We arrive at an evaluation of the environment of each offer. This is an important step in decision making—anticipating how each possible state will interact with each decision alternative, and the resulting satisfaction to the decision maker.

The Popcorn King Example. Assume you may buy popcorn for 5 cents per bag in quantities of 1, 2, 3, 4, or 5 bags. Tomorrow is the day of the Big Game; you will sell popcorn for 10 cents per bag. You may order popcorn only once for each Big Game; you cannot sell stale popcorn. Here is a table which shows the gain (or loss) you have from buying any number of bags of popcorn, then selling up to that many bags:

Bags Bought	\multicolumn{6}{c}{Quantity Sold}
	0	1	2	3	4	5
0	0					
1	(5)	5				
2	(10)	0	10			
3	(15)	(5)	5	15		
4	(20)	(10)	0	10	20	
5	(25)	(15)	(5)	5	15	25

There is a direct computation which leads to the gain or loss if you buy, say, three bags and sell two. The number of bags bought is the alternative selected. The number of bags you sell is the state of the environment. While up to six states are possible, only one may occur. You have no control over what that state is.

Inadequacy of Money. But is the gain a direct measure of your satisfaction? Probably not. If you are satisfied knowing you *tried* to make the largest number of sales (whether you *do* make them or not), then the money earned is not a measure of satisfaction. If you just want to make 10 cents, then gains larger than 10 cents are not meaningful. Although many if not most business decisions are made in pursuit of goals at least partially inexpressible in money, monetary measures, especially of profit, *are* useful and necessary. In management accounting, monetary measures *anticipate* profit. Profit and other monetary measures gauge the satisfaction you expect from making a decision a particular way.

Measurement. The term "measurement" has a specific meaning which is the same in all measurement disciplines. You must understand this meaning: a measurement is not an object, but in certain instances it can *substitute* for an object. When you say a table leg is two feet long, you do not mean that there are two human feet lined up on it, nor must you carry around a two-foot measuring stick or the table leg itself to show others when you inform them of the length of the table leg. "Two feet" stands uniquely for a certain length, but it is not the length itself. The table leg is the length. "Two feet" is a *measurement* of the table leg. As such, "two feet" gives us a different picture of the table leg than does "three feet" or any other length. There is no mistaking one for the other. A measurement refers to a unique quality of an object. This is why the measurement can be a numerical substitute for the object in certain ways. If two objects have the same measurement, then they should have some property in common. (If two tables have legs two feet long, these legs raise both table tops the same height above the floor.) If two objects have the same measurement, we should prefer neither object over the other *on the basis of the measurement itself*. In our popcorn example, the money gain is a measure of the satisfaction you receive. Note that there were two ways to earn 10 cents:

a) Buy two bags and sell two bags, or
b) Buy four bags and sell three bags.

If a gain of 10 cents is the *only* goal, you should not care which of these two situations occur since they both have the same measurement and therefore may be expected to produce the same gain. Of course measurement is rarely so perfect, but this is the objective and definition.

Accounting Profit. Accounting imposes a calculation of a single figure, "accounting profit," on a decision maker. The magnitude of accounting profit is affected by every activity of the decision maker and is taken as a measure of the decision maker's success in achieving its own goals through economic activity. Activities which are expected to increase accounting profit are those a manager will seek to carry out.

INFORMATION AND UNCERTAINTY OF ENVIRONMENT

The astute reader will wonder if two situations giving rise to the same accounting profit are in fact equally preferable. In the Popcorn King example, (*a*) requires purchase of two bags and (*b*) requires double that investment. Either way, we earn 10 cents. Situation (*a*) requires that we sell two units; (*b*), three. Surely we would prefer (*a*) if we *knew* that only two units could be sold. We might prefer (*b*) depending on the assurance that we could sell three bags and our ability to spend the extra nickel. Which will it be: sales of two or of three?

Very rarely we will *know* that a particular state of the environment is going to occur. Then our decision falls into a class called "decisions under uncertainty or risk." For decisions in this class, the major benefit of information is its ability to *reduce uncertainty*.

Let us suppose that we have sold popcorn at six previous Big Games. At these games, popcorn sales went like this:

Game	1	2	3	4	5	6
Bags sold	1	3	2	2	2	4

Since there is no reason to think the present Big Game is any different from previous ones, this historical experience may be relevant. At only two games did we sell as many as three or more bags. At five out of six games we sold two or more bags. This information convinces us there is little chance to sell the three bags to implement (*b*). Accordingly the decision is to take (*a*). The decision depended on the measure of past experience provided by the record of popcorn sales. Information describing the past can predict the future, if forces at work in the past environment continue at work in the future. The reader must judge for himself the extent to which this condition is met.

ECONOMIC DECISIONS

Economic decisions are made by individuals or organizations which have resources. The decisions concern the acquisition, conversion, distribution, and exchange of resources, as summarized by this flow diagram:

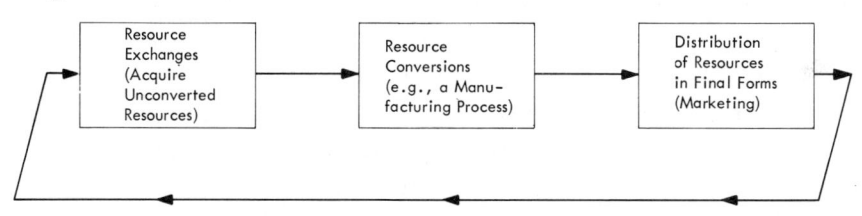

```
┌─────────────┐    ┌─────────────┐    ┌─────────────┐
│  Resource   │    │  Resource   │    │Distribution │
│  Exchanges  │───▶│ Conversions │───▶│of Resources │
│  (Acquire   │    │  (e.g., a   │    │in Final Forms│
│ Unconverted │    │   Manu-     │    │ (Marketing) │
│ Resources)  │    │facturing    │    │             │
│             │    │ Process)    │    │             │
└─────────────┘    └─────────────┘    └─────────────┘
        ▲                                     │
        └─────────────────────────────────────┘
```

The decision concept most people have in mind is of a straightforward choice, self-contained and made at one point in time by a single decision maker who knows all the facts. A real decision is more likely to extend over a period of time, involve many different persons, affect numerous apparently unrelated interests, and be made in the presence of considerable unavoidable ignorance and lack of information.

Economic decision processes are specialized; and to participate in them, managers themselves become specialized. The various specialized functions are difficult to coordinate as entities become larger, yet their internal efficiency permits larger entities to exist.

Economic decisions concern the use of resources for satisfaction. Our consumption-oriented society believes satisfaction can be achieved through massive use of resources. The extent of satisfaction depends on rate of consumption. Most satisfaction does not stem from survival but from acquiring comforts, pleasures, achievement, and enjoyment. Our stress here on material resources does not deny the importance of love, appreciation, attention, and respect as satisfiers—but these are not subject to accounting representation.

Resource Control

Resources endure. They can be kept and used when desired. Entities may establish control over resources they intend to use in the future. Such controlled resources are called *assets*. Accounting can identify assets and the entity which controls them.

Prices. In order to control a resource, an entity must make a sacrifice. This is because there are not unlimited supplies of resources. One gives up a resource already controlled in order to control another. A *price* is an exchange *rate* between one resource and another. If you own two apartment buildings and offer to trade them for eight acres of farmland, you have put a price on your apartments of four acres of farmland each. If anyone accepts, he has put a price of one-fourth apartment building on each acre of his land.

The motivation for resource exchanges is simple. Even as we control, possess, preserve, or convert resources, we perceive that some combinations of resources are more satisfying than other combinations. Given the changing nature of goals, little wonder that we never have the right mix of assets and always want to exchange something for something else.

Scarce Resources

As you attempt to accumulate particular assets (home, car, boat, insurance policies, etc.) you discover that resources are in limited supply. A sacrifice must be made to control a scarce resource. No one is capable of infinite sacrifice. (The ability to sacrifice is also a scarce resource!) You are forced to make decisions about which resources to hold or use.

How Resource Exchanges Happen

You have an excess of one resource and a scarcity of another in terms of the resource portfolio you *want* to have. You seek to exchange the abundant resource for the lacking one. You want bacon for breakfast tomorrow morning; you go to the store to buy bacon. For $1.25 you buy enough bacon for several breakfasts. The storekeeper has plenty of bacon but desires cash to buy clothing.

If everyone wanted bacon for breakfast, there would not be enough to satisfy the demand. Probably the price of bacon would rise. Hog producers, encouraged by the prospect of larger profits, would rush more bacon to market. However, people can only eat so much bacon for breakfast, then they don't want any more. If the hog producers send too much bacon to market, the price of bacon will drop.

Economists have developed concepts of demand and supply relationships that apply to this kind of situation. The basic concept of *demand* is that as the price of a resource falls, less will be brought forward to sell. In terms of the bacon, you might buy only one pound per week at $1.50 per pound but buy two pounds per week at $1 per pound. (Because you get less satisfaction from each successive pound, it does not follow that you will buy a third pound of bacon per week at even $0.10 per pound.) The basic assumption about *supply* is that more of a resource will be supplied as the price of the resource rises. As the price of bacon rose, suppliers prepared to bring more of it to market. When this happened, the price of bacon fell.

This example illustrates the time lag between perceiving an imbalance between supply and demand (signaled by changes in prices) and the effectiveness of steps to gain by such an imbalance. Time lags produce uncertainty because the sacrifices we are willing to make for a particular resource will change over time, with unpredictable effects on our state of satisfaction after the decision is effective. I may want a suit in the latest (at this writing) wide-lapel style so much as to pay $100 for one. In six months such suits are no longer so desirable, and I am then only willing to pay $50 for the same suit. Impermanence of tastes is reflected in prices and makes it difficult to plan efficient transfer of resources onto the market.

Resource Value

All resources are exchangeable for other resources wherever markets exist, usually at known and stable rates. If one unit of resource A may be traded for five units of resource B but for only two units of resource C, then resource C is said to be *more valuable* than resource

B. "Value" is an important concept in planning and evaluating business activity. Resource value *measures* are *relative* and are always based on exchanges past, present, or contemplated future.

Resource Conversion

Most resources are convertible from one form to another. Coal may be burned as fuel, converted to coke for steel-making, or chemically refined to provide essential industrial chemicals. Cotton may be woven into hundreds of different cloths. The allocation of a resource to each application depends on its *value* in each use.

Substitution of Resources

Resources are often substitutable for one another. Copper, steel, aluminum, nickel, and silver have unique applications, but they also have applications in common. Marine fittings are preferably made of stainless steel, but if stainless steel is not available the fittings can be made of bronze. If we cannot get steak, we eat roast; if not roast, ribs; and so on. Substitutability of resources for one another adds to the ways in which demand can be satisfied and lends stability to the value of resources which are highly substitutable. In general, businesses try to create an object with given attributes from the least valuable resources. This does not imply shoddy work; you would not pay for a typewriter made by hand from gold if a manufactured steel and plastic model gives equal service.

Resource Distribution

The use of a resource in any way creates a demand for the resource. If the resource is more valuable in some particular use than in others, the resource will shift into that employment. This happens as follows: those businesses who make copper power transmission cable are willing to pay very high prices to obtain the copper. Toy manufacturers find that the copper they previously used for toy parts now costs more than aluminum or plastic, which do an equivalent job in the toys. Toy manufacturers stop using copper in toys, and more copper is used in electric cable. The cable manufacturers benefit from the greater value of copper in their product and are able to pay the higher prices for it. Here is another example: hardwoods are scarce and expensive because they are highly prized in fine furniture. Utility furniture is no longer made from hardwoods; it is made from the less expensive softwood or wood-grain-imprinted plastic.

Complex specialized management technology has developed to innovate and direct resource conversion and substitution processes. Because it is difficult to anticipate the best uses of resources, a similarly complex technology has developed to perform *these* functions. The accountant is often the originator and manager of this technology.

THE MODERN ECONOMY

The activities of economic entities constitute the *economy*. The economy is extremely diverse—with public and private sectors, service and manufacturing sectors, regulated and unregulated sectors, and so on. Within each sector there may be one to several thousand independent operations organized as partnerships, corporations, government agencies, or proprietorships.

The initiative for economic growth and stable development lies in the private sector of the economy. The responsibility for regulating and supplementing the private sector is in the public sector. In both sectors, exchange activity constitutes a reallocation of resources in response to supply and demand factors and public policy. This arrangement works well enough in the presence of reasonable social stability and international order. A flow of information describing economic opportunities and operations guides the activities of entities in the economy.

The Private Sector

The private sector consists of all entities which are owned by private persons or organizations. The most common forms of organization for entities in the private sector are: proprietorship, partnership, and corporation. A proprietorship is a business owned by a single person; a partnership is a business owned by several persons. A corporation may be owned by many different individuals, has a perpetual life, and the legal rights of a person (except civil rights). Regardless of form, private sector enterprises are characterized as manufacturing or service firms. Examples of service businesses are medical, legal, and accounting partnerships, repair and maintenance firms, consulting firms, and engineering or research companies. Most service firms are small, require few assets, and depend for success on the expert judgment and skill of individuals associated with the firm. Services are the fastest-growing part of the private sector and in 1973 accounted for about half the total volume of that sector. Service businesses present challenges to accounting since the resources of such businesses are intangible skills.

Manufacturing firms tend to be asset-intensive, energy-consuming enterprises converting resources from one form to another using machines and skilled labor. This category includes the extractive industries, transportation, utilities, electronics, textiles, food processing, and consumer goods. Manufacturing is resource-intensive and historically has generated an obvious need for accounting information. Accounting in manufacturing firms describes resource acquisition, conversion, storage, and exchange operations in ways that contribute to control over them.

Management

Most corporations will include these elements in their organizations:

Stockholders, who organize and control the corporation
Board of directors responsible to stockholders
President (chief executive officer) responsible to board of directors
Vice presidents in charge of—
    Finance (one for each country in which capital is used to support operations)
    Marketing (one for each product grouping or market served)
    Manufacturing (one for each product group or country)
    (And also perhaps planning, research and development, and international operations)

Successful corporations have two common features:

1. A unified finance function serving the entire company.
2. An adequate information system including planning and control.

The unified finance function keeps exchange activities moving smoothly; the information system helps management evaluate and choose activities as they affect profit, employees, and public interests.

A corporation must have capital to sustain and extend operations. Capital comes from investors, who receive assurances (e.g., *securities*) of a share in future income and asset distributions of the corporation. The management tries to make securities attractive to investors, just as the firm's products appeal positively to buyers in the market place. The management communicates its accomplishments and plans. In compiling achievements to report and preparing plans for future activities, management also relies on accountants.

Investors

An investor has capital (usually cash, savings accounts, or other asset quickly convertible to cash) and exchanges it for business securities. The term "investor" includes creditors who deliver goods or services and have a claim for payment for them. A lender has a claim for the amount of his loan and unpaid interest against a debtor's assets and income. Some securities are secured by specific assets, such as railway mortgage bonds secured by rolling stock. These claims are arranged such that employee's claims for wages come first and the owners' claims, last. However, the higher ranking a claim, the less certain is it to share in the profits, if any, of the business. Figure 1–1 is a summary of investments and the security they provide.

The investor also has a choice of individual firms, ranging from single-product firms to multi-industry, multinational firms. An example of the former would be a utility such as Houston Lighting & Power; of the latter, International Telephone & Telegraph. Most companies fall between these extremes. Through choice of company and security type the investor can obtain a combination of risk and reward that is acceptable to him.

The investor with his ability to withhold or provide capital becomes a very important person in the private sector; he is at the center of the capital allocation process that determines which goods, services, and risks occur in the private sector; and to whom companies address annual financial statements (prepared by accountants) describing their financial condition and activities.

FIGURE 1–1
Relative Security and Income Shares of Investments

Form of Investment in Order of Claim on Corporate Assets	Security	Precedence Over	Risk	Rewards
Sell to firm on credit, work as employee for firm	All assets of firm	All claims	Low	No share in earnings
Short-term loan	Assets and limited income	All claims below	Moderate	Limited to agreed interest
Loan secured by lien on specified assets	Specified assets and earning power	All claims below	Medium	Agreed interest only
Common stock	Residual assets	No other claims	High	Dividends and capital gains without limits

Investing is criticized because it is risky and because large amounts of money are occasionally lost. However, risk is natural in business; and the losses are small relative to (*a*) the total investments in the economy and (*b*) the losses due to inefficiency if capital were not shifted away from uneconomical businesses. The potential of accounting for informing investors about risk, so that they may make an informed decision whether to bear it, is still being realized.

The Public Sector

The public sector of the economy is characterized by lack of market mechanisms for raising and allocating capital, acquiring raw materials, or disposing of products. Originally the public sector performed only basic functions in society: education, defense, public security, and a judiciary. The public sector has grown, until in the 1970s it accounts for about one third of the total economic activity in the United States. The powers of public sector enterprises derive from governments and their ability to tax. The expanded public sector derives from the apparent inability of market mechanisms to supply certain needs: for example, care of the indigent elderly, parks, recreation, electricity to undeveloped areas, and large national projects such as space exploration.

Accounting has an important and not fully realized role to play in making public sector enterprises manageable and accountable to the public.

The public interest is satisfactory allocation of resources through efficient processes. Transportation, communication, and energy are examples of areas where government-sponsored enterprises perform functions apparently no longer suitable for the private sector because of the associated risk, cost, or magnitude of operation.

Overall

Does this economy have any problems? It is subject to irregular slowdowns and speedups which have never been understood. In 1972, only 72 percent of the nation's productive capacity was in use, notwithstanding recognized shortages of housing, transportation, sewage and waste disposal, and recreation areas—among others. Yet one year later, businesses could not supply the massive demand for goods and services. And inflation constantly threatens the integrity of the currency.

THE ACCOUNTING PROFESSION

There are five major areas of accounting specialization:

1. Independent auditing of financial statements.
2. Managerial advisory services.
3. Tax advisory services.
4. Controllership and managerial accounting.
5. Accounting services within public sector entities.

Three of these areas are normally practiced together by accounting partnerships—auditing, tax advisory services, and managerial advisory services. *Auditing* is the critical examination of evidence underlying published accounting information; it is performed to assure that such statements conform to generally acceptable accounting principles, that they fairly present financial position and results of operations, and that they are prepared on a basis which permits comparability with previous periods' statements of the issuing entity. When engaged in auditing, accountants adhere to rigid standards of evidence and analysis. Accountants accept personal liability for any wrong opinions they issue on financial statements. *Tax advisory services* are rendered to individuals and businesses seeking competent help in computing a present tax liability or determining the tax consequences of proposed future operations. Such help is instrumental in holding tax rates to the minimum. We should point out, too, that the federal income tax is only one tax individuals and businesses are subject to—there are many other federal, state, and local taxes; and for businesses which operate in foreign countries, there are the taxes of those nations. *Managerial advisory services* practice makes available through consultation a range of skills and experience which most businesses alone could not maintain. The principal services are:

1. Information systems design and installation.
2. Operations research studies and recommendations.
3. Computer systems selection.
4. Management development program design and implementation.
5. Executive search.
6. Actuarial consultation in working out pension plans.

Controllership, information technology, and managerial accounting is intended to cover all the activities of accountants in business organizations. The principal activity is operating the accounting-based information system, which includes computers, information storage, and retrieval devices and procedures. Accountants also may be responsible for planning and finance functions, for maintaining a cost accounting system, and for technical services to operating divisions of the business. Finally, *accounting services within the public sector* include the information system operations of public sector organizations. Another category is more diverse and barely adequately described as "law enforcement." The General Accounting Office audits federal agencies to determine whether their expenditures conform to law. FBI accountants examine the accounting records of persons suspected of violating federal laws, such as those dealing with narcotics traffic. IRS agents who are accountants seek to establish compliance with the tax laws. These kinds of work traditionally offer intensive experience as well as satisfaction as a result of the public service rendered.

The professional organization of accountants is the American Institute of Certified Public Accountants, which in 1973 has approximately

80,000 members. Prior to 1973, this organization was responsible for developing and improving the principles which guide preparation of financial accounting statements. In 1973, an independent entity, the Financial Accounting Standards Board, assumed this responsibility. The FASB's opinions will be authoritative definitions of accounting principles. Any member of the American Institute who expresses a favorable opinion on financial statements not prepared in accordance with FASB opinions must justify the points of inconsistency and may be accused of ignoring accounting principles.

In order to become a member of the American Institute of Certified Public Accountants, one must be a Certified Public Accountant. This designation is awarded to individuals under laws in all 50 states and Puerto Rico who pass the four-part, three-day Uniform CPA Examination and (in some states) complete an experience requirement. Increasingly, states require a college degree as a prerequisite to taking the CPA Examination.

Although many CPAs are in public practice (Areas 1, 2, 3), perhaps a majority are in managerial and public sector accounting. These latter provide objective, competent information for decision making by others. They should not become involved in business operating decisions, because such involvement might prejudice their information function.

There are other professional accounting organizations. The National Association of Accountants and its related Institute of Management Accounting, which promotes the professional status of managerial accountants; the Financial Executives Institute; and the Planning Executives Institute are examples of such organizations.

SUMMARY

Managerial accounting provides information for decision making and for evaluating the quality of decision making. To supply such information, accountants rely on a classification and measurement system that can represent resource acquisition, conversion, distribution, and exchange activities.

Decisions themselves arise when a purposive entity is dissatisfied and perceives that its satisfaction may be increased if it is able to achieve certain goals. The entity perceives a connection between alternative choices and goal achievement. Often there are many ways goals can apparently be achieved and decisions must be made to choose acceptable ways.

Scarce resources serve as means to goals. The allocation of scarce resources to achieve satisfaction is called economic decision making. Such allocation is complex because resources may be transformed into different forms, substituted for one another in most applications, and exchanged between entities.

The decision process itself is long and often confusing. The time lag between making and implementing decisions is the origin of the natural uncertainty of economic activity and creates a need for information to guide decision making. Producing this information consumes resources; thus, accountants must be as efficient in their function as any other part of the entity organization.

Accounting develops measurements for the sacrifices and benefits that arise from exchanges in which economic entities participate, as well as for the assets such entities may hold. Economic entities embrace an extraordinary variety of individuals, businesses, and agencies in the public and private sectors of the economy. Lack of knowledge about the activities of these entities creates risk for those whose capital permits business activity to exist. Accounting information helps to describe risk for investors. Within a firm, accounting information describes economic opportunities and business operations.

Accounting information is provided by an independent, competent profession which divides its practice into five major areas: (1) independent auditing of financial statements, (2) managerial advisory services, (3) tax advisory services, (4) controllership and managerial accounting, and (5) accounting services within public sector entities. Entrance into the accounting profession is controlled, if one wishes the designation "Certified Public Accountant," by the state CPA societies.

QUESTIONS

1. How does managerial accounting differ from financial accounting?
2. What kinds of information does managerial accounting provide to managers? What functions does this information perform?

3. What is purposive behavior?

4. What is satisfaction? Why must choices be made in order to achieve satisfaction?

5. What are the general choices which face a business, and how does a business measure its satisfaction which results from its choices?

6. Do accountants make decisions? Why (or why not)?

7. What is measurement? (Harder: does language involve measurement? Is it justifiable to call accounting a language?)

8. What is uncertainty? How does uncertainty affect decisions?

9. Is historical information useful in decisions? If so, how? If not, why not?

10. What is "resource substitutability"? Why does it make business decisions more complex?

11. What is "resource transformation"? Is it ever the same as resource consumption?

12. Suppose that the use of lead in gasoline is summarily banned, and that its octane-increasing function is to be performed instead by a substance known as chemical X. What will happen to the price of lead? The price of chemical X? The profit of lead suppliers? The profit of chemical X suppliers? What should lead suppliers try to do? What should gasoline producers try to do?

13. You are told that the use of certain information in a decision will increase the profit from the decision by $1,000. The information costs $100. Do you buy it?

14. With the same facts as in Question 13, assume you could also spend the $100 on labor which would return $1,500. Which do you acquire, the labor or the information (assume you have only $100)?

15. Imagine that we measure our satisfaction in "utils." We buy a stereo for $500 which produces 10,000 utils per week of satisfaction. After three months, however, this has declined to 1,000 utils per week (we have heard all the tapes we bought). We want a sailboat costing $300 and producing 5,000 utils per week of satisfaction. The sailboat dealer will take the stereo on even trade for the boat. Should we make the trade?

EXERCISES

16. A certain businessman will not choose an investment unless it produces at least $5,000 in profit. Indicate which of the following investment opportunities satisfy this requirement:
  a) Costs of $300; revenues of $5,100.
  b) Trade 8 buffalo for 900 chickens. Buffalo may be bought and sold for $500 each; chickens may be bought and sold for $10 each.
  c) Render consulting advice and receive 5 acres of land valued at $2,000 per acre. Expenses would be $4,000.
  d) Order 100 KP-70 calculators at $30 each and sell them by mail order at $100 each. Costs of each sale (postage, etc.) would be $10.

17. Suppose you can buy calculators at $40 each and resell them at $100 each with no selling expenses. Calculators become obsolete very fast, so any bought must be sold in 30 days, or thrown away. Complete the following table:

Calculators Bought	Calculators Sold	Net Profit (Loss)
1.........	1	$60
2.........	1	?
2.........	2	?
3.........	1	?
3.........	2	?
3.........	3	?

18. Below are two groups of names: one of principals, the other of surrogates (potential measures of principals). Match each principal with its best surrogate.
  a) Sheets of paper printed with pictures and words and stapled together.
  b) A distance approximating the length of one and one-half average human feet.
  c) The condition that it is safe to cross the street.
  d) Control over the existence, possession, and disposal of scarce resources.
  e) A business entity is better off now than it was one year ago.

  1. Legal title.
  2. Magazine.
  3. Green light.
  4. Eighteen inches.
  5. Accounting profit.

19. Here are some events in the business life of an entity. Indicate whether each is *exchange, conversion,* or *distribution:*
   a) Five thousand tons of iron ore are processed into 2,000 tons of pig iron.
   b) Eighty thousand transistor radios are imported from Japan.
   c) Shiny Jewelry Company acquires 200 carats of rough-cut emeralds.
   d) Transmissions and engines are assembled in the auto factory.
   e) Two hundred thousand yards of muslin are sold to an awning manufacturer.

20. Detailed information summaries may perform any of three functions in an ongoing business; they may express plans, describe activities, or allow comparison between plans and activity results. State which function each type of summary below probably performs:
   a) Statement of sources and uses of cash.
   b) Statement of sales forecasts and activities necessary to fulfil sales goals.
   c) Statement showing income in a recent period.
   d) Statement showing predicted and actual costs of selling desk calculators.
   e) Statement describing process for building a dam.

PROBLEMS

21. The Reticle Company produces contact lenses. The lenses are made from a clear plastic called P-1, which costs about $2 per pair of lenses made. Abruptly it is discovered that because of its flexibility, P-1 is a perfect material for automobile windshields, and auto manufacturers scramble to acquire the full production of P-1 for this purpose. The Reticle Company discovers that in order to obtain P-1 for contact lenses it must pay about $5 per pair of lenses made. A search is made for substitute materials, and the following possible substitutes are found:

Substitute	Material Cost per Lens Pair	Other Costs per Lens Pair
P-2	$6	0
P-3	2	$6
P-4	3	1
P-1	Was $2/now $5	$0

Required:

Which material should be substituted for P-1 (if any)?

22. Marty Glass is chief accountant at the Austin Bridge Authority. He is in charge of the accounting system, preparing all accounting reports, helping managers to prepare the annual budget, and maintaining a system of control within the business. The Austin Bridge Authority operates a toll highway and bridge across the Colobrazos River. However, this highway and bridge are old and narrow, and the Authority is considering widening the highway and building a second bridge to complement the original one. Martin Crawford, president of the company, has requested that Glass become a member of the "task force" to determine whether the project should be undertaken.

Required:

- *a)* Should Mr. Glass join the decision-making task force?
- *b)* Formulate a brief statement of what assistance and support Mr. Glass should render in this instance, and also what he should NOT do.

23. Your popcorn business has boomed, and you now pop and sell the corn at all Big Games in the midwest. However, the popcorn still becomes stale if you don't sell it at once, so any unsold excess is lost. You compute that it costs you $0.04 to provide a vendor with a bag of popcorn to sell. The vendor sells the bag for $0.10. You are preparing for this Saturday's games and figure sales will be 100,000, 200,000, 300,000, or 400,000 bags.

Required:

- *a)* Prepare a schedule showing the profit (or loss) at each level of sales if you previously prepared 100,000, 200,000, 300,000, and 400,000 bags to sell.
- *b)* Select the number of bags you would prepare if you have no more information than this.
- *c)* Now suppose you know that on each of the previous five Saturdays you have not sold more than 200,000 bags. Select the number of bags you would prepare.
- *d)* Suppose you know that on each of the previous five Saturdays you sold 400,000 bags, but that there is rain expected this Saturday for the first time. When it rains, popcorn sales fall 75 percent. Select the number of bags you would prepare.

24. Needy College, founded by Mr. I. M. Needy 13 years ago, is a small private community college in a town of approximately 100,000 population. Its sole source of income is tuition from students, a large number of whom are enrolled in evening courses not necessarily leading to a degree. The college has a small faculty which is now planning the fall course offerings. Professor Teach is undecided whether he should offer course A or course B, and to help him, the college accountant provides the following information:

	Course A	Course B
Estimated enrollment.	30	50
Tuition income per student	$ 150	$ 150
Laboratory expense per student.	(20)	(10)
Library expense per student.	(5)	(40)
Expense to set up course.	(500)	(1,000)

Required:

a) Indicate which course the professor should offer by calculating which course will show the largest excess of tuition over expenses.

b) Suppose the faculty member knows that 90 percent of students taking course A will later enroll in course C, which also has tuition of $150 and *no* library, laboratory, or setup expenses. Taking this information into account and assuming course B students do not enroll in other courses subsequently, determine which course Professor Teach should teach.

25. As a young boy, Clyde Hyde became interested in building models of trains, buses, ships, planes—anything that moved. Now, as an adult, Hyde's most valuable possession is the *time* he is able to spend collecting, constructing, restoring, and otherwise working on such models. Unfortunately Hyde must live by his wits. His expenses of living amount to $100 per day, day in and day out. His sleeping and eating activities claim a mandatory 10 hours per day, leaving 14 hours per day in which to pursue both his livelihood and his avocation.

Hyde is proficient in four different activities—speculating, clerking, managing, and consulting. He does not have equal preference for these activities, nor do they all pay equally. Hyde's preferences are, measured in arbitrary units, called *utils:*

	Income (per Hour)	Satisfaction (Utils per Hour)
Model activities		100
Speculating	$20	−50
Clerking	10	−40
Managing.	70	−900
Consulting	30	−70

26　　An Introduction to Accounting for Decision Making and Control

Hyde is self-supporting if he can earn $100 dollars per day and happy if he has a net balance of more than 0 utils for the day.

Required:

a) If Hyde clerks two hours, manages one hour, and works with his models the remainder of the day, will he be self-supporting? Will he be happy?

b) Find a combination of activities that will support Hyde and also leave him happy. Are any concepts from the chapter identifiable in this situation?

26. In 1974 the world copper production figure was about 3,000,000,000 pounds and the price was about $0.50 per pound. In that year, the country of Zolabomba, which had previously developed new and richly productive oil fields, began to use its oil revenues to build up an electrical generating system. The copper requirements were projected at 500,000,000 pounds per year for 10 years, all of which would have to be met out of current world production, steady at about the 1974 figure.

Use of copper in 1974 was as follows:

	(Pounds)	Cost of Best Substitute (per Pound)
Electrical	1,500,000,000	$0.90
Structural	400,000,000	0.60
Reactive	300,000,000	1.20
Plumbing	400,000,000	0.80
Engineering	200,000,000	0.70
Miscellaneous	200,000,000	1.60

Required:

a) Applying the principle of supply and demand, what do you think will happen to the price of copper in 1975 and following?

b) Applying the principles of substitution and distribution, what uses do you think the necessary copper will come from? Will all of Zolabomba's copper requirement be met, or will some of the requirement be met by substitutes? (Assume that the prices of all substitutes are constant regardless of demand changes in this problem.)

c) To approximately what level do you think the price of copper will rise?

27. As a stock market operator, you are widely known for your ability to earn a profit by buying and selling common stocks, which are equities in corporations. Unknown to others, your secret is that extrasensory perception gives you *perfect* knowledge of the price per share movements of *one* business, Occult Services, Inc. Presently, you have before you the Friday closing prices for the next two months:

Friday 6th	$50
Friday 13th	60
Friday 20th	40
Friday 27th	50
Friday 4th	30
Friday 11th	40
Friday 18th	20
Friday 25th	30

Required:

a) Since the price of Occult Services *declines* over this interval, will you be able to make money at all trading in this stock?

b) Assume you *must* trade in the stock. You cannot sell any stock you do not have. You have, on the morning of the 6th, $1,000 available for investment. Compute the maximum trading gain or loss you can show through Friday the 25th, trading only at the Friday prices.

28. Cleanfoot Company operates a rug reconditioning and cleaning service. The company has observed, by experimenting with its price, that the number of calls it receives to do rug work is a function of its advertised cleaning price. Here is how the company's observations look:

Advertised Price to Clean 1,000 Square Feet of Carpet	1,000s of Square Feet of Carpet Business Obtained (per Week)
$100	8
90	11
80	16
70	20
60	23
50	25
40	26

Required:

a) Assuming that the above is the only relevant information, and that Cleanfoot Company can clean a maximum of 16,000 feet of carpet per week, find (to the nearest $10) the price the company should advertise that will produce the most revenue for it.

b) At a cost of $100 per week, Cleanfoot Company can rent enough extra rug cleaning capacity to clean a maximum of 25,000 feet of carpet per week. Do you think the additional capacity should be obtained and the advertised price lowered in order to use it? Why, or why not?

29. Green Finger Copper Company makes copper jewelry for sale in novelty shops and department stores. A management study indicates that the company should be willing to *supply* certain amounts of jewelry depending on the price it can obtain. These amounts, in pounds, are

Pounds to Produce	if	Price Obtained per Pound
1,000		$50
1,200		55
1,500		60
1,800		65
2,000		70

Another survey, conducted by Green Finger's marketing department, showed how many pounds of copper jewelry would be *demanded,* depending on the level of the price:

If the Price per Pound Were—	Then This Many Pounds per Week Would Be Demanded
$50	3,000
55	2,500
60	2,000
65	1,500
70	1,000

Required:

a) Plot on a sheet of rectangular graph paper both sets of data above. Let the horizontal axis be pounds of copper jewelry and the vertical axis be the price in dollars per pound.

b) Identify the price per pound at which the amount Green Finger will supply is equal to the amount novelty shops and department stores are willing to order.

c) If, instead of the production quantity corresponding to the price found in (b), Green Finger produces 2,000 pounds of jewelry, at what price will it have to be sold in order to sell *all* of it?

d) If, instead of the production quantity corresponding to the price found in (b), Green Finger produces 1,000 pounds of jewelry, at what price should all of it be sold to obtain the highest revenue?

DECISION CASE 1–1: FORTHRIGHT FERTILIZER COMPANY

The Forthright Fertilizer Company produces high-analysis fertilizers on the shores of Lake Clearpure, an unspoiled body of water popular for fishing, boating, and other sports. The company's engineers have proposed that gypsum, an inert by-product of fertilizer manufacture, be filtered out of the fertilizer before drying and bagging and discharged into Lake Clearpure. The net effect of doing this would be to save about $200,000 per year in shipping and storage costs. No laws would be broken. However, the volume of gypsum involved would quickly fill up and discolor the lake, making it unsuitable for water recreation. The company is currently losing $20,000 per year, so adopting the proposal would make it profitable. Mr. B. Forthright, president of the company, argues that "After all, we are saving money for 500,000 farmers who buy our products and only two or three thousand persons can use this lake at once." However, the chief accountant replies that "This is like comparing apples and oranges . . . just because accounting shows it would be profitable doesn't mean society necessarily benefits when everything is considered."

Required:

a) Prepare short statements on both sides of this question.
b) If accounting were a perfect measurement system, would computation of a prospective profit on this operation indicate that it was desirable? (Think of the costs *to society* of filling in the lake; try to imagine a way of getting these into the calculation.)

DECISION CASE 1–2: BASE METAL MINT

Base Metal Mint, a private mint specializing in limited editions of engravings, sculpture, medals, and so on executed in bronze, silver, gold, and platinum, is considering reorganization of its decision and information systems.

The company commissions artists to execute various works. The commissions are based on marketing studies of collectors' and potential collectors' preferences and tastes in such things. When the works are complete, the mint's own staff of professional engravers prepares master originals and dies, etc., which are used to strike or otherwise produce between 50 and 1,000 copies. The item is advertised in financial publications and normally priced between $10 and $1,000. Orders are taken only by mail.

Items in the series are stocked up to three years after the original offering; any remaining items are melted down and returned to the storehouse of precious metals used as stock for new items. Additional precious metals are purchased as they are needed on the open market; occasionally the company will speculate by buying or selling short, but the normal procedure is to buy and sell futures in the metals for protection from speculative price changes.

Collecting is a popular pastime. Many mints offer series to collectors, and the competition is vigorous in the area. Consequently, Base Metal Mint must offer the most attractive medals, etc., and must price its offerings attractively, leaving room for value appreciation.

The company was founded 12 years ago. For its first 8 years it was privately held; when the original founder died, his family sold 90 percent of the stock to the public and does not now take an active interest in the business. Sales last year were $12,000,000; profit was $1,500,000. The company considers a 10 percent annual long-run growth rate normal and desirable.

Required:

a) Suggest 10 important decisions that must be made regularly by the management of Mase Metal Mint.
b) Suggest 20 different kinds of information that will be useful or necessary in the decisions listed for (*a*).
c) Discuss generally the sources of such information and name five sources of information the company will use.

BIBLIOGRAPHY

Books

Archer, Stephen H., and D'Ambrosio, Charles A. *Business Finance. Theory and Management.* New York: The MacMillan Co., 1966.

Brandis, Royall. *Principles of Economics.* Rev. ed. Homewood, Ill.: Richard D. Irwin, Inc., 1972.

Mueller, Gerhard G., and Smith, Charles H. *Accounting: A Book of Readings.* New York: Holt, Rinehart, & Winston, Inc., 1970.

Poe, Jerry B. *An Introduction to the American Business Enterprise.* Rev. ed. Homewood, Ill.: Richard D. Irwin, Inc., 1972.

Articles

Churchman, C. West. "The Systems Approach to Measurement in Business Firms," *Accounting in Perspective* (eds. Robert R. Sterling and William F. Bentz). Cincinnati, Ohio: South-Western Publishing Co., 1971.

Donbrovski, Willis J. "Managerial Accounting: A Frame of Reference," *Management Accounting,* August 1965.

Elnicki, Richard A. "The Genesis of Management Accounting," *Management Accounting,* April 1971.

Killough, Larry N. "Does Management Accounting Have a Theoretical Structure?" *Management Accounting,* April 1972.

Shenkir, William G.; Welsch, Glenn A.; and Bear, Jr., James A. "Thomas Jefferson: Management Accountant," *The Journal of Accountancy,* April 1972.

2

The Accounting Description of Business Activity

Evolution of Accounting

IT IS PROBABLE that accounting was known to ancient societies, but the awkward number systems of those days prevented accounting development. One may imagine a pastoral society reckoning its wealth in terms of sheep, chickens, or cattle. Thus a shepherd might calculate the wealth statement in Figure 2–1.

FIGURE 2–1
Illustration of a Wealth Statement
LONG A. GOWE, SHEPHERD
Wealth Statement
As at 3rd Full Moon after
40th Equinox since the
Tree Fell on Big Sister

I have............	XXXV chickens	But of these,	
	L sheep	P. Rehistoric owns.....	XX chickens
	I house	P. Rehistoric owns.....	IV sheep
		Mother owns.........	I house
		So I own...........	XV chickens
			XLVI sheep
Total Things.......	LXXXVI	Total Things........	LXXXVI

This statement *may* have served ancient purposes! It does not permit the comparisons that a statement in currency or the decimal system does. Improved statements were made possible by these developments and the orderly presentation of the double-entry accounting system in books after the invention of the printing press. Luca Paciolo, a Franciscan friar and monk, published *Summa de Arithmetica, Geometria, et Proportionalita* in Venice, Italy, in 1494, only 25 years after the printing press came to that city. This book contained a section on double-entry accounting. There is no evidence that Paciolo invented accounting, but he is one person to whom credit might go for popularizing it.

The environment of accounting in the 15th and 16th century was unlike that of the 20th century. There were no capital or technology intensive industries. The public sector was war minded and rapacious (royalty). Secrecy was a fetish. There was no distinction between business and owner. Dozens of different and inconvertible currencies circulated in all countries. Most business consisted of trading. Yet there were similarities: the private sector was capitalist. There were banks. And there was a managerial class entrusted with the operation of businesses.

Once popular, accounting did not develop rapidly. The simplicity of its structure and the stagnation of technology led many to believe that accounting would not require further refinement. Before judging early accountants harshly, recall that in their times physicians believed bleeding to be an effective medical treatment, astronomers believed the sun revolved around the earth, and kings claimed to be appointed by God. There was plenty of foolishness to go around.

When the industrial development of Europe began in the 18th century, accounting proved adaptable to manufacturing and the new forms of business ownership, especially the corporation which could raise the larger sums of capital manufacturing required. However, the adaptation was in the form of bookkeeping rules thought capable of handling all situations. Because lines of least resistance were followed in developing such rules, there were inconsistencies between rules. As technology revived, allocating costs among many products and time periods became important. The resulting allocation problem accelerated development of managerial accounting, just as the demand for stewardship reports to capitalists on their investments accelerated the development of informative financial statements.

Government institutions began to take an interest in accounting in the early 20th century. World War I, with its attendant business expansion and armaments contracts, stimulated development of accounting in response to questions of cost allocation to enable computation of prices allowing a fair profit. The modern accounting profession and discipline, described in Chapter 1, is thus the product of a long evolution, even as today accounting undergoes the most rapid growth and development as a discipline and profession in its history.

Accounting for Business Activity

In devoting resources to supplying business information, an entity loses the benefits it would enjoy by employing these resources otherwise. These lost benefits are the *cost of information.*

As the knowledge of a decision maker improves from ignorance to perfection (we hope his progress is in that direction!), the expected benefit he can realize from the decision increases. The major goal of accounting is to raise the decision maker's knowledge relevant to the decision until the benefit of further knowledge would be outweighed by the additional cost of the information.

Accounting can increase a decision maker's knowledge in two ways: first, through regularly prepared statement summaries of the information processed through the accounting system; and second, through analysis of the information that would not be included in any single regularly prepared statement.

To illustrate accounting statements and analysis, we create a simple example: the Sundata Electronic Systems Company, engaging in typical activities. We show how accounting describes these activities.

TYPICAL ACTIVITIES OF A BUSINESS ENTITY

Sundata makes a single product called the Delton which is an electronic subassembly used in pollution control devices. The Delton is assembled in a Midville plant from two components: (1) *ceramics* (4 units at $100 each), the basic component; and (2) *skilled labor* (10 hours at $13 each) to assemble and prepare for shipping.

Where do these resources come from? Let us look at all the resource flows within Sundata—at the same time showing the manufacturing process in relation to these, as in Figure 2–2.

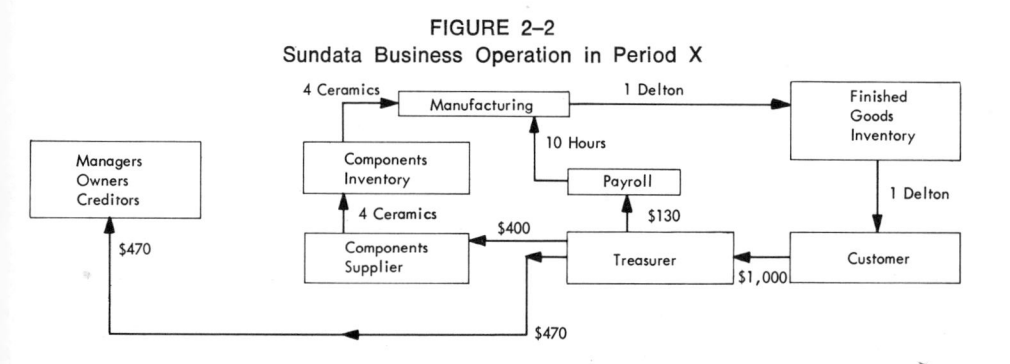

FIGURE 2–2
Sundata Business Operation in Period X

```
                    4 Ceramics                    1 Delton
                   ─────────────► Manufacturing ─────────────►   Finished
                                                                 Goods
                                        ▲  10 Hours              Inventory
  Managers                        Components           │
  Owners                          Inventory            │  Payroll              1 Delton
  Creditors                                            │  $130
                                   ▲ 4 Ceramics                                    │
    $470                                  $400         │                           ▼
                                  Components                                   Customer
                                  Supplier       ◄──── Treasurer    ◄──────
                                                           $1,000
                                    ▲
                                    │  $470
```

The ceramics are purchased from a supplier who delivers them to a "components inventory" where they are kept until issued to the manufacturing departments. The labor is provided by a work force on a regular payroll. Finished Deltons are delivered to a customer who pays $1,000 each for them. The $1,000 is in the custody of the treasurer, who pays employees and the supplier. The residue is distributed to managers, creditors, and owners (not shown).

The Activity Statement

We can produce an "activity statement" for Sundata by showing which assets have increased, which assets have decreased, and the causes of such changes. We use a "spread sheet" schedule in which the asset accounts have column headings, activities occupy rows, and the elements of the matrix thus created are the effects of activities upon assets. Let the activities be:

> Purchase of 100 ceramics
> Manufacture of 100 Deltons
> Sale of 30 Deltons

Beginning of period asset balances are at the top of each column. The complete activity statement is shown in Figure 2–3. This statement summarizes the beginning and ending positions of Sundata and (looking at the rows) the ways in which each activity affected the asset accounts.

36   An Introduction to Accounting for Decision Making and Control

Figure 2-3 is a more detailed accounting statement than you are likely to find in accounting practice, even in managerial information

FIGURE 2-3
SUNDATA ELECTRONIC SYSTEMS COMPANY
Activity Statement
Assets

	Skilled Labor (Hours of Labor)	Ceramics Inventory (Units of Ceramics)	Dollars on Hand ($)	Completed Deltons (Units of Completed Deltons)
Beginning balance	0	400	5,000	100
Period activities:				
Delton sales			+30,000	−30
Ceramics				
purchases		+100	−10,000	
Production	−1,000	−400		+100
Payroll	+1,000		−13,000	
Total Activities........	0	−300	+7,000	+70
Ending balance	0	100	12,000	170

systems. The reason is that it includes so many different kinds of units—labor hours, machine-hours, dollars, and physical units of raw materials and finished product. You can imagine that a really complex set of activities would have even more units, perhaps thousands, to understand. The statement would be in the same form and quite descriptive; it would also be difficult to read without confusion.

Managerial accountants prefer to express activities in terms of physical units when they are telling managers what information describes business events. This can be done by recognizing that each *row* in Figure 2-3 is a separate responsibility and assigned to one manager. The row for each manager can be presented to him as a separate report. For example, *production* might be presented to the manager of that department as in Figure 2-4.

FIGURE 2-4
SUNDATA ELECTRONIC SYSTEMS COMPANY
Activity Report for Period X

You used   ....   400 units of ceramics
and   ....   1,000 hours of skilled labor
To produce   ....   100 completed Delton units

An improvement on Figure 2–4 would be to give some figure or guideline so the manager would know whether he had been efficient during period X. He would appreciate knowing that 550 units of ceramics were normally used to produce 100 Deltons; he would want to find out why he used 150 fewer units than that.

SIMPLIFYING ACTIVITY REPORTS AND BUSINESS PROFIT MEASUREMENT

Imagine an economy utilizing only one economically desirable substance, so flexible and versatile that it can be used to satisfy all wants—eaten, worn, fabricated, etc. Thus, all businesses possess only this one resource. A business would appraise its well-offness and hence its income by its gain or loss of this resource during any period. Since it is always the same resource, an increase in amount possessed would indicate positive income during the period. The quality of performance would be taken from the comparison of planned and actual amounts of income. Obviously, a major simplification of accounting reports would be to express all accounts in a single dimension or unit.

In a real economy each business holds many assets. Businesses are buying and selling assets constantly, so it might be possible to find out how much of some *one* asset a business would equate in one or more exchanges to *all* its assets. We could in effect have a simple single resource economy for accounting purposes and, by determining this complex hypothetical equivalence at two different points in time, determine income *in terms of the selected single resource* for the period between these two points.

We use *cash* as the single asset in which to express all assets and changes in assets for a business. Cash is used because it is a common medium of exchange. Most exchanges involve either cash or a promise to pay or receive cash in the future. The difficulties with cash are:

a) Each country has its own kind, making currency translation a major problem in preparing accounting statements for multinational companies, and

b) Currency is subject to both abrupt and gradual changes in value in exchange (inflation, deflation, and revaluation), making currency at one point in time not equal to the same amount of currency at another point in time.

These difficulties are in fact manifestations of one basic problem: selection of the exchange or conversion ratios to convert various asset quantities into the equivalent magnitudes of currency. There are many different ideas about the proper conversion rates to use. Here are the three most commonly supported:

1. Use the prices received or costs paid for assets (*historical costs*).
2. Use the historical costs of 1 above, adjusted to be expressed in terms of the currency in circulation at the time of statement preparation (*price level or current-dollar accounting*).
3. Use the prices or costs in effect for the assets held by the business at the time of statement preparation (*current exchange value accounting*).

Detailed discussion of these alternatives is postponed until an advanced course. For now, note that 1 above is the accepted basis to convert actual assets into quantities of dollars in financial statements. In simplest terms, this means that businesses report assets in terms of how many dollars were actually paid for them rather than how many dollars would have to be paid to acquire such assets now, or how many dollars could be realized on the open market if the assets were sold. This means that our major emphasis is on accounting information based on historical costs.

STATING ALL ACCOUNT BALANCES IN HISTORICAL UNITS

Here we show you how this may be done by means of a set of agreed exchange rates—prices or costs—for converting all assets into hypothetical cash equivalents. The propositions which permit this *within the accounting context* are:

a) *Equivalence of scarce resources.* All resources do have prices or costs; that is, there is some amount of cash you would consider to *represent* X number of units of another resource. Thus, you might agree that $10 is equivalent to 2.4 hours of plumbing work or to 7 buckets of high-energy detergent.

b) *Linearity.* The cash equivalent (however determined) is the same for each unit of a particular resource; that is, if it is $0.43 for the 2d unit it should be $0.43 for the 34th, 812th, or 1,000,000th unit.

c) *Transitivity of linear equivalents.* If $A is equivalent (under rules [a] and [b] for determining equivalents) to B units of resource I and also to C units of resource II, then B units of I are equivalent to C units of II. As an example, if $10 buys either 2.4 hours of plumbing work or 7 buckets of detergent, you should be able to pay for that much plumbing work with that much detergent.

The extent to which these assumptions are true in economic settings determines the usefulness of accounting statements in a theoretical sense. The assumptions are often violated, but not enough to compromise accounting's overall effectiveness.

a) *Nonexchangeability implies nonequivalence.* Some resources such as a space laboratory or a symphony orchestra have an equivalent in cash only through invocation of the historical cost rule or an arbitrary measure of public welfare; such equivalents cannot be affirmed through exchange activity.

b) *Nonlinearity.* The amount of a resource already held may affect the amount you regard as the cash equivalent of the next unit of it you acquire.

c) *Nontransitivity.* Who, wanting a plumber to work 2.4 hours to repair a plugged drain, would settle for 7 buckets of detergent? What plumber would take soap as payment?

Nevertheless, no one has yet developed a system capable of *as much* descriptive power and communication potential as accounting—for economic decision making. The usefulness of accounting to you depends on your knowing how accounting statements describe a *particular* business' activities and assets; how the assumptions of the accounting model are true and are not true for *that* business; and how the statements are thereby affected or changed. Such awareness is the "art" of accounting—the practical application of the theoretical framework.

Let us review the account balances for the Sundata Company of Figure 2–3, summarized as Figure 2–5.

FIGURE 2–5
Sundata Accounts Balance Summary

	Units	Beginning of Period	End of Period
Cash	$	5,000	12,000
Completed Deltons	Deltons	100	170
Labor	Man-hours	0	0
Ceramics	Ceramics	400	100

Now, convert all these into cash equivalents, using the following equivalences between cash and individual resource types:

Cash	1 $ per $
Completed Deltons	530 $ per Delton
Labor	13 $ per man-hour
Ceramics	100 $ per ceramic

Multiply the account quantities by the appropriate equivalents obtain accounting statements in dollars, as in Figure 2–6.

FIGURE 2–6
Sundata Accounts Restated in Dollars

	Beginning of Period	End of Period
Cash	$ 5,000	$ 12,000
Completed Deltons	53,000	90,100
Labor	0	0
Ceramics	40,000	10,000
Total Assets	$98,000	$112,100

For the first time a comparison is possible of the well-offness of Sundata at each end of the selected accounting period. This comparison shows that Sundata's assets at the end of the period convert into $14,100 *more* than at the beginning of the period. You can't say that the company had that many more dollars, but you *can* say that during this period Sundata had an *accounting profit* of $14,100. We stress to you that this accounting profit is not only a function of the physical assets Sundata controls at the two points in time; it is also a function of the exchange rates—prices and costs—which made the conversion to dollars possible. Change those and you change accounting profit— possibly even to a loss!

How Profit and Activity Are Related

You now know the accounting profit, but do not know how (in terms of dollars) this profit was achieved. An "accounting profit statement" provides this knowledge and comes from the activity statement for Sundata.

First, Sundata cannot increase its well-offness by activities entirely within the business. Thus production (see Figure 2–3) results in no net gain or loss to Sundata because it does not involve Sundata in exchanges with other entities. Accounting profit can only occur as a result of exchanges with other entities; for example, in production:

Increase in Deltons, 100 Deltons @ $530 each.	$ 53,000
Decrease in ceramics, 400 ceramics @ $100 each	(40,000)
Decrease in labor hours, 1,000 units @ $13 each	(13,000)
Accounting gain or loss	$ 0

Second, the purchase of ceramics does not change the number of dollar equivalents representing the firm, as accounting measures this activity.

Third, hiring labor at $13 per hour reduced assets by 1,000 man-hours times $13 per hour equals $13,000. This was offset by the availability of 1,000 labor hours for utilization in Delton production.

Fourth, Sundata's sales activities resulted in acquisition of 30 × $1,000 = $30,000 and loss of 30 Deltons with a dollar equivalent of 30 × $530 = $15,900. These effects are:

Sales	$ 30,000
Less: Cost of sales.	(15,900)
Gross margin	$ 14,100

The activity statement is composed by bringing together all these elements in an appropriate order, as in Figure 2–7.

FIGURE 2–7
Sundata Activity Summary

Gain from sales	$14,100
Gain from hiring skilled labor	0
Gain from purchasing materials	0
Gain from production	0
Total gain (accounting profit) for period	$14,100

A VARIETY OF ACCOUNTING STATEMENTS

There is a large variety of accounting statements. Here we list for you a few of the major ones and their purposes for managers.

Performance Report

This is a statement used within a business, and it compares actual and expected results of economic activity. A hypothetical performance report, based on Sundata and Figure 2-4, is shown in Figure 2-8 below.

FIGURE 2-8
Sundata Production Performance Report

Activity or Item	Planned	Actual	Difference
Ceramics consumption	$55,000	$40,000	$15,000 *less*
Skilled labor used	12,000	13,000	1,000 *more*

"Planned" figures based on actual output of 100 Deltons

A production manager who received this report would wonder why $15,000 less than expected had been spent on ceramics, and why $1,000 more in labor cost occurred than planned. The manager should be able to identify the causes of the departures from plans and be able to take steps to prevent these causes from recurring in the future. This process is called *feed-forward*. It is an important aspect of the managerial process.

Cash Basis Statement

A cash basis statement will tell in which transactions cash was given and in which transactions cash was received during a period. The cash flow statement for Sundata appears in Figure 2-9.

The cash basis statement is used within a business to manage the cash resources. Frequently *projections* are made showing expected inflows and outflows of cash. These projections are compared with actual

2 / The Accounting Description of Business Activity

FIGURE 2–9
SUNDATA ELECTRONICS SYSTEMS COMPANY
Cash Basis Statement

Cash Was Received from—		Cash Was Given for—	
Sale of 30 Deltons	$30,000	1,000 labor hours	$13,000
		100 ceramics units	10,000
Total cash receipts	$30,000	Total cash disbursements	$23,000
		Excess of receipts over disbursements	7,000
Balance	$30,000	Balance	$30,000

inflows and outflows. Maintenance of adequate cash balances is necessary to assure that liabilities, bills, and wages can be paid as they fall due; that dividends can be paid; and that investments can be made as management wishes.

Balance Sheet

This statement is inspired by the "wealth statement" of Figure 2–1. It reflects the assets of the business and the claims upon those assets at a specific moment in time, usually the end of an accounting period. Claims upon assets include the claims of the owners and the creditors to whom the business has promised to pay money. It is used to determine whether the assets of a business are adequate for the activities the business is carrying out, and whether the assets are adequate to satisfy all claims upon them. The Sundata balance sheet at the beginning of the period (derived from Figure 2–6) is shown in Figure 2–10.

FIGURE 2–10
SUNDATA ELECTRONIC SYSTEMS COMPANY
Balance Sheet at 1-1-xx

Assets		Equities (Claims upon Assets)	
Cash	$ 5,000		
Inventories	93,000	Owners' claims	$98,000
Total Assets	$98,000	Total Equities	$98,000

Income Statement

Most knowledgeable businessmen today would point to the income statement as the most important of all accounting statements. It describes in summary form the changes in owners' claims upon assets *between* two balance sheet dates. The income statement for Sundata, based on Figure 2–7, is shown as Figure 2–11.

FIGURE 2–11
SUNDATA ELECTRONIC SYSTEMS COMPANY
Income Statement
For Period from 1-1-xx to 1-1-(xx + 1)

Revenue (sale of 30 Deltons @ $1,000 each)	$30,000
Less cost of sales (30 Deltons @ $530 each)	15,900
Accounting Profit	$14,100

The income statement is used by investors to evaluate the profit performance and potential of a business in their decisions whether to invest in it. Management prepares projected income statements to compare with the actual statements in order to determine whether its plans are having the expected impact on profits as they are carried out.

SUMMARY

In accounting for business activity, each exchange or transformation of a resource is recorded. The activity statement, showing in summary form the effect of each major activity of a business upon each of its assets, is a compact and detailed way of summarizing all information recorded by a business' accounting function. To simplify this information further, it is all converted into units of a single asset—usually cash—and broken down into a series of well-known accounting statements, which include the income statement and balance sheet (supplied to persons outside the business and usually examined and stated to be fair presentations by independent Certified Public Accountants), various performance reports, and cash flow statement. Use of these accounting statements invariably requires their comparison with similar *projected* statements for the same period (or point in time for the balance sheet). Such comparison tells how planned and actual activities compare in the particular respects covered by that accounting statement. From the comparisons come indications of problems requiring future management attention.

The effectiveness of accounting depends not only on its own logical structure and power but also on the understanding and wisdom of management in using it.

QUESTIONS

1. Who is given credit for popularizing accounting? Why do you think accounting then was regarded as a branch of mathematics? Why does a society in which trading is important have a need for accounting?

2. "Accounting reports just confuse me," says a manager. "I try to avoid looking at them." Why might he be confused? What will he NOT learn if he does not understand accounting reports sent to him?

3. What is the "cost of information"?

4. Why are accounting reports not usually prepared in the multidimensional "activity statement" style of Figure 2–3?

5. How do accounting reports measure the quality of economic performance? How are these reports simplified from the style of Figure 2–3?

6. Why is cash used as a single asset in units of which all other assets and changes in assets are expressed?

7. Explain and distinguish between the three major positions for determining conversion ratios in a linear aggregation vector. Do you agree that the generally accepted position today is the superior one? Why or why not?

8. What are the propositions that permit all assets to be stated in historical cash equivalents? Are these propositions perfectly valid? Sufficiently valid to permit accounting to be useful?

9. Suppose that a band of idealists wins control of the government at 3 P.M. this afternoon. At 4 P.M. they abolish currency as a medium of exchange.

a) What do you propose (if anything) to take the place of paper and metal currency?
b) Assume that the idealists establish Beatle record albums as the new currency. Will this pose any special problems for accountants?
c) Suppose Beatle albums don't work out and the next currency is watermelons (fresh ones only). Will this pose any special problems for accountants?

10. Do internal operations of a business increase its well-offness in accounting terms? Why or why not?

11. How is accounting profit calculated?

12. What is a performance report? How does it differ from the activity statement of Figure 2–4? What is feed-forward?

13. What is the difference between a cash flow statement and an income statement? Between an income statement and a balance sheet?

14. What is the difference between the real (economic) income or profit of a business and the accounting measurement that is made of that profit? Can you conceive that a business might have an accounting profit, yet experience a real loss?

EXERCISES

15. Indicate whether each of the following increases or decreases total assets:
    a) Increase of $500 in cash.
    b) Decrease in inventory of 8 units, due to sale of same.
    c) Decrease in raw materials of 20 units, due to manufacturing activity.
    d) Sales of merchandise in exchange for $1,000 (increase in sales).
    e) Increase in payroll liability due to work performed.

16. In each case below, compute the equity of the business' owners.
    a) The business controls 800 dollars, 300 units of inventory, and 50 acres of land. Parties not associated with the business claim 600 dollars, 100 units of inventory, and 3 acres of land controlled by the business.

b) A business controls 1,000 dollars and 20 acres of land. In addition, it claims 400 cows which are controlled by another business entity not otherwise related to it. Finally, 1,500 dollars are claimed by a second business not otherwise related to it.

17. A manager's activity report for a certain period shows that he used 200 units of material A, 400 units of material B, 50 hours of labor type C, and 100 hours of labor type D. The manager's plan at the beginning of the period was to use 300 units of material A, 400 units of material B, 30 hours of labor type C, and 120 hours of labor type D. Planned and actual output was 400 Transitrons. Prepare an activity report for his activities.

18. Brink Company has two assets: property and buildings. Below are this company's asset holdings at the end of each of the last three periods:

	Period 1	Period 2	Period 3
Buildings	3	4	5
Property	9	8	7

If linear cash equivalents are $15,000 for buildings and $20,000 for property, determine the dollar equivalent to assets at the end of each period and the profit during periods 2 and 3.

19. Refer to data in Exercise 18 above. If the linear cash equivalents are redetermined to be $25,000 and $10,000, determine the dollar equivalent to total assets at the end of each period and the profit during periods 2 and 3.

20. Now (refer again to Exercise 18) suppose that a different set of linear cash equivalents applies to each period:

    Period 1 .... ($15,000; $20,000)
    Period 2 .... ($20,000; $20,000)
    Period 3 .... ($25,000; $10,000)

Determine the dollar equivalent to total assets at the end of each period and the profit during periods 2 and 3.

21. Raysun Grape Company sold 400,000 cases of grapes at an average price of $3 each in 1973. In the same period, the company's average

cost of sales was $2 per case. Selling expenses were $0.20 per case. Fixed costs of all sorts were $200,000. Compute the company's accounting profit.

PROBLEMS

22. Hypoid Gear Company is considering introduction of a new power winch. Work on this winch would be done in three departments:

    In department A, 22 hours of labor and 30 pounds of metal form two parts No. 25, which are sent to department B.

    In department B, 13 hours of labor, 10 pounds of plastic, and two parts No. 25 are combined to make one part No. 300. This part is sent to department C.

    In department C, 8 hours of labor and 6 pounds of resin are combined with one part No. 300 to make the completed power winch.

    Required:

    a) Draw a network diagram similar to Figure 2–2 showing the manufacturing process for the new winch.
    b) Suppose that department B can only make available 3,900 hours of labor. Considering only this department, what is the maximum number of power winches that could be made this period?

23. Bryar Bowl is a custom pipe maker in Midville. He buys briar root from a supplier in France, special carving knives at a local hobby shop, and carves pipes to order for a variety of customers. Occasionally, when orders are scarce, he will carve a few pipes for inventory.

    In February, Mr. Bowl bought 150 briar root "blanks" from his supplier at $5 each. He spent 5 hours each on 30 of these, using 8 knife blades. Mr. Bowl pays himself $6 per hour as salary. The knife blades were bought as needed for $3 each. By March 1, all 30 pipes were complete and Mr. Bowl had sold 16 of them for an average cash price of $55 each.

    At February 1, Mr. Bowl had $3,000 cash, no pipe bowls or knives, and 5 finished pipes on hand. None of these were sold during February.

Required:

a) Given a list of the accounts Mr. Bowl needs to record his assets and activities.

b) Prepare an activity statement such as the one in Figure 2–3 which shows activities as rows and principal assets as columns; show February beginning and ending balances of assets and February activities.

24. Here is an activity statement for Marsh Gas Production Company, a gas producer in eastern Oklayoming.

	Cash ($)	Gas Reserves (Millions of Cubic Feet)	Gas Pipeline (Miles)
Beginning balance	800,000	50,000	500
Activities:			
Gas production	+650,000	−3,500	
Exploration	−300,000	+2,500	+20
Total Activities	+350,000	−1,000	+20
Ending balance	1,150,000	49,000	520

Required:

a) What were the activities of Marsh Gas?
b) What are the assets of Marsh Gas?
c) Did the gas reserves increase or decrease in the period depicted?
d) From the information given, is there any way to tell whether or not this firm was profitable during the period depicted?

25. Carter Plow Company has for many years made its own farm implements. Its plant has become old and in need of modernization. Rather than do the job itself, the company decided to give up all production activities and concentrate on marketing. Accordingly, the company sold its manufacturing facility to another firm and is searching for a good supplier of farm implements.

Two firms have indicated an interest in supplying cultivators. Let them be called firm A and firm B. Each has submitted an activity statement for its cultivator production process to Carter Plow, which is trying to determine which firm is the most efficient in cultivator production. Here are the activity statements:

FIRM A
Assets—Cultivator Production

	Cash ($)	Skilled Labor (Hours)	Components (Units)	Completed Cultivators (Units)
Beginning balances	1,500,000	0	500	50
Activities:				
Buy components	−500,000		+800	
Payroll	−300,000	+100,000		
Production		−80,000	−1,000	+400
Total Activities	−800,000	+20,000	−200	+400
Ending balances	700,000	0	300	450

FIRM B
Assets—Cultivator Production

	Cash ($)	Skilled Labor (Hours)	Components (Units)	Completed Cultivators (Units)
Beginning balances	2,000,000	0	0	100
Activities:				
Buy components	−502,500		+1,005	
Payroll	−201,000	+67,000		
Production		−67,000	−1,005	+335
Total Activities	−703,500	0	0	+335
Ending balances	1,296,500	0	0	435

You may assume that firm A and firm B are producing equivalent cultivators, and that the skilled labor hours not used but paid for by firm A represent normal idle time in firm A.

Required:

a) Draw a diagram similar to Figure 2–2 showing what inputs firms A and B require to produce one cultivator.
b) Which firm requires the fewest inputs, including waste, to produce a cultivator?
c) Which firm do you believe is most efficient in cultivator production?

26. The Replete Bubble Company is a domestic champagne maker. Until this time, the firm has only issued multidimensional activity statements. However, the firm has engaged you to formulate a set of linear cash equivalents for use in preparing conventional accounting statements. Right now you are concentrating on the asset accounts and have uncovered the following information:

a) There are four assets: cash (in dollars), grapes (in tons), bottles, and finished product (in gallons).
b) The last few years have been ones of extreme price stability. Recent transactions of the company include these:
 (1) Five hundred thousand bottles bought for $150,000.
 (2) Nine thousand tons of grapes bought for $600,000.
 (3) Seven hundred thousand gallons of bulk champagne bought for $2,100,000.
c) Current asset levels are: cash, 100,000; grapes, 2,000; bottles, 300,000; and champagne, 800,000.

Required:

a) Compute linear cash equivalents to the four assets using position 1 on page 38.
b) Using the above linear cash equivalents, compute the total currency equivalent of Replete Bubble's assets at this time.

27. Six months pass, and Replete Bubble Company's (see Problem 26 above) assets have changed to: cash, 200,000; grapes, 1,000; bottles, 400,000; and champagne, 700,000.

Required:

a) Using the same linear cash equivalents computed for Problem 26, compute the most recent currency equivalent of Replete Bubble's assets and compute accounting profit for the past six months.

28. Many prices changed during that six-month interval, and at Replete Bubble's request (see Problems 26 and 27 above) you prepare a set of linear cash equivalents based on prices at the end of the period. The new linear cash equivalents are 1 $ per $, 70 $ per ton, 0.20 $ per bottle, 2 $ per gallon.

Required:

a) Compute new asset currency equivalents at the beginning and end of this six-month period.

b) Compute a new figure for accounting profit during this period, based on the new linear cash equivalents.
   c) Comment on why there is a difference in income figures even though assets did not change. Is either of these accounting profit figures to be preferred over the other, in your opinion? Is one any more "real" than the other?

29. The Environmental Recycling Company has a contract with the city of Cleantown to collect its garbage and recycle it into reclaimed metal waste, fuel, and compost. The garbage is collected, of course, from homes and businesses. The metal waste is sold to a scrap metal smelter. The fuel is sold to the power plant which provides electrical power for the city. The compost is sold to the city which uses it to fertilize city parks, grounds, and freeway median strips. The separation process requires, per ton of garbage input, 10 hours of labor, 2 gallons of kerosene, 20 kilowatt-hours of electricity, and 150 gallons of water. The results, per ton of garbage processed, are: 100 pounds of scrap metal, 300 pounds of fuel, and 2,500 pounds of compost (high moisture content of compost causes these weights to add up to more than 2,000 pounds).

Required:
   a) Draw a flow diagram similar to Figure 2–2 showing the composting process. Use one ton of garbage as the basic unit for determining other flows.
   b) Cleantown normally produces about 200,000 tons of garbage per year. Based on this, what will be the company's requirement for labor in one year? If the company operates 250 days per year, 8 hours per day, how many employees should the company have?
   c) Basing your answer on 200,000 tons of garbage per year, how many kilowatt-hours of electricity will the company consume? Suppose the city wants to charge 5 cents per kilowatt hour and Environmental Recycling can generate its own electricity for a flat $20,000 per year. Which should the company do—buy from the city or generate its own?

30. Phlow Bus Company operates the rapid transit system in Cleantown. The bus service operates four principal activities: (*a*) suburb-downtown shopping service, (*b*) school bus service, (*c*) suburb-industrial

district service, and (d) charter bus service. The principal assets of the company are (1) bus driver hours, (2) bus hours, and (3) cash.

Required:

a) Prepare an activity statement such as the one in Figure 2–3 which shows activities as rows and principal assets as columns. Include payroll and bus leasing as activities.
b) During the year the bus company paid $400,000 to drivers, who in turn drove 100,000 hours. Fifty percent of these hours were in activity (a); 20 percent in activity (b); 20 percent in activity (c); and 10 percent in activity (d). The buses Phlow used were leased from a leasing company for 120,000 hours at $10 per hour. Each hour driven in activity (a) produced $20 in revenue; in (b), $15; in (c), $25; in (d), $40. Enter the appropriate figures in the activity statement. *Do not* be concerned with beginning and ending asset balances.

31. Flake Vehicles, Inc., makes snowmobiles and beach buggies. The company is aware of modern management techniques; and at the start of the 1973 fiscal year, it prepared projected statements showing the results of its planned operations. Somewhat simplified, here they are:

Projected Income Statement

Sales:		
10,000 snowmobiles @ $1,500 each		$ 15,000,000
5,000 beach buggies @ $2,000 each		10,000,000
		$ 25,000,000
Less:		
Cost of sales of snowmobiles		(10,000,000)
Cost of sales of beach buggies		(8,000,000)
Contribution from sales		$ 7,000,000
Less:		
Selling costs	$3,000,000	
Administrative costs	1,000,000	
Miscellaneous costs	1,000,000	5,000,000
Net Accounting Profit		$ 2,000,000

Projected Balance Sheet

Assets		Equities	
Cash	$1,000,000	Accounts payable	$2,000,000
Inventories	2,000,000	Loans payable	2,000,000
Offices and plant	5,000,000	Owners' equity	4,000,000
Total Assets	$8,000,000	Total Equities	$8,000,000

The year 1974 didn't quite turn out as expected. At the end of the fiscal period, the historical financial statements looked like this:

Income Statement

Sales:		
8,000 snowmobiles @ $1,600 each		$ 12,800,000
6,000 beach buggies @ $2,200 each		13,200,000
Total sales		$ 26,000,000
Less:		
Cost of sales of snowmobiles		(9,600,000)
Cost of sales of beach buggies		(10,800,000)
Contribution from sales		$ 5,600,000
Less:		
Selling costs	$2,000,000	
Administrative costs	1,500,000	
Miscellaneous costs	1,800,000	(5,300,000)
Accounting Profit		$ 300,000

Balance Sheet

Assets		Equities	
Cash	$ 500,000	Accounts payable	$3,000,000
Inventories	2,500,000	Loans payable	2,700,000
Offices and plant	5,000,000	Owners' equity	2,300,000
Total Assets	$8,000,000	Total Equities	$8,000,000

The company president stated, "I am worried that our profit is so much lower than our prediction." But an old director comforted him, saying, "Well, we have just as many assets as we expected to have, so everything's all right."

Required:

a) Take note of as many departures from the planned results as possible. Prepare a list of these.

b) Would you take comfort, if you were the company president, at the old director's advice? Why or why not?

c) If you are the president, in what areas of Flake Company activities do you think you should exert special effort to assure that they run closer to plans in 1975?

DECISION CASE 2–1: YE OLDE ESTATES

"There is no doubt," Sir Michael told the board, "that the figures you see give the status of our estates at the Ides of March in 1044 and again, in 1045." He unrolled a parchment and fastened it to the oaken table with four small hunting knives. On the parchment, in illuminated characters, was the following information.

2 / The Accounting Description of Business Activity

YE OLDE ESTATES
Statement of Assets

	Ides of March 1044	Ides of March 1045
Gold—pounds	100	150
Plowing horses	75	80
Riding Horses	90	60
Castles	1	1
Bushels of wheat	2,500	1,500
Hectares of land	50	70
Total	2,816	1,831

The knights squinted uncertainly at the figures. "And what do they mean?" bellowed Sir Charles, as he realized that 1,831 was less that 2,816.

"The King's scribe has given me some magical numbers which, if I multiply them by the differences between adjacent figures in these columns, then add these differences together, will tell us whether we are better off or not this Ides of March than we were last Ides of March. The magical figures are:

1 pound of gold per pound of gold
3 pounds of gold per plowing horse
5 pounds of gold per riding horse
2,000 pounds of gold for the castle
1/20 pound of gold per bushel of wheat
10 pounds of gold per hectare of land"

"Forsooth! Then tell us our wealth, Sir Michael."

"Alas I cannot. I never got past fourth grade in arithmetic."

Required:

a) Find the amount of change in each type of asset.
b) Using the King's scribe's magical linear cash equivalents, compute the equivalent in pounds of gold of each change in (*a*).
c) Add the equivalents in (*b*) algebraically and state the accounting profit of Ye Olde Estates. What are the advantages and disadvantages of accounting profit so determined?

BIBLIOGRAPHY

Books

Ijiri, Yuji. *The Foundations of Accounting Measurement.* Englewood Cliffs, N.J.: Prentice-Hall, Inc., 1966.

Pyle, William W., and White, John Arch. 6th ed. *Fundamental Accounting Principles.* Homewood, Ill.: Richard D. Irwin, Inc., 1972.

Articles

Capon, Frank S. "Accounting in an Expanding Environment," *Financial Executive,* December 1967.

Carey, John L. "The Origins of Modern Financial Reporting," *The Journal of Accountancy,* September 1969.

Chatfield, Michael. "The Origins of Cost Accounting," *Management Accounting,* June 1971.

Newgarden, Albert. "Accounting and Accountants: An Anthology," *The Arthur Young Journal,* Spring–Summer 1969.

Vatter, William J. "Contributions of Accounting to Measurement in Management," *Management Science,* October 1958.

Part II

Accounting in the Management Process

3

Activity Level Effect on Economic Performance

WHY ARE SOME businesses able to earn an accounting profit and others, apparently very similar, are not?

In this chapter we show you how managerial accounting information can be used to explain the actual or potential profit performance of a business when the management has provided answers to the following important planning questions:

1. What activity level should the firm *be able* to sustain? (How much capacity to have.)
2. What activity level should the firm *actually* sustain? (How much capacity to use.)
3. What products and/or services, and how much of each, should the firm offer?
4. What prices should the firm charge?

You use the record-keeping and control functions of accounting to help you understand *why* a business is or isn't profitable. In this introduction you regard a business as engaging in only one revenue-and-cost-producing activity; however, the methods of analysis you will learn are useful regardless of the size of the business, number of activities, or choice of numbers to use as dollar equivalents to physical resources and assets.

The calculation for income is: Income = Revenue — Expenses. Activity analysis draws upon concepts of economics (the study of resource allocation) applied to the dollar-equivalents, revenue and expense, which accounting uses to measure benefits and sacrifices. For example, an increase in accounting profit that would result from certain operating changes is a *cost* of *not* making the changes. The only way a manager will know about such a cost is to *plan ahead,* anticipating his alternatives and the related accounting profit each is expected to produce.

A decision whether to implement changes would depend on accounting profit forecasts with and without the changes. The success of economic theory applied in business administration depends on the ability of the executive to recognize prospective benefits, sacrifices, and risks—*from accounting data.* And if accounting projections indicate that profits may be increased by certain actions, one expects that real income will actually receive an increment.

COST AND REVENUE CLASSIFICATIONS

Much of the value of accounting derives from its classification of costs and revenues according to their causes, behavior, or effects. These classifications are a bridge between the activities which produce costs and revenues and their overall effect on accounting profits. Classification lets you estimate the effect on future accounting profit of a decision in terms of the decision-related transactions and exchanges.

Here, you consider one particular base for classification—the extent to which revenues and costs are influenced by the level of business activity. Costs and revenues are related to the existence and level of business activity (be that production, research, data processing, auto repairs, or whatever).

Costs can be classified as fixed or variable. A *fixed* cost is or will be a result of the existence of ability to engage in business activity (capacity). A fixed cost is incurred at a constant rate per time period, or not at all. If there is no capability to have business activity, capacity is zero and fixed cost is zero. But if the level of activity can be greater than zero (even if there is no activity now), the fixed cost is set by the maximum capacity available. A *variable* cost is not a function of time but of the actual level of business activity. In the manufacture of fishing reels, the cost of steel and plastic fabrication materials would be a variable cost, whereas the annual salary of the foreman would be a fixed cost.

Revenues would nearly always be variable, expressed at $XX per unit of product or service sold.

Most of activity analysis describes the behavior of costs and revenues as a function of the existence and level of activity during a given interval of time—*cost-volume behavior.*

ECONOMIC THEORY AND COST-VOLUME BEHAVIOR

Assume a firm which measures its level of activity accurately in terms of a single factor: say, direct labor hours, which are the hours its employees spend working directly on products and services. Other resources are required by its production process, but *capacity* is measured by the maximum number of direct labor hours which *can* be worked, and its level of activity in any period is measured by the actual number of direct labor hours which *are* worked. This firm has no inventories and always pays the same prices for the resources which sustain its activities. Figure 3–1 shows how total inputs vary with the level of activity.

As level of activity increases, total inputs also increase. Figure 3–1 shows that even when there is no activity, there are still inputs (mea-

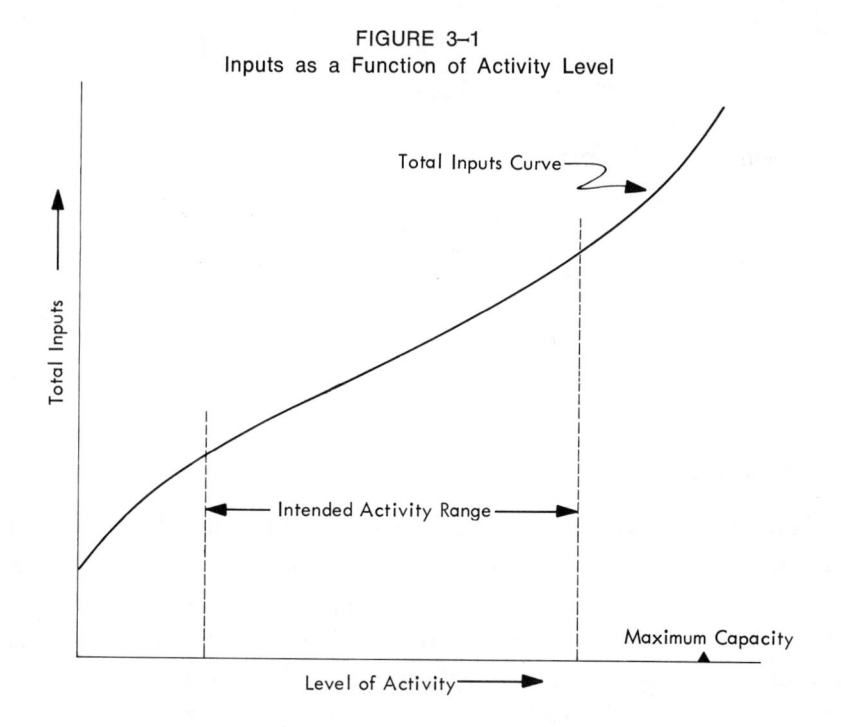

FIGURE 3–1
Inputs as a Function of Activity Level

sured by fixed costs). Then, as a little activity occurs, inputs rise rapidly. This is because the manufacuring process is inefficient when operating at low levels. As activity picks up, total inputs increase at a steady rate that is lower than the initial rate. At last, as activity level approaches its maximum value, the rate of increase in total costs picks up again, for near maximum capacity the process again becomes less efficient. The middle region between the vertical dotted lines in which total inputs rise flatly and moderately is the intended activity range for the process. Within that region, inputs increase at virtually a constant rate per unit of additional activity, and the process is most efficient. If costs are used to measure inputs, the "total cost curve" will have the same shape as the total inputs curve in Figure 3–1.

The total cost curve is easily resolved into fixed (at zero activity level) and variable components. These two curves are plotted on the same coordinates in Figure 3–2.

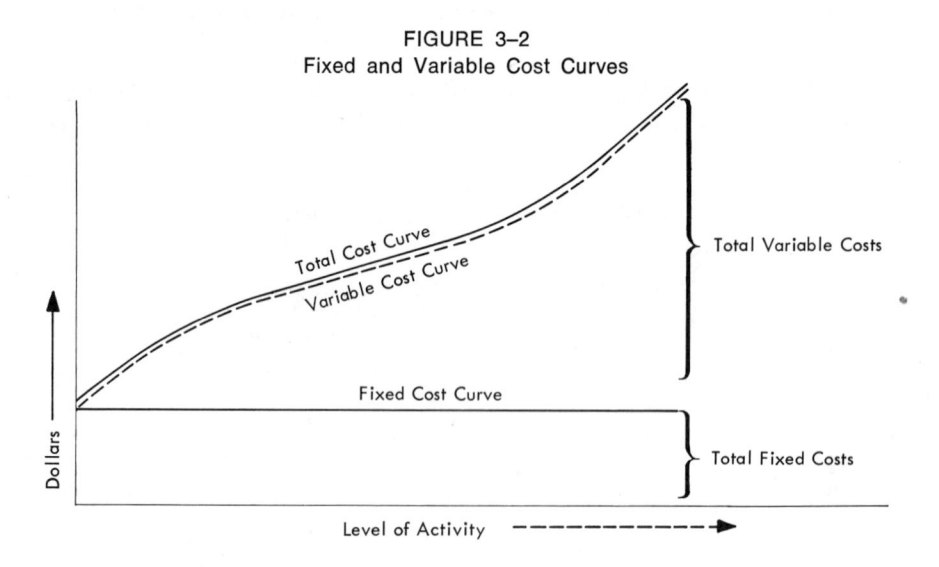

FIGURE 3–2
Fixed and Variable Cost Curves

Marginal Cost

Marginal cost is the total additional cost for one additional unit of activity at any specific activity level. It is the slope of the total cost curve at that activity level. In Figure 3–2, you can see that marginal cost is greatest at very low and very high levels of activity. In the intended operating range, marginal cost is virtually constant.

Average Cost

Generally speaking, average cost is not the same as marginal cost. Average cost per unit is equal to total costs divided by number of units of activity at a specific activity level. Thus, average cost always includes some fixed costs.

Here is a numerical example: Let fixed costs be $12,000; units of activity, 1,000; variable cost of the 1,001th unit, $5; total variable costs, $6,000. Then marginal cost is $5. Average cost per unit is ($12,000 + $6,000) ÷ 1,000 = $18. Average *variable* cost per unit is $6,000 ÷ 1,000 = $6. Average *fixed* cost per unit is $12,000 ÷ 1,000 = $12. Note that average fixed cost plus average variable cost add up to average (total) cost.

The Accounting Approximation to Actual Costs

Accounting assumes that the majority of calculations and decisions will be made in the intended operating range, where marginal costs are virtually constant. In this range, the total cost curve is almost a straight line. The accounting approximation is a straight line that extends in to the vertical axis and outward to the right. Normally, very few errors result from this approximation, and these are made up for by the simplification that also occurs in data analysis. Figure 3–3 shows the true total cost curve and the accounting approximation.

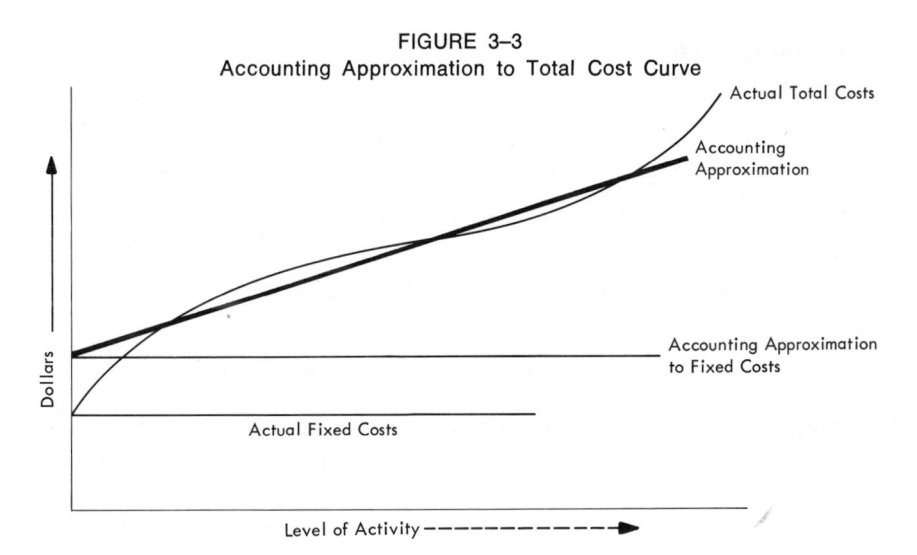

**FIGURE 3–3
Accounting Approximation to Total Cost Curve**

Later, we shall explain how you would obtain the linear accounting approximation to actual costs. At this point, you should accept the notion that the approximation can be made without significant loss of accuracy or of information useful in decisions.

Revenue

Most firms have some control over the prices they charge for their output. If the price set is relatively high, fewer units will be sold than if the price set is relatively low. Normally, all units will be sold at the same price during a sales period (at the end or beginning of a period, a small number of units may be sold at a discount to stimulate buyer interest in the product; we disregard these). Thus, the number of units sold and the total revenue will be determined by the price per unit charged. The revenue curve will be a straight line. If the price charged is relatively higher, the line will be steeper; if the price charged is lower, the line will be less steep.

Marginal Revenue and Average Revenue. Since the price charged is the same for each unit, unit price is equal to both marginal revenue and average revenue.

Figure 3–4 shows a total revenue curve superimposed on a linear total cost curve. No accounting approximation is needed for the revenue curve since it is already linear.

Accounting Profit Estimation

In Figure 3–4, the vertical distance Y between the total revenue and total cost lines at any activity level represents the *profit* at the level—total revenue minus total costs.

Revenue is computed as price (P) times activity level, N. Total variable cost is computed as unit variable cost (UVC) times activity level. Let period fixed costs be FC. Then the calculation of accounting profit is

$$\text{Profit } (Y) = P \times N - FC - UVC \times N$$

In Figure 3–4, the linear relationship makes it appear that profit could be increased without limit. Remember that this graph and the linear

FIGURE 3-4
Revenue and Cost Curves Together

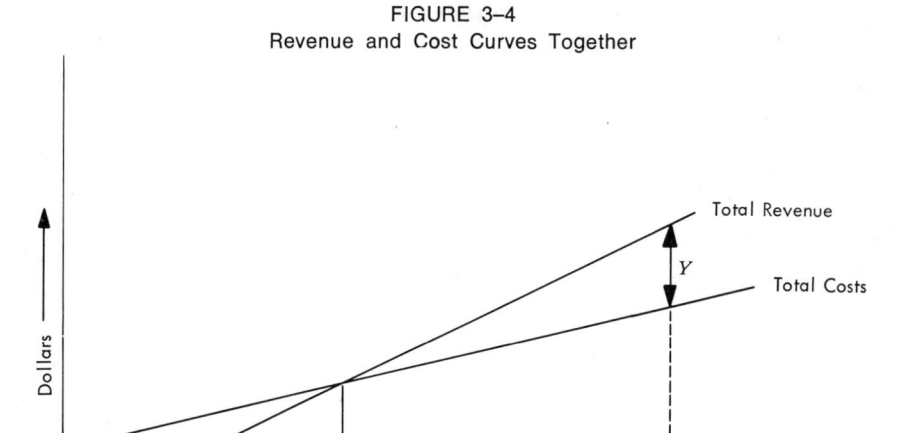

relationships it embodies are intended to be used only inside the intended operating range of the process described.

Numerical Examples

The Blewit Corporation has a particular shoe factory in which stylish boots are made. Fixed costs are a predictable and steady $30,000 per week. Figure 3-5 is the budget committee's best estimates of other costs, revenues, and activity levels, all on a per-week basis.

FIGURE 3-5
Activity Analysis Data for Blewit Corporation

Line No. (i)	Number of Direct Labor Hours N	Total Variable Costs	Total Costs	Total Revenue	Accounting Profit
1	0	$ 0	$30,000	$ 0	$(30,000)
2	1,000	10,000	40,000	30,000	(10,000)
3	2,000	18,000	48,000	60,000	12,000
4	3,000	26,000	56,000	90,000	34,000
5	4,000	34,000	64,000	120,000	56,000
6	5,000	46,000	76,000	150,000	74,000

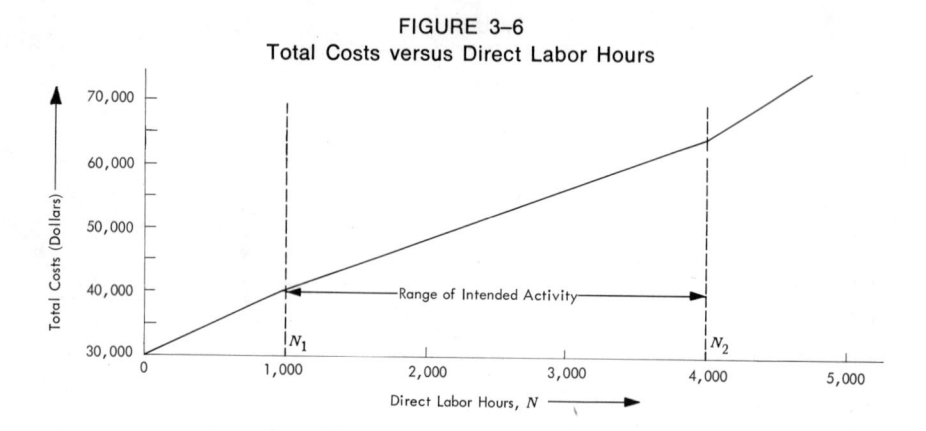

FIGURE 3-6
Total Costs versus Direct Labor Hours

[Graph showing Total Costs (Dollars) on y-axis from 0 to 70,000 versus Direct Labor Hours, N on x-axis from 0 to 5,000. Range of Intended Activity marked between N_1 at 1,000 and N_2 at 4,000.]

To convert these figures (for costs) to a linear basis, you need to find the average variable cost within the intended activity range. To find the intended range, you need to plot total costs versus number of direct labor hours. This is done in Figure 3-6. The range in which total costs form a straight line is the intended activity range.

The intended activity range, within which the total cost line is relatively straight, is from 1,000 to 4,000 direct labor hours per week. In a real situation, you would choose activity levels slightly within these outer limits for the calculation which follows. Here, we use the limits themselves because there are so few data points (deliberately, to retain a simple illustration).

$$\begin{aligned}\text{Average variable cost per unit} &= \frac{\begin{pmatrix}\text{Total cost} \\ @\ N_2 \text{ direct} \\ \text{labor hours}\end{pmatrix} - \begin{pmatrix}\text{Total cost} \\ @\ N_1 \text{ direct} \\ \text{labor hours}\end{pmatrix}}{(N_2 - N_1)} \quad (3\text{-}1) \\ &= \frac{(\$64{,}000 - \$40{,}000)}{(4{,}000 - 1{,}000)} \\ &= \frac{\$24{,}000}{3{,}000} = \$8 \text{ per unit}\end{aligned}$$

At any point, then, if N = the activity level in direct labor hours,

$$\text{Estimated total cost} = \text{Estimated fixed cost} + \text{Estimated average variable cost per unit} \times N \quad (3\text{-}2)$$

Formula (3–2) has an important peculiarity: the "fixed cost" in the formula is the accounting approximation to fixed cost; it is usually higher than the actual fixed cost. Look at Figure 3–3 and see why. To check, let's rearrange (3–2) and compute "fixed costs" from it at the level of 4,000 direct labor hours:

$$\text{Estimated "fixed cost"} = \text{Total cost} - \text{Variable costs} \tag{3-3}$$

$$= \$64{,}000 - 4{,}000 \times \$8$$
$$= \$64{,}000 - \$32{,}000$$
$$= \$32{,}000 \text{ per week}$$

$32,000 per week is the proper fixed cost figure to use when operating the accounting linear dynamic model. So long as you stay inside the intended activity range, you will get accurate, usable results.

What is average cost per unit at, say, 2,000 and 3,000 direct labor hours? The formula for average cost per unit is:

$$\text{Average total cost per unit} = \frac{\text{Total cost}}{\text{Units of activity}} \tag{3-4}$$

$$ATC \text{ @ } 2{,}000 \text{ hours} = \frac{\$32{,}000 + \$8 \times 2{,}000}{2{,}000}$$

$$= \frac{\$48{,}000}{2{,}000} = \$24 \text{ per unit}$$

$$ATC \text{ @ } 3{,}000 \text{ hours} = \frac{\$32{,}000 + \$8 \times 3{,}000}{3{,}000}$$

$$= \frac{\$56{,}000}{3{,}000} = \$18.67 \text{ per unit}$$

Observe that as activity level *increases,* average total cost per unit of activity *decreases.* This is because the same quantity of fixed costs are being divided over more units of activity. Estimated variable costs remain constant at $8 per unit.

Since price per unit is constant, average revenue is constant. If price per unit is greater than average variable cost per unit, the firm will show a constant accounting excess of revenue over cost on each unit of activity, regardless of the level of activity:

$$\begin{array}{c}\text{Contribution} \\ \text{per unit of} \\ \text{activity}\end{array} = \begin{array}{c}\text{Price} \\ \text{per} \\ \text{unit}\end{array} - \begin{array}{c}\text{Estimated average} \\ \text{variable cost} \\ \text{per unit}\end{array} \qquad (3-5)$$

Long- and Short-Run Decisions

Economic theory indicates that so long as contribution per unit of activity is greater than zero, the process should be operated *in the short run*. The short run is a period of time so short that if the process were shut down, the time-related costs associated with it (fixed costs) could not be avoided during that period. Thus, any contribution per unit (excess of revenue over variable costs) will help the business meet its period fixed costs.

In the long run, the process should not be operated unless total revenue exceeds total costs. This point occurs in Figure 3-4 at the level of activity N^*, where total revenue and cost lines cross. N^* is called the *break-even point*.

APPLICATIONS OF THE ACCOUNTING MODEL

While linear relationships provide only approximations to a firm's dynamic behavior, they are used whenever available information is insufficient to compute nonlinear relationships. In practice, the slight loss of accuracy is unimportant compared to the information gained from being able to perform the analysis.

Product Profitability

The Blewit Corporation presently only makes one boot type in the plant we used for the preceding numerical example. Direct labor hours are used to make these boots, which are sold. In order to do the activity analysis in terms of the product (rather than the process inputs), convert direct labor hours to boots by dividing them by the number of labor hours required to make one pair of boots. Let 3.2 labor hours be required per pair of boots. Thus, 1,000 direct labor hours convert to 1,000/3.2 or *312* pairs of boots. At the activity level of 1,000 direct labor hours, each of these pairs are expected to cost

$$3.2 \times \begin{pmatrix} \text{Average variable} \\ \text{cost per direct} \\ \text{labor hour} \end{pmatrix} = \text{Average variable cost per pair}$$

$$3.2 \times \$8.00 = \$25.60$$

Each of these 312 pairs is expected to sell for

$$\left(\frac{\$30{,}000}{1{,}000}\right) \times 3.2 = \$96$$

Revenue per direct labor hour   No. of direct labor hours per boot pair

The contribution per pair of boots is, of course,

$$\$96 - \$25.60 = \$70.40$$

This unit contribution will be the same throughout the intended activity range. To determine the value of N^* in terms of boot pairs, use this formula:

$$N^* \text{ (break-even point)} = \frac{\text{Estimated fixed costs per period}}{\text{Contribution per unit of product}} \qquad (3\text{-}6)$$

$$N^* = \frac{\$32{,}000 \text{ per week}}{\$70.40} = 455 \text{ boot pairs}$$

If Blewit Corporation manufactures 455 or more pairs of boots per week, it will either break even or earn a profit. In the later case, the boot-manufacturing process will produce a *contribution to company profit* in excess of its own fixed costs.

Profit Point

The boot production that will produce a specific desired profit is given by (3-7):

$$YP = \frac{\text{Estimated fixed costs} + \text{Desired profit}}{\text{Contribution per product unit}} \tag{3-7}$$

If Blewit wishes to earn a $40,000 contribution in excess of fixed costs from this process, it can find YP, the number of boot pairs it must manufacture, by substituting into (3-7):

$$YP = \frac{\$32,000 + \$40,000}{\$70.40} = 1,023 \text{ boot pairs}$$

By multiplying by 3.2, you easily convert this back into the number of direct labor hours to be worked: $1,023 \times 3.2 = 3,273$.

Cost and Price Changes

Activity analysis can be used to study effects of changes in fixed and variable costs, units expected to be sold, and product price.

Fixed Cost Change. Fixed cost changes are not common, but suppose Blewit's rise by $10,000. What is the new break-even point N^*? Use equation (3-6).

$$N^* = \frac{\$32,000 + \$10,000}{\$70.40} = 597 \text{ boot pairs}$$

The $10,000 increase in fixed costs caused an increase in the break-even point of $597 - 455 = 142$ boot pairs. This means that if fixed costs or desired profit rise by $10,000, the company must then sell 142 more boot pairs to keep the same profit or to earn the new desired profit.

Variable Cost Change. Variable costs rise from $8 per direct labor hour to $8.80 per direct labor hour, a 10 percent increase. How does this affect the break-even point?

The variable costs per pair of boots will also be 10 percent higher:

$$3.2 \text{ hours per boot pair} \times \$8.80 \text{ per hour} = \$28.16 \text{ per pair}$$

The new contribution per boot pair is $96 - \$28.16 = \$67.84$ *per pair*

The new break-even point is:

$$N^* = \frac{\$32,000}{\$67.84} = 472 \text{ boot pairs}$$

An increase in variable costs increases the level of activity required to break even or earn a specified profit. A decrease in variable cost per unit decreases the level of activity required to break even or earn a specified profit.

Selling Price and Selling Quantity Changes. A change in quantity sold does not affect the break-even point but does affect profit. Let the quantity of boots being sold be 500 pairs. Then the profit is computed as—

$$Y(500) = \text{Revenue} - \text{Estimated fixed costs} - \text{Total variable costs} \quad (3\text{–}8)$$
$$= \$96 \times 500 - \$32,000 - \$28.16 \times 500$$
$$= \$1,920$$

Now, let 550 pair of boots be sold. The profit here is:

$$Y(550) = \$96 \times 550 - \$32,000 - \$28.16 \times 550$$
$$= \$5,312$$

Profit increased substantially on the 10 percent volume increase. The increase was more than 10 percent because profit is the difference between total contribution margin, which is proportional to the volume of activity, and fixed costs, which do not change. Thus a small change in volume (or in fixed costs, unit variable costs, or unit selling price) may produce a large change in profit. This effect is sometimes called "leverage" and occurs most often when fixed costs are several times greater in magnitude than profit. Dramatic profit changes may also occur if price and unit variable cost are nearly the same, and one or both change by even a small amount.

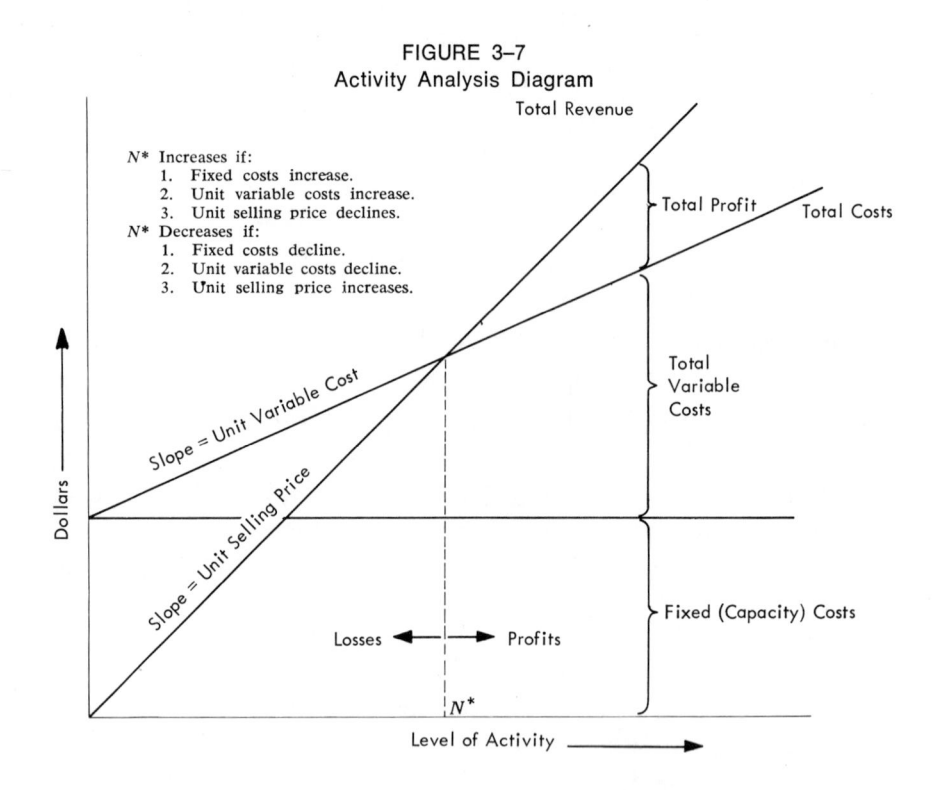

FIGURE 3-7
Activity Analysis Diagram

N^* Increases if:
1. Fixed costs increase.
2. Unit variable costs increase.
3. Unit selling price declines.

N^* Decreases if:
1. Fixed costs decline.
2. Unit variable costs decline.
3. Unit selling price increases.

The effect of a change in selling price would be opposite to the effect of a change in variable cost. Let the selling price per boot pair drop to $90 per pair. The break-even point rises:

$$N^* = \frac{\$32,000}{\$90 - \$25.60} = 497 \text{ boot pairs},$$

which is an increase of 42 pairs over the 455 pairs break-even point at the original price of $96.

Figure 3-7 shows the full activity analysis diagram with all the changes described above drawn in.

Two or More Products

Let the Blewit Corporation make two types of boot—called "Clompers" and "Stompers." Up until now we have been discussing Clompers. Now let us also discuss Stompers. Figure 3-8 gives the direct labor hours required to make each boot.

FIGURE 3-8
Labor Hours in Clompers and Stompers

	Direct Labor Hour Content	Current Period Unit Production
Clompers.	3.2	400
Stompers.	1.6	1,000

Clompers, we know, sell for $96; and Stompers sell for $24 per pair. What will be the profit earned by the schedule in Figure 3-8?

```
Revenue:
  Clompers 400 pair × $96 per pair  . . . . . . . .  $ 38,400
  Stompers 1,000 pair × $24 per pair . . . . . . .    24,000
    Total. . . . . . . . . . . . . . . . . . . . .  $ 62,000
Less variable costs:
  Clompers 3.2 hours per pair × $8 per
    hour × 400 pair . . . . . . . . . . . . . . .   (10,240)
  Stompers 1.6 hours per pair × $8 per
    hour × 1,000 pair . . . . . . . . . . . . . .   (12,800)
    Total Contribution. . . . . . . . . . . . . .  $ 38,960
    Less estimated fixed costs . . . . . . . . . .  (32,000)
    Net Total Profit. . . . . . . . . . . . . . .  $  6,960
```

Let sales of both Clompers and Stompers decline by 10 percent. What would be the new profit?

Since sales of both styles decline by the same percent, their respective total contributions also decline by a similar percent. The new total contribution will be 10 percent less than the old one, or $38,960 — $3,896 = $35,064. Now, profit is

```
Total contribution . . . . . . . . . . . . .  $ 35,064
Less estimated fixed costs . . . . . . . . .   (32,000)
Profit. . . . . . . . . . . . . . . . . . .  $  3,064
```

Activity Analysis Using Percentages

Occasionally you will find variable costs expressed as a percentage of revenue. A retail store may report that "our variable costs are 45 percent of our sales revenues." In this case, the proper formula to use for profit is:

$$Y = \begin{matrix}\text{Total}\\ \text{sales}\\ \text{revenue}\end{matrix} \times \left(1 - \begin{matrix}\text{Fraction of}\\ \text{each \$ that is}\\ \text{variable cost}\end{matrix}\right) - \begin{matrix}\text{Estimated}\\ \text{fixed}\\ \text{costs}\end{matrix} \quad (3\text{--}9)$$

To illustrate, let Stonehenge Rent-A-Car have variable costs of 60 percent of revenue. Last year, the firm made $50,000 on sales of $300,000. What are the estimated fixed costs of Stonehenge?

You rearrange (3–9) so that "estimated fixed cost" is on the left-hand side:

$$\begin{matrix}\text{Estimated}\\ \text{fixed}\\ \text{costs}\end{matrix} = \begin{matrix}\text{Total}\\ \text{sales}\\ \text{revenue}\end{matrix} \times \left(1 - \begin{matrix}\text{Fraction of}\\ \text{each \$ that is}\\ \text{variable cost}\end{matrix}\right) - Y$$

Substituting known information gives

$$\begin{matrix}\text{Estimated}\\ \text{fixed}\\ \text{costs}\end{matrix} = \$300{,}000 \times (1 - 0.60) - \$50{,}000$$

$$= \$70{,}000 \text{ per year}$$

Many other calculations of this sort, including the break-even point and volume required to earn a desired profit, can be made using percentages.

MAXIMIZING PROFIT

The accounting linear approximations are easy to use but are limited to the expected activity range; and within this range, they literally indicate that the largest profit is earned by producing and selling at the highest volume. Every businessman knows that this is not always true. To understand why, return to the nonlinear total cost curve of Figure 3–2, this time with a linear total revenue curve such as that in Figure 3–6 drawn over it. The result appears as Figure 3–9.

FIGURE 3-9
Nonlinear Dynamic Analysis

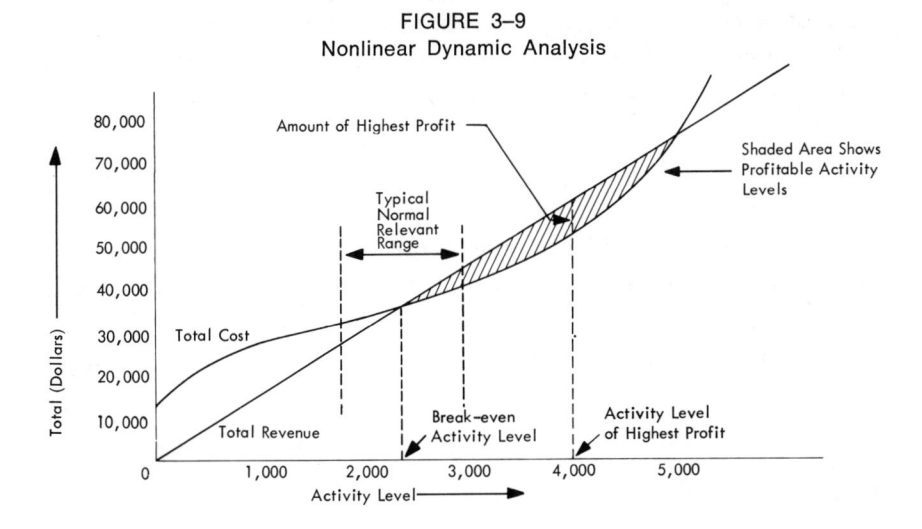

In Figure 3-9, which does not correspond to any previous examples, the normal break-even point is at an activity level of 2,400 units. There is another point, at very high activity levels, at which inefficiency and waste would cause total costs to rise above total revenue. Find this point.

The striking feature of Figure 3-9, however, is the shape of the area below the total revenue curve and above the total cost curve. Any vertical distance between these two curves represents the profit at the corresponding activity level below on the horizontal axis. For example, at an activity level of 3,000 the profit is about $7,500. Although at first, as activity level surges past 2,400 units, the profit increases, *it eventually reaches a maximum* at 4,000 units, *then begins to decline.* This business would want to produce, if possible, no more or less than 4,000 units per period.

Condition for a Profit Maximum

Briefly stated, the major condition for a profit maximum is:

Marginal cost = Marginal revenue (price)

There are other conditions which are important and are discussed in economics and advanced accounting texts. The condition that marginal cost be equal to marginal revenue is the most important condition and the easiest to discuss in an introductory text. Its rationale is this: If marginal cost is greater than marginal revenue, the firm will want to operate at a lower level, since it is losing money on the last unit it is producing and selling, and can increase its profit by cutting back some. If marginal cost is less than marginal revenue, the firm will want to operate at a higher level, since it is making money on the last few units it is producing and selling, and can increase its profit by going to a higher activity level. If marginal revenue equals marginal cost, it can neither increase nor decrease its activity level without lowering profit.

Numerical Example

An example using Figure 3–8 will make this clear. Recall that marginal cost is the slope of the total cost curve, and marginal revenue is the slope of the total revenue line (i.e., unit price). Marginal revenue is constant in Figure 3–8 and equal to $15. We computed $15 from the graph by choosing an activity level, finding the corresponding total revenue, and dividing. Thus,

$$\$15 = \frac{\$36{,}000}{2{,}400}$$

Any other level would do as well. The slope of the total cost line fluctuates along its length. We compute its slope anywhere along its length using an approximation formula:

$$\frac{\text{Marginal cost @ }N\text{ activity units}} = \frac{\text{Total costs @ }N+\Delta\text{ units of activity} - \text{Total costs @ }N-\Delta\text{ units of activity}}{(N+\Delta)-(N-\Delta)} \quad (3\text{–}10)$$

The value $N - \Delta$ is less than N; the value $N + \Delta$ is greater than N. The difference "Δ" is as small as can be conveniently read from a graph. For this example, let Δ be equal to 200 activity units.

Now, compute the slope of the cost curve at three points: 3,600; 4,000; and 4,400 activity units.

3 / Activity Level Effect on Economic Performance

Values of N	Total Costs at:		
	$(N - \Delta)$	(N)	$(N + \Delta)$
$N = 3,600$	3,400 $46,000	3,600 $48,000	3,800 $50,000
$N = 4,000$	3,800 $50,000	4,000 $53,000	4,200 $56,000
$N = 4,400$	4,200 $56,000	4,400 $60,000	4,600 $64,000

We may insert these data into (3–10) to obtain the approximate slopes and marginal costs.

$$\text{Marginal cost @ 3,600 units} = \frac{\$50,000 - \$46,000}{3,800 - 3,400} = \frac{\$4,000}{400} = \$10 \text{ per unit}$$

$$\text{Marginal cost @ 4,000 units} = \frac{\$56,000 - \$50,000}{4,200 - 3,800} = \frac{\$6,000}{400} = \$15 \text{ per unit}$$

$$\text{Marginal cost @ 4,400 units} = \frac{\$64,000 - \$56,000}{4,600 - 4,200} = \frac{\$8,000}{400} = \$20 \text{ per unit}$$

At the 4,000 activity unit level, marginal cost equals marginal revenue, so this must be the maximum-profit activity level. Figure 3–10 shows how marginal cost increases and finally exceeds constant marginal revenue. The actual maximum profit itself is either measured from the graph in Figure 3–10 or computed. It is $60,000 − $53,000 = $7,000.

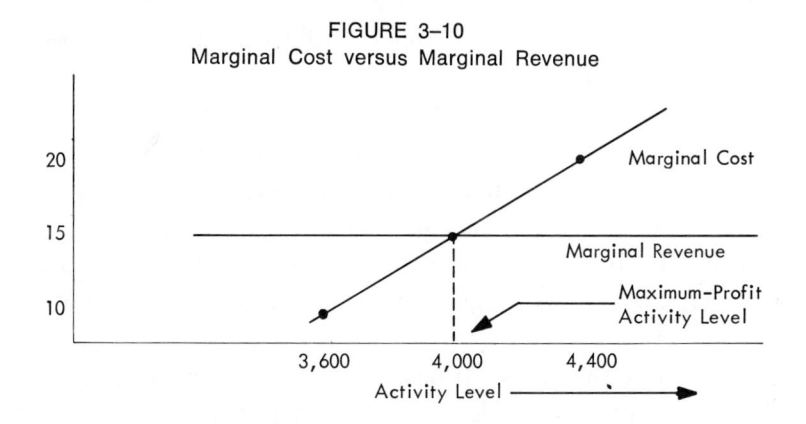

FIGURE 3–10
Marginal Cost versus Marginal Revenue

A Strange Fallacy

When nonlinear activity analysis is appropriate, some businessmen insist that the best activity level is one at which average costs are a minimum. This activity level will not be the same as the one at which profit is a maximum, so it is impossible to accept their reasoning. To produce at the lowest average cost per unit will always result in a lower activity level and lower profits than producing where marginal cost equals marginal revenue.

Let us compute average cost at several points in the interval from 3,400 to 4,600 activity units in the current example:

Activity Level	Total Costs	Average Cost
3,400	$46,000	$13.53
3,600	48,000	13.33
3,800	50,000	13.16 *lowest av. cost*
4,000 (max. profit)	53,000	13.25
4,200	56,000	13.33
4,400	60,000	13.64
4,600	64,000	13.91

Average costs are of little interest in business planning; you will use marginal costs and revenues and other cost classifications there. Average costs and revenues, however, are of interest in financial reporting.

SUMMARY

This chapter presented the basic elements of activity analysis. You first learned how costs change with activity level. As activity increases, the cost to make one additional unit (marginal cost) typically declines, remains almost constant, then rises again. The range of expected activity includes the interval in which marginal cost is constant. The accounting analysis is made by approximating the entire total cost curve by a straight line with constant marginal cost along its entire length. Estimated fixed costs (intersection of this line with zero activity level) will be a little higher than real fixed costs when this approximation is used. The total revenue line is straight, implying all units are sold at the same price.

The accounting analysis permits computation of break-even activity level and activity level required to earn a target profit. It also permits one to calculate the effect on these two activity levels of changes in unit variable cost, estimated fixed cost, quantity sold, and unit selling price.

However, accounting analysis (which is linear) does not permit computation of the activity level corresponding to maximum profit. The maximum profit point occurs when marginal cost and marginal revenue are equal. The nonlinear activity model will, if sufficient data are available, permit you to find the largest profit and the activity level at which it occurs.

An understanding of activity analysis is basic to an understanding of how resource allocation is planned in a firm. In the next chapter, we show you details of cost flow and classification as they must be understood in order to plan for resource-using processes, a common application area for activity analysis.

QUESTIONS

1. What is the "range of intended activity"? Why is it identified?

2. Does a business have to make a conscious decision about the amount of capacity to maintain? Why is it important for a business to make this decision carefully?

3. "We can save $50,000, the total costs of these building modifications, if we don't make them," says Mr. Pennywise. "We'll save $20,000 a year for 4 years in building heating costs if we *do* make them," says Mr. Gamgee. What is the economic cost of the building changes? What is the accounting cost of the building changes?

4. The president of Blewit Corporation was addressing a luncheon meeting of security analysts. "We earned $500,000 last year—double the previous year's income. My presidency has been good for our stockholders," he said. In the subsequent question and answer period, an analyst charged, "You should have been able, with any competence, to *triple* the previous year's income. Therefore, your incompetence has cost your stockholders $250,000." Assume both men have correct figures. How do you evaluate Blewit's president, in terms of his benefit or cost to stockholders?

5. What is a fixed cost? A variable cost?

6. Why is "estimated fixed cost" higher than the actual level of fixed costs?

7. "Mass production leads to lower costs." Reconcile this statement with Figure 3–1, which shows that higher production activity ultimately leads to prohibitively high total *and* unit costs.

8. What is a marginal cost? Explain the difference between marginal cost and average cost.

9. Shannon Services offered babysitting service for $1.25 per hour. At that rate its sitters sat 2,000 hours per week. Then the company increased its rate to $1.75 per hour. At the new rate its sitters sat 1,600 hours per week. Was additional revenue produced by the new price?

10. As business activity increases and total fixed costs remain the same, what happens to the magnitude of average fixed cost per activity unit?

11. Neighborhood Security Corporation is contemplating extra services that will bring in an additional $1 per hour worked by its private patrolmen. A total of 850 hours per week are worked. What is the maximum increase in costs that can occur without making these extra services unprofitable?

12. Do you think it might be possible for marginal cost to *never* be equal to or less than marginal revenue? What would this mean in terms of amount of profit?

13. What is the difference between long-run and short-run decisions to maintain business activity?

14. When marginal cost is greater than average cost and activity level is rising, is average cost increasing or decreasing?

15. Greeb-beep Company makes children's toys and industrial dynamos. The president of the company wants a single activity analysis diagram for the entire company. Suggest and justify a better plan.

16. Puffer Motor Company wants to use its productive capacity as profitably as possible. It makes two truck models—the H/34 and H/44. The H/34 model requires two hours on the assembly line and sells for $5,000. The H/44 model requires three hours on the assembly line and sells for $7,000. One hour on the assembly line

costs $1,500 per truck. Which truck costs most to produce? Which truck has the largest contribution per unit? Which truck gives the largest contribution per hour of assembly line time? Which truck would you recommend producing?

17. The Brick Bakery uses hours of oven time as its measure of business activity. At 1,000 hours per week, revenue is $40,000. At 4,000 hours per week, revenue is $70,000. Within this range, what is average revenue per oven-hour?

18. The Brick Bakery total costs at the 1,000 hours per week level are $30,000. At the 4,000 hours per week level, total costs are $60,000. What are estimated fixed costs when operating in this range? What is average variable cost per unit?

EXERCISES

19. Let fixed costs = $10,000; variable costs = $20,000; units of activity = 4,000. What is unit variable cost? What is unit total cost? Is it possible to compute marginal cost per unit from this information? If selling price per unit is $6, what is the profit or loss in this operation?

20. Two points on a curved total cost line are:

	(1)	(2)
Activity level	2,000	7,000
Total costs	$10,000	$30,000

What are average variable costs per unit? What are estimated fixed costs per unit?

21. A company sells its product for $10 per unit, and this period sells a total of 5,000 units. Fixed costs are $15,000, and the variable costs are a constant $2 per unit. What is the company's profit or loss? If unit price is raised $1, what is the new profit or loss? What is the contribution per unit when selling price is $10? When the price is raised by $1?

22. Beowulf Company has fixed costs of $50,000. The contribution per unit is $4. What is the break-even point? Suppose that unit variable costs fall by $3, and at the same time fixed costs decline by $1,000. What is the new break-even point?

23. Proudfoot Company has fixed costs of $50,000 and wishes to earn a profit of $70,000. How many units must it sell in order to do this if selling price is $3 per unit and unit variable costs are $1?

24. Green Company has a choice of producing one of two products. The first product includes two units of activity and sells for $10; the second product includes four units of activity and sells for $25. The company has a total of 1,000 units of activity to use in production. Which product should it produce? If a unit of activity has variable costs of $5, what will be the company's total contribution?

PROBLEMS

25. The Bodacious Auto Repair Company is attempting to develop useful planning information to guide future operations. The company is aware that costs are affected by the volume of repair work done. The volume of work done is measured by the number of mechanic work hours performed. An inspection of records over the past few weeks shows:

Mechanic Work Hours Performed	Total Costs Incurred
0	$ 800
100	1,500
200	2,200
300	2,600
400	3,000
500	3,400
600	3,800
700	4,200
800	5,200
900	6,200

The principal source of revenue for this company is billings for mechanics' work done on cars and trucks. The current billing rate is $7 per hour (i.e., the customer is charged $7 for each hour a mechanic works on his car).

Required:

a) On a sheet of graph paper, plot the data above in a format similar to Figure 3–6. Also plot the total revenue line.

b) If the mechanics work 600 hours next week, what will be the total revenue? Total costs? Net profit?

c) Assume that the relevant range is 200 to 700 hours worked. Using equations (3–1) and (3–3), compute estimated fixed cost, and estimated variable cost per hour.

26. For this problem, use the data of Problem 25. The Bodacious Auto Repair Company presently operates at an activity level of about 600 mechanics' work hours per week. Mr. Iyam Bodacious, the company president, has asked you if there is any reason this should not be increased, through advertising, promotions, and maintenance contracts, to the level of 900 hours.

a) Give and support your answer to this question.
b) What is the minimum profitable activity level in terms of work hours performed, if the billing rate remains at $7 per hour? If the billing rate rises to $8 per hour? If the billing rate drops to $6 per hour?
c) In your opinion, what might be responsible for a cost structure such as that of the Bodacious Auto Repair Company?
d) What average billing rate would cover all costs and allow a $400 weekly profit for Bodacious at the 600-hour-per-week level? At the 900-hour-per-week level?

27. The Pure White Milk Company operates a dairy, milk processing plant, and wholesale milk delivery service. At present, Pure White only services the River City area but is thinking of extending service to Waterloo, a neighboring town of considerable size. Such an extension of service would drastically alter the cost and revenue structure of the company. The present and probable cost structures are summarized below:

	(A) If No Service Expansion Is Undertaken	(B) If Service Is Extended to Waterloo
Total fixed costs per year	$100,000	$150,000
Variable cost per gallon of milk	0.50	0.47
Average selling price per gallon of milk	0.75	0.75
Expected sales of milk in gallons per year	600,000	850,000

Pure White feels that it must earn a minimum $40,000 per year profit.

Required:

a) What is profit per year under (A) and (B)?
b) Should milk service be extended to Waterloo?
c) What milk price would just barely guarantee the minimum profit if service is extended to Waterloo?

84   An Introduction to Accounting for Decision Making and Control

    d) Suppose milk sales under (B) are 600,000 gallons in River City and 250,000 gallons in Waterloo, but that the milk sales in Waterloo are all at a price of $0.60 per gallon.
        (1) Do you still recommend extending service to Waterloo?
        (2) What is the lowest price that could be charged in Waterloo without impairing the minimum acceptable profit?

28. Roscoe Department Store computes its profitability as $0.05 per dollar of sales. Fixed costs are $200,000 annually. Last year profit was $100,000.
    a) What was total revenue for Roscoe last year?
    b) What were total variable costs for Roscoe last year?
    c) What is the break-even dollar sales volume for Roscoe?
    d) This year fixed costs are expected to rise to $220,000. Compute the new break-even point and the new sales level that must be achieved in order to make the same profit as last year.

29. Sturdy Packing Company makes paperboard shipping containers. At present the product line includes the S model and the T model. The basic input to each container model is the machine-hours of cutting time. The S model requires 0.3 hours; the T model requires 0.1 hours.

    The S model sells for $3; the T model sells for $1. Each cutting machine-hour used requires $5 in variable costs. Total fixed costs are $5,000. Last month the Sturdy Packing Company sold 1,000 S boxes and 4,000 T boxes.

Required:

    a) How many hours of machine cutting time were used?
    b) What were total costs last month?
    c) What was the profit on last month's activity?
    d) What is the revenue per hour of machine cutting time?
    e) Sturdy Packing is contemplating a price decrease: the S model price would be cut $0.50 and the T model price would be cut $0.10. The expected result of these price cuts would be to increase by 15 percent the unit sales of each product. Would making the price cuts increase total profit?
    f) Sturdy Packing is considering a change in manufacturing method which would increase fixed costs to $6,000 and at the same

time reduce the cost of a cutting machine-hour to $4.25. Would you recommend this change (assume original prices in effect)?

30. Nuff College is considering adding a coffee-and-snack bar to its present faculty lounge. Since the college is in poor financial condition, it insists that the snack bar be profitable. The lounge is open 250 days per year. On the average, 200 faculty members visit it each day. The average item sold by the snack bar would cost 20 cents. Half of the faculty visiting the lounge would make a purchase each day at the snack bar. The snack bar would be operated by a commercial caterer whose terms are that the college must pay him $50 per week (50 weeks per year) to operate the snack bar; he in turn will give the college 25 percent of his total snack sales.

Required:

Should the college accept these terms? If so, what will its profit probably be? If not, how much additional profit must it have in order to install a snack bar?

31. Boxy Company makes shipping containers through two divisions. The cutt division provides corrugated paper cartons at a price of $0.09 per pound. The direct cost of making these cartons runs about $0.07 per pound. The gash division provides heavy-duty foamed-plastic cartons for fragile items; these sell for about $0.20 per pound and have direct costs of $0.175 per pound. The cutt division's administrative and other fixed costs are $145,000 per year; the gash division's fixed costs are $200,000 per year.

At the present time, cutt division sales are running at a rate of 12 million pounds per year; gash division sales, at a rate of 9 million pounds per year. Boxy Company has unexpectedly won a judgment in a patent-infringement case; the judgment is for $80,000. The company management wants to spend this money to increase profits. If it is spent in the cutt division, sales will rise 30 percent; in the gash division, 40 percent.

Required:

a) Compute the present revenue, variable costs, and profit of each division.
b) Compute the profit of each division if the $80,000 is spent to increase its sales and is counted as part of that division's fixed expenses.
c) Indicate in which division the $80,000 should be spent.

86   An Introduction to Accounting for Decision Making and Control

32. The Curvy Company's statisticians have calculated that the company's dollar revenues are

$$500X - 0.1X^2 \quad (X = \text{total units sold})$$

Curvy's total costs are

$$30,000 + 100X + 0.9X^2$$

Required:

a) Compute the break-even point at which revenue equals total cost. Use graph paper and choose values of X between 0 and 400. Y should range from $-30,000$ to $+30,000$.

b) Is it possible for Curvy Company to earn a $30,000 profit? What is the largest profit Curvy can earn (use calculus)? At what value of X is this largest profit earned?

33. Astral Coal Company has developed a new technology for strip mining coal without ecological damage to the environment. This technology's costs are not known with any certainty and depend to a large extent on the characteristics of the coal seam under development. However, a trial run has produced some preliminary data which Astral Coal has asked your help in analyzing. The data show total variable cost, total cost, and total value of coal mined, all in dollars, and all as a function of the number of hours of operation per week. Here are the data:

Line No.	Number of Hours Worked per Week (N)	Total Variable Costs	Total of All Costs	Total Revenue
1	10	$ 30,000	$ 50,000	$ 40,000
2	20	55,000	75,000	80,000
3	30	80,000	100,000	120,000
4	40	105,000	125,000	150,000
5	50	135,000	155,000	180,000
6	60	170,000	190,000	205,000

Required:

a) Prepare a table showing marginal cost, marginal revenue, and profit at 10-hour increments in number of hours worked per week, using Eqn 3–10.

b) At what level of work time is profit from this technology the highest?

c) Is there any range within which revenue and costs appear to be approximately linear?

d) For the 10–60 hours per week range, give the average variable cost per hour and average revenue per hour.

DECISION CASE 3–1: WILLIAM WETHERS AND FRIENDS

Mr. William Wethers and several of his friends are developing a venture to sell conch salad in franchised highway stands near seacoast communities. They envision four stands initially, each operating 360 days per year, each selling 200 orders per day. One order will sell at $1. The variable costs of filling an order are $0.25. In addition, each stand is expected to experience $20,000 per year in costs not related to the volume of business, and the central administrative and marketing costs of the business are expected to be $120,000.

Required:

a) If affairs develop exactly as expected by Wethers, what will be the venture's profit (or loss) the first year of business?

b) What will be the "break-even point" of the venture in its first year?

c) In the second year of the venture, sales volume will increase 10 percent. The same price per order will be charged and cost per order will remain the same. All other costs will be the same. By what percentage does profit (or loss) change? Why is this percentage not the same as the percentage increase in revenues?

BIBLIOGRAPHY

Books

Bierman, Jr., Harold, and Dyckman, Thomas R. *Managerial Cost Accounting.* New York: The Macmillan Co., 1971.

Leftwich, Richard H. *The Price System and Resource Allocation.* New York: Holt, Rinehart & Winston, Inc., 1961.

Articles

Bhada, Yezdi. "Dynamic Cost Analysis," *Management Accounting,* July 1970.

Black, Thomas N., and Modenbach, Donald J. "Profit Planning for Action and Results," *Management Accounting,* January 1971.

Jaedicke, Robert K., and Robichek, Alexander A. "Cost-Volume-Profit Analysis under Conditions of Uncertainty," *The Accounting Review,* October 1964.

Jenkins, David O. "Cost-Volume-Profit Analysis," *Management Services,* March–April 1970.

4

Accounting for Economic Activities

ECONOMIC ACTIVITY is a term that applies to the whole array of business and social processes such as mining, refining, smelting, rolling, stamping, extrusion, grinding, casting, forming, assembly, distribution, horticulture, husbandry, health care, and related functions which provide us so many of the food, clothing, housing, luxury, entertainment, recreational, police and fire protection, defense, education, welfare, public works, and other products and services we consume in search of satisfaction. In this chapter we show how accounting and activity analysis permit description of the many changes in the form and substance of resources as the result of organized economic activity. The purposes of such descriptions are to—

a) Enable planning of the best economic strategies and resource conversion technologies,
b) Signal decision makers when economic activities can be made more economical,
c) Identify responsibilities for specialized managerial functions and activities, and
d) Record the history of the actual operations as they take place.

Accomplishing these purposes has led to specialized features of accounting such as standard costs, budgets, and performance reports.

Such features may have developed in primarily manufacturing operations, but they have merit in nonmanufacturing operations as well. Accountants treat all economic activities as one or more changes in assets arising out of such activities. Accounting records each such change, the type and amount of asset(s) affected, and the activity causing the change. Thus assets are classified, and changes themselves are classified, to correspond to the specific needs of individual entities. No two economic entities are likely to have identical accounting functions.

Public Sector

In the public sector, an economic entity participates in one or more *programs*. Each program calls for achievement of specific goals and the utilization of specific human and material resources in specific ways to achieve these goals. A public sector entity's accounting system spells out these goals and resource utilizations and records activities to permit comparison of actual activity with that called for in the programs in which the entity participates. Significant deviations from program plans require corrective action; compliance with the program plans implies efficient entity performance.

Private Sector

The ultimate result of business processes is one or more products to be sold for revenue. Products are made in expectation of an accounting profit. To know whether a profit can be earned, there must be forecasts of the costs of a particular set of business operations. Accounting developed originally for purpose (*d*) above—to construct a product cost. There will be an accounting profit if the total revenue proceeds from product sales are *greater* than the sum of the accounting costs of product sold plus those business costs which occur as a function of time's passage. The conventions governing the cost-accumulation and cost-revenue matching processes enable us to develop forecast information and diagnostic and control signals as well as product costs and income calculations.

THE FACTORS OF PRODUCTION

This is an imposing term which applies to those identifiable scarce resources that are inputs to an economic process. There may be hundreds of factors of production; all can be classified in one of these groups:

Labor   Materials   Management   Capital

Labor is, of course, the work one does in person. You can think of the obvious examples—ditchdigging, typing, a station on an assembly line—but you should also think of "labor" as virtually any activity that takes time to carry out—such as monitoring an automatic factory, computer programming, surgery, writing, and law enforcement duty.

Materials are tangible and generally visible. Steel, plastic, fiber, lubricants, fuels—all are materials that may enter an economic process. The paint on a new car is a material, so is the abrasive that polished the paint until it is shiny, the food in the company cafeteria where employees eat subsidized meals, and the stationery on which the foreman issues memos.

Management is the contribution of supervisors. Commonly there are alternative ways to perform even simple operations—beginning with the choice of processes, technology, organization and layout, distribution network, materials, labor skills, and even maintenance schedules. All of these choices will have an impact on measures of economic performance. The right choices lead to higher profits, environmental harmony, and social responsibility. The wrong choices produce trouble. Someone (you, if you are educated and willing) must face these choices responsibly, and when doing so is performing the management function.

Capital is represented by the entity's control of land, buildings, machines, improvements, patents, copyrights, and inventories. Capital is depleted as time passes, so the entity seeks to recover capital through operations. Capital recovery occurs over more than one operating period. Public sector entities need not recover capital through operations, if they are able to justify its depletion as producing otherwise unobtainable beneficial effects on the public interest. The contribution of capital is rarely visible in a product, service, or program; however, greater efficiency, speed of production, and corresponding lower price are among the intangible utilities contributed by capital.

RESPONSIBILITY CENTERS

A responsibility center is a point in an organization at which production factor allocation and usage decisions are made. A responsibility center is accountable, in terms of both information and stewardship, for its activities. For example, a business may include responsibility centers specializing in some or all of these functions:

Finance	Public relations
Sales	Personnel
Research and development	Engineering
Administration	Customer service
Information systems (accounting, budgeting, planning, etc.)	Purchasing
	Inventories
	Manufacturing

All responsibility centers function as production, service, or investment centers, or as combinations of these.

Production Center

A production center is a responsibility center which accepts materials, labor, and capital to be converted into entity outputs of goods or services. These centers operate directly on one or more products or render services to other entities. For example, at a production center in a furniture company you could expect to find pine, walnut, mahogany, and other woods being combined directly into pieces of furniture. A carpenter's time would be directly required also to shape, fasten, and finish the wood.

A production center will be responsible for acquiring the necessary inputs for its work in proper quantities, combining them in the approved manner with as little waste as possible, in accordance with the agreed timetable (if there is one), and issuing the completed result to a storage point or to the next production center, or rendering the service to appropriate parties.

Service Center

A service center renders essential services to other responsibility centers, but *does not* do work directly with the entity's products or services outputs. Examples of service operations include machinery maintenance, security, plant utilities (such as electricity, compressed air, steam, water, gas, heat, cooling), quantity control, instrumentation, plant cleanup, waste disposal, stores and supplies depots, data processing, engineering, and employee medical care. Most of these services are rendered to the production centers; some of them go to other service centers.

Investment Center

An investment center is a focus or concentration of activities which jointly utilize invested capital. Typically, an entity will include more than one investment center, and these centers will in turn be composed of service and production centers. In the public sector, each major department of a government level might be regarded as an investment center (city government: parks, utilities, tax assessment–collection, police, fire, sanitation, streets, planning). In the private sector, a business might regard manufacturing, information systems, research, marketing, administration, and possibly others as investment centers. Each investment center would have to justify its use of capital to carry out programs consistent with entity economic goals. Figure 4–1 is a diagram of a simple economic entity which consists of one investment center, one service center, and two production centers. This entity produces one product. The service center renders services to each production center; both production centers work on the final product of this entity.

Control at Responsibility Centers

Control of responsibility centers is obtained by requiring each center: production, service, and investment, to state its plans and programs, and operations necessary to carry out those plans and programs during a given interval of time. Information describing actual activities is com-

FIGURE 4–1
Responsibility Centers in an Organization

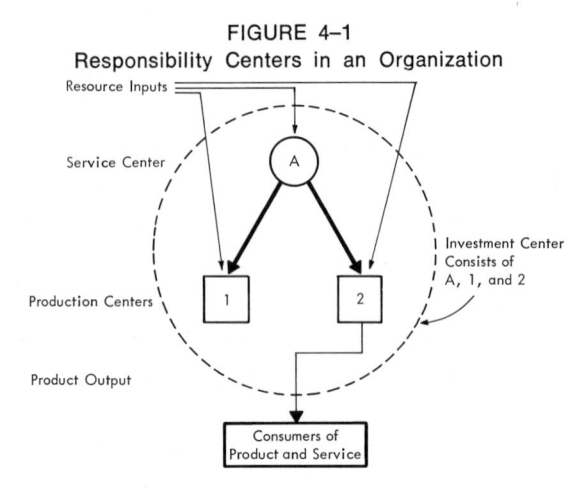

[Diagram showing: Resource Inputs flowing into a Service Center (A) which connects to Production Centers (1 and 2). Product Output from center 2 flows to Consumers of Product and Service. Investment Center Consists of A, 1, and 2.]

pared with these plans. Deviations from plans require attention. "Control" is taken to be consistency with the prepared plans of operations and achievement of the goals those plans express.

COST AND REVENUE CLASSIFICATIONS

In order to plan entity activity by responsibility centers, you must know how different activities can be expected to affect the costs and revenues accounting will, during the operating period, associate with each responsibility center as a *result* of its activities. Then if the same cost and revenue figures occur as are contained in the plans, you may reasonably conclude that the activities were substantially those that were planned.

In planning activities, you will routinely use different cost and revenue classifications. In Chapter 3, you learned about fixed and variable costs. Here are other cost and revenue classes you need to know:

Controllable Cost

If the use of a factor of production is regulated by a responsibility center, its cost is a *controllable cost* of that responsibility center. Controllable costs should be controllable at a single specific center. A cost is controllable at a center if it is attached to a resource which that center decides whether (and how) to use. Costs which are controllable at *one* responsibility center are *noncontrollable costs* so far as other responsibility centers are concerned.

Relevant Costs and Revenues

When a decision is made, only certain specific activities, processes, inputs, and outputs will be affected. The costs of these items are called *relevant costs* to the decision; revenues associated with them are *relevant revenues*. If a cost or revenue will not be changed by a decision, it is not relevant to the decision and its future occurrence must not be allowed to influence the decision.

The distinction between controllable costs and relevant costs is this: controllable costs are attached to organizational units; relevant costs are attached to individual decisions. If a decision affects several responsibility centers, certain costs at each center will be relevant to the decision, even though no single center can regard all the relevant decision costs as its own controllable costs.

Discretionary and Committed Costs

Some costs can be changed more quickly than others. If a cost can be changed during a given time interval, it is said to be a discretionary cost of that interval. Methods of altering a cost may include activity level changes, program termination, equipment purchase or sale, and/or product mix changes. If a cost cannot be changed during a specified time interval, it is said to be *committed* for that interval.

In a sense all revenues should be discretionary, since one need only withhold the product or service causing the revenue in order to stop it. However, contractual obligations, slow response to changing market conditions, or market necessity may require some revenues to be regarded as nondiscretionary.

Direct Costs

A cost may be *direct* in either of two ways: (*a*) with respect to responsibility center, and (*b*) with respect to product or service. A responsibility center direct cost is one that is incurred at that center—whether it is controllable there, or whether it is direct with respect to product.

A product or service direct cost is a cost representing some direct component of the product or service or some operation that is part of the product or service. Consider a shoe: the leather uppers, the metal last, the composition sole, the packing carton, and the work of cutting and sewing are all direct shoe inputs; and their costs are all direct costs of the shoe. However, the packing carton cost is not a direct cost of the responsibility center that cuts the uppers from animal hides.

Indirect Costs

Costs are accumulated at the responsibility center directly responsible for the activities the costs represent. Those costs accumulated at service responsibility centers cannot be controlled except by reference to the level of activity in the production responsibility centers, which in turn generates a demand for the services that service centers render. In Figure 4–1, the costs incurred at service centers are all indirect costs with respect to the production centers, and their total amounts depend on the demand for center A services at centers 1 and 2. It is important to be able to predict service center costs from expected production center activities in order to control them.

As a short example, suppose that center 2 expects to make 1,000 units of a product. Each unit of this product requires 2 hours of time on a certain type of machine—a total of 2,000 machine-hours. Each 100 hours, this type of machine must be dismantled and maintained. The direct costs of maintenance are $50 per overhaul. There will be 2,000/100 = 20 overhauls. The total overhaul cost should be $50 per overhaul × 20 overhauls = $1,000. If center A performs the overhauls, this center can expect to have $1,000 in extra costs as a result of center 2's production of 1,000 units of product. In a sense, center 2 is responsible for this $1,000 in costs and the consumption of resources in overhaul activity it represents.

The attribution of product-indirect costs to production centers and then to units of product or service would not be difficult, if it were not that each service center serves many production centers, and each production center may do work on many different products and services. The control of indirect costs is extremely complex and important, since such costs are a very high proportion of the total costs of many economic entities.

VALUATION AND CONTROL USING ACCUMULATED COSTS

In Figure 4–1 the flow of responsibility center inputs and outputs is shown by arrows. Accounting in practice assumes that the costs paid for the inputs (materials, labor, capital, management) when they were acquired can be associated with each one and consequently with the outputs into which they are progressively incorporated. For example, the product at production center 1 is represented in the accounting system by the factors of production added to it there, and also with a share of the costs of the factors used by service center A to provide services to production center 1. When the incomplete product is physically transferred from production center 1 to production center 2, these costs are transferred with it in the accounting records and become part of the cost input to production center 2. The simplified diagram of Figure 4–2 indicates how these costs are accumulated and applied to the product.

In Figure 4–2, we use a device called a *T-account* (from its T shape) to show how costs are accumulated and distributed. The left-hand side of a T-account shows costs by source or cause as they are accumulated at a center; the right-hand side shows the purpose or allocation of these costs from the center. The T-accounts are drawn in heavy lines to distinguish them from the finer-lined cost flows between them. Each arrow is a flow or reclassification of costs from one T-account to another. Each arrow links the right-hand side of one T-account with the left-hand side of another T-account. The significance is that such relationships as the output of service center A becoming inputs to the two production centers are thereby accurately portrayed. When an accounting system is under development, accountants use diagrams of T-accounts corresponding to responsibility centers and arrows corresponding first to production factor flows, then to cost flows, to determine how the accounting system must accumulate information.

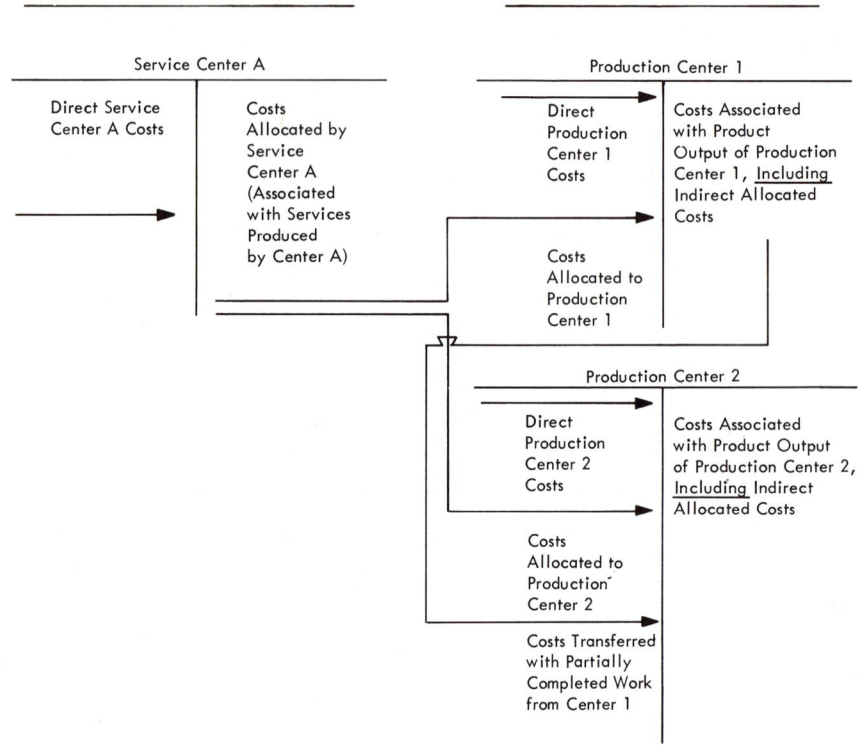

FIGURE 4-2
Cost Flows through Service and Production Centers

```
Service                              |  Production
─────────────────────────────────────|──────────────────────────────────────
         Service Center A            |         Production Center 1
─────────────────────────────────────|──────────────────────────────────────
 Direct Service  │ Costs             |  Direct       │ Costs Associated
 Center A Costs  │ Allocated by      |  Production   │ with Product
                 │ Service           |  Center 1     │ Output of Production
    ───────────▶ │ Center A          |  Costs        │ Center 1, Including
                 │ (Associated       |               │ Indirect Allocated
                 │ with Services     |    ─────────▶ │ Costs
                 │ Produced          |               │
                 │ by Center A)      |  Costs        │
                 │                   |  Allocated to │
                 │                   |  Production   │
                 │                   |  Center 1     │
                                     |         Production Center 2
                                     |──────────────────────────────────────
                                     |  Direct       │ Costs Associated
                                     |  Production   │ with Product Output
                                     |  Center 2     │ of Production Center 2,
                                     |  Costs        │ Including Indirect
                                     |               │ Allocated Costs
                                     |    ─────────▶ │
                                     |  Costs        │
                                     |  Allocated to │
                                     |  Production   │
                                     |  Center 2     │
                                     |               │
                                     |  Costs Transferred
                                     |  with Partially
                                     |  Completed Work
                                     |  from Center 1
```

Cost Allocation Basis

Cost allocation occurs at two significant points in Figure 4–2. *First,* costs at the production centers must be allocated among units of production output. If there are 400 units of production output during a period at center 2 and an accumulated total of $2,200 in costs, then the costs allocated to each unit will be $5.50. *Second,* costs at the service center must be allocated to production centers. This allocation is done to reflect as nearly as possible the use of services from that center by the production center. For example, maintenance services may be allocated according to the number of hours machines are used in various production centers. From the previous example, center 2 was allocated $1,000 in costs for machine overhauling, and this $1,000 is included in the total $2,200 of costs allocated to completed product.

Detail at Production Center 2

At center 2 the T-accounts and flows of costs between accounts as shown in Figure 4–3 is representative of what you might find in practice in similar situations. This illustration shows the increasing amount of detail required at individual responsibility centers.

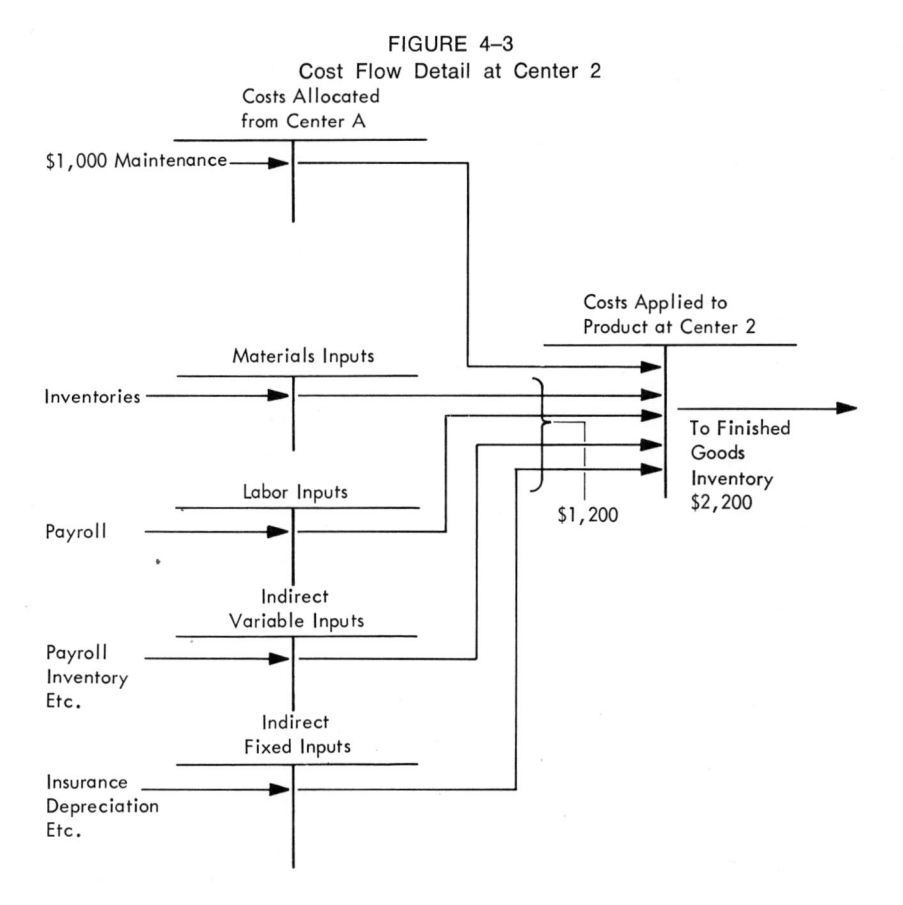

FIGURE 4–3
Cost Flow Detail at Center 2

```
                    Costs Allocated
                     from Center A
$1,000 Maintenance ─────▶│
                         │
                         │
                         │                      Costs Applied to
                         │                     Product at Center 2
                    Materials Inputs        ┌──────▶
Inventories ────────────▶│           ┐      │
                         │           │──────▶    To Finished
                         │           │           Goods
                    Labor Inputs     │──────▶    Inventory
Payroll ────────────────▶│           ┘           $2,200
                         │        $1,200
                       Indirect
                    Variable Inputs
Payroll
Inventory ──────────────▶│
Etc.                     │
                       Indirect
                     Fixed Inputs
Insurance
Depreciation ───────────▶│
Etc.                     │
```

As you can see in Figure 4–3, each T-account in the first column accumulates a particular sort of cost on its left-hand side. The left-hand side of some account should be increased any time a factor of production comes under the control of center 2. When a factor of production is actually *used* in production, the right-hand side of its account is increased, *and at the same time,* the left-hand side of the T-account

"Costs Applied to Product at Center 2" is increased. The latter T-account is called an *in-process inventory* account since its left-hand side shows total resources committed to production at that center.

When production work on product is completed, the product is physically transferred to a storage area. At the same time, the right-hand side of the in-process inventory account is increased, and the left-hand side of an account called "Finished Goods Inventory" is increased. The amount of the increase is the total amount of costs associated with the inputs in the completed product.

Center 1 transferred partially completed product to center 2 for completion. Center 1 will increase the right-hand side of its in-process inventory account at the time of the transfer of control, and center 2 will increase the left-hand side of its account, "Materials Inputs." Thus, center 2 regards partially completed work transferred in as direct materials.

Effect of Including Fixed Costs in Product Costs

All product-direct costs are variable costs. Product-indirect costs include both fixed and variable costs. Fixed costs are product-indirect costs because they cannot be associated directly with units of product. Although for financial accounting purposes these costs must somehow be included in unit product cost, they should *not* be associated with product units in the managerial accounting system and reports.

Fixed costs have a misleading effect on unit product cost when production rate fluctuates. Consider a garden hose company which has $100,000 in fixed costs annually and in 1973 produced 1,000,000 feet of hose. In 1974 business is worse and only 200,000 feet of hose were produced. Observe the effect on unit total cost:

Year	Fixed Costs	Variable Costs	Total Production	Unit Cost
1973	$100,000	$200,000	1,000,000	$0.30
1974	100,000	40,000	200,000	0.70

The fluctuation is meaningless since it does not correspond to any change in the manufacturing process, design of the hose, or resources required per unit of hose.

Effect of Time Period on Cost Classification

Whether a cost is controllable by a responsibility center may depend on the time period for which control is considered. In a one-year period, the cost of a 5-year fire insurance policy cannot be changed; over a 10-year period, the cost of fire insurance is controllable. The longer the time period considered, the more costs become subject to manipulation and therefore are controllable. Economists are fond of saying, "In the long run there are no uncontrollable costs"; this is a valid statement of our point. Good engineering in a process seeks to keep all costs controllable over as short a time period as possible, to give the greatest flexibility to the firm in planning its operations. Note that over short time intervals, some costs are not controllable; that is, not all costs are controllable.

TYPICAL ILLUSTRATIONS

The concepts described in this chapter apply to production and service operations, businesses, and governments alike. To give you a better grasp of this important point, we give here some illustrative examples of investment, production, and service centers in a variety of economic entities. Figure 4–4 summarizes these examples.

SUMMARY

Responsibility centers, which are points in an organization where decisions are made, are divided into production, service, and investment centers. Production centers accept materials, labor, and capital to be converted into entity outputs of goods and services. Service centers facilitate the work of production centers, which create the entity's outputs. Investment centers control and establish the need for long-lived assets.

Every cost is direct and controllable with respect to one responsibility center out of those comprising the entity. Each responsibility center is expected to regulate the costs and revenues which it controls.

This chapter listed four purposes of managerial accounting in economic processes: enable planning, signal possibility of improvement,

FIGURE 4-4
Responsibility Centers Composing Economic Entities

Entity	Investment Centers	Service Centers	Production Centers
Manufacturing business	Inventories, plant, current assets, markets	Administrative, accounting, quality control	Marketing, assembly, painting, packing
Hospital	Health care programs	Pathology, diagnostic, food preparation, janitorial services, accounting	Surgery, maternity, emergency room, etc.
Law office	Offices in each city (or, alternatively, practice specializations)	Secretarial, legal research, investigative	Staff lawyers advising clients and carrying out client directives
City utility department	Generators, storage system, distributing system	Billing, maintenance, customer service, meter reading	Generating, pumping
Railroad	Routes	Equipment and track maintenance	Trains
Fire department	Stations	Truck and equipment maintenance, firemen training programs, public information program, communication system	Fire fighting units
Research and development organization	Research programs or projects	Utilities, testing, computer, janitorial	Experimental centers and research teams

identify responsibilities, and record activity. Economic processes themselves combine labor, materials, capital, and management—the factors of production—into new products and services that are, in the private sector, produced and offered for sale in the expectation of earning accounting profits; and in the public sector, provided to the public in hopes of this creating a net benefit to the public's total satisfaction. To control profits and benefits, it must be possible to compute costs. In order to compute present, past, or future costs, the accounting system distinguishes between direct and indirect costs, between fixed and variable costs, between controllable and noncontrollable costs, and between decision-relevant and decision-irrelevant costs and revenues. The accounting system thus makes it possible for managers to identify the costs and revenues that must be known to them in order to carry out any specific responsibility.

The accounting system tracks resource flows by recording the cost of each resource unit acquired, used in economic activity, and made part of completed outputs. The accounts used to record these cost flows are unique to the type of entity and type of activities. These features are common to all economic entities and accounting systems.

QUESTIONS

1. What are the purposes of managerial accounting in manufacturing operations?

2. Do you believe that the purposes of accounting in manufacturing operations are substantially different from accounting's purposes in other economic activity classes?

3. What are the factors of production? What asset and expense accounts would describe *capital* as a factor of production if you added them to Figure 4–3?

4. What is a service center? How can a cost be direct to a service center yet indirect to a production center?

5. Indicate which of the following are direct costs, and which are indirect costs, for a clothing manufacturer:
   a) Income taxes.
   b) Cloth bolts.
   c) Maintenance of cutting machines.
   d) Advertising.
   e) Electrical utility.
   f) Property taxes.
   g) Labor to operate cutting machines.
   h) Supervisor salaries.

6. Indicate which of the following are relevant costs for the stamping mill center of Highland Steel Products:
   a) Rolling mill supervisory costs.
   b) Costs transferred in from other centers.
   c) Stamping mill supervisory costs.
   d) Maintenance costs of rolling mill machinery.
   e) Cost of direct labor to operate rolling mill.
   f) Insurance for all Highland Steel facilities.

7. What does a management learn about operations from the allocation of indirect costs to units of product or service?

8. May a production responsibility center incur relevant costs which are also indirect costs?

9. Indicate which of the following are discretionary costs for Highland Steel Products during (*a*) the year 1974 and (*b*) the decade 1970–80:
    (1) Cost of three-year property and facilities insurance policy.
    (2) Cost of stamping machine, estimated lifetime 25 years.
    (3) Cost of personnel paid on a monthly basis.
    (4) Cost of maintenance responsibility center activities.
    (5) Cost of foreman's salary, paid monthly and based on a three-year contract.
    (6) Cost of research program paid monthly and including projects not expected to be completed for 3–20 years.

10. In a flowchart, arrows symbolize accounting entries and T-accounts symbolize accounts. Draw flowcharts to represent these situations:
    a) Department X processes materials received from the Storeroom, using labor paid from Payroll. The completed work is sent to Inventory. When it is sold, Cash is received which is used to pay for labor and materials.
    b) Department Y furnishes indirect services to departments K and L, which in turn furnish indirect services to departments M, N, and P. Product I is worked on at M and N; product II at M only, and product III at N and P. All products pass to Inventory upon completion.

11. Reconsider the example illustrated by Figures 4–1, 4–2, and 4–3 in this chapter. Why is the cost of fuel used to generate electricity at service center A a direct cost for this center but an indirect cost for all other responsibility centers?

12. How many accounts should a responsibility center have?

13. "I don't bother with accounting information since my accountant told me all the costs wound up in one big pile that was divided up among units of product produced," said Herman Bungle, president of Quality Products, Inc. Comment on this statement and appraise the truth of it as well as the consequences of Bungle's policy for his company.

14. You are controller of Nova Cosmetics Company and you produce accounting statements for manufacturing management at weekly intervals. One of your new young employees comes to you with a proposal: "Let's measure the amount of powder base that goes into each ounce of our products until we know what a reasonable amount is. Then, let's add that information to our weekly reports, so managers will not only know how much powder they actually used but also what a reasonable use of powder is." What do you think of this idea? What do you think managers could do with the new information?

EXERCISES

15. In order to make 100 filter cases, the finishing department requisitioned and received from the storeroom 75 cases of material 101 with a cost of $100 each and employed 12 men a total of 44 hours each, at an average wage of $4 per hour. Draw a diagram showing T-accounts affected and the arrows that connect them. On each arrow write the amount of the resource flow and its cost equivalent.

16. Product 56 must pass through departments B, D, and H—in that order. In each department, $500 in materials and labor are added. Prepare T-accounts and arrows showing transfers from one department to another and addition of resources in each department.

17. The service center has incurred $40,000 in allocable costs. There are two production centers. Service center costs are *passed on* to production centers at the rate of $8 per direct labor hour actually worked in the production centers. Production center A worked 2,000 direct labor hours; production center B worked 3,000 direct labor hours. How much service department cost is passed on to each production center?

18. A particular department received $6,000 in indirect allocated costs during a period. It allocates these costs to units of product at the rate of $0.50 per direct labor *dollar*. Two products were in process during the period: product A, with 40 direct labor dollars per unit, and product B, with 30 direct labor dollars per unit. One hundred fifty units of product A were made; 200 units of product B were made. How much indirect cost will be allocated to a unit of each type of product? How much indirect cost will be allocated to the total amount of each product?

19. Costs may be classified many ways: controllable, relevant, direct, variable. In a decision to reduce stamping mill *capacity* by 150 units, indicate the classification(s) of each of the following items:
    a) All stamping mill costs.
    b) Cost of maintaining 150 units of capacity *ready* to use.
    c) Increase in stamping mill costs if one additional unit of capacity is *used*.
    d) Salary of manager of stamping mill.
    e) Salary of manufacturing vice president.

20. Bright Company is considering including some manufacturing fixed costs in unit total costs. Last year, production was 100,000 units; this year, 50,000 units are produced. Variable cost per unit is $10. Fixed costs each year are $300,000. Compute unit total cost each year and comment on the significance of the variation therein, if any.

PROBLEMS

21. The Aquarius Fertilizer Company manufactures chemical organic plant food in its plant at Smellsbad in the central United States. There are three responsibility centers in the plant: the services department, the mixing department, and the bagging department. The services department provides indirect services to the other two departments, which are production centers. During March, 1973, only one fertilizer was made, named Phosphon. The services department incurred $30,000 fixed costs and $30,000 variable costs. The mixing department incurred $200,000 direct costs and no indirect costs. The bagging department incurred $100,000 direct costs and no indirect costs. The costs of the services department are all allocated (both fixed and variable) to production centers in proportion to direct costs at production centers.

    During March, 20,000 tons of Phosphon were processed at the mixing department and bagged at the bagging department.

    Required:
    a) Draw a network or flowchart showing the three departments and the flow of factors of production through this plant.
    b) Compute the amount of indirect costs allocated to each production center, assuming all indirect costs are allocated.
    c) Compute the cost per ton of Phosphon processed at each production center—and the total cost to produce one ton of Phosphon.

d) At the suggestion of the supervisor of the mixing department, the services department total costs in April 1973 were allocated this way: one half to the mixing department and one half to the bagging department. At the end of April (during which activity was exactly the same as in March) what will be the cost per ton of Phosphon processed at each production center?

e) Pursuant to (d) above, the supervisor of the bagging department was criticized for allowing his per-ton processing costs to rise. Was this fair? Discuss relevant costs in your answer.

22. The Bravo Watch Company has recently introduced a new quartz crystal model and is undergoing test production runs to determine the cost to produce the new watch. This information will be used to help determine a sales price. During the run, 15,000 watches were produced. Direct materials costing $75,000 were used. Direct labor costing $105,000 was employed. Overhead representing indirect services amounted to $210,000; this was 20 percent of total overhead during the month of the test run. During normal production of 22,500 watches per month, it is estimated that 30 percent of all indirect services would be used up by the production of quartz crystal watches. All costs of indirect services are *fixed*.

Required:

a) What is the cost per watch of direct materials and direct labor?

b) If all indirect services costs are fixed, will varying the production rate of quartz watches change the amount of indirect costs? (If not, production of other watches is reduced or increased as quartz watch production is increased or reduced respectively.)

c) How do you recommend that the overhead costs be treated in computing a tentative per-unit production cost for the quartz crystal watch?

23. Fabrication Devices, Inc. produces prefabricated framing components for residential homes. These components are manufactured in a plant which incurs annual indirect costs of $100,000. All of these indirect costs are allocated to units of product through the cost accounting system. A typical framing component, for example, in 1974 has a total accounting cost of $34.10, of which $16 represents allocated indirect costs. During 1974 the plant operated at 50 percent of capacity.

In 1975 the company added a new line of commercial construction components. The company president reasoned, "Now that we have two product lines, each of them must absorb half of total manufacturing indirect costs." Accordingly, he directed the controller to assign $50,000 of indirect costs to residential framing component units and $50,000 of indirect costs to commercial framing component units.

At the end of 1975, 6,250 residential components had been produced—the same number as in 1974. However, the unit cost of each was now $26.10.

Required:

a) The sales vice president proposed that since the residential components operation had become so much more efficient, the selling price of these units should be decreased. He argued that this would increase sales from 6,250 units to 7,500 units. The proposed price change would be a reduction of $5 per unit. Considering only residential components, do you support this change?

b) In 1975, only 500 instead of the expected 2,000 commercial framing components were produced and sold. What was the total expected and actual accounting cost per unit if variable costs were $30 per unit?

c) Commercial components are sold for $100 each. If a realistic estimate of 1976 production and sale of these components is 1,000 units, do you recommend that production be continued? Would you recommend continued production if sales are reliably estimated at only 500 units? Why?

24. Asphalt Shingle Company manufactures composition shingles for homes. Each shingle contains 4 ounces (¼ lb.) of tar (costing $20 per ton), 4 ounces of asbestos fiber (costing $40 per ton), and 2 ounces of facing (costing $10 per ton). All the operations to manufacture shingles occur in one responsibility center, which incurs $70,000 per year in indirect costs to provide itself essential services such as maintenance and repair.

During 1973 the following selected operations associated with shingle manufacture occurred:

(1) Issued 80 tons of tar to production.
(2) Issued 90 tons of asbestos fiber to production.
(3) Issued 50 tons of facing to production.

(4) Employed men who worked 2,800 hours at $3 per hour as direct labor to produce shingles.
(5) Produced and sold 560,000 fully completed shingles.

There were *no* beginning inventories of any material in process.

Required:

a) Compute the materials inventories in production at the end of 1973. If a physical count is made and reveals the proper amount of asbestos fiber but less tar and facing than calculated, what would be probable causes for the discrepancies?
b) How many shingles does one direct labor hour produce? What is the cost per shingle of direct labor?
c) Compute the cost of goods (shingles) manufactured by Asphalt Shingle in 1973, allocating all indirect costs to production.
d) Draw a linear cost-revenue diagram showing profit, total costs, direct costs, indirect costs, and revenue (assume that shingles may be sold for $0.05 each).
e) If 60,000 shingles remained in finished goods inventory at the end of 1973 (and there were *none* in finished goods inventory at the beginning of 1973) compute the difference between revenue and cost of goods sold and mark this point on the diagram prepared in (*d*).

25. The Alpha Beta Company imports watch parts to the Virgin Islands, assembles them into watches, then imports the assembled watches to the United States, where they are sold as "house brands" by smaller department and variety store chains. Although the Virgin Islands were selected as the plant site to save on manufacturing and assembly costs, in the year since the operation was begun on June 1, 1972, there have not been any remarkable economies. The manager of the plant is furnished this statement on a weekly basis:

ALPHABETA WATCH COMPANY
Week of ____
Statement of Manufacturing Costs

Watch parts issued to production	$ 22,000
Direct labor in production	50,000
Overhead allocated	35,000
Total	$107,000
Watches completed	21,000
Cost per watch	$5.10
Projected cost per watch	$4.00

You are a prominent Virgin Islands consultant. The plant manager summons you and says, "I don't know what is the trouble; I am all over this plant watching my department heads but there simply are too many things to do at once. No, I do not give my department heads statements of costs. Why bother?"

Your inquiry establishes that there are four production centers, each using 7 to 10 material inputs and 2 to 5 specialized direct labor inputs. There is one service center, which provides services to the production centers. There are six types of watches produced. Each type goes through two production centers; no two types go through the same pair of production centers.

Required:

a) Suggest reasons why department heads should be furnished cost information regarding their centers' activities.

b) During week 18, production center B works on watch styles 1, 2, and 6, making 3,000, 1,000, and 1,000 of them respectively. Style 1 requires 1 direct labor hour; style 2, 2 hours; and style 6 requires 3 hours—all at $1.20 per hour. There are no beginning or ending inventories. Record the transfer of the labor portion of these completed watches to finished inventory.

26. AB Company operates two divisions, named division A and division B. Each division makes two products. These products are sold in a constant product mix. Performance figures for the most recent year are:

Division A:		
Sales, Bldgets 1,000 units @ $34 each		$ 34,000
Sales, Gunches 2,000 units @ $40 each		80,000
Total sales.		$114,000
Less: Cost of sales (including fixed costs):		
Bldgets	$30,000	
Gunches	50,000	(80,000)
Division A margin		$ 34,000
Division B:		
Sales, Blobs 8,000 units @ $10 each		$ 80,000
Sales, Brands 1,000 units @ $15 each		15,000
Total sales		$ 95,000
Less: Cost of sales (including fixed costs):		
Blobs.	$50,000	
Brands	30,000	(80,000)
Division B margin		$ 15,000
Total margin.		$ 49,000
Less: General and administrative costs		60,000
		$ (11,000)

Fixed costs in division A were $50,000. Of this total, $20,000 were clearly due to production of Blidgets; $20,000 more were clearly due to production of Gunches, and the rest is nonallocable but is distributed anyway to Blidgets and Gunches in proportion to the total contribution margins of these two products. Fixed costs in division B were $40,000. None of the total is clearly due to either Blobs or Brands; however, the division allocates half the total to each product in the above performance statement.

Planning for the next year is now in process. Next year is expected to be similar to the current year so far as economic environment and productive efficiency are concerned.

Required:

Consider each proposition below carefully and separately from the others.

a) The manufacturing vice president proposes that Brands should be discontinued. If you can do this without affecting sales of other products, would you support him?
b) Company economists suggest that if the prices of Blidgets and Gunches are each raised 10 percent, sales in units will decline 5 percent. If this is done, what will be the effect on income?
c) The engineering vice president has proposed a plant improvement that will add $10,000 per year to division A unallocable fixed costs. If this is done, per-unit variable costs will decline (on both products) by 8 percent. Should the improvement be considered further?
d) Suppose that (b) and (c) are considered together. Is the "package" acceptable? Would you consider aggregating change proposals in this way a logical procedure?

27. The Wet Water Hose Company produces 1,000,000 feet per year of garden hose. Fixed costs (not direct product costs and not variable costs) run $100,000 per year. Variable costs are always $0.03 per foot of hose. Inventories are negligible.

Last year was a bad year. The company only produced 500,000 feet of hose. Next year, the company expects to produce 1,500,000 feet of hose. The company wants to sell at a price which is $0.07 above total manufacturing cost.

The sales committee of Wet Water is concerned about pricing the hose. "After all," says Herman Commonsense, a director of long standing, "our cost per foot of hose went up last year from

$0.13 to $0.23 per foot. And we lost money selling hose for $0.20 cents per foot. I say, charge $0.30 per foot."

"We shouldn't have to charge so much if we can control prices," answers Credit. P. Terrific, the only accountant on the sales committee. "We should sell at the lowest price, which is $0.07 above our *average* total manufacturing cost."

Required:

a) What is average total manufacturing cost per unit in an "average" year? What is average total manufacturing cost expected to be next year? What was it last year?
b) Do you think average unit manufacturing cost should fluctuate with manufacturing volume? Should market price go up as volume declines, and down as volume increases?
c) How much fixed cost would be allocated to a foot of hose in an average year?
d) Over all the three years considered in this problem, what would be average unit manufacturing cost of a foot of hose?

28. The State of Arkalina would like to establish a series of roadside parks. Because of political considerations, at least 15 parks *must* be built if *any* are built. Because of budget considerations, no more than $5,500,000 may be spent on all parks built.

Each park is to be 3.3 acres. The land will cost an average $40,000 per acre. Direct improvements on each site will require 750 hours of manual labor at $3.50 per hour and 100 hours of supervisory labor at $7 per hour. Each site will require four shelters at $3,000 materials cost per shelter and two restrooms at $4,000 materials cost each, and one-fourth mile of macadam roadway at $30,000 per mile. Finally, the roadside parks will require that $120,000 be invested in special maintenance machinery, equipment, and supplies, and that additional personnel be hired at an annual cost of $25,000.

Required:

Determine whether the proposed system of parks can be built. Support your conclusions with figures showing the direct costs of one park, of all the parks, and the indirect costs of the park system, and finally, the total cost of the system.

29. Airline Food Service caters in-flight meals at the Midville Airport, which is served by Sayure Prairie Airlines and Sedmyne Airlines. The airlines each have different meals requirements. Airline Food

Service is paid $3 per meal by Sayure and $3.50 per meal by Sedmyne. The former are calculated by Airline Food to cost $2 and the latter, $3.50 each. The diagram below shows the steps by which the meals are prepared and the cost Airline Food assigns to that step:

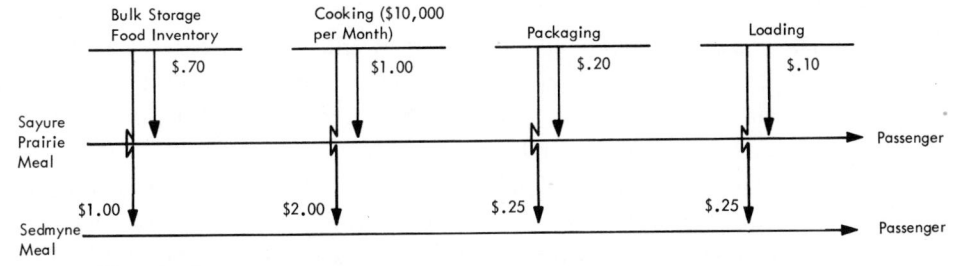

```
              Bulk Storage        Cooking ($10,000
              Food Inventory      per Month)          Packaging            Loading
                     $.70                $1.00             $.20                 $.10
Sayure
Prairie       ─────┬──────────────────┬──────────────────┬───────────────────┬──────────────► Passenger
Meal
              $1.00                $2.00              $.25                 $.25
Sedmyne       ─────┴──────────────────┴──────────────────┴───────────────────┴──────────────► Passenger
Meal
```

Required:

a) If 2,000 meals per month are catered for Sedmyne Airlines, how many were catered for Sayure Prairie Airlines? Is cooking, which is done by four cooks using large ovens in which both airlines' meals are cooked at once, a direct or indirect cost per meal?

b) What was the total cost of bulk food used in meals in the month in which $10,000 cooking costs were incurred?

c) If cooking expense is $10,000 per month regardless of the number of meals cooked, is a contribution earned on meals prepared for Sedmyne Airlines?

d) How many meals must be prepared (in the same ratio as in [a]) to earn a $32,000 contribution above all costs listed above?

DECISION CASE 4–1: TORNADO FENCE COMPANY

Tornado Fence Company makes galvanized wire-mesh fencing for use in residential neighborhoods and by industry. This fence is fastened to galvanized metal poles thrust into the ground and set in concrete. The company manufactures these poles in a separate responsibility center. The operating statement of this center for April, a typical month, shows:

Direct costs:		
Metal pipe, 50,000 feet	$20,000	
Galvanizing solution, 2,000 pounds	3,000	
Labor, 640 hours @ $4 each	2,560	$25,560
Indirect costs:		
Stockroom	$ 1,000	
Utilities	3,000	
Labor	1,000	
Allocated by plant administration	8,000	13,000
		$38,560

Fence posts made, 10,000. Cost per fence post: $38,560/10,000 = $3.86. Tornado has been approached by Hustler Steel Corporation, which promises to sell fence posts to Tornado identical to those the company is now making for $3.30 each.

Required:

   a) Assume that all allocated costs would be incurred regardless of whether fence posts are made or not. Which of the costs above are avoidable and therefore relevant to a decision whether or not to purchase rather than make fence posts?

   b) Tornado's president tells the fence post foreman: "For now, we will continue to make our own fence posts under your supervision. But if the average cost per fence post is ever over $3.30 for two months in a row, we will stop making fence posts and start buying them." Three months later, cost per post has been $3.53, $3.50, and $3.45. The president orders production of posts halted and purchases posts from Hustler steel. Did he do the right thing? Why, or why not?

BIBLIOGRAPHY

Books

Anthony, Robert N. *Planning and Control Systems: A Framework for Analysis.* Boston, Mass.: Harvard Business School, 1965.

———. *Management Accounting: Text and Cases.* 4th ed. Homewood, Ill.: Richard D. Irwin, Inc., 1970.

Beyer, Robert, and Trawicki, D. J. *Profitability Accounting.* 2d ed. New York: Ronald Press Co., 1972.

Fremgen, James M. *Accounting for Managerial Analysis.* Rev. ed. Homewood, Ill.: Richard D. Irwin, Inc., 1972.

Rossell, James H., and Frasure, William W. *Managerial Accounting.* 2d ed. Columbus, Ohio: Charles E. Merrill Publishing Co., 1972.

Articles

Bergquist, Richard E. "Direct Labor v. Machine Hour Costing," *Management Accounting,* May 1971.

King, Barry G. "Cost-Effectiveness Analysis: Implications for Accountants," *The Journal of Accountancy,* March 1970.

Netten, E. W. "Responsibility Accounting for Better Management," *The Canadian Chartered Accountant,* September 1963.

Prenger, Al J. "Divisional Controllership," *Management Accounting,* November 1972.

Wells, M. C. "Profit Centers, Transfer Prices, and Mysticism," *Abacus,* December 1968.

5

Fundamental Planning Using Accounting Information

As COMMERCE has developed, the size of economic units participating in commerce has increased. With the increases in size has come emergence of specialized functions within the firm. These specialized functions exist better to perform their limited set of operations, or make their limited number of decisions. By and large specialization succeeds in increasing the economic efficiency of a firm by reducing the uncertainty of operations. However, it is achieved at the cost of a reduced natural ability to communicate and coordinate intrafirm activities. Consequently one of the first responsibilities of a firm's top management is to provide formal channels, processes, and incentives for communication and cooperation within the firm between specialized functions.

In most firms the accounting information system is used as the vehicle to encourage communication and cooperation, and as you might expect it has developed a specialization especially for this purpose. This specialized function is called *budgeting* or *profit planning*. The budgeting process continues year-round. Its nominal output is a set of pro forma (looking forward) financial statements which describe the financial position and results of operations of the company during the next operating interval. The real product, however, is a detailed set of supporting performance statements showing the activities expected of each responsibility center within the business. These performance statements can be compared later with actual performance statements; the results, condensed through variance analysis, enable pinpointing problems while at the same time promoting management efficiency.

In this chapter we shall explain the budgeting process and the planning decisions which it incorporates. Budget preparation is a fundamental activity of the managerial accountant; nothing else he does can be so intimately involved with fundamental business processes or have such a profound influence on the operating profitability of the firm.

BUDGET PROCESS ORGANIZATION

Responsibility for the budgeting process is divided among the components of an organization structure (review Chapter 1 for organizational components of a private corporation):

—The budget committee of the board of directors is responsible for financial and planning policy for the firm.
—The president's budget committee oversees the budgeting process and makes certain that there is high-level support and enthusiasm for the budgeting process.
—The chief budget officer or budget director must execute budget policies through his administrative services and coordination of the budgeting process.
—The budget advisers are scattered through the profit centers and functional areas and provide staff services to operating vice presidents, enabling them to prepare their parts of the overall budget.

Figure 5-1 shows the general relationships between these various segments of a firm.

Within a firm, budget preparation proceeds continuously throughout each operating period. Each segment of the firm must prepare detailed proposed operating plans. In a small business, the process is the same except that many steps are simpler and functions combined.

Initial Budget Policies

These policies will be based upon initial assumptions which are formulated by the board of directors, the board of directors' budget

FIGURE 5–1
Corporate Organization Structure

```
                    Stockholders
                         |
                  Board of Directors
                         |
        Budget Committee─┤
                         |
                     President
                         |
   ┌──────────┬──────────┼──────────┬──────────┐
   |          |                     |          |
Vice        Vice           Vice Presidents   Vice Presidents
President   President        Domestic        International
Finance*    Research*        Operations*     Operations*
   |          |                     |          |
Treasurer    |                      |          |
             |                      |          |
         Controller*                |          |
             |                      |          |
         Chief                      |          |
         Budget  ─ ─ ─ ─ ─ ─ ─ ─ ─ ─┼─ ─ ─ ─ ─ ┤
         Officer       |            |          |
                       |            |          |
                   Budget        Budget     Budget
                   Adviser       Advisers   Advisers
```

─────── Line Authority

─ ─ ─ ─ Staff Authority

*Member of President's Budget Committee

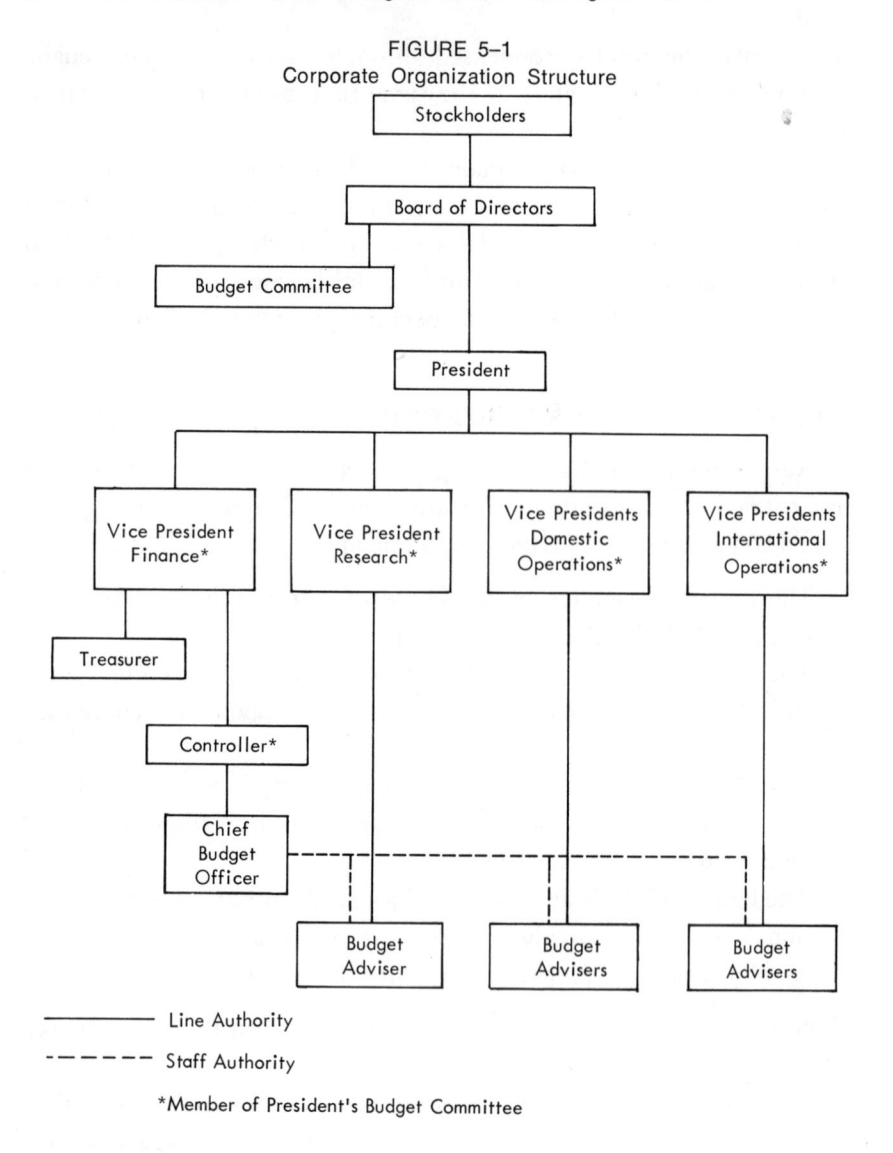

committee, and the president's budget committee. These policies should deal with:

1. *Major economic trends* that will be assumed to operate in the firm's environment during the forthcoming budget period.
2. *Major goals* of the firm during the coming period (rate of return on investment, sales volume, profit level, equity readjustment, em-

ployment level, pricing policies, share of the market, emphasis on exports, environmental protection, and other goals).
3. *Mechanics and sequence* of the budgeting process.

Major economic trends should be developed through *long-range planning*. Such planning would be assisted by an economic analysis staff advising the president and other top-level executives. To forecast trends, you would call in expert statisticians and economists, as prediction must be carried out with some precision to be reliable. The predictions of the economists and statisticians would be compared with the intuitive predictions of operating management. For example, the chief marketing officer of each of the profit centers may be asked his opinion of marketing trends and developments. His opinion will serve both as a check on the statistical predictions and as input to the ongoing process of revising such predictions.

Major goals would be part of budget policy so that the plans prepared by the various profit and cost centers have in common some fundamental assumptions about the firm. The budget committees, in formulating these general goals, do not take the initiative for proposing change in operations from lower responsibility levels. One purpose of the budget process is to encourage a flow of such ideas upwards through the administrative structure to higher levels of management.

Mechanics and sequence may be delegated to the chief budget officer. This person should be sure that common forms are supplied and consistent documentation required whenever budgeting takes place. Because budgeting may not be a familiar process to many new employees, the CBO operates several training schools or management development programs during the year to explain the budgeting process in his company. A few managers (and especially the CBO himself) will attend outside seminars and programs to trade budgeting experiences with other managers in other companies. The CBO will also consult with operating executives and set a schedule for completion of the various steps of the budgeting process.

The First Draft Budget

The result of the first round of steps will be a complete "first draft" budget. This budget will be assembled and scrutinized for inconsistencies or projected results which are obviously not acceptable to higher management. (For example, one department may have exceeded a tentative ceiling on its projected expenditures.) When such are found, the CBO informs the responsible departmental executives and offers his services in helping prepare an improved budget. The CBO can never order revision of a proposed budget. If an impasse develops between himself and a department executive, it must be passed up the line of responsibility to the executive's superior for resolution.

The "first draft" budget will receive close examination from the president's budget committee. It is probable they will suggest revisions to produce a more acceptable plan. The board of directors budget committee, and finally the board of directors,[1] would examine the revised budget. All parties recognized that budgeting is an iterative process; that is, that it should not be expected to produce an acceptable result right away; several trials will be necessary. The result of each trial will be an improvement on the result of the previous trial. Finally a trial will produce pro forma financial statements which appear satisfactory to the board of directors; this trial will be adopted as the formal budget and the processes and policies leading to those pro forma statements will become the *expected operations* of the business, and the benchmark against which actual operations are compared.

BUDGET COMPONENTS

The components of a total budget may be viewed in two ways: (1) with regard to the period of time covered and (2) with regard to the function or responsibility covered.

Period of Time

There will be two or possibly three distinct budget periods. The first has already been mentioned—the *long-range budget*. The long-range budget covers a period of time running from the present forward to a point in time perhaps 7 to 15 years distant. The purpose of this

---

[1] Usually the board looks at only the "final" budget.

budget is to anticipate long-range needs or opportunities which require specific steps to be taken now or in the near future. The company should not be taken by surprise by any developments which occur gradually over an extended period of time. Prospective restrictions on the sales of cigarettes or leaded gasoline are examples of events which have cast long shadows before them, which were (or could have been) foreseen, and for which preparation could be made. Long-range planning should be more than trend projection; trends rarely project to the extremes. Consequently long-range planning and budgeting must involve operating executives in the firm, possibly through retreats or regularly scheduled conferences. But because operating executives are not fundamentally planners, a staff of trained planners—statisticians, mathematicians, economists, and accountants—attends such meetings and interprets their results as input into a process of defining long-run problems, opportunities, environmental conditions, and company weaknesses which can be fed back to operating managers for further reaction at another meeting. The level of detail in long-range budgets is not high. There are pro forma financial statements, but they are condensed statements. Functional areas may be combined for these planning purposes, and much of the budget will consist of economic reports, scenarios, analysis, and narrative.

The *intermediate range budget* covers a period of time from the present forward perhaps three to six years. Its purpose is to schedule the continuance of programs already underway and the startup of programs necessary to achieve long-range objectives. The construction of a larger plant or systematic introduction of a new product line might be shown in such a budget.

The *operating budget* covers a relatively short time interval—normally equal to one year (or to one financial reporting period). It is prepared in considerable detail—as much detail as is necessary to compare the major operations of the firm with the plans made for them.

All of these budgets articulate together very closely. In fact, the intermediate range budget is simply the first few years of the long-range budget, and the operating budget may be the first year of both of these. This is possible because as the point in time budgeted for becomes closer, progressively more information is collected and included in the budget. Figure 5–2 illustrates these relationships.

FIGURE 5-2
Budgeting through Time

| 19X0 | 19X1 | 19X2 | 19X3 | 19X4 | 19X5 | 19X6 | 19X7 |

19X0 Long-Range Budget

19X0 Intermediate-Range Budget

19X0 Operating Budget

19X1 Long-Range Budget

19X1 Intermediate-Range Budget

19X1 Operating Budget

19X2 Long-Range Budget

19X2 Intermediate-Range Budget

19X2 Operating Budget

Level of Detail

Operating Budget

INTERMEDIATE-RANGE BUDGET

LONG-RANGE BUDGET

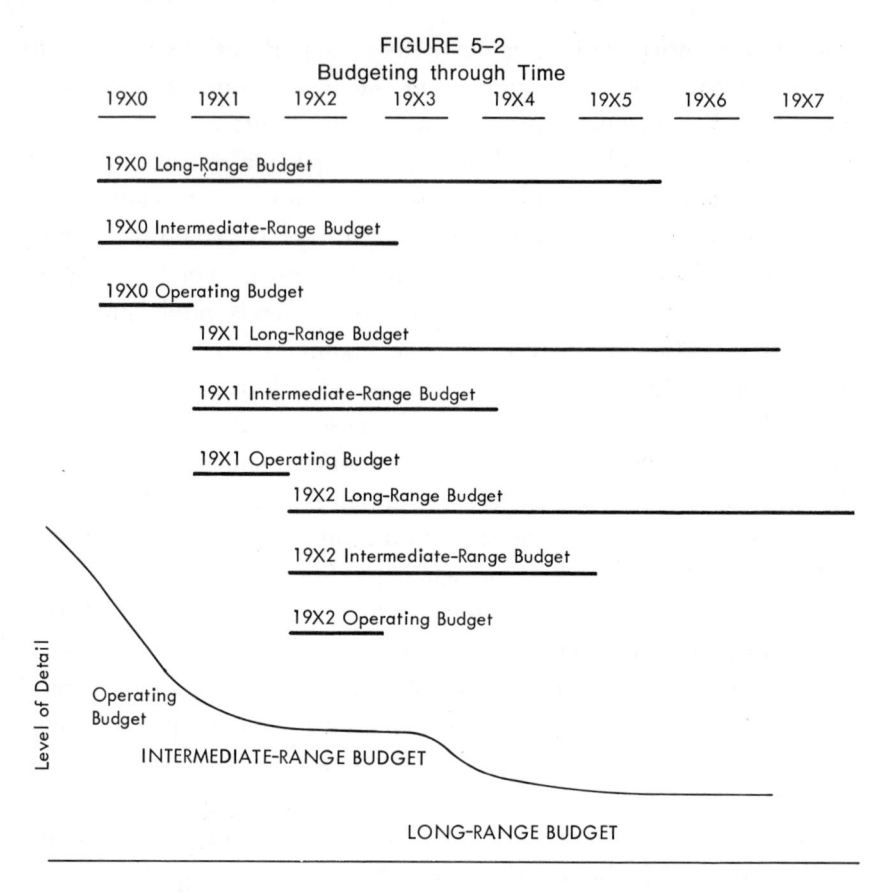

Function or Responsibility

The components of an operating budget will include (but may not be limited to):

Sales forecast and plan	Administrative budget
Sales budget	Capital budget
Inventory policy	Research and development budget
Purchases budget	Cash flow schedule
Manufacturing budget	Pro forma financial statements

In all cases, the budgets follow a form that will permit later comparison with operating results of the responsibility center involved. These comparisons lead to control over operations.

Let us discuss each component in turn.

Sales Forecast and Plan. It is most difficult to look ahead and develop reliable predictions of sales during a future interval because of the large numbers of variables involved. This task will fall upon the economic planning group and the marketing specialization, with the former acting as staff to the latter. Two methodologies will be used together to develop forecasts: statistical analysis and intuitive methods. Statistical techniques may include plotting on graph paper all sales in previous periods and extending the trend thereby revealed. More exact statistical methods such as regression analysis, moving averages, and exponential smoothing are employed by many businesses. When a business management does not itself possess these skills, it is as a rule able to engage outside consultants to provide statistical sales forecasts. Intuitive methods may include the judgments of individuals whose hunches have proven reliable on previous occasions, telephoning a few major customers to determine their buying plans, or exchanging views with marketing executives in other firms. If the two methodologies produce radically different pictures of future sales, the budget staff must try to bring them closer together. Usually one methodology confirms the other and most businesses will accept the redundancy to obtain the additional assurance of reliability in the sales forecasts. The sales *plan* is based on the most reliable sales forecast. Sales plans are prepared by month, by quarter, or other useful subperiod within the overall operating budget interval. In addition, the plan should be broken down into sales by products (or, where there are many products, by product groups) and by selling regions, if there is more than one region. Sales should be expressed in physical units and also in dollars.

Sales Budget. The sales budget is the marketing function's proposed expenditures and activities in support of the sales plan. It may include an advertising budget, a sales administration budget, a direct selling expenses budget, and other subbudgets which detail each activity in this function. A sales budget is always related to a particular sales plan; it should be understood that if either the sales plan or budget is materially changed (to reduce by half the number of calls by salesmen on purchasing agents, for example), the other should be scrutinized for possible revision.

Inventory Policy. The inventories policy will be largely the work of the manufacturing function, which will share responsibility with the marketing and finance functions for determining inventories of finished goods. The purpose of inventories is to provide service—quick deliveries of orders to customers, few or no delays in intraplant transfers, raw materials available as needed. The purpose of the inventories policy is to specify the levels of service inventories will provide. The level of service has to be balanced against the cost involved—and inventories maintenance represents capital which might be better invested elsewhere in a firm. In Chapter 12 you will learn ways of developing sensible inventory policies; here you only need to know that the inventory policy will specify *inventory levels* at the beginning, interim points, and end of the operating budget interval.

Purchases Budget. The purpose of the purchases budget is to schedule materials and supplies acquisition during the year to support the inventory policy and sales forecasts as well as manufacturing schedules. It is easy to compute purchases:

Purchases = Desired ending inventory + Withdrawals by production − Expected beginning inventory (5−1)

Since inventories are specified at several interior points during the budgeting period, we can show at what times materials and supplies have to be delivered to the firm (and, if there is more than one plant, at what locations). If there is a delay period between the time an order is placed and the time the goods arrive at the plant, this period can be subtracted from the desired delivery time, an additional safety factor subtracted, and the necessary order date determined. If suppliers have been tentatively picked, now is the time to alert them and to inquire whether they are able to meet the firm's anticipated needs. The expected costs of purchases are used to prepare dollar estimates of purchases also.

Manufacturing Budget. The manufacturing budget may be the most complex of all the budgets in the firm. It will show the quantities of finished products to be manufactured, the quantities of in-process materials, and the units to be started. From the latter information the purchases budget takes its starting point. The manufacturing budget can be extremely complex when there are many plants and outputs of some of these are inputs for the others. However, many firms have relatively simple manufacturing operations for which there is little difficulty in preparing budgets.

A manufacturing plant should budget at each of its responsibility centers, measuring activity in terms of a major key resource input such as direct labor hours or machine-hours. Other variable costs may be keyed to these major resource inputs. If production responsibility centers are budgeted first, service responsibility centers may be budgeted based on the services they would provide production centers operating at those budgeted levels. When manufacturing activity cannot be forecast very far ahead, the "flexible budget" described in Chapter 10 will be used.

Administrative Budget. The administrative budget sets out the activity levels and expenditures of the major nonmanufacturing, nonsales activities of the firm. Some of these are:

- Accounting and finance
- Public relations
- President's staff
- Economic planning
- Purchasing
- Merger and acquisition staff
- Legal counsel and litigation

These responsibility centers submit budgets in which are detailed—

- Number of employees, rank of employees, salaries
- Supplies expenses
- Travel and entertainment (if any)
- Indirect costs and departmental fixed costs

The budgets should cover the programs to which administrative centers are committed. Although program budgeting is most widely accepted in the public sector, it is also appropriate wherever there is no clear-cut criterion of efficiency (such as standard costs provide in the factory and profit margins provide in marketing) by which to judge scarce factor input utilization. Thus, finance may have to report its operations research, computer software development, debt management, and budgeting *programs* and show how each responsibility center in finance contributes to these programs. Program budgeting lets management judge the effect on all responsibility centers of changing the pace of a specific program.

Capital Budget. Capital budgeting decision making is intended to provide the firm with long-lived assets to deploy in future situations with profit potential. Long-lived (capital) assets require a relatively long lead time for getting into place and use (they cannot be ordered up or replenished as can inventory, for example); at any given moment the business must use the long-lived assets it has on hand. Consequently a major consideration in capital budgeting is to plan the acquisition of assets which have enough flexibility in use to meet all of the future profit opportunities that are likely to occur.

The business pays a price in achieving such flexibility. Multipurpose assets are unlikely to be as profitable in any specific use as assets designed especially to be profitable in that particular use alone, and the more uses an asset is designed to have, the less efficient it will be in any one of them.

The capital budgeting process begins at several levels. Efficiency improvements that require capital expenditures will originate at operating responsibility centers. Proposals for new plants, major capacity expansion, or replacement of one production process by another may originate in the manufacturing function at the highest staff levels or in the economic planning staff. Proposals for capital expenditures in support of marketing, distribution, or research and development will originate within those respective functions—usually at a high level. Proposals for mergers and acquisitions will originate in the finance function, the president's office, or even with the board of directors.

As capital expenditure proposals accumulate, their disposition cannot wait for the budgeting process to be completed. Decisions on proposals are made as they arise. (The selection processes themselves are reviewed in Chapter 11.) The budgeting process attempts to anticipate major categories of capital spending and the functional or profit areas which will receive the benefit of the expenditures. Each area vice president may be asked to make a capital expenditures forecast for his area; these forecasts will be reviewed in the CBO's office. Any revisions or changes will be cleared with the vice presidents involved.

Research and Development Budget. This may be a difficult area to budget since much R&D cannot be directly related to profits earned or to be earned. Fortunately, much research is of the applied variety and may be related to a forthcoming product line, adaptation of equipment to new purposes, and other programs which can be accounted for and controlled. The R&D budget measures the resources going into R&D and the consistency of their use by R&D responsibility centers with planned use. Although there is no logical justification for doing so, some businesses tie their overall R&D expenditure to total revenue, total profit, return on investment, or some other measure of business activity. This attempt to limit R&D costs may be reasonable if it is applied with regard for the programs underway in R&D; it would make little sense to cut back programs with strong promise of increasing future revenue simply because current revenues were falling.

Cash Flow Schedule. From all the budgets prepared, the treasurer identifies cash receipts and disbursements within the budget period. The receipts and disbursements should be identified as to source and sub period so that cash position during the budget period is anticipated.

For example, 94 percent of sales may be on credit; of this percentage, 80 percent is collected in the month following sale, 10 percent is collected in the second month following sale, and 4 percent is uncollectible or paid out in returns and allowances. The 6 percent noncredit sales are for cash, which of course is collected immediately.

Once a sales forecast is developed, cash receipts from sales can be scheduled. The purchases and manufacturing budgets will show the timing and amounts of accounts payable and wages payable liabilities; from these are computed the amount and timing of cash disbursements. To operating disbursements add disbursements for dividends, interest, and capital expenditures. Naturally, the firm may discover a substantial excess of receipts over disbursements (or disbursements over receipts) at times which may be invested in short-term securities to earn extra interest income for the firm. A cash shortage projection is the signal to reduce or defer some activities which lead to cash expenditures, increase activities which lead to cash receipts, or seek additional sources of cash through issue of stock or credit equities.

Pro Forma Financial Statements. These statements are the final rigorous test of the budget process's success in producing an acceptable plan of operations. The pro forma statements present the picture of the business that investors will see at the end of the budgeting period, after the budget has been transformed into history by the firm's operations. If this picture is favorable to the firm, in the opinion of investors, the business will continue to receive capital and support from the financial community. If it is not favorable, capital may be withheld or withdrawn, and the firm will fall upon difficult days.

You have already seen that financial statements present a precise but not always complete description of a firm, and it is quite possible that the firm's operations will be sound, yet this will not be reflected by the financial statements. The firm which realizes this knows that its choices are *limited to those productive activities which will "look good" in the financial statements.*

If the financial statements projected by the budgeting process do not present a picture of the firm which in the opinion of the board of directors will be attractive to outside capital sources (stockholders and creditors), a new budget may have to be prepared which does produce such statements. Thus financial reporting rules and principles do influence the planning and activities of management by channeling them away from business processes which do not look good in financial statements. Examples of such processes might be (until recently) environmental preservation, labor skill upgrading, and waste material recycling.

Activities which may be contrary to the public interest but are encouraged by the rules of financial reporting may include business combinations (certain types), stock options, and market monopolization (restraint of trade).

Accountants are aware of potential for abuse in financial reporting and have established authoritative bodies to minimize it. The foremost of these is the Financial Accounting Standards Board, which attempts to spot abusive financial reporting and eliminate it before it becomes an embarrassment to the accounting profession. Through such activity the quality of financial reporting is being steadily improved; it is approaching the goal of being an objective channel of information to permit efficient capital allocation between firms.

PREPARATION OF AN OPERATING BUDGET

The budgets and schedules you have just read about are best prepared in a recognized sequence, which is illustrated in Figure 5–3.

FIGURE 5–3
Budget Preparation Sequence

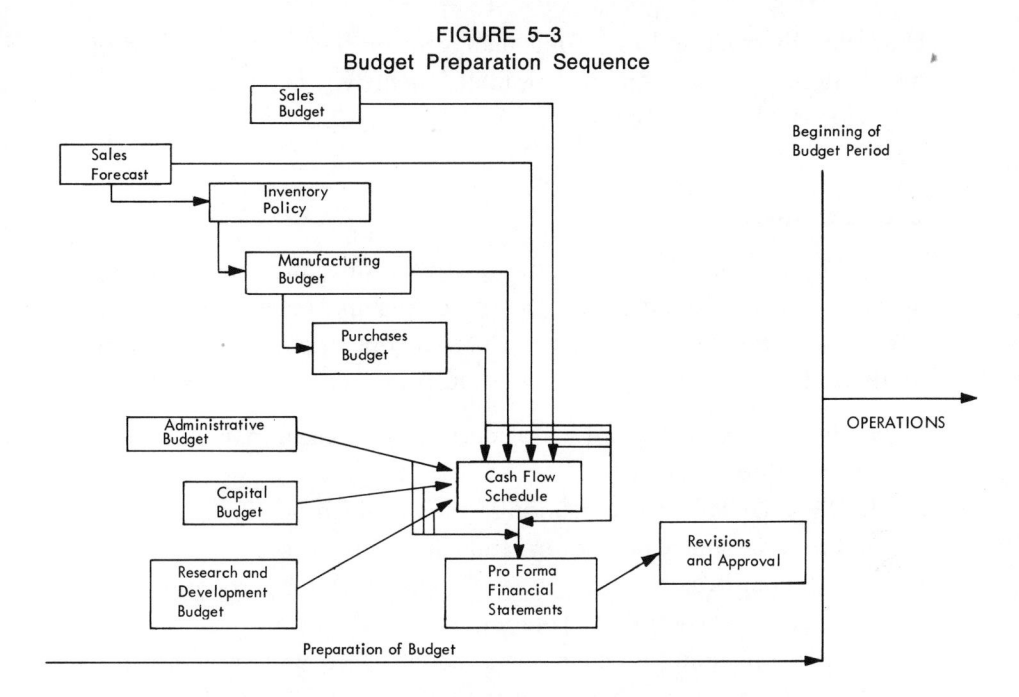

Figure 5–3 could be more detailed since there are many unshown connections and feedback loops between individual budgets. For example, the capital acquisitions budget may be revised based on the results of preparing the cash flow schedule; the manufacturing budget may be revised if a supportive purchases budget cannot be developed. Not shown is the "financial budget" which will be the treasurer's schedule of proposed investments and borrowings to maintain a smooth and adequate cash flow.

BUDGET INSTALLATION

Surprisingly, many businesses large and small do not have budget systems in operation. This section will give you some idea of what such a business must do to develop a useful budget.

Motivation

Some managers will view a budget as a potential threat to their security rather than as a way for them to be rewarded for their efficiency. To encourage their cooperation, a top-level committee of the board of directors and operating management should oversee budget installation. Such a committee's establishment will be the first step a firm should take towards a budget.

Systems Study

The top-level committee of the board of directors and operating management should supervise a study, employing outside consultants if necessary, to determine what the present operations and budgeting needs of the firm are. Points that should be especially checked are:

1. Is there a clear-cut definition of decision responsibility in all operations of the firm?
2. Is there an effective accounting system which produces accurate and timely management information system reports?
3. Are standard costs[2] used wherever appropriate for accounting simplification and control of operations?
4. Is there a planning function operating efficiently within the firm?
5. Is the entire management substantially free of internal conflict?

If these questions can be affirmatively answered, the process of budget installation may proceed.

First Steps. Perhaps one first step is to prepare an annual profit plan. As this plan is in process, the business ought to be preparing sales forecasts, cash flow schedules, capital budgeting procedures, and inventory policies.

Additional Steps. If a standard cost system is appropriate for the business and doesn't yet exist, this would be the time to install it. Using standard costs and production scheduling techniques, a manufacturing budget should be developed. Administrative and research and development budgets can be begun.

Finally. From there, budget installation is a matter of refinement and improvement. Continuously throughout the installation stage, the budget committee must maintain the interest and enthusiasm of all managers for the budget. They should especially understand that the budget is not imposed on them from above but is prepared from the lowest decision-making levels of the firm and travels upward in the

---
[2] Covered in Chapter 6.

organization. It is a formal communication process in which these levels tell top management what can be done, and top management evaluates whether this is acceptable—and if it isn't, provides operating management with the tools to do better.

SUMMARY

A business is organized in a systematic manner, with logical separation of specialized functions such as research, finance, production, and sales. Responsibilities within these functions are clear-cut. Accounting reports permit descriptions of the ways responsibilities are discharged by executives.

Budgeting provides a planning benchmark for comparison with accounting reports to determine how well a responsibility center is performing. Budgets are complex representations of business plans for future operations. The preparation of a budget is not simple. Budget preparation is supported at the highest levels within a business, but the budget itself must be prepared by all levels of responsibility across all functional areas. The budget staff, which is usually responsible to the controller, provides advisory services in assisting executives prepare their budgets.

The first part of the operating budget to be prepared is usually the sales forecast, followed by the sales, inventories, manufacturing, purchasing, research, capital additions, and administrative budgets. These budgets result in many performance schedules, a cash budget, and pro forma financial statements. Such financial statements and budget summaries are forwarded to the board of directors for their study and approval or criticism. It is not uncommon for a budget to be revised or even rejected by the directors if they feel that it doesn't represent an effective operating plan for the business.

The operating budget, described above, is not the only part of the budgeting process that is important. In fact, budgeting can be regarded as going on for a period of time extending into the future as much as 15 to 20 years, with the detail becoming more and more involved and explicit as the plan approaches the present moment—until the budget for the next period is in fact the operating budget.

It is still common to find firms without budgets; however many of these are moving over to some sort of budgeting process to facilitate planning. Computers in many firms simplify and speed up preparation of budget schedules.

APPENDIX 5A: AN EXAMPLE OF BUDGET FORMS AND PROCESS

This section shows you one way different budget components are prepared and assembled. The Gowingplaces Company sells two products, A and B. These products are made in a single plant and sold in the northern and southern sales regions. Budgeting is by quarters

TABLE 5A-1

Schedule S-1
Ref: Sales forecasting support folder

GOWINGPLACES COMPANY
Budget for Year Ending 12-31-74
Sales Plan

	Quarter 1	Quarter 2	Quarter 3	Quarter 4	Year
PART 1—UNITS					
Northern region:					
Product A	1,000	1,200	1,600	1,200	5,000
Product B	2,000	2,000	2,000	2,000	8,000
Southern region:					
Product A	1,000	1,000	1,000	1,000	4,000
Product B	1,500	1,200	1,200	1,600	5,500
Quarterly unit totals:					
Product A	2,000	2,200	2,600	2,200	9,000
Product B	3,500	3,200	3,200	3,600	13,500
PART 2—UNIT SELLING PRICES					
Northern region:					
Product A	$ 100	$ 120	$ 120	$ 125	
Product B	200	200	200	200	
Southern region:					
Product A	90	90	100	100	
Product B	200	200	200	200	
PART 3—DOLLARS					
Northern region:					
Product A	$100,000	$144,000	$192,000	$150,000	$ 586,000
Product B	400,000	400,000	400,000	400,000	1,600,000
Subtotal	$500,000	$544,000	$592,000	$550,000	$2,186,000
Southern region:					
Product A	$ 90,000	$ 90,000	$100,000	$100,000	$ 380,000
Product B	300,000	240,000	240,000	320,000	1,100,000
Subtotal	$390,000	$330,000	$340,000	$420,000	$1,480,000
Total sales	$890,000	$874,000	$932,000	$970,000	$3,666,000
Product A both regions	$190,000	$234,000	$292,000	$250,000	$ 966,000
Product B both regions	700,000	640,000	640,000	720,000	2,700,000

for a one-year budget period. Sales forecasting for the next budget period begins in June preceding beginning of the next year in January. Final forecasts are prepared by September.

Standard cost assumptions are finalized in November preceding the January 1 effective date of the new budget. During November, contacts are made with suppliers and Gowingplaces' bankers and auditors are briefed on the budget. The board of directors acts informally on the budget in draft in late November and formally on the official version sometime before Christmas.

The *sales plan* is prepared with primary reliance on the sales estimates of salesmen in the two sales regions. Selective contacts with major customers and forecasts using two computer programs developed by the economic planning staff are used to validate the data from salesmen. The sales plan which was produced is shown as Schedule S–1 in Table 5A–1. The *sales budget* supporting this plan is shown as Schedule S–2 in Table 5A–2. The assumptions underlying the sales budget are these:

```
Direct selling cost per
    sales dollar:
    Northern region..........  $0.03
    Southern region..........   0.02
Indirect fixed selling costs:
    Northern region..........  $45,000
    Southern region..........   60,000
```

TABLE 5A–2

Schedule S–2
Ref: S–1 and other support

GOWINGPLACES COMPANY
Budget for Year Ending 12-31-74
Sales Budget

	Quarter 1	Quarter 2	Quarter 3	Quarter 4	Whole Year
PART 1–DIRECT SELLING EXPENSES					
Northern region............	$15,000	$16,320	$17,760	$16,500	$ 65,580
Southern region............	7,800	6,600	6,800	8,400	29,600
Total...............	$22,800	$22,920	$24,560	$24,900	$ 95,180
PART 2–FIXED SELLING EXPENSES					
Northern region............	$11,250	$11,250	$11,250	$11,250	$ 45,000
Southern region............	15,000	15,000	15,000	15,000	60,000
Total...............	$26,250	$26,250	$26,250	$26,250	$105,000
Grand total costs.........	$49,050	$49,170	$50,810	$51,150	$200,180

The *inventory policy* is, roughly speaking, to hold at the end of any quarter an inventory equal to 30 percent of the expected transfers out of that inventory during the next quarter. This policy applies to both finished goods and raw materials. The Gowingplaces Company manufacturing process is very rapid and produces virtually no "work in process"; the latter will therefore be ignored in the budgeting schedules. The next budget, shown in Table 5A–3 as Schedule M–1, is the production schedule, which is prepared only in terms of physical units and shows the requirement for production in each quarter as a function of the inventory policy and expected demand for finished goods.

TABLE 5A–3

Schedule M-1
Ref: S-1
inventory policy

GOWINGPLACES COMPANY
Budget for Year Ending 12-31-74
Manufacturing Schedule

	Quarter 1	Quarter 2	Quarter 3	Quarter 4	Whole Year
PART 1–PRODUCT A					
Sales (units)	2,000	2,200	2,600	2,200	9,000
Add: Ending inventory for quarter	660	780	660	600	600
Less: Beginning inventory for quarter	(600)	(660)	(780)	(660)	(600)
Required production	2,060	2,320	2,480	2,140	9,000
PART 2–PRODUCT B					
Sales (units)	3,500	3,200	3,200	3,600	13,500
Add: Ending inventory for quarter	960	960	1,080	960	960
Less: Beginning inventory for quarter	(1,050)	(960)	(960)	(1,080)	(1,050)
Required production	3,410	3,200	3,320	3,480	13,410

Any particular unit of A or B has a "standard composition" in terms of direct inputs. It is necessary to extend these inputs to the scheduled production in order to determine the total input (materials and labor) requirements. Table 5A–4 contains the expected direct inputs to A and B and their expected prices during 1974.

The physical units column is multiplied by the quarterly production requirements for the respective product to obtain the physical units

TABLE 5A-4
Expected Inputs to A and B

Product	Input Identity	Physical Units	Cost per Unit
Product A	Raw material X	6	$5
	Type I direct labor hours	10	3
Product B	Raw material Y	10	3
	Type II direct labor hours	20	4

TABLE 5A-5
Total Direct Production Inputs

Quarter	Quarterly Production Product A (Schedule M-1)	Units Raw Material X Required	Hours Type I Direct Labor Required
1	2,060	12,360	20,600
2	2,320	13,920	23,200
3	2,480	14,880	24,800
4	2,140	12,840	21,400

Quarter	Quarterly Production Product B (Schedule M-1)	Units Raw Material Y Required	Hours Type II Direct Labor Required
1	3,410	34,100	68,200
2	3,200	32,000	64,000
3	3,320	33,200	66,400
4	3,480	34,800	69,600

of S, Y, and the two types of direct labor which are required as inputs each quarter. The results are shown in Table 5A-5.

These requirements can be used as support for a schedule of materials inventories and purchases and a schedule of labor skills requirements. We first prepare these schedules in terms of physical units just as we did Schedule M-1—except of course that labor cannot be inventoried. Schedule M-2 in Table 5A-6 presents these schedules for materials.

5A-7 presents as Schedule M-3 the quarterly requirements for labor.

To complete the description of manufacturing operations, you need a statement of indirect manufacturing costs other than labor.

Indirect materials and supplies are estimated to be 10.6 percent of

TABLE 5A-6

Schedule M-2
Ref: M-1, inventory policy, direct inputs tables, quarterly production computation

GOWINGPLACES COMPANY
Budget for Year Ending 12-31-74
Schedule of Materials Inventories and Purchases

	Quarter 1	Quarter 2	Quarter 3	Quarter 4	Whole Year
PART 1—MATERIAL X					
Needed for production	12,360	13,920	14,880	12,840	54,000
Add: Ending inventory for quarter	4,200	4,500	3,900	3,700	3,700
Less: Beginning inventory for quarter	(3,700)	(4,200)	(4,500)	(3,900)	(3,700)
Required purchases	12,860	14,220	14,280	12,640	54,000
Times purchase price per unit	×5	×5	×5	×5	×5
Purchases material X	$ 64,300	$71,100	$ 71,400	$ 63,200	$270,000
PART 2—MATERIAL Y					
Needed for production	34,100	32,000	33,200	34,800	134,000
Add: Ending inventory for quarter	9,600	10,000	10,400	10,200	10,200
Less: Beginning inventory for quarter	(10,200)	(9,600)	(10,000)	(10,400)	(10,200)
Required purchases	33,500	32,400	33,600	34,600	134,100
Times purchase price per unit	×3	×3	×3	×3	×3
Purchases material Y	$100,500	$97,200	$100,800	$103,800	$402,300

total direct labor. Fixed costs total $55,000 per quarter. All results are shown as Schedule M-4 in Table 5A-8.

We're now ready to prepare the pro forma cost of goods manufactured and cost of goods sold statements.

As presented, these statements are prepared in *contribution analysis* form; they do not report any allocation of fixed costs to units of product. Such allocation is necessary in actual financial statements but is undesirable in budgets, which are intended to be used within the firm.

TABLE 5A-7

Schedule M-3
Ref: M-1, direct inputs tables, quarterly production computation

GOWINGPLACES COMPANY
Budget for Year Ending 12-31-74
Schedule of Labor Hours and Dollars

	Quarter 1	Quarter 2	Quarter 3	Quarter 4	Whole Year
Direct labor hours:					
Type I	20,600	23,200	24,800	21,400	90,000
Times wage rate.	×3	×3	×3	×3	×3
Type I wages	$ 61,800	$ 69,600	$ 74,400	$ 64,200	$ 270,000
Type II.	68,200	64,000	66,400	69,600	268,200
Times wage rate.	×4	×4	×4	×4	×4
Type II wages	$272,800	$256,000	$265,600	$278,400	$1,072,800
Direct labor wages	$334,600	$325,600	$340,000	$342,600	$1,342,800
Indirect labor hours (.20 × total direct labor hours)	17,760	17,440	18,240	18,200	71,640
Times wage rate for indirect labor	×3	×3	×3	×3	×3
Indirect labor wages	$ 53,280	$ 52,320	$ 55,720	$ 54,600	$ 215,920
Total wages	$387,880	$377,920	$395,720	$397,200	$1,558,720

Indirect variable costs amount to $215,920 (labor) and $142,340 (materials, supplies, etc)—a total of *$358,260*. From Table 5A-7, the total number of direct labor hours worked (of which variable indirect costs are primarily a function) is 90,000 + 268,200 = *358,200* hours. From these two figures, you can compute a reasonable budget allocation rate for indirect variable costs of $358,260/358,200 hours = *$1* per direct labor hour. Since 10 direct labor hours are used to make one unit of product A, $10 of indirect variable costs will be included in the manufacturing cost of each unit product A made. Similarly, the 20 direct labor hours included in each unit of product B require $20 of indirect costs in the manufacturing cost of each unit of that product made.

TABLE 5A-8

Schedule M-4
Ref: M-3

GOWINGPLACES COMPANY
Budget for Year Ending 12-31-74
Indirect Manufacturing Costs

	Quarter 1	Quarter 2	Quarter 3	Quarter 4	Whole Year
Depreciation	$20,000	$20,000	$20,000	$20,000	$ 80,000
Insurance, etc.	5,000	5,000	5,000	5,000	20,000
Other fixed expenses	30,000	30,000	30,000	30,000	120,000
Total fixed costs	$55,000	$55,000	$55,000	$55,000	$220,000
Indirect labor wages	$53,280	$52,320	$55,720	$54,600	$215,920
Indirect materials and supplies	35,470	34,510	36,040	36,320	142,340
Total variable indirect costs	$88,750	$86,830	$91,760	$90,920	$358,260

The statement of cost of goods manufactured is Schedule CGM-1, shown as Table 5A-9. Remember that quarterly fixed manufacturing costs are given in Table 5A-8.

Schedule CGS-1, shown in Table 5A-10, is the projected cost of goods sold statement. It assumes unit prices of $70 for A and $130 for B.

Another important budget statement will show the performance of sales regions, each of which is a responsibility center. Table 5A-11 presents such a statement as Schedule CGS-2.

As another example of a performance statement, suppose that each product line is a profit center. We may prepare Schedule CGS-3, shown in Table 5A-12, to budget their respective performances. This statement does not suffer from the same defect as Schedule CGS-2—the cost of goods manufactured in Table 5A-12 is separated into fixed and variable components. The "Total net margin" line is the most important in this statement.

Although additional performance statements could be prepared, we will go on now and illustrate the remaining budgets for the Gowingplaces Company. There is a central administrative office. The major

TABLE 5A-9

Schedule CGM-1

GOWINGPLACES COMPANY
Budget for Year Ending 12-31-74
Cost of Goods Manufactured

	Quarter 1	Quarter 2	Quarter 3	Quarter 4	Whole Year
Product A:					
Material X inputs (M-2)	12,360	13,920	14,880	12,840	54,000
Times cost per unit	×5	×5	×5	×5	×5
Material X value	$ 61,800	$ 69,600	$ 74,400	$ 64,200	$ 270,000
Labor type I (M-3)	61,800	69,600	74,400	64,200	270,000
Total direct costs A	$123,600	$139,200	$148,800	$128,400	$ 540,000
Direct labor hours (alloc. basis)(M-3)	20,600	23,200	24,800	21,400	90,000
Indirect costs (rate = $1 per DLH)	$ 20,600	$ 23,200	$ 24,800	$ 21,400	$ 90,000
Total costs product A	$144,200	$162,400	$173,600	$149,800	$ 630,000
Units manufactured (M-1)	2,060	2,320	2,480	2,140	9,000
Cost per unit (to nearest $)	$ 70	$ 70	$ 70	$ 70	$ 70
Product B:					
Material Y inputs (M-2)	34,100	32,000	33,200	34,800	134,100
Times cost per unit	×3	×3	×3	×3	×3
Material and value	$102,300	$ 96,000	$ 99,600	$104,400	$ 402,300
Labor Type II (M-3)	272,800	256,000	265,600	278,400	1,072,800
Total direct costs B	$375,100	$352,000	$365,200	$382,800	$1,475,100
Direct labor hours (alloc. basis)(M-3)	68,200	64,000	66,400	69,600	268,200
Indirect costs (rate = $1 per DLH)	$ 68,200	$ 64,000	$ 66,400	$ 69,600	$ 268,200
Total costs product B	$443,300	$416,000	$431,600	$452,400	$1,743,300
Units manufactured (M-1)	3,410	3,200	3,320	3,480	13,410
Cost per unit (to nearest $)	$ 130	$ 130	$ 130	$ 130	$ 130

TABLE 5A–10
Budgeted Cost of Goods Sold Statement

Schedule CGS-1
Ref. as noted

GOWINGPLACES COMPANY
Budget for Year Ending 12-31-74
Cost of Goods Sold—Assuming
Oldest Units in Inventory
Are Sold First

	Quarter 1	Quarter 2	Quarter 3	Quarter 4	Whole Year
Northern region:					
Product A (S-1)	$ 70,000	$ 84,000	$112,000	$ 84,000	$ 350,000
Product B (S-1)	260,000	260,000	260,000	260,000	1,040,000
Total cost	$330,000	$344,000	$372,000	$344,000	$1,390,000
Southern region:					
Product A (S-1)	$ 70,000	$ 70,000	$ 70,000	$ 70,000	$ 280,000
Product B (S-1)	195,000	156,000	156,000	208,000	715,000
Total cost	$265,000	$226,000	$226,000	$278,000	$ 995,000
Total cost of A:					
Both regions	$140,000	$154,000	$182,000	$154,000	$ 630,000
Total cost of B:					
Both regions	$455,000	$416,000	$416,000	$468,000	$1,755,000

Note: Cost of sales was computed by multiplying unit sales times unit price from Schedule CGM-1.

functions of administration are accounting, security, and staff. These are shown as Schedule A–1 in Table 5A–13.

There is no research function at Gowingplaces, so naturally there is no research budget. If there were one, it would look a great deal like the administrative budget. We proceed here to an illustration of the capital budget, shown in Table 5A–14 as Schedule CB.

With all these schedules in hand, the firm is able to prepare pro forma financial statements.

There are also other budget schedules, such as the asset additions and retirement schedule and the cash receipts and disbursements schedule which are beyond the scope of an introductory treatment. To conclude this presentation of typical budget schedules, therefore, we select the pro forma income statement (Table 5A–15). We do not prepare the balance sheet because it would introduce factors into the budget other than activities already described.

TABLE 5A-11
Budgeted Regional Sales Performance

Schedule CGS-2
Ref. as noted

GOWINGPLACES COMPANY
Budget for Year Ending 12-31-74

	Quarter 1	Quarter 2	Quarter 3	Quarter 4	Whole Year
Northern region:					
Revenue (S-1)	$ 500,000	$ 544,000	$ 592,000	$ 550,000	$2,186,000
Cost of sales (CGS-1)	330,000	344,000	372,000	344,000	1,390,000
Gross margin	$ 170,000	$ 200,000	$ 220,000	$ 206,000	$ 796,000
Less: variable selling expenses (S-2)	(15,000)	(16,320)	(17,760)	(16,500)	(65,580)
Net margin	$ 155,000	$ 183,680	$ 202,240	$ 189,500	$ 730,420
Less: Fixed selling expenses (S-2)	(11,250)	(11,250)	(11,250)	(11,250)	$ (45,000)
Net contribution, northern region	$ 143,750	$ 172,430	$ 190,990	$ 178,250	$ 685,420
Southern region:					
Revenue (S-1)	$ 390,000	$ 330,000	$ 340,000	$ 420,000	$1,480,000
Cost of sales (CGS-1)	(265,000)	(226,000)	(226,000)	(278,000)	(995,000)
Gross margin	$ 125,000	$ 104,000	$ 114,000	$ 142,000	$ 485,000
Less: Variable selling expenses (S-2)	(7,800)	(6,600)	(6,800)	(8,400)	(29,600)
	$ 117,200	$ 97,400	$ 107,200	$ 133,600	$ 455,400
Less: Fixed selling expenses (S-2)	(15,000)	(15,000)	(15,000)	(15,000)	(60,000)
Net contribution, southern region	$ 102,200	$ 82,400	$ 92,200	$ 118,600	$ 395,400
Total net contribution	$ 245,950	$ 254,830	$ 283,190	$ 296,850	$1,080,820

TABLE 5A–12

Schedule CGS-3
Ref. as noted

GOWINGPLACES COMPANY
Budget for Year Ending 12-31-74
Product Line Performance Budgets

	Quarter 1	Quarter 2	Quarter 3	Quarter 4	Whole Year
Product A:					
Sales (S-1)	$ 190,000	$ 234,000	$ 292,000	$ 250,000	$ 966,000
Variable cost of sales (CGS-1)	(140,000)	(154,000)	(182,000)	(154,000)	(630,000)
Gross margin—A	$ 50,000	$ 80,000	$ 110,000	$ 96,000	$ 336,000
Product B:					
Sales (S-1)	$ 700,000	$ 640,000	$ 640,000	$ 720,000	$ 2,700,000
Cost of sales (CGS-1)	(455,000)	(416,000)	(416,000)	(468,000)	(1,755,000)
Gross margin—B	$ 245,000	$ 224,000	$ 224,000	$ 252,000	$ 945,000
Total gross margin	$ 295,000	$ 304,000	$ 334,000	$ 348,000	$ 1,281,000
Less: Direct selling expenses (S-2)	(22,800)	(22,920)	(24,560)	(24,900)	(95,180)
Total net margin	$ 272,200	$ 281,080	$ 309,440	$ 323,100	$ 1,185,820
Less:					
(1) Fixed manufacturing expense	(55,000)	(55,000)	(55,000)	(55,000)	(220,000)
(2) Fixed selling expense	(26,250)	(26,250)	(26,250)	(26,250)	(105,000)
Total net contribution	$ 190,950	$ 199,830	$ 228,190	$ 241,850	$ 860,820

TABLE 5A–13

Schedule A-1

GOWINGPLACES COMPANY
Budget for Year Ending 12-31-74
Administrative Budget

	Quarter 1	Quarter 2	Quarter 3	Quarter 4	Whole Year
Accounting:					
Professional salaries	$ 22,000	$ 22,000	$ 22,000	$ 25,000	$ 91,000
Assistants' salaries	11,000	11,000	11,000	11,000	44,000
Equipment rental	9,000	9,000	9,000	9,000	36,000
Supplies	3,000	4,000	5,000	4,000	16,000
	$ 45,000	$ 46,000	$ 47,000	$ 49,000	$187,000
Security:					
Guard salaries	$ 1,500	$ 1,500	$ 1,500	$ 1,500	$ 6,000
Other expenses	3,000	3,000	3,000	3,000	12,000
	$ 4,500	$ 4,500	$ 4,500	$ 4,500	$ 18,000
Staff:					
Executive salaries	$ 25,000	$ 25,000	$ 25,000	$ 25,000	$100,000
Secretarial salaries	5,000	5,000	5,000	5,000	20,000
Professional salaries	10,000	10,000	10,000	10,000	40,000
Supplies	2,000	2,000	2,000	2,000	8,000
Other expenses	1,000	2,000	4,000	1,000	8,000
	$ 43,000	$ 44,000	$ 46,000	$ 43,000	$176,000
Other expenses:					
Depreciation— offices	$ 6,000	$ 6,000	$ 6,000	$ 6,000	$ 24,000
Various amortizations	5,000	5,000	5,000	5,000	20,000
	$ 11,000	$ 11,000	$ 11,000	$ 11,000	$ 44,000
Total administrative budgets	$103,500	$105,500	$108,500	$107,500	$425,000

TABLE 5A–14

Schedule CB
Supporting
detail on
indicated
schedules

GOWINGPLACES COMPANY
Budget for Year Ending 12-31-74
Capital Additions Schedule

	Quarter 1	Quarter 2	Quarter 3	Quarter 4	Whole Year
Marketing:					
Transport vehicles (CB-1)	$28,000	$ 0	$ 20,000	$10,000	$ 58,000
Warehouse in Cleveland (CB-1)	0	10,000	55,000	0	65,000
Total	$28,000	$10,000	$ 75,000	$10,000	$123,000
Manufacturing:					
Versing machine in plant	$ 0	$ 0	$150,000	$10,000	$160,000
Total	$ 0	$ 0	$150,000	$10,000	$160,000
Administration:					
Architectural studies for new offices (CB-3)	$ 0	$ 7,000	$ 0	$ 0	$ 7,000
Total capital	$ 0	$ 7,000	$ 0	$ 0	$ 7,000
Total capital expenditures	$28,000	$17,000	$225,000	$20,000	$290,000

TABLE 5A-15
Budgeted Income Statement

Schedule FS-1

GOWINGPLACES COMPANY
Budget for Year Ending 12-31-74
Income Statement

	Quarter 1	Quarter 2	Quarter 3	Quarter 4	Whole Year
Sales (S-1)	$ 890,000	$ 874,000	$ 932,000	$ 970,000	$ 3,666,000
Less:					
Variable cost of sales	(595,000)	(570,000)	(598,000)	(622,000)	(2,385,000)
Variable selling costs	(22,800)	(22,920)	(24,560)	(24,900)	(95,180)
Net margin	$ 362,200	$ 281,080	$ 309,440	$ 323,900	$ 1,185,820
Less:					
(1) Fixed manufacturing expense	(55,000)	(55,000)	(55,000)	(55,000)	(220,000)
(2) Fixed selling expense	(26,250)	(26,250)	(26,250)	(26,250)	(105,000)
Net contribution	$ 190,950	$ 199,830	$ 228,190	$ 241,850	$ 860,820
Less: Administrative expenses (A-1)	(103,500)	(105,500)	(108,500)	(107,500)	(425,000)
Profit before taxes and dividends	$ 87,450	$ 94,330	$ 119,690	$ 134,350	$ 435,820
Less:					
Estimated taxes	(30,000)	(30,000)	(30,000)	(30,000)	(120,000)
Estimated dividends	(20,000)	(20,000)	(20,000)	(20,000)	(80,000)
Estimated addition to retained earnings	$ 37,450	$ 44,330	$ 69,690	$ 84,350	$ 235,820

QUESTIONS

1. What are some reasons that the use of budgets has grown over the years among businesses?

2. Does the chief budget officer have the authority to order changes in an unacceptable department or division budget? Why is authority distributed this way?

3. The Ajax Corporation decided not to have a president's or director's budget committee "because it will waste too much of our valuable

time to be snooping into every department in this firm," said the president. Comment.

4. The manager of the computer components division refused to accept his budget adviser, saying, "The man is nothing but a spy and a factotum for the controller." What could you say that might disabuse the manager of this quaint notion?

5. On the other hand, suppose the manager in Question 4 above is correct. Who should take what steps to correct the situation?

6. The Granoff Company decided to install a budget. Their first step was to direct the preparation of pro forma financial statements by the public relations officer. Criticize this approach.

7. In which budgets is the greatest level of detail found? Why is this so?

8. Each year the Smith Company prepares a totally new five-year budget, starting from scratch in all forecasts and assumptions. In addition, a separate staff works on the operating budget. Can you suggest any efficiencies that might be realized from changing these policies?

9. In the Bell Company the sales forecast is prepared by the manufacturing division. The company has a chronic oversupply of several hard-to-sell, easy-to-make items in its product line. Suggest relationships between these situations.

10. The Hasti Company budgets its complex manufacturing division very carefully, but has no sales or administrative budgets "because those are such simple things compared to manufacturing." The latter two operations spend as much money combined as does manufacturing. Comment.

11. When the Welsch Company decided to establish a profit planning and control system, the management employees became very upset. Why? What should be done to alleviate their distress?

12. The Roosevelt Company board of directors wishes to establish a budget system. The company management at this time is in the midst of a bitter argument whether to locate a new production facility overseas. This argument has caused considerable bad blood between factions in the management. The board of directors hopes

the new budget will "get our boys pulling together again." What do you think—and why?

13. Why should the operating budget information be comparable with actual operating data?

14. Why should the operating budget be expressed as a series of performance statements?

15. Why should performance statements not lump together fixed and variable costs, if the statements are going to be of maximum utility?

16. Why is the board of directors interested in the pro forma financial statements as a major criterion of budget acceptability?

17. How might a budget take into account such nonprofit objectives as environmental preservation?

EXERCISES

18. It is time to prepare the 1976 operating budget. The intermediate range budget shows, for 1976, the following figures:

Sales	$ 45,000,000
Cost of sales	(30,000,000)
Administrative costs	(10,000,000)
Profit	$ 5,000,000

Review of the assumptions underlying this budget show that they should be revised as follows: sales up 10 percent, cost of sales up 15 percent, administrative costs down 5 percent. Compute the new budgeted profit.

19. The sales forecast is to sell 10,000 units of product A and 50,000 units of product B. There are seven regional sales offices. The sales budget is: $50,000 indirect costs at each sales office, $100,000 in central administration, and $5 for each unit of product A sold, $3 for each unit of product B sold. Compute the total sales budget.

20. Purchases of raw materials for use in manufacturing must be made (orders placed) three months before the materials are scheduled for use in manufacturing. The manufacturing schedule is:

January: 10,000 units
February: 20,000 units
March: 30,000 units
April: 40,000 units

Each unit includes 7 pounds of material 56, costing $20 per pound. All orders are on credit and are paid for two months after the order is placed. Prepare a schedule showing when orders should be placed for material 56, and a second schedule showing when material 56 will have to be paid for in cash.

21. The capital budgeting staff is reviewing proposals for capital expenditures. There are six proposals, all calling for costs of $100,000 each and a useful lifetime of five years. The rates of return are 10, 20, 30, 25, 35, and 15 percent. The capital budget is only $300,000; choose the projects which will offer the highest rate of return for a $300,000 expenditure.

22. Savage Company does not mind borrowing money if it can anticipate doing so and negotiate a lower rate of interest. The rate for unscheduled borrowing is 12 percent per year; the rate for scheduled borrowing is 9 percent per year. In an average year, $44,000,000 is borrowed for an average period of time of 90 days. Compute the potential savings if Savage Company can schedule (budget) all of its borrowing activities.

23. Dim Company is preparing to install a budget. Below are some steps being considered for the installation process. Select those which are properly part of this process and put them in proper sequence:
    a) Forecast sales.
    b) Develop a system of standard costs.
    c) Appoint a top-level committee to oversee installation.
    d) Prepare an annual profit plan.
    e) Develop an organization chart for the business.
    f) Establish regional manufacturing plants.
    g) Acquire a computer.

24. Cling Company has a margin on sales which is, year in and year out, constant at 50 percent. Cling is developing a research budget and estimates that research increases sales in the following way:

    Research expenditures up to $100,000 increases sales $3 for each $1 spent on research.
    From $100,001 to $200,000, research expenditures increase sales $2.50 for each $1 spent on research.
    From $200,001 to $300,000, research expenditures increase sales $1.75 for each $1 spent on research.

From $300,001 to $400,000, research expenditures increase sales $1 for each $1 spent on research.

What is the ideal-size research budget to produce the largest total contribution minus research expenditures?

PROBLEMS

25. River City Community Center, located in a growing medium-size town, is preparing to expand its facilities but first must have some notion of future demand for facilities—in other words, it must do some planning. Use of the community center is closely related to the number of families in River City. City fathers believe that the center must contain 500 square feet for each 1,000 families living in the city. For each 1,000 families, the center will be used 200 hours per year. Each hour of use requires 0.08 hours of supervisory time at $4 per hour, and other expenses of $1.50.

    A forecast from the local university department of demography showed the following annual numbers of families in River City:

Year	19x4	19x5	19x6	19x7
Families	8,000	9,000	11,000	11,000

    The center's fixed costs are negligible. The city reimburses the center for any operating losses.

    Required:
    a) Prepare a forecast of expenses for the years 19x4 through 19x7.
    b) If expansion can be in multiples of 1,000 feet of floor space and present floor space is 5,000 square feet, will an expansion be required by or before 19x7? If one year is required to design, approve, and construct an addition, in which year should any needed addition be begun?

26. Burnoose Manufacturing Company makes headlamps for small automobiles. These lamps are for the new and replacement markets. You were hired last June to become assistant controller, and since that time have become familiar with the company. The controller has asked you to prepare the next quarterly sales budget. You have the following information:

    Sales are forecast as 70 percent of last quarter's sales plus 5 percent of automobile production three years ago. Last quarter's sales were 300,000 lamps. Auto production three years ago was 1,200,000 cars. Selling price of lamps is estimated by this formula:

$$\begin{matrix}\text{Selling}\\\text{price}\\\text{this}\\\text{quarter}\end{matrix} = \begin{matrix}\text{Selling}\\\text{price}\\\text{last}\\\text{quarter}\end{matrix} \times \left\{1.05 - \frac{\begin{matrix}\text{Last}\\\text{quarter's}\\\text{sales}\end{matrix} - \begin{matrix}\text{This}\\\text{quarter's}\\\text{forecast}\end{matrix}}{1,000,000}\right\}$$

Selling price per lamp last quarter was $0.90 per lamp.

The sales department has fixed costs of: supervisory salaries, $20,000; office administration, $10,000; and institutional advertising, $30,000. In addition, a commission of 2 percent is paid to salesmen, and travel and entertainment run about $0.02 for each lamp sold.

Required:

a) Prepare a sales forecast.
b) Prepare a sales budget.
c) Prepare a pro forma income statement, assuming that direct manufacturing expenses are $0.20 per lamp, fixed manufacturing expenses are $30,000, and that administrative and other expenses are $50,000.

27. Budding Contractors, Inc. is a growing construction firm. Much of its construction is done on credit, and recently the firm's traditional source of credit, the Money State Bank, has been urging the firm to develop a budget system as a basis for supporting loan requests. As controller of the firm, you have decided to develop a cash budget for the month of June.

During June, billings are expected to be $300,000. These billings are due upon receipt by customers, but most customers procrastinate; only 30 percent of a month's billings are actually collected in cash that month. Sixty percent are collected the following month, and 10 percent are uncertain of collection, subject to adjustment, and so on. Billings in May were $200,000.

Employees are paid in cash at the end of each week. There are four paydays in June. Employees work about 3,000 hours per week and earn wages which in cash payments amount to about $5.50 per hour. In addition, there are six management personnel whose average salary (paid monthly) is $1,000 per month each.

During June, the firm will acquire for cash a new bulldozer costing $22,000 and will have other expenses of $45,000. Depreciation on building and equipment will be included in this amount to the extent of $10,000. Other noncash expenses are negligible.

Three months ago, Budding sold a piece of land originally held for development and accepted at $30,000 90-day note bearing 8 percent interest as partial payment. This note plus interest should be collected in June. The cash balance at the beginning of June is $40,000, and the company owes $120,000 on which interest of 1 percent per month or fraction of a month is paid in cash.

Required:

a) Prepare a schedule showing on one side all cash receipts and on the other side all cash disbursements expected for June. To the receipts side add beginning cash balance; to the disbursements side add ending cash balance such that the two sides are equal.
b) If Budding prefers to maintain a cash balance at the end of June of no less than $50,000, how much can the company borrow or pay back and still meet this constraint?
c) The bank has determined that it will not loan Budding any more than 150 percent of an average month's cash collections. If June is taken as the average month, what amount is the ceiling on total loans to Budding?

28. Commercial Garages, Inc. performs maintenance work on commercial vehicles on a contract basis. There is a central shop into which cars, trucks, and special-purpose vehicles are scheduled for the required work. It is possible to predict work level and resource requirements to a high degree of precision, although the company has never done this. One problem as a result of no planning has been periods of inordinate delay in getting vehicles back out of the shop—so the management has determined to prepare shop budgets, hoping that later these will lead to sequences and schedules.

There are three work centers in the shop: A, drive train; B, steering and chassis; and C, body. For the month of July, A will have available 500 mechanic hours, B will have 800 mechanic hours, and C will have 200 mechanic hours.

An average vehicle requires 4 hours at A, 3 hours at B, and 10 hours at C. Not all vehicles require work at all stations.

During July, the following jobs have been scheduled:

Job	No. Vehicles	Work Required at Center A	B	C
1.......	10	Yes	Yes	No
2.......	50	No	Yes	Yes
3.......	30	Yes	Yes	No
4.......	40	Yes	Yes	Yes

Required:

a) Determine the expected July work load at each center.

b) If one center has more work than another, so that a center has idle mechanic hours, these mechanics can be used at the overloaded center. However, the mechanics are only able to work *half* as fast since they are unfamiliar with the type of work done. Show which centers should reassign their personnel. Can all the work accepted for July be completed that month?

29. The Peurile Soap Company has heard about profit planning and would like to try it. You are the company's controller. You are asked by the president to draw up some quick schedules "so we can see how much of a problem would be involved."

As your first try at budgeting, you decide to prepare some simple second-quarter schedules—April, May, and June, 1974. Sales at Peurile are quite seasonal, and the seasonal indices are

March	100	Actual March sales, $100,000
April	110	
May............	115	
June	120	

The average variable cost of production is 40 percent of retail selling price; the average variable selling costs are 22 percent of selling price. Manufacturing fixed costs are $12,000 per month. All of the variable costs and 75 percent of the fixed costs are out-of-pocket costs; the remainder are accruals such as depreciation and prepaid insurance.

About 80 percent of sales are on credit, resulting in accounts receivable. Half of the new accounts receivable are collected in the month of sale; the remainder are collected the following month. The remaining 20 percent of sales are for cash, which is of course collected on the spot.

Administrative expenses are $8,000; $10,000; and $9,000 as budgeted for April, May, and June respectively, and are paid in cash the month incurred.

All out-of-pocket expenses are credited to accounts payable. All accounts payable are paid the month after they are incurred. In April the company intends to buy more land for the plant, paying $20,000 for it (this is not a tax-deductible expense). In June the company must repay a loan which with accumulated interest amounts to $58,000; of this total, $5,000 is interest expense. The company is subject to a 40 percent tax on net income. Tax installments are due each month, based on that month's net income estimate.

If end of month cash balance is less than $50,000, the company will borrow in multiples of $10,000; if cash balance is greater than $60,000, the company will repay any such short term loans, again in multiples of $10,000. You may ignore interest charges on such loans.

Required:

a) Prepare a cost of goods sold schedule, assuming full application of fixed overhead to units of product produced. Since Peurile soap doesn't keep too well, there are no beginning or ending inventories to consider.

b) Prepare an income statement by months for this quarter for Peurile Soap Company.

c) Assume the beginning cash balance on April 1 will be $50,000. Prepare a statement of cash receipts and disbursements for this quarter, including tax payments, borrowings, cash expenses, accounts receivables collections, etc.

30. Randy's Typewriter Store handles typewriters, calculators, dictating machines, and copiers. The store is in the midst of the downtown area and does a very brisk business, but is also quite limited for space. Since the items sold are bulky, the store likes to limit its inventories to the minimum possible quantities by ordering from its suppliers as needed every two weeks. Such an order will be placed on March 10, for delivery on Monday, March 13.

On March 10, inventories are

Typewriters	22
Calculators	4
Dictating equipment	12
Copiers	3

On March 24, Randy's wishes to have five fewer typewriters, four more calculators, the same number of dictating sets, and one more copier in stock.

Sales during the next two weeks are expected to be higher than usual. Randy expects that typewriter and calculator sales will be 20 percent higher than in the corresponding interval a year ago; dictating equipment, 10 percent higher; and copiers, 30 percent higher.

Sales one year ago were, in the corresponding interval:

Typewriters	120
Calculators	20
Dictating equipment	40
Copiers	10

Required:

a) Compute the order quantities for Randy's Typewriter Store.
b) How do you think Randy's arrived at the sales estimates; that is, what factors were taken into consideration?

31. Spare-Time Hobby Company operates under a budgeting plan which calls for the board of directors to review an annual budget once each quarter. The budget reviewed adds a new quarter each time. It is unusual for a budget to be rejected, but this time it has happened; the board of directors has ordered a new budget prepared which would show at least a 10 percent return on present owners' equity of $22,000,000.

Spare-Time makes two product lines for use by home craftsmen. The rejected budget called for sales in line A of $30,000,000 and in line B of $40,000,000. The percentage of variable costs in line A is 60 percent and in line B, 80 percent. Fixed factory costs are budgeted at $10,000,000; selling and administrative costs would be $9,000,000.

After considerable reworking of forecasts and estimates, two alternative plans were developed:

Plan 1: Line A sales up 10 percent over original budget.
Line A variable costs 58 percent of sales.
Line B sales and variable costs unchanged.
Fixed factory costs unchanged.
Selling and administrative costs up by $300,000.

Plan 2: Line A sales up 2 percent over original budget.
Line A variable costs 60 percent of sales.
Line B sales up 20 percent.
Line B variable costs 87 percent of sales.
Fixed factory costs up $100,000.
Selling and administrative costs up $500,000.

Required:

Determine whether either of these plans will produce a profit that meets the board of directors' specification.

32. Hoary Age Clock Company makes floor clocks (grandfather clocks) which it sells either as finished clocks or as build-it-yourself kits. The finished clocks require 80 hours of direct labor to complete; the kits require 30 hours of direct labor. The present plant facility employs 200 men who perform direct labor, each working 40 hours per week. No overtime is permitted.

In 1973 the plant completed and shipped an average of 50 finished clocks and 100 kits per week. The contribution per unit, considering only selling price and direct costs, was $20 per finished clock and $16 per kit.

Allen Upe, the marketing vice president, has proposed a plan to market the company's clocks and kits by mail, as well as through the conventional channels. Estimated costs of the mail marketing effort would be $750 per week. Mr. Upe believes that 5 finished clocks and 50 clock kits could be sold each week through the mail.

Required:

a) Determine whether there is enough plant capacity (labor hours available) to make as many clocks as were made last year *plus* the clocks that may be distributed by mail this year.

b) Assume that capacity is available. Can enough clocks be sold by mail to justify the additional marketing costs? Answer this question by preparing a statement comparing the contribution on clocks to be sold this way with the costs of selling by mail.

33. Biel Corporation makes and sells medical-surgical supplies. Last year the company established a new division to introduce a line of prepackaged operating room "kits." One of these kits, completely sterile and ready, could be used for one operation, then discarded.

156   An Introduction to Accounting for Decision Making and Control

The cut-and-run division, as it is called, has conducted test-marketing and has prepared the following budget for the year 1975:

Sales, deluxe model, 5,000 @ $90 each.	$ 450,000
Less:	
Cost of sales 5,000 @ $30 each	(150,000)
Variable selling expense, 5,000 @ $20 each	(100,000)
Contribution	$ 200,000
Sales, standard model, 15,000 @ $60 each.	$ 900,000
Less:	
Cost of sales, 15,000 @ $25 each	(375,000)
Variable selling expense, 15,000 @ $20 each	(300,000)
Contribution	$ 225,000
Total contribution.	$ 425,000
Less:	
Manufacturing fixed costs	(150,000)
Fixed selling costs	(200,000)
Administrative costs	(100,000)
Contribution to Biel Corporation margin (loss)	$(25,000)

This budget was rejected by the budget committee. Cut-and-run executives decided that fixed selling expense could be reduced by 25 percent without affecting sales levels. While the budget was being revised, a rival firm announced that it also was introducing a line of similar operating room kits. If Biel kept its prices the same, the rival firm would probably get 30 percent of Biel's kit sales. But if Biel lowered its prices by $10 on each kit, sales would, in spite of the competition, probably actually increase by 10 percent.

Required:

a) If there were no competing operating room kits, and fixed selling expense is reduced, what would cut-and-run division's contribution be?

b) If there is competition from the rival firm, which set of prices—unchanged or dropped by $10—will produce the largest profit or least loss?

c) Even with competition, Biel expects to sell 120,000 operating room kits over the next three years. What will the average annual profit or loss be if this estimate is correct? (Assume 25 percent of these sales will be the deluxe model, and all sales at $80 and $50 respectively, and all other costs as shown above, *with* the fixed selling expense reduction.)

d) In 1975, actual sales are 2,000 deluxe kits and 5,000 standard kits. Should you consider this information when deciding whether to continue the kit program? Assume all fixed and indirect costs are avoidable if the program is terminated.

DECISION CASE 5–1: MIDTOWN HOTEL

The Midtown Hotel operates as a travel and convention center in the city of Midtown. Midtown Hotel's budget chief, William A. (Feather) Bedd, believes that all of the hotel's activities depend in level on the general economic condition of the surrounding geographic region. This region is primarily agricultural and wood product-oriented. The prosperity of agriculture depends on rainfall, and the prosperity of wood products depends on home building nationwide. Both of these industries schedule conventions, annual meetings, and sales presentations at the hotel. Mr. Bedd believes that this equation relates the occupancy to the economy:

$$\text{No. of rooms to be occupied by one person for one night each (room-person-days)} = 1{,}000 \times \left(\begin{array}{c}\text{No. of inches of rain-}\\ \text{fall the preceding year}\end{array}\right) + 0.05 \times \left(\begin{array}{c}\text{No. of family dwelling}\\ \text{units built in region}\\ \text{the preceding year}\end{array}\right)$$

In 1975 the average rainfall for the Midtown area was 30 inches (on the low side). Four million family dwelling units were started nationwide, 20 percent of them in the Midtown region.

The hotel's functions all key on the occupancy of its rooms. Each room occupied by one person one night brought in $10 in room charge, $6 in meal charges, and $5 in bar charges in 1975. Mr. Bedd has been informed by various managers that room rates will rise 5 percent, food prices will stay the same, and bar charges will go down 10 percent in 1976. The hotel has about $300,000 in annual fixed charges, and in addition, about 40 percent of room charges, 70 percent of meal charges, and 30 percent of bar charges are variable costs to the hotel. Taxes are 30 percent of net income.

The hotel's owners have received an offer for the hotel of $2,000,000 from a national chain; however, they have determined not to sell if this is less than nine times expected 1976 earnings.

Required:

a) Prepare the 1976 budget.
b) Determine whether, if Mr. Bedd is asked, he should recommend that the owners accept the national chain's offer to buy the hotel.

BIBLIOGRAPHY

Books

Chamberlain, Neil W. *The Firm: Micro-economic Planning and Action.* New York: McGraw-Hill Book Co., 1962.

Copulsky, William. *Practical Sales Forecasting.* New York: American Management Association, 1970.

Heckert, J. Brooks, and Willson, James D. *Business Budgeting and Control.* 3d ed. New York: The Ronald Press Co., 1967.

N.A.A. Research Report No. 42, *Long Range Planning.* New York: National Association of Accountants, 1964.

Miley, Arthur L. *Directory of Planning, Budgeting, and Control Information.* Oxford, Ohio: Planning Executives Institute, 1969.

Report of the President's Commission on Budget Concepts. Washington, D.C.: U.S. Government Printing Office, 1967.

Welsch, Glenn A. *Budgeting: Profit Planning and Control.* 3rd ed. Englewood Cliffs, N.J.: Prentice-Hall, Inc., 1971.

———, and Sord, Burnard H. *Business Budgeting.* New York: Controllership Foundation, 1962.

Articles

Ansoff, H. Igor, and Brandenburg, Richard C. "A Program of Research in Business Planning," *Management Science,* February 1967.

Osler, Paul W. "Long-range Forecasts: Where Do We Go from Here," *Management Accounting,* January 1971.

Prestbo, John A. "Budgeting Business," *The Wall Street Journal,* December 20, 1965, p. 1.

Schiff, Michael, and Lewin, Arie Y. "Where Traditional Budgeting Fails," *Financial Executive,* May 1968.

6

Standard Costs and Control of Activities

IN CHAPTER 4 you learned how costs can be accumulated and attached to activities. There were two processes involved: one, the *flow of resources* through an economic entity; the other, the *flow of costs attached to resources*. The present chapter introduces an accounting concept which is a departure from strictly representing the costs attached to a flow of resources. The concept is *standard costing*. Standard costing has these important advantages:

1. Simplifies accounting records of activity.
2. Increases the number of activities that can be controlled by one manager.
3. Provides goals or benchmarks for responsibility centers to evaluate their performance and contribution to overall company profitability.
4. Provides consistent income and asset measurement for financial reporting.
5. Simplifies planning future activity.

A standard cost is used in product costing or cost accumulation at responsibility centers *instead of* the actual or historical cost. In Chapter 2 you learned that costs are used in the information system to signify inputs and finished products. Actual historical costs may be hard to compute, especially if resource prices fluctuate and resource units are hard to distinguish from one another. A standard cost is a single cost figure used in place of historical costs that might correspond to units of a particular resource. As an example, you might have these historical cost figures for successive repetitions of an activity:

$$345 \qquad 320 \qquad 300 \qquad 350 \qquad 340$$

While these figures have some slight documentary significance, they require time to compute and would obscure the significance of inventory valuation and income calculation, for the accounting system would have to keep track separately of the inventory and cost of sales corresponding to each different product cost figure. There is insignificant, unavoidable natural variation in cost per unit among different units of the same item. It isn't reasonable to expect the accounting information system to be cluttered this way with natural variation. Identical units of the same product should not be carried at insignificantly different costs in inventory; nor, if sold at the same time, same price, and to the same buyer, should they indicate different contributions to profit.

To avoid these difficulties, standard costs have been widely accepted. For the activity above, you might designate the average cost, $331, as the standard to be used whenever a cost is needed. The figures above would be modified like this:

Historical cost.........	345	320	300	350	340
Standard cost	331	331	331	331	331
Difference or variation	+14	−11	−31	+19	+9

The historical cost has really been resolved into two components: the standard cost of $331 and a variation from the standard cost. Standard costs can be used for documentation, valuation, planning, and control. *Variations* from standard costs, called variances, act as signals for the control function to use in determining when management action is needed.

USES OF STANDARD COSTS

Simplify Accounting Records

Imagine that you are accounting for costs in a machine shop. If you do not have standard costs, you must record the cost of all materials and supplies passing through the shop. You must record all labor wages and cause them to follow the work performed through the shop. Each period new product costs, new indirect cost allocations, and new work in process costs will be computed.

If you use standard costs, you need only record the standard costs for all materials, labor, and indirect costs as they are acquired and associate these with work performed. Differences between standard and actual costs are noted for later analysis.

For example, suppose you buy for $4,000 cash some materials with a standard cost of $3,500. The cost valuation of materials in inventory will be increased by $3,500 (added to left-hand side of T-account); cash will be decreased by $4,000 (added to right-hand side of Cash T-account), and there will be an unfavorable "purchasing variance" of $500 (added to left-hand side of a Purchase Variance T-account).

The particular items in inventory are then carried at the same unit prices as all similar items placed there at all other times as a result of earlier purchases. You do not need to trace the invoice price for this particular batch of materials as it is issued to the machine shop; you use the standard cost per unit. Further, the unfavorable purchasing variance relates to the act of *purchase* rather than to the *use* of these materials.

The same reasoning applies to wage rates. If a standard rate is used for each type of labor, that rate will be used to compute an accounting cost for that labor at whatever time it is incorporated into products—even if actual wage rates disagree with the standard (an example of the latter would be a substitution of another type of labor for that specified).

Increase Management Span of Control

Historical costs give subjective indications of the control state of a process, since the manager must provide his own standard of comparison—and managers are not consistent in such standards or their application. Without standard costs and variances from them, managers investigate each process or activity to determine if it is operating satisfactorily. If standard costs are used in management performance reports, many processes can undoubtedly be shown to be operating satisfactorily and not in need of corrective attention. The manager can devote his talents to processes requiring attention. This is called *management by exception* and is a foundation principle of efficient management. When management by exception is possible, a manager may take responsibility for more activities.

Goals or Benchmarks

An important contribution of standard costs is the description they furnish of satisfactory performance. If studies have shown that 2.0 yards of material are sufficient to produce a pair of pants and one cutter regularly requires 2.5 yards, a strong presumption is created that this cutter's efficiency can be improved.

The first performance standards were "work norms" or quotas developed for employees by "efficiency experts" whose objectives were honorable but often misinterpreted. Modern performance standard formulation practices take into account the effect of standards on employees and involve employees in the standard setting process. When employees help set the standards, they are willing to accept performance evaluations based on them.

You should establish separate standards for each activity. For example, a coffee table may require:

wood	1	$4 \times 4 \times \frac{1}{2}''$ panel
sanding	3	hours
nailing	1	hour
finishing	1	hour

If the latter three operations are done at different responsibility centers, it would not be proper to combine them into a single five-hour labor standard for coffee tables. Only through separate standards could you appraise each center's efficient use of labor. A "joint" standard shared by several centers is loss of control, since no center is singly answerable for complying with it.

Well-prepared standards do more than spur workers and managers to efficiency. They provide an opportunity for satisfaction in legitimate achievement. Well-prepared standards will prevent a supervisor from pushing his department beyond reasonable limits, protecting human and material resources from exploitation.

Rational Income and Asset Measurement

We have mentioned the unavoidable fluctuation of actual costs. In most cases standard costs will produce an expected cost of production per unit that can be used as a basis for inventory valuation, pricing decisions, activity analysis, and income measurement (computing cost of goods sold).

Cost consistency produces understandable financial statements and managerial reports. A manager will be unable to measure his own department's effectiveness if its inputs are "costed" at different amounts from period to period. His concern is not with cost variations that occur in other departments and processes, but with those that he can control as part of his own responsibilities. Standard costs focus his attention on these.

Standard Costs in Planning

Standard costs simplify planning operations by serving as estimates of future costs. In planning, a standard cost may be regarded as a cost of resource input per unit of output. The standard cost consists of two parts:

	(1)	(2)	
Standard cost of resource required per unit of output	= Physical units of resource required per unit of output (called an *activity standard*)	× Standard cost of one unit of input resource	(6–1)

The product of these two parts provides a direct inputs budget useful for operational control, record-keeping, and valuation.

In the most common case, a resource input is used both directly and indirectly at a responsibility center to create output. A secretary, for example, spends some time directly typing contracts, and some time indirectly carrying messages, locating supplies, and at coffee. Both direct and indirect use of time must be considered in determining the activity standard and standard cost of producing a contract, or the total time to produce 100 contracts.

Suppose you want to estimate the secretarial labor budget of typing 200 contracts of a certain kind. Your estimate might make these reasonable assumptions:

1. Direct inputs are proportional only to output level (i.e., number of contracts typed).
2. Indirect inputs are not a function of output level (i.e., are fixed).

These assumptions lead to a linear estimation equation:

$$\begin{matrix}\text{Total} \\ \text{typing} \\ \text{budget}\end{matrix} = \begin{matrix}\text{Indirect} \\ \text{secretarial} \\ \text{costs}\end{matrix} + \begin{matrix}\text{Standard cost} \\ \text{to type one} \\ \text{contract (left-hand} \\ \text{side of (6-3) above)}\end{matrix} \times \begin{matrix}\text{Number of} \\ \text{contracts} \\ \text{to be typed}\end{matrix} \quad (6\text{-}2)$$

Or, in briefer notation,

$$Y = A + B \times X \quad (6\text{-}3)$$

In (6-3), Y would be the standard budget for typing X contracts. The constant B would be the direct standard cost of secretarial typing of one contract. The constant A would be the indirect cost of typing any number of contracts.

To further illustrate, let the activity standard be 2.102 hours to type one contract, and the secretarial wage rate be $5 per hour. Then the direct standard cost of secretarial typing of one contract would be:

$$B \doteq 2.102 \text{ hrs./contract} \times \$5/\text{hr. standard wage}$$
$$= \$10.51$$

Finally, the indirect costs of having a secretary able to type contracts are $952. The total typing budget for 200 contracts is:

$$Y = \$\ 952 + \$10.51 \times 200$$
$$= 3{,}054$$

If you do not believe that the standards hold true for this estimation, you may modify them. Common causes which should be considered as possibly necessitating modification are:

Learning effects
Worker productivity increases or decreases
Working condition changes
Material specification changes (substituting materials easier or harder to work with)
Large turnover in work force (making it difficult to train employees)
Product design changes (making the operation more or less difficult to perform)

The wage rate may change as a result of cost-of-living wage adjustments or an agreement negotiated with a union.

Linear estimation equations such as (6–3) are the basis for "formula budgets" which estimate costs, revenues, and profits for combinations of activities, and which are useful in the overall strategic and operational planning and control processes. Formula budgets are discussed in Chapter 10.

CONTROL USING VARIANCES FROM STANDARDS

The significance of the *difference* between standard and actual cost depends on the way the standard cost was chosen. We have suggested that the most significant comparison a business can make is the one between actual and expected performance. If standard costs represent expected performance in some sense, then the difference between standard and actual costs is a measure of the difference between expected and actual performance. It measures the firm's departure from expected performance.

Control using standard costs and variances assumes that the variances do in fact represent deviations of actual from expected performance, that these deviations may be eliminated by specific actions which can be taken by managers at responsibility centers, and that disappearance of the variance in subsequent periods is evidence that the deviations themselves have been corrected.

Suppose a responsibility center operates a process which generates actual costs. If the process is *in control,* these actual costs will deviate little if at all from expected (standard) costs. But if the process goes *out of control,* an indication that it is out of control will be that actual costs deviate significantly from the standard cost values. The actual significance of being "out of control" is that the process is misusing resources—using too much or too little of various resources and/or combining them inefficiently, with a corresponding reduction of profits.

Since accounting costs are reported by periods, you learn after a period is over that a process was in or out of control then. One assumes that a process in control tends to stay in control, and that a process out of control tends to stay out of control. Managers do not interfere with a process which reports no significant differences between actual and standard costs; they do attempt to bring back into control a process which reports significant differences between actual and standard costs.

Figure 6–1 shows how accounting actual and standard costs are used to diagnose the state of a system and how they behave when a system's

FIGURE 6–1
Illustration of Control Process

Data are available after end of this week:	April 17-22	April 24-29	May 1-6	May 8-13	May 15-20
Standard cost	4,000	4,000	4,000	4,000	4,000
Actual cost	5,000	4,000	4,000	6,000	4,000
Difference	−1,000	0	0	−2,000	0
Control action taken?	Yes	No	No	Yes	No

state of control changes. Thus in the week April 17–22 the process is out of control as evidenced by the actual-standard difference of $1,000. A corrective action is taken; its success is reflected in the next period's zero actual-standard difference. Since this is an indication the process is in control, no corrective actions are necessary. The process is apparently still in control in the week of May 1–6; but in the week of May 8–13, it goes out of control again. Once more corrective action is taken, and the accounting system reports the process is in control again in the final week covered.

In a real process "out of control" might designate many departures from normal behavior. Ideally, the accounting system would be able to identify each way the system is out of control. The accounting system signals many kinds of differences between actual and standard costs. The computation and study of these signals—or *variances*—is called *variance analysis*. The analysis of accounting variances produces much of the control information available through an accounting system.

Standard cost accounting systems try to provide a separate variance for each possible thing that can go wrong. Management tries to have a corrective action or remedy to stop the "wrong" and prevent it from recurring. These statements give two rules:

Rule of information: For each way that a responsibility center can operate unsatisfactorily, there should be a unique significant variance or combination of variances.

Rule of control: For each way that a responsibility center can operate unsatisfactorily, there should be a corrective action that brings the responsibility center back into a state of satisfactory operation.

Here is an example that should give you a feel for specific variances and how they contribute to the control process:

Raw material Y is used by the Superior Boat Company as part of the hulls of its boats. The purchasing department has agreed that it will be responsible for securing as much Y as necessary at $1 per pound. The hull department has agreed to be responsible for using Y at a standard rate of 1,000 pounds per 10,000 pounds of hull weight.

The purchasing department acquires 10,000 pounds of Y and pays $1.10 per pound for it. In a later period, the hull department uses 1,500 pounds of Y; simultaneously a total weight of 13,000 pounds is added to the weight of hulls under construction.

Price Variance

The first responsibility was that of the purchasing department:

Total price paid: $1.10 × 10,000 =	$11,000
Standard price: $1 × 10,000 =	10,000
Unfavorable variance (purchase price)	$ 1,000

This variance is unfavorable because the price paid was more than the standard price. Here is a formula for price variance which will give a positive answer if the variance is favorable and a negative answer if the variance is unfavorable:

$$\text{Price variance} = \text{Quantity purchased} \times \left(\text{Standard price per unit} - \text{Actual price per unit}\right) \quad (6\text{–}4)$$

$$\$-1{,}000 = 10{,}000 \times (\$1.00 - \$1.10)$$

Efficiency Variance

The Y stayed in storage for a while. Since we use standard costs, there is no need to distinguish this shipment of Y from other shipments. We are not sure from where the Y we are now using came. The issue to the hull department is 1,500 pounds of Y at $1 each. The accounting office calculates:

$$\begin{array}{ll}
\text{Actual consumption of Y} = & 1{,}500 \text{ lbs. @ } \$1/\text{lb.} = \$1{,}500 \\
\text{Standard consumption of Y for actual period output level} = & \\
\dfrac{13{,}000 \text{ lbs. added to hulls}}{10{,}000 \text{ lbs.}} \times 1{,}000 \text{ lbs. Y} \times \$1/\text{lb.} & = \underline{1{,}300} \\
\textit{Unfavorable} \text{ variance (efficiency)} & \$\ \ \ 200 \\
\end{array}$$

This variance is unfavorable because the amount used exceeded the standard. The standard for 13,000 pounds of hull construction is 1,300 pounds. Here is a formula for efficiency variance which will give a positive result if the variance is favorable and a negative result if the variance is unfavorable:

$$\text{Efficiency variance} = \text{Standard cost per unit} \times \left(\text{Standard input for actual output} - \text{Actual input for period}\right)$$

$$-\$200 = \$1 \times (1{,}300 - 1{,}500) \quad (6\text{–}5)$$

The latter two quantities are both expressed in the common physical units of measure (hours, pounds, tons, gallons, MCF) for the resource.

Thus, the hull department is not penalized for the higher price at which Y was purchased, nor is the purchasing department penalized for the inefficient way in which the hull department used the Y! The heads of both departments will (if these are significant variances) have to explain how the inefficiencies occurred.

Standard to Actual Costs

Standard and actual costs are reconcilable using the computed variances, through this relationship:

$$\frac{\text{Standard}}{\text{cost}} = \frac{\text{Actual}}{\text{cost}} + \frac{\text{Favorable}}{\text{variances}} - \frac{\text{Unfavorable}}{\text{variances}}$$

In the example, this reconciliation holds true:

$$\begin{aligned}\text{Purchasing: } \$10{,}000 &= \$11{,}000 - \$1{,}000 \\ \text{Use: } 1{,}300 &= 1{,}500 - 200\end{aligned}$$

The equation also holds true for a mixture of price and efficiency variances if the number of units is the same in all cases. For example, let the purchase price variance on 1,500 pounds of Y be $150, and apply the relationship:

$$\begin{aligned}1{,}300 \text{ lbs.} \times \$1/\text{lb.} &= 1{,}500 \text{ lbs.} \times \$1.10/\text{lb.} - \$150 - \$200 \\ \$1{,}300 &= \$1{,}650 - \$150 - \$200 \\ \$1{,}300 &= \$1{,}300\end{aligned}$$

This relationship is sometimes useful for finding a missing variance (see Exercise 27).

Is a Variance Significant?

If a variance is designated as "significant" it will be investigated and if a cause is found, the cause will be corrected. The investigation of a variance entails costs. These costs are offset by benefits only if the cause of the variance is found and corrected.

Not every variance indicates an out of control state for a process. However, the larger a variance is, the more likely it is to signify an out of control state warranting investigation. The objective is to establish significance limits for variances that will result in a *net benefit* from investigating variances exceeding these limits and not investigating variances that lie within them.

Here is a simple numerical example: By investigation, study, statistical analysis, and experience, it is established that a variance of $50 indicates an out of control state 20 percent of all the times it occurs, and a variance of $100 indicates an out of control state 80 percent of all the times it occurs. Assume only these two variances—$50 and $100—can occur. It is established further that to investigate a variance costs $20 (whether or not an out of control state is found and corrected), and to allow a process to continue in an out of control state costs $80.

Should the $50 variance be investigated? If it is, there will be a cost of $20 each time it occurs. If it is not investigated, there will be a cost of $80 just 20 percent of the time, or 0.20 × $80 = $16 average cost. Since $16 is less than $20, it would be economical *not* to investigate the $50 variance; it is therefore *not significant*.

Should the $100 variance be investigated? It will cost $20 to do this each time it occurs. If it is not investigated, there will be a cost of $80 fully 80 percent of the time, or 0.80 × $80 = $64 on the average. Since $20 is less than $64, it would be economical to investigate the $100 variance; it is therefore *significant*.

Reasoning such as that above may lead to preparation of a simple *control chart* that shows the significance limits and permits plotting period variances as they occur to determine trends and magnitudes of variances:

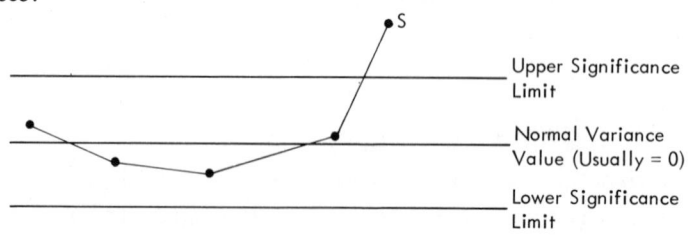

Only the variance represented by the point S above the upper significance limit would be investigated. The other points are within "normal" limits and don't trigger investigations.

ESTABLISHING STANDARD COSTS

There are several ways to estimate standard costs such as *A* and *B* in (6–3). Let us continue this contract-typing example to develop two such ways. The data in Figure 6–2 describe previous instances in which this same contract was typed.

FIGURE 6–2
Standard Data Set for Cost Finding

(Y) Secretarial Costs Incurred	(X) Number Times Contract Typed
$2,050	100
1,870	90
1,750	75
2,090	115
2,830	180
2,475	140

The simplest ways to estimate A and B are:

> Guess
> "Eyeball" estimate
> High-low method

A more elaborate way is:

> Least squares regression analysis

Simple Estimation Methods

Since anyone can guess or eyeball and disagree with anyone else using the same methods, we don't encourage you to adopt these estimation methods. The high-low method is the simplest *objective* estimation method. It designates two points to use in determining the equation (6–3). Anyone using this method would choose those same two points. The method is not very good because if there are more than two points, all the information contained in the extra points is ignored by the resulting equation. The high-low method is this:

> Pick out the largest and smallest values of X. Compute a straight-line expression for Y that will pass through the points these two values represent.

You may not remember how to find the equation for a line passing through two points. First, remember that two points *define* a line. Now, think of the constant B as being the rate of change of Y per unit of X as X goes from its lowest to its highest value. Let the lowest value of X be "XL" and the corresponding value of Y be "YL"; then the highest value of X is "XH" and the corresponding value of Y, "YH." The constant B is defined by the formula:

$$B = \frac{YH - YL}{XH - XL} \qquad (6\text{-}6)$$

What about the constant A? A is the value of Y when X is zero. Multiply your new value of B by XL and subtract the product from YL; the remainder is A. You would get the same value of A by subtracting $B \times XH$ from YH.

Try the high-low method on the Figure 6–2 data.

High point is $XH = 180$ $YH = 2{,}830$
Low point is $XL = 75$ $YL = 1{,}750$

Using (6–6),

$$B = \frac{YH - YL}{XH - XL} = \frac{2{,}830 - 1{,}750}{180 - 75}$$

$$= \frac{1{,}080}{105}$$

$$= \$10.29 \text{ per contract typed}$$

Now,

$$\begin{aligned} A &= YL - B\,XL \\ &= 1{,}750 - (\$10.29 \times 75) \\ &= 1{,}750 - 771 \\ &= 979 \text{ dollars} \end{aligned} \qquad (6\text{-}7)$$

To check this, let us compute A using (XH, YH):

$A = 2{,}830 - \$10.29 \times 180 = \$979$, which is convincing.

The complete estimation equation is then,

$$Y = 979 + 10.29X$$

You should plot this line on graph paper along with the data in Figure 6–2. This method will be accurate enough for many estimation situations. It may, however, *not* be accurate enough for estimating budget figures, for which you need all the information available for your estimate.

Least Squares Regression Analysis

More elaborate estimation procedures take into account information from all the data points you have, while retaining objectivity. "Least squares" is a method of statistically computing a line that comes closest to *fitting* or representing a group of points. It is a flexible method, easy to use but requiring some knowledge of calculus and courage in the face of symbolic notation (both are harmless).

Regression analysis uses all the information represented by all the pairs of values which you have. The equation is, as before, $Y = A + BX$. Although you have probably seen summation signs before, we have not used them in this book. The notation

$$\Sigma X_i$$

means "add up all values of X." We use this summation notation in these formulas for the equation constants A and B:

$$A = Y_{\text{average}} - B(X_{\text{average}}) \qquad (6-8)$$

$$B = \frac{n\Sigma X_i Y_i - \Sigma X_i \Sigma Y_i}{n\Sigma X_i^2 - (\Sigma X_i)^2} \qquad (6-9)$$

Let us use these equations to compute constants for Figure 6–1.

In this data set, n is the number of pairs and is 6.

$\Sigma Y_i = 2{,}050 + 1{,}870 + 1{,}750 + 2{,}090 + 2{,}830 + 2{,}475 = 13{,}065$
$\Sigma X_i = 100 + 90 + 75 + 115 + 180 + 140 = 700$
$\Sigma X_i^2 = 100^2 + 90^2 + 75^2 + 115^2 + 180^2 + 140^2$
$ = 10{,}000 + 8{,}100 + 5{,}625 + 13{,}225 + 32{,}400 + 19{,}600$
$ = 88{,}950$
$X_i Y_i = 2{,}050 \times 100 + 1{,}870 \times 90 + 1{,}750 \times 75 + 2{,}090 \times 115$
$ + 2{,}830 \times 180 + 2{,}475 \times 140$
$ = 205{,}000 + 186{,}300 + 131{,}250 + 240{,}350 + 509{,}400$
$ + 346{,}500$
$ = 1{,}600{,}800$

Solve first for B, since you need B before you can solve for A:

$$B = \frac{6 \times 1{,}600{,}800 - 700 \times 13{,}065}{6 \times 88{,}950 - 700 \times 700} = 10.51$$

$$A = \left(\frac{13{,}065}{6}\right) - \left(10.51 \times \frac{700}{6}\right) = 952$$

Much other information can be obtained from regression analysis. Statistical references such as those listed in this chapter's bibliography give additional details.

The assumptions underlying least squares regression analysis require precautions by accountants and others using it in planning. In summary, these cautions are:

1. The operation represented by the regression equation should be linear, or sufficiently close to linear to permit a reasonable approximation. Thus, the first contract should have the same expected typing time as the 100th or 200th contract; the secretary should be paid at the same hourly rate whatever the number of contracts typed.
2. The factors which influenced the time required to type a contract and the hourly wage paid a secretary during the previous contract-typing instances, as summarized in Figure 6–2, must continue to operate during any contract-typing instance for which the estimation equation will be used to develop a budget. Thus, a new and inexperienced secretary replacing the original one would at once make the old relationship useless.
3. The estimation relationship should not be used outside the range of the independent variable (X) for which it was developed (in this case, from 75 to 180 contracts). To use the equation to estimate the cost of typing 200 contracts runs the risk of an inaccurate estimate due to unknown factors influencing cost at that value of X.

Comparison of Methods

Least squares regression analysis is the preferred estimation method whenever you have the computation power to apply it, because it uses data in the most efficient manner. High-low estimation is simple but does not use all the available data and may produce error if the high and low points aren't typical of the data.

As a comparison of these two methods, using the contract-typing example, here are values of Y as in Figure 6-2, along with the value of Y for each value of X, as computed using the appropriate estimation procedure. These values are in Figure 6-3. It is interesting to note that when a statistical measure of estimation error—the variance of the observations around the estimation line—is computed, it is less (42.8) for the least square estimation equation than for the high-low estimation equation (43.4). No estimation procedure will give a lower value for this error measure than least squares.

FIGURE 6-3
Comparison of Estimation Methods

Basic Data Observed Y	High-Low Method $Y = 979 + 10.29X$ Calculated Y	Difference	Least Squares Method $Y = 952 + 10.51X$ Calculated Y	Difference
2,050	2,008	42	2,003	47
1,870	1,905	−35	1,898	−28
1,750	1,750	0	1,740	10
2,090	2,162	−72	2,160	−70
2,830	2,830	0	2,844	−14
2,475	2,420	55	2,423	52

The substantial computations necessary to use least squares must nearly always be done by computer. Smaller problems may be done by the manager himself, or his secretary, using a "time-sharing" service; larger problems will be given to computer programmers, run by them through a computer facility, and returned to the manager, usually the same day. The time and error factors which loom so large in hand calculations have dwindled away in the computer age.

MAINTENANCE OF STANDARD COSTS

Since a manufacturing operation will have thousands of standards, or possible standards, the maintenance of an up-to-date and accessible standard cost file is a major accounting responsibility.

Particularly in the 1970s, prices and technology are changing rapidly. The result is a short expected lifetime for standard costs. And, old standard costs run the risk of being so far away from the real costs as to distort product costs and create meaningless variances.

When standard costs could be relied upon to remain valid for relatively longer periods of time, a management could review them on a rotating basis, revising perhaps 20 percent of them each year. No standard would be more than five years old, and many of them much less. The fewer cost standards which were rapidly changing would be reviewed more often. To determine which cost types were changing most rapidly, the firm could "sample" a few of each type at random and compare them with currently effective standards.

As prices and technology change at increasing rates, the rotating review has become, for many firms, inadequate to permit useful standards. Such firms resort to computer review and revision of standards on the basis of published indices. For example, if the price of raw material Y was $6.75 per unit at the time the standard was last revised, and the industry price index for raw material Y was then 120, and is now 150, we may program a computer to compute a new Y standard of $6.75 $\times$ (150/120) = $8.43. There are bound to be some goof-ups in a set of thousands of such recalculations, but their cost overall is likely to be less than the cost of a massive hand recalculation in the conventional way.

The factor other than price and technology changes which may obsolete cost standards is human nature. Chapter 10 discusses behavioral phenomena impinging on the practice of managerial accounting, so we only note this factor in passing. For example, a standard cost set low to encourage efficiency (we aren't endorsing the wisdom of doing this) has been "found out" by the responsibility center involved and no longer has the desired effect; then it's time to revise the standard.

SUMMARY

Standard costs provide a major improvement in management information systems by making them more efficient, more informative, and more rational. A product's inventoriable cost may be constructed using uniform quantities and costs for all the factors of production included in the product. Variances from these standards provide the basis for extending the management by exception principle even to very complex, sensitive production procedures. Standard costs serve as efficiency goals and protect employees and managers from exploitation in the form of unreasonable goals.

Costs with fixed and variable components may be analyzed to determine how cost components are influenced by the volume of production or other activity. The simpler methods are best when the data do not present unusual features—essentially linear data, enough points to establish that a relationship actually exists, and reasonable looking results. Regression analysis is used when standard costs or resource inputs for many products must be determined at once or when efficiency in extracting information from the raw data is desired.

The linearity assumption employed in this chapter is so often used that it is hardly any longer questioned. Nevertheless you remember Chapter 3 and the nonlinear behavior of costs presented there. Thus the "relevant range" within which a standard is defined should be observed as the range for its use and application. If a linear relationship cannot be assumed within a useful relevant range, nonlinear regression analysis formulas will give good estimation for nonlinear standards.

APPENDIX 6A: THE LEARNING EFFECT

The learning effect refers to the efficiency obtained from repetition of a manufacturing procedure, process, or operation. The learning effect has a significant effect on resource input quantities and thus on unit production costs.

One commonly observed learning effect shows the resources required per unit produced decreasing by 20 percent (or some other figure) each time the total cumulative production quantity is doubled. Thus, if the first unit cost $100, the second unit would cost $100 $\times$ 0.80 = $80; the fourth unit would cost $80 $\times$ 0.8 = $64; $Y_{2N} = 0.8Y_N$ generally. These costs, when plotted on a vertical axis against total units produced on the horizontal axis, produce a declining unit cost curve as in Figure 6A–1.

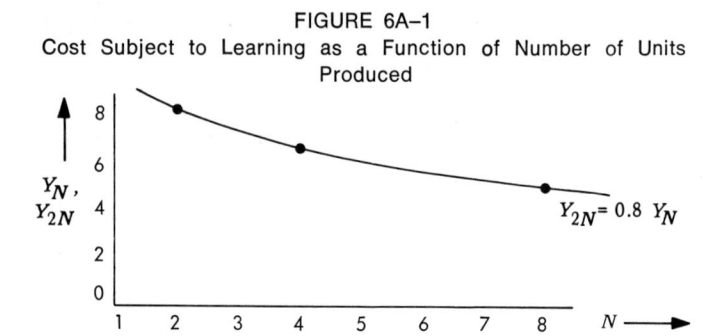

FIGURE 6A–1
Cost Subject to Learning as a Function of Number of Units Produced

Y_N, Y_{2N} plotted against N; $Y_{2N} = 0.8\ Y_N$

Learning Effect and Standard Costs

A standard cost is considered constant, subject to effects of management decisions and external cost changes. The cost of a unit produced is *also* affected by variables controllable by the firm. As a production run lengthens, production efficiency increases so that many operations and inputs are continuously subject to the learning effect and unit costs decline. However, the rate of decline becomes small in a long production run; most of the benefit is realized early in the run.

If the learning effect is not considered, a standard cost may be excessively liberal as an operational standard. Performance variances may be misleading. As an example, let us consider a process subject to a 20 percent unit cost reduction each time total production quantity doubles (this is called a "20 percent learning effect"). The first unit costs $100, and the standard cost is set at $75. In Figure 6A–2 there are

FIGURE 6A–2
Variances from Standard That Ignores Learning Effect

Unit No.	Actual Cost	Standard Cost	Overall Variance
1	100	75	25 Unfavorable
2	80	75	5 Unfavorable
4	64	75	11 Favorable
8	51	75	24 Favorable
16	41	75	34 Favorable
32	33	75	42 Favorable

actual and standard costs and overall variances for selected units in the production run.

Since the learning effect is present naturally, the reported variances will occur to the puzzlement of management if they are unaware of it. The production management will labor to eliminate the initial unfavorable variances, then watch in amazement as the favorable variances become larger and larger. The danger is that they will not realize that the standard is excessively liberal, and that waste and inefficiency will creep into the process even while large favorable variances exist. For example, the 32d unit could cost $66 instead of $33—*twice* what is should cost—yet the favorable variance would still be $9, and management without knowledge of learning effects will interpret this as a signal that the system is in control.

Classifying Activities

Activities of a firm subject to learning effects are:

1. Activities that are new or recently revised. In contrast, long-familiar activities will not exhibit the learning effect.
2. Activities performed by new workmen or others not familiar with the activity. Activities performed by workmen familiar with them will not exhibit the learning effect.
3. Activities requiring use of unfamiliar raw materials. Activities specifying familiar and regularly used raw materials will not exhibit the learning effect.
4. Production runs of short duration, especially if there are follow-on runs. A long-running production line (auto assembly, for example) may not reflect a learning effect.

Computing Learning Effects

The majority of learning effects can be described and applied with a minimum of mathematics. The technique employed is to plot certain selected values on "log-log" paper (graph paper on which the scales are spaced as logarithms rather than scalar values). The learning effect

180   An Introduction to Accounting for Decision Making and Control

forms a straight line on log-log paper instead of the curved line of Figure 6A–1. Each point plotted will represent values for a pair of variables—the dependent variable (the measure in dollars or other units of the resource used) and the independent variable (the measure of output—usually the number of units produced). The terms "resource used" and "number of units produced" require definitions appropriate to each particular application.

In Figure 6A–3, for example, are the data of Figure 6A–2 plotted on log-log paper. The first unit cost is $100. The learning effect is 20 percent—which means that each time production quantity doubles,

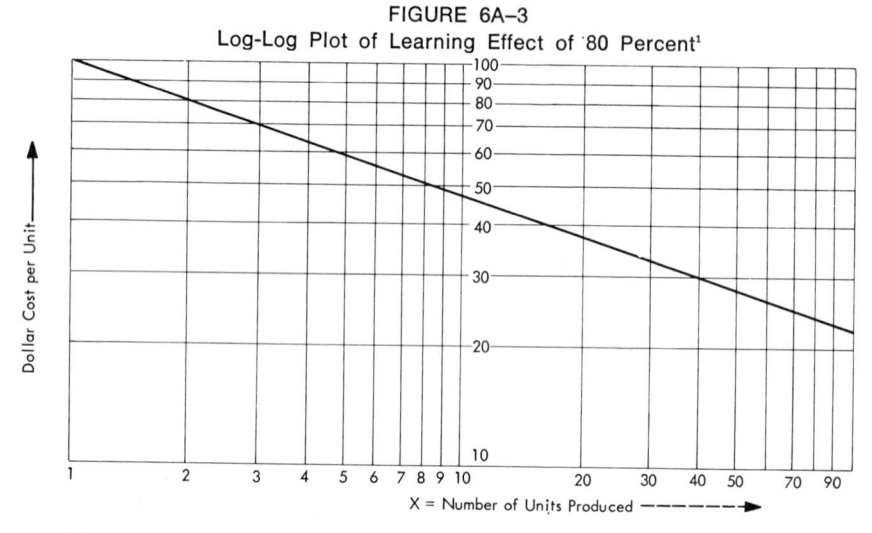

FIGURE 6A–3
Log-Log Plot of Learning Effect of 80 Percent[1]

[Graph: Dollar Cost per Unit vs. X = Number of Units Produced, showing a straight descending line on log-log axes]

[1] Here is a formula to compute the cost of producing *any* unit in the production run without drawing a graph:

$$Y_x = Y_1 X^k \qquad (6\text{--}10)$$

Here are the meanings of the symbols:

X = unit for which Y is calculated
Y_x = inputs to xth unit since production began
Y_1 = actual or estimated inputs to first unit produced
$k = \dfrac{\log(1-r)}{\log 2}$ (Use logarithms to base 10 for simplicity. Note $\log_{10} 2 = +0.301$)
r = learning effect (fractional reduction in required resources for each 100 percent increase in total units produced)

cost per unit declines 20 percent. Note the extremely low costs of units produced at the end of a long production run.

The learning effect is one factor affecting cost behavior which managers are more often taking into account. A generation ago, the learning effect was not completely understood and rarely considered.

Although a learning-effect expert should do the actual work of measuring the learning effect, you should understand the work done and its contribution to business efficiency.

TABLE 6A–1
Common Logarithms: 100–549

N	0	1	2	3	4	5	6	7	8	9
10	0000	0043	0086	0128	0170	0212	0253	0294	0334	0374
11	0414	0453	0492	0531	0569	0607	0645	0682	0719	0755
12	0792	0828	0864	0899	0934	0969	1004	1038	1072	1106
13	1139	1173	1206	1239	1271	1303	1335	1367	1399	1430
14	1461	1492	1523	1553	1584	1614	1644	1673	1703	1732
15	1761	1790	1818	1847	1875	1903	1931	1959	1987	2014
16	2041	2068	2095	2122	2148	2175	2201	2227	2253	2279
17	2304	2330	2355	2380	2405	2430	2455	2480	2504	2529
18	2553	2577	2601	2625	2648	2672	2695	2718	2742	2765
19	2788	2810	2833	2856	2878	2900	2923	2945	2967	2989
20	3010	3032	3054	3075	3096	3118	3139	3160	3181	3201
21	3222	3243	3263	3284	3304	3324	3345	3365	3385	3404
22	3424	3444	3464	3483	3502	3522	3541	3560	3579	3598
23	3617	3636	3655	3674	3692	3711	3729	3747	3766	3784
24	3802	3820	3838	3856	3874	3892	3909	3927	3945	3962
25	3979	3997	4014	4031	4048	4065	4082	4099	4116	4133
26	4150	4166	4183	4200	4216	4232	4249	4265	4281	4298
27	4314	4330	4346	4362	4378	4393	4409	4425	4440	4456
28	4472	4487	4502	4518	4533	4548	4564	4579	4594	4609
29	4624	4639	4654	4669	4683	4698	4713	4728	4742	4757
30	4771	4786	4800	4814	4829	4843	4857	4871	4886	4900
31	4914	4928	4942	4955	4969	4983	4997	5011	5024	5038
32	5051	5065	5079	5092	5105	5119	5132	5145	5159	5172
33	5185	5198	5211	5224	5237	5250	5263	5276	5289	5302
34	5315	5328	5340	5353	5366	5378	5391	5403	5416	5428
35	5441	5453	5465	5478	5490	5502	5514	5527	5539	5551
36	5563	5575	5587	5599	5611	5623	5635	5647	5658	5670
37	5682	5694	5705	5717	5729	5740	5752	5763	5775	5786
38	5798	5809	5821	5832	5843	5855	5866	5877	5888	5899
39	5911	5922	5933	5944	5955	5966	5977	5988	5999	6010
40	6021	6031	6042	6053	6064	6075	6085	6096	6107	6117
41	6128	6138	6149	6160	6170	6180	6191	6201	6212	6222
42	6232	6243	6253	6263	6274	6284	6294	6304	6314	6325
43	6336	6345	6355	6365	6375	6385	6395	6405	6415	6425
44	6435	6444	6454	6464	6474	6484	6493	6503	6513	6522
45	6532	6542	6551	6561	6571	6580	6590	6599	6609	6618
46	6628	6637	6646	6656	6665	6675	6684	6693	6702	6712
47	6721	6730	6739	6749	6758	6767	6776	6785	6794	6803
48	6812	6821	6830	6839	6848	6857	6866	6875	6884	6893
49	6902	6911	6920	6928	6937	6946	6955	6964	6972	6981
50	6990	6998	7007	7016	7024	7033	7042	7050	7059	7067
51	7076	7084	7093	7101	7110	7118	7126	7135	7143	7152
52	7160	7168	7177	7185	7193	7202	7210	7218	7226	7235
53	7243	7251	7259	7267	7275	7284	7292	7300	7308	7316
54	7324	7332	7340	7348	7356	7364	7372	7380	7388	7396

Taken by permission from Ernest Kurnow, Gerald J. Glasser, and Frederick R. Ottman, *Statistics for Business Decisions* (Homewood, Ill.: Richard D. Irwin, Inc., 1959), pp. 507–8.

TABLE 6A-1—(Continued)
Common Logarithms: 550–999

N	0	1	2	3	4	5	6	7	8	9
55	7404	7412	7419	7427	7435	7443	7451	7459	7466	7474
56	7482	7490	7497	7505	7513	7520	7528	7536	7543	7551
57	7559	7566	7574	7582	7589	7597	7604	7612	7619	7627
58	7634	7642	7649	7657	7664	7672	7679	7686	7694	7701
59	7709	7716	7723	7731	7738	7745	7752	7760	7767	7774
60	7782	7789	7796	7803	7810	7818	7825	7832	7839	7846
61	7853	7860	7868	7875	7882	7889	7896	7903	7910	7917
62	7924	7931	7938	7945	7952	7959	7966	7973	7980	7987
63	7993	8000	8007	8014	8021	8028	8035	8041	8048	8055
64	8062	8069	8075	8082	8089	8096	8102	8109	8116	8122
65	8129	8136	8142	8149	8156	8162	8169	8176	8182	8189
66	8195	8202	8209	8215	8222	8228	8235	8241	8248	8254
67	8261	8267	8274	8280	8287	8293	8299	8306	8312	8319
68	8325	8331	8338	8344	8351	8357	8363	8370	8376	8382
69	8388	8395	8401	8407	8414	8420	8426	8432	8439	8445
70	8451	8457	8463	8470	8476	8482	8488	8494	8500	8506
71	8513	8519	8525	8531	8537	8543	8549	8555	8561	8567
72	8573	8579	8585	8591	8597	8603	8609	8615	8621	8627
73	8633	8639	8645	8651	8657	8663	8669	8675	8681	8686
74	8692	8698	8704	8710	8716	8722	8727	8733	8739	8745
75	8751	8756	8762	8768	8774	8779	8785	8791	8797	8802
76	8808	8814	8820	8825	8831	8837	8842	8848	8854	8859
77	8865	8871	8876	8882	8887	8893	8899	8904	8910	8915
78	8921	8927	8932	8938	8943	8949	8954	8960	8965	8971
79	8976	8982	8987	8993	8998	9004	9009	9015	9020	9025
80	9031	9036	9042	9047	9053	9058	9063	9069	9074	9079
81	9085	9090	9096	9101	9106	9112	9117	9122	9128	9133
82	9138	9143	9149	9154	9159	9165	9170	9175	9180	9186
83	9191	9196	9201	9206	9212	9217	9222	9227	9232	9238
84	9243	9248	9253	9258	9263	9269	9274	9279	9284	9289
85	9294	9299	9304	9309	9315	9320	9325	9330	9335	9340
86	9345	9350	9355	9360	9365	9370	9375	9380	9385	9390
87	9395	9400	9405	9410	9415	9420	9425	9430	9435	9440
88	9445	9450	9455	9460	9465	9469	9474	9479	9484	9489
89	9494	9499	9504	9509	9513	9518	9523	9528	9533	9538
90	9542	9547	9552	9557	9562	9566	9571	9576	9581	9586
91	9590	9595	9600	9605	9609	9614	9619	9624	9628	9633
92	9638	9643	9647	9652	9657	9661	9666	9671	9675	9680
93	9685	9689	9694	9699	9703	9708	9713	9717	9722	9727
94	9731	9736	9741	9745	9750	9754	9759	9763	9768	9773
95	9777	9782	9786	9791	9795	9800	9805	9809	9814	9818
96	9823	9827	9832	9836	9841	9845	9850	9854	9859	9863
97	9868	9872	9877	9881	9886	9890	9894	9899	9903	9908
98	9912	9917	9921	9926	9930	9934	9939	9943	9948	9952
99	9956	9961	9965	9969	9974	9978	9983	9987	9991	9996

QUESTIONS

1. What is a standard cost? Can you give some reasons why managers and accountants turn to standard costs?

2. Standard costs have found wide acceptance in manufacturing operations. Why do you think they are not accepted for planning and controlling, let us say, medical and surgical practice, or the educational process?

3. You normally perform an operation in 99 minutes. The standard for this operation has been 110 minutes. Abruptly the standard

is changed to 90 minutes. What is your subsequent reaction and performance?

4. The Shiny Auto Paint Company paints automobiles. There are five major operations, each performed by an independent work station. However, the management recognizes only one standard cost for the entire operation—4.5 hours and 1.1 gallons of paint. Any deviation from these standards results in a loss of salary bonuses for all employees in the paint shop. Comment on this system of control.

5. What is a "significant variance"? What is a "significance limit"?

6. When you arrive at an intersection of streets, you look at the traffic light, which can be red, yellow, or green. For what states do these messages stand? Can you think of any other states not represented by such signals? Is the rule of information adequately fulfilled? Is your answer the same if you are color-blind?

7. As a manager, you receive a performance report which says "significant variance" or "not significant variance." You know that the former means the process is not in control, and the latter that it is in control. If the process is in control you do nothing, if it is not in control you write a memo to that effect to the performance center manager, who never reads memos. Is the rule of control adequately fulfilled? Is your answer the same if a copy of the memo goes to the division vice president, who follows through successfully on such matters?

8. How does a price variance differ from an efficiency variance? What is the message each is trying to carry?

9. How do simple cost-estimation procedures differ from more complex estimation procedures?

10. Of the two estimation procedures illustrated in this chapter for the equation $Y = A + BX$, which seemed to produce the best agreement with the data in Figure 6–2?

11. Why must an output standard cost consist of an activity standard and a cost per resource input unit?

12. When planning using standard costs, why must output costs be assumed to have indirect and direct components?

13. What is computer time sharing? Find out if your college or university has a time-sharing service for students.

14. What are some factors which may tend to modify or upset standard cost predictions based on regression analysis or other mathematical estimation techniques using historical costs?

15. The learning effect becomes less evident as the length of a production run increases. Explain in simple language why this is so.

16. A cost is supposed to be subject to a learning effect. During one year, the cost declined from 80 to 70, but learning theory predicted the cost would decline from 80 to 64. What was the rate of price inflation that year, for that cost?

17. What kinds of activity are most subject to the learning effect?

18. The Reserve Company operates a computer-based, rapid-access information storage system. One item in the system is a file of 32,000 standard costs of operations performed by the company. A specially prepared computer program relates each of these costs four times a year to current prices, technology changes, wage rates, and inflation. Explain why such detailed monitoring of standard costs is necessary.

EXERCISES

19. Below are series of actual costs recorded in successive periods at constant activity levels. The standard cost for the activity is given for comparison purposes. Indicate in which series there is evidence that the underlying process got out of control:
    a) Standard cost: $1,000.
       Actual costs: $1,000; $1,010; $990; $1,000; $980.
    b) Standard cost: $879.
       Actual costs: $850; $900; $880; $1,100; $1,150.
    c) Standard cost: $1,450,000.
       Actual costs: $1,600,000; $1,650,000; $1,550,000; $1,600,000.
    d) Standard cost: $56,346.
       Actual costs: $42,000; $45,000; $47,000; $49,000; $50,000.

20. Below are two sequences of costs: standard cost and actual cost for the same period. Indicate at which points the underlying process

appeared to be out of control, and the points at which control appears to have been regained over the process:

Period	Standard Cost	Actual Cost	Difference
1	4,000	5,000	−1,000
2	4,500	4,490	+10
3	3,500	3,500	0
4	4,500	5,500	−1,000
5	5,000	5,700	−700
6	5,000	6,200	−1,200
7	4,000	3,900	+100
8	4,000	4,100	−100
9	4,000	4,200	−200
10	4,000	4,400	−400

21. The manufacture of a prefabricated door jamb calls for the following inputs:

        32 board feet of No. 1 white pine
        80 nails
        2 hours carpenter's apprentice time

No. 1 white pine is available for $0.40 per board foot, nails sell for $0.50 per pound (400 nails per pound), and carpenter's apprentices are paid $4 per hour. Find the direct standard cost of a door jamb.

22. One hundred door jambs as described in Exercise 21 are manufactured. These door jambs had the following *actual* costs: white pine, $0.38 per board foot; nails, $0.80 per pound; carpenter apprentice wage, $4.50 per hour. The following *actual* inputs occurred: 3,500 board feet of pine; 23 pounds of nails; and 180 hours of carpenter apprentice time. Compute all price and efficiency variances, assuming inputs were purchased as needed.

23. A publishing company wishes to print 5,000 copies of a 500-page book. The standard cost of paper is $0.004 per page. It is normal to waste or damage 10 percent of the pages in printing, so an allowance is made for this much waste in setting the standard for the book. Find the standard cost of the paper to be used in this printing project.

186   An Introduction to Accounting for Decision Making and Control

24. The book in Exercise 23 is published. Three million pages are purchased and used. The cost of these pages was $15,000. Find the purchase price and efficiency variances for paper on this project.

25. Indicate in each situation below whether the rule of information and the rule of control are valid:

Situation	Number of Ways Responsibility Center Can Get Out of Control	Number of Variances Reported to Manager	Number of Effective Corrective Actions for Manager
a)	4	3	6
b)	4	6	2
c)	4	6	6
d)	4	4	4
e)	4	3	3

26. A certain operation's input is related to its output by the equation:

$$Y = 4,500 + 60X$$

What standard total inputs would be required by each of the following output levels:

   a) 100   b) 50   c) 200

27. Refer to the data in Exercise 26. The total inputs that correspond to each case were, respectively: (a) 11,000; (b) 7,000; and (c) 15,000. Compute efficiency variances, assuming that all indirect cost spending variances are zero.

28. A regression analysis estimation procedure produces the following values:

$$\Sigma Y_i = 20,000 \qquad \Sigma X_i = 1,000$$
$$\Sigma X_i Y_i = 4,000,000 \qquad \Sigma X_i^2 = 200,000 \qquad n = 10$$

Find the regression equation.

PROBLEMS

29. The Midtown Radiological Clinic specializes in gastrointestinal X-rays. The source documents for the last quarter show that Midtown Radiological's purchasing department ordered 6,000 photographic plates at a cost of $1 each. The X-ray department used

5,000 plates in the course of the quarter, completing a total of 4,500 X-ray series. Technician time required was 9,000 hours at a wage rate of $10 per hour. The applicable standards are as follows:

Standard cost of plates.	$1.10 each
Standard number of plates per X-ray series	1
Standard technician hourly wage	$9.50
Standard hours of technician time per X-ray series	2

Required:

a) Compute and show the costs—actual and standard—of operating the Clinic last quarter.

b) Compute price and efficiency variances for plates and technician time.

30. One year after the situation described in Problem 29 above, the Midtown Radiological Clinic decided to review its standards for gastrointestinal X-ray series. For three successive quarters the clinic observed the relation between the number of X-ray series completed and the number of technician hours and photographic plates used. Here are the results:

Qtr. No.	X-ray Series	Plates Used	Technician Hours
1	4,000	4,200	7,000
2	5,000	5,100	8,900
3	6,000	6,100	10,500

Required:

a) Using the high-low method, compute an equation to estimate plates used as a function of the number of X-ray series and give the standard number of plates per additional X-ray series.

b) Using the high-low method, compute an equation to estimate the technician hours required as a function of the number of X-ray series and give the standard number of hours per additional X-ray series.

c) If the cost per plate and wage rate which were standard last year are still valid, compute the new standard cost of an additional gastrointestinal X-ray series.

31. The Smooth-Cruise Motor Shop provides a variety of services to motor yachtsmen. A relatively new service is the overhaul of large outboard motors. Since billing is on the basis of skilled repairmen's

time required, the company is keeping careful records to determine a reasonable standard for such overhauls. Each week for seven weeks the number of hours recorded by the mechanics as worked on these overhauls is related to the number of motors overhauled. Here are the results:

Week	Mechanic Hours	Motors Overhauled
1	120	35
2	100	33
3	130	37
4	140	42
5	80	21
6	90	24
7	90	22

Required:

a) Using the high-low method, compute an equation estimating total mechanic hours as a function of motors overhauled per week. Put the lowest three values of the independent variable in one group and the others in another group. What is the standard number of direct hours required per overhaul?

b) Normally three mechanics work on motor overhauls up to 40 hour each. Next week, 45 motors are promised out after overhauls. Do you think another mechanic should be transferred to this activity for that week?

32. This motor shop (see Problem 31 above) also installs new inboard engines in boats not originally constructed to receive them. This is a difficult operation, requiring much skill and time. Nevertheless, the company wonders whether it can develop estimation parameters. Over a six-month period these data were collected:

Month	Mechanic Hours	Number Inboards Installed
1	2,050	105
2	1,500	80
3	2,500	180
4	1,850	100
5	2,350	150
6	1,750	70

Required:

a) Using least squares analysis, compute an equation estimating total mechanic hours as a function of inboards installed per month.

b) Express your opinion whether this equation fits the data well enough to permit using the "B" value from it as a standard direct labor input for inboard installations.

33. Phil Mason, manager of the Mason Machine & Grinder Company, has become interested in least squares analysis as a result of your campaign to budget time for billing operations in the accounting department, in which you are a new employee. The controller of the accounting department gives you the following information for the six weeks just ended:

Hours Spent in Billing Operations	Number of Billings Performed
2,000	10,000
2,200	13,000
1,820	8,000
1,500	6,000
2,330	14,000
1,750	7,000

Required:
a) Develop an equation for estimating the number of accounting hours required for a given number of billings to be performed.
b) What is the estimated time required to perform one additional billing?
c) Why cannot you multiply number of billings required times average time per billing and obtain the total hours required for billing?

34. The first unit of an experimental accounting course requires 38 lecture hours to teach. Assuming a 75 percent learning constant applies to accounting instruction, how many lecture hours (round *up* to nearest hour) will be required to teach the second unit? The third unit? The fourth unit?

35. Hercules Powderhorn Company makes dynamite caps used by farmers to blow up tree stumps and, occasionally, themselves. The company's engineers have developed a foolproof cap which is more complex than the present cap and therefore more expensive. The company hopes manufacturing costs can be brought down over time to make this cap competitive and has called in Peter T. Priceright, a learning theory specialist. You are Priceright's assistant and do all his work for him.

Study of recent manufacturing records for the Hercules Powderhorn Company lead you (for Mr. Priceright) to conclude that r, the learning effect, is 0.20 for this company (making $1 - r = 0.80$ and $ln(1 - r)/ln2 = -0.322$). The learning equations are applied to 1,000 cases as a single batch.

Initially, market conditions dictate that the selling price for the new model cap be $0.60 each. But the average unit cost in the first batch manufactured will be $2.

Required:

a) Using no more information than is given here, perform calculations to show whether the 50th batch of redesigned caps will be profitable.

b) Using the equation $Y_x = 2.00x^{-0.322}$ plotted on log-log paper, determine the first batch which will be profitable.

36. Crashmaster Aircraft Company is developing a new passenger plane. The company expects to manufacture 500 of the new craft, which will sell for $3,000,000 apiece. The total cost of the first unit is $3,800,000. The 500th unit is expected to cost $1,500,000. Crashmaster's learning function has the unique characteristic that it is *linear* and *not* exponential; hence it can be plotted on rectangular cartesian graph paper. Thus, cost per unit plotted against total units produced gives a straight-line relationship on ordinary graph paper.

Required:

a) After how many planes produced will the company break even?
b) What is the average cost per plane?

37. Greg Arious, a young lawyer in Midville, is planning to be a candidate in his party's primary for the office of U.S. congressman representing his district. Greg is not wealthy and must solicit campaign contributions. To estimate the cost of his campaign, he contacts the state chairman of his party, Mr. G. Ladd Hander.

GREG: I don't know how much a run for office will cost me.

LADD: Well, we have developed some estimates over the years for young bucks like you in the primaries.

GREG: Our district has some 300,000 voters.

LADD: And 200,000 of them are registered with our party. You'll probably make two mailings to each registered party member and one mailing to all other voters. Postage is a nickel, and the message is about four cents.

GREG: What about television?

LADD: Most primary candidates make about five spots. The agencies will charge about $1,000 to make a spot. And to show a spot once will cost $200.

GREG: Show each spot once?

LADD: No, you idiot, show each spot 30 times! And then there's your staff.

GREG: I thought my wife could do staff work.

LADD: Maybe she can, but you'll need a campaign manager who'll cost you $15,000 for the primary and three secretaries for 40 hours a week for 6 weeks before the primary date at $2.50 an hour.

GREG: Uh, and what about travel expenses?

LADD: Rent a car. That's $100 a week for 6 weeks plus 10 cents a mile. You'll probably drive about 20,000 miles. And make a trip to Washington to have your picture taken with somebody. Make it $500 for that.

GREG: Good grief. Anything else?

LADD: Speechwriters. We'll supply you with position papers and speeches—same ones we give your opponent in the primary—you use what you want—pay us for it—about $2,500.

GREG: What if I win this primary?

LADD: The general election'll cost you 250 percent of what you spend in the primary. That's our rule of thumb.

Required:

a) Assuming that Mr. Hander's estimates are objectively determined standard costs, estimate the total primary campaign expenses of Greg Arious.

b) If Greg wins the primary, how much will he have to spend in the general election?

DECISION CASE 6-1: WHOVILLE OIL COMPANY

To help combat the energy crisis, Whoville Oil Company is preparing to place a new domestic oil field into production. The company, however, is unsure how to operate the new field efficiently. "What if our costs don't conform to the standards?" the production supervisor, Mr. Chilton, asked. "Well, from our experience with other producing fields of this same general nature," replied Mr. Slick, chief engineer and cost analyst, "we know that a good standard for production at this field is 1,000 barrels per day. And goods standards for labor cost per barrel and fuel usage per barrel are $0.12 and 1.1 gallons respectively. We should be able to obtain the fuel at its standard cost of $0.15 per gallon." "Yes," Chilton said, "but my point is: when are variations from those standards *significant?*" Slick shrugged, "I always investigate any variance that is more than 10 percent of the standard."

At the end of the first month of production, the Whoville chief accountant produced the following historical figures for the new oil field:

>Actual production: 1,200 barrels per day.
>Actual labor cost: $0.11 per barrel.
>Fuel usage: 1.3 gallons per barrel at $0.17 per gallon.

Required (all variances on a *per-day* basis):

a) How should the significance of a variance be determined?
b) Compute the total price variance on fuel used in oil production (assume fuel used = fuel purchased).
c) Compute the total efficiency variance on fuel used in oil production.
d) Compute the total variance in labor cost of oil production. Explain why this variance is less useful than those computed for fuel in *(b)* and *(c)*.
e) Compute the efficiency variance for oil production, in units of barrels.
f) Discuss the additional advantages Whoville may realize from applying standard costs to oil production, and the factors that may tend to change these standards as time passes.

BIBLIOGRAPHY

Books

Hare, Jr., Van Court. *Systems Analysis: A Diagnostic Approach* New York: Harcourt, Brace & World, Inc., 1967.

Shillinglaw, Gordon. *Cost Accounting: Analysis and Control.* 3d ed. Homewood, Ill.: Richard D. Irwin, Inc., 1972.

Articles

Benston, G. J. "Multiple Regression Analysis of Cost Behavior," *The Accounting Review,* October 1966, pp. 657–72.

Calas, Robert. "Variance Analysis in Profit Planning," *Management Accounting,* July 1971.
Dopuch, Nicholas; Birnberg, Jacob S.; and Demski, Joel. "An Extension of Standard Cost Variance Analysis," *The Accounting Review,* July 1967.
Grace, William E. "Planning and Organizing a Work Measurement Program," *Management Accounting,* July 1970.
Likert, Rensis, and Seashore, Stanley E. "Making Cost Controls Work," *Harvard Business Review,* November–December 1963.
McClenon, Paul R. "Cost Finding through Multiple Correlation Analysis," *The Accounting Review,* July 1963.
Parsons, Vincent A., and MacDonald, George A. "Standard Cost and Control System," *Management Accounting,* November 1970.
Seaton, Jr., Lloyd. "Standard Costing Developments and Applications," *Management Accounting,* July 1970.
Summers, Edward L. and Welsch, Glenn A. "How Learning Curves Can Be Applied to Profit Planning," *Management Services,* March–April 1970.

7

Treatment of Indirect Costs

A MAJOR basic problem in accounting is to control costs which do not have a direct association with the product. These product indirect costs are called *overhead*. Some obvious categories in which *overhead costs* are accumulated are:

Maintenance	Engineering
Security	Quality control
Utilities	Supervision
Stores	Sanitation
Pollution control	

The costs of these functions can develop into one fourth, two thirds, or more of the total costs incurred. How such costs are assigned to production departments and to individual units of product and service makes an important difference in the decisions and performance evaluation of the firm. The important issues are:

The flow of overhead
Performance measurement at service departments
Performance measurement at production departments
Direct and full absorption costing
Overhead allocation and decision making

THE FLOW OF OVERHEAD

Overhead costs originate in responsibility centers. The outline below illustrates fixed and variable overhead in service and production centers:

I. Service centers
   A. Fixed costs
      1. Depreciation
      2. Insurance
      3. Engineering
      4. Supervisory salaries
      5. Lease payments
      6. Property taxes
      7. Skeleton crew
   B. Variable costs
      1. Hourly salaries
      2. Materials and supplies

II. Production centers
   A. Fixed costs
      1. Depreciation
      2. Insurance
      3. Quality control
      4. Supervisory salaries
      5. Lease payments
      6. Property taxes
      7. Skeleton crew
   B. Variable costs
      1. New supplies
      2. Hourly salaries of indirect labor

The flow of service center costs through the accounts is shown in Figure 7–1 on page 196. On the left, various indirect costs are incurred:

                Indirect materials costs
                Indirect wages
                Depreciation
                Miscellaneous indirect costs

FIGURE 7–1
Flow of Overhead Costs

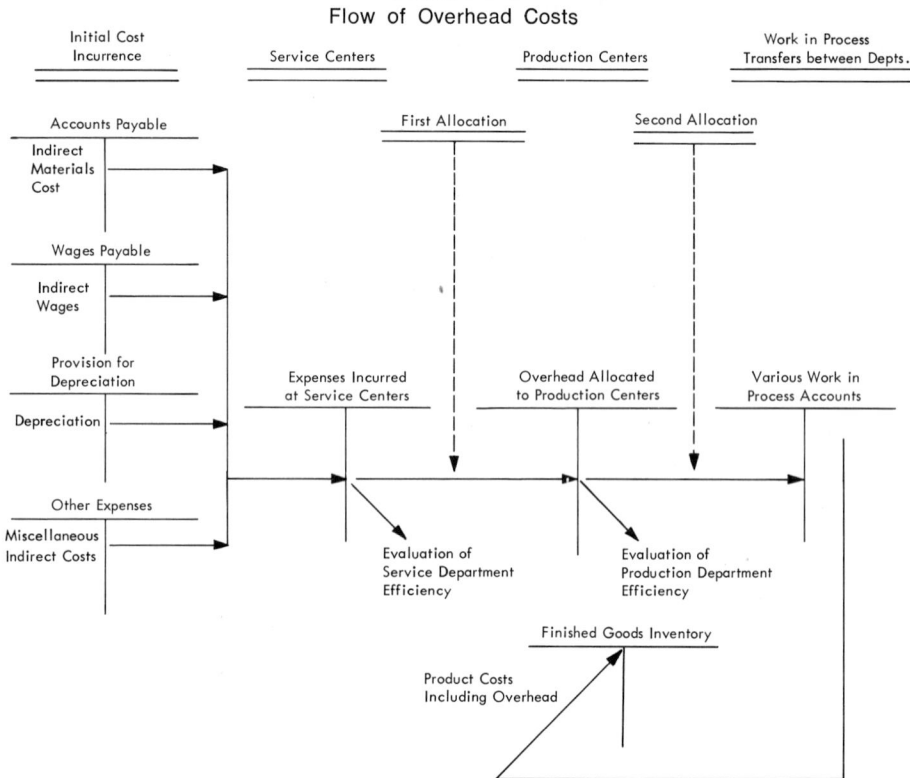

Initial Cost Incurrence	Service Centers	Production Centers	Work in Process Transfers between Depts.

Accounts Payable — Indirect Materials Cost

Wages Payable — Indirect Wages

Provision for Depreciation — Depreciation

Other Expenses — Miscellaneous Indirect Costs

First Allocation → Expenses Incurred at Service Centers

Second Allocation → Overhead Allocated to Production Centers

Various Work in Process Accounts

Evaluation of Service Department Efficiency

Evaluation of Production Department Efficiency

Finished Goods Inventory

Product Costs Including Overhead

These service center costs are accumulated in accounts according to the particular service center which is responsible for using the resources associated with each cost. Since the service centers do not produce inventoriable products to which the costs may attach, they must pass on their costs to production centers, which *do* use the outputs of service centers and incorporate them indirectly into inventoriable products. In a real situation the production centers would have inventoriable costs too, but we are ignoring these here to keep the picture simple.

The first allocation of indirect costs is from service centers to production centers. This allocation permits you to evaluate service centers' efficiency in meeting production center *demand* for indirect services. The production centers perform the second allocation of indirect costs—this time to units of their own output. This second allocation helps produce a product cost and also permits you to evaluate the production centers' efficiency in utilizing the indirect services they have demanded. These two evaluations of service and production center efficiency will be described by means of an illustrative example.

ILLUSTRATIVE EXAMPLE

The following example of the Bender Company will be used to illustrate the concepts of performance measurement at service and production centers with respect to variable overhead costs.

The Bender Company maintenance department (a service center) calculates variable costs as a function of total machine-hours worked in two production centers—the sanding and bending departments. The current operating budget of the maintenance department indicates that if 9,000 machine-hours are run, variable maintenance expenses should be $27,000.

During the month of March, the following events occurred:

1. Six thousand machine-hours were run in the sanding department.
2. Five thousand machine-hours were run in the bending department.
3. The maintenance department actually spent $20,000 of fixed costs when it planned to spend $11,000.
4. The actual variable expenses of the maintenance department were $30,000.
5. The sanding department produced 1,000 units with a standard machine-hour input of five hours each.
6. The bending department produced 1,400 units with a standard input of five machine-hours each.

PERFORMANCE MEASUREMENT AT SERVICE CENTERS

At service centers, both fixed and variable costs are incurred in the process of rendering indirect services. At this point we defer consideration of service department fixed costs and consider *only* indirect *variable* costs.

Choice of Activity Base

There must exist some measure of activity in production departments which largely determines their demand for indirect services. An electrical power generating center's activity would be determined by, say, the number of machine-hours run in production departments. A maintenance center's activity might be determined by direct labor hours worked in production departments. Insurance and fringe benefits might be determined by payrolls in production departments, and so on. Let us designate whatever measure is agreed upon as the *activity base*. At Bender Company the activity base is machine-hours.

Variable Overhead Rate

When the operating budget is prepared, the level of indirect variable costs is related to the activity base by a *variable overhead rate* which may be computed as

$$\text{Variable overhead rate} = \frac{\text{Expected variable overhead costs}}{\text{Expected value of activity base}} \quad (7\text{--}1)$$

For Bender Company, this rate is

$$\frac{\$27,000}{9,000} = \$3 \text{ per machine hour}$$

Allocable Overhead

When the actual value of the activity base for an operating period is determined, it can be multiplied by the variable overhead rate to compute the overhead allocable to production departments.

$$\text{Variable overhead allocable to production centers} = \text{Variable overhead rate} \times \text{Actual value of the activity base} \quad (7\text{--}2)$$

For Bender Company, overhead allocable to production centers is:

$3 per hour × (6,000 + 5,000) actual machine-hours = $33,000

Service Efficiency Variance

At the same time the allocable overhead is determined, a variance is computed which measures the efficiency of the service center in using resources (labor, materials, supplies, etc.) to meet the production demand for indirect services.

$$\begin{array}{c}\text{Service cen-}\\ \text{ter efficiency}\\ \text{variance}\end{array} = \begin{array}{c}\text{Variable overhead}\\ \text{allocable to}\\ \text{production centers}\end{array} - \begin{array}{c}\text{Actual variable}\\ \text{expenses of}\\ \text{service center}\end{array} \quad (7\text{--}3)$$

This variable will be positive if favorable and negative if unfavorable.

At Bender Company, the maintenance department efficiency variance is

$$\$33,000 - \$30,000 = \$3,000 \; favorable$$

PERFORMANCE MEASUREMENT AT PRODUCTION CENTERS

Again, consider only variable overhead. The production department, which may receive overhead allocations from 2 to 10 or even more service departments, must distribute this overhead among the units of product upon which it works. It is, after all, the production work or product or service output which alone can justify the consumption of indirect services. The production department may choose a measure of its own output as an activity base that is different from the activity base of the service department(s). Common production department activity bases are direct labor hours, direct labor dollars, or units of some direct material. In the Bender Company, the base for allocation from maintenance to production departments is the same as the base for allocation from production to product (both are machine-hours).

Standard Value of Activity Base

When standard costs are prepared, the standard content of a product unit with respect to direct components is established. The standard value of the production department activity base is then—

$$\begin{array}{c}\text{Standard value}\\ \text{of production}\\ \text{activity base}\end{array} = \begin{array}{c}\text{Units of}\\ \text{product}\\ \text{worked on}\end{array} \times \begin{array}{c}\text{Standard quantity of}\\ \text{activity base included}\\ \text{in each product unit}\end{array} \quad (7\text{--}4)$$

At Bender Company the standard value of the production activity base (machine-hours) is:

$$1{,}000 \times 5 \quad + \quad 1{,}400 \times 5 \quad = 12{,}000 \text{ machine-hours}$$
$$\text{(Sanding dept.)} \quad \text{(Bending dept.)}$$

Variable Overhead Rate

When the operating budget was prepared, the level of indirect variable costs allocated to the production department was anticipated and related to the *expected* standard value of the activity base as:

$$\text{Variable (production) overhead rate} = \frac{\text{Expected level of indirect variable costs allocated to production center}}{\text{Expected standard value of production activity base}} \quad (7\text{--}5)$$

Since the base for allocation from maintenance to production is the same as the base for allocation from production to product (both are machine-hours), the variable production overhead rate will be $3, the same as the variable maintenance overhead rate.

Product-Allocated Overhead

The amount of production-allocated overhead which may be transferred to units of product is called *product-allocated overhead*.

$$\text{Product-allocated overhead} = \text{Variable (production) overhead rate} \times \text{Standard value of production activity base} \quad (7\text{--}6)$$

In the sanding department, the amount of product-allocated overhead is

$$\$3 \text{ per hour} \times 5{,}000 \text{ standard hours} = \$15{,}000$$

In the bending department, the amount of product-allocated overhead is

$$\$3 \text{ per hour} \times 7{,}000 \text{ standard hours} = \$21{,}000$$

Production Efficiency Variance

At the same time, you can compute a variance which measures the efficiency of the production center in using indirect services provided to manufacture product.

$$\begin{array}{c}\text{Production center}\\\text{efficiency variance}\end{array} = \begin{array}{c}\text{Product-}\\\text{allocated}\\\text{overhead}\end{array} - \begin{array}{c}\text{Variable overhead}\\\text{allocated to}\\\text{production center}\end{array} \qquad (7\text{--}7)$$

This variance will be positive if favorable and negative if unfavorable.

The production efficiency variances at Bender Company are:

Sanding: $15,000 − $3 per hour × 6,000 actual hours
= $3,000 *unfavorable*

Bending: $21,000 − $3 per hour × 5,000 actual hours
= $6,000 *favorable*

The Fixed Overhead Spending Variance

Fixed costs are:

a) The costs of maintaining *capacity* to produce, and
b) Costs which are committed (must be incurred) for the operating period under consideration.

Determination of the capacity a business should have is a high-level decision for which service center managers should not be held responsible. Utilization of capacity may depend on market factors and thus be only partially controllable. The most useful fixed overhead variance is thus a spending variance, which shows the difference between planned fixed costs and actual fixed costs. Waste, inflation, economy, etc., are factors which may cause planned and actual fixed costs to vary.

The fixed overhead spending variance is computed as shown in (7–8):

$$\begin{array}{c}\text{Fixed overhead}\\\text{spending variance}\end{array} = \begin{array}{c}\text{Planned}\\\text{fixed costs}\end{array} - \begin{array}{c}\text{Actual}\\\text{fixed costs}\end{array} \qquad (7\text{--}8)$$

This variance will be positive if favorable and negative if unfavorable.

At Bender Company, this variance is:

$11,000 − $20,000 = $9,000 *unfavorable*

Performance Reporting

A summary performance report showing how overhead costs and allocations and variances are related might look like Figure 7–2. A flow-of-costs diagram corresponding to this report is shown in Figure 7–3.

FIGURE 7–2

BENDER COMPANY
Performance Report
March

	Maintenance	Sanding	Bending
Total costs incurred	$ 50,000	...	...
Less: Spending variance	(9,000) U	...	...
Other capacity costs	(11,000)	...	...
Add: Maintenance			
Efficiency variance	3,000 F		
Allocable costs	$ 33,000		
Allocated to sanding	(18,000)	$18,000	
Allocated to bending	(15,000)		$15,000
	$ 0		
Less: Sanding efficiency variance		(3,000) U	
Add: Bending efficiency variance			6,000 F
Total product-allocated overhead		$15,000	$21,000

In Figure 7–2, we take advantage of the equality of incurred costs with product-allocated costs plus favorable variances and minus unfavorable variances:

$$\text{Product-allocated overhead} = \text{Variable overhead incurred} + \text{Favorable variances} - \text{Unfavorable variances} \quad (7\text{–}9)$$

This equality is used twice: first, to obtain allocable costs, and second, to obtain product-allocated overhead.

DIRECT AND FULL ABSORPTION COSTING

You have seen illustrated in this chapter what is termed *direct costing*. When direct costing is used, no fixed costs are included in the cost valuation of manufactured products. For financial reporting pur-

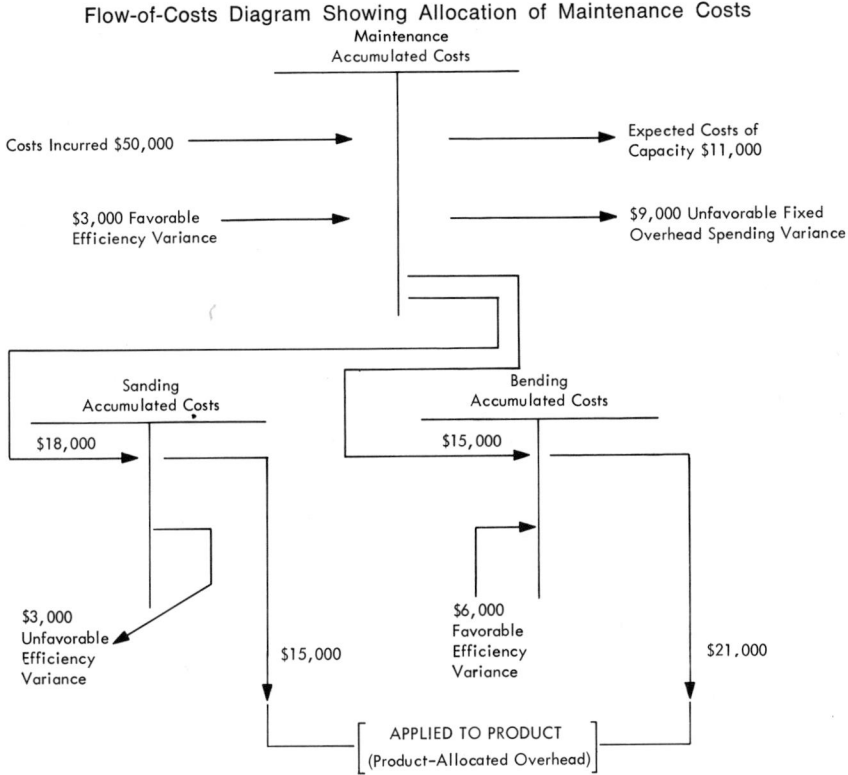

FIGURE 7–3
Flow-of-Costs Diagram Showing Allocation of Maintenance Costs

```
                    Maintenance
                 Accumulated Costs

Costs Incurred $50,000 ──────────▶           ──────────▶  Expected Costs of
                                                          Capacity $11,000

 $3,000 Favorable   ──────────▶              ──────────▶  $9,000 Unfavorable Fixed
 Efficiency Variance                                      Overhead Spending Variance


      Sanding                                Bending
 Accumulated Costs                      Accumulated Costs

    $18,000                                 $15,000


                                            $6,000
   $3,000                                   Favorable
   Unfavorable                              Efficiency          $21,000
   Efficiency        $15,000                Variance
   Variance

                        ┌  APPLIED TO PRODUCT  ┐
                        └ (Product-Allocated Overhead) ┘
```

poses, fixed costs must be included in the reported cost of goods sold and in ending inventory. When volume of production fluctuates, and fixed costs become part of product cost, unit product cost can fluctuate, causing income to vary as a function of production volume as well as of sales volume. This method of costing, called *full absorption costing,* is not desirable for managerial performance reporting.

Imagine a business which incurs *no* variable costs but does incur a steady $100,000 in fixed costs each year, regardless of production volume. Production volume may be up to 10,000 units per year. Each unit may be sold for $15.

In the first year of operations, 10,000 units are manufactured and 5,000 units are sold. In the second year of operations, 10,000 units are manufactured and 6,000 are sold. In the third year of operations,

1,000 units are manufactured and 10,000 are sold. Figure 7–4 illustrates reported income using both direct and full absorption costing.

FIGURE 7–4
Comparison of Calculated Income Using Direct and Full Absorption Costing

	Year 1	Year 2	Year 3	All 3 Years
Direct costing:				
Revenue @ $15 per unit sold...........	$ 75,000	$ 90,000	$ 150,000	
Less: Direct variable cost of sales............	0	0	0	
Contribution margin............	$ 75,000	$ 90,000	$ 150,000	
Less: Fixed costs.......	(100,000)	(100,000)	(100,000)	
Revenue less direct cost of sales and manufacturing fixed costs..........	$ (25,000)	$ (10,000)	$ 50,000	$15,000
	Loss	Loss	Profit	Profit
Full absorption costing:				
Revenue @ $15 per unit sold...........	$ 75,000	$ 90,000	$ 150,000	
BOP inventory........	0	50,000	90,000	
Add: Cost of goods produced..........	100,000	100,000	100,000	
Units produced.....	10,000	10,000	1,000	
Cost per unit produced.......	$10	$10	$100	
Less: Cost of goods sold @ $10 per unit.......	(50,000)	(60,000)	(190,000)	
Revenue less cost of sales.............	$ 25,000	$ 30,000	$ (40,000)	$15,000
	Profit	Profit	Loss	Profit

Examine Figure 7–4 and note the differences between these two product-costing methods for income determination. Also note that for these three years, *for which as a whole* production equaled sales, both methods produced identical accounting profit measurements. Full absorption costing will, relative to direct costing, defer fixed costs recognition as expense until a future period if production level is greater than sales level. If production level is lower than sales level, fixed costs of previous periods plus all the fixed costs of the current period will be matched against revenue. The former effect occurred in year 1 and year 2; the latter effect occurred in year 3. Only if sales level equals production level, as was true for the three-year period, will both methods give the same result.

In performance evaluation, you would be interested in production efficiency and sales efficiency, and would require performance information on each function separately in order to manage them. Full absorption costing makes it difficult to acquire this separate information and is not preferred for internal management use. Direct costing has the advantage there.

OVERHEAD ALLOCATION AND DECISION MAKING

To see why, follow us through this example. Exemplary Furniture Company operates a plant in River City in which two lines of furniture are produced: Spanish and Contemporary. Here is information about the two product lines, which are produced in separate departments under the same roof:

Direct variable costs of Spanish	$ 45,000
Direct variable costs of Contemporary	28,000
Indirect variable and fixed costs	125,000
Revenue from sale of Spanish	90,000
Revenue from sale of Contemporary	112,000

One day the management decided to have a round table and discuss ways of allocating indirect costs to the product lines. The accounting office prepared Figure 7–5, which shows product line profitability statements under two different indirect cost allocation procedures:

1. Allocate costs equally to each product line.
2. Allocate costs to each product line on basis of floor space devoted to its manufacture.

Naturally, the manager of the Spanish department would not accept (1), and the manager of the Contemporary department would not accept (2). Further, *both* men were unable to agree on a way of allocating the indirect costs that was "fair" to each department.

You must accept that there is no clear-cut way to attach overhead costs to units of product. The benefit to overhead allocation was not

FIGURE 7–5
Allocation Basis Comparison

	Spanish		Contemporary	
	(1) Equally	(2) Floor	(1) Equally	(2) Floor
Sales revenue	$ 90,000	$90,000	$112,000	$112,000
Less: Direct variable costs	45,000	45,000	28,000	28,000
Operating margins	$ 45,000	$45,000	$ 84,000	$ 84,000
Less: Allocated indirect costs	62,500	12,500	62,500	112,500
Margin after allocation	$(17,500)	$32,500	$ 21,500	$ (28,500)

to produce information useful in determining product profitability, but to determine the efficiency of production and use of overhead services.

For planning purposes, you would never allocate overhead in any way that distorts the relative profitability of a product, since planning requires knowledge of the contribution margin—the difference between unit price and unit direct costs.

Here are those margins at Exemplary Furniture:

$$\text{Spanish} \dots \dots \dots \dots \$45,000$$
$$\text{Contemporary} \dots \dots \dots 84,000$$

Their ratio is $45/84 = 0.536$. Here is an allocation of overhead which adds up to $125,000 and also is in the *same* ratio:

$$\text{Spanish allocated overhead} \dots \dots \dots \$ 43,605$$
$$\text{Contemporary allocated overhead} \dots \dots 81,395$$
$$\text{Total overhead} \dots \dots \dots \dots \$125,000$$

There is no distortion of *relative* contribution margins, either:

Spanish contribution margin $= \$45,000 - \$43,605 = \$1,395$

$$\text{Ratio } \frac{1,395}{2,605} = 0.536$$

Contemporary contribution margin $= \$84,000 - \$81,395 = \$2,605$

Probably no allocation process that also satisfies the performance evaluation requirements will produce precisely this allocation. However, the *relative-contribution-margin* approach to overhead allocation can provide a rule of thumb for evaluating the "fairness" of an existing allocation method.

The essential fact about Spanish and Contemporary manufacture is that *taken together,* both product lines show a profitable plant. Neither of the allocation methods proposed in Figure 7–5 show both product lines as profitable, and therefore neither method is acceptable. We return to this topic in a broader context in Chapter 9.

SUMMARY

The process of overhead allocation permits a reconciliation of overhead costs incurred with overhead actually allocated to units of product. The allocation occurs in two stages:

1. Distribution of service center costs to producing departments.
2. Distribution of costs allocated to producing departments to units of product.

Control information about spending, capacity, and efficiency may be generated at each allocation. Without a standard cost system, overhead allocation will not produce control information. Overhead allocation does produce a unit cost for a product, necessary for income determination and inventory valuation. For managerial purposes, it is not necessary to allocate fixed costs to product units; it *is* necessary to do this for financial reporting purposes, producing confusing shifts in fixed costs between reporting periods.

For decision making, no overhead allocation methods are fully acceptable; however, relative-contribution-margin allocation produces a benchmark for evaluating the fairness of allocation processes used for control purposes.

QUESTIONS

1. Why are indirect costs such a large part of any complex modern undertaking?
2. Zee Company makes 17 products in its plant. One of these has direct costs of $50 and allocated (overhead) costs of $70. The

product sells for $100 per unit. There is a proposal to discontinue the product since it is produced and sold at a loss. Do you endorse the proposal? Why?

3. In view of the drawbacks of overhead allocation, why do it?

4. A company has no variable costs but does have $120,000 annually in fixed costs. In 1973 it produces 40,000 units with a cost of $120,000/40,000 = $3 each. These are sold for $5 each. In 1974 it produces 20,000 units with an average unit cost of $6. The marketing manager wants to leave the price alone, but the manufacturing manager insists that since unit cost has doubled, the company must sell the product at double last year's price—or $10. What do you think?

5. What information would be lost if indirect costs were allocated directly to units of product by service departments, ignoring the customary allocation to production departments first?

6. Why not use one rate to allocate both fixed and variable costs from service to production centers? Would this be a deficiency if no standard allocation rate existed?

7. What is an "efficiency" variance? Explain how overhead efficiency variances are related to the efficiency variance described in Chapter 6. Are standard overhead allocation rates in any sense related to standard costs?

8. In what sense do fixed costs relate to or represent established capacity? Why cannot capacity be changed quickly to accommodate fluctuating demand?

9. What is the importance of the distinction between the service efficiency and the production efficiency variances? Why is it impossible to combine the two into one efficiency variance?

10. What are the characteristics of a good overhead application basis? Answer from the perspective of both service department and production department. (Remember that a basis used to allocate from service to production need not be the same as the basis used to allocate from production to product units.)

11. Consider the performance report in Figure 7–2. Describe how you would break up this table into individual performance reports, each intended for *one* service or production department.

12. Why is there no production department overhead spending variance?

13. Who in a business would decide how much capacity to maintain (and thus set the level of planned fixed costs)?

14. Cruse Company produces two products. Revenue from product A was $30,000; variable costs were $15,000. Revenue from product B was $40,000; variable costs were $35,000. Fixed and indirect variable costs totaled $12,000.
    a) Suggest the best way to allocate these costs to A and B.
    b) The manufacturing department assigned half the overhead to A and half the overhead to B. Subsequently the marketing manager recommended that B be discontinued. Why?

15. University faculty members may find themselves involved in "sponsored research" supported by government foundation grants. The university administration will normally impose a "tax" on the grant, claiming that the amount appropriated helps to cover indirect costs to the university of allowing the faculty member to perform the research. Faculty members themselves often resent this policy of universities. Discuss.

EXERCISES

16. Which of the following would be likely to be classified as overhead costs:
    a) Depreciation.
    b) Cost of skeleton crews.
    c) Direct materials costs.
    d) Insurance.
    e) Electricity to operate airconditioning machinery.
    f) Gasoline to operate plant manager's plant car.
    g) Property taxes.

17. Green Company expects to have $34,000 in total overhead costs, of which $14,000 represents fixed overhead. The plant has a capacity of 20,000 direct labor hours, but this period expects to work only 16,000 direct labor hours. What will be the *variable* overhead rate?

18. Neil Company's variable overhead rate is $5 per direct labor hour. In January, 1,000 direct labor hours were worked and actual indirect

variable costs were $5,500. Compute the efficiency variance and state whether it is a service or production efficiency variance.

19. Neil Company's production during January (see Exercise 18 above) was 500 units, each with a standard direct labor content of 3 hours. Compute the efficiency variance and state whether it is a service or production efficiency variance.

20. The winding department has the following indirect costs:

Allocated from service departments	$15,000
Indirect variable labor	3,000
Indirect variable materials	4,000

During the period these costs occurred the department completed 1,000 units of work, each with a standard direct labor hour content of 7 hours. Indirect variable costs are allocated to product at the rate of $4 per standard direct labor hour. Compute the production efficiency variance of the winding department.

21. Grain Company incurred fixed overhead costs in 1973 of $110,000. Capacity of Grain Company's plant is storage of 40,000 tons of wheat. This capacity was planned to have annual fixed costs of $2.50 per ton. Compute the fixed overhead spending variance.

22. Young Company has been in operation for three years. Here are data on various aspects of these operations:

	Year 1	Year 2	Year 3
Capacity (units)	1,000	1,000	1,000
Fixed costs	$10,000	$10,000	$10,000
Production (units)	500	700	800
Sales (units)	400	700	900

Compute income if there were no variable costs, each unit sold for $50; use full absorption and direct costing, and compare.

PROBLEMS

23. The Helpin Laundry operates a central cleaning station and three neighborhood pickup-delivery stations. Customers bring clothes to these stations to be picked up by truck and taken to the central station. At the central station, commercial cleaning equipment cleans

the clothes, after which they are returned to the neighborhood stations.

Because laundry is washed in large batches, all of the central station's costs are treated as indirect overhead. In February, these costs were $11,000 fixed costs and $23,000 variable costs. *Budgeted* total central station costs are:

Monthly expenses = $12,000 + $0.20 per pound of laundry processed

In February, 100,000 pounds of laundry were processed. Of these, 30,000 pounds came from station A, 40,000 pounds came from station B, and 30,000 pounds came from station C. In a normal month, up to 150,000 pounds of laundry may be processed.

Required:

a) Compute the total central station costs for February which are allocable to neighborhood stations.
b) Compute the spending variance for fixed costs in February.
c) Compute the service efficiency variance for February.
d) Why would management be more interested in the variances than in the absolute amounts of expenses?

24. Beke Welding Service has a record of excellent quality welding but very poor cost control. For example, in the last quarter, jobs were completed which had an estimated cost of $80,000 but an actual cost of $100,000. "I don't understand it," said Mr. Beke; "I keep absolute track of everything that goes into a welding job—metal, rods, work hours. Why do my costs keep getting away from me?"

Your investigation shows that there is one service center which provides all utilities, security, administration, and other indirect services. The quarterly expenses of this single service center were:

	Actual	Expected
Fixed:		
Supervisory salaries.......	$15,000	$14,000
Depreciation............	4,000	4,000
Security	1,000	500
Total..............	$20,000	$18,500
Variable:		
Utilities	$24,000	
Maintenance............	3,000	
Other services	10,000	
Total..............	$37,000	

You find that there is one production center and that the best of several measures of its activity level is the number of labor hours worked on production jobs. Last quarter there were 6,000 direct labor hours worked on jobs. The standard number of labor hours that *should* have been worked was 5,000. The total expected variable overhead when a normal 10,000 direct labor hours are worked is $60,000.

Required:

a) Compute the variable costs for the service center last quarter which are allocable to production centers.
b) Compute the overhead that was applied to units of product last quarter, assuming only variable overhead is allocated.
c) Compute the fixed overhead spending variance, the service efficiency variance, and the production efficiency variance.
d) How much of Beke Welding's cost overruns may be attributed to (1) underutilization of plant capacity? (2) inefficiency in the service center? and (3) inefficiency in the production center? How much is not attributable to overhead variations and therefore lies elsewhere in the operation?

25. The Davis Manufacturing Company has the following departments: (1) general factory administration, (2) machining, and (3) assembly. At the end of each period the general factory administration overhead costs are apportioned to the producing departments on the basis of actual man-hours used by the respective producing departments. The overhead costs and man-hours used for the period are as follows:

	General Factory Administration	Machining	Assembly	Total
Overhead:				
Fixed	$100,000	$10,000	$20,000	$130,000
Variable	380,000	5,000	20,000	405,000
Man-hours:				
Expected		24,000	12,000	36,000
Actual		25,000	10,000	35,000

Required:

a) Reapportion the service department's variable overhead costs to the machining and assembly departments. Compute the service department efficiency variance if the variable overhead is normally $400,000 at the level of 40,000 labor hours worked.

b) Give the total overhead of the producing departments, including allocation of variable general factory administration costs.

26. U-Watch Company manufactures home television systems. The technology in this area changes very rapidly, and the company must continuously review all its manufacturing procedures, standard costs, and overhead allocation policies. There are two manufacturing centers—electronics and assembly—and three service centers—utilities, maintenance, and quality control.

At the present time, U-Watch is recomputing the standard overhead content of its standard model video system. Utilities costs are allocated at the rate of $3 per transister used, maintenance costs are allocated at the rate of $3 per pound of weight in the product, and quality control is allocated at the rate of $4 per direct labor hour.

Here are the standard values for these components in the production departments per unit system produced:

	Electronics	Assembly
Transistors used	50	14
Pounds added to weight	10	18
Direct labor hours	6	7

In a typical week, each department will complete 150 systems.

Required:

a) Compute the standard overhead cost content of a standard unit system. How much of this is added in each production department?

b) In a typical week, how much total overhead will be added in each production department?

c) In a typical week, how much overhead will each service department be able to allocate to both production centers?

27. Brain Software creates custom computer programs for clients. Brain owns an Error Mark II Computer and incurs annual fixed costs related to the computer of $84,000. The company began operations in 1972.

The level of business at Brain varies remarkably. When a project is undertaken, the direct costs associated with the project are attached it while it is in process. Normally, variable costs are $6 per hour worked by programmers on a project. All fixed costs are attached to work done during a year. The basis of allocation is actual programmer hours worked.

Lately, the volume of work done has been picking up—but profits have, in the opinion of Brain's puzzled president, mysteriously lagged behind.

Specifically, in 1972 the firm worked 6,000 programmer hours, with 3,000 of these hours (and the attached fixed overhead) attached to "work in process" or unfinished projects at the end of 1972. In 1973 the firm worked 10,000 programmer hours to finish the projects begun in 1972 and to start new projects. Five thousand of these hours (and attendant fixed overhead) were attached to projects still incomplete at the end of 1973. In 1974 the company plans to work 14,000 programmer hours to finish jobs begun in 1973 and begin additional projects. The company estimates that 2,000 of these hours (and attendant fixed overhead) will be attached to projects still in process at the end of 1974. Billings for work *completed* were: 1972, $90,000; 1973, $150,000; and 1974, $210,000 (estimated).

Required:

a) Assuming that programmer wages are the only direct cost and that computer costs are the only fixed cost, compute Brain Software's income in 1972, 1973, and 1974 (estimated). Use full absorption costing.
b) Repeat (a) but use *direct* costing.
c) Compare (a) and (b). Which gives higher income figures? Which is preferred by managers? Which is preferred by users of financial statements?

28. U-Findit Calculator Company makes small solid-state calculators. The calculator is assembled by one department, which uses 12 labor hours at $5 each and direct materials with standard cost of $40. This assembly department receives indirect services from the factory department, which distributes $4 in costs for each labor hour actually worked in the assembly department. Last month 4,100 calculators were assembled. Forty-nine thousand direct labor hours were worked. Total wages were $250,000. The factory department in-

curred $190,000 in variable costs in addition to fixed costs of $80,000; planned fixed costs are $85,000.

Required:

a) Compute the standard cost of work performed.
b) Compute and interpret all variances related to last month's manufacturing activity.

29. The Pyle Corporation manufactures and sells an industrial communicator unit, using a standard cost system for costing and control purposes. The standard cost of a single communicator unit is:

Material, 1 pound plastic @ $2	$ 2.00
Direct labor, 1.6 hours @ $4	6.40
Variable overhead cost	3.00
	$11.40

The overhead cost per unit was calculated from the following annual overhead cost budget for a 60,000-unit volume:

Indirect labor, 30,000 hours @ $4	$120,000
Supplies—oil, 60,000 gallons @ $0.50	30,000
Allocated variable service department costs	30,000
Total variable overhead costs	$180,000

The actual figures for November, when 5,000 units were produced, are:

Material, 5,300 pounds @ $2	$10,600
Direct labor, 8,200 hours @ $4.10	33,620
Indirect labor, 2,400 hours @ $4.10	9,840
Supplies—oil, 6,000 gallons @ $0.55	3,300
Allocated variable service department costs	3,200
Total	$60,560

Required:

a) Prepare a report showing standard and actual variable overhead costs for November.
b) Compute and identify the variances associated with variable overhead in November.

(Adapted from the December 1972 Certificate in Management Accounting Examination)

30. The Draft Manufacturing Company has three departments: general factory administration (service), machining (production), and assembly (production). At the end of each period, the general factory administration department's fixed costs are apportioned to the producing departments on the basis of total man-hours used by the respective producing departments. The fixed costs and proportion of man-hours used for the period are as follows:

	General Factory Administration	Machining	Assembly	Total
Fixed costs	$480,000			
Man-hours used		24,000	12,000	36,000

Required:

Reapportion general factory administration fixed costs to the two producing departments.

31. Flyclean Company operates on a contract basis to tidy up airliners at the end of a flight, before they are sent out again. Crews descend on an airliner and sweep, scrub, empty, and wash until the interior looks and smells clean. (This is especially hard to do after a night cargo flight with livestock aboard!)

The crews consist of five persons each, each earning $3 per hour. Direct materials for a cleanup of a typical 150-passenger plane cost $55. The cleanup lasts 1.5 hours.

Flyclean management allocates indirect variable costs at the rate of $60 per cleanup. In June, 400 flights were cleaned; this was considered to be a normal number. Fixed costs of operation are $15,000 per month, normally. Flyclean charges $220 for a cleanup.

In July, the company performed 500 cleanups, in the process working 700 hours of overtime on cleanup crews. Indirect variable costs including overtime premium were $35,000. The overtime premium is $1.50 per hour. Flyclean's July profit was $21,250, and the company president sent a message to all department chiefs, saying "Congratulations to all on a fine performance based on comparison with the previous month."

Required:
- a) What was June profit?
- b) In your opinion, was the president's message justified in respect to indirect-services responsibility centers? Why or why not?

DECISION CASE 7–1: VALIANT COMPANY

Valiant Company is a small manufacturer of specialized tree-surgery equipment. The company has suffered from lower-than-normal profits for two or three years and has fired the man who was president during that period. Now, the directors have chosen Mr. B. Ware as president, and have arranged that his compensation be equal to 10 percent of the company's before-tax margin. Here is a summary of financial information about Valiant for the year before Ware became president:

Balance Sheet

Cash and accounts receivable	$ 50,000	Current liabilities	$200,000
Inventories	200,000	Long-term debt	200,000
Net fixed assets	600,000	Owners equities	450,000
	$850,000		$850,000

Income Statement

Sales revenue			$1,200,000
Inventory BOP		250,000	
Add: Direct costs of manufacturing		800,000	
Plus: Fixed costs of manufacturing		600,000	
		$1,650,000	
Less: Inventory EOP		200,000	
Cost of goods sold			1,450,000
Margin before taxes		(Loss)	$ (250,000)

"Obviously we must increase production to fully absorb fixed costs!" exclaimed Mr. Ware. And he did increase production. In fact, the next year's condensed accounting statements looked like this:

Balance Sheet

Cash and accounts receivable	$ 50,000	Current liabilities	$ 200,000
Inventories	600,000	Long-term debt	200,000
Net fixed assets	600,000	Owners equities	850,000
	$1,250,000		$1,250,000

Income Statement

Sales revenue			$1,800,000
Inventory BOP		$ 200,000	
Add: Direct costs of manufacturing		1,200,000	
Plus: Fixed costs of manufacturing		600,000	
		$2,000,000	
Less: Inventory EOP		600,000	
Cost of goods sold			1,400,000
Margin before taxes			$ 400,000

At the end of this year, Mr. Ware resigned as president of Valiant Company and stated, "I have restored this company to a state of pristine business vigor. I must seek other challenges equal to my talents!" And he did leave, collecting his $40,000 bonus as he went.

Required:

a) What would have been the profit of Valiant Company using direct costing (note that direct costs of sales are roughly two thirds of sales revenue)?

b) Do you think that Valiant's financial position has been improved? Why or why not?

c) If you were a member of the board of directors of Valiant Company, would you favor an arrangement similar to this one for the next president of the company? Can you think of a better way to determine compensation and still preserve an incentive to improve the company?

BIBLIOGRAPHY

Books

Horngren, Charles T. *Accounting for Management Control.* 2d ed. Englewood Cliffs, N.J.: Prentice-Hall, Inc., 1970.

Matz, Adolph, and Currey, Othel J. *Cost Accounting: Planning and Control.* 5th ed. Cincinnati, Ohio: South-Western Publishing Co., 1972.

Articles

Arcus, Albert L., and Pietsch, William H. "Planned Performance and the Product Cost Controversy," *Management Accounting,* September 1970.

Broster, E. J. "The Folly Called Absorption Costing," *Certified Accountants Journal,* April 1971.

Fremgen, James H. "The Direct Costing Controversy—An Identification of Issues," *The Accounting Review,* January 1964.

Frye, Delbert J. "Combined Costing Method: Absorption and Direct," *Management Accounting,* January 1971.

Largay, III, James A. "Microeconomic Foundations of Variable Costing," *The Accounting Review,* January 1973.

Sharp, Harold E. "Control and Management of Indirect Expenses," *Management Accounting,* February 1973.

Witt, Wallace E. "Work Measurement of Indirect Labor," *Management Accounting,* November 1971.

8

Accounting for Manufacturing Activity

THIS CHAPTER gives you the methods and significance of accounting used in planning and controlling manufacturing processes: (1) You learn two important methods of producing forecasted or real unit costs: by *job,* or by *process.* Although many product costs will be estimated or accumulated by methods not purely either of these, such methods can always be understood as combinations of job and process costing. A key to designing a cost accumulation system and understanding its messages is familiarity with job and process costing. (2) You find that *all* manufacturing information systems have the elements described in Chapters 3–7: accounting by responsibility centers, production and service centers, standard costs, and allocation of overhead. You will not find radically unfamiliar material here.

JOB AND PROCESS COSTING

Job and process costing are methods of reporting and controlling manufacturing costs—and through costs, the operations which generate the costs and consume resources. Job costing is found in industries such as custom shipyards, construction companies, hospitals (for structuring a patient's billing), and contract research companies whose work is in the form of sequential, irregular, often made-to-order items—or jobs. In job costing, costs flow through production and service centers to individual jobs and become cost of sales when the job is complete and delivered to the buyer.

Process costing is best for mass-production processes whose output is standardized identical units of product. Chemicals, petroleum products, consumer appliances, electronic units, and clothing may be produced by such processes. One unit of output is the same as any other. For example, no one gallon of a refinery's daily 500,000-gallon gasoline output is distinguishably different from the other 499,999 gallons. In process costing, costs are accumulated at production centers and allocated to all work done by the process in a given time period. Each unit of work done is assigned an average cost. Thus, if a center completes 100 units and period costs are $2,500, each unit is allocated $25 of costs.

In this chapter we develop job costing in detail. Process costing's distinguishing features will be described less elaborately.

PLANNING A JOB

When a new job enters the plant, a job specification sheet for it is developed. This specification is a budget for the job and shows the components of the job by production centers, and at each production center by kinds of mterials, labor, and machine time to be required. These specifications serve as prompters to production centers to make timely requisitions and have available the required machine and labor time. When the specification is complete, the job will be scheduled. All schedules are tentative but nevertheless useful in helping production center supervisors plan activities. The service center supervisors review production schedules and estimate what the requirement will be for indirect services.

A typical job specification sheet showing expected requirements at one production center where three types of labor, two types of machine-hours, and three types of material are added to jobs might look like Figure 8–1.

The materials requirements in the job specification sheet provide a guide to inventory levels in the storeroom and to placing orders by the company purchasing office in order to have adequate stocks of re-

FIGURE 8–1
Job Specification Sheet

PRODUCTION CENTER 42
Job No. 12345

	Period 10	Period 11	Period 12	Period 13

Labor hours type A
Labor hours type B
Labor hours type F
Machine-hours type 2
Machine-hours type 4
Chronium clad sheet
  10 Ga.
Copper rod (feet)
  ¼"
  ½"
Assembly from center 31
Send to center 43				

quired items on hand. The mix of labor skills required by all jobs during planning periods provide a guide to the personnel office in hiring new workers and retraining present employees.

THE FLOW OF JOB COSTS

Job costs are described through the special documents identified in Figure 8–2. These documents are as follows:

Materials and supplies report, which shows the materials and supplies issued from the storeroom to the various centers. Each center receives the report for its own materials and supplies received.

Labor report, which shows the labor hours worked in each center.

Overhead allocation report, which shows the distribution of overhead to production centers. Each service center receives a report showing overhead incurred, overhead allocated, and related variances. Each production center receives a report showing overhead allocated *to* it by all service departments and overhead allocated *by* it to jobs, and related variances.

Materials assignment report, which shows how materials and related costs at a production center are allocated to jobs. Only standard or scheduled amounts as in the job specification may be allocated to jobs; assorted variances (spending and efficiency) account for any difference.

Labor assignment report, which shows how labor and related costs at a production center are allocated to jobs. Only standard or scheduled amounts as in the job specification may be allocated to jobs; assorted spending (wage rate) and efficiency variances account for any difference.

Job control report, which for a single job shows all the inputs and standard costs cumulatively, and other information about the current status of the job.

Job transfer ticket, which is a receipt for a job passed by one production center to another.

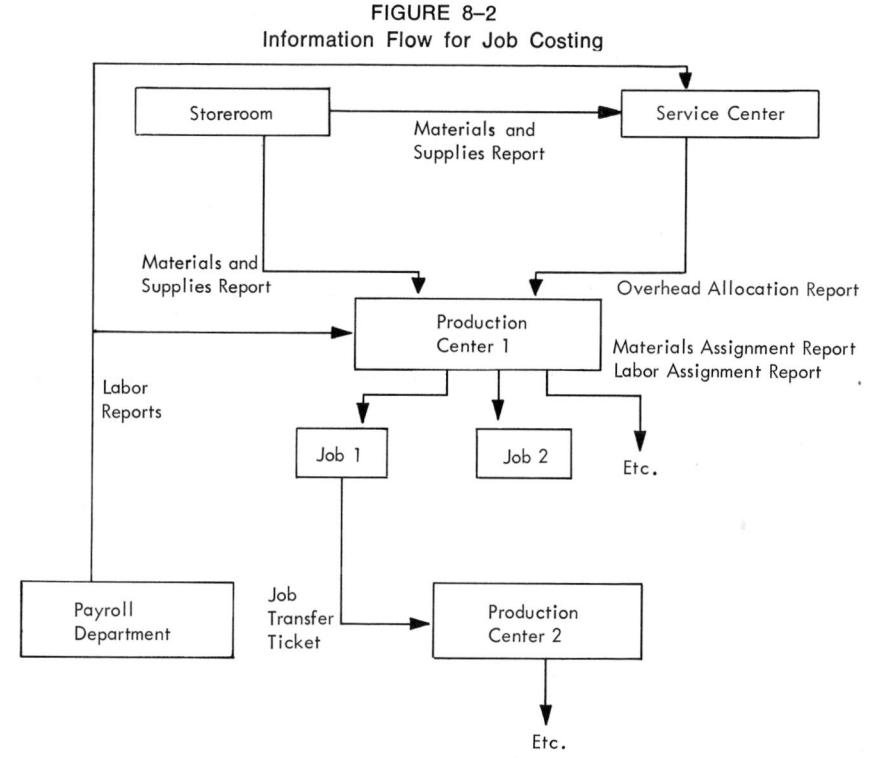

FIGURE 8–2
Information Flow for Job Costing

Materials and Labor Assignment Reports

Cost flow through responsibility centers follows Figure 8–2. The account categories themselves are shown in Figure 8–3, with arrows representing accounting entries.

FIGURE 8–3
Accounts Needed for Job Costing

JOB DOCUMENTATION

Here is an example which illustrates some typical job-manufacturing cost flows and reports. The Superior Boat Company makes custom fiberglass yachts. These boats are designed to the specifications of individuals by naval architects. Each yacht is different from all others, yet there is similarity in the operations required to make any hull, any deck, to outfit any interior, or to install rigging. The Superior Boat Company recognizes this and is organized according to Figure 8–4 for purposes of manufacturing and using the job order costing system.

During the week April 17–22, the hull department will start its work on job 198. The job specification sheet for this job calls for these inputs to the job in the hull department that week:

200 yards woven roving @ $2 each, total	$ 400
600 yards cloth @ $1.50 each, total	900
200 gallons resin @ $8 each, total	1,600
120 hours skilled labor @ $5 each, total	600
80 hours utility labor @ $3 each, total	240

These inputs are the standards for work on job 198 that week. In the example, only variances related to this job will be identified.

FIGURE 8–4
Organization Chart of Superior Boat Company Plant

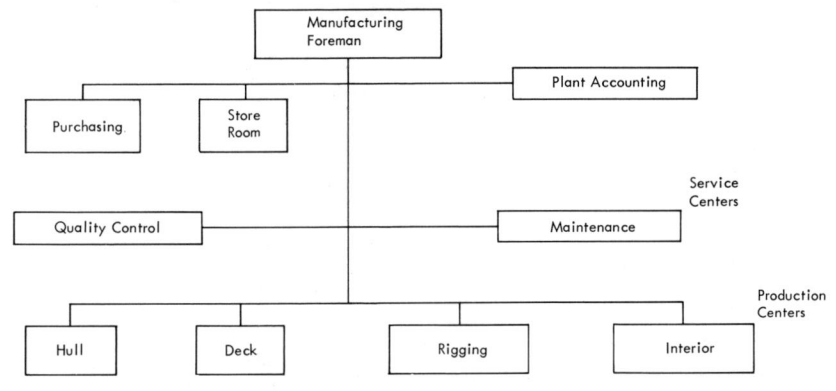

A materials requisition submitted by hull to storeroom for materials and supplies appears in Figure 8–5.

FIGURE 8–5
Hull Department Materials Requisition

No. *4567*

HULL DEPARTMENT
Materials and Supplies Requisition

Issue the following supplies:

I.D. No.	Description	Quantity	(Issued)	(Accepted)
1. # 45	Roving	200 yds.		
2. # 05	Cloth	600 yds.		
3. # 123	Resin	200 gals.		

Comments or
Special Instructions

Authorized Signature Hull Department

Date

The documentation for labor is similar. The labor report (Figure 8–6) shows *actual* hours worked on each job in process, standard hours, and the job labor efficiency variances. The "indirect" column is for within-center overhead.

FIGURE 8-6
Hull Department Labor Report

April 17–22	HULL DEPARTMENT Labor Report			No. 199
Type Labor	Hours Worked	Indirect	Job 198	Job 152
Skilled				
Actual	120	16	80	24
Standard	160	16	120	24
Variance			40 F	
Unskilled				
Actual	90		90	
Standard	80		80	
Variance			10 U	

Each production center will also receive a materials report. Because this report is similar to the labor report we will not show it. Materials standards for job 198 were observed, except for a favorable resin variance of 20 gallons. The labor and materials reports enable each center to account for all the labor, materials and supplies received as assigned to jobs, "indirect," or efficiency variances.

The service departments assign their costs to production centers, which in turn assign them to jobs. An assignment sheet for allocating overhead to production centers looks like Figure 8–7.

In Figure 8–7, you reconcile incurred overhead with allocated overhead. There is one entry in each column under "production centers." Each entry will be added to that production center's internal overhead to give the total indirect costs that center must assign to jobs or recognize as production overhead efficiency variance.

The accounting office will record the work done and compute the standard costs of each job and any related variances, using the labor, materials, and overhead reports and standard wages, costs, and allocation rates as guides. These new job standard costs will be recorded on departmental cumulative cost control reports, such as the hull department report in Figure 8–8. On this report, actual quantities at standard costs are recorded in the "total" and "indirect" columns. Each job column records first the standard cost (using standard input quantities) of that job, then any efficiency variance related to that job and input. The bottom row gives standard cost totals for each job, total variances on each job, and total costs attached to jobs in process in

FIGURE 8–7
Maintenance Department Overhead Allocation Report

April 17–22	MAINTENANCE DEPARTMENT Overhead Allocation Report			No. 3422
		Production Centers		
		Hull	Deck	Rigging	Interior

		Hull	Deck	Rigging	Interior
Overhead assignments (based on actual direct labor hours)	$ (990) (1,210) (880) (1,870)	$990	$1,210	$880	$1,870
Total overhead assigned	$ 4,950	$990	$1,210	$880	$1,870
Overhead incurred: Labor cost report . . . . Material cost report . . . . Indirect variable costs	$ 2,350 1,100 1,050				
Total overhead incurred	$ 4,500				
	450 Maintenance efficiency variance (*favorable*)				
	$ 4,950 Agrees with total overhead assigned				

that department. *Note* that the variances must be added to the "end of this week" total to make it agree with the total of standard job costs.

The cumulative cost assignment reports will be used by the accounting office to prepare job control report for each job. The organization of a job control report for job 198 is reflected in Figure 8–9. A job control report should also give the state of completion of the job and the variances related to the job in each production center. Such information may help to identify a troublesome job or a balky production department.

The accounting department will maintain a revised schedule for the job, showing which departments are ahead or behind the most recent schedule.

Documentary Support

All accounting for manufacturing is done in the accounting office based on documentary support furnished by the manufacturing centers. The reference to appropriate documentary support is provided to iden-

FIGURE 8–8
Hull Department Cumulative Cost Assignment Report

HULL DEPARTMENT
Cumulative Cost Assignment Report

April 17–22

Reference	Total	Indirect	Job 198 Std. Cost	Job 198 Variance	Job 152 Std. Cost	Job 152 Variance
End of previous week	$ 8,100				$ 8,100	
Transfers in	0					
Labor report (Figure 8–6):						
120 hrs. @ $5 ea.	600	$ 80	$ 600	$200 F	120	$ 0
90 hrs. @ $3 ea.	270		240	30 U		
Materials report (Figure 8–5):						
200 yds. ro. @ $2 ea.	400		400			
600 yds. cl. @ $1.50 ea.	900		900			
180 gals. res. @ $8 ea.	1,440		1,600	160 F		
Overhead report (Figure 8–7):						
Maintenance	990	990				
Quality control	94	94				
	$12,794	$ 1,164				
Overhead assignment:						
Job 198 (rate = $6 per std. DLH)		(1,020)	1,200	180 F		
Job 152 (rate = $6 per std. DLH)		(144)			144	
Job totals		$ 0	$4,940	$510 F	$ 8,364	$ 0
Less: Transfers out	(8,364)				$(8,364)	
End of this week	$ 4,430	$ 0	$4,940	$510 F	$ 0	$ 0

FIGURE 8-9
Superior Boat Company Job Control Report

SUPERIOR BOAT COMPANY
Job Control Report
Job. No. 198

Cost Center	April 17-22	April 24-29	May 1-6	May 8-13	May 14-20
Hull (Figure 8-8):					
Direct	$3,740	$3,457	$ 1,425		
Overhead	1,200	1,142	954		
Deck:					
Direct		2,135	3,022	$1,567	
Overhead		778	1,110	1,089	
Rigging:					
Direct				3,211	
Overhead				2,300	
Interior:					
Direct			3,566		$2,128
Overhead			1,641		992
Period totals	$4,940	$7,512	$11,718	$8,167	$3,120

tify any costs attributed to a responsibility center or job in process. Thus, managers know who in the manufacturing function is responsible for any manufacturing resource input. This detail is taken care of simply in practice through use of prenumbered forms, maintenance of orderly supportive files in the accounting office, and computer programs to process all the data and prepare reports.

For example, the cumulative cost assignment report of Figure 8-8 provides documentary support for addition of costs to job 198 (and others) and receives documentary support for its figures from—

1. Labor assignment reports.
2. Materials assignment reports.
3. Overhead allocation reports.
4. Data processing by the accounting office recording overhead allocation.

Each of these items is in turn supported: 1 is supported by completed labor pool requisitions and time clock tickets; 2 is supported by completed materials requisitions; 3 is supported in part by 1 and 2 and also by the expense documentation at service centers; and 4 is supported by expense documentation in the central manufacturing office.

APPRAISAL OF JOB COSTING

Job order costing is at its best if a firm makes a sequence of nonstandard products. The efficiency of job order costing can be improved when the number of possible operations and materials which can be combined can be expressed as standard inputs and costs. In effect, products can be made from a set of standard components. The advantage is that the cost characteristics of these standard components and operations can be studied and reported much more accurately.

Job costing requires arbitrary allocations of overhead. The overhead on job 198 ran perhaps one third of the total cost. If this job will be sold on a cost-plus basis, the allocation of overhead is a matter of critical interest to manufacturer and buyer alike. No particular rationale exists for one system of allocation over another. Because all methods are arbitrary, cost-plus agreements often include limits which allocated overhead cannot exceed.

COMPARISON OF JOB COSTING WITH PROCESS COSTING

Process manufacturing is organized into service and production cost centers, just as a job plant is. The production cost centers each carry out a process which brings one or more products closer to completion. There may be more than one product, and products may proceed through the plant in dissimilar sequences. At the same production center, each product undergoes identical processing.

In process manufacturing there is just one job. Costs do not attach to specific orders or projects, but to all of the work done in some agreed time interval. Some general measure is required to represent the total work done at a production center in one time interval. The accepted measure is equivalent units.

Concept of Equivalent Units

The key to understanding process costing is the concept of equivalent units. Each production center's work can be resolved into units of its own output. In other words, suppose a center receives a unit of product and performs its work on it, then passes it on to the next center. This is one unit of work. Now if the center receives *two* units of product and does *half* the work it is supposed to do on *each* of them, the center has done the *equivalent* of one unit of work. This concept is important because in process costing, each equivalent unit of work done at a center in a period will be assigned the same cost, whether that equivalent unit of work was done on 1 unit of product or 20.

Here is a numerical example. The facing department has beginning inventory of 42 units, each one-fourth complete. Costs of $1,050 are attached to this beginning inventory. During the period 58 units are started and 70 units (not necessarily all drawn from those started or those in beginning inventory) are completed. An end-of-period check shows that the 30 remaining units are each one-fourth completed. The costs attached to manufacturing inputs to the facing department during the period are $6,700. What is the cost per unit of items completed? What is the value of ending in-process inventory?

$$
\begin{aligned}
\text{Total equivalent units performed during period} &= \text{Units completed and transferred out} + \text{Equivalent units @ end of period} - \text{Equivalent units @ beginning of period} \\
&= 70 + \tfrac{1}{4} \times 30 - \tfrac{1}{4} \times 42 \\
&= 70 + 7.5 - 10.5 \\
&= 67
\end{aligned}
\tag{8-1}
$$

$$
\begin{aligned}
\text{Cost per equivalent unit} &= \text{Costs incurred during period} \div \text{Equivalent units} \\
&= \frac{\$6,700}{67} \\
&= \$100 \text{ per unit}
\end{aligned}
\tag{8-2}
$$

$$
\begin{aligned}
\text{Value of units completed} &= \text{Units completed} \times \text{Cost per equivalent unit} \\
&= 70 \times 100 \\
&= \$7,000
\end{aligned}
\tag{8-3}
$$

$$
\begin{aligned}
\text{Value of in process inventory @ end of period} &= \text{Equivalent units @ end of period} \times \text{Cost per equivalent nuit} \\
&= (\tfrac{1}{4} \times 30) \times \$100 \\
&= \$750
\end{aligned}
\tag{8-4}
$$

The steps in process costing are:

1. Accumulation of costs at responsibility centers.
2. Allocation of service department costs to production departments.
3. Determination of equivalent units of work done at each production center.
4. Assignment of costs to equivalent units.
5. Determination of product and in-process inventory costs.

Steps 1 and 2 are as described for job costing earlier in this chapter. Let us briefly explain and illustrate 3, 4, and 5.

Determination of Equivalent Units

Two relationships are required to determine equivalent units. The equivalent unit relationship has been already given; it is repeated with the physical unit relationship in Figure 8–10.

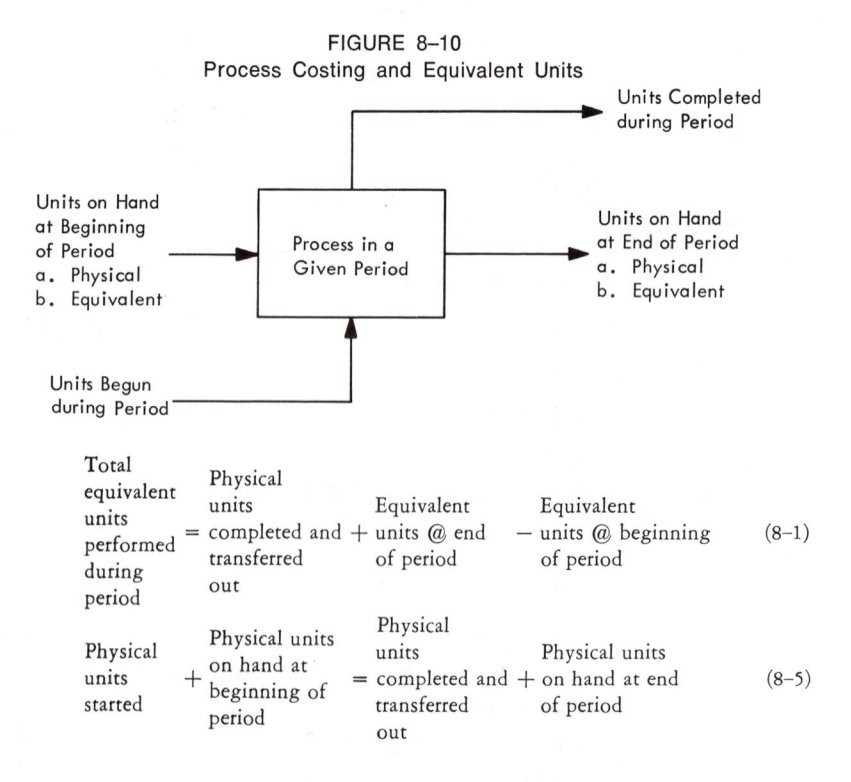

FIGURE 8–10
Process Costing and Equivalent Units

$$\begin{pmatrix}\text{Total equivalent} \\ \text{units performed} \\ \text{during period}\end{pmatrix} = \begin{pmatrix}\text{Physical units} \\ \text{completed and} \\ \text{transferred out}\end{pmatrix} + \begin{pmatrix}\text{Equivalent} \\ \text{units @ end} \\ \text{of period}\end{pmatrix} - \begin{pmatrix}\text{Equivalent} \\ \text{units @ beginning} \\ \text{of period}\end{pmatrix} \quad (8\text{--}1)$$

$$\begin{pmatrix}\text{Physical} \\ \text{units} \\ \text{started}\end{pmatrix} + \begin{pmatrix}\text{Physical units} \\ \text{on hand at} \\ \text{beginning of period}\end{pmatrix} = \begin{pmatrix}\text{Physical units} \\ \text{completed and} \\ \text{transferred out}\end{pmatrix} + \begin{pmatrix}\text{Physical units} \\ \text{on hand at end} \\ \text{of period}\end{pmatrix} \quad (8\text{--}5)$$

The appropriate cost relationship to accompany (8–1) and (8–5) is:

$$\begin{array}{l}\text{Costs attached}\\ \text{to BOP inventory}\end{array} + \begin{array}{l}\text{Costs attached}\\ \text{to components}\\ \text{entering department}\\ \text{during period}\end{array} \quad (8\text{–}6)$$

$$= \begin{array}{l}\text{Costs attached to}\\ \text{completed units}\end{array} + \begin{array}{l}\text{Costs attached}\\ \text{to EOP inventory}\end{array}$$

Let us become more familiar with (8–1) and (8–5). Assume a single-component product in one department. The physical units on hand at the beginning of the period are 200; these are one-half complete. Two hundred eighty additional units are started during the period. There are 220 units on hand at the end of the period; they are judged to be one-fourth complete. How many units were completed? How many equivalent units of work were performed?

How many physical units were completed comes from a rearranged (8–5), which is a simple material balance:

$$\begin{array}{l}\text{Physical}\\ \text{units}\\ \text{completed}\end{array} = 280 + 200 - 220 = \textit{260}, \text{ all transferred out}$$

Equivalent units performed comes from (8–1):

$$\text{Equivalent units} = 260 + 220 \times \tfrac{1}{4} - 200 \times \tfrac{1}{2} = \textit{215}$$

SUMMARY

This chapter has provided your first in-depth look at the information accumulation and classification that must be performed by any cost system. You should expect in subsequent chapters to learn more about the interpretation of the resultant output data and its use in planning and decisions.

Job order costing begins when materials, supplies, and labor services are combined in controlled ways with the services of long-lived assets at responsibility centers which fabricate custom assemblies called jobs. Jobs are analyzed and scheduled before work begins on them, and they pass from one responsibility center to another until work on them is completed.

Service centers expenses are allocated each period among the production centers. A secondary allocation of this overhead, along with production overhead, is to jobs in process. The allocations of costs are done in the accounting office and supported by documentation originating with the service and production centers and describing their activities.

Process costing applies to continual-production industries. It uses the same flow of cost assumptions as job costing, except that costs are averaged among all work done. A variation on these two methods is "job-process costing" which is used when processes are operated sequentially in a plant. For example, your shoe factory may make boots for three weeks, then wing-tip shoes, then loafers. While these are separate jobs, they have all the characteristics of processes and are accounted for as processes.

Equivalent units are the key to understanding process costing. Arithmetic balances must be made between

1. Equivalent units on hand at the beginning of the period plus equivalent units produced AND equivalent units on hand at the end of the period plus equivalent units transferred out (completed units transferred out);
2. Actual units on hand at the beginning of the period plus actual units started AND actual units on hand at the end of the period plus completed units transferred out; and
3. Dollars in beginning of period inventory plus costs of components transferred in AND dollars in end of period inventory plus dollars allocated to completed units transferred out.

QUESTIONS

1. Indicate whether job or process costing would be most appropriate for the following manufacturing operations:
    a) Custom order small print shop.
    b) Company specializing in erecting fences for suburbanites.
    c) Petroleum refinery.
    d) Factory making passenger car tires.

e) Company fabricating large machine tools.
f) Interior decorators supplying furnishings for mobile homes to manufacturer.
g) Cutting industrial diamonds.
h) Catering meals at a large airport motel to convention groups.

2. What is the essential difference between job and process costing?
3. What are the similarities between job and process costing?
4. Why do you think it is necessary that a job be carefully planned before work is begun on it? Would a process be planned before it was constructed, set up, and operated?
5. In a job-manufacturing plant, how does the purchasing division know what, how much, and when to order?
6. Why must there be documentation for all significant manufacturing input transfers and conversions?
7. What is the labor assignment report? What is the flow of labor costs from the time they first occur until they appear in Finished Goods Inventory?
8. What is a job control report? Who prepares the job control report? How would it be used, if at all, when
    a) The job is behind schedule?
    b) Job costs are above the expected costs?
    c) The service centers have large unfavorable efficiency variances?
9. In a two-department plant, department A has $5,000 in costs and 200 labor hours. Department B has $3,000 in costs and applied 1,500 pounds of material to jobs. Four jobs were worked on during the period, as follows:

Job	Department A (Hours)	Department B (Pounds)
1146	30	500
198	80	300
95	50	450
597	20	250

What is the cost of each job? Did one department waste anything? What was the cost of the waste? How would you suggest accounting for the cost of he waste?

10. Do you think that manufacturing centers should report their activities in terms of physical units rather than historical or standard costs?

11. In a one-department plant, 100 units each one-half complete were on hand at the beginning of the week. During the week 500 more units were started into production. At the end of the week there were 200 units still in process, each one-eighth complete. How many units were completed and transferred out? How many equivalent units of work were done?

12. In a one-department plant, 300 equivalent units of work were done. Ending inventory contained 200 units each one-fourth complete. Costs in process at the beginning of the period were $6,000. Costs incurred during the period were $14,000. Beginning inventory was 200 units, each one-half complete. How many units were completed and transferred out? How many units were started during the period?

    What was the total cost of goods transferred out? Of goods remaining in process at the end of the period?

13. A job calls for 500 direct labor hours in the blunging department. It actually receives 450 direct labor hours. The standard cost of a labor hour is $6. The blunging department was expected to incur 5,000 direct labor hours during that week, but actually incurred 5,500. Compute the job labor efficiency variance and the blunging department labor efficiency variance. Is it reasonable that one is favorable and the other is unfavorable? How would you explain this (speculatively)?

14. The bending department of a process-manufacturing firm completes 1,000 equivalent units in a given week. The standard labor content of each unit is 3.2 direct labor hours. During that week, 3,500 direct labor hours are worked. Compute the direct labor efficiency variance, in hours. If the standard cost of an hour of labor is $6, what would be the dollar amount of the variance? Which would you report to the bending department—hours or dollars? Why is no labor rate (spending) variance computed for the bending department, even if the actual wage rate is $5 per hour?

15. Consider the data in Question 14 above. The service department incurred variable overhead of $40,000 at standard costs (there was no fixed overhead). This overhead is normally allocated at the standard rate of $11 per direct labor hour. If the bending department is the only production center, what is the service efficiency variance?

The production efficiency variance: The standard overhead content of one equivalent unit?

EXERCISES

16. Identify which of the following are NOT documents used to describe or control the flow of manufacturing costs:
    a) Materials and supplies report.
    b) Job control report.
    c) Pro forma financial statements.
    d) Materials assignment report.
    e) Sales forecast.
    f) Labor report.
    g) Research and development budget.
    h) Administrative budget.
    i) Job transfer ticket.

17. Here are the specifications for job 345 at work center G during week 23:

    400 lbs. material 66 @ $4 each
    50 hrs. type 2 specialists labor @ $4 each
    20 hrs. type 5 finishing labor @ $5 each

    The materials and labor assignment reports for these jobs indicate the following actual inputs:

    40 hrs. type 2 specialists labor @ $4 each
    400 lbs. material 66 @ $5 each
    25 hours type 5 finishing labor @ $4 each

    What variances will arise from these facts? What is the significance of each variance?

18. The stores foreman at Rance Metals Company is in charge of issuing supplies upon request to production centers. At the start of the month, he had 56 cases of additive 678 on hand. His files show the following activity for the month:

    5th: 30 cases to center 6.
    7th: Shipment received of 144 cases; 24 sent back as defective.
    15th: 86 cases to center 5.
    22nd: 10 cases returned unopened by center 6.
    28th: 15 cases to center 7.

    Compute the end-of-month balance in stores of additive 678.

19. The skid department labor report shows 500 hours worked on jobs last week. Jobs in process were job A (standard input 100 hours), job B (standard input 300 hours), and job C (standard input 200 hours). On job A, 80 hours were actually worked. On job B, 350 hours were actually worked. The records for job C were lost. Compute the actual number of hours worked on job C and the efficiency variances for each job, and for the skid department as a whole.

20. Prepare a flow diagram to show cost information in Exercise 17 above. The diagram should reflect the acquisition of materials and labor by work center G, the use of these inputs in job 345, and all variances except price or rate variances.

PROBLEMS

21. Perfect Poultry Products, Inc., is a large-scale chicken farm. Ten thousand eggs are bought each month; and a corresponding number of chickens are hatched, fed to maturity, and processed into various chicken products. The process is continuous and predictable, although its economy depends on chicken feed prices and the efficiency of various operations. The company has grown rapidly and recently acquired a new process costing system. In the feeding division, for example, there may be as many as 80,000 chickens, each eating a standard 6 ounces of chicken feed daily, or 15 tons of feed. Chicken feed costs fluctuate, but the standard cost is $100 per ton. (A business spending $1,500 per day on hen food isn't chicken feed!) There is a central labor pool from which employees are assigned to hatching, feeding, packing, etc., as needed.

In May, 400 tons of chicken feed were consumed. The equivalent of 60,000 chickens were fed during that month by the feeding division.

Required:

a) Compute the standard cost of feeding one chicken for one month (May). Remember that chickens eat *every* day.)
b) Compute the feeding division feed efficiency variance for May.
c) Each chicken is believed to require 0.005 labor hours to feed each day. Compute the standard direct labor allowance for the feeding division during May.
d) Compute the standard cost of feeding a chicken sent to the pro-

cessing division if a chicken is normally fed for 240 days after hatching and the wage rate is $3 per hour.

22. Custom Paint Company mixes large batches of paint for customers who must have specific unique colors or properties in their paints. Mixing is accomplished very quickly, requiring only a day or two. There is only one responsibility center in the plant, and it handles all operations, including testing the resulting paints to assure that they meet customer specifications.

In February, nine jobs were handled.

1	5,000 gallons	heat resistant two colors
2	5,000 gallons	weatherproof one color
3	6,000 gallons	three colors
4	12,000 gallons	heat resistant one color
5	7,000 gallons	special base heat resistant two colors
6	10,000 gallons	metallic one color
7	3,000 gallons	acid resistant weatherproof one color
8	4,000 gallons	acid and heat resistant one color
9	8,000 gallons	special base weatherproof one color

The standard costs for paint mixing are as follows:

Property	Cost per gallon
Heat resistant	$1.00
Color	0.50
Weatherproof	0.25
Special base	2.00
Acid resistant	1.50
Metallic	0.40
Mixing charge	2.00

Required:
a) Compute the standard cost of each of these batches.
b) If an indirect-cost standard charge is made of $0.20 per gallon, what should total indirect costs have been in February?
c) If the actual direct and indirect costs associated with batch No. 7 were $9,375, what was the difference between actual and standard costs for this batch?

23. Slopoke Construction Company makes heavy-duty construction equipment to order. There are three production departments: blueprints, fabrication, and finishing. A single service department provides indirect services. Job 300 is a large crane, used to lift beams

and other heavy items to the top of tall structures. This job is now in fabrication. The specifications there are:

Direct labor type A	1,000 hours @ $10 per hour
Direct labor type B	2,000 hours @ $13 per hour
Direct labor type C	2,500 hours @ $8 per hour
Structural steel	28 tons @ $250 per ton

Overhead is allocated to fabrication by the service department at the rate of $3 per *actual* fabrication department types A, B, and C direct labor hour. This overhead plus internal indirect costs are allocated to jobs by fabrication at the rate of $5 per *standard* types A, B, and C direct labor hour. (Thus, $5 — $3 = $2 = the part of the application rate intended to cover fabrication's own indirect costs.)

Job 300 has lasted for several months, and during that period, it has been the only job worked on by fabrication. The job is now complete. Material requisitions were:

Structural steel	31 tons
Supplies (indirect)	$4,500

The labor cost report showed

Direct labor type A	1,100 hours
Direct labor type B	2,000 hours
Direct labor type C	2,300 hours
Indirect labor	$13,000

Required:

a) What is the total amount of cost the fabrication department may attach to this job?
b) Give the labor and material efficiency variances in the fabrication department, for job 300.
c) Give the fabrication department overhead efficiency variance.

24. The Uknowit Company is a regional furniture manufacturer which has grown by marketing its furniture through franchised "discount" furniture retail warehouses. In anticipation of opening many more warehouses soon, the company has built up large inventories. The company president is concerned about the effect of these large inventories on reported profits and has asked you to look into the matter for him. Here are the essential cost data summarizing the manufacturing and sales activity of the year (projected to year-end), expressed in terms of hypothetical "equivalent units" of furniture,

which may be taken as approximating the furnishings of an ordinary three-bedroom house:

	Units	Costs
Beginning of year, on hand	4,000	$ 3,200,000
Produced during year	30,000	36,000,000
On hand, end of year	8,000	
Sales		32,500,000

Required:

a) Using process costing as explained in the text, compute the projected income of Uknowit Company.
b) Why is "cost of units sold" during the year different from "cost of units produced" during the year?
c) Indicate whether the company president should be concerned about the situation in (a) and (b) or not, and why.
d) Imagine that Uknowit's costs above are all standard costs, and that there were a total of $3,000,000 in unfavorable manufacturing variances during the year. What would you recommend be done with them?

25. Bryant Solvent Company makes custom solvents for various industrial applications. Many of the solvents are made in large batches for inventory; others are produced to special order for customers. One customer has ordered a batch for which the following basic inputs have been established:

Acetone	12,000 gal. @ $1.10 per gal.
Benzene	40,000 gal. @ $0.90 per gal.
Mixing (labor)	40 hrs. @ $6 per hr.
Mixing (nonlabor costs)	40 hrs. @ $2 per hr.
Variable indirect cost	$10 per hr. (applied on the basis of direct labor hours)

Actual inputs are:

Acetone	12,250 gal. @ $1.12 per gal.
Benzene	40,850 gal. @ $0.89 per gal.
Mixing (labor)	44 hrs. @ $6 per hr.
Mixing (nonlabor costs)	44 hrs. @ $2.20 per hr.

Required:

a) Compute the indirect costs production efficiency variance for this order.
b) Compute price and efficiency variances on all direct inputs for this order.

c) Compute the standard cost of this order and arrange these standard costs alongside actual costs on job control sheet (use only one time period column).

d) Bryant Solvent Company is asked to consider bidding on an order for an identical batch of this solvent by another customer. Bryant knows that another company will bid $50,500. Bryant is willing to underbid provided it can still realize some revenue on the order in excess of its direct costs.

    (1) Should Bryant bid, if the standard quantities and costs are accepted?

    (2) Should Bryant bid if the price of benzene is expected to drop $0.01 per gallon, and at the same time the company decides to increase its fixed overhead allocation to $30 per direct labor hour?

26. Leaf'n'Bark Nurseries is an establishment specializing in custom plantings of formal gardens. Although such plantings and landscaping can become quite elaborate, Leaf'n'Bark has developed a series of standard costs covering activities on most jobs:

Digging	$10 per hour
Plant one bush	$12
Plant small tree	$21
Plant large tree	$35
Use of truck	$15 per day or fraction of a day

Billing is 150 percent of these costs.

In March, Leaf'n'Bark successfully secured a contract to landscape the grounds of the local county courthouse. Here is some information about the job:

Activity	Actual Cost
66 hours of digging	$ 525
Plant 100 bushes	995
Plant 50 small trees	1,125
Plant 20 large trees	650
Truck, used 23 days	300
Total	$3,595

"We did pretty good on this job," said Charles Leaf, the partner in charge of the courthouse job. "Our actual costs are in every case below what I expected for this job." "Ah!" returned William Bark, the other partner, "Don't forget that the original job specification called for 30 hours of digging, 80 bushes, 40 small trees, 12 large ones, and for the truck to only be used 20 days. This job cost us a lot more than it should have, had we done the work as we agreed to do it."

Required:

a) Compute the standard costs for this courthouse job (1) as it was actually done and (2) as Mr. Bark claims it should have been done.

b) Assume that the job could have been done using the inputs specified by Mr. Bark. Compute efficiency and spending variances for each of these five inputs.

c) If the courthouse job was won in competitive bidding, and the bid price was 150 percent of the standard cost of Mr. Bark's estimated inputs, did Leaf'n'Bark earn a profit on this job?

27. Catskinner Construction Company builds roads. The company builds light-duty, medium-duty, and heavy-duty roads. The light-duty road requires 200 hours per 1,000 feet; the medium-duty, 300 hours; and the heavy-duty, 400 hours. Each hour has a standard cost of $8.75.

Last month Catskinner worked on these jobs:

Job	Feet Completed	Hours Worked
Road 1325 (medium duty)	36,500	11,000
Road 2222 (heavy duty)	19,000	7,500
Road 1960 (light duty)	25,000	4,900

The company's accountant recorded total costs of $221,000. He reported $4,000 price variance (unfavorable) on Road 1325 and a $3,000 price variance (favorable) on Road 1960. The performance report for Road 2222 was lost. Naturally, the foreman on that job was anxious to know his costs and variances.

Required:

a) Compute the standard cost of each road construction project for last month.

b) Compute the efficiency variances for each road for last month.

c) Compute the Road 2222 price variance for last month.

d) Comment on these variances. Do they generally present a picture of a company that is controlling its activities?

28. Onerous Systems Company specializes in contracting to prepare property tax assessments, mail them out, and collect and deposit the remittances as they come in. This work is normally done by

tax assessor–collectors at the local government level, and Onerous competes effectively by using modern computer/data processing equipment, efficient procedures, and strong cost control. The company uses the process method of cost accumulation. The direct costs of statement preparation are $0.115 each.

Winter is the busiest time of year for OS, with 80 percent of the total work coming in November and December. The company's fixed costs amount to about $2,400,000 per year. At the present time, one twelfth of these costs are applied to work done in each month.

In November, 40,000 statements were one-half prepared at the beginning of the month and 70,000 statements were one-fourth prepared at the end of the month. During the month, 400,000 statements were started. The number of statements completed in November amounted to 40 percent of the annual total.

Required:

a) Compute the standard direct cost of work in process at the beginning and end of November, and the standard direct cost of work transferred out during November.

b) Compute the fixed costs which would be applied to each equivalent billing during November. If 2 percent of the total year's work is done in June, what would be the fixed costs applied to one billing in that month?

c) Compute the total number of billings performed during a typical year and the average amount of fixed cost allocable to one billing.

d) Recommend whether the present system of overhead allocation is preferable to the method implied in (c).

29. Seabrook Center is an oceanside hotel-convention center which specializes in providing facilities for executive conferences. The conferences typically last one or two weeks and involve 10 to 30 persons each. The center provides lodging, meals, recreational opportunities, and meeting rooms. Normally, the center is asked to name a price in advance of a conference, and the eventual conference cost is expected to be within 1 percent of the estimate. Seabrook has developed a series of standard costs for a conference cost estimation. The total estimated cost is increased by 30 percent to give the cost quoted to prospective customers.

Last week, Grant Slacks Company held its annual executive conference at Seabrook Center. The advance information given the center was: 32 executives in attendance for 6 days, 17 meals, 3 conference rooms.

The center's standard costs are: single room, $12; supper, $3; lunch, $2; breakfast, $1; conference rooms, $25 per day. In addition, $3 per day per person is figured as a cost of recreational facilities. No fixed cost allocations appear in any of these figures.

Seabrook Center's actual costs, as figured this week after the conference was over, were: 5 breakfasts, $170; 6 lunches, $380; 6 suppers, $600; rooms (all single), $2,270. Recreation costs actually were $500; conference rooms were $450.

Required:

a) Compute the price quoted to Grant Slacks.
b) Compute the actual cost to Seabrook of the conference and the amount of the billing sent to Grant. Did Seabrook earn more or less than its customary margin?
c) Compute variances which reconcile actual costs and standard costs. Assume all variances are due to price or rate fluctuations (no efficiency variances).
d) Assume that Seabrook Center incurs $5,000 debt service; $20,000 fixed indirect labor, supplies, and management; and wants a $3,000 profit per month. How many 32-participant, 6-day conferences must the center host to cover all of these items?

30. The H. B. Jackson Company produces busts of famous men, carving them from monkey pod wood imported from the Phillipines. The busts require two types of labor: 20 hours of carving at $4.50 per hour and 10 hours of finishing and polishing at $3.50 per hour, for each bust completed. Production data for January show:

        100 busts produced
        1,900 hours carving labor; total payroll $9,120
        1,200 hours finishing and polishing labor;
            total payroll $4,440

Required:

a) Assuming there can be no substitution of one type of labor for another, compute efficiency variances for January.
b) Compute wage rate variances for January.
c) Can you see a pattern in these variances? Would you consider

them as indicative of any out-of-control situation and if so, how would you deal with it?

DECISION CASE 8-1: BOATSMAN CONSULTING COMPANY

Mr. Grymes Boatsman is president of his own growing consulting company. Recently, as the firm has grown, there have been problems in coordinating the substantial amount of work done and delivering promised results on schedule.

The company is situated in a large Eastern city. In a typical year, 5,000 consulting engagements may be considered; 1,000 may be taken. The engagements taken range from computer selection, information systems design, employee compensation plans, executive search, and similar personnel-related activities to engineering plant layout, plant site selection, new product evaluation, and pollution control systems installations to various continuing education programs. The basic skills required in consulting are virtually as varied as Boatsman's 250-person professional staff; the major ones are education, engineering, mathematics, psychology, and economics—as well as accounting, finance, and management and marketing. The firm operates its own computer system and does all its own programming for internal information purposes.

When a consulting engagement is accepted, a partner in the firm is given responsibility for it. The partner appoints a small "task force" representing different skills in the firm, which appraises the engagement and defines the objectives, methods of achieving objectives, and a schedule for completing the engagement. Periodically the partner-in-charge reviews progress on the engagement, and when it is completed, he reviews the firm's report with the client. Only when the client is satisfied is the engagement closed and the client billed. The contribution from each engagement is computed as the amount billed minus the hourly costs of each staff member who has worked on the engagement, and minus an allowance for indirect (secretarial, computer, rental of offices, etc.) costs. At the present time there are no responsibility centers in Boatsman Consulting Company and no reports or schedule other than those a partner-in-charge may prepare for his own use.

Required:

Prepare a proposal for internal organization of this consulting firm and indicate an appropriate information system concept for scheduling and controlling engagements and the work necessary to complete them. Even though this is not a manufacturing business, point out the similarities between Boatsman Consulting Company and a typical manufacturing business.

BIBLIOGRAPHY

Books

Cantor, Jerry. *Profit Oriented Manufacturing Systems*. New York: American Management Association, 1969.

Henrici, Stanley B. *Standard Costs for Manufacturing*. 3d ed. New York: McGraw-Hill Book Co., 1960.

Klugston, Richard. *Estimating Manufacturing Costs*. Boston: Cohners Publishing Co., 1972.

Articles

DeCoster, Don T. "The Unit Cost Denominator in Process Costing," *The Accounting Review,* July 1964.

Walker, Charles W. "Profitability and Responsibility Accounting," *Management Accounting,* December 1971.

9

Contribution Analysis of Planning Decisions

NATURALLY, not all information is of equal value in decision making. Much information is collected as a necessary historical record rather than for use in decision making. In this chapter, you continue the developments begun in Chapters 1 and 3 which detailed the formal structure of decision models and showed how changes in activity level affect the accounting measures of business profit. You learn how to identify needed information, extract it from accounting files and reports, and use it to make proper decisions. You begin to learn the difference between needed and unneeded information.

The models of decisions discussed in this chapter are preferred whenever they can be clearly established as appropriate. The structure of real decisions is so complex that often a formal model or analysis cannot be established. Nevertheless, the information you would use with a relevant decision model is probably also useful in any substitute decision process, although we cannot prove this.

All decision models have in common that they depend upon development of the *differences* between decision alternatives. Each alternative is said to make a contribution (measured in dollars) to the operation, and so decision analysis based on economic information has come to be known as contribution analysis. We shall present several examples of contribution analysis: make-or-buy decisions, sunk-cost decisions, joint-production decisions, and decisions on the further processing of products and setting the production level of products.

WHAT A DECISION MODEL IS

You have already examined a very general model of decisions (in Chapter 1). The decision model is a way of generating a business policy, or *decision-making rule,* from whatever is known about the environment and the consequences of the decision alternatives.

A decision-making rule is always in this form:

>If A happens, do I
>If B happens, do II, etc.

Such a rule presupposes that we can identify all the things (A, B, etc.) that can happen as well as all our alternatives (I, II, etc.). In order to develop and evaluate decision-making rules, you must assess what will happen to the decision maker if he chooses I and A happens, or B happens; or if he chooses II and A happens, or B happens; and so on. This is not easy but it *is* the way of deciding in advance what to do.

Decision Models Compared to Real Decision Processes

Here you may ask, "How did executives make decisions before they had decision models?" The answer is that a few executives came to be very good at logical and intuitive analysis to produce an acceptable or even outstanding solution to an inventory holding and ordering, resource allocation, or waiting line problem. It is also true that many costly and avoidable decision errors were made. "On the job trial and error" best describes such instinctive decision making.

Significance to Accountants of Decision Model Analysis

Accountants participate in use of decision models even though their primary function is that of information suppliers. As information suppliers, accountants are most interested in the kinds of information persons using the decision models need. If you are an accountant you may not want to be an accomplished authority on, for example, linear programming models (though if you *do* want to be, you will find many rewarding paybacks to you as accountant or manager). An accountant will want to know enough about linear programming to understand what kinds of information to provide persons using linear programming.

ACCOUNTING INFORMATION AND OTHER INFORMATION USED IN ECONOMIC DECISIONS

Information describing past activities is useful in decisions only if you expect that future decisions will be made under the same conditions that governed similar past decisions.

Decisions deal with *changes* from a present or contemplated way of doing things. The *"rules of information and control"* (Chapter 6) help identify useful information for decisions:

Information useful in a decision will describe a benefit or cost for each change the decision would cause if implemented.

Totals and averages are not especially useful in decisions: the effects of changes can be buried in a total. For example, there are any number of combinations of price and volume which might produce $1,000,000 in revenue; the single total figure does not tell us which combination actually produced the $1,000,000.

The accounting information we will emphasize (and which can be used in decision models) helps you distinguish between alternative solutions to a problem, identify out-of-control states, and measure the gain or loss from individual business operations.

CONTRIBUTION ANALYSIS ILLUSTRATED: MAKE OR BUY

A common nonroutine decision that confronts most organizations is whether to make or buy a required input. To make this decision properly, you must compute the cost to the business of making the input, and the cost of buying the input. The alternative with the lowest cost is preferred.

The trick to this decision lies in knowing which costs to associate with the manufacture of the input. These should be the costs *which will not occur* if the input is purchased. Here is an example:

The Answer-U Telephone Answering Device Manufacturing Company has designed a new model automatic telephone answerer which requires a series of etched circuits. These circuits could be produced on existing idle equipment for these costs:

1 hour direct labor	$ 5.50
2 KW electrical power	0.08
1 circuit board	0.50
Allocated fixed overhead	10.00
Total, per unit	$16.08

A commercial manufacturer of these boards has offered to provide them for $12 each.

The proper decision is to manufacture the circuit boards internally. The reason is: the allocated fixed overhead represents resource commitments that are independent of volume of activity; these commitments and their associated costs would continue regardless of whether circuit boards are manufactured internally. The general rule in applying contribution analysis is to disregard costs that are not affected by any alternative under consideration.

The only costs affected by Answer-U's decision are those of labor, power, and the circuit board: $5.50 + $0.08 + $0.50 = $6.08. Since this cost is considerably less than the $12 price quoted by the outside supplier, his offer should be declined. If 10,000 circuit boards are required, the savings or contribution of internal manufacture is 10,000 × ($12.00 − $6.08) = $59,200.

In summary,

Alternative I: Make board . . . . $ 6.08 cost per unit–proper choice
Alternative II: Buy board . . . . $12.00 cost per unit

TIME DIMENSION OF CONTRIBUTION ANALYSIS: SUNK COSTS

Imagine your bicycle cost you $100 new and has been a real dog: you have spent $300 in repairs for it. Now one more thing goes wrong which will cost $50 to repair, but that repair will make the bicycle equivalent to a brand new one, with absolutely no more repairs needed. Do you make the repair? Or do you junk your bike and buy a new one for $100?

You should say that you will make the $50 repair. It is an important principle of decision making that "sunk" costs (money which has been irrevocably spent and is unrecoverable) are not considered in decision making. This principle is reasonable enough; we do not allow the "dead past" to influence our activities. Nevertheless, it leads to some strange situations that, superficially at least, do not appear reasonable.

> The Kallus Shoe Company has just invested in a large automated shoemaking machine. You were the person who persuaded Corn J. Kallus, president, to buy the machine. The machine cost $800,000 and will make 1,000,000 pairs of shoes over its one-year useful life at $9.50 per pair in direct variable costs.
>
> The week after the machine is delivered, installed, paid for and put to work, you pick up a shoe industry trade publication and see an advertisement for a new automated shoemaking machine costing $800,000 and able to make 1,000,000 pair of shoes over its useful life for *$1.40* per pair in direct variable costs.
>
> You turn pale and begin to shake, because you know that you must now tell Mr. Kallus that the machine you told him to buy is *junk;* that he must dispose of it for a pittance; that he must at once spend *another* $800,000 for the new shoemaking machine; that if he does not do so he will be unable to remain competitive in the shoemaking business.

The direct savings of the new machine will be $9.50 − $1.40 = $8.10 per pair of shoes. These savings will, over the lifetime of either machine, total to $8.10 × 1,000,000 pair = $8,100,000. Even though this is enough to pay for the second shoemaking machine 10 times over, you are not at all sure Mr. Kallus will understand that.

In fact, the new machine could be priced up to $8,100,000 and the decision would still have to be to acquire it—so long as the purchase price is less than the savings it will produce.

The sunk-cost principle illustrates why large development contracts are often continued even though there have been large-scale cost overruns.

> The State of Oklayoming let a contract to the Home Development Corporation to produce a prototype low-cost mass-production

home. The contract amount was $500,000. Six months after the contract was let, the company told the State that unexpected difficulties would cause the cost to rise by $200,000, but that it was expected the contract would be fulfilled at that price. Twelve months later, giving the same assurances, the company requested an additional $300,000. Each time the State satisfied itself the difficulties were bonafide and made the commitment to reimburse Home Development for the extra costs. The reason it did so was that the additional costs were still less expensive than starting over with a new contractor.

When you approach a decision which may involve sunk costs, it is important that you identify these costs and determine that they are really unrecoverable. Costs of long-lived assets, past wages and materials, and taxes are examples of sunk costs. However, some costs may be recoverable through sale of the asset to which they attach. If the Kallus Shoe Company's "old" shoemaking machine could be sold for $300,000, then the actual sunk cost would only be $800,000 − $300,000 = $500,000.

DECISIONS INVOLVING JOINT PRODUCTS

One of the important axioms of accounting is that causal relationships link events, and therefore the costs and revenues related to these events. When a causal relationship is identified, accountants take advantage of it to combine specific costs and revenues together if they attach to the related events. The sale of dental services and subsequent receipts of payment are causally related to one another, permitting a dentist to conclude that your payment came as a direct result of filling your cavities. Such direct causal relationships might be represented by the arrows in Figure 9–1, which shows events as caused by other events.

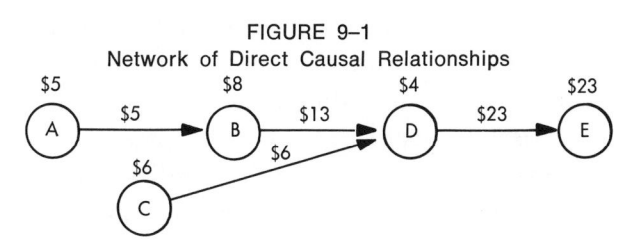

FIGURE 9–1
Network of Direct Causal Relationships

In this diagram, event A causes event B, which together with event C causes event D, which itself causes event E. This network might describe a manufacturing process in which A, B, C, D, and E are individual steps. The number beside each event is the dollar sacrifice in order for that event to take place; the number on each arrow is the sum of these costs for events occurring *before* the event to which the arrow leads. For example, $8 is the sacrifice in order that event B occur. Because this sacrifice causes B to occur, the cost of B is $8. Since A causes B to occur, the cost of A is really part of the cost of B and is transferred to it by the arrow. If E is the final event (the completed product), the cost of all events leading up to E are associated with E ($23) and are referred to as the product cost. In this sense, the $23 figure sums up the chain of events which culminated in the production of E.

Joint Products Illustrated

Not all chains are so easily dealt with as shown in Figure 9–1. Consider the chain in Figure 9–2. Here a single event A has caused two

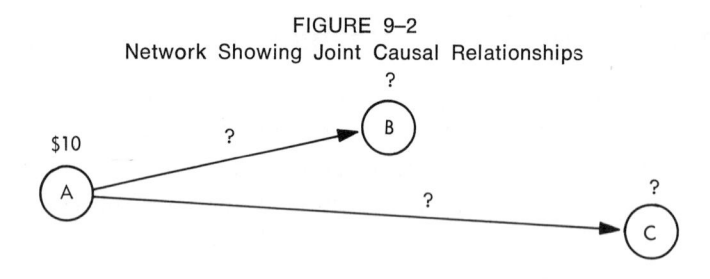

FIGURE 9–2
Network Showing Joint Causal Relationships

events B and C. The cost of A is $10. What costs are transferred to B? What costs are transferred to C? Perhaps a classic example of this kind of process is the petroleum refinery, which includes a massive reaction chamber called a "catalytic cracking tower" into which crude oil is fed and where, in the presence of catalysts, heat, and pressure, it changes into a variety of hydrocarbon fractions including bunker fuel, kerosene, gasoline, naptha, and cooking gases. What cost should be assigned to each of these products? In the diagram of Figure 9–2, B and C are an illustration of *joint products;* and the bunker fuel, kerosene, and other products of the cracking tower are also joint products. Here are some more examples:

—Peanuts (and other agricultural products such as sorghum, cattle, and hogs) produce a variety of foods, chemicals, and other substances with economic value.
—Coal is the source of many hydrocarbons ranging from ordinary blast furnace coke to dyes.
—Many ores contain more than one valuable metal, most of which are economically recoverable through an integrated process.
—A public expenditure on education has joint benefits: crime reduction, unemployment reduction, earning power enhancement.

You have already studied an example of a process producing joint products—the operation of service centers. Their costs were allocated more or less arbitrarily to those who received the benefits of their services—production centers.

Our concern in studying joint products will be that costs which are truly joint be allocated to the joint products in ways that preserve the actual contribution of all the joint products as a group to business profitability. In other words, decisions to continue, increase, or decrease these products have to be made about all the products as a group—and not about each of them individually.

Costing Joint Products

The Copy-It Company has a large, fast copier which is the firm's principal asset. Time on this copier is rented to various companies in 30-minute increments. The copier is available 24 hours a day and, to encourage off-hours use, the rate after 5 P.M. and before 8 A.M. is 50 percent of the regular rate. The company is open five days per week—5 × 24 = 120 potential hours of use. Many companies rent two or more segments of off-hours time and one segment during regular hours, doing their rush work during daylight hours and the less important copying at night. The Copy-It Company spends $1,200 per week in direct and indirect costs to keep the copier running and available. Of these costs, $900 are regarded as fixed. The company charges $18 per hour for daylight time and $9 per hour for off time.

Recently the Copy-It Company's vice president, Hiram Shortsight, pointed out that the company's costs came to $10 for each and every hour that the firm was open for business, yet the billing rate on two thirds of this time was only $9 per hour. He proposed making the billing rate $18 for all hours, day and night. This was done. Night business fell off by two thirds, from an average 15 hours per night to only 5 hours per night. Daily revenue declined by $45 (why?).[1] The company management was very upset, so they call Frank Debitcredit, your accounting partner, to tell them what they did wrong.

"First of all," Debitcredit says, "your copier time is a joint product. It is made, minute by minute, by all those expenditures which are necessary in order to run the copier 24 hours per day. You cannot say that it costs $10 to run the copier between 2 and 3 A.M.; it costs $1,200 per week to run the copier one hour or 120 hours. Therefore it is foolish to try to price the time so that in some way an allocation of costs is covered and a profit is made. Either you make a profit every week, or you don't. There is no such thing as making a profit on one hour during the week and not on another."

"But," interrupted Shortsight, "how can we know what a good pricing policy is?"

"That isn't easy," Debitcredit replies, "your pricing policy must follow the market factors of supply and demand. When you raised prices on night work, your business fell off very sharply. That is because your customers decided they would rather do without some copying they had been getting, or they took their business to a copying service with lower prices and equivalent services. Prices are set by the market and not by costs. Since you had so much business under your original pricing policy, return to it, and make price changes only after some forethought in the future." After presenting his bill, he left.

Continuing a Joint Product

Now look at the Trash-It Company, which has the contract to collect garbage from a medium-size city. The company brings the garbage to its plant, separates out the recyclable items—cans, bottles, and

---

[1] [8 hrs. × $18/hr. + 15 hrs. × $9/hr.] − [8 hrs. × $18/hr. + 5 hr. × $18/hr.] = $45
    $279 − $234 = $45

paper—and uses the rest for land fill. Prices for processed waste are set strictly by the markets for the respective items. The present practice of the Trash-It Company is to assign the costs of its separation operation to cans, bottles, and paper by weight. Thus, in a recent month, collections and cost allocations were as shown in Figure 9–3.

FIGURE 9–3
Trash-It Cost Allocations

		Cans	Bottles	Paper
Pounds recovered		45,000 lbs.	75,000 lbs.	60,000 lbs.
Total costs	$ 36,000	(No Direct *product* costs at all)		
Allocation	(9,000)	$9,000		
	(15,000)		$15,000	
	(12,000)			$12,000
	$ 0			
Cost per pound		$0.20	$0.20	$0.20

Trash-It prepares product-line statements, and for that same month, the figures appeared as in Figure 9–4 (inventories are negligible).

FIGURE 9–4

TRASH-IT COMPANY
Product Line Profit Statement

	Total	Cans	Bottles	Paper
Sales	$ 42,000	$20,000	$ 8,000	$ 14,000
Less: Cost of sales	(36,000)	(9,000)	(15,000)	(12,000)
Profit (loss)	$ 6,000	$11,000	$ (7,000)	$ 2,000

After being fired by the Copy-It Company, Mr. Shortsight was employed by Trash-It. His review of the statement in Figure 9–4 caused him to propose that the company stop separating and selling bottles; that instead the bottles be buried in the land fill and no longer sold on the open market. "I am positive," he stated, "that this will save $7,000 per month, increasing our profit to $13,000 per month." There was not much discussion; the idea was approved and the men in the separation process were instructed to no longer take bottles out of the trash. The first month under this new system was similar to the month described above except that the $36,000 in costs were allocated only to cans and paper. The allocation was:

Cans—45,000 lbs.; costs of $15,429 assigned
Paper—60,000 lbs.; costs of $20,571 assigned

This allocation produced the condensed monthly profit and loss statement of Figure 9-5.

FIGURE 9-5

TRASH-IT COMPANY
Condensed Product Line Profit Statement

	Total	Cans	Paper
Sales	$ 34,000	$ 20,000	$ 14,000
Less: Cost of sales	(36,000)	(15,429)	(20,571)
Profit (loss)	$ (2,000)	$ 4,571	$ (6,571)

Mr. Shortsight, upon being asked for an explanation of the $2,000 loss, points out that somehow now there is a loss on the paper operation which he attributes to "unforeseen factors." He proposes that the company stop separating paper and concentrate on cans only. Skeptical, the directors of Trash-It turn to Mr. Debitcredit for advice. His report: "Obviously the only effect of discontinuing bottle separation and sale was the loss of the $8,000 you received as a result. Your costs did not change at all. This leads me to believe that cans, bottles, and paper are all joint products which must be considered together. In the last month in which you separated and sold all three, you had a fine profit of $6,000. My advice is to resume bottle separation and continue paper separation."

"But," said Shortsight, "that doesn't explain the loss on bottles as reported in the financial statement for that month. . . . ?"

"I explain it this way," Debitcredit explains. "You made an arbitrary allocation of costs. Your cost allocation made it appear that bottle separation was unprofitable. I suggest that you allocate your costs in proportion to product contributions. That would assure that each joint product received a cost allocation less than the revenue it produced, which would assure that each joint product appears to be profitable—

which is consistent with my contention that the entire separation process is profitable."

Debitcredit produced, after a few moments, the computations of Figure 9–6 to support his argument.

FIGURE 9–6
TRASH-IT COMPANY
Properly Prepared Product Line Performance Statement

Percent of total sales due to cans:	$20,000/$42,000 = 0.476 × 100 = 47.6%
Percent of total sales due to bottles:	$8,000/$42,000 = 0.190 × 100 = 19.0%
Percent of total sales due to paper:	$14,000/$42,000 = 0.334 × 100 = 33.4%

Costs to be allocated to product lines: $36,000 total.
Cans	$36,000 × 0.476 = $17,142
Bottles	36,000 × 0.190 = 6,858
Paper	36,000 × 0.334 = 12,000
Total	$36,000

Profit margin on each product line:
Cans:
Sales	$20,000	
Less allocated costs	17,142	
	$ 2,858	$2,858

Bottles:
Sales	$ 8,000	
Less allocated costs	6,858	
	$ 1,142	1,142

Paper:
Sales	$14,000	
Less allocated costs	12,000	
	$ 2,000	2,000
Total margin		$6,000

Debitcredit also pointed out that there was not the slightest value for planning and control purposes to any figure in this calculation except the "total margin" which, he said, applied to the separation process *as a whole* and not to any of its components. "The separation process is a single responsibility center. It must be evaluated to show overall output's effect on Trash-It profits."

FURTHER PROCESSING OF PRODUCTS

Frequently a situation will arise in which there is an opportunity to further process one or more products in order to sell them at higher prices. The question that must be answered before such an opportunity is a single responsibility center. It must be evaluated to show overall processing exceed the extra cost of such processing?"

If the opportunity arises in a process in which there are no joint products, there is seldom any question what to do. The Soft-Sit Chair Company manufactures a metal lawn chair which is purchased unfinished by various retail stores who do the finishing themselves. The typical monthly operating statement of SoftSit looks like this:

```
Sales:  1,000 chairs @ $10 each. . . . . . . . . . . . .  $10,000
Less:   Direct cost of sales @ $5 each . . . . . . . . . . .   5,000
Contribution margin . . . . . . . . . . . . . . . . . .  $ 5,000
Less:   Monthly fixed manufacturing costs. . . . . . . .    1,500
        Selling and administrative costs . . . . . . . . . . . . .    2,000
Income before taxes . . . . . . . . . . . . . . . . . .  $ 1,500
```

Soft-Sit is considering finishing the chairs itself. If it did so, there would be additional direct costs of $2 per chair and additional fixed manufacturing costs of $500 per month. The chairs could be sold for an additional $3 each. The proposal may be analyzed as follows:

```
Extra revenue:  1,000 chairs × $3 =                      $3,000
Less:   Additional direct costs
        1,000 chairs × $2 =                 $2,000
        Additional fixed costs . . . . . . . . . .    500    2,500
        Additional contribution margin. . . . . . .         $  500
```

Since the additional contribution margin is positive, the proposal should be adopted.

However, now consider a joint-product situation. The Soft-Sit Company is making two metal chairs. They are stamped out together from one piece of sheet metal by one machine. However, one chair requires about twice as much finishing work as the other. The costs of the whole operation are reported to management as they are shown in Figure 9–7.

The quantity of chair A which produced the costs in Figure 9–7 is sold for $65,000; the corresponding quantity of chair B, for $55,000. There is an overall profit of $65,000 + $55,000 − $75,000 − $35,000 = $10,000. The company is satisfied with this.

FIGURE 9-7
SOFT-SIT COMPANY
Product Profit Statement

		Metal Chair A	Metal Chair B
Total joint costs of stamping operation	$50,000		
Allocated according to weight of chairs	(35,000)	$35,000	
	(15,000)		$15,000
Cost of finishing chairs (direct costs)		40,000	20,000
Total costs		$75,000	$35,000

However, the Hard-Sit Company comes to Soft-Sit and proposes to buy the unfinished chair A production, finish it, and sell them itself. The price offered is $30,000.

"No," argues the ubiquitous Mr. Shortsight, just breaking in at another management position after being terminated at the Trash-It Company. "The allocated cost at the stamping machine is $35,000. How can we possibly sell $35,000 of production for $30,000?"

By now you scarcely need Mr. Debitcredit as a helper; you recognize that these allocated costs are not necessarily valid as any basis for a decision. You develop the network diagram in Figure 9-8 showing the stamping operations and subsequent finishing operations.

FIGURE 9-8
Cost Analysis of Soft-Sit Company Sell-or-Process-Further Decision

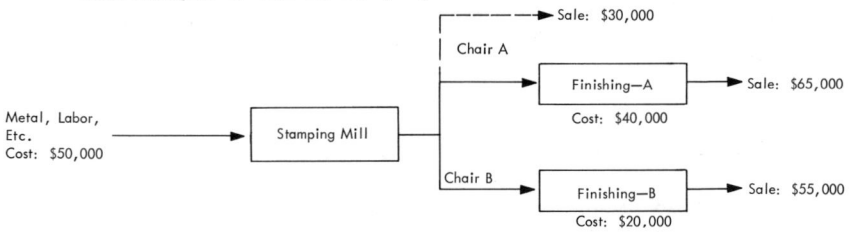

```
                                          ----→ Sale: $30,000
                                         |
                                       Chair A
                                         |
                                         →  Finishing—A    → Sale: $65,000
Metal, Labor,                               Cost: $40,000
Etc.           →  Stamping Mill
Cost: $50,000
                                       Chair B
                                         →  Finishing—B    → Sale: $55,000
                                            Cost: $20,000
```

"The purpose of this diagram," you say, "is to make clear the real contribution of this decision's alternatives to Soft-Sit's overall profits. Let us disregard the stamping mill costs entirely, for they are necessary to produce either chair and we all know there is no way to allocate them to chair A and chair B that is useful in a decision. Instead, let us concentrate on the profitability of further processing. Note that at present, the finishing operation contributes to profits as follows:

Sales of chair A	$ 65,000
Cost of further processing	(40,000)
Contribution to profit	$ 25,000

"Now imagine that we accept the Hard-Sit proposal to sell them all our unfinished chair A production for $30,000. We still have the joint stamping mill costs; they are not affected by this decision. However, we fully and completely avoid all the $40,000 of finishing costs for chair A! In other words, the entire $30,000 is a contribution to profit. To me, then, it appears that the proper comparison and choice should be on this basis:

Contribution to profit of finishing chair A	$25,000
Contribution to profit of selling chair A to HardSit	30,000
Excess in favor of selling to HardSit	5,000"

Of course, Soft-Sit fired poor Mr. Shortsight and adopted your proposal as outlined above—to sell unfinished chair A to Hard-Sit. The principle that we employed here is, stated in more formal language, that—

> A choice among alternatives is to be made to produce the greatest contribution to profit *regardless* of costs incurred prior to the point in processing at which the choice is to become effective.

We followed this principle by refusing to consider the joint stamping costs in our decision since that operation and its costs had to occur before there would be any unfinished chair A about which to make a decision.

AT WHAT LEVEL SHOULD JOINT PRODUCTION BE SET?

Frequently decisions regarding joint products are made more difficult because they are sold in quite different markets, in which prices move up and down in an unrelated fashion, producing uncertainty as to the best level of operation of the joint process. The analysis outlined here assumes that you know how prices in each market will change with volume changes in the total market, and that you know how your own costs will change as your level of production changes. Furthermore, your total volume is too small to affect any market price by itself.

Let us suppose there are two joint products, A and B, and that during the planning period A is expected to sell for $20 per unit while B is expected to sell for $30 per unit. The nature of the joint process is such that for each one unit of A produced, three units of B are produced. The production level decision will, of course, be so as to equalize marginal cost and marginal revenue at the level chosen (see Chapter 3 to review this rule). The available cost and revenue data are summarized as Figure 9–9. It is clear that *no allocation* of joint

FIGURE 9–9
Joint Production Level Data Summary

Joint Costs	Units A Produced	Units B Produced	Marginal Costs	Revenue from A and B	Marginal Revenue	Marginal Revenue Less Than Marginal Cost?	Profit
$10,000	100	300		$11,000			$ 1,000
			$ 9,000		$11,000	No	
19,000	200	600		22,000			3,000
			8,000		11,000	No	
27,000	300	900		33,000			6,000
			8,000		11,000	No	
35,000	400	1,200		44,000			9,000
			10,000		11,000	No	
45,000	500	1,500		55,000			10,000
			12,000		11,000	Yes	
57,000	600	1,800		66,000			9,000
			14,000		11,000	Yes	
71,000	700	2,100		77,000			6,000

costs to individual products is necessary in order to decide the proper level of production. In this case the proper level lies between 500A/1,500B and 600A/1,800B. As an exercise you should plot this data and determine the optimum level of production.

If a forecast of market conditions in the A market or the B market indicates a price change coming, the "Revenue from A and B" column can be refigured based on the new price, and a new level of production determined. You should be on notice that if marketing these two products becomes the responsibility of two separate marketing organizations (which is logical considering the unrelated natures of the two markets), these organizations will often disagree with each other as to whether production should be increased or decreased. It is possible that prices in one market would rise, as prices in the other market dropped, and that the net effect would be a production decrease. You can easily imagine the "stab in the back!" cry of the person in charge of marketing the product for which prices were rising.

WHEN COST ALLOCATION CAN'T BE AVOIDED

Occasionally managers will insist on some cost allocation to joint products, and certainly the requirements of financial accounting for an inventory valuation and income measurement will necessitate joint cost allocation. Such allocation is permissible *if the joint costs are allocated in proportion to the individual product total contribution margins*. We'll give you an illustration based on the SoftSit Company and its two chairs. Here, for convenience, is the contribution-margin information on these two chairs:

Chair A: Sales − Costs after stamping = Contribution margin
$65,000 − $40,000 = $25,000
Chair B: Sales − Costs after stamping = Contribution margin
$55,000 − $20,000 = $35,000
Total contribution margin = $25,000 + $35,000 = $60,000
Total joint costs = $50,000.
Joint costs allocable to chair A: $50,000 × (25,000/60,000) = $20,800
Joint costs allocable to chair B: $50,000 × (35,000/60,000) = 29,200
    Total allocated $50,000

What is the effect of these allocations? Let us show product-line profitability statements:

	Chair A	Chair B
Sales revenue	$ 65,000	$ 55,000
Less: Costs after stamping	(40,000)	(20,000)
Contribution margin before allocating joint costs	$ 25,000	$ 35,000
Less: Allocated joint costs	(20,800)	(29,200)
Contribution margin after allocating joint costs	$ 4,200	$ 5,800

If the decision is whether to process one or more joint products further or to sell them in an unfinished state, the key line in such a performance statement is still "Contribution margin *before* allocating joint costs." If the contribution margin is larger than the revenue which could be gained from sale unfinished, then the company should not sell the product unfinished.

If the decision is with respect to the process as a whole, then the key line is the final line, "Contribution margin *after* allocating joint costs." If the sum of figures in this row is positive, the joint process should be continued. If the sum is negative, the process should be discontinued. The individual column totals are useless in such a decision. These are general guides and do not take into account the possibility of not processing some product with negative contribution margin before allocating joint costs, improving process efficiency, or other options which may have to be considered before a broad decision to discontinue an entire process. Nor do we consider changing technology which may make it possible to replace one joint process with two or more nonjoint processes. If that change is a possibility, the apparent unprofitability of a joint product after fixed-cost allocation may be a signal to management to encourage development of nonjoint process technology.

SUMMARY

A decision model is a way of generating a selection among alternatives using whatever is known and is relevant about the decision and the environment. Decision models are useful for studying decision information requirements even when the model does not strictly conform to an actual decision process. Information useful in decisions will predict a benefit or cost for each change the decision would cause if implemented.

The major sources for information used in contribution analysis are the historical accounting system and its reports, the flexible budget, and external economic measurements and opinions. These sources produce *decision-relevant costs and revenues.*

Contribution analysis is a process of associating costs and revenues or cost savings with relevant alternatives of a decision. Only those costs, revenues, and cost savings which will occur as a direct result of an alternative's adoption should be associated with it. These are the same costs that will be avoided if the alternative is rejected. Normally, the alternative will be selected which has the largest contribution, so calculated, to profit.

Opportunities to apply contribution analysis occur in decisions to make or buy some required input; in decisions involving the foregoing of asset services already bought and paid for (sunk-cost analysis); joint product costing, pricing, and further processing; and setting production level.

When it is necessary to allocate joint costs over several products, it should be done so as to preserve the contribution margin relationships among joint products that exist before the allocation occurs.

QUESTIONS

1. What is a decision model? What is a "contribution" associated with a decision alternative? Why do you think such a contribution is sometimes called an *avoidable* cost or revenue?

2. Why are total costs and average costs not very useful in decision making? When is historical information of maximum use in decision making?

3. The Flip-Flop Company's management must decide whether to make or buy a component. You are the controller. The president asks you to provide information as a basis for the decision. He says, "We are going to all get around the table and decide what is best for us to do." How do you know what information to provide?

4. The Moore Company has bought typewriters for the typing pool for $5,000. A new automatic typing machine that types from voice tape is being offered for $26,000. The machine would last five years and save $4,000 per year. It would replace all the new typewriters, which have an expected life of five years. What do you recommend doing?

5. The Kallus Shoe Company (see page 252) buys the *new* $800,000 shoemaking machine. However, unit costs turn out to be $5 per pair rather than $1.40 as expected. Was the machine a good buy?

6. In 1971, Sockheed Corporation nearly became bankrupt as a result of cost overruns on a government contract. At the same time the company was deciding whether to proceed on a commercial jetliner. Costs on the jetliner had at that time already run $300 million

above budget. Costs yet to be incurred were expected to run $8 million per plane. The new plane would sell for $20 million apiece. In view of its shaky financial situation, should Sockheed continue the commercial jetliner project?

7. What is "sunk cost"? Give a brief illustration.

8. What are joint products? Why do joint products present a special problem to accounting and management? How can this problem be handled properly? Give examples of joint products.

9. The P-Nut Company buys peanuts and sells shelled peanuts and empty peanut shells. The cost of peanuts is $100 per ton. All of this cost is allocated to the shelled peanuts, which account for about two thirds of all sales revenue. Criticize this process and indicate what harm it may do.

10. The Copy-it Company (see page 255) sells daylight copying time for $18 per hour and evening copying time for $9 per hour. The company requires that a purchaser of daylight time buy an equal amount of evening time. The Welsch Company buys 30 minutes of each type of time, then does all its copying in the evening, "because the charge is less for that time and therefore our copying is more economical." Comment.

11. The city of Midville constructs a new lake near town. The lake is used to cool a power generation plant, for flood control, irrigation, drinking water, and recreation. The $1,000,000 cost of the dam is allocated entirely to drinking water and is being recovered through the charge for use of city water. This charge is based on the direct costs of pumping and supplying water plus 10 percent of the investment in the water system (including the cost of the dam). The year the dam was built, water bills doubled. You live in Midville and use a lot of city water. What arguments would you make to reduce your water bill?

12. Midville City Hospital operates three divisions: surgery, maternity, and emergency. Fixed costs are allocated to each division in proportion to the number of square feet of floor space it occupies. The hospital manager wants to eliminate emergency because it only brings in $300,000 per year as opposed to $500,000 in total costs ($200,000 of which are direct costs). The empty space would be

used for miscellaneous purposes. Do you support the manager? Why?

13. Now refer to Question 12 above. Same facts, except that the extra space would be used for a staff lounge, office space, etc., which are badly needed and would cost $150,000 per year in fixed costs to build if the emergency division is retained. Now what do you recommend? Why?

14. The Bay Ferry operates one ferryboat across a 20-mile channel. Because the crossing is long, the boat has a restaurant aboard. The fixed costs of operating the restaurant are $3,000 per month. Variable costs are about $0.40 per dollar of sales. Sales amounted to $8,000 in each of the last six months—which is normal. The Bay Vending Company has offered to replace the restaurant with a set of vending machines for which revenues would be about $7,000 monthly. The Bay Ferry Company would receive 12 percent of total revenue as rental income, and would avoid all restaurant fixed and variable costs. What should Bay Ferry do?

15. If overhead or other indirect costs must be allocated to joint products, how can it be done? Does it make any difference whether the purpose of allocation is to prepare a statement to determine whether to process a single product further, or whether to continue operating an entire process?

EXERCISES

16. The Roberts Company assembles television sets. Indirect variable manufacturing costs are $3,000,000 per year; they are allocated at the rate of $10 per direct labor hour. The company makes one subassembly which has $50 worth of materials and 4 direct labor hours at $6 each as inputs. The nature of this assembly is that 50 percent of the indirect variable costs could be avoided if the subassembly is not made. An outside supplier can provide the identical subassembly for $99. Should Roberts make or buy this subassembly?

17. Contrast TV Broadcasting Company operates KGUM-TV in Midville. The firm 90 days ago budgeted a local special at $20,000. The project is half completed, and $10,000 has been spent. The

station has just learned of a network special on exactly the same topic that can be shown for $12,000. "Since this special is so much cheaper than ours, we must buy it and show it, and cancel our project," says the station manager. Comment.

18. I, II, and III are independent sets of joint products. In each set, the contribution of each product is set forth. The joint costs of all products are shown separately for each set. Indicate whether each set should be continued or discontinued. May products within a set be discontinued individually?

	Set I	Set II	Set III
Joint costs	$50,000	$30,000	$60,000
Product A contribution	10,000	10,000	10,000
Product B contribution	−20,000	10,000	15,000
Product C contribution	10,000	5,000	30,000
Product D contribution	30,000	1,000	5,000
Product E contribution	30,000	1,000	0

19. Jones Company must use full absorption costing to evaluate its inventories and cost of sales for financial reporting purposes. In 1972, fixed indirect manufacturing costs were $160,000. Three products were made. Here are data for them:

	Product A	Product B	Product C
No. of units made.	6,000	2,000	8,000
Selling price per unit	$50	$80	$60
Direct variable costs per unit . . .	$30	$60	$40

Were manufacturing operations profitable? Suggest the quantity of overhead to allocate to total production of each product, then the amount to allocate to each unit of each product.

20. Tolkien Company makes two products, A and B. A sells for $50 and costs $45 in variable costs; B sells for $30 and has variable costs of $35. If B is discontinued, the sales of A will drop by 20,000 units. At present, 100,000 units of A and 50,000 units of B are sold. Should B be discontinued? Should A *and* B be discontinued?

PROBLEMS

21. Dingbat Company is a small Kentucky firm which manufactures baseball bats and stuffing for inexpensive furniture from white ash

wood. The ash is purchased from a local lumber yard (whose motto is, "we have the whitest ash in town") for $0.50 per board foot. Each board foot of ash yields 0.2 bats and 2.0 pounds of shavings. The bat-turning operation costs $1 for each two bats produced. Further processing of the shavings into furniture stuffing costs $0.02 per pound for fireproofing, fumigating, and cleaning. A diagram of this process is as follows:

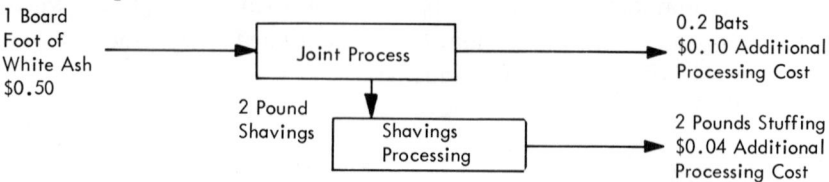

```
1 Board                                              0.2 Bats
Foot of        ┌──────────────┐                      $0.10 Additional
White Ash ────▶│ Joint Process│──────────────────────▶ Processing Cost
$0.50          └──────────────┘
                      │
                 2 Pound
                 Shavings   ┌──────────┐              2 Pounds Stuffing
                            │ Shavings │              $0.04 Additional
                            │Processing│──────────────▶ Processing Cost
                            └──────────┘
```

Meathead Company, located nearby, normally takes all the furniture stuffing output of Dingbat Company; however, this year they are proposing that the normal $0.05 per pound price be dropped to $0.025 per pound. The two alternatives are (a) burn the shavings (no cost) or (b) lease a sizer which will convert the shavings into an organic mulch which sells for $0.03 per pound. The sizer will cost $1,200 per year to lease. Operating costs are $0.02 per pound of shavings input; one pound of shavings produces 1.2 pounds of mulch.

Required:

a) If Dingbat normally consumes 200,000 board feet of white ash per year in its operations, should the firm sell to Meathead, burn the shavings, or make mulch?

b) If bats are sold for $3.10 each, compute the total contribution of the whole process.

22. Water Products Company makes 21,600 rubber dinghies annually for use as yacht tenders, camping boats, and day recreation. The process is to cut rubberized cloth to sized patterns, "tack" it together, and finally vulcanize all seams and test for airtightness. Water Products has always performed all these operations itself, but this year has received two proposals: A—to provide precut, tacked-together forms for further processing; and B—to use an automated machine to cut cloth prior to tacking.

The present process for a typical model would require inputs with costs of $8 for materials, $1 for cutting, $1 for tacking, and

$3 for vulcanizing. Alternative A would supply the form cut, tacked, and ready for vulcanizing for $12. The automated cutting machine would reduce material cost (by cutting waste) to $6 and reduce cutting cost to $0.80. The machine would cost $50,000 and cut 20,000 rubber dinghys before wearing out.

Required:

a) Based on only the information given, select an alternative. Remember that Water Products is not obligated to select either A or B.

b) The two men who do the cutting receive $5 per hour each. If the cutting machine or the precut forms were selected, these two men would be transferred to the special products division to increase the capacity there. In that division, these men would return a net contribution to profit of $2 per hour each. A 180-hour month is standard. Would this information change your decision in (a) and if so, how?

23. Cityville is a town of 300,000 population. At present it is divided into four quadrants. Residential property in each quadrant is assessed once every four years. Thus, each year one quadrant is assessed. Property is assessed at the market value. The tax rate is 2 percent of the market value. Property values rise about 2 percent annually. In 1974, property valuations in each quadrant and the year of last assessment are given here:

Year of Last Assessment	Value	Quadrant
1974	$300,000,000	1
1973	400,000,000	2
1972	500,000,000	3
1971	200,000,000	4

The city council is considering a proposal which would assess half the entire city every two years. A serious problem with this proposal would be its additional cost. The tax assessor's office now has a budget like this:

Supervisory salaries	$ 50,000
Allocated indirect costs	60,000
Assessor salaries (direct cost)	40,000
Various direct costs	110,000
Total budget	$260,000

Assessment every two years would require doubling the direct cost of property assessment. The city council is not sure the city could afford the proposed system.

Required:

a) Compute the direct cost of assessing $1,000,000 worth of property in 1974. Assume that this cost will remain constant during the next four years.
b) Compute the valuation of property in Cityville in 1975, 1976, 1977, and 1978, using the present quadrant system and using the proposed system each two years, evaluating 3 and 4 in 1975, 1 and 2 in 1976, etc.
c) Compute the budget of the tax assessor's office in 1975, 1976, 1977, and 1978 under both the present quadrant system and under the proposed system.
d) Determine whether the extra cost of the proposed system is justified by the additional revenue it generates.

24. Bonanza Mines operates an open-pit mine in Wyoming which produces 30,000 tons per day of Lignumvitae, an ore which contains (per ton) 100 pounds recoverable copper, 20 pounds recoverable lead, 1 pound recoverable silver, and 5 pounds recoverable zinc. Long ago, the company stopped recovering silver during processing. However, the price of silver has risen to $30 per pound and Bonanza is considering resuming recovery of silver.

Here is a performance statement for March, a typical month:

Item	Copper	Lead	Zinc	Total
Revenue	$4,500,000	$1,800,000	$350,000	$6,650,000
Less:				
Selling and administrative				500,000
Allocated joint costs of mining ore	792,000	158,000	40,000	990,000
Direct cost of further refining	2,400,000	1,100,000	300,000	3,800,000
Product contributions	$1,308,000	$ 542,000	$ 10,000	$1,360,000

Mining proceeds 30 days per month. The facilities for silver processing which have been idle have fixed costs of $100,000 per month which have been absorbed by the other metals extracted. Silver extraction would entail direct costs of $28 per ton of ore treated. In addition, new fixed costs of $600,000 per month would be incurred to operate new storage and shipping facilities connected with silver production.

Joint costs are allocated based on the percentage by weight of metal in the ore.

Required:

a) Prepare a new performance statement which shows the proper relationships between direct and joint costs.
b) Determine whether silver should be processed and, assuming that it is, what the profit or loss would be.

25. Etruscan Marketing Corporation sells unusual specialties in wholesale markets. Over the years the company has found three markets in which it is effective: antique furniture, recreational vehicles, and pharmaceuticals. Because of the unique approach used by Etruscan, the sales force cannot be expanded without a great deal of search, training, and time. There are presently 16 salesmen.

In the table below, total sales commissions earned as a result of sales activity (as days of selling time) are shown for each product line. For example, for recreational vehicles, 120 days of selling activity resulted in $15,000 in commissions, and 160 days, in $18,000 in commissions.

Salesmens' Total Time (Days)	Furniture	Vehicles	Pharmaceuticals
40	$ 4,000	$ 5,000	$ 3,800
80	7,800	10,000	7,500
120	11,500	15,000	11,100
160	15,000	18,000	14,600
200	18,000	19,000	18,000
240	20,600	19,500	21,300
280	22,600		24,500
320	24,100		27,600

You are manager of the sales force and you are planning for the next 320 selling days (20 calendar working days).

Required:

a) Suggest how selling days should be allocated in order to maximize total salesmen's commissions.

b) Consider only the 880 days for which data are presented above. Do you think time was allocated properly during that period? Why?

c) Consider a 520-day selling plan. Present a sales plan showing allocation of salesmen's time which maximizes sales commissions. Why are the times not in the same proportions as in the 320-day plan?

d) Does this problem suggest a reason to you why sales commissions should be proportional to profit margins on products? What is it?

26. Foodstuff Supermarkets operates a chain of high-volume grocery stores. Although the company began by selling only food, each store now offers check cashing, drugs and cosmetics, and clothing. A typical 6,000-square-foot store produces these figures:

Department	Feet	Revenues	Direct Costs
Fresh meat............	500	$ 300,000	$ 250,000
Other groceries	5,000	2,025,000	1,900,000
Drugs and cosmetics	500	280,000	240,000
Totals	6,000	$2,605,000	$2,390,000

There is a proposal to add hardware to the departments in Foodstuff Supermarkets. The proposed typical hardware department would occupy 500 square feet. Revenues are forecast to be $220,000 and direct costs, $205,000. The typical store overhead runs about $120,000 and is allocated on the basis of floor space.

Required:

a) If each department would have to contribute one twelfth of its floor space (and thus lose one twelfth of its contribution), should the hardware department be added?

b) If the necessary floor space must be taken from only one department (but not fresh meat), would you recommend addition of the hardware department?

c) What is the minimum profit per square foot any new department must earn in order to be added to an existing store?

27. You are the budget officer for the Crashem Airplane Works and your firm has in the last 10 years spent $100,000,000 developing a new passenger airliner. When the project began, your company only planned to spend $10,000,000—so there has been a 1,000 percent overrun on the budget. The project was expected to return $50,000,000 in sales—so there is no chance whatever that all the money will be returned, much less a profit. This year the chief of development asks for $10,000,000 to complete development of the plane and to begin production.

Required:

a) Assume that if you agree to the request, that will actually complete the plane and there will be sales of $50,000,000. Prepare budgets for this project as if (1) you did not grant the latest request, and (2) you did grant the latest request.
b) What are the "sunk costs" in this problem?
c) If at the end of this year yet *another* $10,000,000 is, against all expectations requested, what would you recommend?
d) What factors other than the straightforward sunk-cost analysis might bear on your decision in (c)?

28. The Neil Corporation, which produces and sells to wholesalers a successful line of cosmetics, has decided to diversify into seasonal products. This winter, the company will market "Chap-off," a lip balm to be sold in a lipstick-like tube. The product will be sold to wholesalers in boxes of 24 tubes for $8. There is excess capacity, meaning no additional fixed costs to produce the product. However, $100,000 of existing fixed costs will be allocated (as a "fair share") to the new product.

Estimated sales and production of 100,000 boxes of Chap-off for the winter season are forecast. This forecast led to the following standard costs per box:

Direct labor	$2.00
Direct materials	3.00
Total overhead	1.50
Total	$6.50

Neil has approached a cosmetics manufacturer about purchasing the lipstick tubes for Chapoff. The purchase price of the empty tubes from the cosmetics manufacturer would be $0.90 per 24 tubes. If the Neil Corporation accepts the purchase proposal, it is estimated that direct labor and *variable* overhead costs (included with the fixed cost allocation in "total" overhead above) would be reduced by 10 percent and direct material costs would be reduced by 20 percent.

Required:

a) Should Neil Corporation make or buy the tubes? Why?
b) What would be the *maximum* price Neil could pay for the tubes?
c) Revised sales estimates show sales of 125,000 boxes. At this higher level, additional equipment at an annual rental of $10,000 *must* be acquired to manufacture all tubes required. However, this would be the *only* additional fixed cost required even if sales increase to 300,000 boxes. Under this circumstance, should Neil make or buy the empty tubes?

(This problem adapted from December 1972 CMA Examination)

29. Sam Smith is a furniture craftsman whose furniture business has long since passed the time when he made primarily custom furniture. Most of his work now goes into the standardized bedroom and dining room sets most buyers seem to want and are able to afford. These sets require 48 hours of work each, which costs $6 per hour; and hardwoods and hardware costing approximately $80. A bedroom or dining room set sells to the distributor for $600 and is resold by him for $1,000–$1,200. To help him, Smith uses a chosen experienced group of 20 associates. There is never any overtime; each man works approximately a 40-hour week spread over six days.

Recently, a small distributor asked Mr. Smith to make him a special order of the old custom-style furniture. The order would be for eight bedroom suites requiring 150 hours of labor each and six dining room suites requiring 200 hours of labor each. Mr. Smith estimated that the bedroom suites would each require $120 worth of materials; the dining room suites, $150 worth. The distributor has offered to pay $1,500 each for the bedroom suites and $2,200 each for the dining room suites. Mr. Smith is inclined to accept the order, because he likes the challenges of that kind of work, but he has told his accountant, "I won't take it if the profit is less than 75 percent of the profit I get on the regular work."

Required:

a) As the accountant, determine whether Mr. Smith should accept the order, using contribution-per-hour as the criterion.

b) Determine the prices for the custom work at which Smith would be indifferent whether he did the order or not.

30. George Lellis operates a small machine shop. He manufactures one standard product available from many other small businesses and also manufactures products to custom order. His monthly performance report is prepared by product lines, and appears below:

	Custom Sales	Standard Sales	Total
Sales	$50,000	$25,000	$75,000
Materials	$10,000	$ 8,000	$18,000
Labor	20,000	9,000	29,000
Depreciation	6,300	3,600	9,900
Power	700	400	1,100
Rent	6,000	1,000	7,000
Heat and light	600	100	700
Other miscellaneous (all indirect)	400	900	1,300
Total costs	$44,000	$23,000	$67,000
	$ 6,000	$ 2,000	$ 8,000

The depreciation charges are for machines used to manufacture both custom and standard products; the apportionment is roughly proportional to the fractions of time for each use. The power charge is apportioned on the estimate of power consumed. Rent, heat, and light are apportioned to the product lines as Mr. Lellis thinks they should be apportioned.

Gauge Hardware Supply Company has asked Mr. Lellis if he would manufacture 5,000 special units for them. Mr. Lellis is working at capacity; he would have to give up some other business in order to take this business. He can't renege on custom orders already agreed to but he could reduce the output of his standard product by one half for one month in order to produce the 5,000 special units. Gauge will pay $7 for each part. Materials and labor cost per special unit will be $5.60. Mr. Lellis will have to buy a precision meter for $2,000 which will be discarded when the job is done.

Required:

a) Examine the "performance report" above carefully, then redo it in an acceptable form showing the true contribution of each product, and of manufacturing operations to total profit.

b) Determine whether Mr. Lellis ought to take the order. Explain your reasoning.

(Adapted from December 1972 CMA Examination)

DECISION CASE 9–1: WELFARE ADMINISTRATION AGENCY

The State of Arkalina, concerned about its rising welfare costs, is considering a proposal by the governor of money grants directly to persons who qualify for welfare. "It costs us $5,000 in administrative costs to pay a welfare recipient $2,500 per year," complains the governor. The money for the grants would come from

a) Cancellation of all present welfare programs, and
b) Disbanding the present Welfare Administration Agency, transferring any nonwelfare programs to other agencies.

Critics maintain that the $5,000 cannot be right and in any case it could not all be saved. The governor seeks your impartial counsel. You find that the Welfare Administration Agency (WAA) has a total budget of $210,000,000. And of this, $70,000,000 is disbursed as welfare payments to the 28,000 qualified recipients of welfare in the state each year.

The WAA employs 2,000 persons, each earning an average salary of $12,000. The agency rents space in the state's office complex for $20,000,000 annually (paid to state office building agency). The agency's records are processed on the state-owned computer system, which bills the agency $30,000,000 annually for that service. WAA maintains official automobiles which are heavily driven in the course of welfare investigations; transportation expenses amount to $12,000,000 annually. The WAA supports research programs in sociology, psychology, and adult education; this research runs $25,000,000 annually and is considered essential to the quality of higher education in the state. Finally, the WAA operates three of the state's hospitals; support for these is $29,000,000 annually.

Required:

a) Prepare a summary budget for the WAA using the information you have uncovered. The budget should show the governor exactly how much he can save by canceling welfare payments and disbanding the welfare organization.

b) Do you think the same principles of contribution analysis (and overhead allocation!) are applicable in government agencies as in the private sector? Why (not)?

BIBLIOGRAPHY

Books

Bower, Joseph L. *Managing the Resource Allocation Process.* Boston: Harvard Business School, 1970.

Horngren, Charles T. *Cost Accounting.* 3d ed. Englewood Cliffs, N.J.: Prentice-Hall, Inc., 1972.

Thomas, Arthur L. *The Allocation Problem in Financial Accounting Theory,* Studies in Accounting Research No. 3. Evanston, Ill.: American Accounting Association, 1969.

Articles

Brady, Daniel W. "The Strategic Forces of Profit," *Management Accounting,* February 1971.

Davidson, H. Justin, and Trueblood, Robert M. "Accounting for Decision-Making," *The Accounting Review,* October 1961.

Harris, Jr., William T. and Chapin, Wayne R. "Joint Product Costing," *Management Accounting,* April 1973.

Hobbs, III, William. "Contribution Reporting for Consumer Products," *Management Accounting,* November 1970.

Rawcliffe, George A. "Accounting Concepts for Managerial Decision Making," *Management Accounting,* April 1972.

Solomons, David. "Flexible Budgets and the Analysis of Overhead Variances," *Management International,* 1961–1. Reprinted in *Contemporary Issues in Cost Accounting,* (eds. Hector Anton and Peter Firmin) 2d ed. New York: Houghton Mifflin Co., 1972.

10

Preparing Information Reports for Management

ACCOUNTING information measures activity and analyses decisions. A planned activity may be considered from many points of view. Each will be the subject of an appropriate accounting analysis which can be prepared and used, as you saw in the last chapter, to help you judge whether the activity should be pursued. There is also a unique accounting representation which will be most useful in *controlling* an activity once it begins to occur. Accounting is essential to control of activities.

To many executives, "control" has the connotation of restrictions on managerial discretion. To you, "control" should mean *full information*. Restrictions and restraints are necessary in any operation, but they have little to do with control. Control exists when a manager is fully informed about the probable consequences of each alternative he is contemplating.

In this chapter you learn to plan for an operating period by using the budgeting process and standard costs as a study whose purpose is to *remove uncertainty* about the future operating period; to relate in dollar-and-cents terms what will be expected of you if you elect given alternatives.

In particular, we show how flexible budgeting, standard costs, and dynamic analysis give a basis for evaluating performance that is superior to the fixed-budget concept. We show how to establish sensible fixed-cost levels through planning and how to report performance through variances from a flexible budget. Finally, we discuss effects that accounting and budgeting information may have on the attitudes and behavior of individuals and organizations.

FLEXIBLE BUDGETING AND PLANNING

Questions to Ask

The Gowingplaces Company budget of Chapter 5, Appendix 5A showed only the *results* of the budgeting process, based on specific policies for business activity during the coming operating period. Managers ask these questions about budgets:

1. How do policies translate into a budget?
2. What if these policies are changed?

"How do . . . ." You saw how a sales forecast led to manufacturing and purchase budgets. The dollar amounts in these budgets were based on quantities of physical resources, production distribution and sales technology, and prices for each unit of input. The "standard cost" of each unit of product A was built up as in Figure 10–1. Standard

FIGURE 10–1
Standard Cost of Product A

1.	Six units material × @ $5 each	$30
2.	Ten hours type I direct labor @ $3 each	30
3.	Variable overhead $1 per hour × 10 hours	10
	Total Variable Standard Cost.	$70

costs per unit were used to prepare manufacturing, purchase, and other budgets. The process then was for tentative operating policies to be translated into costs and revenues per unit activity or per time period, then combined to produce projected operating statements for the budget period.

"What if . . . ." Unsatisfactory projected operating statements imply the need for revision of underlying policies. Imagine that Schedule CGS–2 on page 141 is examined by an executive who says, "I doubt

that we can sell 1,000 units of A each quarter in the southern region. If we sell 500 units of A each quarter there, how does our contribution on A look then?"

The quick way to see the answer is to recall that in the southern region the price of A, by quarters, is scheduled to be: $90, $90, $100, and $100. The contribution margin by quarters will be:

(1)	(2)	(3)	(4)	(quarter)
90	90	100	100	(unit price)
−70	−70	−70	−70	(unit cost excluding fixed overhead)
$ 20	$ 20	$ 30	$ 30	
× 500	× 500	× 500	× 500	(volume per quarter)
$10,000	$10,000	$15,000	$15,000	(contribution margin in southern region from A)

We must add these figures to the contribution margin on A in the northern region:

$30,000	$60,000	$80,000	$66,000	(contribution margin in northern region from A)
$40,000	$70,000	$95,000	$81,000	(Total contribution margin from A)

The bottom line of figures compares directly with the "gross margin—A" line from Table 5A–12. Our executive can decide whether the differences are substantive.

FLEXIBLE BUDGETING AND CONTROL

Operations actually occur, and sure enough actual sales of A in the southern region are only 500 units per quarter. Here are the rules you must follow:

1. Revise all pertinent budget schedules (sales forecast, sales budget, cost of goods manufactured, etc.) to reflect the actual level of sales. All parties who participated in making the original budget should accept the changes in their budgets necessitated by the actual sales level.

2. Judge the performance of all responsibility centers strictly on the new budget schedules.

If actual sales were 500 instead of 1,000 units of A in the southern region, it is unrealistic to judge southern region sales performance based on the 1,000-unit forecast. The comparison of actual sales with the 1,000-unit budget will be unfavorable and unfair. If production is cut back, lower production rates will make the total direct cost variances from the original budget favorable. The basis for control, which is comparison of reasonable expectations with actual events, will be destroyed unless all performance variances are computed from the standard inputs or costs for the actual levels of outputs.

Sales Variances

A performance report for the southern region should stress failure of this region to sell as many units of A as it agreed to sell in the operating budget. The contribution per unit of A multiplied by the difference between budgeted and actual sales will give the contribution margin lost to the company because of failure to achieve sales goals. Unless there are obvious justifications for the variance (such as unexpected change in economic conditions, market oversupply, etc.), the budgeting and selling processes should both be examined with an eye to producing future budgets and performance that are more in agreement with each other.

In this case, the sales variance for product A, southern region, would be:

Quarter 1: $(1,000 - 500) \times (\$90 - 70) = \$10,000$ unfavorable
Quarter 2: $(1,000 - 500) \times (\ 90 - 70) = \ 10,000$ unfavorable
Quarter 3: $(1,000 - 500) \times (100 - 70) = \ 15,000$ unfavorable
Quarter 4: $(1,000 - 500) \times (100 - 70) = \ 15,000$ unfavorable

Recomputing an Expense Budget

In the Gowingplaces Company, selling costs are computed by region and include fixed costs and costs which are a function of the number of units sold and selling price of each product. A formula which summarizes the southern region sales budget is:

$$\begin{aligned}\text{Total selling}\\ \text{costs—southern}\\ \text{region}\end{aligned} = \begin{aligned}\text{Fixed selling costs,}\\ \text{southern region}\end{aligned}$$

$$+ \begin{bmatrix} \text{Total unit sales} & & \text{Unit price} \\ \text{southern region} & \times & \text{southern region} \\ \text{product A} & & \text{product A} \end{bmatrix}$$

$$+ \begin{bmatrix} \text{Total unit sales} & & \text{Unit price} \\ \text{southern region} & \times & \text{southern region} \\ \text{product B} & & \text{product B} \end{bmatrix} \times \begin{bmatrix} \text{Southern region} \\ \text{direct selling} \\ \text{costs per sales} \\ \text{dollar} \end{bmatrix} \quad (10\text{--}1)$$

Formulas of this sort are called *formula budgets*. This formula (10–1) can be used to create a new standard of comparison for the southern region sales office based on its actual sales of A and B.

Performance Analysis

Table 5A–2 in Appendix 5A to Chapter 5 includes the sales budget for the southern region. Under the original sales forecasts, this budget would have appeared as in Figure 10–2.

FIGURE 10-2
Sales Budget for Southern Region

	Quarter 1	Quarter 2	Quarter 3	Quarter 4
Unit sales:				
A	1,000	1,000	1,000	1,000
B	1,500	1,200	1,200	1,600
Sales dollars:				
A	$ 90,000	$ 90,000	$100,000	$100,000
B	300,000	240,000	240,000	320,000
Total	$390,000	$330,000	$340,000	$420,000
Direct selling expenses:				
$0.02 per sales dollar	$ 7,800	$ 6,600	$ 6,800	$ 8,400
Fixed selling expenses	15,000	15,000	15,000	15,000
Total	$ 22,800	$ 21,600	$ 21,800	$ 23,400

As soon as the actual sales were known, this sales budget would be revised, using equation (10–1) and information in Appendix 5A to Chapter 5. The revised sales budget appears as Figure 10–3.

FIGURE 10-3
Revised Sales Budget for Southern Region

	Quarter 1	Quarter 2	Quarter 3	Quarter 4
Unit sales:				
A	500	500	500	500
B	1,500	1,200	1,200	1,600
Sales dollars:				
A	$ 45,000	$ 45,000	$ 50,000	$ 50,000
B	300,000	240,000	240,000	320,000
Total	$345,000	$285,000	$290,000	$370,000
Direct selling expenses:				
$0.02 per sales dollar	$ 6,900	$ 5,700	$ 5,800	$ 7,400
Fixed selling expenses	15,000	15,000	15,000	15,000
Total	$ 21,900	$ 20,700	$ 20,800	$ 22,400

It is Figure 10–3 that would be used for performance evaluation in the southern region. To see how, imagine that the first quarter of operations has occurred. The actual performance was: 500 units of A sold at $90, 1,500 units of B sold at $200, direct selling expenses of $7,200, and fixed selling expenses of $15,500. These facts are compared with the performance standards of Figure 10–3 as Figure 10–4.

Other formulas, such as (10–2) and (10–3) below may be used to calculate expected performance based on actual levels of activity in the firm:

$$\begin{aligned}\text{Total manufacturing costs} = &\ \text{Fixed manufacturing costs} + \text{Direct costs of making A} \\ &\ + \text{Direct costs of making B} \\ &\ + \text{Indirect variable labor costs} \\ &\ + \text{Indirect variable materials costs}\end{aligned} \quad (10\text{--}2)$$

$$\text{Profit (direct costing basis)} = \text{Sales revenue} - \text{Total variable costs} - \text{Total fixed costs} \quad (10\text{--}3)$$

FIGURE 10–4
Southern Region Sales Performance Report

Category	Budget	Actual	Variance	Remarks
Unit sales:				
A	1,000	500	500 units **unfavorable** $10,000 contribution loss	Note 1
B	1,500	1,500	0	
Selling price:				
A	$ 90	$ 90		
B	200	200		
Sales revenue (for computing direct selling expenses)	345,000			
Direct selling expenses	6,900	7,200	$300 **unfavorable**	Note 2
Fixed selling expenses	15,000	15,500	$500 **unfavorable**	Note 3

Note 1: Unexpectedly large imports of Tasmanian A apparently reduced unit sales; this level of sales was maintained without price reductions.

Note 2: Extra costs represent expense of revising sales presentations to stress advantages of our A over Tasmanian A.

Note 3: Cold weather and higher utilities expenses for first quarter.

The detail of these formulas prevents their illustration here, but be assured that in a practical administrative setting they would be regularly used (computers would accelerate calculations) for appraising the profit and cost effects of changes involving markets, technology, and activity levels; and to compute standards of comparison for operations control.

PRESENTING AND EXPLAINING BUDGET VARIANCES

Budget variances should be part of regular performance reports. Let us take an example of simple variances. Figure 10–5 is the second quarter administrative performance report with budget figures in the first column, actual performance figures in the second column, and the variances in the third column. These administrative costs, although all "fixed" in the sense that they don't vary with production, do vary with administrative events such as unexpected salary changes, equipment rental changes, or addition of new continuing operations.

FIGURE 10-5

GOWINGPLACES COMPANY
Administrative Performance Report
April, May, June, 1974

Expense Category	Budget	Actual	Variance Favorable (Unfavorable)	Remarks
Accounting:				
Professional salaries	$ 22,000	$ 22,000	$ 0	...
Assistants' salaries	11,000	11,800	(800)	Note 1
Equipment rental	9,000	8,800	200	Note 2
Supplies	4,000	4,100	(100)	Note 0
Total	$ 46,000	$ 46,700	$(700)	
Security:				
Guard salaries	$ 1,500	$ 1,000	$ 500	Note 3
Other expenses	3,000	2,800	200	Note 0
Total	$ 4,500	$ 3,800	$ 700	
Staff:				
Executive salaries	$ 25,000	$ 25,000		
Secretarial salaries	5,000	5,250	$(250)	Note 4
Professional salaries	10,000	10,000		
Supplies	2,000	2,500	(500)	Note 5
Other expenses	2,000	1,700	300	Note 0
Total	$ 44,000	$ 44,450	$(450)	
Other expenses:				
Depreciation—offices	$ 6,000	$ 6,000	0	
Various amortizations	5,000	5,000	0	
Total	$ 11,000	$ 11,000	$ 0	
Total administrative	$105,500	$105,950	$(450)	

Note 0: Variance is insignificant.
Note 1: New assistant authorized for controller to serve as deputy budget coordinator. Hired 5-1-74 effective 6-1-74 @ monthly salary of $800 per month.
Note 2: Rental on tape drive units lowered by lessor to reflect competitive conditions in this market. Effective 5-1-74 rental will be lower by $100 per month on all units leased from this company. Lessor will give 30 days' notice before posting higher rates.
Note 3: Guard quit at end of May and has not yet been replaced.
Note 4: All staff secretaries given 5 percent salary increase in first quarter; budget figure has not yet been changed to reflect the increase.
Note 5: No reason known why supplies expense should increase.

No doubt there will be an investigation to determine why supplies expense for the staff have increased. You may have already thought that the budget figure for staff secretarial salaries should have been revised so as not to show this variance.

This performance report would in practice be a summary of reports going to each of the four responsibility centers shown in the report. Each responsibility center would learn in detail from its report how its operations compared with the current budget standards for its operations. The administrative supervisor—perhaps a vice president for administration—would receive the overall report of Figure 10–5.

PLANNING FIXED COSTS

Let us imagine that Gowingplaces Company is currently operating at nearly its full total capacity, and accordingly is planning to expand its plant (increasing its fixed costs). At the present time plant profitability and capacity are both related to total direct labor hours which can be worked per period. For the year 1974, budgeted direct labor hours add up to 90,000 + 268,200 = 358,200. The contribution to fixed costs and profits resulting from this many labor hours is $1,192,500. Thus the profit per direct labor hour is

$$\frac{\$1,192,500}{358,200} = \$3.33$$

The expansion contemplated will add capacity to work an additional 1,000,000 direct labor hours. Administrative costs remain at the present level, but fixed manufacturing and selling costs will increase approximately in proportion to the capacity increase itself—from $325,000 to $1,200,000; an increment of $875,000. However, sales *volume* will not at first require the total capacity. In fact, in the first year after the plant is expanded, only 200,000 direct labor hours above present capacity will be worked—only 20 percent of the new capacity will be used. In the second year of use, 30 percent will be used; and in the third year, 40 percent. A profitability analysis will appear thus:

Year	New Capacity Used	Contribution Generated	− Additional Fixed Costs =	New Plant Addition to Profits
1975	200,000	$ 666,000	$(875,000)	$(209,000)
1976	300,000	999,000	(875,000)	124,000
1977	400,000	1,332,000	(875,000)	457,000

The expansion will not contribute to profits until its second year of operation. Further, the first year loss is big enough to knock 50 percent off the current level of profits.

This is a phenomenon known as *semifixed costs* which you can anticipate using contribution analysis. A cost-volume-profit chart for the company as shown in Figure 10–6 indicates that semifixed costs are those

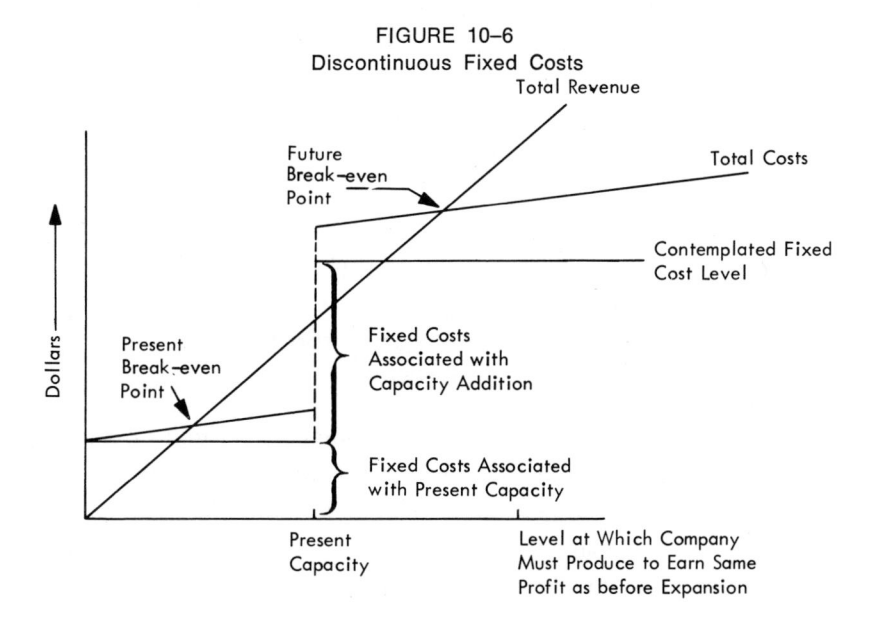

**FIGURE 10–6
Discontinuous Fixed Costs**

related to a change in capacity. Since capacity changes in relatively large increments, corresponding fixed (capacity) costs will rise in corresponding large jumps.

The Gowingplaces Company will have to use about 26 percent of its new capacity if it is to be profitable from the beginning, which is computed using (10–4) and (10–5).

$$\text{Break-even capacity increment} = \frac{\text{Fixed costs associated with addition}}{\text{Profit contribution per unit of capacity used}} = \frac{\$875,000}{\$3.33}$$

$$= 263,000 \text{ hours } (break\text{-}even \text{ } point) \quad (10\text{–}4)$$

$$\text{Break-even percentage of new capacity} = \frac{\text{Break-even capacity}}{\text{Size of planned addition}}$$

$$= \frac{263,000}{1,000,000} = 26 \text{ percent} \quad (10\text{–}5)$$

A Business Pitfall

The capacity increment decision is a critical one to businesses which, expanding as the consequence of growth, do not want to sacrifice cash position to the maintenance of capacity for future use. If Gowingplaces Company wants to add capacity that will earn an additional $100,000 income increment the first year it is in use, it can compute the maximum capacity increment from this formula:

$$\text{Maximum capacity increment} = \frac{\text{Capacity to be used} \times \text{Expected contribution margin per unit} - \text{Desired income increment}}{\text{Fixed operating cost per unit of capacity increment}} \quad (10\text{-}6)$$

The only new variable here is "fixed operating cost per unit of capacity increment" which is a function of the size of the increment (since capacity usually costs less per unit to operate as more of it is acquired). To simplify matters, compute fixed operating costs per unit of capacity as the increment in fixed operating costs divided by increment size.

$$\frac{\$875,000}{1,000,000 \text{ hours}} = \$0.875 \text{ per hour}$$

Computation with (10-6) now gives

$$\text{Maximum capacity increment} = \frac{200,000 \text{ hours to be used in first year} \times \$3.33 \text{ Expected margin} - \$100,000}{\$0.875 \text{ per hour operating costs per year}}$$

$= 646{,}857$ *hours*. No more capacity than this should be added at once if 200,000 hours will be used the first year and Gowingplaces Company insists on a $100,000 income increment from the addition.

Reduce Capacity, Increase Income

The same phenomenon—semifixed costs—also works in reverse. Suppose a firm is operating below or slightly above its break-even point.

If operating costs are semifixed, it may be possible to reduce them by reducing capacity and earn considerably more profit. That is why one of the first things a new management may do after taking over a troubled firm is try to reduce fixed costs.

BEHAVIORAL DIMENSION OF ACCOUNTING REPORTS

Many persons believe that accounting derives its real significance *not* from the accuracy of its descriptions of historical events but from the influence that accounting reports can have on the behavior of individuals. Here are examples of such influence:

—Ben Howe, noting that the Soft-Sit Chair Company has increased its earnings in each of the last three years, invests his life savings in the common stock of this company.

—Ronald Bennett, foreman of the day shift in the stamping division of Soft-Sit Chair Company, is staying up late tonight working on a new equipment layout he believes will increase the stamping rate and enable him to comfortably exceed the "standard" stamping rate for the first time this month.

—Gloria Smith, secretary for Howard H. Soft-Sit, president of the chair company bearing his name, is doing a slow burn at her typewriter because the monthly performance report shows poor performance on the part of the three billing clerks under her supervision. As a result, she has made mistakes in each of the four letters she has managed to type since the report came out.

—Edward Slansky, TV repairman, has just run his repair truck up a telephone pole. He was exceeding the speed limit and had to swerve to avoid a child on a bicycle. At the time he was thinking of the lecture the shop boss gave him about completing too few service calls per day. The shop boss was referring during the lecture to an accounting performance report.

In each case an accounting report refers to historical events in such a way as to connote approval or disapproval of them to the readers. These persons feel that their satisfaction is affected by their reaction (or the reaction of other persons) to the report. You should be able to identify these elements in each example above. Figure 10–7 gives a diagram to help you do this.

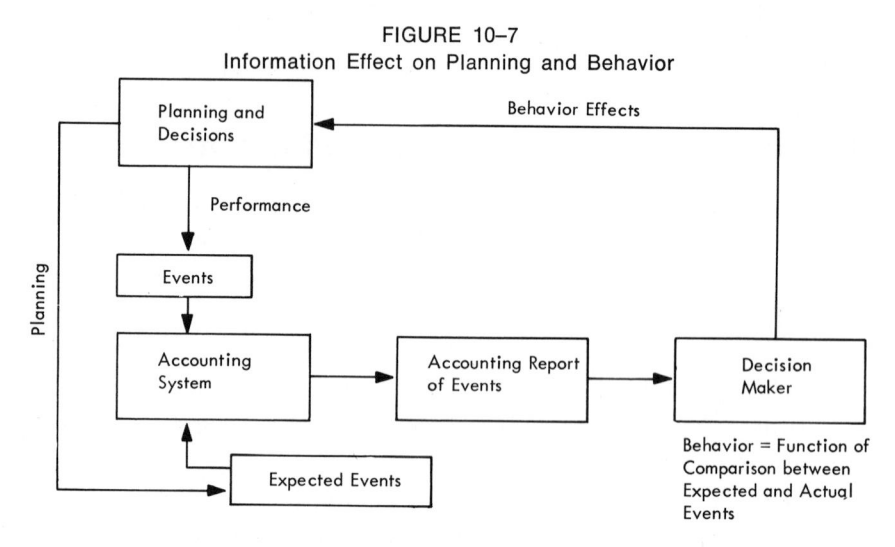

FIGURE 10–7
Information Effect on Planning and Behavior

```
                            Behavior Effects
    ┌─────────────┐ ◄──────────────────────────────────┐
    │ Planning and│                                     │
    │ Decisions   │                                     │
    └─────────────┘                                     │
           │ Performance                                │
           ▼                                            │
    ┌─────────────┐                                     │
 P  │   Events    │                                     │
 l  └─────────────┘                                     │
 a         │                                            │
 n         ▼                                            │
 n  ┌─────────────┐   ┌──────────────┐   ┌───────────┐  │
 i  │ Accounting  │──►│ Accounting   │──►│ Decision  │──┘
 n  │ System      │   │ Report of    │   │ Maker     │
 g  └─────────────┘   │ Events       │   └───────────┘
           ▲          └──────────────┘
           │                           Behavior = Function of
    ┌─────────────┐                    Comparison between
    │ Expected    │                    Expected and Actual
    │ Events      │                    Events
    └─────────────┘
```

Most modern organizations utilize collective decision processes. Figure 10–7 also applies when the "decision maker" is more than one person. Study of the response of decision makers, individual and collective, to reports of their performance which imply or permit an evaluation of that performance by comparing it with a previously stated standard, is called the "behavioral dimension" of accounting. Anyone dealing with accounting information should be aware of this behavioral dimension.

The Pressure Model

There are many models describing individual and collective behavior. All of them possess some validity. Here we select one which is suitable for explaining responses to control efforts applied through performance reports. It assumes that individual behavior is motivated by a desire to keep "pressure" below a long-term bearable level. If you want to know what "pressure" is, you can regard it as the strain and anxiety you feel as you prepare for a difficult examination on which you must do very well in order to obtain a grade you want in a course. No one likes that feeling. While you will accept high levels of pressure for a short time, if the pressure is maintained you will find a way to reduce it.

Individuals become members of various organizations in order to reduce pressure. You join a business organization to reduce the pressure of finding food, clothing, and shelter. You join social organizations to reduce the pressure of needing human association and companionship. Once a member of an organization, additional pressures may arise through the organization. Specifically, standards of performance may be set with the implication that nonconformance with such standards may result in ostracism, punishment, or even severance from the organization. These standards may be the result of economic necessity—pressure for those most responsible for the organization's survival and continued ability to satisfy the needs of its members.

Natty Bumppo[1] is an executive in the middle ranks of the Midwest Resources Company, which he joined after pathfinding his way across the country from the East Coast (no charge for this kind of pun). He is pleased with his position. One of his sources of security is that his function in Midwest Resources is defined as bargaining for 1,000 animal hides per month from the dozens of trappers who range the midcontinent countryside. These hides must be secured for an average price of $1 each. Mr. Bumppo takes pride in knowledge that he secures these hides for, on the average, only $0.90 each. This $0.10 per hide saving makes Mr. Bumppo feel that he is contributing significantly to Midwest Resources, Inc., and enables him to deal with the challenges of his job without experiencing unbearable pressure.

One day, however, a new president arrives at Midwest; and after studying the situation, announces, "Our agents must deliver hides to us at lower prices. The trappers are getting rich from our generosity and this must stop. Hereafter the standard price for hides is $0.70."

Mr. Bumppo is dismayed. He has never offered a trapper such a low price. If this is indeed the price Midwest Resources expects him to pay, it leaves him no room at all for the comfortable, pressure-reducing favorable variance to which he is accustomed.

Sure enough, after two months of operation under the new standard, Mr. Bumppo's average price per hide paid is $0.85, all the trappers

---

[1] American literature buffs will recognize the protagonist of J. F. Cooper's *Leatherstocking Tales*.

are angry at him, and he is reporting a $0.15 per hide unfavorable variance. He is angry and frustrated. At first he did try very hard to obtain the new price. He felt as if he had failed the company when his best efforts did not get it. He has visited the company headquarters in Pittsburg, talked with other agents, and discovered that none of them are getting the new standard price. This made him feel better, for if he has failed, he at least is not alone.

After two more months with the new standard, the average price per hide is still $0.85 and the company management is threatening him with punishment if he does not come closer to the standard. Mr. Bumppo hates his job and hates Midwest Resources, Inc.

On his next visit to headquarters, he finds the other agents share his feelings, and over beverages in a Pittsburg tavern, they reach an agreement: among themselves they will honor the old $1 standard. They know Midwest cannot fire them all. They feel that joint action might prevent the company from moving against any of them. They agree to write each other periodically and tell each other how the hide market is in their territories.

Over the next few months, Mr. Bumppo actually pays as much as $1.10 for hides. He no longer feels that the company merits his effort or contribution; instead, he feels his loyalty is to his fellow agents, and he wants to make sure that he does not pay a lower price than they are paying. When the new president, an ex-writer named J. F. Cooper, personally inquires why the prices paid for hides cannot be reduced, Mr. Bumppo replies, "Market conditions. There are not enough deerslayers in the territory and the scarcity of hides has driven up the price." And feeling like the last of the Mohicans, but no longer under the unbearable pressure of the lower price standard, Mr. Bumppo continues to serve as Midwest's agent.

The Example Interpreted. This example illustrates some important responses of individuals to pressure. The pressure was kept to a manageable level when performance was in a controllable relationship to the standard. In the example, this was the comfortable and maintainable margin of the 90-cent price paid to the $1 standard.

Pressure rose to a level unbearable in the long run when the standard was changed. When unbearable pressure is present, something will be done to reduce it. In the example, two things happened:

1. Bumppo and the other agents turned to an *informal organization*. The purpose of this informal organization was to provide substitute goals for those of the formal organization (Midwest Resources) which were causing the pressure. These substitute goals actually were the nonachievement of the formal goals. The substitute goals had to be achieved since the goal of the very low price was impossible to reach anyway.
2. The informal organization set up its own *informal information system*. This information system reported on progress toward the goals of the information organization. The information system of the formal organization, which reported on achievement of the formal organizations goal of the unreasonably low price paid per hide, was increasingly disregarded.

When the informal organization was successful in achieving its initial goals, it developed additional, noneconomic, self-serving goals—its own survival, for one; and protection of all the agents even if Midwest Resources was damaged by the high prices paid for hides. We add this dimension to the illustration to make sure you understand that informal organizations need not be virtuous, altruistic, or even particularly wise—any more than are the formal organizations they counter.

Of course, informal organizations nearly always exist in a business entity. When pressure is generally at tolerable levels, an informal organization will be weak because there is no need for it. It is only when pressure rises that the informal organization becomes strong.

Informal information systems will also exist. They carry rumor, speculation, and much of value that cannot be included in the accounting reports, personnel records, and other components of an organization's formal information system. Informal information systems are dangerous to a business entity primarily when they serve the purposes of strong informal organizations formed to resist pressure.

A General Model

The reader may ask, "Can we change goals and performance standards without arousing the informal organization?" Much can be done if those whose performance will be judged participate in the standard-setting process. This point was made in Chapter 5 and bears repeating here. However, there is a point beyond which such participation will not produce agreement on a proposed standard, and that is the point at which one expects that the proposed standard will not allow one to receive a pressure-reducing evaluation of performance. In other words, if Mr. Bumppo must have at least a $0.05 favorable price paid per hide variance in order to maintain a tolerable level of pressure, and if he can produce such a variance when the standard is lowered to $0.90 per hide, then he will (or should) cooperate with such a change. But since he cannot obtain such a variance when the standard is lower, no amount of participation will cause him to agree to further reductions of the standard below $0.90.

Additionally, persons can withstand more pressure for short periods of time than is possible over the long run. Mr. Bumppo might have agreed to a standard of $0.70 for, say, three months, and would have conscientiously tried to achieve it. But such a prospect becomes unacceptable when proposed on an indefinite basis.

Finally, as the informal organization relieves pressure, one's productivity in the formal organization decreases. Figure 10–8 summarizes this model.

Point 1 on Figure 10–8 shows where pressure begins to rise as productivity is increased by raising the standard of performance—the point at which productivity is no longer increasable without a rise in pressure. At point 2, pressure becomes unbearable and the informal organization appears, followed by a reduction of pressure. (Such a reduction may not always occur; there may be such active conflict between formal and informal organizations that pressure is increased. It is really the *expectation* that pressure will be reduced that leads to the formation of the informal organization and its survival.)

The effects described here may be conditionally reversible if a business takes steps to reduce pressure through the formal organization. This may occur by incorporating all or part of the informal organization into the formal organization. An example would be recognition of a union and deduction of union dues from paychecks. The union actually becomes part of the company; it has been "institutionalized." If a business removes whatever caused the pressure initially, the informal organization may no longer be powerful. This will occur if

FIGURE 10–8
Productivity and Pressure as Functions of Performance Standard

(Figure: curves showing Productivity in the Formal Organization peaking at point 2 then dropping sharply, and Pressure Felt by the Individual rising to point 1 then leveling off, plotted against Standard of Performance from a Flexible Budget or Standard Cost System)

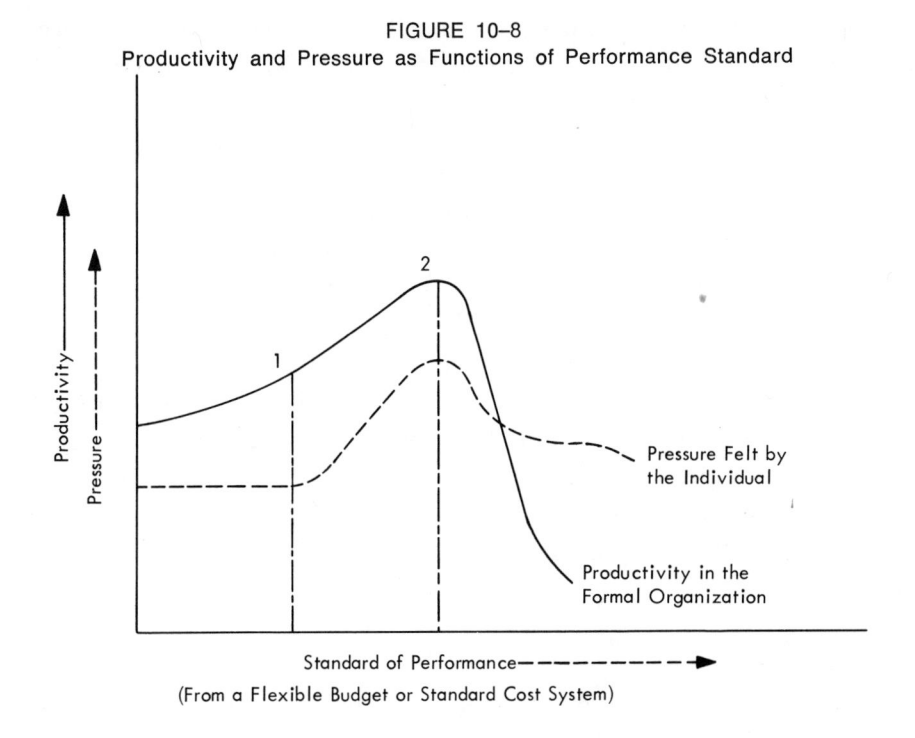

employees believe there is no further need to seek the informal organization's protection. On the other hand, the informal organization may, in order to survive, provoke pressure against its members to stimulate their loyalty and support.

In some organizations the threshold of hostile response to attempts to increase productivity by increasing standards is very low. No one is quite sure why this is true. Sometimes, the point of resistance to such moves can be changed significantly through incentives offered by a skillful management. Motivation of salesmen is intended to increase their efforts and result in higher sales, which may be accompanied by an increased standard. Retraining employees may increase their productivity. Increasing fringe benefits or wages may make employees willing to perform consistently at levels which they otherwise would resist vigorously.

When to Change Expectations. Organizations should seek ways to increase productivity and therefore strengthen their right to exist economically. In some instances, manipulation of standards may prove to be a temporarily effective method of doing so. The accountant, however, regards standards as objective descriptors of what is possible under given conditions. While he agrees that accounting is important because it influences behavior, he objects to the literal destruction of standards to achieve temporary productivity or behavior changes, especially when distortion of standards holds peril and potential for harm to the organization. The accountant argues that accounting should influence behavior through its comparisons of what is *possible* with what actually *occurs*. The accountant protects the standards from change motivated by the desire to provide cheap incentives for increased productive activity. Only when productivity increases are possible through positive motivation, retraining, upgrading capital equipment, learning effects, wage incentives, working condition changes, and the like may standards reflecting expected performance be legitimately revised.

SUMMARY

Flexible budgeting permits quick recomputation of the operating budget to fit the most valid assumptions or recently adopted business policies, even when these are different from the ones existing when the budget was first computed. Flexible budgeting requires knowledge of fixed and variable costs, as well as semifixed costs—costs which are fixed over some range of activity, then rise or fall to a new level abruptly when activity leaves this range. Use of flexible budgeting permits managers to anticipate the consequences for profits of adding or reducing capacity to produce and sell.

Performance reporting requires comparison of budget with actual operating figures. The resulting variances, if any, must be classified as "not significant" or "significant;" and if the latter, they must be explained. If the variance will tend to be a repeating one, either the budget for future periods should be modified to reflect it (uncontrollable variance or favorable controllable variance) or the cause of the variance removed (unfavorable controllable variance).

Operating control depends on management knowledge of what is happening in the business, why it is happening, and how to secure cooperation to change unsatisfactory situations. Performance reporting provides this management knowledge, and can influence responsible persons to work for the benefit of the organization.

QUESTIONS

1. What is the principle of flexible budgeting?
2. A particular flexible budget shows $30,000 in fixed costs, $4 per direct labor hour, $5 per pound of raw material, and variable overhead of $6 per hour. If 120 units, each requiring one direct labor hour and two pounds of raw material are to be produced, what is the flexible budget?
3. Why in planning must fixed and variable costs be kept separate?
4. What is a "formula budget"? Is such a budget useful for planning, performance evaluation, or both?
5. The Forsythe Company makes two products, A and X. Total expenses are T = $50,000 + $22 A + $44 X. What is budgeted production cost if 800 A and 1,200 B are produced? If 900 A are actually sold for $50 each and 1,000 B are sold for $60 each, what is the budgeted profit? If your budget looked like this, would you be satisfied?
6. What are semifixed costs? With what factors other than actual activity level may a cost vary?
7. How is it possible for a company to reduce its productive capacity and at the same time increase its income? Can *any* company do this?
8. Brown Company wishes to enlarge its plant. New capacity costs $30 per unit; fixed operating costs amount to $3 per unit (of annual capacity). Each unit produced will contribute $9 towards profit and fixed costs. If the company wishes to earn $15,000 from the expansion in the first year and expects to sell 10,000 units that year, what is the largest expansion (in units of annual capacity) which the company should consider?
9. Why are budget variances reported to the persons most directly responsible for them? Would you report capacity variances to a manufacturing foreman, a marketing supervisor, or a budget staff officer—or none of these?

10. As staff supervisor of the Kry Day Care Center you supervise three employees in the care of 100 children under the age of 5. An economy move by your city government reduces your staff to two, yet 50 more children are expected soon. How would you react—immediately? and after a few weeks?

11. You are a happy B-movie producer. Your budget is about $200,000 per film. Your pictures are satisfactorily successful, and your studio expects you to do more. They give you a $700,000 per picture budget. You produce additional pictures under the bigger budgets, but they are not notably more profitable than the $200,000 pictures. The studio cuts you back to $200,000 budgets. Describe your feelings at each stage of this process.

12. Mr. Bumppo (see chapter narrative) has just received word that he must pay no more than $0.70 per hide. In those first trying weeks after he receives this news, he learns two things: (*a*) the president, Mr. Cooper, actually expects the average price per hide to be $0.85, and (*b*) a competing trading concern wants to hire him at double his present salary, promising that he can set the standard himself. Discuss the effect on Mr. Bumppo's state of mind and behavior upon learning each of these facts.

13. What is pressure? How can an accounting report create or alleviate pressure? Can pressure be altered *without* communication in an organization?

14. What is a formal organization? A formal information system? An informal organization? An informal information system?

15. Your Students' Association has organized a series of peaceful demonstrations against a particular university administration policy. As a result the Students' Association, long a weak influence on campus, is at a new peak of strength and prestige. You are the university president. What single most effective thing could you do to weaken the Students' Association? Be objective about this question. What would be the likely sequence of events after you did it?

16. When pressure begins to rise within an organization, what is the first response of individuals in the organization? The second response?

17. When may standards of performance be changed?

EXERCISES

18. Lincoln Company has prepared two different budgeted income statements which differ only in their treatment of fixed and indirect costs. Here is one:

Budgeted Income Statement 1

	Product A	Product B
Sales revenue:		
4,500 units @ $50	$ 225,000	
3,000 units @ $70		$ 210,000
Less: Cost of sales	(135,000)	(180,000)
Gross margin	$ 90,000	$ 30,000
Less: Selling and administrative expense	(50,000)	(50,000)
Profit (total $20,000)	$ 40,000	(20,000)

You find that $97,500 in fixed indirect manufacturing costs have been allocated to cost of sales at the rate of $15 per unit of A and $10 per unit of B, and that $30,000 of selling and administrative expense allocated equally between the two products is in fact indirect (joint) expense. Prepare "budgeted income statement 2" reflecting your findings.

19. Brighton Company uses a formula budget. This budget is:

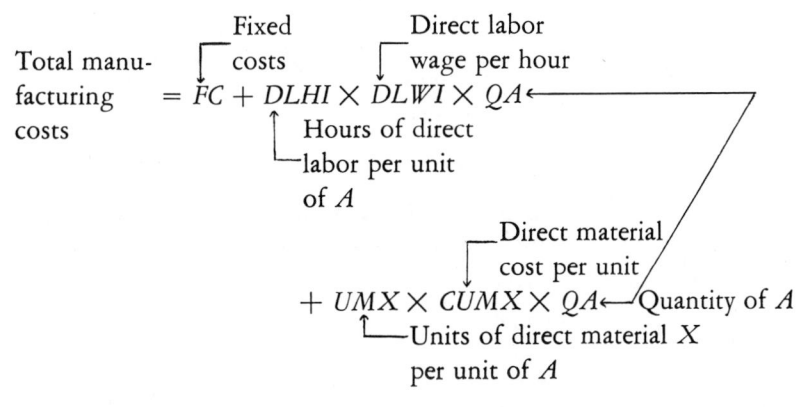

$$\text{Total manufacturing costs} = FC + DLHI \times DLWI \times QA + UMX \times CUMX \times QA$$

where FC = Fixed costs; $DLHI$ = Hours of direct labor per unit of A; $DLWI$ = Direct labor wage per hour; QA = Quantity of A; UMX = Units of direct material X per unit of A; $CUMX$ = Direct material cost per unit.

The symbols have these values: FC = $80,000 per year; $DLHI$ = 4 per unit of A; $DLWI$ = $5 per hour; UMX = 100 per unit of A; $CUMX$ = $0.50 per unit X. What is the level of QA at which manufacturing operations break even if the price of A is $110 per unit? If total selling and administrative costs = $80,000, what is the break-even point of the firm?

20. The tax rate on Howard Company is 50 percent; that is, half of its income must be paid to the federal government. In 1972 this company's total fixed costs of all sorts were $100,000. It sold three products, in the quantities and with the contributions shown below:

	Product 1	Product 2	Product 3
Units sold	1,000	1,000	1,000
Unit contribution	$50	$210	−$10

Compute the tax on Howard Company's 1972 income.

21. The Howard Company feels that it must pay a minimum dividend of $50,000 per year and have retained earnings increase by $70,000 per year. If the sales of all products can be increased equally without additional fixed costs, what percentage increase in sales will produce the desired amounts? (See Exercise 20 above for details.)

22. Blue Bonnet Company wishes to increase productive capacity. The smallest increment available is 10,000 units per year, at a fixed indirect cost per year of $50,000. The company's product has direct variable costs of $40 and sells for $60. Blue Bonnet can sell 2,000; 3,000; 5,000; and 6,000 additional units in the first, second, etc. years after the capacity is added. Compute the effect on income of adding this capacity for each of these four years.

23. Ames Company is considering three different sizes of capacity increment:

Size of Increment	Cost per Year to Operate
10,000 units per year	$50,000
20,000 units per year	80,000
30,000 units per year	99,000

The company can use 5,000 additional units of capacity per year, thus: 5,000; 10,000; 15,000; etc. Over a six-year period, the company could add 10,000 units of capacity three times; 10,000 and 20,000 units each once; or 30,000 units now. Compute which alternative is least expensive. Contribution per unit is $8, and constant.

24. Shaw Company is able to determine exactly the type of capacity increment to add. It can use 6,000 units of capacity in the first year it is available. Its products have an average contribution margin per unit of $80. It desires to earn at least $10,000 from the increment in its first year of service. The annual operating cost per unit of capacity increment is $20. What is the largest increment that can be added?

PROBLEMS

25. See-Thru Carpet Company was started 11 years ago and has grown steadily throughout that interval. Recently it bought the Hemp Carpet Company plant in a nearby town at what appeared to be a bargain price. Now See-Thru has discovered why it was so cheap: the fixed costs will eat the owner up alive. Present sales are $200,000; variable costs are $140,000; fixed (capacity) costs are $60,000. The plant is operating at 50 percent of capacity. Fixed costs are proportional to the capacity of the plant.

Required:

a) What reduction in fixed costs will produce a $10,000 profit in the new plant, assuming sales remain constant? At what percentage of capacity will the plant then be operating, assuming capacity available is proportional to fixed costs?

b) If the present level of operation were 95 percent of capacity instead of 50 percent, would it be possible to achieve a $10,000 profit by the manner suggested in (a)? By how much (amount and percentage) would variable costs have to be reduced to produce the desired profit?

c) It is possible to make a capital expenditure which would increase fixed costs in the former Hemp Company plant by 20 percent and reduce variable costs by 10 percent. Would you recommend this expenditure? Would you recommend it if the criterion of acceptability is that the new plant must earn a $10,000 profit?

d) If all of the above measures fail to produce a $10,000 profit, what do you think See-Thru should do with its bargain plant?

26. The Bumper Fender Company produced and sold 1,000 units in February. The original budget, prepared in December, called for 1,200 units to be made and sold. The standard cost of B-F's product, a water-filled bumper, has variable components as follows:

Direct labor, 3 hrs. @ $2 each	$ 6
Direct materials, 16 lbs. @ $4 per lb.	64
Variable overhead @ $8 per d.l.h.	24
Total variable costs	$94

The budgeted fixed costs were $40,000; actual fixed costs were $38,000. Actual production costs in February, compared with the original budget figures, are given below in the company's manufacturing performance statement.

	Total $ Budgeted	Total Actual Units	Total Actual $	Variance
Direct labor	$ 7,200	3,000 hrs.	$ 6,300	$ 900 F
Direct materials	76,800	16,500 lbs.	68,000	8,800 F
Variable overhead	28,800		26,000	2,800 F
Total variable	$112,800	n/a	$100,300	$12,500 F

Required:

a) The president, Mr. Fender Bumper, is quite pleased with all the favorable variances in February. Write a critical analysis of operations in February, utilizing the concept of the flexible budget to compute spending and efficiency variances for the three variable components.

b) The water bumpers sell for $150 each. Describe and compute a variance which will call attention to the fact that the sales goal for February was not met.

c) Refer to (b) above. How will this variance be treated for income measurement purposes (on the monthly income statement)?

27. The Gowingplaces Company (see Chapter 5 and this chapter) is analyzing some alternative plans for the next budget period. One alternative plan would change the manufacturing process layout and sequence so that certain costs were altered. The amounts of the *changes* are:

Variable cost of A . . . . −$ 8.20
Variable cost of B . . . . +   4.00
Fixed costs . . . . − 8,000

Also,

Quantity of A = 9,000
Quantity of B = 13,500

Assuming that sales volumes and prices do not change, compute the effects of these changes on budgeted profit and recommend whether to consider them further.

28. The Reversible Rivet Company is a small firm, founded three years ago by two engineering faculty professors. The company has successfully marketed a special rivet which reduces riveting time by 60 percent.

Last year's volume was 60,000 cases of rivets, produced at average direct cost of $12 each—all variable. Total fixed costs were $80,000.

The cases were sold for $900,000—leaving a gross profit of $100,000 before taxes. At that time the company was working at top capacity. Because business prospects seemed good, the firm's owners decided to expand. The expansion tripled capacity, to 180,000 cases per year. However, borrowing costs and operating costs of the new equipment and additional administrative functions connected with the new capacity pushed total fixed costs to $250,000 annually. During this year, the first full year of operations using the new capacity, sales rose to 75,000 cases. Selling price and unit variable cost remain unchanged.

Required:

a) Compute the Reversible Rivet Company's income last year and this year. Explain what happened to the company.
b) Assume that the sales for this year may be forecast *before* committing the company to a capacity expansion. If the company desires the same profit as last year, what would be the maximum increase in annual fixed costs the company should incur in order to obtain enough additional capacity to sell 75,000 cases of rivets in total?
c) Why would capacity be added at all when it cannot increase profits at once?

29. The Bearingdown Company's prodding department has been a problem to the company for the past year, ever since Goering Legree became its manager. The department was informed, in Legree's first memo, that "I intend to improve the productivity of this department by establishing high standards of endeavor."

Subsequently, standards were raised and productivity, as measured by output per direct labor hour, increased. Here is the record:

Month	Productivity Index
January	90
February	92
March	95
April	102
May	103
June	103
July	102
August	95
September	85
October	70
November	75
December	75

In June, the safety record in prodding began to worsen. Record absenteeism began in July. In August, several employees protested the new standards to Legree. In September and October, wildcat strikes occurred. In November and December, Legree raised standards again and gave several talks to employees exhorting them to do better and demanding disbanding of the "employee's complaint committee."

Required:

Explain what is happening and what Legree will have to do to restore productivity. How should he have tried to improve productivity initially?

30. The City Council of Midville is considering a plan for a new civic center. If built, a civic center would attract tourists and conventions. Each person coming to Midville would create, according to Chamber of Commerce estimates, $200 per day in business for city merchants.

A team of outside specialists estimate that for each $1,000 spent on a civic center, one person will spend one day per year in Midville. An architect prepares plans for two possible civic center concepts estimated to cost $6,000,000 and $25,000,000 respectively. The city accountant announces that annual operating costs for the centers would be $500,000 and $1,500,000 respectively. Service of the debt to finance construction would be 9 percent of the center cost annually. Finally, the tax office estimates that because of additional commercial business, a civic center would increase the property tax *base* in Midville by 70 cents for each dollar of total business produced by the center. The property tax is the only source of city revenue and is 4 percent of assessed valuation.

Required:

a) Prepare a schedule for each civic center concept showing (i) its effect on the city economy, and (ii) its effect on city tax revenues.
b) In addition to what is stated above, unemployment in Midville is high. When operative, the center would reduce unemployment by 50 persons for each $1,000,000 invested in it. Each unemployed person costs the city $1,500 in direct costs. Add this information to each schedule above.
c) By how much would city taxes have to be increased or reduced to make a center break even? Do you think a center should be built? If yes, which one? Why?

d) Assume that the $6,000,000 center is built. In its first year of operation (a typical year) it employs 400 persons, 8,000 persons each spend an average of 3 days in Midville, creating business of $160 per day each, and operating costs are $600,000. Debt financing service is $500,000. The effect on tax base is as expected but the tax rate is now 5 percent. Prepare a performance report comparing this performance with that expected. Make recommendations for improving performance.

31. Thorp Shoes Company began as a single high-volume, middle-price shoe store in downtown Midville. Mr. Thorp, a hyperactive and entirely self-made man, decided to expand his operation. He now owns 36 shoe stores in Midville and surrounding region. Each store has a full-time manager. Mr. Thorp personally selects the shoe styles each store will sell, sends the shoes to each store in what he considers to be the proper quantity and at the proper times, and says, "It is the responsibility of each store manager to move the shoes out." Mr. Thorp establishes the shoe selling prices. Several times a year, he will hold sales on selected lines and at selected stores.

Mr. Thorp believes in modern management techniques and has developed a performance report format which he believes helps him determine the efficiency of a store manager. As an income standard, Mr. Thorp thinks that before taxes, each store should show a 20 percent return on investment (Mr. Thorp selects store sites and approves architectural plans). The report format is typified by the report below for January in store 22: Sales by product line:

Mens dress	$ 12,000
Ladies dress	23,000
Mens sport	2,000
Ladies sport	3,000
Childrens	14,000
Miscellaneous	4,000
Total sales	$ 58,000
Less: Cost of sales	(38,000)
Less: Store overhead and administrative	(9,000)
Less: Central office overhead and administrative (allocated)	(8,000)
Store profit	$ 3,000
Normal profit: one-twelfth of 20% of investment in store ($250,000)	$ 4,167
Variance	$ 1,167 *Unfavorable*

Each store manager received each other store manager's performance report. The variance was in big red letters if unfavorable and in regular black letters if favorable. Managers' year-end bonuses were based on total favorable minus unfavorable variances. However, few store managers stay with the firm as long as a year.

Required:

a) List as many things wrong with Mr. Thorp's management policies as you can.
b) List as many things wrong with the store performance report and its use as you can.
c) Briefly outline what you think might be improved management and reporting procedures for Thorp Shoes.

32. Intercity Bus Company operates bus transit systems in cities of 100,000–300,000 population. Each system is a separate responsibility center, actually organized as a company all of whose stock is held by Intercity. Each company is named after the city it operates in.

The Midtown Company has 50 buses which it is not using. Annually, it incurs $200,000 in fixed costs and $50,000 in direct variable costs to own these buses, even though they are not in service. Midtown has offered Capewood Company, another system owned by Intercity, the use of these buses at $0.06 per mile; Capewood needs 50 buses for its system and has been considering leasing from a commercial leasing company at a cost of $0.03 per mile. Capewood system's buses are normally driven 90,000 miles per year.

Midtown system's management says, "We cannot lease the buses to the Capewood system for less than 6 cents per mile or we will lose money. Capewood should lease at our price from us because if they lease the buses from the commercial company, the cash they pay will be lost to Intercity Bus Company, whose overall profit will drop."

Capewood's management says, "How can we pay 6 cents per mile to Midtown when we need only pay 3 cents per mile to the commercial leasing company? Our profit will be much less if we are forced to deal with Midtown on its own terms!"

Puzzled, Intercity management turns to you, the independent CPA who expresses an opinion on the annual financial statements, for advice.

Required:

a) Assume Midtown leases the buses to Capewood at 3 cents per mile. What will be Midtown's loss on owning buses?

b) Assume that Capewood leases the buses from Midtown at 6 cents per mile. How much lower will its profit be than if it had leased from the outside commercial company?
c) Now, consider Intercity. How much better off would it be, if any, if Capewood leases from Midtown at 6 cents than from the outside company at 3 cents?
d) If the suggestion in (c)—Capewood lease from Midtown at 6 cents per mile—is followed, what will be the effect on Capewood management? How can something so good for the company be so "bad" for one of its divisions? Can you suggest any performance reporting scheme which would eliminate this effect?

33. A. Able Gunnslinger was hired as investments manager of the Gogo Mutual Fund. His contract calls for him to receive no salary; however, he will receive percentages of the profits his management brings the fund. These percentages are:

Of the first $1,000,000 increase over January 1 assets.	5%
Of the next $1,000,000 increase over January 1 assets.	2
Of the third $1,000,000 increase over January 1 assets.	0.5
Of anything over a $3,000,000 increase	0.1

On January 1 the fund's assets stood at $6,000,000. On July 1, the fund's assets were $9,500,000. On July 3, Mr. Gunnslinger, upon being shown a summary of assets at July 1, said, "Well, that's the ball game!" He converted all assets into cash and went fishing until January 1, next year. The stock market rose steadily throughout this period. The puzzled Gogo Mutual Fund directors are at a loss to understand Mr. Gunnslinger's behavior.

Required:

a) Compute Mr. Gunnslinger's compensation for the year as at July 1.
b) Imagine that Gogo's assets at year-end would have been $16,000,000 instead of $9,500,000 if Mr. Gunnslinger had not gone fishing. How much income did Mr. Gunnslinger forego in order to take his six-month vacation?
c) Suppose you were devising an incentive plan for managers. Indicate how your plan would differ from Gogo's plan.

DECISION CASE 10-1: TRAILS MOTOR COACH COMPANY

Trails Motor Coach Company accepted a contract from the Department of Transportation to develop a small new electric railway car. The technological and developmental problems posed by the specifications were unique. Trails Company established a separate division to perform the contract and placed Mr. Barrett Journalbox in charge of it. Mr. Journalbox had been with Trails for 12 years, and had successfully carried through other programs for the company.

The initial budget was $25,000,000 with performance to DOT satisfaction in 25 months. Quite early in the contract, Mr. Journalbox decided that the contract could be fulfilled quite easily; that somehow the specifications were not as rough as had been supposed.

But when he told government officials this, they reviewed and renegotiated the contract to produce a new $14,000,000 figure and completion within 15 months. The new schedule was extremely tight; in fact, Trails did not make the new completion date. Sometime after completion and acceptance by DOT, it was discovered that the final report was in some ways falsified; the claimed performance for the electric car could not be obtained. Although Journalbox disclaimed responsibility for the falsifications, he was blamed, and shortly thereafter left the company.

Required:

Discuss all the factors of judgment and behavior that may have contributed to this situation. What specific mistakes were made by the various parties?

BIBLIOGRAPHY

Books

Caplan, Edwin H. *Management Accounting and the Behavioral Sciences.* Reading, Mass.: Addison-Wesley Publishing Co., Inc., 1971.

Joplin, Bruce, and Pattillo, James W. *Effective Accounting Reports.* Englewood Cliffs, N.J.: Prentice-Hall, Inc., 1969.

Lev, Baruch. *Accounting and Information Theory,* Studies in Accounting Research No. 2. Evanston, Ill.: American Accounting Association, 1969.

Articles

Chambers, R. J. "The Role of Information Systems in Decision Making," *Management Technology,* June 1964.

Dyckman, T. R. "The Investigation of Cost Variances," *The Journal of Accounting Research,* Autumn 1969.

Figler, Homer R. "Goal-Setting Techniques," *Management Accounting,* November 1971.

Fremgen, James M. "Transfer Pricing and Management Goals," *Management Accounting,* December 1970.

Horngren, Charles T. "Motivation and Coordination in Management Control Systems," *Management Accounting,* May 1967.

Kirby, Fred M. "Variance Analysis—the 'Step-Through' Method," *Management Services,* March–April 1970.

Krueger, Donald A., and Kohlmeier, John M. "Financial Modeling and 'What if' Budgeting," *Management Accounting,* May 1972.

Malcom, Robert E. "Sales Variances—A Further Look," *Management Adviser,* March –April 1971.

Ridgway, V. F. "Dysfunctional Consequences of Performance Measurements," *Administrative Science Quarterly,* September 1956.

Part III

Accounting Information in Specialized Decisions

11

Planning Capital Investments

IN CHAPTER 5, we showed the form of the "capital" budget (Table 5A-14, page 144) and indicated that decisions to acquire long-lived assets are handled in a unique way. In this chapter you look closely at the process of selecting long-lived assets for acquisition. You identify important variables affecting such decisions, and learn simple procedures for capital asset decision making.

Capital asset acquisition decisions must be considered apart from other purchasing decisions because a business keeps and uses capital assets over an extended period of time—5, 10, or even more years. Capital assets cost a great deal of money, which often is borrowed and repaid out of future revenues. Capital assets are intended to help produce revenues to cover their own cost and operating expenses, plus an excess which shows up as accounting profit. If the wrong assets are acquired, a firm's earning power is crippled for many operating periods. If the proper assets are acquired, the firm is in an advantageous operating and profit-making position.

Typical capital expenditures might include:

Efficiency improvements in a manufacturing plant or distribution network.
An extended research program.
Entirely new manufacturing or distribution facilities.

Some persons argue that all expenditures are capital expenditures since they contribute to shaping the firm's future ability to compete. Thus, manpower training programs, customer service programs, advertising programs, and environmental control programs are all capital expenditures. You may decide for yourself how far to extend the capital expenditure designation; we shall consider a method of analysis which applies to *any* acquisition you wish to regard as "capital" in nature.

The basis of this method, called the "present value" method, is a comparison of *net cash inflows* resulting from operating a long-lived asset with the *current cash outlay* to acquire the asset.

THE TIME VALUE OF MONEY

The principle behind the time value of money is: *A dollar received now is more desirable than a dollar received at any future date.* As an obvious illustration, consider your savings account, which is an agreement with a financial institution under which you pay the institution \$X now, and the institution will pay you \$X+ at a future date—the amount of the "+" depending on the interest rate and the precise future date. The "+" is called *interest* and is intended to be your compensation for foregoing use and enjoyment of your money.

Similarly, if you have the opportunity to receive a \$10 payment today or a \$10 payment one year hence, you will surely choose the immediate payment. But if your choice is between \$10 today and \$12 one year hence, you will have to stop and decide if the additional \$2 compensates you for not having the use of \$10 for one year. (You would *not* have hesitated if your choice were between \$10 now and \$8 a year from now!)

Determination of Investor's Target Rate of Return

When you consider capital investments, you expect to receive more cash receipts in the future than the present cash cost of the investment. This excess may be attributed to the *investor's target rate of return* (abbreviated ITRR). The ITRR is critical to successful evaluation of proposed capital expenditures. Four factors determine ITRR:

1. Basic profit obtainable.
2. Adjustment for inflation.
3. Rate of growth or expansion desired.
4. Compensation for risk desired.

Basic Profit. There is a basic minimum return which anyone can obtain as a compensation for letting others use and benefit from his money or capital. It is not high; probably 2 or 3 percent per year and possibly less.

Adjustment for Inflation. Inflation is an increase in the number of currency units equivalent to a representative collection of marketplace commodities—in other words, a general increase in the price level.[1] It is caused by a money supply which increases faster than the number of things available on which to spend money. The annual inflation rate in the United States has fluctuated since World War II from almost nothing in the 1950s and early 1960s to 6 and 7 percent in the late 1960s and early 1970s. Economists disagree over how much inflation our economy can tolerate. Some economists feel that modest amounts of inflation are harmless; in fact, essential to stimulate growth and investment. Others feel that even slight inflation distorts resource allocation processes and is damaging to investor confidence and consumer psychology. Anticipated inflation is discounted by current interest rates covering loans due in the future. If inflation is expected, interest rates will be higher than if inflation is not expected. If the rate of inflation is expected to rise, interest rates should also rise.

This was observed to happen during a recent inflation, 1967–73. In 1967 and in 1968, most interest rates rose approximately 2 percent. Further increases were experienced in 1969 and 1970. The interest rate increases were determined in money markets and reflect an unwillingness by capital suppliers to forego the use of their money without added compensation for the effect of inflation on monetary value in exchange.

To understand how inflation reduces the return to a lender, consider your situation if you have $100 today. A 5 percent inflation exists. One year from today $105 will only have the purchasing power of about $100 today. You are strongly tempted to spend your money today,

---

[1] A discussion of price changes and the ways accountants measure and report them is contained in Chapter 16.

when its value in exchange is highest. Instead, a borrower offers to take your money and pay you 8 percent interest—pay you $108 one year from today. But if you accept, you will not make $8 profit. Of the eight extra dollars, five will be accounted for as necessary to make up the $105 year-from-now equivalent to the purchasing power of $100 today. The real compensation to you for lending is only $3.

Rate of Growth. Most investors aren't satisfied to receive only inflation compensation plus the barest basic return on their investments. For reasons rooted in sound business practice or deriving from personal motivations, they want a return that is higher. Two reasons for wanting a higher-than-minimum rate of return on investments are:

The industry in which the investor participates is growing faster than the economy as a whole.

The investor has a growth rate goal which requires that new investments earn at a higher rate.

Compensation for Risk. If it is impossible to know exactly all the relevant details about a proposed capital investment, the investment is said to involve *risk*. The *more* risk an investment entails, the higher additional profit or return the investor expects.

The problem of risk anticipation in capital investment planning is one of the most interesting and formidable in all of business administration. Yet risk must be successfully identified if the investor is to decide whether an investment's expected return justifies his accepting the associated investment risk. It derives from the hidden nature of the future, which no one can know with certainty. You can make estimates about the future, but these estimates may be wrong.

Error may occur in estimates of investment useful lifetime, investment cost, investment operating costs, investment cost savings or revenue, or even the tax rate. Such errors are caused by misreading economic conditions, making biased estimates, or simple ignorance of what makes the world tick. Errors are to some extent unavoidable, unpredictable, and in capital budgeting decisions expose a firm to loss and possible termination.

Managers have ways of measuring or estimating error and the associated risk in capital budgeting decisions. One of the simplest is to classify investment proposals into three categories: (1) low risk, (2) medium risk, and (3) high risk.

A *low* risk investment is one for which you believe all the estimates will prove to be accurate in the future. A *medium* risk investment is one in which many of the estimates may prove not to be accurate. A *high* risk investment is one in which many of the estimates may prove to be extremely inaccurate. Of course, these characterizations are approximate and subjective.

A practical procedure for evaluating risk would require risk categories and conditions for accepting or rejecting proposals falling in each category.

Let R_1 = the minimum expected compensation for investing in a project of *low risk*.
Let R_2 = the minimum expected compensation for investing in a project of *medium risk*.
Let R_3 = the minimum expected compensation for investing in a project of *high risk*.

Compensation Must Be Proportional to Risk. By common sense, you want more compensation to attract investment in a proposal of higher risk; less compensation will attract investment in a proposal of lower risk. The financial world bears out this prediction: savings accounts, which are low risk, return less interest than church bonds, which are high risk. Consequently R_1 is less than R_2, and R_2 is less than R_3.

Here is how you would use the risk categories:

1. Designate proposal as high, medium, or low risk (*after* collecting all essential data describing it).
2. Select appropriate value of R (R has been previously determined for high, medium, and low risk proposals). This value represents compensation for risk.

Investor's Target Rate of Return Illustrated

Suppose that the investor's target rate of return is 10 percent. Then any sum of money set aside now as a capital investment would have to earn a return equal to 10 percent annually to satisfy the investor.

A capital investment returns sums of money in the future. It is these *future sums* that a business purchases when it makes a capital investment. The investment now must be small enough that the future sums will produce at least a 10 percent return.

For example, let a capital investment be one which will pay a future sum of $100 at the end of two years. What sum would, if set aside to earn 10 percent interest compounded annually, be equal to $100 in two years?

The amount is:

$$\frac{\$100}{(1.00 + 0.10)^2} = \$82.64 \text{ (See footnote 2.)}$$

You can verify this by letting $82.64 earn 10 percent interest for two years:

Principal at present time	$ 82.64
Interest first year	8.26+
Principal + interest at end of one year	$ 90.90+
Interest second year	9.09+
Principal + interest at end of two years	$100.00

You would not pay more than $82.64 for this future payment if your ITRR is 10 percent. The less than $82.64 you pay, the better you will like your investment.

INFORMATION TO CONSIDER IN PLANNING CAPITAL INVESTMENT DECISIONS

In planning capital investment decisions you will need certain information. By means of an example, let us illustrate this information and how it is used in decision making.

You are executive vice president of Mildew Mining Corporation, a firm operating several open-pit limestone quarries. Stone is cut from

---

[2] The formula used is

$$\frac{\text{Present}}{\text{equivalent}} = \frac{\text{(Future receipt in Period } N\text{)}}{(1 + \text{ITRR})^N}$$

or

$$\frac{\text{Present}}{\text{equivalent}} = \frac{\text{Future receipt}}{\text{in period } N} \times \frac{\text{Factor in Figure 11–1 for period } N \text{ and ITRR}}$$

FIGURE 11-1
Factors for Converting Future Receipts to Present Equivalents

$$\text{Present equivalent} = \text{Future receipt in period } N \times \text{Table factor for period } N$$

Investor's Target Rate of Return

Period N	2	4	6	8	10	12
1	0.9804	0.9615	0.9434	0.9259	0.9091	8.8929
2	0.9612	0.9246	0.8900	0.8573	0.8264	0.7972
3	0.9423	0.8890	0.8396	0.7938	0.7513	0.7118
4	0.9238	0.8548	0.7921	0.7350	0.6830	0.6355
5	0.9057	0.8219	0.7473	0.6806	0.6209	0.5674
6	0.8880	0.7903	0.7050	0.6301	0.5648	0.5066
7	0.8706	0.7599	0.6651	0.5835	0.5136	0.4523
8	0.8535	0.7307	0.6274	0.5403	0.4665	0.4039
9	0.8368	0.7026	9.5919	0.5002	0.4241	0.3606
10	0.8203	0.6756	0.5584	0.4632	0.3855	0.3220

Investor's Target Rate of Return

Period N	14	16	18	20	22	24
1	0.8772	0.8621	0.8475	0.8333	0.8197	0.8065
2	0.7695	0.7432	0.7182	0.6944	0.6719	0.6504
3	0.6750	0.6407	0.6087	0.5787	0.5507	0.5245
4	0.5921	0.5523	0.5158	0.4823	0.4514	0.4230
5	0.5194	0.4761	0.4371	0.4019	0.3700	0.3411
6	0.4556	0.4104	0.3704	0.3349	0.3033	0.2751
7	0.3996	0.3538	0.3139	0.2791	0.2486	0.2218
8	0.3506	0.3050	0.2660	0.2326	0.2038	0.1789
9	0.3075	0.2630	0.2255	0.1938	0.1670	0.1443
10	0.2697	0.2267	0.1911	0.1615	0.1369	0.1164

The table factor is the amount that, if invested now at the ITRR interest rate at the head of its column, would increase to $1 in N periods.

these quarries and pulverized, then heated to make "calcined lime," used in cement making and other industrial applications. It is heavy, chemically active, and presents important handling problems. Recently a large machine has been developed which creeps along a limestone pit, ingesting limestone at one end and ejecting bagged calcined lime at the other end. A salesman is urging you to purchase one as a *replacement* for the existing facilities. But how do you know this machine, called a "sublimer" would be a desirable investment for Mildew Mining Company? In other words, what information must you have about the proposed equipment acquisition and about your own business—in order to make the decision?

322   An Introduction to Accounting for Decision Making and Control

The kinds of information you should want are these:

1. Net cash revenue or cost savings per unit activity and per time period.
2. Number of periods acquisition may be expected to last.
3. Tax effect of the acquisition.
4. Initial cost of acquisition.
5. *Risk* of the acquisition.
6. Target rate of return for your firm.

Let us examine each of these types of information in turn.

Net Cash Revenue or Cost Savings

For the sub-limer, a unit of activity is "one ton of limestone mined, crushed, calcined, and bagged" and the method of computation would be to compare the variable cost per ton of the new process with the variable cost per ton of the existing process. (This suggests a need to know Mildew's present cost structure.) When a proposed capital acquisition would produce revenue, the excess of revenue over variable costs is taken as the measure of benefit. We may imagine that you have analyzed the sub-limer and compared its costs with those of the facilities it would replace as shown in Figure 11–2. Total savings are computed by multiplying the savings per ton by the number of tons

FIGURE 11–2
Operating Cost per Ton Comparison of Sub-limer and Existing Plant

Cost in Dollars per Ton of Bagged Lime	Sub-limer	Existing Plant
Excavation	$2.50	$2.75
Transportation to crusher	0	0.20
Crushing	0.35	0.35
Calcining	0.40	0.45
Transportation to bagger	0	0.10
Bagging	1.20	1.80
Transportation to warehouse	0.20	0.10
Total	$4.65	$5.75
Excess of existing plant costs over sub-limer costs		$5.75 − $4.65 = $1.10 per ton [savings if sub-limer acquired]

expected to be produced. Since utilization of the sub-limer may vary from year to year, to compute total savings you need to know (a) the useful lifetime of the sub-limer, and (b) the utilization Mildew Mining plans to make of it. For convenience and simplicity assume that the sub-limer would be used to produce 200,000 tons of bagged lime per year. Then the savings on operating costs per year would be

200,000 tons per year × $1.10 per ton = $220,000 *per year*

In addition to the variable costs, there will be fixed costs that you will have to consider.

Additional Fixed Costs. Fixed costs are those costs which must be incurred whether or not the equipment is used, including:

Depreciation (not a cash expense in period taken)
Insurance (may be a cash expense in period taken)
Preventive maintenance (cash expense in period taken)
Supervisory salaries (cash expense in period taken)

Figure 11-3 compares the sub-limer's annual fixed costs with the annual fixed costs of the existing technology.[3]

FIGURE 11-3
Fixed Cost Comparison

Fixed Costs in $ per Year for 200,000 Tons Capacity	Sub-limer	Existing Plant
Depreciation (noncash)	$ 90,000	$ 70,000
Insurance (cash)	5,000	4,000
Preventive maintenance (cash)	14,000	8,000
Supervisory salaries	20,000	25,000
Total	$129,000	$107,000

Acquisition Lifetime

Considerable study and consultation with engineers leads to the conclusion that the sub-limer would last 10 years, the same length of time

---

[3] This is an important point. You are comparing the sub-limer to an existing facility which it would *replace*.

the existing plant should last. Knowing the lifetime of the acquisition lets you schedule its incremental savings or costs by periods.

Additionally, the engineers estimate that neither the sub-limer nor the conventional plant would have any appreciable market value at the end of this period of time.

Depreciation and Tax Effects

As you know, depreciation is not a cash expense. It is a systematic transference of historical asset cost to the category of a current expense, symbolizing the using up of asset services as time passes. The significance of depreciation in capital decisions is as a deduction from income for purposes of computing the federal income tax. The income tax must be paid in cash—and the cash tax expense the company must pay is reduced by depreciation. The amount of the reduction depends on the tax rate—and of course, if there is no income, there is no income tax and no depreciation as a deduction.

Depreciation Expense Reduces Tax Payments. If Mildew Mining Company will continue having income, consider the effect of the additional depreciation deduction available on the sub-limer over the existing assets. The annual excess is $90,000 — $70,000 = $20,000. This extra depreciation reduces taxable income by $20,000 and with a 50 percent tax rate reduces the tax which must be paid by $20,000 × 0.50 = *$10,000 per year*. This is a cash saving attributable to the additional depreciation available on the sub-limer.

Why is this important? In capital budgeting, you compare *cash* expenses and *cash* savings. Obviously even though depreciation does not affect cash flows *its tax effect does*. The procedure to compute one period's net cash savings after taxes is:

Step no:

(1) Add together all cash revenues and/or cash savings.
(2) Add together all cash expenses, including fixed cash expenses.
(3) Compute net operating cash savings before taxes by subtracting (2) from (1).
(4) Subtract depreciation and other noncash expenses from (3).
(5) Compute taxes by multiplying (4) times the tax rate.

(6) Compute estimated net cash savings after taxes by subtracting (5) from (3).

Let us use the expected first year of operation of the sub-limer as an example of these steps (the number in the right-hand column refers to the column number of Figure 11–4):

	Proposed Addition (Sub-limer)	Existing Plant	Difference
Step 1:			
Net sub-limer cash operating savings	$220,000	$ 0	(1)→ $220,000
Step 2:			
Annual operating expenses (Figure 11–3)	$129,000	$107,000	$ 22,000
Less: Noncash expenses (Figure 11–3)	(90,000)	(70,000)	(20,000)
Total annual fixed cash expense	$ 39,000	$ 37,000	(2)→ $ 2,000
Step 3:			
Net sub-limer cash operating savings	$220,000	$ 0	$220,000
Less: Total annual fixed cash expense	(39,000)	(37,000)	(2,000)
Net cash operating savings before taxes	$181,000	$ (37,000)	$ 218,000
Step 4:			
Less: Noncash expenses	(90,000)	(70,000)	(3)→ (20,000)
Taxable operating savings	$ 91,000	$(107,000)	(4)→ $198,000
Step 5:			
Estimated tax effect [50% of (4)]	$ (45,500)	$ 53,500	$ (99,000)
Step 6:			
Net cash operating savings before taxes	$181,000	$ (37,000)	$218,000
Less: Estimated tax effect	(45,500)	53,500	(5)→ (99,000)
Net cash savings after taxes	$135,500	$ 16,500	(6)→ $119,000

The difference in favor of the sub-limer is $135,000 − $16,500 = $119,000. If the sub-limer were not replacing existing equipment, the first column above would be all you'd need. You should study the effect of taxes on estimated cash flows until you understand the computation. *The key point is that depreciation and other noncash expenses do reduce taxes (increasing cash flow) but do not count in any other* way. Net operating cash savings are increased by the savings from the depreciation deduction, but depreciation itself is not a cash expense. Figure 11–4 is a tabular computation of net savings after taxes for

FIGURE 11–4
Computation by Periods of Net Cash Savings

| | \multicolumn{6}{c}{Subheading Corresponds to Step No.} |
Year	(1) Gross Savings	(2) Cash Expenses	(3) Depreciation	(4) Taxable Savings (1) – (2) – (3)	(5) Tax 0.5(4)	(6) Net Cash Savings (1) – (2) – (5)
1	$220,000	$2,000	$20,000	$198,000	$99,000	$119,000
2	220,000	2,000	20,000	198,000	99,000	119,000
3	220,000	2,000	20,000	198,000	99,000	119,000
4	220,000	2,000	20,000	198,000	99,000	119,000
5	220,000	2,000	20,000	198,000	99,000	119,000
6	220,000	2,000	20,000	198,000	99,000	119,000
7	220,000	2,000	20,000	198,000	99,000	119,000
8	220,000	2,000	20,000	198,000	99,000	119,000
9	220,000	2,000	20,000	198,000	99,000	119,000
10	220,000	2,000	20,000	198,000	99,000	119,000

each year in the proposed investment's lifetime. Each row follows the calculation above. For simplicity and convenience, assume that each year's net cash saving will all occur at once, on the anniversary of the sub-limer's purchase.

Initial Cost of Acquisition

The acquisition cost of a capital asset includes the following expenditures:
—Cash price of the asset.
—Shipping and freight.
—Setup costs.
—Startup costs.
—Modifications to new asset or old assets to make them compatible with the new asset.
—Any other costs which are incurred once-only and would not be incurred if the new asset were not acquired.

When comparing an existing facility with a proposed replacement, you must use the *net* cost, which is total acquisition cost of the replacement *less* the salvage or resale value of the equipment replaced. The net cost of the sub-limer is computed in Figure 11–5. The costs in Figure 11–5 include no sums which would be incurred if the sub-limer were

FIGURE 11–5
Net Cost of Sub-limer

Item	
Cash price	$ 2,300,000
Shipping and freight	0
Setup costs	20,000
Startup costs	20,000
Modifications	10,000
Other	40,000
Total cost	$ 2,390,000
Less resale value of existing plant	(1,610,000)
Net cost of sub-limer	$ 780,000

not purchased. Theerfore, the acquisition cost difference of $780,000 truly represents the additional cost of the sub-limer over the alternative of keeping the present plant. If you combine this extra cost with the information about annual net cash savings, you have a schedule consisting of *one* cash payment now (time of purchase) and 10 equal cash receipts, one on each of the next 10 anniversaries of the acquisition date:

Year		Cash Receipt (Payment)	
(now)	(from Figure 11–5)	$(780,000)	← Payment
1		119,000	
2		119,000	
3		119,000	
4		119,000	
5	(from Figure 11–4)	119,000	Future
6		119,000	receipts
7		119,000	
8		119,000	
9		119,000	
10		119,000	

The question you must ask yourself now, as a decision maker for Mildew Mining Company, is, "Is this extra $780,000 in expenditures justified by the additional $119,000 per year we will receive for 10 years?" If yes, you recommend purchase; if not, you recommend against purchase.

Risk of Acquisition

Mildew classifies proposals according to perceived risk: low, medium, and high. The sub-limer proposal meets criteria for the low-risk category. The corresponding compensation for risk is $R_1 = 3$ percent.

Mildew's Target Rate of Return

Mildew Mining Corporation has adopted, as a matter of company policy, the following target rate of return:

Basic return desired.............	3%
Adjustment for inflation...........	5
Rate of expansion	5
Compensation for risk	3
Total....................	16%

In other words, any investment made by Mildew Mining will be expected to return at least this rate of interest, or rate of return.

The Present Equivalent of Sub-Limer Future Sums. How can you tell if the proposed sub-limer offers this rate of return? You must compute the amount which would have to be set aside now, to earn at the rate 16 percent, to produce the future sums shown in the schedule above. An equivalent statement is: If you invest $780,000 today at a 16 percent rate of interest and at the end of each of the next 10 years draw off $119,000, would the last withdrawal leave a positive balance? If "yes" then the sub-limer does offer a return equal to or greater than 16 percent. To give a "yes" or "no" answer to this question, you compute the amounts of money you have to set aside NOW *and* which would grow to $119,000 in 1 year, grow to $119,000 in 2 years, and so on for all 10 years. The sum of these amounts is the *present equivalent* of the proposed investment's net future cash flows, if this sum earns at the assumed investor's target rate of return.

In Figure 11–1 are factors to make this calculation easier. Each factor is the dollar amount which will, if allowed to earn at the column target rate of return, grow to $1 in the row number of periods. Thus, $0.4104 invested at 16 percent will grow to $1 after six periods. To find out how many dollars are equivalent *now* to $119,000 in six periods, multiply $119,000 by 0.4104 and get $48,840. Figure 11-6 applies this calculation to all the expected cash flow associated with the sub-limer, then sums them to find the sub-limer's present equivalent or present value.

FIGURE 11-6
Present Equivalents of Sub-limer Savings

(N) Year	Present Equivalent of $1 in N Years at 16%(F[N, 16])	Present Equivalent of $119,000 in N Years at 16%($119,000 × F[N, 16])
1	0.8621 × $119,000 =	$102,590
2	0.7432 × 119,000 =	88,440
3	0.6407 × 119,000 =	76,240
4	0.5523 × 119,000 =	65,720
5	0.4761 × 119,000 =	56,660
6	0.4104 × 119,000 =	48,840
7	0.3538 × 119,000 =	42,100
8	0.3050 × 119,000 =	36,300
9	0.2630 × 119,000 =	31,290
10	0.2267 × 119,000 =	26,980
Total present equivalent.		$575,160

It is common to all present equivalent calculations that a smaller present equivalent occurs as the number of periods before receiving the cash flow becomes larger (because there are more periods in which interest accumulates). Look for this in Figure 11-6. Thus, $65,720 set aside now at 16 percent interest compounded annually would amount to $119,000 in four years. The sum of all 10 numbers such as $65,720 is the total amount of cash that would have to be set aside now at 16 percent interest in order to produce 10 annual payments of $119,000 each. The sum of all these present amounts is $575,160. This is the *present equivalent* to the 10-year sequence of payments the proposed sub-limer is expected to produce. It is the "fair price" you should be willing to pay now in exchange for receiving the $119,000 payments annually for 10 years, provided you are willing to earn exactly 16 percent return on the $575,160.

The present equivalent will be larger if the ITRR is smaller and smaller if the ITRR is larger. If the ITRR happens to be selected so that the present equivalent exactly equals the present cost, it is said to be the *rate of return* on that proposal. This is another criterion for investment decisions but we will not discuss it here.

MAKING THE DECISION

If you invest more that $575,153—for example, invest $780,000—your actual return would be less than 16 percent. Therefore, the sublimer, whose net cost is $780,000, *cannot* be regarded as a desirable investment at this time.

The rule is: If the present equivalent of the future cash flow the investment is expected to produce (computed as described in Figure 11–6) is *less* than the present cost of that future income, *an investment should not be considered further*. If, on the other hand, the present equivalent of future income is *greater* than the expected cost of the investment, *the investment merits further consideration*. You can put this into a diagram such as Figure 11–7.

FIGURE 11–7
Capital Investment Decision Rule

	Present Equivalent of Investment Income GREATER THAN Expected Investment Cost	*Present Equivalent of Investment Income LESS THAN Expected Investment Cost*
Favorable to investment	Yes	No
Unfavorable to investment	No	Yes

OTHER FACTORS IN INVESTMENT DECISIONS

Often projects do not compete with each other or are not proposed at the same time and cannot be considered in direct comparison with one another. If this is the case, you should consider investments one at a time in sequence as they are proposed, evaluating each using the methods of this chapter. Projects whose present equivalent exceeds their cost should be considered further.

"Further consideration" will be influenced by these important factors:

—A limit on total funds which can be spent on capital projects.
—Compatibility of proposed projects with existing facilities.

—Changes in investor's target rate of return expected in future periods.
—Different lifetimes of proposals which compete with each other for funds.
—Different investor's target rates of return proposed for different responsibility centers in a firm; that is, the problem of allocating scarce capital among competing entities in the firm.

Because of the extreme complexity of these variables' interactions with one another, many researchers and businessmen have suggested use of business-wide computer-based planning models to produce fast, comprehensive answers to capital allocation questions. In addition, linear programming models are occasionally useful in selecting investments. Although sophisticated refinements are helpful, be assured that great improvements in the efficiency of capital deployment can be achieved through the simple methods of this chapter.

SUMMARY

Capital investments are those expenditures to acquire long-lived assets. The benefits from these expenditures extend through more than one accounting period. Capital investment decisions require specific types of information: estimates of investment cost, annual cash investment revenue or cost savings, annual cash investment expense, investment lifetime, and investment risk. In addition, the economic situation, tax structure, and growth goals of a firm will influence the type of investments it chooses.

Because returns from a capital investment are received in the future, they must be converted into present equivalents for comparison with the expected present cost of the investment. This is done by computing the amount of cash to be set aside now which would, if it earned interest at a rate equal to the investor's target rate of return, be sufficient to produce all of the future returns expected of the proposed investment. If this present equivalent is more than the present cost of the investment, the investment may receive further consideration.

Tax structure of a firm influences capital investment decisions because depreciation and other noncash expenses of capital assets produce reductions in cash tax expense. Risky capital investments must promise a higher return in order to be attractive. Inflation tends to discourage long-term investment by requiring a higher return than would otherwise be necessary.

However helpful procedures are in evaluating investment proposals, they do not *originate* proposals. It is still up to management to produce high quality promising investment proposals if a business is to prosper.

QUESTIONS

1. What is a capital expenditure? Why are capital investment decisions regarded as different from other decisions?

2. Accounting associates, Inc., a consulting firm, is considering buying an electronic calculator for $2,000. The firm would sell two mechanical adding machines, receiving $500. The calculator would last two years and would save a net of $1,000 each year. What factors must be considered in this decision besides those given?

3. If the ITRR of Accounting Associates for the proposal in Question 2 is 20 percent, decide whether to recommend its purchase. Ignore taxes.

4. Which of the following would you designate as capital expenditures?
    a) Wages paid to production line employees.
    b) Overhead allocated to production departments.
    c) Cost of office supplies and stationery.
    d) Cost of an advertising campaign to sell candy at Mother's Day.
    e) Cost to make a movie expected to play in theaters for three years.
    f) Cost of dies and molds for a new car model.
    g) Lease payments on a passenger jet airplane; the lease runs from month to month up to five years.

5. Which of the following would be operating costs for a fleet of taxicabs in a decision to replace the taxis with new ones?
    a) Gasoline.
    b) Tires.
    c) Salary of dispatcher.
    d) Salary of cab drivers.

e) Advertising costs.
   f) Taxi depreciation.
   g) Income tax expense.

6. Why must all costs, cost savings, and expenses considered in a capital investment decision be in cash?

7. A particular proposal shows annual depreciation expected to be $32,000 per year. The expected tax rate is 40 percent. Net cash savings before considering the tax effect are $40,000 per year. What will the net cash savings after considering tax effect be?

8. Which of the following would be acquisition costs of a fleet of new taxicabs?
   a) Freight and delivery charge.
   b) License fees.
   c) State sales tax.
   d) Washing and waxing of taxicabs.
   e) Taxi depreciation.
   f) Trade-in allowance on used taxicabs.

9. Why would you settle a debt owed to you in the amount of $1,000 due two years from now for less than $1,000 (ignore interest)?

10. If you are using an investor's target rate of return of 20 percent and a proposed investment does not qualify for further consideration, would an investor's target rate of return of 10 percent make that proposed investment more or less likely to qualify for further consideration?

11. You are considering three proposals for investment. Your budget is tight, so you can only choose one of them. They are equivalent in all respects, including present cost, except that their present equivalents are, respectively, $35,000, $40,000, and $30,000. Which do you choose and why?

12. Brown Properties has developed a shopping center at a cost of $600,000, and work is now 90 percent complete. When finished (at an additional cost of $67,000) the center will produce an after-tax cash flow of $40,000 annually. The company is considering buying the equity in another shopping center for $67,000; the cash flow on this investment after taxes would be $45,000 annually.

State your preference between these investments if only one can be selected and (*a*) there is the same degree of risk in each; and (*b*) the second investment is considered much more risky.

13. Rank these investments in order of ascending risk:
    a) Ninety-day savings certificate at a savings and loan association.
    b) The second mortgage bonds of the 1,000-member Town Church.
    c) Five-year savings certificate at a savings and loan association.
    d) Debentures of Penn Central Railroad.
    e) Drill 10 oil wells in an established Middle East field.
    f) Drill 10 exploratory wells in Massachusetts.
    g) Develop and produce a nonpolluting electric steam car.

14. The Error Instrument Company is preparing to modernize its product line. Any changes in this line are considered risky. Two proposals have survived initial screening. The risk analysis of them shows:

	Proposal A	Proposal B
Probability that present equivalent is $800,000	0.2	0.5
Probability that present equivalent is $1,000,000	0.7	0.2
Probability that present equivalent is $1,600,000	0.1	0.3

    Which proposal do you recommend? Why?

15. Proposal A will cost $100,000 and return $15,000 per year for 10 years; proposal B will cost $100,000 and return $5,000 per year for 30 years. Which do you think should be selected? Why?

EXERCISES

16. Which of the following companies have the same target rate of return?

	A	B	C	D	E	F
Basic profit	3	2	4	1	5	0
Inflation	3	3	2	5	4	0
Expansion	3	5	0	6	2	5
Risk	3	1	6	0	5	7

17. A 10 percent inflation exists. One year from now, what will be the purchasing power of $100, in dollars of the present time? If

the tax rate is 50 percent, approximately what pre-tax rate of return is necessary in order to just cancel out the effect of inflation on purchasing power? Approximate answers are acceptable.

18. For the Rountree Company, $R_1 = 6$ percent, $R_2 = 10$ percent, and $R_3 = 20$ percent. Below are the *net present equivalents* (present equivalent minus initial investment) for some projects under consideration by Rountree Company:

Project	Net Present Equivalent Using R_1	Net Present Equivalent Using R_2	Net Present Equivalent Using R_3
A........	$ 50,000	$ 0	$-60,000
B........	-10,000	-30,000	-70,000
C........	90,000	70,000	30,000

Indicate the highest degree of risk which is acceptable to warrant further consideration of each proposal.

19. Arabella Company has a fertilizer plant that will make 400,000 tons of fertilizer per year. Allebara Company has offered to build a new plant for $4,000,000 and buy Arabella's old plant for $1,500,000. The new plant would reduce the cost of fertilizer manufacture by $1.40 per ton, and would last five years. Assuming either plant would be operated at capacity, and that Arabella has a target rate of return of 4 percent, determine whether this offer should be considered further.

20. Caminski Company's present plant computes its profit contribution from the formula $P = -\$400,000 + \$30X + \$40Y + \$20Z$. A contractor offers to build a new plant whose profit would be computed as $P = -\$500,000 + \$40X + \$35Y + \$50Z$. Expected production and sales figures are: $X = 5,000$; $Y = 8,000$; $Z = 5,000$. All figures represent cash flows. Neglecting the effect of taxes and depreciation, compute the net increment or decrement in cash flows that would result each year if the contractor's plant replaces the existing one.

21. Neely Company has before its management a capital proposal showing net cash inflow per year before taxes or depreciation of $50,000. Depreciation will be $30,000 per year, and the tax rate is 40 percent. Compute the annual net cash inflow after taxes and depreciation.

PROBLEMS

22. The Larson Company produces magic and illusion-creating props for stage magicians. Until the present, the company has employed relatively unskilled workers to assemble the equipment, much of it made to the custom specifications of performing magicians.

    Recently, an engineer of the company has proposed an array of small machines which could do much of the work now done by the unskilled workers if operated by a small number of trained employees. The machines are inexpensive; the major cost is training for the operators. This training would run about $2,000 per employee in tuition to a technical institute. Ten employees would be trained. The equipment would cost $11,000 and have a five-year lifetime. It would have no salvage value. Certain present equipment could be sold for $1,000.

    Expenses from use of the equipment would result as follows:

Annual salaries of trained employees.	$95,000
Operating costs of machines per year.	20,000
Fabrication materials costs per year.	20,000

    Costs of continuing as at present would be:

Annual wages of 40 untrained employees	$120,000
Fabrication materials costs per year	25,000

    The company is not subject to income taxes.

    Required:

    a) Prepare a five-year schedule of cash flows for the proposal on an incremental basis; that is, as they would differ from cash flows if the proposal is not adopted.

    b) If the Larson Company requires a 15 percent return on investment, should this proposal be adopted; that is, should the machines be built and 10 employees trained?

23. Gandalf Swords, Inc., manufactures mithril swords in an automated plant near the Misty Mountains. The automated machinery is wearing out. Mr. Gandalf is interested in replacing the equipment and has decided on a special type of equipment which will cost $1,200,000. This equipment will have a three-year life and a salvage value estimated at $300,000.

    Mr. Gandalf is uncertain how to depreciate this equipment. The tax rate in Middle-Earth is 60 percent. Mr. Gandalf knows that accelerated depreciation produces higher cash flows in the early years of an asset's useful life—and therefore larger cash tax savings—but he believes that the tax rate will soon be increased to 70 percent and wonders "if I shouldn't save my depreciation for then?"

Required:

a) Prepare depreciation schedules on a straight-line and also on a sum-of-the-years'-digits basis. (The latter is an accelerated depreciation method. The first year's depreciation is three sixths of the difference between initial cost and salvage value; the second year's depreciation, two sixths; the third year's, one sixth.)

b) Assume that the tax rate may change for the second and third years to 70 percent. Show the cash savings which would result under each depreciation schedule if (1) the tax rate remains at 60 percent and (2) the tax rate increases as indicated.

c) Using a 10 percent ITRR, compute the present equivalent of each stream of cash savings after taxes computed in (b) above.

d) Recommend to Mr. Gandalf what depreciation method he should use.

24. Cushing Capital Tools, Inc., is offering your company a machine tool you need at a current price of $250,000. You estimate that next year the tool's price will have risen to $275,000. You believe that if you buy the tool this year, it will save $40,000 in operating costs this year. Inflation during the coming year will average 5 percent.

Required:

a) Assume that if the tool is bought now, all savings will occur at the end of the year in end-of-year dollars. Prepare a schedule which shows, in *current* dollars (to get current dollars, divide end-of-year dollars by 1.05), whether it is preferable to buy the tool now or one year from now.

b) With the same assumptions as in (a), also assume that the rate of return the company requires is 18 percent, *including* the allowance for inflation. Determine on the basis of present equivalents in *current* dollars whether it is preferable to buy the tool now or one year from now.

25. The Midtown Publishing Company is considering two new ways to print the chain of small-town daily and weekly newspapers it

publishes: a computerized typesetter and a new offset process. Here is a comparison of the two:

	Computerized Typesetter	Offset Process	
Initial cost without trade-in	$150,000	$220,000	⎫ more equipment
Trade-in of old equipment	10,000	80,000	⎬ traded in for
Net cash operating savings per year before taxes	20,000	25,000	⎭ offset process
Operating cost per year (noncash)	17,500	25,000	
Expected lifetime (years)	4	4	
Expected salvage value	10,000	20,000	

Midtown Publishing pays income taxes which amount to 60 percent of its net income. The company's banker has advised that a basic interest rate is 1 percent, that inflation is expected to average 3 percent, and that the local region's economy is expanding at a rate of 4 percent per year. The company has no additional growth goals.

Required:

a) Assume that the old equipment is wearing out and must be replaced. With which of these systems would you replace it?

b) Assume that the old equipment can go on another few years. Would you replace it with either of these systems at the present time?

26. Gold Seal Tire Company has a reputation as a maker of fine commercial and passenger car tires. These tires have always been bias-ply tires. However, other tire manufacturers' radial tires are taking an increasing share of the market. Gold Seal Tire is certain there will always be a market for bias-ply tires and plans to update the plant in which they are produced. A modernization plan has been proposed by the engineers with these characteristics:

Cost of new equipment	$300,000
Plant renovation	300,000
Employee retraining	100,000
Startup period extra costs	200,000
Trade-in value of old equipment	400,000

The newly renovated plant would be useful for four years and have no scrap or residual value. Gross cash savings would be $300,000 the first year, $350,000 the second year, and decline thereafter by $20,000 each year. Gross cash variable expenses would be 40 percent of gross cash savings each year. Fixed cash expenses would be

$40,000 per year. Depreciation on the net cost of the plan would be by the sum-of-the-years'-digits method. (See Problem 23, Requirement (a) for an explanation of this method of computing depreciation. Here the first year's depreciation is four tenths.) The ITRR, including a risk factor of 2, is 16 percent. The tax rate is 50 percent. However, one executive has pointed out that this factor assumes the renovation is a low-risk investment. He feels that since it will commit the company to bias-ply tire production for another four years, it is a very risky proposal and should receive a high risk factor of 9. The management disagrees with this appraisal. They argue that the renovated plant could be converted to radial tire production at any time, at no extra cost—except that gross cash variable expenses would increase to 60 percent of gross cash savings. The investment is, management maintains, for this reason still a low-risk proposal.

Required:

a) Determine whether the investment proposal should be considered further if it is low risk and radial tires are not built.

b) Determine whether the investment proposal should be considered further if it is low risk and radial tires must be built beginning at the start of the second year.

c) Determine whether the investment proposal should be considered further if it is high risk and radial tires are not built.

d) Based on the calculations you have made, express your opinion whether the plant should be renovated in accordance with the modernization plan.

27. Tollafsen Trinket Company is considering an investment that will cost $100,000. It will replace existing machinery with a market value of $20,000 and will have a salvage value in three years of $30,000. Net cash savings in each of the three years of its lifetime are:

```
1 . . . . . . . .  $50,000
2 . . . . . . . .   30,000
3 . . . . . . . .   30,000
```

Tollafsen's ITRR is 10 percent.

Required:

Determine whether this investment should be considered further.

28. Sord Enterprises is an American firm which has specialized in developing products, then seeking manufacturing firms to make them.

Its margin is normally about 5 percent of an item's retail selling price.

Last year the firm sent a representative to the trade fair of a nation with which the United States recently resumed trade relations and spotted a product concept it feels has potential in the U.S. market. Sord estimates that 10,000 of the product could be sold per year for five years for $150 each. However, the foreign government insists that Sord forego its entire 5 percent margin on the first 10,000 units, rebating it all directly to that government. In exchange for this "token of good will" the foreign government will allow Sord a $3 bonus on each of the remaining 40,000 units, in addition to the normal margin.

Assume that any margin or bonus related to a year's sales is realized all at once at the end of that particular year (thus, the sacrifice of the first year's margin occurs at the end of one year, the second year's bonus occurs at the end of two years, etc.).

Sord Enterprises considers this venture to be high risk, and assigns such projects a risk factor of 6. The inflation rate is 3 percent, the nominal return on money is 2 percent, and the extra return is 5 percent.

Required:

a) What margin is sacrificed by Sord? What payments will flow in to compensate for this sacrifice?
b) What is the total present equivalent of the government's proposal?
c) State whether the proposal should be accepted as a condition for trade.

29. The Threadneedle Street Bakery, owned by Mr. Horace Yeast (whose diminutive wife is known as the Little Old Lady of Threadneedle Street), has been aware that the demand for its bread outruns its ability to produce. Mr. Yeast has reviewed alternative methods of increasing capacity. At the present time he is reviewing a combination radar and infrared oven which bakes bread in one fourth the time required by conventional ovens.

The new oven would last three years, have no salvage value, cost $15,000 and be depreciated by the straight-line method. Mr. Yeast expects that he could make 50,000, 60,000, and 80,000 loaves of bread in the first, second, and third years of this oven's life. Each loaf would produce a contribution of 15 cents before taxes, which are 40 percent of taxable income.

Required:

Use the present value method to determine whether the Threadneedle Street Bakery should invest in this oven. The investors' target rate of return must be equal to or greater than 15 percent to justify an investment. (Do not attempt to find the actual ITRR.)

30. Escargot Amusement Park operates a 100-acre family entertainment center at Midville. Three years ago, the family operating the park approved plans for a $10,000,000 expansion of the park. The budget for the expansion, and the actual results, are shown below:

	Budgeted	Actual
Initial cost	$8,000,000	$9,000,000
Annual depreciation	800,000	900,000
Additional revenues from new attractions (per year)	6,840,000	8,000,000
Direct variable expenses of new attractions (per year)	⅔ of additional revenues	¾ of additional revenues
Cash fixed costs of new attractions per year	$ 400,000	$ 500,000

Looking at these figures, the president of Escargot said, "We have had the expansion in operation for two years now, with no improvement in the operating picture. Our target rate of return was 10 percent, but I do not think we are making it."

Required:

a) Assume that Escargot figured on a 10-year life for the addition. Assume further that the tax rate is 50 percent. Did the addition appear to meet Escargot's investment criterion when it was approved?

b) All as in (a) above. Now, assume that operating data for the entire 10-year life will be as it appears in the first two years. Does it appear that the addition actually will meet Escargot's criteria?

c) If it appears that a project is not living up to the projections which originally justified it, what steps might a management take to bring it back under control? Specifically, suggest *five* actions Escargot should consider to make this addition perform satisfactorily, assuming it is not now doing so.

31. Wolters Corporation owns a number of fried-chicken-to-go stands and is planning to franchise others. The company will charge 10 percent commission on all sales of the franchisee, and is also considering buying and developing the site of a franchisee's stand, then leasing it back to him. Wolters is wondering whether the proposed leases would be profitable. Here are typical figures for a site purchase-leaseback:

Purchase cost to Wolters of land (year 0)	$ 60,000
Lessor's cash expenses per year (starting in year 1)	15,000
Lessor's noncash expenses per year (starting in year 1)	10,000
Expected selling price of land (year 7)	100,000
Expenses associated with selling land (including taxes)	15,000
Lessor's receipts from lessee (per year, starting in year 2)	20,000

Wolters Corporation expects an inflation rate of 5 percent over the coming decade. The basic interest rate, according to the banker, is 3 percent. The risk in land ownership is slight—meriting only 2 percent additional return. The additional growth goal of Wolters Corporation is 5 percent, but the firm is willing to forego this growth in order to help franchisees get into business.

Required:

a) Compute the investors' target rate of return for Wolters.
b) Compute annual cash flows, assuming a 40 percent tax rate.
c) Discount these cash flows to their present equivalent value.
d) Determine whether, on the basis of these figures, Wolters ought to buy and lease back property to its franchisees.

DECISION CASE 11-1: CAMPGO COMPANY

The CampGo Company makes its own branded line of camping equipment, which it sells through stores that are franchised to display the CampGo name and agree to carry only CampGo products. Due to the camping boom, the company has operated at full capacity for several years and should continue to do so.

A national department store chain has approached CampGo and asked the company to provide a line of camping equipment to sell under the department store label. The company would have to spend $200,000 on new equipment, $200,000 on setup costs, and $100,000 on employee training in order to sell the department store chain $900,000 worth of equipment per year. Of this $900,000, $400,000 would represent direct and indirect variable costs and $100,000 would represent cash fixed costs. Because the equipment would compete with its own branded products, CampGo expects that it would lose $100,000 in cash contribution on sales made in its own stores annually. CampGo, because until recently not a profitable company, is not expected to pay income taxes during the next five years.

CampGo's management believes there will be a 6 percent annual inflation through the next five years, a 2 percent basic interest rate, and holds a target extra growth rate of 3 percent. The company will accept a 3 percent compensation for low risk, 5 percent compensation for medium risk, and 9 percent compensation for high risk. After some deliberation, the management decides the department store's proposition is a medium risk investment.

Required:

a) How is each major function: marketing, manufacturing, finance, and accounting—affected by this investment proposal?
b) Compute the annual cash net inflow if the proposal is accepted.
c) Determine whether the proposal should be considered further. What is the function of the ITRR in this determination?
d) Suppose after accepting and implementing the proposal, everything is as expected except that CampGo decides this was a high-risk proposal and should have been evaluated as such. What does this mean to CampGo?

BIBLIOGRAPHY

Books

Bierman, Harold, and Smidt, Seymour. *The Capital Budgeting Decision.* 3d ed. New York: The Macmillan Co.: 1971.

Edwards, James W. *Effects of Federal Income Taxes on Capital Budgeting,* NAA Research Monograph No. 5. New York: National Association of Accountants, 1969.

Kempster, John H. *Financial Analysis to Guide Capital Investment Expenditure Decisions,* NAA Research Report No. 43, New York: National Association of Accountants, 1967.

Articles

Coughlin, John W. "Accounting and Capital Budgeting," *The Business Quarterly,* Winter 1962.

Edge, C. G. "Capital Budgeting: Principles and Projection," *Financial Executive,* September 1965.

Edwards, James B. "Adjusted DCF Rate of Return," *Management Accounting,* January 1973.

House, William C. "Use of Sensitivity Analysis in Capital Budgeting," *Management Services,* September–October 1967.

Wellington, Roger. "Capital Budgeting," *The Journal of Accountancy,* May 1963.

12

Inventory Management

MANAGEMENT literature abounds with references to inventory and the need for its economical administration. For example, the annual cost of keeping inventory worth $1 on hand may be as much as 25 cents. A firm with total assets of $1,000,000 and inventories of $200,000 may be spending as much as $50,000 annually on insurance, pilferage, obsolescence, shrinkage, damage, and other costs of maintaining inventory—a considerable sum. It often happens that inventory analysis using accounting information can *cut in half* the amount of inventory the firm has on hand and the costs of inventory maintenance. In this example, the $25,000 thus saved would raise return on total assets by 2.5 percent (somewhat more on owners' equities)—no small boost to any business.

Inventories serve a valuable function by smoothing out short-run disparities between the supply of an item and the demand for it. Although the advantages of inventory management are demonstrable, and superior methods have been available during most of the 20th century, few firms make use of them. Introducing you to such methods early in your professional education may help correct this peculiar situation.

INVENTORY MANAGEMENT AND POLICY

The management of inventory is to provide service and convenience to the company and its customers at reasonable cost. An inventory policy to perform this function is expressed in this form:

When inventory gets down to a predetermined replenishment point of S units (S may be negative, indicating a shortage), replenish inventory with an order of Q additional units.

The inventory policy guides inventory management performance.

Inventory Models Lead to Inventory Policy

Inventory policies are developed by creating a model of the inventory situation, then using the model to create a policy which meets some criterion for being most acceptable. Without inventory models, it is difficult for a firm to relate its inventory policy to its real needs for inventory service and convenience. Using inventory models, a firm can decide what service it does require in each kind of inventory it keeps—raw materials, work in process, finished goods (it isn't unusual to see a firm which has 10,000–100,000 different *types* of items in inventory)—and compute an inventory policy that gives the level of service for each kind of inventory. Figure 12–1 shows the inventory model graphically.

FIGURE 12-1
Model Showing Inventory Level as a Function of Time, Q, S, and Demand

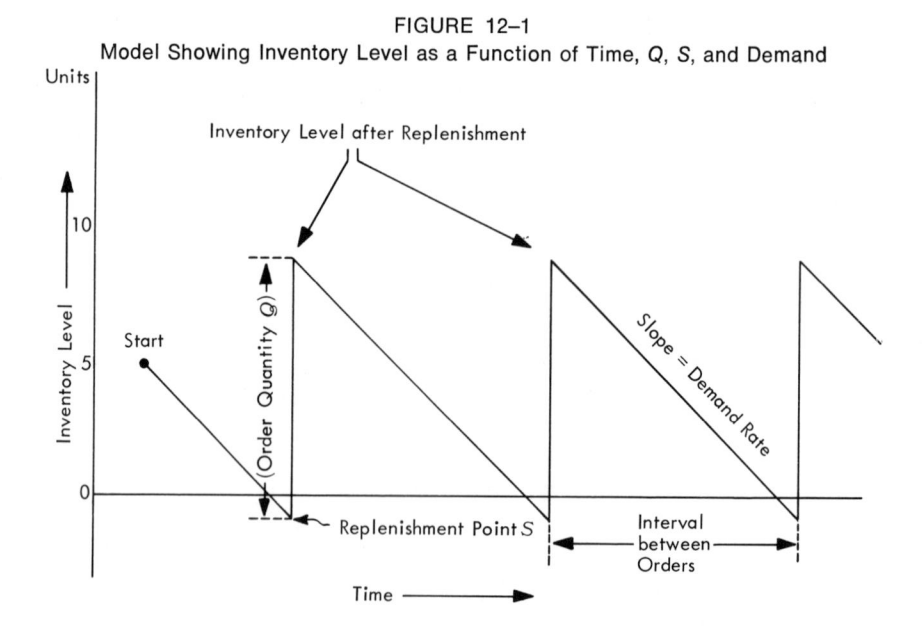

PARAMETERS AFFECTING INVENTORY MANAGEMENT

The inventory environment includes these parameters which affect inventory management:

1. Ordering costs—costs of ordering or replenishing inventory.
2. Carrying costs—costs of keeping or storing inventory on hand.
3. Shortage costs—costs of not being able to satisfy demand from inventory on hand.
4. Demand—future rate of withdrawals from inventory per period.

Let us list costs which could occur in categories 1, 2, and 3.

1. *Costs of Ordering or Replenishing Inventory*
   a) Cost of setting up plant to produce a batch of product for inventory (setup costs).
   b) Cost of preparing and placing an order with a supplier (if item cannot be produced; these are called order costs).
   c) Cost of preparing space for storage of inventory if this must be done each time an order is placed.
2. *Cost of Keeping or Storing Inventory on Hand*
   a) Cost of maintaining the storage area (utilities, heat, light, cooling).
   b) Cost of security for storage area.
   c) Depreciation, taxes, insurance for storage area structure.
   d) Taxes, insurance on value of inventory itself.
   e) Theft, shrinkage, accidental damage to inventory.
   f) Cost of obsolescence.
   g) Lost income due to inventory investment not earning a direct cash return.
3. *Shortage Costs*
   a) Expenses of readjusting production line after a shortage.
   b) Extra costs of expediting inventory orders to alleviate a shortage.
   c) Margin on lost sales to customers alienated by existence of shortage.

The following isn't a cost category, so instead of costs we list sources of information to help you estimate the future demand for withdrawals from inventory.

4. *Future Rate of Withdrawals from Inventory*
   a) Records of previous withdrawal rates.
   b) Predictions of future sales, production, etc., prepared during the budgeting process.
   c) Specialized forecasting models utilizing regression analysis, moving averages, exponential smoothing, etc., and which calculate inventory demand rates as a function of overall business policies and environment.

The accounting system provides a *starting point* for accumulating the cost information you need. A word of caution: you are only interested in the variable costs of ordering, carrying, or being short of inventory. For example, if there is a security patrol of the inventory storage area irregardless whether inventory is stored there, then the security patrol cost is not a relevant cost. If the depreciation and taxes on the storage area don't vary with the inventory quantity stored, they aren't relevant costs either.

The cost of inventory itself didn't enter the inventory model information requirements. The cost of inventory may determine some of the other costs: insurance, for example. But the omission of inventory cost as an information input to inventory decisions is not accidental. You may best understand this by realizing that withdrawals must be paid for whatever the inventory policy is. The demand to be satisfied is not a function of the inventory policy.

Typical Inventory Management Method

Visualize the total quantity of some article as kept in a large container or bin. When this article is requisitioned, the clerk goes to the bin and takes out the quantity requisitioned. One day he goes to the bin and sees a red line emerging on the inside of the bin. This signals him that the article's supply has become so low that it must be reordered. The clerk completes a purchase form and sends it to the purchasing department, retaining a copy that is placed at the article's bin to show it is reordered. The quantity below the red line should be sufficient to meet demand until the new order arrives and replenishes the bin.

This "bin" method is a reasonable system which does not require management of employee sophistication to work smoothly. But—how do you know where to draw the red line inside the bin? The average investment in inventory and inventory costs are determined by the height of the reorder mark above the bottom of the bin and the size of the reorder quantity.

The next section explains one way to find a place to "draw the red line."

SIMPLE ECONOMIC ORDER QUANTITY MODELS

These models were developed generations ago to determine inventory management through reorder points, replenishment points, and reorder quantities. In the form you study here, they are simple, yet capable of producing improvements over inventory management already existing. Sophisticated economic order quantity (EOQ) models accommodate to complex inventory situations. Figure 12–2 contrasts the assumptions of typical simple and sophisticated models.

FIGURE 12–2
Economic Order Quantity (EOQ) Model Assumptions

Simple Model Assumptions	Sophisticated* Model Assumptions
1. Demand is steady during a period, occurring uniformly throughout.	1. Demand is irregular and fluctuates uncertainly.
2. A new order arrives a predictable time after it is placed.	2. Delays in delivery are often and irregular.
3. All inventory-related costs are known and constant.	3. Very few costs are known.
4. Average unit cost is independent of order size or production run length.	4. Discounts are given for large orders; long production runs have learning effects and other economies which lower average unit cost.

*Only simple models are discussed in this text.

Inventory management will consist of finding the values of Q and S that minimize costs while satisfying demand.

Influence of Inventory Parameters on Inventory Management

Figure 12-3 shows how order quantity and replenishment point will be influenced by relatively higher or lower values of demand, carrying cost, shortage cost, and order cost in the simple models covered in this chapter.

FIGURE 12-3
Inventory Parameters and Inventory Management

	Effect on—	
Parameter	*Reorder Quantity*	*Replenishment Point*
Order cost:		
1. Higher	Larger	More negative
2. Lower	Smaller	Less negative
Carrying cost:		
1. Higher	Smaller	More negative
2. Lower	Larger	Less negative
Shortage cost:		
1. Higher	Smaller	Less negative
2. Lower	Larger	More negative
Demand		
1. Higher	Larger	More negative
2. Lower	Smaller	Less negative

You can express the relationships in Figure 12-3 more usefully with symbols. Here are symbolic definitions:

S = replenishment point.
Q = reorder quantity.
c_o = the direct cost of placing one order (order cost).
c_h = the cost of holding one unit in inventory for the period with which you are dealing (carrying cost).
c_s = the cost of being unable to fill an order for one unit from inventory for one period (shortage cost).
D = the demand to be filled from inventory during the period with which you are dealing.

Cost of Inventory Policy

With the symbols above you can describe the cost of an inventory policy. The following is not a derivation but an explanation of the parts of an expression for total inventory function costs.

Total   Total   Total   Total
cost   =   carrying + ordering + shortage
(TC)   costs   costs   costs

$$TC = \text{Average inventory level} \times c_h + \text{Number of orders} \times c_o + \text{Average inventory shortage} \times c_s$$

$$TC = \frac{(Q+S)^2}{2Q} c_h + \frac{D}{Q} c_o + \frac{S^2}{2Q} c_s \tag{12-1}$$

Economic Order Quantity Models for Q* and S*

An asterisked symbol denotes the *optimum* (least-cost) value of a decision variable. The use of differential calculus permits (12–1) to yield expressions for the optimal Q and S. These expressions are

$$\text{Order quantity: } Q^* = \sqrt{\frac{2c_o D}{c_h}} \times \sqrt{\frac{c_h + c_s}{c_s}} \quad \left.\begin{array}{l} Q^* \text{ and } S^* \\ \text{define the} \\ \text{least-cost} \\ \text{inventory} \\ \text{policy} \end{array}\right. \tag{12-2}$$

$$\text{Replenishment point: } S^* = -\sqrt{\frac{2c_o D}{c_s}} \times \sqrt{\frac{c_h}{c_h + c_s}} \tag{12-3}$$

To illustrate the uses of these formulas, assume you are in charge of the resin inventory at the Fiberglass Boat Company. Resin is used continuously and can be replenished by going next door to the resin factory to pick it up—requiring no time at all.

Applying the Models to Compute Inventory Policy

Working with the cost accountant, you have determined that the cost of making an order, going over and picking it up, and stacking it on the shelves is $8. Similarly, you have determined that the cost of storing 1 unit of resin for one year is $10. This covers insurance, spoilage, interest on investment in resin, and several other minor factors. The Fiberglass Boat Company mass produces standard boats, hence there is a steady and constant demand for the resin. Demand in the coming period is estimated at 3,422.5 units. Finally, you figure that being short of resin costs $100 per year per unit short, in terms of upsetting production schedules and other inconveniences.

You are therefore able to assign the variables in the economic order quantity models the following variables:

C_o = $8 per order.
D = 3,422.5 units per year.
C_h = $10 per unit per year.
C_s = $100 per unit short per year.

You insert these numbers into (12–2) and obtain:

$$Q^* = \sqrt{\frac{2 \times \$8 \times 3{,}422.5}{\$10}} \times \sqrt{\frac{\$10 + \$100}{\$100}}$$

= 74 × 1.054 = 78 *units*. This is the amount to be ordered whenever an order is placed.

Now, solving with (12–3) for the replenishment point,

$$S^* = -\sqrt{\frac{2 \times \$8 \times 3{,}422.5}{\$100}} \times \sqrt{\frac{\$10}{\$10 + \$100}}$$

= −23.4 × 0.301 = −7.01   or about   −7   *units*.

The replenishment point S^* will never be greater than zero. When it is negative, that means it is cheaper in terms of the overall inventory policy to run slightly short before receiving the next order.

The proper policy is to arrange for delivery of 78 units of resin when you are 7 units short. The cost of this policy will be the lowest possible total cost for this inventory situation, and can be figured from (12–1):

$$\begin{aligned}\text{Total cost} &= \frac{(78-7)^2}{2 \times 78} \times \$10 + \frac{3{,}422.5}{78} \times \$8 + \frac{7^2}{2 \times 78} \times \$100\\ &= \$323.14 \qquad\quad + \$351.03 \qquad\quad + \$31.41\\ &= \$705.58\end{aligned}$$

When the Shortage Cost Is Very High

If you examine (12–3), you will see that a very high shortage cost would cause the expression under the second square root sign to approach zero, implying that the replenishment point also approaches zero. When the shortage cost is very large relative to the carrying cost, a new and simpler set of formulas may be used to find the least-cost inventory policy.

$$\text{Total cost} = \underbrace{\frac{Q}{2} c_h}_{\text{Carrying cost}} + \underbrace{\frac{D}{Q} c_o}_{\text{Ordering cost}} \qquad (12\text{--}1\text{A})$$

$$Q^* = \sqrt{\frac{2c_o D}{c_h}} \qquad (12\text{--}2\text{A})$$

$$S^* = 0 \qquad (12\text{--}3\text{A})$$

If you apply these formulas to the Fiberglass Boat Company resin inventory situation, you obtain:

$$Q^* = \sqrt{\frac{2 \times \$8 \times 3{,}422.5}{\$10}} = 74 \text{ units}$$

$$S^* = 0$$

$$TC = \frac{74}{2} \times \$10 + \frac{3{,}422.5}{74} \times \$8$$

$$= \$740$$

This cost is not directly comparable with the cost of the previous policy since it assumes an infinitely high cost of being unable to satisfy demand for resin from inventories. However, if you use the policy ($Q = 74$, $S = 0$) when shortage cost is actually $100 per unit short per year [making the policy ($Q = 78$, $S = -7$) optimal], you will spend an extra $740 — $705.58 = $34.42 per year maintaining resin inventories.

Generality of Cost Formulas

Note that the cost formulas (12–1) and (12–1A) may be used to compute the cost of any inventory policy, even if it is not the optimal policy. This makes them useful for calculating the savings that may occur if an optimal policy replaces an existing policy.

Cost Savings

Suppose the Fiberglass Boat Company current resin inventory policy is to order 200 units of resin to arrive when the inventory level is 50 units on hand.

The cost of this policy is

$$TC = \frac{(200 + 50)^2}{2 \times 200} \times \$10 + \frac{3{,}422.5}{200} \times \$8 + \$0 \quad \begin{bmatrix} \text{Since this policy} \\ \text{has no shortages,} \\ \text{there is no short-} \\ \text{age cost!} \end{bmatrix}$$

$$= \$1{,}699.40$$

A change to the optimal policy would save $1,699.40 − $705.58 or $993.82 annually. Such savings are representative of those available when appropriate operating procedures are applied.

Delay in Restocking after Ordering

Now suppose that delivery of resin occurs exactly one working day after Fiberglass Boat Company's order is received. You must place your order for resin well before the replenishment point is reached in order to implement the optimal inventory policy. The inventory level at which an order is *placed* is called the *order point*.

The period during which 3,422.5 units of resin are consumed is one year, which includes 244.5 working days at Fiberglass Boat. Thus, 3,422.5/244.5 = 14.00 units of resin are consumed each working day. If the replenishment point is −7 units of resin, you should dial the resin company and order 78 more units at the exact time that 14 − 7 = 7 units of resin remain in inventory. The order should arrive the following day just as you are 7 units of resin short. This shortage is immediately filled and remaining part of the order—71 units—is placed in inventory to satisfy future demand.

If the replenishment point is 0 units of resin, your order should be placed one day before the current inventory is exhausted, or when 14 units remain in inventory.

Safety Stock

You may not trust the resin factory to deliver exactly on schedule. No matter. It will cost you a little more, but you can still be reasonably assured of having enough resin on hand by determining a safety stock and *adding* it to the demand during the time lag between ordering and replenishment to get the proper order point. Here is how that would work.

You have noticed that about one time in five the resin factory gets its dates fouled up and delivers after two working days rather than one. This means that 20 percent of the time your shortage before replenishment is 21 units rather than 7—and this shortage also exists over a longer period of time than the smaller shortage. These extra shortage costs are slightly offset by the lower levels of inventory and associated lower carrying costs, but the overall effect is higher costs which you'd like to avoid.

If you are not permitting any shortages at all, the safety stock problem is easy. Simply order when inventory level reaches 28 units. Then, about 20 percent of the time the new order will arrive at an inventory level of zero, and 80 percent of the time, at a level of 14. The extra cost will be approximately the same as the cost of carrying 14 extra units in stock at all times (they are not in stock only about nine days per year—try to figure out why!),[1] or $10 × 14 = $140 per year. Note that preventing stockouts cost you ($140/$706) × 100 or about 20 percent of the total optimal cost of the inventory function. You may interpret this as the extra cost of assuring uninterrupted supply. If it seems excessive, you could look for a more reliable source of resin supply.

Safety Stock when Shortages Are Permitted. Shortages are permitted only when they are controlled. You are thus willing to be 7 resin units short when you are seeking a least-cost inventory operation—but may not be willing to be 21 units short when that is not your plan and is caused by an unreliable supplier. This section explains how you might adjust inventory policy to minimize the effects of an uncontrollably irregular supply of resin.

---

[1] There are $3{,}422.5/74 \approx 46$ orders per year, of which 20 percent or 9.2 are delivered late—causing the safety stock to be exhausted.

Irregular deliveries create uncertainty for the inventory policy maker. The simplest approach to analyzing this uncertainty is to recognize that there are really two situations: delivery when the shortage is 7 units, which occurs 80 percent of the time; and delivery when the shortage is 21 units, which occurs 20 percent of the time. Your assignment is to find an inventory policy that covers both situations at the lowest total cost.

You already know the cost of the policy ($S = -7$, $Q = 78$) when deliveries are normal; it is $705.58. When deliveries are a day late this policy's cost rises to $841.98 (calculated using [12–1] and $S = -21$, $Q = 78$). The total cost is a weighted average of these amounts: $TC = (0.20 \times \$841.98) + (0.80 \times \$705.58) = \$732.86$.

Further use of calculus on a modified (12–1) reveals that if Q remains at 78, the single best replenishment point is $S = -4.29$ units of resin. Let S be rounded off to -4 units of resin. The cost of this policy when deliveries are regular is $712.31; when deliveries are a day late, $789.50. The total cost of this policy under all conditions is $(0.2 \times \$789.50) \times (0.8 \times \$712.31) = \$727.75$. The new policy costs $732.86 - \$727.75 = \$5.11$ less per year than the original one. A summary of these results appears in Figure 12–4.

FIGURE 12–4
Comparison of Least-Cost Inventory Policies for Resin under Different Conditions

c_o = $8 per order	c_h = $10 per unit per year D = 3,422.5 units per year	c_s = $100 per unit per year
	Delivery of Orders after One Day (80% of Time)	Delivery of Orders after Two Days (20% of Time)
A. CONTROLLED SHORTAGES ALLOWED		
1. Q = 78; order point = 7; average TC = $732.86.	$S = -7$ TC = $705.58	$S = -21$ TC = $841.98
2. Q = 78; order point = 10;. average TC = $727.75. . . .	$S = -4$ TC = $712.31	$S = -18$ TC = $789.50
B. NO SHORTAGES ALLOWED		
1. Q = 78; order point = 14;. average TC = (very large) . .	$S = 0$ TC = $740	$S = -14$ TC = (very large)
2. Q = 78; order point = 28;. average TC = $880.	$S = 14$ TC = $880	$S = 0$ TC = $880

The calculations to support this demonstration are happily beyond the scope of an introductory course.[2] The purpose of the demonstration is to establish the importance of costs and other information developed through an accounting system in making inventory policy decisions. Although $5.11 may not seem like much, this saving on each item in a 10,000 item inventory amounts to $51,100 per year. The actual savings may vary as circumstances determine.

SENSITIVITY ANALYSIS

Suppose you fail to measure one or more parameters of the economic order quantity model correctly. How wrong will your inventory policy be? Your errors will increase roughly as the square root of the ratio of correct to incorrect parameter value. For example, in formula (12–2A) for Q^*, if actual carrying cost is 2 times your estimate, the order quantity will be understated by $(\sqrt{2} - 1) \times 100 = 41$ *percent*.

Let us assume that in the Fiberglass Boat Company example, you estimate carrying cost as $10 when it is actually $20. The true order quantity should have been 57.29 units. The true replenishment point should have been −9.56 units. Inserting these values into (12–1) gives a cost of *$955.21*. This is the cost of the optimal policy if c_h is actually $20; to find out the cost of erroneous information, compare it with the cost of your erroneous policy. This cost is not $705.58; that was based on the wrong carrying cost. The cost of the erroneously calculated inventory policy $(Q = 78, S = -7)$ is actually *$1,028.74*.

The opportunity cost of using the erroneous policy when $(Q = 57.29, S = 9.36)$ is optimal is $1,028.74 − $955.21 = *$73.53* per year. This is a small extra cost compared to the substantial savings the economic order quantity policy $(Q = 78, S = -7)$ offers over the hypothetical original policy's cost of (using the correct carrying cost $c_h = \$20$):

$$TC = \frac{(200 + 50)^2 \times \$20}{2 \times 200} + \frac{3{,}422.5 \times \$8}{200} = \$3{,}262!$$

---

[2] But see the Appendix 12A if you want to know anyway.

This relative insensitivity of the economic order quantity model to errors in estimating its independent parameter values makes it useful in practice even if you do not have perfect information or if the assumptions about demand or reorder time are not true. Accounting efforts should be directed toward estimating most accurately those parameters which have the greatest impact on inventory policy cost. With a little care, you can be virtually certain that your policy's cost will be within, say, ±50 percent of the lowest possible cost, and well below the cost of the policies it will replace.

INVENTORY MANAGEMENT SYSTEMS

An inventory management *system* is based on analysis similar to that conducted above. Such systems exhibit vast differences, depending on the needs they serve. In a typical manufacturing firm which has 10,000 different items in inventory, the inventory management system would be expected to monitor the levels of all the fastest-moving items (it has been observed that about 20 percent of all the items will account for 80 percent of the capital investment and activity in inventory), monitor demand for these items, to determine a replenishment point in light of the latest information about expected demand, compare the actual level of inventory with the computed replenishment point, and give the signal for placing an order for items in need of replenishment (reorder point higher than inventory level on hand). Computers are used extensively to implement inventory systems. If items are contracted to be purchased from known suppliers, the computer can even print out an order addressed to the supplier for the appropriate number of additional units. Such systems, when they are economically feasible, remove the clerical burden from management and free persons for concentration on business strategies and responsibilities.

SUMMARY

The economic order formulas are among the most commonly used models for analyzing an inventory situation. They make use of estimates of costs of carrying, ordering, and being short of inventory, and of demand for a commodity from inventory. The economic order quantity formulas allow computation, when the assumptions underlying them are met, of inventory policy cost, amount to be ordered at one time, and the inventory level at which replenishment should occur.

Inventory management systems based on economic order quantity analysis seek to make as small as possible the sum of ordering, holding, and shortage costs, while at the same time providing an acceptable level of service from inventory—provision of items from inventory at the convenience of users—with no more shortages and ensuing delays than are acceptable to customers.

Inventory management is an important function in the business because so much money may be invested in inventories. Typically, inventory management is decentralized to the users of inventory; however, the financial and accounting functions perform important services by defining the financial restraints on inventory and the important measures and forecasts of costs and future demands.

APPENDIX 12A

How the Optimal Economic Order Quantity Policy Was Computed When Controlled Shortages Are Permitted and 20 Percent of Deliveries Are a Day Late

$$TC \text{ (irregular deliveries)} = 0.8TC(Q = 78, S)$$
$$+ 0.2TC(Q = 78, S - 14) = 0.8\left[\frac{(Q+S)^2 c_h}{2Q} + \frac{Dc_o}{Q} + \frac{S^2 c_s}{2Q}\right]$$
$$+ 0.2\left[\frac{(Q+S-14)^2 c_h}{2Q} + \frac{Dc_o}{Q} + \frac{(S-14)^2 c_s}{2Q}\right]$$

If this expression is differentiated with respect to S, the result set equal to zero and solved for S, the resulting value of S will be that which produces the lowest value of TC when deliveries are irregular.

$$\frac{\partial TC}{\partial S} = 0.8 \left[\frac{(Q+S)c_h}{Q} + \frac{Sc_s}{Q} \right] + 0.2 \left[\frac{(Q+S-14)c_h}{Q} + \frac{(S-14)c_s}{Q} \right]$$

$$0 = 0.8 \left[\frac{(78+S)10}{78} + \frac{100S}{78} \right]$$

$$+ 0.2 \left[\frac{(78+S-14)10}{78} + \frac{(S-14)100}{78} \right]$$

$$S = -4.29$$

APPENDIX 12B: SQUARE ROOTS OF NUMBERS 1–100

Instructions: To find the square root of a number in this table, follow these steps:

a) Multiply or divide the number by 10 an *even number of times* until the number is between 1 and 100.
   Example: Let the number be 45,000. When divided 4 times by 10, the result is 4.5, which is between 1 and 100.

b) Find the number N in the table which is closest to the result of (*a*). If the number in (*a*) lies between two table entries, note both entries.
   Example: 4.5 is between 4 and 5.

c) Find the square root of the table entry and record it. If two table entries were noted above in (*b*), record both square roots, then take their average.
   Example: Square root of 4 is 2. Square root of 5 is 2.236. The average is $(2.000 + 2.236)/2 = 2.118$.

d) Number found in (*c*) should be divided by 10 (if the original number was multiplied in [*a*] or multiplied by 10 (if the original number was divided by 10 in [*a*]) *half the number of times* the opposite operation was carried out in (*a*). The result is the desired square root.
   Example: 45,000 was divided 4 times by 10 in (*a*). Therefore, multiply 2.118 by 10 two times: $2.118 \times 10 \times 10 = 211.8$. To check, 211.8 squared is 44,859, very close to 45,000.

This procedure will give sufficiently accurate results to solve all problems in this book, and most practical problems as well. A slide rule also gives good square roots. The true square root of 45,000 is 212.1—the error was 0.14 percent.

N	$\sqrt{N}$	N	$\sqrt{N}$
1	1	51	7.141
2	1.414	52	7.211
3	1.732	53	7.280
4	2.000	54	7.348
5	2.236	55	7.416
6	2.449	56	7.483
7	2.645	57	7.549
8	2.828	58	7.615
9	3.000	59	7.681
10	3.162	60	7.745
11	3.316	61	7.810
12	3.464	62	7.874
13	3.605	63	7.937
14	3.741	64	8.000
15	3.872	65	8.062
16	4.000	66	8.124
17	4.123	67	8.185
18	4.242	68	8.246
19	4.358	69	8.306
20	4.472	70	8.366
21	4.582	71	8.426
22	4.690	72	8.485
23	4.795	73	8.544
24	4.898	74	8.602
25	5.000	75	8.660
26	5.099	76	8.717
27	5.196	77	8.774
28	5.291	78	8.831
29	5.385	79	8.888
30	5.477	80	8.944
31	5.567	81	9.000
32	5.656	82	9.055
33	5.744	83	9.110
34	5.830	84	9.165
35	5.916	85	9.219
36	6.000	86	9.273
37	6.082	87	9.327
38	6.164	88	9.380
39	6.244	89	9.433
40	6.324	90	9.486
41	6.403	91	9.539
42	6.480	92	9.591
43	6.557	93	9.643
44	6.663	94	9.695
45	6.708	95	9.746
46	6.782	96	9.799
47	6.855	97	9.849
48	6.928	98	9.899
49	7.000	99	9.950
50	7.071	100	10.000

QUESTIONS

1. What is the replenishment point? A shortage? A safety stock? A carrying cost? An order cost? A shortage cost?

2. Goodall Company has a certain item for which one order is placed, for 2,000 units per period. Reordering and replenishment both occur when inventory level is 100 units. What is the average level of inventory?

3. Clank Equipment Company has discovered, as a result of a study, that its cost to hold a certain item in inventory is $5 per unit per month. Which is more economical, (a) a policy of ordering 1,000 units when inventory drops to 200, or (b) a policy of ordering 500 units when inventory drops to 350? Disregard order costs.

4. What are some sources of information about inventory order or replenishment costs? What are some specific costs you might include in this category?

5. Which of the following situations are opportunities to apply inventory models?
    a) Space Age Wing Company has a contract with Lockjaw Aviation to supply tail assemblies for its new business jet; they are to be shipped within seven days after notification is given that an assembly is needed.
    b) Midville Community Hospital hopes to have enough beds so that no one is turned away who needs one.
    c) Midville Pharmacy has a reputation of never being out of any ethical drug a doctor prescribes.
    d) The University Co-op wishes to know how many texts of a certain variety to have on hand before the first day of classes.
    e) Crumbley Motors salesmen have vowed to sell 400 cars before month's end.
    f) The National Park Service is concerned that it will run out of camping sites in park areas open to the public.

6. What is demand? What are some factors which determine demand? Which is the normal situation: steady demand, or unsteady demand? What complications are introduced by unsteady demand?

7. Bell Company has a certain item in stock which is up for inventory policy review. Carrying cost is $5 per unit, and stockout cost is

$10 per unit (for a full period). Which will be the cheaper policy: (*a*) order 1,000 units when inventory level is 50, or (*b*) order 1,000 units when inventory level is —50? Period demand is 1,000 units. Inventory runs out when 95 percent of the period has elapsed if (*b*) is chosen, and there are shortages for 5 percent of the period.

8. What are some of the costs of carrying inventory? Why are only the *variable* costs of carrying inventory considered?

9. What is the purpose of carrying inventory?

10. A certain firm is, because of an inventory stockout, unable to produce a certain item for three days. The lost production could not be made up, since the firm was already operating at top capacity. Suggest a measure of the cost of this stockout.

11. Considering the situation in Question 10, would the stockout cost be positive if the firm were operating at 50 percent of capacity and the lost production was easily made up over the two days following resumption of production?

12. Colfax Company must wait three periods after an order is placed for replenishment to occur. The highest demand ever experienced in one period was 90 units. The company's replenishment point is always —10 units. Suggest a reorder point.

13. Upon hearing that the accounting section could not estimate inventory costs closer than plus or minus 30 percent, the president of Deaf Smith Company discontinued the inventory analysis project, saying, "I'll just guess at the right policies and save us a lot of money on the investigation!" Comment on the wisdom of this action.

14. Cobb Component Company has 250,000 different items in inventory. Several computer salesmen have told the firm that no computer made is large or fast enough to handle all these items. In fact, about how many items should a computer-based inventory management system for this firm concern itself with and what fraction of maximum possible gross savings will this produce?

15. In the Harris Company, inventory management is the responsibility of inventory users. In the Travis Company, inventory management is the responsibility of the finance function. Speculate about the differences in inventory policies between these two firms.

EXERCISES

16. Edwards Company's inventory of a certain item reflects the following activity:
    Week 1: Inventory level 5,000 units.
    Week 3: Order and receive 10,000 units.
    Week 4: Issue 3,000 units.
    Week 5: Issue 3,100 units.
    Week 7: Issue 5,900 units.
    Week 8: Order and receive 11,000 units.
    Week 9: Issue 3,000 units.
    What is average order size? Approximate reorder and replenishment point?
    Average inventory during the nine weeks covered?

17. Chambers Company maintains an average inventory of a certain item of 5,000 units. It reorders when inventory level reaches 1,000 units. The quantity ordered is 10,000 units, which arrives when inventory is exactly zero. It is necessary to reorder exactly every 10 days. The cost of carrying inventory is $4 per unit per year. The company estimates that the costs of ordering amount to $50 per order. Compute the total cost of the inventory function.

18. Doyle Company has a particular item in inventory that occasionally runs short. The facts are these: 90 percent of the time there is an average inventory of 100 units; 10 percent of the time there is a shortage of 20 units. An order for 240 units is placed regularly; demand is 48,000 units per year. To be short costs $60 per unit short per year; to carry a unit in stock costs $10 per unit per year. Direct costs of placing an order are $10. Compute the total cost of Doyle's inventory function.

19. Morris Company estimates that its inventory of plywood costs $9,500 per year in total costs to maintain. A new plan is presented which calls for an order quantity of 30,000 board feet every 30 days, and no shortages. Cost of ordering would be $100; cost of storing plywood is $8 per 100 board feet per year. Will the new plan be an improvement, cost-wise, over the old one?

20. Chilton Company has an inventory function that is now costing it $70,000 per year. The company's demand for the item comprising the bulk of inventory is 500,000 units per year. A study just com-

pleted shows that the cost of carrying one unit in stock one year is $2, and the cost of placing an order, receiving it, etc., is $200. Should the present inventory policy be changed? If so, what are the maximum potential savings? Assume no shortages are permitted.

21. Harvey Company is trying to establish a reorder point. Orders take up to 10 days to arrive after being placed. Demand can unpredictably rise 50 percent above its average level of 1,000 units per day for short periods. The maximum shortage is 4,000 units, but the company does not want any shortages of more than 1,000 units. Determine a reorder point.

PROBLEMS

22. Refer to the "EOQ" formula (equation [12–2A]). Assume $Q = 2,500$ units per order.

    Required:
    a) If D increases by 100 percent, what will be the new value of Q?
    b) If c_o decreases by 50 percent, what will be the new value of Q?
    c) If c_h approaches zero, what will happen to the value of Q? What is a reasonable practical interpretation of this peculiar result?

23. Refer to the formula for S, the replenishment point (equation [12–3]). Assume $S = 500$ units.

    Required:
    a) If D increases by 100 percent, what will be the new replenishment point?
    b) If c_s approaches infinity, what happens to the value of the replenishment point? How do you interpret this result in practical terms?

24. The Resounding Crash Company, Inc., which specializes in nostalgic recordings pressed from the original master disks, has experienced a prolonged and steady demand for an album recorded in 1955 by rock and roll star Big George. It costs $1,000 to set up for production of this record, regardless of the number of records produced. The cost of storing one disk for one year is $0.50. Demand is a steady 50,000 disks per year. At the present time Resounding Crash produces the full 50,000 disks in January, essentially all at

once. The company is considering using an EOQ model to determine inventory production quantity.

Required:

a) Use the appropriate EOQ formula to determine production quantity for the Big George record. Let $S = 0$.
b) Explain why it is not necessary to know the selling price of the record or its direct production cost in order to compute this quantity.
c) A consumer study shows that if a fan orders Big George's record and must wait for it, the cost to the company is $100 per year due to customer ill will. Compute the production quantity and the point at which inventory replenishment must occur.
d) Assume that one month is required to set up and produce the record. At what inventory level must this production setup begin?

25. Mr. Hackinn Kauph, president of Kauph Supply Company, is concerned by the existence of a very large inventory of transistor radios in his warehouse in Los Angeles. These radios are distributed in a predictable manner to secondary warehouses around the country. The radios are received from Taiwan, and may be ordered and received airfreight within 24 hours in any quantity desired.

At the present time, the replenishment point is 50,000 cases of radios. Each case costs $75. The cost of receiving and stacking a single case is $1. Insurance, shrinkage, obsolescense, and battery deterioration cause holding costs to run at a level of $5 per case per year. In addition, Kauph Supply allocates $2 per case of indirect general overhead to holding cost.

Orders are presently for 20,000 cases at one time; for an order this size a jet freighter is chartered. The freighter could carry up to 50,000 cases for a one-way flight from Taiwan to L.A. airport; a fleet of trucks is rented there to transport the order to the warehouse at $0.10 per case. Mr. Kauph's accountants tell him that the direct paperwork and freight costs of an order are about $7,000. At the present time 10 orders are placed per year.

Required:

a) Compute the cost of the present inventory policy.
b) Compute the cost of an optimal order policy with replenishment just at zero inventory.

c) Assume that a change in inventory policy will cost $5,000. Would this amount be saved in three years or less if a switch is made to the optimal policy?

26. King Rag Company supplies various grades of "rag" (from which fine paper is made) to publishers and other users. Demand for this rag fluctuates over a considerable range, but averages 36 tons per week.

Because of the chemical instability of rag before it is made into paper, there is a high spoilage rate and consequently a high cost of storing rag for any length of time: $10 per ton per week. To prepare a batch of rag entails direct setup costs of $500 per batch. Inability to ship an order is not greatly serious; King rag estimates a cost for being short of about $200 per ton per week.

It takes two days to make a batch of rag. No more than 100 tons of rag can be made at one time.

Required:

a) You are the controller of King Rag and the president has asked you to prepare a simple study showing the optimum size batch of rag to make up, at what inventory level a new batch should begin production, and at what inventory level the new batch should be added to inventory.

b) The production manager in King Rag is unhappy about the shortage "cost" of $200 per week. He maintains that the cost is much, much higher than this. Re-do part (a) assuming c_s = $2,000 per week per ton shortage per week.

c) Compute the costs of policies (a) and (b) and compare them. Would you argue strongly for one policy or the other, based on the difference in cost between them? Why?

27. Ryan Company manufacturers fertilizer using a two-stage process. First, phosphoric acid is produced by treating calcium phosphate rock with sulphuric acid. Second, the phosphoric acid is combined in a reactor with ammonia and potash to produce balanced fertilizers of varying compositions.

Only one type of fertilizer may be produced at a time, yet each type of fertilizer is demanded continuously by customers. As a first step toward determining production quantities and number of runs for each fertilizer, Ryan has accumulated this information about the fertilizer process:

Direct costs to operate first stage . . . . $100 per hour
Direct costs to operate second stage . . . . $200 per hour
Indirect plant costs . . . . $9,000 per month
Cleanup after required amount of one type of
   fertilizer is completed $500
Waste fertilizer while adjusting process to proper
   fertilizer composition when starting production. . $2,000
Air conditioning fertilizer storage warehouse . . . . $0.50 per ton stored per month
Security for warehouse. . . . . $1,200 per month
Depreciation on warehouse . . . . $2,000 per month
Fertilizer production rate (any type). . . . . 50 tons per hour

Required:

a) Using EOQ inventory theory as your guide, classify the costs above into three categories: unrelated to problem, related to direct carrying costs, and related to direct production setup (order) costs.

b) If Ryan cannot fill an order for fertilizer as a customer specifies, the firm buys the appropriate type from a competitor at $96 per ton and delivers it to the customer. Note that Ryan's cost per ton is approximately $6. Let $90 be the stockout cost, c_s. Compute the optimal inventory policy and interpret it in terms of the amount and frequency of production runs for a fertilizer type of which 300 tons per month are demanded.

28. Ring Telephone Company staggers the distribution of telephone directories so that the printers can work at a constant rate all year around. Recently an executive suggested that this policy, which minimizes inventory on hand, might not be the most economical with respect to overall costs. He suggests that the company investigate using high-capacity presses to print many telephone directories about three times per year and store them until they are needed for distribution.

Under the present system, there are essentially no inventories, and production costs per directory are: $0.60, data accumulation; $0.50, printing; and $0.15, distribution. Additional relevant indirect costs are $30,000 per month. Three million directories per year are printed.

The proposed system would print 1,000,000 directories each four months. The directories would each cost $0.01 cents per month to store, would cost $0.60 for data accumulation; $0.48 for printing; and $0.14 to distribute. Indirect costs will run $100,000 per printing. It is not conceivable that the company not distribute directories.

Required:
a) Compare the proposed and existing system costs.
b) If directories may be printed on a batch basis, and $100,000 is the setup cost to print a batch, what is the most economical size batch to print? Can you think of any reason why this policy should NOT be adopted?

29. The Newases River Authority operates a series of dams on the Newases River. These dams are primarily for irrigation of downriver farmland. One particular pair of dams is operated together as follows:

Dam A, downstream, releases up to 1,000,000 gallons per day. When the reservoir is down to its minimum level, it is replenished from dam B, which is upstream.

It costs $1,000 to open the gates on dam B. Thus, the NRA wants to do this as seldom as possible. On the other hand, water in the dam A reservoir evaporates, accumulates pollution, and otherwise deteriorates so that 1 percent of the water held in the dam A reservoir becomes unusable each day. If it were not unusable, this water could be sold for irrigation at $50 per 100,000 gallons. The replenishment level of the reservoir behind dam A is 50,000,000 gallons; its maximum capacity is 200,000,000 gallons.

Required:
a) Assuming water is released at dam A at the maximum rate, find the amount of water that should be released into the dam A reservoir at any one time, and how frequently this will be done.
b) If 1 percent of the water in the dam B reservoir became unusable each day, would inventory analysis models be applicable to the water release problem? Would there even *be* a water release problem?
c) Might there be other uses of the water, such as for recreation, which might also have to be considered in the real world?

30. Fiber Newsprint Company is a distributor of newsprint in the southeastern quadrant of Arkalina. Although newsprint demand does fluctuate somewhat, it can be assumed steady over periods of 60–90 days, and changes over longer intervals are gradual. Currently demand is higher than expected—4,000 tons per day versus an expected 3,000 tons. No shortages are permitted.

The standard out-of-pocket costs of holding one ton of newsprint in inventory one day are $0.01. Newsprint is ordered from several suppliers; the standard out-of-pocket cost of ordering is $60 per order. Fiber's warehouse can hold any reasonable amount of newsprint; since delivery is virtually instantaneous, the replenishment and order points are identical.

In April, an order quantity was computed on the basis of expected demand of 3,000 tons per day, and this quantity was ordered whenever newsprint was required during the month. The expected cost of the inventory function was $1,800; the actual cost was $2,100. "I am sure it's just that demand was 25 percent above what we expected," commented the inventory center supervisor. "I do not think any of our costs are out of line."

Required:

a) Verify the standard cost of inventory function *expected* in April is correct. To do this, you will have to compute Q^*.
b) Determine, using equation (12–1A), whether the entire cost increase above expected cost is attributable to increased demand, and if not, how much extra cost (or savings) is attributable to ordering and holding activities.

31. Mr. D. Mann Cash is treasurer of a manufacturing-distributing firm. It is the policy of the firm to regularly advance cash to its dealers. Normally this cash comes back, but the growth of the business is such that each month the company advances about $60,000 more than its collections. Mr. Cash has typically borrowed this amount each month. Two weeks ago, he attended a continuing education seminar at which his group discussed the application of inventory EOQ models to cash management. Now, he has decided to test his present borrowing policy against that which the inventory model, which treats cash as any other inventoriable commodity, would determine.

The current interest rate for the firm is 1 percent per month. There are no other costs of borrowing except that of taking a loan. The bank charges lenders' fees of $100 for issuing a loan of any amount. Finally, Mr. Cash has an understanding with dealers that if there is a delay before cash is advanced, he will pay any penalties the dealer may incur while he is waiting. The typical penalty is for late payment of trade account payables and is 6 percent per month of the shortage.

Required:

a) Using the EOQ model with shortages, determine the optimal amount for Mr. D. Mann Cash to borrow, and how often he will borrow that amount.
b) Determine the monthly average cost of the policy in (*a*).
c) Determine the savings of this policy over his present policy on an *annual* basis, assuming no delays for dealers at present.

DECISION CASE 12–1: CANDLE ELECTRIC COMPANY

Candle Electric Company uses gas-fired generating plants to provide electricity to a wide area. To obtain cheap gas, the company accepted a low priority from the gas gathering and pipeline utility. As a result, service is interrupted fairly regularly. When gas deliveries are interrupted, the Candle Electric Company burns No. 2 fuel oil as an alternative means of generating electricity. The fuel oil is expensive, hard to obtain, and difficult to store. However, it is unthinkable that electricity not be generated, and Candle Electric has constructed 10 tanks, each holding 100,000 gallons of fuel oil. During a curtailment of natural gas deliveries, 50,000 gallons of fuel oil are burned each day. Candle Electric has arranged for delivery of this same amount daily during a curtailment to keep a maximum supply on hand (tanks all full).

The fuel oil company charges $250 for a delivery of any amount of fuel oil. Storage of oil involves costs due to seepage, evaporation, and safety precautions of $0.0001 per gallon per day.

Although curtailments can be of any duration, once a curtailment of gas deliveries begins, it is assumed that it will continue indefinitely. To calculate comparative costs in the requirements below, assume a curtailment of 30 days' duration. Disregard storage costs of fuel oil when natural gas deliveries are not curtailed.

Required:

a) Compute the cost of the present inventory policy with respect to fuel oil of Candle Electric Company.
b) Compute an economic order quantity inventory policy for fuel oil for Candle Electric Company.
c) What considerations determine how much fuel oil is stored between gas delivery curtailments? Does the availability of fuel oil have any bearing on the amount stored?

d) There is no penalty to Candle Electric Company if its generators are stopped for lack of fuel. Why is it "unthinkable" for this to happen? Can you think of any way to get a concept of social responsibility into the fuel oil inventory policy?

BIBLIOGRAPHY

Books

Brown, Robert Goodall. *Statistical Forecasting for Inventory Control.* New York: McGraw-Hill Book Co., 1959.

Green, James H. *Production and Inventory Control Handbook.* New York: McGraw-Hill Book Co., 1970.

Naddor, Eliezer. *Inventory Systems.* New York: John Wiley & Sons, Inc., 1965.

Articles

Brady, Edward, and Babbitt, J. C. "Inventory Control Systems," *Management Accounting,* December 1972.

Bruns, William J. "Inventory Valuation and Management Decisions," *The Accounting Review,* July 1965.

Eden, Donald F. "Computerized Inventory Control in a Small Company," *Management Accounting,* August 1972.

Rinehard, Jack R. "Economic Purchase Quantity Calculations," *Management Accounting,* September 1970.

Toy, James H. "Controlling Sales Goods Inventory," *Management Accounting,* September 1972.

13

Cost Analysis for Project Planning and Control

NOT ALL BUSINESS activity is routine manufacturing work. Construction of a home or building, development of a subdivision site, completion of an audit, closing the books of a large company, changing the machine layout in a large plant, launching a communications satellite, and hundreds of other tasks have nothing routine about them. They are unique. There is much opportunity to capitalize on knowledge of accounting in planning and carrying out unique projects if procedures especially developed for them are used.

These procedures allow you to perform the following planning and control steps:

1. Identify the steps or subactivities which together comprise the overall activity to be planned and controlled.
2. Identify and estimate:
    a) Costs which will be incurred as a direct result of performing a step. These costs may be:
    (1) Independent of step completion time, that is, basic materials in pouring a building foundation; or
    (2) Related to the time taken to perform the step, that is, extra costs of overtime and special equipment if the foundation is to be completely cured by artificial means after it is poured in order to save time. In general, costs related to the planned time to perform a step may be

lowered if the planned time is increased and raised if the planned time is decreased.

 b) Costs which will be incurred as a result of undertaking the activity as a whole. These costs also consist of:

  (1) Costs independent of project completion time; and

  (2) Time-related costs. An example of a time-related project cost would be the interest expense on funds borrowed to finance the project. These costs tend to increase as planned project completion time increases.

3. Determine the step and project completion times which will produce the lowest total overall project cost.
4. As the project is underway, monitor rate of activity completion and activity costs; variations from your plans give clues to the need for extra managerial attention.

The accounting function supplies expected values for step and project costs independent of and related to time. These costs serve as building blocks for a budget to control the entire project. The accounting function reports rate of progress and cost accumulation compared with plans to project the step managers.

IDENTIFYING PROJECT COSTS

The key to project planning and control is to identify steps comprising the project and identify time-related and time-independent costs for both individual steps and the project as a whole.

Step Costs

Most unique activities or projects consist of many individual operations or steps. Some of these steps occur simultaneously; others, in a distinct order or sequence. Each step has an identifiable beginning and end. Normally, a step will be assigned to a manager who can identify when the step begins and when it is completed. When a step is identified in this manner, the step-related costs associated with it can also be identified.

Step Costs Independent of Time. Certain costs will be incurred regardless of the step completion time. Imagine a hole to be dug for a pump site foundation. The hole dimensions will have to be surveyed and marked, and the cost of this will not vary with the planned excavation time. Generally, costs of direct materials are time independent, as are administrative costs and some labor costs.

Step Costs Related to Time. Other step costs do vary with time. For example, if one man with a shovel could dig the foundation in 10 days, it does not follow that 10 men with 10 shovels could dig the hole in 1 day. The 10 men would get in each other's way, efficiency would be reduced, and some time period between 1 and 10 days would be required to dig the hole. Thus, when a step is made shorter, the cost of the step may be expected to increase. The actual relation between completion time and total step costs may be complex, but for simplicity we assume a linear relationship. In Figure 13–1, the dotted line is a typical actual cost-time relation and the solid line is the assumed linear relationship that is used for project planning and control.

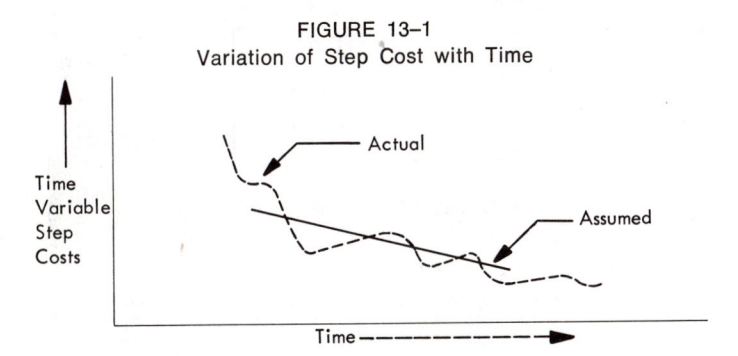

FIGURE 13–1
Variation of Step Cost with Time

Project-Related Costs

Some portion of the total cost of a project is not directly relatable to component steps. These project-related costs are estimated, controlled, and accounted for without reference to steps. Project-related costs in turn consist of time-related and time-independent costs. Obvious time-related costs are interest charges on money borrowed and penalty or bonus amounts written into a contract and related to a normal completion time. Although such costs don't relate to any particular step, they do relate to the project as a whole and have to be analyzed as such.

376   An Introduction to Accounting for Decision Making and Control

The *total* project costs are then determined as

$$\begin{array}{c}\text{Total}\\\text{project}\\\text{costs}\end{array} = \begin{array}{c}\text{Project-}\\\text{related}\\\text{costs}\end{array} + \begin{array}{c}\text{Step-}\\\text{related}\\\text{costs}\end{array} \qquad (13\text{–}1)$$

Or, adding the classification of costs according to their relation to step and project completion time,

$$\begin{array}{c}\text{Total}\\\text{project}\\\text{costs}\end{array} = \begin{bmatrix}\text{Time-}\\\text{independent}\\\text{project-related}\\\text{costs}\end{bmatrix} + \begin{bmatrix}\text{Time-}\\\text{related}\\\text{project}\\\text{costs}\end{bmatrix}$$

$$+ \begin{bmatrix}\text{Time-}\\\text{independent}\\\text{costs for}\\\text{step 1}\end{bmatrix} + \begin{bmatrix}\text{Time-}\\\text{related}\\\text{costs for}\\\text{step 1}\end{bmatrix} \qquad (13\text{–}2)$$

$$+ \begin{bmatrix}\text{Time-}\\\text{independent}\\\text{costs for}\\\text{step 2}\end{bmatrix} + \begin{bmatrix}\text{Time-}\\\text{related}\\\text{costs for}\\\text{step 2}\end{bmatrix} + \begin{array}{c}\text{etc., for all}\\\text{other steps}\\\text{in project}\end{array}$$

The relations developed in this section are summarized in Figure 13–2.

FIGURE 13–2
Summary of Project Cost Classification and Behavior

| | Costs ||
	Step Related	Project Related
Time Related	Decrease as step completion time extended	Increase as project completion time extended
Time independent.	Should not change	Should not change

ESTIMATING STEP COSTS

Now you have defined the time and cost elements of a project and are ready to use these elements in a project description, as you estimate step costs.

Project Description

After steps are identified and defined, you find the sequence of steps—what steps have to be completed before others can begin, and what step(s) begin the project and what step(s) complete the project. As an example, you might be considering construction of a house. A simplified list of steps and planned or expected completion times t_e is:

Step	t_e (Days)
Foundation	7
Framing	14
Electrical	4
Plumbing	8
Roofing	9
Appliance installation	3
Painting	15
Flooring	5
Cleaning	2

Let us expand on the information in this list by showing what the sequence of steps is:

Step	Step before—	Step after—
Foundation	None	Framing
Framing	Foundation	Electrical, Plumbing, Roofing
Electrical	Framing	Appliance installation
Plumbing	Framing	Appliance installation
Roofing	Framing	Painting
Appliance installation	Electrical, Plumbing	Flooring
Painting	Roofing	Flooring
Flooring	Appliance installation	Cleanup
Cleanup	Flooring	None

This is sufficient information to allow you to make a *network* describing the relationships of steps within the project. The network, which is used extensively in planning the project, is shown in Figure 13–3. Each arrow corresponds to a step. The two dotted arrows do not correspond to real steps; they are only there to show the sequence of steps. "Dummy 1" shows that appliance installation cannot begin until electrical work is finished. "Dummy 2" shows that until painting is completed, flooring cannot begin. All dummy steps have zero completion time; no dummy has any costs associated with it.

It is easier to refer to a step in a network by the numbers at the head and tail of the arrow corresponding to the step. These numbers

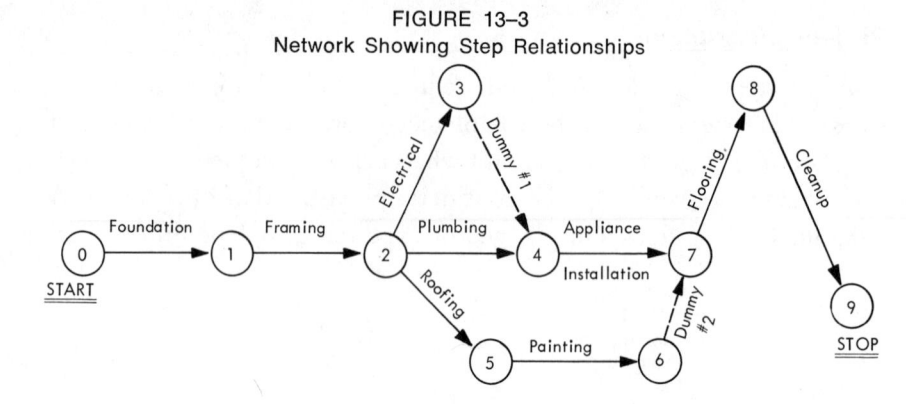

FIGURE 13–3
Network Showing Step Relationships

are related to the network structure. Notice that the numbers are arranged so that—

1. The number at the *head* of the arrow is larger than the number at its *tail*.
2. The *lowest* number is at the tail of the *first* step.
3. The *highest* number is at the head of the *last* step.

The numbers corresponding to steps are then

Foundation	01	Appliance	47
Framing	12	Painting	56
Electrical	23	Dummy II	67
Plumbing	24	Flooring	78
Roofing	25	Cleanup	89
Dummy I	34		

Hereafter we shall refer to these steps by the appropriate numbers.

Step Completion Times

Since a substantial part of project costs are related to step completion time, it is important to secure reliable step cost estimates as a function of step completion time. Here is a simple way to work out linear relationships:

1. Secure estimates for the longest reasonable or *upper* step completion time t_u and the cost of the step if completed in this time.

2. Secure estimates for the shortest reasonable or *lower* step completion time t_l and the cost of the step if completed in this time.
3. Using the two data points thus secured, compute the equation of the straight line joining them.

These estimates should come from persons responsible for carrying out the steps. Their performance will be judged according to how well the step completion time and costs conform to their own estimates.

The interval from t_l to t_u is the interval in which you expect the step completion time eventually chosen to fall. It is the relevant range for the cost estimates. That is, the cost estimates for steps have to be good representations of actual costs within this range of step completion times.

Now let's consider the completion times for the steps of our project. Figure 13–4 below represents step completion time estimates by each

FIGURE 13–4
Completion Times for Steps

Step No.	Step Name	t_l	t_e	t_u
01	Foundation	4	7	9
12	Framing	10	14	21
23	Electrical	2	4	8
24	Plumbing	6	8	9
25	Roofing	4	9	12
34 (dummy)		0	0	0
47	Appliance	1	3	5
56	Painting	10	15	25
67 (dummy)		0	0	0
78	Flooring	4	5	8
89	Cleanup	1	2	4

of the contractors on this particular house. The estimates are for lowest reasonable completion time, expected completion time, and upper reasonable completion time.

Concept of Critical Path. In order to perform the cost-reducing process which will be described shortly, you must understand the idea of a critical path. Consider the short network in Figure 13–5.

The numbers at the midpoints of the arrows represent t_e, the expected time required to complete the step corresponding to the arrow.

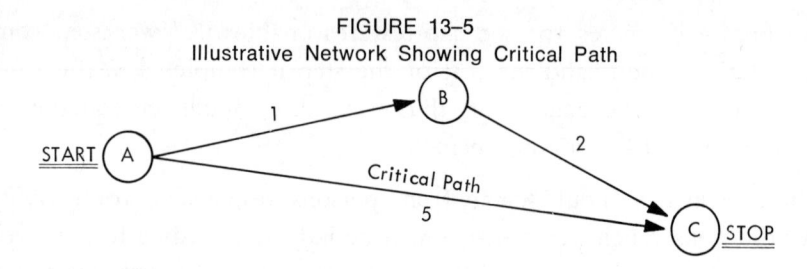

FIGURE 13–5
Illustrative Network Showing Critical Path

```
                    B
              1         2
START  A          Critical Path
                       5              C  STOP
```

You can see that both steps AB and AC can be started at once. Step AB will be finished in one day and when it is finished, step BC may begin.

Step AC, meanwhile, is still in progress even when both AB and BC are finished. If two crews were working, the ABC crew will sit idle for two days until the AC crew finishes. The project cannot be considered complete until both steps BC and AC are completed. Therefore, it is *critical* that step AC be completed as quickly as possible. *The steps forming the path through the project network which together require the greatest time to complete are the critical path.* The project cannot be completed until all steps on this path are complete. Delay in completing any step on this path will delay the entire project.

That is not true of steps not on the critical path. Here, steps AB and BC are not on the critical path. These steps could be delayed up to two days without lengthening the time required to complete the entire project. If savings result from so doing, these steps' planned completion times should be stretched out by two days. You will find it important to identify the critical path and devote extra planning and control to steps included in it.

Step Completion Costs

We have explained that step costs decline as step completion time is lengthened. Figure 13–5 shows the *variable costs* associated with each step (fixed costs do not change as completion time is varied). The third column is the savings per day if the step is lengthened (this is, of course, the same as the extra cost per day if the project is shortened). In addition, the second column is the *total cost* of each step, if it is completed in its expected time t_e, to serve as a base point.

13 / Cost Analysis for Project Planning and Control   381

To illustrate the information content of Figure 13–6, imagine an equation like (13–3) that applies to an individual step:

$$\begin{array}{l}\text{Step cost}\\\text{if performed}\\\text{in time } t\end{array} = \begin{array}{l}\text{Step cost}\\\text{if performed}\\\text{in time } t_e\end{array} + (t_e - t)\begin{bmatrix}\text{Incremental change}\\\text{in step cost per}\\\text{unit time}\end{bmatrix} \quad (13\text{–}3)$$

where $t_l \leq t \leq t_u$.

FIGURE 13–6
Step Cost as a Function of Completion Time

Step No.	Step Name	Step Cost if Completed in t_e	Incremental Change in Step Cost: $ per Day
01	Foundation	$ 4,000	$150
12	Framing	6,000	200
23	Electrical	1,000	50
24	Plumbing	1,500	100
25	Roofing	2,000	200
34 (dummy)		0	0
47	Appliance	2,200	60
56	Painting	3,000	120
67 (dummy)		0	0
78	Flooring	1,500	80
89	Cleanup	300	30
	Total	$21,500	

For step 23, numbers would make (13–3) look this way:

$$C_{23,t} = 1,000 + (4 - t)50$$

where $2 \leq t \leq 8$.

Figure 13–7 shows some values of t for step 23 and the corresponding step cost, $C_{23,t}$.

PLANNING COSTS FOR PROJECT AS A WHOLE

You may ask, "If all step costs can be reduced by stretching out step completion times, why cannot we simply require all steps to be done in the longest possible time and thereby minimize project cost?"

The answer is that there are costs for the project as a whole which increase as time passes. In our home construction case, let the construction company incur project-related penalty, interest, and insurance costs

FIGURE 13-7
Step 23 Cost and Completion Time

	$C_{23,t}$
$t_l = 2$	$1,100
3	1,050
4	1,000
5	950
6	900
7	850
$t_u = 8$	800

Cost of Step 23 as a Function of Completion Time

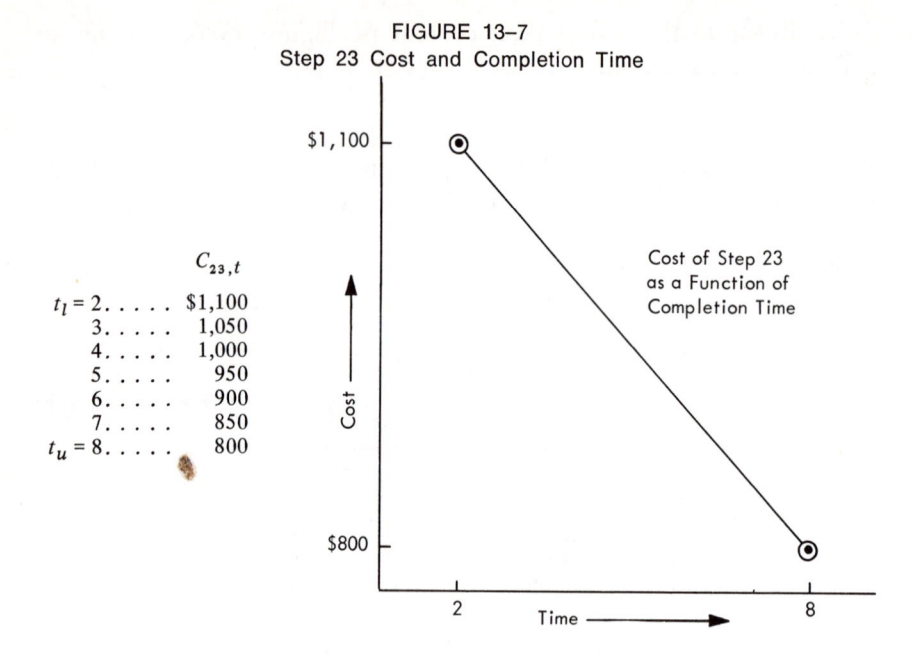

of $300 per day for each day the home remains uncompleted. *Our problem now is to find the completion schedule which has the smallest sum of step-related and project-related costs,* as shown in Figure 13–8.

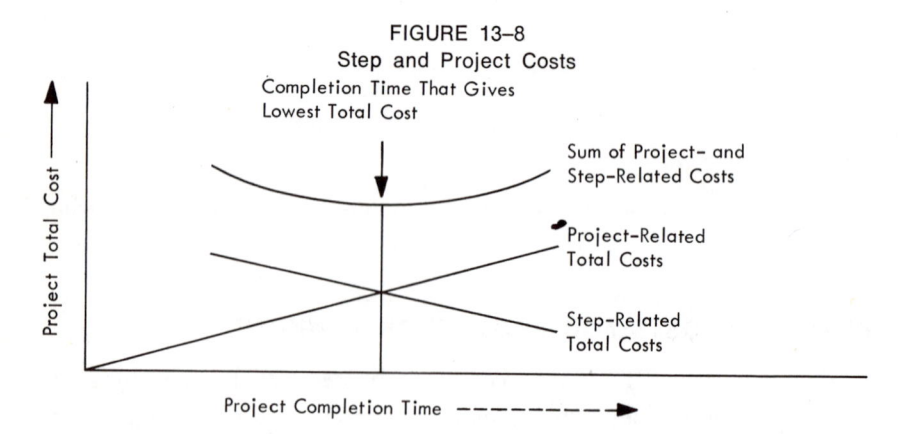

FIGURE 13-8
Step and Project Costs

Completion Time That Gives Lowest Total Cost

Sum of Project- and Step-Related Costs

Project-Related Total Costs

Step-Related Total Costs

This lowest total project cost occurs when lengthening the project an additional time unit would incur more project-related costs than would be saved by reducing step-related costs, and shortening the project would incur more additional step-related costs than the corresponding reduction in project-related costs. This condition is shown in Figure 13–9.

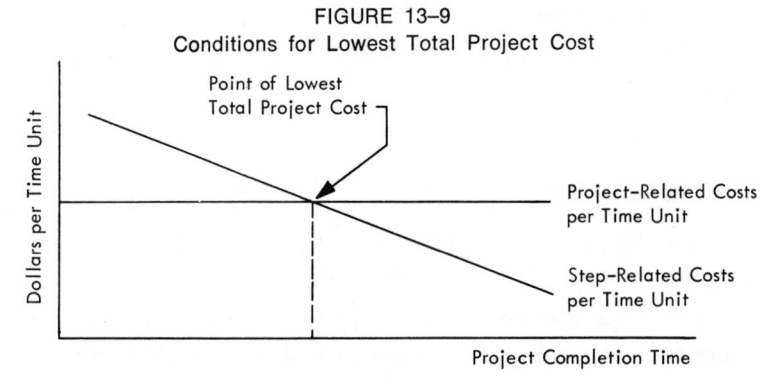

FIGURE 13–9
Conditions for Lowest Total Project Cost

As a starting point, find the project total cost and completion time if all steps are completed in their respective initial t_es. To help, we show in Figure 13–10 the original diagram of the construction project with projected completion times, expected costs, and the incremental change in dollars per day shown in the middle of each step arrow.

FIGURE 13–10
Network Showing Expected Completion Times and Costs

Total cost = $37,100; Total time to complete = 52 days.

Here are all three possible paths from *start* to *stop*:

1. 01234789   requires 35 days to complete.
2. 0124789   requires 39 days to complete.
3. 01256789   requires 52 days to complete.

Obviously, path 3 is the critical path since it requires 52 days to complete, which is longer than any other path. The entire construction project will cost $21,500 (the sum of step costs from Figure 13–10) and 52 days times $300 equals $15,600 in project costs—a total of $37,100.

Stretching Out Steps

The first thing that should occur to you is that there is no point in hurrying through the steps which only appear on path 1 or path 2 since these steps do not affect the project completion time. We can save money by stretching out the steps which are unique to these paths.

Rule 1. Look for the steps that will save the *most* money when they are stretched out. Stretch these steps *first.*

The steps unique to path 1 are: 23 and 34. Step 34 is a dummy step and is not considered here. However, step 23 can be stretched out from 4 days to 8 days. The savings will be 4 × $50 = $200. Then both paths 1 and 2 will arrive at node 4 at the same time.

The step unique to path 2 is 24 (47 is also on path 1). This step may be extended by one day, at a saving of $100.

Step 47 is not unique to any path, but it is not on the critical path. It may be lengthened two days at a saving of $120.

Ideally, you stretch all paths to the same length as the critical path. That is not possible here. We have obtained all the benefits possible from stretching out steps not on the critical path. The revised project cost, step completion times, and overall completion time stand as shown in Figure 13–11.

Shortening the Critical Path

The remaining way to save money is to reduce the length of the critical path. This will run up costs associated with completing steps more rapidly, but also result in a savings of $300 of *project* time-related costs for every day the critical path (and therefore the project) is shortened. This will be desirable so long as the savings exceed the extra expense. The point to stop is where marginal cost ≤ marginal savings;

FIGURE 13-11
Revised Project Configuration

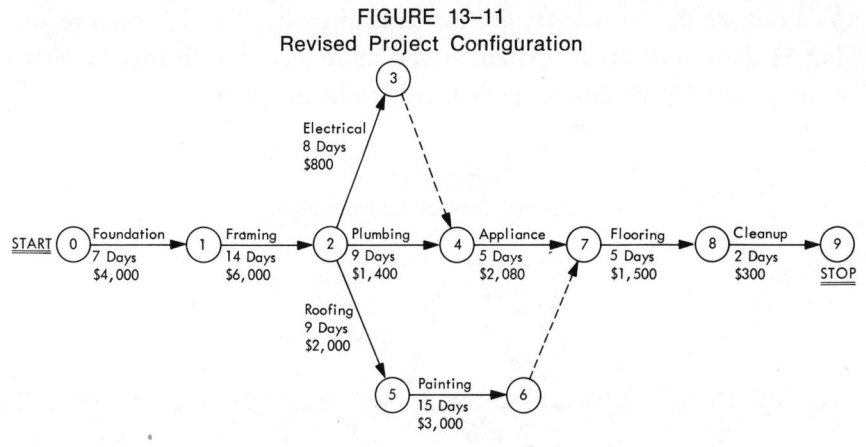

```
START →(0) Foundation →(1) Framing →(2) Plumbing →(4) Appliance →(7) Flooring →(8) Cleanup →(9) STOP
        7 Days      14 Days     9 Days       5 Days       5 Days       2 Days
        $4,000      $6,000      $1,400       $2,080       $1,500       $300
```

Electrical (2→3→4): 8 Days, $800

Roofing (2→5): 9 Days, $2,000
Painting (5→6→7): 15 Days, $3,000

Total revised cost = $36,680; Total completion time = 52 days.

that is, any further step shortening would cost more than $300 per day in this illustration. Examine Figure 13-9 again and locate this point.

Rule 2. Look for the steps that cost the *least* money to shorten, and reduce their length first. Shorten *only* steps on the critical path(s).

Step 89 will cost only $30 to shorten by 1 day ($t_e - t_l = 2 - 1 = 1$).[1] Since this step also shortens the critical path, we go ahead and shorten it. The net saving is $270.

Step 78 may be shortened by one day ($t_e - t_l = 5 - 4 = 1$) at a cost of $80, so we shorten it next. The net saving is $220.

Step 56 may be shortened by 5 days ($t_e - t_l = 15 - 10 = 5$), for a cost increment of $600 and a saving of $900 (net).

Step 01 may be shortened 3 days for a net saving of $450.

Step 12 may be shortened 4 days for a net saving of $400.

Step 25 may be shortened 5 days for a net savings of $500.

These changes produce new times to complete the critical and other paths:

Path	Time to Complete (Days)
1. 01234789	32
2. 0124789	33
3. 01256789	33

---
[1] t_e and t_l are shown in Figure 13-4.

You can see that now there are two critical paths: 2 and 3, each requiring 33 days to complete. There are no more steps which may be shortened. Figure 13–12 shows the final version of the project.

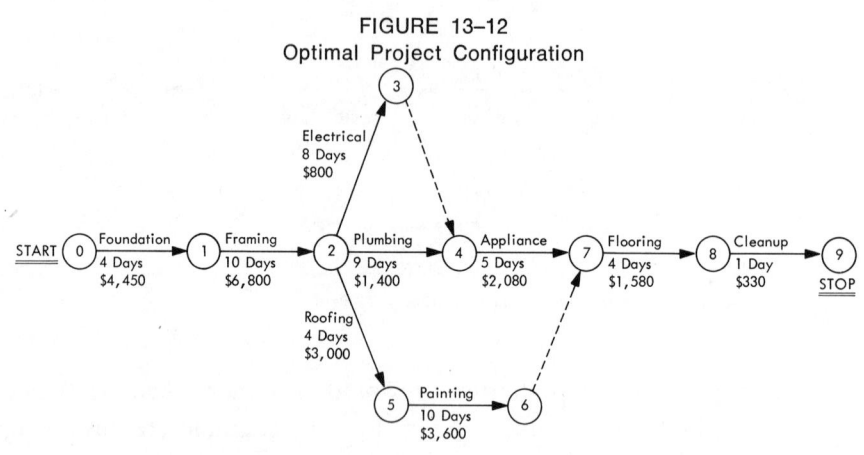

FIGURE 13–12
Optimal Project Configuration

```
START (0) --Foundation--> (1) --Framing--> (2) --Plumbing--> (4) --Appliance--> (7) --Flooring--> (8) --Cleanup--> (9)
            4 Days           10 Days         9 Days            5 Days            4 Days           1 Day         STOP
            $4,450           $6,800          $1,400            $2,080            $1,580           $330

         (3) Electrical 8 Days $800  — from (2) to (3) to (4) dashed
         (5) Roofing 4 Days $3,000 — from (2) to (5)
         (5) --Painting--> (6)  10 Days $3,600, dashed to (7)
```

Total optimal cost = $33,940; Total optimal completion time = 33 days.

Compare the optimal completion time of 33 days with the original completion time of 52 days; compare the present lowest completion cost of $33,940 with the original estimated completion cost of $37,100. You expect to build the house faster and save money doing it. This is not the same thing as making water run uphill; you did it by making commonsense judgments, based on accounting information estimates, about which steps in the project to expedite and which to delay and stretch out.

COMPUTER APPLICATIONS

The form of analysis we have demonstrated was developed in the 1950s as a way of expediting completion of military weapons systems. Cost control and analysis features were added when the technique came to be applied to nonmilitary projects.

The calculations quickly become overwhelming if you try to do them by hand on a project of any size. Even special work sheets do not guarantee you will keep track of every path and every step. Luckily, there are computer programs available for commercial computers and through computer centers that perform the calculations for you, turning out tables of step completion times and cost in only a few seconds. Therefore, you need not be an expert about the theory or technique of critical path computational routines before applying them.

CONTROL USING CRITICAL PATH ANALYSIS RESULTS

This chapter has discussed the planning phase of critical path analysis. After the planning, of course, comes the implementation. The principle of comparing actual results with planned expected results applies to project control. You use the plan to determine whether any steps are falling so far behind as to jeopardize scheduled project completion. Naturally, steps on the critical path(s) receive closest scrutiny. Responsibility center managers will compare the costs incurred on steps with the budget estimates, and if necessary implement cost control measures to curb cost overruns. Computer programs are used to make the time and cost comparisons and calculations and print out performance reports in good form which go to responsibility centers supervising the various steps. The computer programs will even indicate which if any future steps in a project should be expedited to keep the project as a whole on schedule.

SUMMARY

Critical path analysis is the most effective means known of organizing, planning, and controlling complex projects when the necessary information input is available. Its calculations are routinized and can be performed by computers, freeing managers to act on the consequences of computer output. To use critical path analysis, you must know the steps in a project, their sequence, their shortest and longest feasible completion times, and the structure of step and project costs as a whole. Critical path analysis assumes (at least in its simplest forms) linear decrease in step costs with increasing step completion time and linear increase in project-related costs as project completion time increases. Solution procedures work to achieve a minimum cost for a project by selectively expediting and stretching out steps. The output of critical path analysis contributes to operational control by providing a realistic project "budget" for comparison with actual project experience.

QUESTIONS

1. Why is there a need for project planning and control? Do you consider the information requirements for planning and control reasonable or excessive?

2. Which of the following activities might require critical path analysis:
    a) Automobile production.
    b) Office building production.
    c) Feed lot operation.
    d) Real estate office.
    e) Golf course construction.
    f) End-of-year closing of corporate accounts.
    g) Preparation of annual budget.

3. How does the behavior of a step cost differ from the behavior of mixed costs as described in Chapter 6? How are these two similar?

4. A particular step has the step total cost equal to $13,000 plus $300 for each day under 40 days required to complete it. What is the cost to complete the step in 30 days? 36 days? 42 days?

5. Which of the following costs would probably be functions of step completion time?
    a) Direct materials.
    b) Direct labor.
    c) Perishable materials.
    d) Overhead applied to the step on the basis of direct labor.
    e) Progress inspection costs.
    f) Quality control inspections.

6. Which of the following costs are probably *project* related and which are probably *step* related:
    a) Insurance on partly completed work.

b) Work or building permit and legal fees related to drawing contract.
c) Subcontractor payments.
d) Direct materials.
e) Interest expense on money borrowed to finance project.
f) Project site preparation.

7. This question illustrates computation of T_e when step completion time is a random event. Let $p(t_l) = 0.25$, $p(t_u) = 0.25$, and $p(t_e) = 0.50$. T_e is the weighted average of three time estimates. Let $t_l = 30$, $t_e = 33$, $t_u = 42$. What is T_e? What kind of probability distribution does T have?

8. Professor Smith prepares semester grades in a two-step process. The first step is to collect and average homework grades. The second step is to collect and average test grades. Smith notes the following completion times for these steps from his past records (expressed in hours):

Homework	Tests
4	3
5	3.5
3	2.5
6	5
2	1.5

Give t_l and t_u for these two steps. Do you think that these two step completion times are related in any way?

9. How would you recognize a step as a distinct entity in a project?

10. What is a critical path? What is a noncritical path? Is it possible for a project to have *no* critical path? To have more than one critical path?

11. You are a highway contractor. You have agreed to build 50 miles of four-lane concrete highway at $1,500,000 per mile. The contracting authority wants you to agree to do it in 50 working days with a 3 percent penalty for each day over that. Since under ideal conditions your crew can lay 5,280 feet of four-lane highway per day, you are inclined to agree to these terms. Can you think of any reasons you should not? (Your profit on the overall job will be, ideally, $5 million.)

12. What is a "dummy step"? Why are dummy steps necessary?

13. At node 3 of a particular project which is being planned using critical path analysis, you have this situation:

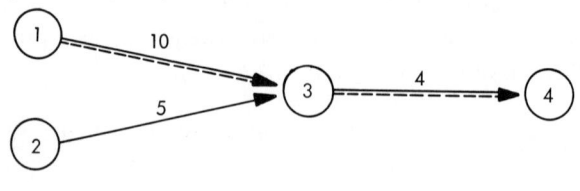

```
    (1)
       ╲  10
        ╲═════╗
         ╲    ▼
          ╲  (3) ════4════▶ (4)
         5╱
        ╱
    (2)
```

========= = Critical Path

The critical path is 1–3–4. Step 2–3 can be stretched to last 13 days, saving $100 per day. What is the maximum length for 2–3 without affecting project completion time?

14. When optimizing the total cost of a project, why is the procedure to first stretch other noncritical paths to the same length as the critical path (or as nearly so as possible), *then* compress all paths until no more savings can be achieved?

15. How is control achieved using critical path analysis? If you were asked to develop a method for applying critical path analysis, to be used by a large construction company on its projects, what would be the steps in your method?

EXERCISES

16. A certain step has costs independent of time = $32,000; costs dependent on time of $2,500 per week; and a normal completion time of 10 weeks. Compute the normal cost to complete the step.

17. Consider the step in Exercise 16. This may also be completed in any number of weeks from 8 to 12; the corresponding costs per week dependent on time are:

Completion Time for Project	Cost per Week Dependent on Time
8	$3,625
9	3,000
10	2,500
11	2,091
12	1,750

Find the total costs dependent on time for each completion time above. What is the rate of *total cost* increase per week as completion time varies?

18. A certain project consists of two activities carried out one after the other. Here are important cost data on these two steps:

Step	Completion Time	Time-Independent Costs	Time-Dependent Costs per Week
A	10 weeks	$10,000	$2,000
B	20 weeks	5,000	3,000

Step A was completed on time, at a total cost of $32,000; Step B was completed on time at a total cost of $70,000. What are the overall cost variances associated with each step? If the *actual* time independent costs were $9,000 for A and $6,000 for B, what are the variances associated with the *time-dependent* costs?

19. Refer to the data in Exercise 18. Imagine that A's completion time may vary from 8 to 12 weeks, with a total time-dependent cost of $26,000 at 8 weeks and $14,000 at 12 weeks. B's completion time may vary from 18 to 22 weeks, with a total time-dependent cost of $64,000 at 18 weeks and $56,000 at 22 weeks. What completion times for each step, considering only these costs, give the lowest total time-dependent cost?

20. Refer to the data in Exercises 18 and 19. There are costs for the project which increase as project completion time lengthens. These costs are given below:

Project (A + B) Completion Time (Weeks)	Total Costs that Increase with Passing Time
26	$ 78,000
30	90,000
34	102,000

Find the total project duration and step durations that give the lowest total project cost.

PROBLEMS

21. Nueches River Authority operates a string of lakes known for the purity of their waters. In recent years, land developers have dis-

covered this purity and built about 50,000 homes along the shores of the lakes. Tests have shown that the lake water contains *e. coli*, and the NRA has determined that septic tanks along the lakes must be inspected for proper operation. Fifty thousand septic tank inspections are a great many, and even small inefficiencies if repeated could prove expensive. Accordingly a procedure has been developed for septic tank inspection and applied in a sample of 100 homes. The results of the sample will be used to judge the reasonableness of companies bidding for the septic tank inspection contract.

The results of the sample are summarized this way (all *t*'s in hours):

Step	Start	Stop	t_l	t_e	t_u
Dummy step	3	5	0	0	0
Identification	0	1	0.20	0.30	0.45
Close-up	4	5	0.11	0.20	0.28
Sounding	1	3	0.08	0.22	0.30
Measuring	2	4	0.30	0.45	0.80
Pacing	1	2	0.19	0.39	0.70

Required:

a) What is the expected time required in all steps of one septic tank inspection if all steps are completed in their respective t_e's?

b) Draw a diagram or flowchart showing all steps in their proper relationship to one another.

c) Identify the critical path of this inspection procedure if all steps are completed in their respective t_e's. What is the elapsed time for one inspection?

d) What would be cheaper in this inspection procedure: (1) to send one man and let him do all steps, one after the other, paying him $6 per hour; or (2) to send two men and let the second man (a helper) do steps on paths other than the critical path? The first man receives $6 per hour; the helper receives $3 per hour. Remember that the helper is paid whether he is idle or not.

e) Would your answer to (d) change if all steps were done in their respective t_u's? (Remember that the critical path steps may not be the same.)

22. Master Builders, Inc., a builder and developer of large subdivisions, has created a critical path analysis of the "Bedford," its new best-selling model. This analysis is summarized as follows:

Step No.	Step Name	Average Time to Complete (Days)	Extra Cost per Day to Shorten	Extra Savings per Day to Extend
01......	Foundation	10	$ 80	$ 40
12......	Framing	20	50	40
23......	Roofing	5	150	100
24......	Interior	20	100	60
45......	Carpeting	4	200	100
35......	Painting	12	90	40
56......	Finishing	8	70	40

Required:

a) Find the critical path. How many days will the "Bedford" normally require to complete?

b) Suppose that a rainstorm delays start of the roofing operation for 10 days (this does not affect the Interior operation, which proceeds). Has the critical path from that point forward changed? If so, to what?

c) For each day in excess of 62 days that a "Bedford" requires for completion, Master Builders must pay a $100 penalty to the buyer. Keeping this in mind, Master Builders puts you, the critical path expert, to work during the rainstorm to figure the most economical schedule for completing this home when the rain stops (such a schedule need not require 62 days to completion). Give the new schedule. You may lengthen or shorten any steps by as much as three days each.

d) Under the new schedule developed in (c), how much will the penalty be? How much will the home cost over or under what its cost would have been with no rainstorm and all steps completed in the average time?

e) Suppose that you were ill during the rainstorm and could not work on this problem for Master Builders. What would be the difference between the total cost of the home and penalties using the (c) schedule and the total cost of the home and penalties if the rainstorm delay was simply accommodated into the normal schedule without changing any of the subsequent steps?

f) If the critical path analysis cost $100, did it pay for itself? What was the net benefit of using critical path analysis?

23. The Littleton Oil Company has developed a plan for "cleaning up" its oil refinery. The changes must be made in a proper sequence since the refinery operates as a system. The State Environmental Control Agency has obtained a court order threatening Littleton with $2,000 per day in fines after April 30 for every day the refinery operates in its present polluting state. The project begins on March 11. The steps in making the changes are:

Step No.	t_l	t_o	Cost if Completed in t_e	Cost per Day to Shorten t_e
14	10	16	$ 9,000	$ 130
01	2	3	500	20
02	6	9	2,000	100
03	4	8	1,000	100
23	0	0	0	0
15	18	24	40,000	1,000
24	10	19	30,000	1,500
46	20	28	60,000	1,400
56	26	32	50,000	2,500
35	8	12	35,000	1,800

Step costs are increased if a step is shortened and decreased if a step is lengthened.

Required:

a) Find each possible path through this project.
b) Designate the critical path. Designate the length of each path. Assume each step completed in its own t_e.
c) If each step is completed in its respective t_e, what will be the fine (if any) paid?
d) If the critical path is to be reduced by three days, which step on it will be expedited first? If the project is to be reduced by nine days, which steps will be expedited? DO NOT try to find the project minimum cost!
e) If the amount of the fine represents a fair measure of the social costs of this plant operating in a polluting manner, is it socially responsible for Littleton Oil to so operate and pay the fine?

24. Freebies Service Company provides maintenance of large electrical generators. One step, the disassembly, cleaning, and reassembly of windings, is labor-intensive and can be completed in more or less time depending on the desires of the maintenance manager. However, if the step is performed too quickly, there are equipment losses, misplacement of parts, and other inefficiencies. On one type of generator, the manager has prepared this table showing labor hours as a function of the number of days in which the step is completed:

Total Labor Hours Required to Maintain Windings	Number of Days in Which Winding Maintenance Done
100	2
90	3
80	4
82	5
85	6
90	7

Required:

a) Plot these figures on a sheet of graph paper, assuming that *days* (D) is the independent variable and that *hours* (H) is the dependent variable.
b) Determine two equations (which are linear of the form $H = A + BD$ and intersect between $D = 3$ and $D = 6$) representing the relationship.
c) Determine one equation of the same form representing the relationship.
d) Indicate which of the above, (b) or (c), you would prefer for use in a critical path analysis.
e) If maintenance work costs Freebies Service $50 per hour to perform, what is the additional cost of going from three days to two days for this step? What is the cost of going from three days to five days for this step? Use the equations in (b) to compute your answers.

25. Stuthers Margolean Company remodels restaurants. The crew moves from restaurant to restaurant, applying pretty much the same process and decor in each one. Because the process is routine, the company's bids are modest and profit good. The company has discovered that if its remodeling crew works at a rate of 36 hours per day, the profit is $14 per hour above direct and indirect costs. As the number of hours the crew must work per day goes up, the profit changes as shown here:

Hours Worked per Day	SM Profit per Hour
30	$13.33
32	13.43
34	13.60
36	14.00
38	12.90
40	12.00
42	10.95

Just as work begins on a new 720-hour job on April 2, the company is offered an additional 792-hour job. This job would offer a profit of $11,880—more than usual for this size job. The only condition is that work *must begin* on the new job on April 19 (leaving only 18 days for the present job).

Required:

a) Determine whether the new job ought to be undertaken.
b) What total profit on the proposed new job would make it just barely acceptable?

26. Divers Salvage Company made an agreement with the Colozuela government to salvage sunken Spanish galleons lying offshore its coast. The agreement called for work to be completed in 60 days, with the government reimbursing the company only for costs incurred as a result of bad weather. The salvage company would take as compensation 10 percent of all treasure recovered. If the work took longer than 60 days, the agreement was canceled and Divers Salvage would receive no treasure, only reimbursement for bad weather delays.

The salvage proceeded in three steps:

Step No.	Step Name	Estimated Duration (Days)	Minimum Duration	Maximum Duration	Expected Cost
01	Location	10	8	15	$14,000
12	Setup	20	15	25	30,000
23	Recovery	30	20	50	45,000

If any step is shortened, extra costs are $2,000 per day. But if a step is extended past the estimated duration, there are savings of $500 per day. There are no project-related costs.

Of course the weather acted up, and the company suspended operations on the fifth day of the setup step. After a 10-day delay, the step was resumed. The salvage project was completed on the 60th day. Total costs were $90,000.

Required:

a) Compute the total cost of the salvage project if completed in the estimated step durations.

b) Compute the total cost of the salvage project considering the delay. What is the difference between this figure and the one in (a)?

c) When Divers Salvage billed the Colozuelan government for the difference computed in (b), the government responded with an offer of $1,000, saying, "That is the difference between your actual costs and the costs you predicted before you started; that must be what the bad weather cost you." Comment on the positions of the government and the salvage company. Why do you suppose actual costs of salvage were so much less than the estimate in (b)?

27. Stampic Construction Company is the contractor for a government office building in an African nation. Plans have been made for the building's foundation. Before the foundation was begun, the costs were estimated as follows, based on completion time of 90 days.

Direct materials*	$700,000
Direct labor†	900,000
Supervision	1,000 per day
Indirect variable overhead (incurred for this job)	2,000 per day
Financing and insurance	2,000 per day

* The company estimates that due to a local shortage of building materials, $600 per day worth of materials will be stolen from the site. The figure above takes this into account for 90 days.

† As part of its contract with the government, Stampic must hire local workers for the entire completion time of the building. There is a shortage of skilled workers. Stampic would like to hire fewer workers (who would be more efficient) and take longer to build the foundation. The company believes this would reduce direct labor costs by $10,000 per day of completion time extension beyond 90 days. If the company must expedite the foundation, it will have to hire additional low-skill workers, and its labor costs will *rise* by $1,000 per day.

Stampic actually completed the foundation in 95 days, at a total cost of $2,100,000.

Required:

a) If the company had planned a 90-day completion time, determine whether any of the cost of completion could be attributable to the 5-day construction delay.

b) If the company had planned to complete the foundation in 95 days, might it have saved money as compared with the actual completion cost (that is, compare expected cost for 95 days with actual cost at 95 days)?

c) Do you see any value in comparing actual performance with a standard prepared *after* the event is over—with an *expost* standard?

28. Fynewyne Company is developing a new winery in Arkadelphia, a state with considerable vintnerian potential. Ivan Bluetoes, the chief winemaker, has developed a short plan for getting the winery going:

Step No.	Step Name	Average Time to Complete	Extra Cost per Week to Shorten	Extra Savings per Week to Extend
01	Harvesting	14 weeks	$300	$100
12	Fermenting	10	500	200
23	Bottling	4	100	100

No step in this process can be accelerated or extended more than two weeks from the average time.

Required:

Find the completion times for each step that produce the lowest cost, assuming that the costs of operating the winery are $400 per week.

29. Treetop Airlines has bought some new jets and must train its flight crews to operate them. Connie Trail, in charge of personnel, has decided to design a program for this purpose. In the program are seven modules to be covered. *Navigation* must precede all other modules, and *emergency procedures* must be the last module covered. After navigation, both *landing* and *instruments* begin together. *Preflight checks* and *inflight checks* must start at the same time. *Postflight checks* must directly follow preflight checks. Inflight checks and instruments must both directly precede emergency procedures. No other module may be covered at the same time as navigation or emergency procedures. Landing must directly precede preflight checks. Each module will receive a five-week treatment.

Human learning rates cannot be hurried, but the modules could be made more intensive by using learning machines, computer instruction, etc., at a cost per week saved of $3,000. No module may be reduced to less than three weeks' duration. No savings occur if a module is stretched.

If a crew is out of service in the school, the airline is losing about $5,000 per week in profits from passengers who would be attracted by the jets. Thus, Connie Trail would like to get the program over with the pilots on the line as quickly as possible.

Required:

a) Draw the network diagram for the program and label each module.
b) Determine the length of the program if each module is taught in five weeks.
c) Determine the length of the program which produces the maximum savings and identify the modules which are reduced, and how much they are reduced.

30. Robert Keding has agreed to supervise the Midville Water Festival. Part of this festival is a water parade in which decorated floats pass by stands full of spectators. Last year, the water parade was a disaster as boats jammed the launching area, rammed each other jockeying for a position in line, and ran out of gas or caught fire due to last minute hurrying and carelessness. Mr. Keding is determined to avoid any such thing this year through careful planning.

Once a boat is in its position in the parade line, there are no more problems. Here is a diagram showing how that is done:

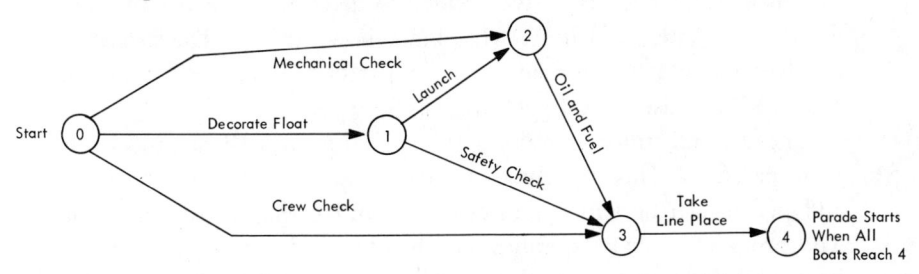

The estimated average time for each step is given below. Unless otherwise stated, any number of floats may do a step at the same time.

	(Hour per Float)
Mechanical check	0.3
Decorate float	5.0
Crew check	0.5
Launch (two floats may be launched at once)	0.4
Safety check	0.2
Oil and fuel replenishment	0.4
Take line place (one float at a time)	0.1

There are 20 floats scheduled to be in the parade, which will start about 7 P.M. Mr. Keding needs to answer the questions below.

Required:

a) How long will the average float require to become ready for the water parade?
b) How long will the floats require to organize into a line?
c) When will the first float have to begin launching if the parade does start at 7 P.M.?
d) If all the boats are to be safety-checked in a period of 1 hour, how many crews must be available to do the checking if each crew checks one boat at a time?

DECISION CASE 13–1: ELECTRONIC DIGITS, INC.

Electronic Digits, Inc. is a diversified consulting firm which has long advised other companies how to improve their management processes, but only recently realized how inefficient its own management has been. The management officials have decided to determine whether the company needs a computer, and if so, what kind, how big, etc. The determination involves many steps, and in order to perform it properly the company has decided to use critical path analysis.

One step identified is writing the special-purpose data processing program packages. This step comes after a computer system has been selected and before actual delivery, installation, and operation of the computer. The program package specifications would be drawn up; general guidelines and rules to assure the compatibility of all programs with each other would be decided. Then each package would be flowcharted, written in a programming language, tested and revised until all errors were eliminated, and added to the computer-available set of programs for general use later when the computer was fully operational.

Electronic Digits' information systems management reported that these programs could be done in 40 days at a total cost of $30,000, or over 90 days at a total cost of about $20,000. The tentative plan was to write the programs in 50 days. The costs cited consisted of computer rental time to checkout programs and the net contribution on consulting fees lost because the programmers were working for the company and not for clients who could be billed for the work.

Required:

a) Identify t_l, t_e, and t_u for this situation.
b) Give an expression for the cost of this step as a function of completion time t and expected completion time t_e.
c) Give the cost to complete the step in t_e days.
d) Imagine that the step is scheduled for completion in 50 days, as indicated. After 30 days a specialized program-writing firm offers to complete the step for a fee of $12,000 in 20 more days. Should this offer be accepted? Assume that all time-independent costs amount to $10,000 and have already been incurred, and that time-dependent costs are incurred in equal amounts each day throughout the duration of the step.

BIBLIOGRAPHY

Books

Stilian, Gabriel N., et al. *PERT: A New Management Planning and Control Technique.* New York: American Management Association, 1962.

Wiest, Jerome, and Levy, F. K. *Management Guide to PERT-CPM.* Englewood Cliffs, N.J.: Prentice-Hall, Inc., 1972.

Articles

Bawly, Dan A., and Dotan, Joseph M. "Using PERT in Accounting Reports," *Management Services,* July–August 1970.

DeCoster, Don T. "Pert-Cost: The Challenge," *Management Services,* May–June 1964.

Schoderbek, Peter P. "Is PERT/Cost Dead?" *Management Services,* November–December 1968.

14

Production Mix and Profit Maximization

CHAPTER 3 presented the dynamic analysis of a business entity. There you learned the basic formulas and concepts that enable businessmen to predict the accounting profit response of companies to new products, selling price changes, capacity changes, direct cost changes, and the economic phenomena which are the cause of such events. That analysis works only when there is just one product or activity. Normally, many activities are carried out together. The activity mix is a major controllable variable in most companies. To assume it is constant is to forego use of a powerful profit-influencing tool, and also unnecessary.

In this chapter you discover linear programming, a simple and useful method of relating accounting profit to degree of participation in different alternative business activities. Here are some of the questions you will see linear programming help answer for a company:

1. What activity mix will produce the largest contribution margin?
2. What is the least expensive way to carry out specific required activities?
3. If the contribution margins on different activities change, should the activity schedule be changed to obtain more profit?
4. Should activities be dropped from or added to a program?
5. How should production capacity be increased or decreased to improve total contribution margin?

Computer programs to solve linear programming problems are widely available; you may never have to solve such a problem of any size yourself, and you will be able to use linear programming in decisions before you understand all the calculations involved. But you must know (and this chapter tells you) how to successfully approach a problem using linear programming and how to identify information describing these problems with corresponding elements of the linear programming model.

Simplifying Assumption—Linearity

The simplifying assumption that makes linear programming models possible is *linearity*. This assumption manifests itself in two ways:

1. The profit or cost associated with one unit of product or activity is the same regardless of when during a period that unit occurs, or whether it is the first, last, or other unit of the period.
2. The resource inputs to a unit of activity are the same regardless of when during a period that unit occurs, or which units of resource inputs are actually included in the activity.

An economist has a way of stating these effects: "Constant returns to scale and no production efficiencies or disefficiencies." Real situations are full of exceptions, but often these can be ignored in order to obtain an easily solved model that gives useful information.

CONSTRAINTS AND CAPACITIES

A linear programming model consists of three sections—

1. A set of constraints describing availabilities, limitations, and relationships of resources to products.
2. Constraints requiring that all variables have values equal to or greater than zero.
3. An objective function—maximized or minimized—which is a weighted linear sum of all the decision variables in the problem.

Constraints are explained in this section; the objective function is explained in the following section.

Illustrative Example

Let us take an illustrative situation involving the Richer Chemical Corporation, which makes commercial organic fertilizers. There are three steps to the manufacturing process: *cooking, drying,* and *packing.* Each process has its own capacity, and each organic fertilizer made has its own slightly different production process. Each fertilizer requires these same three basic steps, however.

Constraints Arising from Productive Capacity

Fertilizer production is planned for one week at a time. Only one 40-hour shift is worked. The cooking and drying processes therefore each have 40 hours per week of operating time. Fertilizer is made by the ton. At the present time, Richer Chemical Corporation is only making two kinds of fertilizer, which we shall refer to as type X and type Y. Both of these fertilizers go through cooking and drying but require different amounts of time. Figure 14–1 gives the times required for cooking and drying per ton of type X and type Y fertilizer made.

FIGURE 14–1
Cooking and Drying Times for Fertilizers X and Y

	Fertilizer	
	Type X	*Type Y*
Cooking	0.1 hour	0.2 hour
Drying	0.2 hour	0.1 hour
Packing	0.16 hour	0.16 hour

Each fertilizer process may operate up to 40 hours per week. We can make "time balances" which account for all the time available for cooking, drying, and packing:

Cooking:

    Hours spent   Hours spent
    cooking type X + cooking type Y ≤ 40 hours per week   (14–1)
    fertilizer   fertilizer

Drying:

Hours spent drying type X fertilizer + Hours spent drying type Y fertilizer ≤ 40 hours per week (14-2)

Packing:

Hours spent packing type X fertilizer + Hours spent packing type Y fertilizer ≤ 40 hours per week (14-3)

The actual number of hours spent cooking type X fertilizer is $0.1 \times$ (number of tons of type X fertilizer made). Similarly, the actual hours spent cooking type Y fertilizer is $0.2 \times$ (number of tons of type Y fertilizer made).

Let us choose the symbol X to mean the number of tons of type X fertilizer made per week, and the symbol Y to mean the number of tons of type Y fertilizer made per week. Then the cooking time balance will be:

$$0.1X + 0.2Y \leq 40 \qquad (14\text{-}4)$$

You can quickly construct the symbolic representation of the drying and packing time balances using the same principles:

$$0.2X + 0.1Y \leq 40 \qquad (14\text{-}5)$$
$$0.16X + 0.16Y \leq 40 \qquad (14\text{-}6)$$

Constraints Describing Nonnegativity

Now, X and Y might either or both be zero, but neither could ever be negative—logic, experience, and the second law of thermodynamics forbid it, but mathematics will not unless we expressly so state. So you also have the statements:

$$X \geq 0 \qquad (14\text{-}7)$$
$$Y \geq 0 \qquad (14\text{-}8)$$

Equations (14-4), (14-5), (14-6), (14-7), and (14-8) describe the technology and physical characteristics of Richer Chemical's fertilizer production process. Because the relations they describe act to

406   An Introduction to Accounting for Decision Making and Control

constrain the ways in which that process can operate, we name these equations and others like them, *constraints*.

A *constraint* is a symbolic representation of a restriction on the values which the controllable variables in a linear programming model may assume.

The system of constraints for Richer Chemical can be plotted on rectangular coordinates, such as those in Figure 14–2. Let X be the hori-

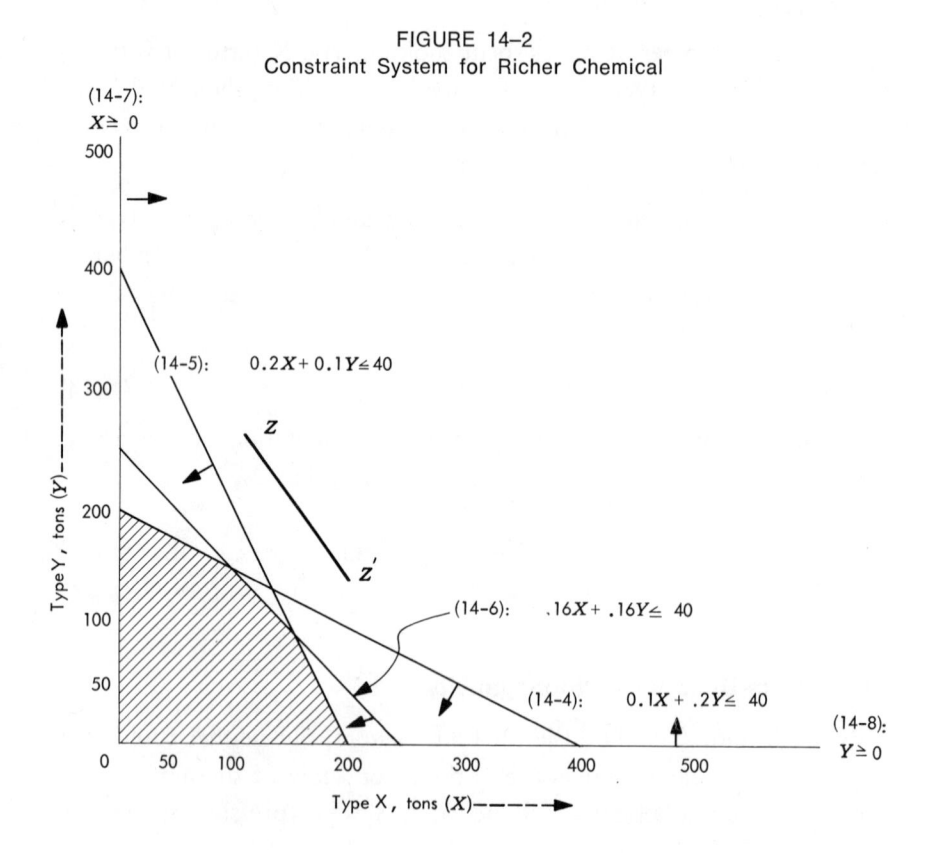

FIGURE 14–2
Constraint System for Richer Chemical

zontal axis and Y be the vertical axis. The graph shows *regions* or areas that correspond to the constraints. For example, all the area *above* the X-axis corresponds to the constraint $Y \geq 0$. All the area to the *right* of the Y-axis corresponds to the constraints $X \geq 0$. Thus, the upper right quadrant is the area that satisfies the two "nonnegativity" constraints, (14–7) and (14–8). Similarly, the area below and to the left of the line labeled (14–4) is the area represented by the inequality $0.1X + 0.2Y \leq 40$. The area below and to the left of the line labeled (14–5) is the area which satisfies the inequality $0.2X + 0.1Y \leq 40$. The area below and to the left of (14–6) satisfies *that* constraint.

All of these areas come together and overlap each other in the cross-hatched area in the lower left-hand corner. The points on the border of and inside this cross-hatched area satisfy all the inequality constraints. Any of them would be a possible plan of operation for Richer Chemical Corporation's fertilizer plant. For example, the point $X = 50$, $Y = 50$ is within this cross-hatched area. You can insert these values for X and Y into the equations and verify that the plant could indeed produce 50 tons of type X and 50 tons of type Y fertilizer:

$$0.1(50) + 0.2(50) = 15 \text{ hours} \leq 40 \text{ hours cooking time}$$
$$0.2(50) + 0.1(50) = 15 \text{ hours} \leq 40 \text{ hours drying time}$$
$$0.16(50) + 0.16(50) = 16 \text{ hours} \leq 40 \text{ hours packing time}$$

Thus under this plan there would be *slack capacity*—25 hours of idle time for the cooker, 25 hours for the dryer, and 24 hours for the packer.

This is not the best plan for operating the fertilizer plant. But in order to know the best plan, we need to know more about the cost and price structure of Richer's fertilizer products.

OBJECTIVE FUNCTION

The selling prices of types X and Y fertilizer are:

```
Type X . . . . . . . . . .   $120 per ton
Type Y . . . . . . . . . .    130 per ton
```

The variable costs of manufacturing these fertilizers, to the extent they can be identified with a specific fertilizer, are:

```
Type X . . . . . . . . . .   $ 80 per ton
Type Y . . . . . . . . . .    100 per ton
```

By subtracting the variable costs from the selling prices, we compute the *contribution margin* on each fertilizer:

```
Type X . . . . . . . . . .   $40 per ton = C_x
Type Y . . . . . . . . . .    30 per ton = C_y
```

The total contribution Z is given by the function:

$$Z = 40X + 30Y \tag{14–9}$$

We are at last ready to make a formal statement of the problem:

Maximize	$Z = 40X + 30Y$	(14–9)
Subject to	$0.1X + 0.2Y \leq 40$	(14–4)
	$0.2X + 0.1Y \leq 40$	(14–5)
	$0.16X + 0.16Y \leq 40$	(14–6)
	$X \geq 0$	(14–7)
	$Y \geq 0$	(14–8)

This statement says that the problem is to find values of X and Y which satisfy the first three constraints (called *technological* constraints since they describe the technology of the fertilizer production process) as well as the last two *nonnegativity* constraints, and also maximize (14–9), the objective function. If Z is made as large as possible, the contribution from fertilizer activities will be maximized by the corresponding values of X and Y. Note that fixed costs, which are a function of time rather than activity mix, are not considered when constructing linear programming models.

GRAPHICAL SOLUTION

Return to the graphical solution of this problem in Figure 14–2. The line ZZ' in the center of the graph has the same slope as the equation $Z = 40X + 30Y$. A line such as ZZ' is plotted by assuming a value for Z, finding any two points corresponding to this equation, plotting those two points on the graph, and drawing the straight line corresponding to them.

> Thus, we let $Z = 12,000$. Two points which satisfy $40X + 30Y = 12,000$ are $(X = 0, Y = 400)$ and $(X = 300, Y = 0)$. Any other two points satisfying the equation would also be satisfactory. When these two points are plotted on Figure 14–2 and connected, the line ZZ' is seen to be part of that line.

The significance for the graphical solution of the line ZZ' and its slope is this: the further to the right or upward a line with the same slope as ZZ' is drawn, the larger is the value of Z, the objective function. *The only limit to how high or how far to the right the objective func-*

tion line may be pushed is the requirement that it pass through at least one point in the shaded area or on its boundaries, which represent the limitations of the constraints on the solution.

Clearly, the point which produces the largest value of Z must lie on the boundary of the shaded area, for if it lay inside the shaded area Z could be pushed higher or further to the right. In short, to solve the problem *find the Z line which is highest and furthest to the right and still just touches the boundary of the shaded area. The point of tangency gives the values of X and Y which are the solution.*

Let us proceed to the graphical solution of the problem before us. Do this by slowly bringing ZZ' downward and to the left until it *just touches* the area of acceptable solutions (use a ruler or index card to get a straight line; move the ruler down until it just touches the shaded area; keep it parallel to ZZ'). This *tangency* occurs at the corner caused by the intersection of (14–5) and (14–6) and is the point ($X = 150$, $Y = 100$). Therefore the solution to this linear programming problem is $X = 150$ and $Y = 100$; that is, in the real world, produce 150 tons per week of type X fertilizer and 100 tons per week of type Y fertilizer. To show that these values satisfy the technological constraints, insert them into (14–4) (14–5), and (14–6).

$$0.1(150) + 0.2(100) = 35 \leq 50 \quad (14\text{–}4)$$
$$0.2(150) + 0.1(100) = 40 \leq 40 \quad (14\text{–}5)$$
$$0.16(150) + 0.16(100) = 40 \leq 40 \quad (14\text{–}6)$$

The constraints are all satisfied. Note that (14–4) is satisfied as an inequality; that is, there are five hours of idle time in the cooking process. This idle time is unavoidable if contribution is to be maximized by producing type X and type Y fertilizers. A reasonable step for management to take would be to sell or lease this surplus capacity to others or attempt to eliminate it and its corresponding period-fixed costs.[1]

---

[1] The solution will always be on the boundary of the area containing the points satisfying the constraint system. In fact, this is critical in solving complex linear programming problems. We can go even further and say that the solution will lie at a "corner" of the area satisfying all constraints. Thus, in complex problems you need only systematically identify all the "corners" of the area satisfying all constraints, compute the value of Z for each one, and choose the variable values corresponding to the "corner" which produces the highest value of Z.

ADDITIONAL PLANNING INFORMATION

What additional information can we gain from the linear programming model of the Richer Chemical Company? All of the questions on page 402 can be answered.

1. Activity Mix Producing Largest Contribution Margin. Refer to the preceding section and the solution, $X = 150$ and $Y = 100$.

2. Least Expensive Way to Carry Out Required Activities. In the illustration as carried to this point, there is no "required" activity. But suppose Richer Chemical Company was obligated by contract to supply 200 tons of type X fertilizer, and the direct costs of the three input processes were known. Then the objective would be to make the required amount of fertilizer at the lowest total cost. This is called a *minimization problem*. The constraints are usually of the form (left-hand side) $\geq$ (a constant). The line representing the objective function must be moved as close as possible to the point (0, 0) and still pass through one point in the area of points satisfying all constraints. The latter area does *not* include the origin in a minimization problem.

3. Adjusting Activity Mix to Changes in Activity Contributions. First of all, you can determine whether a change in the selling price or manufacturing cost of type X or type Y fertilizer would affect the weekly production mix. To illustrate, let us choose two new sets of values for the contribution margins on type X and type Y and recompute the optimum product mix. These sets are:

	Type X	Type Y
Contribution set I	40	53.3
Contribution set II	40	35
(Original contribution set)	(40)	(30)

In Figure 14-3 we have plotted ZZ', the original objective function, II' ($Z_I = 40X + 53.3Y$), and II II' ($Z_{II} = 40X + 35Y$).

We have moved the original objective function line ZZ' down to pass through the solution point in Figure 14-3. The objective function II II', which has a contribution margin per ton of type Y of $35 instead of $30, also passes through the same solution point as ZZ'. This means that despite the $5 increase in margin per ton of type Y, the weekly

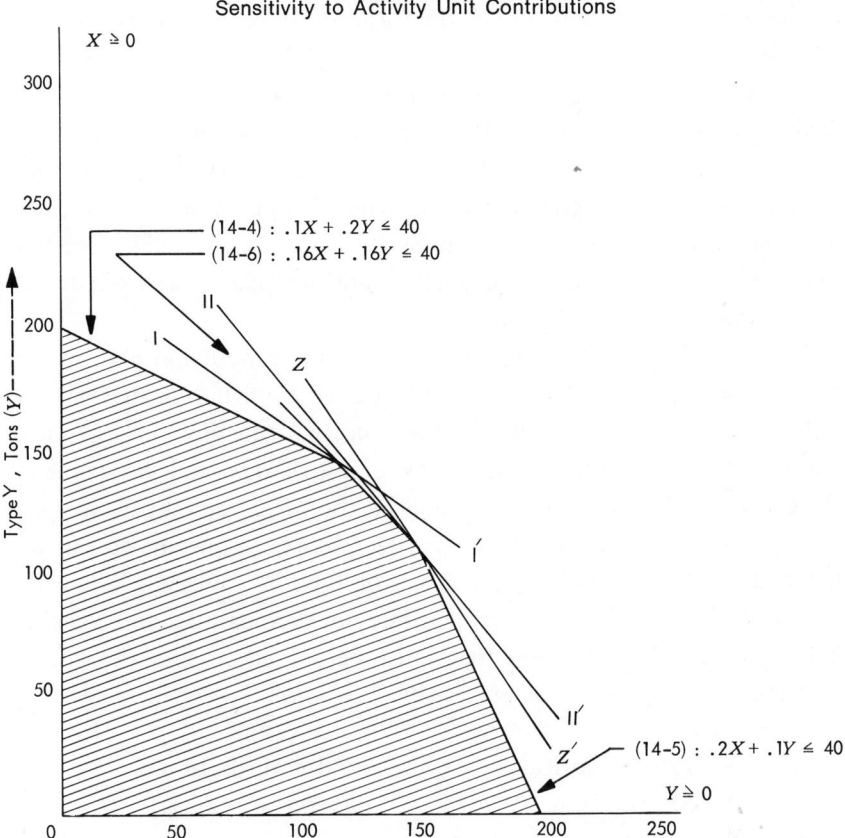

FIGURE 14-3
Sensitivity to Activity Unit Contributions

$X \geq 0$

(14-4) : $.1X + .2Y \leq 40$
(14-6) : $.16X + .16Y \leq 40$
(14-5) : $.2X + .1Y \leq 40$
$Y \geq 0$

production mix should remain unchanged. The value of Z increases from 9,000 to 9,500 dollars, but the mix itself is unchanged at $X = 150$ and $Y = 100$.

The objective function II' passes through a different point; however, $X = 100$ and $Y = 150$. This corresponds to changing the production mix from 150 to 100 tons of type X and from 100 to 150 tons of type Y. This change was brought about by a $13.30 increase in the contribution margin for type Y.

When the contribution margin per ton of type Y increased to a critical point when compared with the contribution margin on type

X, the production mix was shifted. Before this critical point was reached, no shift was made. After the critical point, the *entire* shift was made.

The shift also changed the utilization of capacities. Before the shift, cooking capacity was idle. After the shift, all cooking capacity is in use but drying capacity is idle. Thus, shifts in relative contribution margins may, if not critical, produce no change in production mix; or, if critical, require a change in production mix as well as changes in capacity utilization which may have to be anticipated well in advance of the production mix change.

Can you identify the contributions when the production plan should change? At the critical point, the relation of contribution margins for type X and type Y is such that the objective function line is exactly parallel to the line representing constraint (14–6)—and *any* point on the constraint line would have produced the *same* value of Z. Imagine that the contribution on type X fertilizer remains constant at $40 per ton and that the contribution per ton of type Y increases. When the slopes of ZZ' and (14–6) are equal, the lines are parallel and coincide. The appropriate proportion that must be solved to find the critical contribution on type Y that makes this happen is

$$\frac{\text{Type Y critical contribution}}{\underbrace{0.16}_{\substack{\text{(Coefficient of } Y \\ \text{in [14-6])}}}} = \frac{\overbrace{\$40}^{\substack{\text{(Old contribution} \\ \text{per ton of type X)}}}}{\underbrace{0.16}_{\substack{\text{(Coefficient of } X \\ \text{in [14-6])}}}} \qquad (14\text{--}10)$$

$$\text{Type Y critical contribution} = \$40$$

For any type Y contribution over $40, 150 tons of Y would be produced (of course, there is also a value for type Y contribution which would cause NO type X to be produced and 200 tons of type Y to be produced). It is important that the management information system be able to distinguish when this or other critical changes have occurred, to permit adjustments in production mix. It is similarly important not to think the changes have occurred if they haven't—with the attendant unnecessary production mix changes.

To complete this illustration, let us find the *lower* critical limit on the type Y contribution margin. The appropriate proportion this time is:

$$\frac{\text{Type Y critical contribution}}{0.1 \text{ (Coefficient of Y in [14–5])}} = \frac{\$40 \text{ (Old contribution per ton of type X)}}{0.2 \text{ (Coefficient of X in [14–5])}} \quad (14\text{–}11)$$

$$\text{Type Y critical contribution} = \$20$$

Recall that (14–5) is the constraint whose boundary is below and to the right of the original solution point. Its slope is more negative than that of the equation for Z. The range of contribution on type Y when type X contribution is constant at $40 is

$$(\text{Lower}) \ \$20 \leq \text{Margin on type Y} \leq \$40 \ (\text{upper})$$

and so long as the margin on type Y remains within these limits, the original optimal production mix will remain at ($X = 150, Y = 100$).

To show how these limits can be related to decisions, here is the decision rule assuming type X contribution is constant:

Type Y Contribution	Weekly Production Schedule	
	Tons of X	Tons of Y
0–$20	200	0
$20–$40	150	100
$40–$80	100	150
$80+	0	200

These bounds are valid only if *one* margin is changed (that of Y) and *all* others are held constant. Advanced techniques exist for determining the ranges of validity for margins when two or more change at the same time.

The advantage of knowing these ranges is illustrated by this brief episode from the history of Richer Chemical Company:

Richer Chemical's major competitor was Green Valley Fertilizer Company, which also makes and sells type X and type Y fertilizer.

On March 1, Green Valley announced a major decrease in the price of type Y fertilizer. Since Green Valley sold nearly 90 percent of all the type Y fertilizer sold in the market, Richer Chemical would have to follow the price leader and decrease its price also. The price decrease worked out to a new margin on type Y for Richer of $22 per ton.

"Well," said the president of Richer Chemical, "now that type Y is so much less profitable, perhaps we should attempt to make and sell a great deal less of it than we were when the margin on it was $30. After all, the margin on type X fertilizer remains unchanged—so it seems that a more efficient use of our facilities would be to use them to make more type X fertilizer, and less type Y fertilizer."

You are familiar with linear programming analysis. Quickly you show the president that no change from the present production mix of 150 tons of type X and 100 tons of type Y is necessary; that this production mix still produces the largest possible total contribution margin.

Active businesses are often faced with such decisions, precipitated by changes in market prices for products or product inputs. Linear programming gives decision makers information they can obtain no other way—information concerning the profitability of proposed production mix changes in such circumstances. The accounting responsibility is to define the basic cost and price information required by the linear programming model, then interpret the model output (through decision rules) to management.

4. *Adding New or Dropping Old Activities.* Often the decision arises: should an old product continue to be made? Should a new product be added to the line currently marketed? Assume that all the products, old and new, are earning revenues in excess of their direct costs and that in one or more respects the company is operating at capacity. Then the decision rule to follow is:

Decision Rule: If an activity change (adding or dropping activities) will *increase* the value of Z, the change should be made.

In a problem of the sort represented by the Richer Chemical Company, scarce resources such as drying and packing time (remember that there is a surplus of cooking capacity) are being employed to produce the maximum total contribution margin. Each scarce resource contributes its share (by imparting value to the products) to the total contribution margin. In a linear programming model this value can be identified for each scarce resource represented by a constraint in the problem formulation.

Example. Let C = value per hour of cooking capacity, D = value per hour of drying capacity, and P = value per hour of packing capacity, all for Richer Chemical when the optimum program as explained earlier is implemented. Further, we know (by a process to be partly explained later) that the values of these variables are:

C = $0 (remember not all cooking capacity is used)
D = $100 per hour
P = $125 per hour

To assure yourself that these are correct values, you might hypothesize that the total contribution margin must be the same as the value it imparts to all the resources used to produce it. The value of Z, the total contribution margin, is:

$40 per ton of type X × 150 tons of type X
+ $30 per ton of type Y × 100 tons of type Y = $9,000   (14-12)

The value of all resources, using C, D, and P as defined above, is:

$0 per hour of cooking capacity × 40 hours
+ $100 per hour of drying capacity × 40 hours
+ $125 per hour of cooking capacity × 40 hours = $9,000   (14-13)

Further, no product may have resources included in it which have a value larger than its contribution margin. For type X,

$0 per hour of cooking capacity × 0.1 hours per ton type X
+ $100 per hour of drying capacity
× 0.2 hours per ton type X
+ $125 per hour of packing capacity
× 0.16 hours per ton type X
= $40 *per ton type* X = margin on type X   (14-14)

For type Y,

$0 per hour of cooking capacity × 0.2 hours per ton type Y
+ $100 per hour of drying capacity
× 0.1 hours per ton type Y
+ $125 per hour of packing capacity
× 0.16 hours per ton type Y

= *$30 per ton type Y* = margin on type Y   (14–15)

The values of C, D, and P are sometime called *shadow prices* because they tell the additional contribution of units of scarce resources in a linear programming problem.

Now imagine that Richer chemical is considering a new product: let it be called type Z fertilizer. This material would have to be made with existing capacities, and would require these inputs:

Cooking	0.2 hours per ton
Drying	0.3 hours per ton
Packing	0.2 hours per ton

Except for cooking, these resources would have to be obtained by *not making* type X and type Y mixes, which would entail a loss of contribution margin. The original decision rule then becomes:

Make a change in the activity mix if the benefit from the change is greater than the loss from the change.

The loss per ton of type Z fertilizer made is:

0.2 cooking hours per ton × $0 per cooking hour
+ 0.3 drying hours per ton × $100 per drying hour
+ 0.2 packing hours per ton × $125 per packing hour

= *$55 per ton of type Z*   (14–16)

Remember, this loss is due to decreased ability to make type X and type Y fertilizers.

The benefit per ton of type Z is its contribution margin. If this benefit is more than $55 per ton, Richer Chemical should make type Z. If this benefit is less than $55 per ton, type Z should not be made. Thus, if the margin per ton of type Z is $50, type Z should not be made; capacities are being more effectively used to make type X and type Y fertilizer.

Re-solving the program would tell you how much type Z to make and what the new X and Y quantities will be if the margin were more than $55.

It should be apparent that accounting systems must distinguish between direct and indirect costs, and provide standard costs of sufficient accuracy to permit decisions such as this one to be made properly. Note that if the unit contribution on the proposed product is quite high or low (say $100, or $20), the accounting measurement does not have to be nearly so discriminating as if the first estimates put it in the neighborhood of $55!

5. Changing Production Capacities to Improve Contribution Margin. The "shadow prices" developed above are also useful in determining whether to add capacity. The shadow prices C, D, and P may be regarded as the *contribution* to total contribution margin that would be made if *one* additional unit of a resource is made. (Now you can better understand why $C = \$0$; adding more cooking capacity would not permit more fertilizer of type X or type Y to be made and sold.) *If an additional unit of a resource will cost less than this contribution, it may be acquired.* Thus, if one additional unit of packing capacity will cost $125 or less per week, it should be acquired. If a unit of packing capacity will cost more than $125 per week, it should not be acquired.

SHADOW PRICES IN OPERATIONS CONTROL

Because shadow prices do represent sacrifices of profit if resources are not used optimally, as well as additions to profit if resources are used optimally, they can be used to prepare an unusual operating budget for the Richer Chemical Company. Let a single responsibility center have control of the drying operation. This center's budget is as shown in Figure 14–4.

Now, during the week, the drying department does not quite adhere to this budget, and actual production is 60 tons of type X and 160 tons of type Y. The performance report would appear as shown in Figure 14–5.

This sort of performance report shows the contribution to company performance in terms of scarce capacity utilization. Try to understand

FIGURE 14-4

DRYING DEPARTMENT
Weekly Budget

	Drying Hours per Ton	Total Drying Hours	$ per Hour	Total Contribution
Tons of type X to process: 150	0.20	30	$100	$3,000
Tons of type Y to process: 100	0.10	10	100	1,000
		40		$4,000
				(Planned contribution)

FIGURE 14-5

DRYING DEPARTMENT
Weekly Performance Report

Activity	Planned Contribution	Actual Contribution	Variance
Type X	$3,000	$1,200*	$(1,800) Unfavorable
Type Y	1,000	1,600†	600 Favorable
Total	$4,000	$2,800	$(1,200) Unfavorable

* Twelve hours (to dry 60 tons of type X) multiplied by $100 per hour of drying time.

† Sixteen hours (to dry 160 tons of type Y) multiplied by $100 per hour of drying time.

where all the numbers come from in both Figures 14–4 and 14–5. The latter is simplified by considering only production mix variations, and the entire total variation is due to production changes from the original budget which result in idle drying time. Efficiency variances (use of more or less than 0.10 hours per ton of type Y, for example) would be handled as described in Chapter 8, using $100 as the standard cost.

Shadow Prices in Companywide Control

The shadow prices, as the value per unit of optimally used resource, may be used to describe losses of contribution margin due to nonoptimal operations. The linearity of the programming model somewhat restricts this use, but the information is useful if understood. Any nonoptimal use of capacity will produce a total contribution that is *less* than the total value of resources used. The difference represents the loss due to nonoptimal operations—departures from the plan. Because this is a difference of actual from planned contribution rather than actual from planned cost, it is unique. Figure 14–6 shows how a performance statement for the entire company might look.

FIGURE 14–6

RICHER CHEMICAL COMPANY
Weekly Performance Report

Total contribution from operations:	
60 tons Type X × $40 per ton	$ 2,400
160 tons Type Y × $30 per ton	4,800
	$ 7,200
Total value of resources used in production:	
Cooking time 40 hours × $0 per hour	$ 0
Drying time 40 hours × $100 per hour	4,000
Packing time 40 hours × $125 per hour	5,000
	$ 9,000
Unfavorable variance	$(1,200)

The unfavorable variance in Figure 14–6 is superficially attributable to idle capacity in the drying and packing departments. The real culprit is the improper product mix, which does not allow the departments to use their capacity optimally. Again, efficiency variances have been omitted from Figure 14–6.

Be sure you understand that Figures 14–4, 14–5, and 14–6 do take into account the actual and expected costs of materials, labor, and other inputs as shown on page 407. The control you get through use of contribution figures based on these costs and expected selling prices is significant because it is *direct control of profits*. All activities and variances are reported in terms of their effect on profits. Shadow price analysis is complementary to cost accounting control and control based on budgets and costs directly; it does not replace other types of control or reporting.

SUMMARY

Linear programming offers an extremely powerful analytical and decision model for describing resource allocation problems in terms of accounting and technological information. A linear programming model consists of—

1. A set of constraints which describe resource availabilities, limitations, and relationships to products;
2. Constraints which require all variables to have values equal to or greater than zero; and
3. An objective function which is to be maximized or minimized and is a weighted linear sum of all the decision variables in the problem.

All these relations are linear.

A more efficient method of solving linear programming problems is the *simplex* method; however, when there are only two variables, the graphical method of solution employed in this chapter may be used. In terms of a numerical example, we answered three of the questions posed in the beginning of the chapter. These questions were: best activity mix, changes in activity schedule if relative activity profits change, and adding or dropping activities from the schedule of those performed.

Linear programming models also have an interesting similarity to accounting: although the criterion function is expressed in a single type of unit, such as dollars, the decision variables are each in their own dimension—such as units of type A and units of type B fertilizer, and the constraints are each in a different dimension—units of cooking and units of drying capacity. This recalls the many different units (or dimensions) of fundamental accounting processes as described in Chapter 2. The criterion function's single dimension recalls the linear aggregation of physical units and prices or costs used to develop a single-dimension measure of entity welfare. Thus, accounting techniques of aggregation and summation to record historical events and evaluate them in terms of a single entity must be used to prepare a linear programming decision model intended to find optimum decisions for a single entity. This similarity may be the reason that so many accountants and managers use linear programming for business planning, operating

14 / Production Mix and Profit Maximization

directly from accounting data and expressing the results in the form of accounting statements.

APPENDIX 14A: WHERE DO SHADOW PRICES COME FROM?

Profit Balance

The key to understanding and computing shadow prices is the notion that the total combined contribution margin produced by products such as type X and type Y fertilizers is equal to the total value *imparted to these products* by the combined cooking, drying, and packing capacities available. Express this equality as

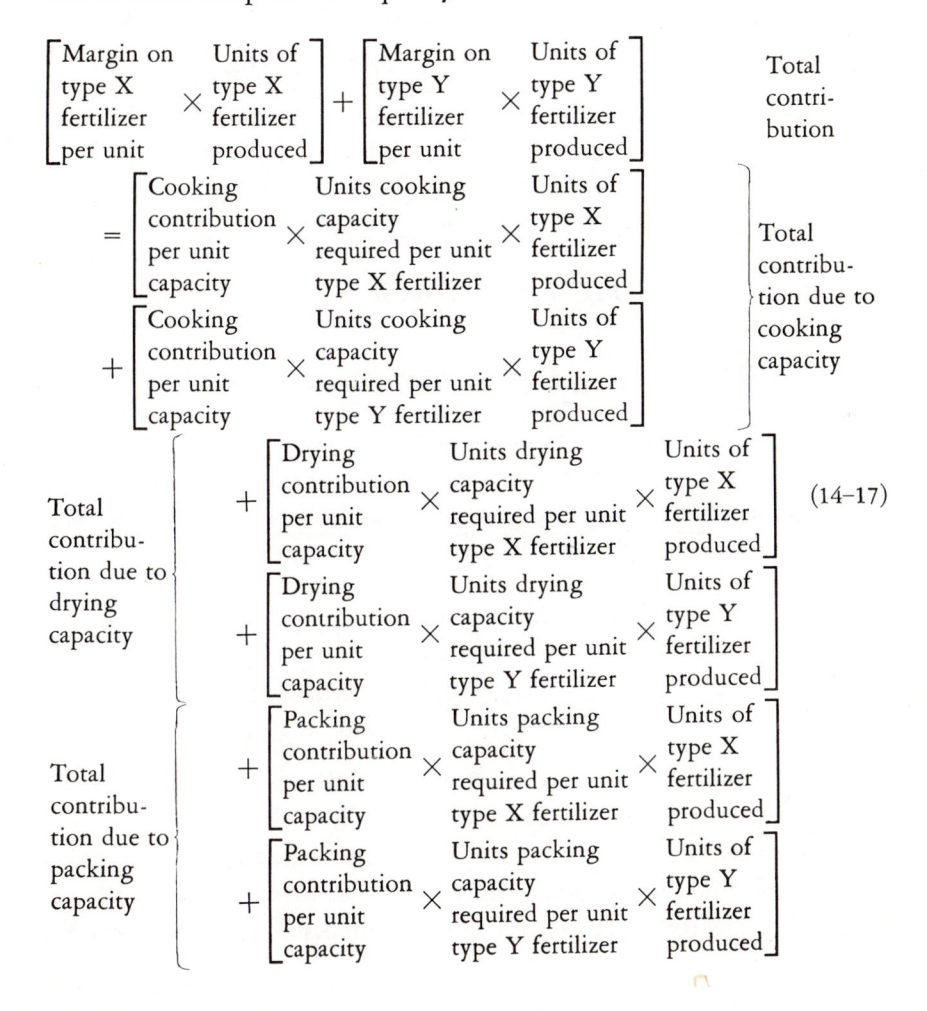

$$\begin{bmatrix} \text{Margin on} \\ \text{type X} \\ \text{fertilizer} \\ \text{per unit} \end{bmatrix} \times \begin{bmatrix} \text{Units of} \\ \text{type X} \\ \text{fertilizer} \\ \text{produced} \end{bmatrix} + \begin{bmatrix} \text{Margin on} \\ \text{type Y} \\ \text{fertilizer} \\ \text{per unit} \end{bmatrix} \times \begin{bmatrix} \text{Units of} \\ \text{type Y} \\ \text{fertilizer} \\ \text{produced} \end{bmatrix} \quad \begin{matrix} \text{Total} \\ \text{contri-} \\ \text{bution} \end{matrix}$$

$$= \begin{bmatrix} \text{Cooking} \\ \text{contribution} \\ \text{per unit} \\ \text{capacity} \end{bmatrix} \times \begin{bmatrix} \text{Units cooking} \\ \text{capacity} \\ \text{required per unit} \\ \text{type X fertilizer} \end{bmatrix} \times \begin{bmatrix} \text{Units of} \\ \text{type X} \\ \text{fertilizer} \\ \text{produced} \end{bmatrix}$$

$$+ \begin{bmatrix} \text{Cooking} \\ \text{contribution} \\ \text{per unit} \\ \text{capacity} \end{bmatrix} \times \begin{bmatrix} \text{Units cooking} \\ \text{capacity} \\ \text{required per unit} \\ \text{type Y fertilizer} \end{bmatrix} \times \begin{bmatrix} \text{Units of} \\ \text{type Y} \\ \text{fertilizer} \\ \text{produced} \end{bmatrix} \quad \begin{matrix} \text{Total} \\ \text{contribu-} \\ \text{tion due to} \\ \text{cooking} \\ \text{capacity} \end{matrix}$$

$$\begin{matrix} \text{Total} \\ \text{contribu-} \\ \text{tion due to} \\ \text{drying} \\ \text{capacity} \end{matrix} \begin{cases} + \begin{bmatrix} \text{Drying} \\ \text{contribution} \\ \text{per unit} \\ \text{capacity} \end{bmatrix} \times \begin{bmatrix} \text{Units drying} \\ \text{capacity} \\ \text{required per unit} \\ \text{type X fertilizer} \end{bmatrix} \times \begin{bmatrix} \text{Units of} \\ \text{type X} \\ \text{fertilizer} \\ \text{produced} \end{bmatrix} \\ + \begin{bmatrix} \text{Drying} \\ \text{contribution} \\ \text{per unit} \\ \text{capacity} \end{bmatrix} \times \begin{bmatrix} \text{Units drying} \\ \text{capacity} \\ \text{required per unit} \\ \text{type Y fertilizer} \end{bmatrix} \times \begin{bmatrix} \text{Units of} \\ \text{type Y} \\ \text{fertilizer} \\ \text{produced} \end{bmatrix} \end{cases} \quad (14\text{-}17)$$

$$\begin{matrix} \text{Total} \\ \text{contribu-} \\ \text{tion due to} \\ \text{packing} \\ \text{capacity} \end{matrix} \begin{cases} + \begin{bmatrix} \text{Packing} \\ \text{contribution} \\ \text{per unit} \\ \text{capacity} \end{bmatrix} \times \begin{bmatrix} \text{Units packing} \\ \text{capacity} \\ \text{required per unit} \\ \text{type X fertilizer} \end{bmatrix} \times \begin{bmatrix} \text{Units of} \\ \text{type X} \\ \text{fertilizer} \\ \text{produced} \end{bmatrix} \\ + \begin{bmatrix} \text{Packing} \\ \text{contribution} \\ \text{per unit} \\ \text{capacity} \end{bmatrix} \times \begin{bmatrix} \text{Units packing} \\ \text{capacity} \\ \text{required per unit} \\ \text{type Y fertilizer} \end{bmatrix} \times \begin{bmatrix} \text{Units of} \\ \text{type Y} \\ \text{fertilizer} \\ \text{produced} \end{bmatrix} \end{cases}$$

The contribution of a resource per unit capacity *must* be the same regardless of which product it is used in. If this were not so, then resource units would be shifted from the low-contribution products to the high-contribution products, and since you already have an optimum production mix, this cannot happen.

The massive equality above may be expressed much more compactly using the already-introduced symbolic notation of the chapter:

$$40X + 30Y = 0.1CX + 0.2CY + 0.2DX + 0.1DY \\ + 0.16PX + 0.16PY \quad (14\text{–}18)$$

You may rearrange the right-hand side of this equation to produce:

$$40X + 30Y = (0.1C + 0.2D + 0.16P)X \\ + (0.2C + 0.1D + 0.16P)Y \quad (14\text{–}19)$$

Now, make two equations from this one by noticing that the same two variables appear on each side—X and Y, and that the coefficients of X and Y on the left side of (14–18) should be the same as the corresponding coefficients on the right-hand side.

$$0.1C + 0.2D + 0.16P = 40 \quad (14\text{–}20)$$

and

$$0.2C + 0.1D + 0.16P = 30 \quad (14\text{–}21)$$

We have greatly simplified the development of these relationships. (14–20) and (14–21) become constraints in a new linear programming problem, a *minimization* (because C, D, and P are costs of resources and you want to minimize costs) problem. This new problem is:

$$\begin{aligned}
\text{Minimize} \quad & 40C + 40D + 40P \\
\text{Subject to} \quad & 0.1C + 0.2D + 0.16P \geq 40 \\
& 0.2C + 0.1D + 0.16P \geq 30 \\
& C, \quad D, \text{ and } P \geq 0
\end{aligned}$$

This problem may be solved in 3-dimensional space using the same graphical concepts used to solve the original problem. You plot the constraints as volumes, then note the volume of acceptable solutions *above* the boundary lines and to the *right* (since these are "greater-than-or-equal-to" constraints). Since you are minimizing, you would choose the point on the boundary plane which was lowest and furthest to the left. In this particular case, that point is:

$$C = \$0 \quad D = \$100 \quad P = \$125$$

as assumed in the body of the chapter.

QUESTIONS

1. What is linear programming? What can linear programming do that ordinary cost-volume-profit analysis cannot do?
2. What does "linear" mean as applied to making a linear model of a real situation? Why is a linear model usually preferred over nonlinear models?
3. What is an equality? An inequality? A nonnegativity condition? Give an example from your own experiences of each of these.
4. To what kinds of problems are maximizing models applied? Minimizing models? In your opinion what important criticism might be made of optimizing models in general?
5. Let an inequality be of the form $3X + 8Y \leq 48$. Which of the following objective functions is parallel to this constraint?
    a) $8X + 3Y$.
    b) $6X + 16Y$.
    c) $4X + 1.5Y$.
    d) None of these.
6. In a particular problem the objective function is $5X + 5Y$. If the objective function is changed to $5X + 6Y$, is the problem solution necessarily changed? Explain.
7. Which of the following appear to be potential applications of linear programming?
    a) Computing job cost.
    b) Finding product mix.
    c) Blending cattle feed.
    d) Computing inventory order quantities and levels.
    e) Planning a unique project.
    f) Computing significant variances.
    g) Preparing budgets.
    h) Planning sausage production.

8. Suppose a linear programming model has two variables and eight constraints. Can it be solved graphically? Give examples of problems which *can* and *cannot* be solved graphically. Generally speaking, how are problems solved which cannot be solved graphically?

9. How are the contributions or costs of variables in the objective function developed? Do they include indirect allocations? Why?

10. What does the *right-hand side* of a constraint represent? How might the value of the right-hand side be determined or measured?

11. How would you decide what constraints and variables to include in a linear programming model?

12. Is it possible that constraints and/or variables in a linear programming model are controlled exclusively by certain responsibility centers? Assume this is true; how would you collect information required to set up the model and report information obtained from solving the model?

13. What is a "shadow price"? In what sense is it a "price" at all?

14. A particular application of linear programming includes two technological constraints representing maximum available quantities of scarce resources. Two solutions to the problem have been posed. The "shadow prices" associated with each solution are:

	Shadow Price Set 1	Shadow Price Set 2
Resource A	30	50
Resource B	20	25

Which set of shadow prices is associated with the better solution? How do you know this?

15. A particular application of linear programming has four constraints representing maximum available amounts of scarce resources. The optimal solution to the problem has produced shadow prices of these resources of 10, 20, 30, and 40. A new product has been proposed which would have a contribution margin of 120 and require 2, 1, 1, and 1 units of the scarce resources, respectively. Should this product be considered for inclusion in the product mix?

EXERCISES

16. Harper Company is considering a new product which will require resources that are scarce to the company. Each unit of the proposed

product will require three units of resource I; four units of resource II; and five units of resource III. The company has available 120 units of I, 152 units of II, and 150 units of III. What is the maximum quantity of this product that can be made? If a $5 profit would be made on each unit, what is the maximum profit that can be made? If "tooling up" to make the new product will cost $100, should the new product be started?

17. Proctor Company makes three products: X, Y, and Z. Two resources are used in each product, I and II. Here are the inequalities showing how product quantities are related to resource availability (constraints):

$$\text{I: } 3X + 4Y + 5Z \le 120$$
$$\text{II: } 6X + 8Y + 9Z \le 216$$

The company wants to make: 10X, 15Y, and 5Z. Can it do so? If not, which resource is in short supply? If so, how much of each resource is left over?

18. Storey Company is making three products: X, Y, and Z. All three products are made from Derium, a scarce resource. Each product requires two units of Derium. There are 3,000 units of Derium presently available, and all of it is used. The company makes 300X, 600Y, and 600Z. The profit per unit is $10 on each product. How much should Storey be willing to pay for additional units of Derium (at the maximum)?

19. The following constraint system describes two products made by Caraway Company:

$$(1) \quad 3X + Y \le 400 \text{ (resource 1)}$$
$$(2) \qquad\quad Y \le 100 \text{ (resource 2)}$$

The profits per unit are $12 per unit of X and $20 per unit of Y. At present, 120 units of X and 40 units of Y are made. Suggest a product mix that produces a better total profit. How much would you pay for additional units of the resource in constraint 2?

20. Consider the facts in Question 19. An additional 150 units of the resource in constraint 2 are purchsed at $15 apiece. By inspection, find the new solution to the problem. Then, assume that a minimum of 80 units of X must be produced to meet contractual obligations made when Caraway Company did not think any more resource (2) would be available. How much might the company be willing to pay in order to produce only 50 units of X?

PROBLEMS

21. Using graph paper on which one axis is labeled X1 and the other axis is labeled X2, solve the following linear programming problem:

$$\text{Maximize} \quad Z = 3X1 + 7X2$$
$$\text{Subject to (1)} \quad 4X1 + 2X2 \leq 16$$
$$(2) \quad 2X2 \leq 11$$
$$(3) \quad 3X1 + 4X2 \leq 24$$
$$X1, X2 \geq 0$$

22. Using graph paper on which one axis is labeled X1 and the other is labeled X2, solve the following linear programming problem:

$$\text{Minimize} \quad Z = X1 + X2$$
$$\text{Subject to (1)} \quad 2X1 + 4X2 \geq 48$$
$$(2) \quad X1 \geq 10$$
$$(3) \quad X2 \leq 5$$
$$X1, X2 \geq 0$$

23. The Hearty Sausage Company is a meat-processing concern. The company produces a variety of meat products (by slaughtering and processing cattle and hogs) such as sausage, bologna, lunch meat, and dog food. Prices of these products fluctuate, so that some months it is more profitable to make one or the other. Hans Schultz, the sausage master for Hearty Sausage, has directed the preparation of the company's products for 48 years; however, last month he announced he would retire at the end of the year. In his announcement, he urged the company management to develop a linear programming model to decide which products to make from which component meats. As an illustration, he included this example:

"Let $X1$ = the pounds of sausage made per month and $X2$ = the pounds of dog food made per month. Now, these two products are made from bone shavings and organ meats, which in any month are available in specific amounts. My experience tells me we require 0.4 pounds bone shavings and 0.9 pounds organ meats to make one pound of sausage, and 0.8 pounds bone shavings and 0.3 pounds organ meats to make one pound of dog food. This month I expect to have 20,000 pounds of bone shavings and 40,000 pounds of organ meats. I know that we must have at least 5,000 pounds of sausage and no more than 20,000 pounds of dog food. In addition, our accountants tell me that we make $0.20 per pound of sausage and $0.02 per pound of dog food. This leads to the following equation system:

Maximize $0.20 X_1 + 0.02 X_2$
Subject to $0.40 X_1 + 0.80 X_2 \leq 20{,}000$ (bone shavings)
$0.90 X_1 + 0.30 X_2 \leq 40{,}000$ (organ meats)
$X_1 \geq 5{,}000$ (minimum sausage)
$X_2 \leq 20{,}000$ (maximum dog food)
$X_1, X_2 \geq 0$

"This system, when solved, will produce as values for X_1 and X_2 the amounts of sausage and dog food we ought to make from materials on hand."

Required:

a) Using the graphical method, find the values of X_1 and X_2.
b) If the model is to be expanded to include all products of the Hearty Sausage Company, how would you propose that the model be incorporated into the planning process? Assume that bone shavings and organ meats are produced by separate responsibility centers in the packing company, but that sausage and dog food are marketed by the same center.

24. George Sausage, president of the Hearty Sausage Company described in Problem 23, was reviewing the memo from Hans Schultz, the retiring sausage maker, in which Schultz gave these profit margins on sausage and dog food:

Sausage. . . . . $0.20 per pound
Dog food. . . . . 0.02 per pound

Mr. Sausage was impressed by the memo (which you can read in Problem 23) and decided to verify these profit figures as a preliminary step toward the kind of decision model Schultz proposed as his replacement. Mr. Sausage asked Bob Bologna, the controller, to prepare product line performance statements for him for these two products. Here are the essential elements of these statements:

	Sausage	Dog Food
Selling price per pound.	$0.90	$0.20
Less:		
1. Allocated "costs" of bone shavings and organ meats (only whole animals are bought)	0.07	0.13
2. Ageing and seasoning	0.20	0.00
3. Packaging	0.20	0.02
4. Allocated advertising and overhead	0.18	0.01
5. Distribution.	0.05	0.02
Contribution margin	$0.20	$0.02

Required:

a) Determine whether Mr. Schultz was correct in his statement of the profit or contribution margins.

b) Without prejudice to your answer in (*a*) above, assume that the actual contribution margins are $0.52 on sausage and $0.16 on dog food. Substitute these values for the $0.20 and $0.02 respectively in the equation system of Problem 23 and solve. Determine the proper quantities of sausage and dog food to be made.

c) What was the potential cost of using the wrong information, based on your answer to (*b*)? (Remember to use the correct contribution margins.)

25. Midville Investment Corporation is a quasi-public enterprise which loans money to high-risk businesses, especially those whose proprietors or managers have unconventional backgrounds such as ex-convicts, former narcotics addicts, and educationally or economically disadvantaged persons. The company must obtain the highest possible return on its money as well as observe certain constraints on its lending policies. The actual model is complex, but a simpler version of it would be:

$$\text{Maximize} \quad 0.04 X_1 + 0.08 X_2$$
$$\text{Subject to} \quad (1) \quad X_1 + X_2 \leq 60{,}000$$
$$(2) \quad X_1 \geq 10{,}000$$
$$(3) \quad X_2 \geq 10{,}000$$
$$(4) \quad 2 X_1 + 5 X_2 \geq 100{,}000$$
$$X_1, X_2 = 0$$

Constraint (1) is a budget constraint, indicating that in this period X_1 and X_2, the amounts of money loaned in districts 1 and 2 of Midville respectively, cannot exceed $60,000; (2) and (3) give minimum amounts to be loaned in each district; and (4) is a constraint based on the relative population and income of the two districts.

Required:

a) Solve this problem graphically to determine the amount of money which should be loaned this period and in which districts it should be loaned.

b) If the return on loans in district 2 rises to 0.12, what will be the new solution?

c) If the return on loans in district 1 rises to 0.09 (and the return in district 2 remains at 0.08), what will be the new solution?

26. Food Processing Company makes frozen French fried potatoes and packaged Idaho baking potatoes. The potato raw materials come from two large suppliers. This month the suppliers announce that as a result of drouth, they are only able to supply 400 tons of grade A potatoes and 320 tons of grade B potatoes. Food Processing can sell all of the French fries and baking potatoes it makes, and it wants to make the highest profit from these limited raw materials. The profit margin on French fries is $30 per ton and on baking potatoes, $60 per ton. The yields are:

	Tons Required for One Ton of French Fries	Tons Required for One Ton of Baking Potatoes
Of grade A potatoes	3	2
Of grade B potatoes	1.6	3

Required:

a) Find the optimal number of tons of French fries and of baking potatoes to make.
b) Formulate the *dual* to the above problem and solve it to find the shadow prices of grade A and grade B potatoes.
c) One supplier offers Food Processing the opportunity to buy one more ton of grade B potatoes for $35. Should this offer be accepted?
d) Assume that instead of the optimal production plan, 10 percent fewer of each product is actually produced. Did the company earn an accounting profit? Prepare a performance statement based on shadow prices and contribution margins which shows how the company performed. Does this statement show a profit or a loss?

27. Go-Fast Boat Company concentrates its boatbuilding efforts on three models: the GF-15, GF-20, and GF-25. Go-fast is a small company that can sell all the boats it makes. At the present time it is making and selling:

        0 .... GF-15s
      100 .... GF-20s
  and 100 .... GF-25s per month

Boatbuilding proceeds in two stages at Go-Fast: forming and finishing. The forming process can work 1,000 hours per month; the finishing process, 1,800 hours per month.

Each of the three models requires forming and finishing work in the following amounts:

	Forming (Hours)	Finishing (Hours)
GF-15	2	2
GF-20	3	6
GF-25	7	14

An hour of work in forming has direct costs of $100; an hour of work in finishing has direct costs of $200. The selling prices of the three models are:

GF-15	$1,200
GF-20	1,900
GF-25	4,000

Required:

a) Compute the contribution margins on each boat model.
b) Compute the total contribution from the present production quantities.
c) Compute a production schedule for Go-Fast assuming that the GF-15 and GF-20 will be produced. What is the total contribution margin from this arrangement?
d) The Go-Fast production manager says, "My goal is to keep all our capacity busy producing." How important is this? What else (if anything) should he consider?

28. The Wizzo Corporation manufactures and sells three grades, A, B, and C, of a single wood product. Each grade must be processed through three phases—cutting, fitting, and finishing—before it is sold. The following unit information is provided:

	A	B	C
Selling price	$10.00	$15.00	$20.00
Direct labor	5.00	6.00	9.00
Direct materials	0.70	0.70	1.00
Variable overhead Allocated	1.00	1.20	1.80
Fixed overhead arbitrarily	0.60	0.72	1.08
Materials required in board feet	7	7	10
Labor required in hours:			
Cutting	3/6	3/6	4/6
Fitting	1/6	1/6	2/6
Finishing	1/6	2/6	3/6

Only 5,000 board feet of wood can be obtained per week. The cutting department has 180 hours of labor available each week.

The fitting and finishing departments each have 120 hours of labor available each week. No overtime is allowed.

Contract commitments require the company to make 50 units of A per week. In addition, company policy is to produce at least 50 additional units of A, 50 units of B, and 50 units of C each week to remain actively in each of the three markets. Because of competition, only 130 units of C can be sold each week.

Required:

Formulate and label the linear objective function and the constraint functions necessary to maximize the contribution margin for Wizzo Corporation; DO NOT attempt to solve the resulting problem.

(Adapted from the December 1972 Certificate in Management Accounting Examination)

29. The graph below presents the constraint functions for a chair manufacturing company whose production problem (deciding how many kitchen chairs and how many office chairs to manufacture each period, using limited resources) can be solved using linear programming. The company earns $8 for each kitchen chair sold and $5 for each office chair sold.

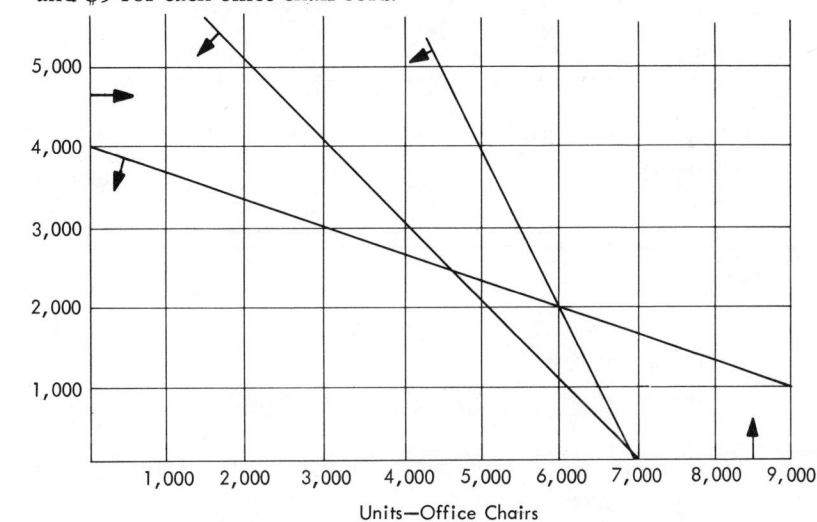

Required:

a) What is the profit maximizing schedule? (To answer this question, you should trace the graph above onto a separate sheet of paper, identify the area satisfying all constraints, plot the line representing the objective function, and the appropriate point of tangency with the area satisfying all contraints.)

b) Explain *why* this schedule maximizes profit.

(Adapted from the December 1972 Certificate in Management Accounting Examination)

30. Perfect Poultry Products, Inc. operates a poultry farm which raises chickens. The company spends a great deal on chicken feed and recently became aware that linear programming could help reduce the cost of chicken feed without endangering the chickens' nutrition. This is called the "diet" problem in linear programming, and it works like this: You must determine the nutrition content for each major nutrient in each available chicken feed, and the amount of each nutrient a well-nourished chicken should have. Then you find the cheapest diet that nourishes the chicken.

PPP has determined that there are three major nutrients chickens need: protein, vitamins, and bulk. Two feeds contain these nutrients in amounts and at costs as follows:

Feed	Cost per Ounce	Protein per Ounce	Vitamin per Ounce	Bulk per Ounce	
Gro-bird	$0.02	30	2	6	(Each column becomes a constraint)
Bird-gro	0.01	3	5	8	
Daily amount needed		90	60	120	

Required:

a) Let $X1$ = amount of Gro-bird per chicken per day in the minimum cost diet.

Let $X2$ = amount of Bird-gro per chicken per day in the minimum cost diet.

Find the number of ounces of Gro-bird and Bird-gro in the minimum cost diet and the cost per chicken per day.

b) Now, other nations discover that chickens are a cheap, economical food and that there are no religious scruples against eating it, so everyone starts to raise chickens—and to buy the chicken food in the United States—so that the cost of chicken

food rises. What is the ideal nutritious diet if the prices become $0.03 for Gro-bird and $0.04 for Bird-gro per ounce?
c) Consider only the diet in (a). Are chickens getting *too much* of any one nutrient? If so, can this be helped?

DECISION CASE 14–1: DRANE COMPANY

The Drane Company manufactures bathroom fixtures. Until two years ago, the company manufactured the traditional lines of fixtures—basins, tubs, showers, and toilets. Two years ago the company abruptly switched to "modular" bathrooms—completely self-contained bathrooms, requiring only external connections to function as part of a dwelling. These are popular in apartments, motels, and mobile homes, but have not been as profitable to Drane as the original lines were. The company can still make the old products in its present plant, and is wondering whether it should do so. It can sell all it makes of modular and old-style bathrooms.

Let the unit of production be one bathroom. Let TB = "*t*raditional *b*athroom" units made and sold and MB = "*m*odular *b*athroom" units made and sold. Both products pass through two departments, whose major input is direct labor hours. Here are estimated resource requirements for the products:

	One TB	One MB
Department I	20 DLH	30 DLH
Department II	30 DLH	20 DLH

In a typical week each department has available 1,200 direct labor hours to use in production. The modular bathroom sells for $1,000 and has direct costs of $300 in department I and $400 in department II. The traditional bathroom sells for $1,200 and has direct costs of $200 in department I and $600 in department II.

Required:

a) Using the graphical method, find the mix of product which produces the highest contribution margin and state whether it is different from the present product mix.
b) In one week, what is the additional contribution margin that would be earned by switching to the optimum product mix?
c) Imagine that making this switch will require a one-time setup cost of $201,600. For how many weeks would the new product mix have to continue in production? Would this seem to be a capital budgeting decision?

BIBLIOGRAPHY

Books

Driebeek, Norman J. *Applied Linear Programming*. Reading, Mass.: Addison-Wesley Publishing Co., Inc., 1969.

Gass, Saul I. *An Illustrated Guide to Linear Programming*. New York: McGraw-Hill Book Co., 1970.

Levin, Richard I. and Lamone, Rudolph P. *Linear Programming for Management Decisions*. Homewood, Ill.: Richard D. Irwin, Inc., 1969.

Loomba, N. Paul. *Linear Programming, An Introductory Analysis*. New York: McGraw-Hill Book Co., 1964.

Articles

Demski, Joel S. "An Accounting System Structured on a Linear Programming Model," *The Accounting Review*, October 1967.

Ijiri, Yuji; Levy, F. K.; and Lyon, R. C. "A Linear Programming Model for Budgeting and Financial Planning," *Journal of Accounting Research*, Autumn 1963.

Moore, Joe F. "What Operations Research Means to the Accountant," *Management Advisor*, November–December 1966.

Palmer, B. Thomas. "Management Reports for Multiproduct Plants," *Management Accounting*, August 1970.

Samuels, J. M. "Opportunity Costing: An Application of Mathematical Programming," *Journal of Accounting Research*, Autumn 1965.

Summers, E. L. "The Audit Staff Assignment Problem," *The Accounting Review*, July 1972.

Wilson, J. R. M. "Profitability as a Tool in Product Planning," *The Arthur Young Journal*, Winter 1966.

15

Decision Making and Information System Performance

THUS FAR in Part III of this book you have studied four important recurring managerial decisions—capital budgeting, inventory planning and management, large-scale project planning and control, and production mix analysis. Each decision has its information requirements, which accounting analysis and accounting systems help to satisfy. In this chapter, you learn the conceptual relationships between decisions and information systems.

Some Basic Terminology

In Chapter 1 you were exposed to the Popcorn King's decision: how much popcorn to buy for sale at football games. This decision will be used to illustrate the points of the present chapter. To refresh your memory, Figure 15-1 gives the matrix of payoffs occurring for each combination of number of bags of popcorn bought and number of bags demanded at the Big Game.

The range of bags of popcorn you can buy before the game is called your *set of alternatives*. Your alternatives consists of all the values of all the variables you control. For example, you may have any number of popcorn suppliers arrive up to one hour before game time and charge any price per bag you wish. Here we are assuming that you already have determined the price per bag (10 cents), have selected

FIGURE 15–1
Popcorn King Payoffs
(in cents per bag)

Bags of Popcorn Bought	Number of Bags Demanded at Game					
	0	1	2	3	4	5
0	0	0	0	0	0	0
1	(5)	5	5	5	5	5
2	(10)	0	10	10	10	10
3	(15)	(5)	5	15	15	15
4	(20)	(10)	0	10	20	20
5	(25)	(15)	(5)	5	15	25

a supplier of popcorn who charges you 5 cents per bag, and begin to sell popcorn exactly as the game begins. Thus the only remaining variable whose value must be set is the number of popcorn bags you will buy.

The range of the number of bags that may be demanded at a game is called the *set of states* (those who appreciate a touch of the metaphysical will say "the set of states of nature"). Your states of nature contain variables you cannot control. For example, the number of bags demanded at a game may depend on the weather or how many season ticket holders come to the game. The state of nature that actually occurs—how many bags of popcorn you sell—is composed of all the variables and factors you as a decision maker must accept as "given" and uncontrollable.

Your objective in deciding how many bags of popcorn to buy is to obtain the largest *payoff* possible. The payoffs are the figures you have worked out in the body of the matrix table, Figure 15–1.

As a decision maker you will find there are two types of decisions depending on the availability of the information you have to work with—decisions under certainty and decisions under uncertainty. These decisions together with their information systems are discussed in the sections that follow.

WHEN ONLY ONE STATE IS POSSIBLE

A decision under certainty is characterized by the unique circumstances of there being possible only *one* state, which is fully and completely known in advance. All of the decisions studied in Part III were decisions under certainty. Here is an elaboration:

Decision	Variables Defining State
Capital allocation	Proposed investment's lifetime, cost, net cash flows, and appropriate investor's target rate of return (ITRR) explained in Chapter 11. Your alternatives were possible capital investments. You found it easy to compute each one's current equivalent, then to select those whose current equivalents were highest.
Inventory management	Demand, order cost, carrying cost, shortage cost. When certain assumptions are valid, you just "plug" these figures into formulas and compute the least-cost inventory policy, which was the preferred alternative.
Project planning and control	Project and step completion times, time dependent and time independent costs. By use of special algorithms you selected the schedule which completed a project at lowest total cost.
Product mix analysis	Resource availabilities and capacities, technological coefficients, and product contribution margins. Graphical and numerical methods allow you to calculate a maximum-profit or least-cost product mix.

With decisions under certainty, the decision steps are to develop all the information needed, compute the payoff associated with each alternative, and choose the alternative with the highest payoff. As an example, if you know that demand for popcorn at the game will be precisely four bags, you would see from Figure 15–1 that the highest profit of 20 cents would then be earned if four bags were purchased. In other words,

If this many bags are bought:	0	1	2	3	4	5
The payoff is:	0¢	5¢	10¢	15¢	20¢	15¢

By inspection you quickly decide to buy four bags to sell.

Expectations and Reality

Of course, when you are planning, the numbers 0, 5, 10, 15, 20, 15 are only your best **expectations** about the payoffs of the respective alternatives. Until you actually buy popcorn and try to sell if you won't know the *true* payoff.

Your information about expected payoffs was derived from your decision information system. If this information is not completely accurate, you may or *may not* be led into a wrong decision. So long as the information leads you to select the alternative "buy four bags of popcorn," the information system for decision making is operating

438   An Introduction to Accounting for Decision Making and Control

satisfactorily. If you are led to choose some other alternative, the information system is not operating satisfactorily and it *may* be in your interest to improve it.

Effect of Information System Error on Decisions

Due to price fluctuations, weather, etc. which are known to you but which your information system improperly evaluates, your decision is based on the predicted payoffs in the second column below. The actual payoffs observed later appear in the third column.

Number of Bags Bought	Information System Predicts This Payoff	Actual Payoff Would Be This
0	0	0
1	5	8
2	10	16
3	15	24
4	20	32
5	15	24

Using the predicted payoffs, you would come to the same decision as you would if you knew the actual payoffs. There would be no point in attempting to improve this information system, for it leads to optimal decisions. But below is the output of a system which would mislead you:

Number of Bags Bought	Information System Predicts This Payoff	Actual Payoff Would Be This
0	0	0
1	6	8
2	10	16
3	16	24
4	20	32
5	24	24

Your information system leads you to buy five bags rather than four, causing you to forego 8 cents (not 5 cents) of profit a better information system might have brought you. Worse still, you compare the predicted 24 cents of profit with the actual 24 cents of profit and conclude that your decision worked well. Thus, you were not only deprived of additional profit, but also of the feedback that would have helped you discover something was wrong with your decision and decision information.

Cost of Information

The cost of information has a critical bearing on whether you attempt to improve a malfunctioning information system. In the data immediately above, you would be willing to spend up to 8 cents to discover the proper number of popcorn bags to buy (equal, of course, to the gain in contribution that would result from the improved information).

In repeating decisions, the problem whether to improve the information basis is itself an important resource allocation decision that should be regarded as a capital budgeting decision. To illustrate, let your firm have an ITRR = 20 percent and let the popcorn decision be made 10,000 times per year for five years. An information systems consultant has offered to provide completely accurate data describing the payoff of all such decisions, given only the demand for popcorn at each game. You expect this would produce the average 8 cents per game improvement, or $0.08 \times 10,000 = \$800$ per year. There would be no direct costs of the additional improved information, only a one-time charge of $2,000. Should you pay this charge and shift to completely accurate data?

The current equivalent of five annual payments of $800 each with a 20 percent ITRR is $2,392. This is greater than $2,000 and therefore should receive favorable consideration. Had the current equivalent of the improved information been less than $2,000, the information would not produce enough improvement in decisions to justify its cost. A similar evaluation would apply if the improved information produced a direct cost, say $0.01, that had to be deducted from the contribution increment of $0.08. Your annual payment due to improved information would then be ($0.08 − $0.01 = $0.07) × 10,000 = $700.

Decision Models Sensitivity to Information

All of the decision models you have studied in this section are sensitive to changes in the information used to describe the existing state of nature. Here are brief examples, taken from the numerical illustrations already presented.

Capital Allocation. Suppose that your information system misestimates annual cash operating savings on the sub-limer investment decision discussed in Chapter 11. The true figure turns out to be $180,000 (rather than the expected $119,000) annually. The current equivalent of this sum is $870,000, making the sub-limer more attractive in operation than it was in contemplation.

If the sub-limer was rejected on the basis of available information, Mildew Mining Company would in effect have foregone the benefit of having the sub-limer: $870,000 − $780,000 = $90,000.

The decision is also sensitive to changes in ITRR. Given the cash flows in Chapter 11, their current equivalent varies with ITRR as indicated:

ITRR	Cash Flow Current Equivalent
8	$798,000
16	575,153
18	534,810

However, if the information error involves just a few of the cash payments, the significance of the error is greater if it occurs early in the proposed investment's lifetime. A $10,000 overestimate of net cash flow, using a 20 percent ITRR, will overstate current equivalent by $8,333 if it occurs in the first year, but only by $1,615 if it occurs in the 10th year.

Inventory Management. In Chapter 12 we indicated that the inventory model is relatively insensitive to measurement errors of its major variables. The stress there was on the value of the model even when information to support it did not appear of especially high quality. Now, we show the benefit that could be achieved by "cleaning up" this information.

Recall that in the Chapter 12 discussion of sensitivity analysis, the information system was assumed to estimate carrying cost as $10 when it was actually $20. The result was an inventory policy which cost $1,028.74 per period rather than $958.38, the optimal policy cost. The loss due to imperfect information was $1,028.74 − $958.38 = $70.36 per period. You should be willing to pay up to this amount per period in order to obtain perfect information about the carrying cost. This $70.36 should not be confused with the savings realized by going from the original non-EOQ policy to an EOQ policy based on imperfect information, which was much larger.

Project Planning and Control. The steps in the critical path(s) of a project are those for which information errors can produce the most spectacular delays and costs. A cost estimation error cannot be exaggerated or minimized regardless of the step in which it occurs, but an error in fixing the completion time of a critical path step may produce scheduling errors and attendant correction costs in many other steps. These errors arise because you plan to complete a step in, say, 40 days, then discover that the rate of work you thought would yield this completion time actually produces a 45-day completion time.

To try to anticipate this sort of information error, planners may, after the ideal schedule has been established, seek estimates of the longest and shortest completion times. The former will occur under pessimistic assumptions about the activity; the latter, under optimistic assumptions. If a probability distribution is assumed to govern the distribution of step completion times, you can compute estimates of *expected* (in the probabilistic rather than the planned sense) step completion time and the *variance* of this expected completion time. You can add together the expected completion times of all steps along a path and obtain an expected completion time for that path, and by adding variances obtain a variance for the completion time of the path. Some illustrative results of such analysis appear in Figure 15–2. The thing to notice is that any of the paths in this project *could* be critical paths and lack of perfect information prevents you from identifying one as unquestionably the critical path.

FIGURE 15–2
Illustrative Results of Analysis of Variation in Step and Path Completion Times

Path	Expected Path Completion Time (Days)	Standard Deviation of Path Completion Time (Days)
1	100	20
2	90	30
3	115	25

If path 1 is delayed, for example, due to information system error in relating rate of completion to resource input, it may easily extend beyond the 115 days path 3 is expected to last, and replace the latter as the critical path. Or if paths 1 and 3 proceed unexpectedly rapidly, path 2 may be the critical path. Path 3 itself may be delayed and extend the entire project.

The costs of the imperfect information would be those costs incurred to avoid the worst of its effects. You may decide to expedite *all* paths by 10 days to assure that the entire project may be completed in 115 days. Such expediting would not be necessary if your information was known to perfectly anticipate the project's dynamics; and so its cost would be avoidable if you had perfect information. If the cost of expediting is estimated at $1,000 per day, you would spend up to $10,000 to obtain improved information.

Of course, expediting in the absence of pinpoint estimates doesn't guarantee project completion in *any* chosen time frame—just makes it more likely.

Product Mix Analysis. In Chapter 14, you saw how sensitivity analysis could show you the proper solution to a product mix problem when the contribution per unit of the different products changed. The same methods may be used to show how information errors lead to additional costs in such decisions.

The original contributions in the Chapter 14 illustrative problem were $40 per unit of X and $30 per unit of Y. Let these be the actual contributions. Now, let the information system erroneously estimate C_y as $35 per unit. Despite the error, the Z-line in Figure 14–3 still passes through the same solution point as the actual Z-line, and the solution that is optimal with the estimation error turns out to be optimal when the decision is implemented.

If C_y is estimated at $53.30 per unit, the estimation error is large enough to cause a nonoptimal solution to be selected. In Figure 15–3 we give the two solutions and the loss of contribution (measured by using the actual C_y rather than the erroneous estimate) from choosing the nonoptimal solution.

Let us examine the problems arising from the information error and nonoptimal product mix chosen as a result.

The first problem arises when actual results are compared with ex-

FIGURE 15-3
Cost of Information Error in Product Mix Analysis

True Values	Information System Values	Optimal Total Contribution	Total Contribution Realized
$C_x = 40$ $C_y = 30$	$C_x = 40$ $C_y = \$53.30$	$9,000	$8,500

pectations. The plan called for 100 units of X and 150 units of Y to be produced. Assume this occurred; the total contribution *expected* would be 100 × $40 + 150 × $53.30 = *$11,995*. The actual contribution observed will be $8,500, and the $3,495 difference would be regarded as a most puzzling unfavorable variance. This variance might be attributed to production, sales, uncontrollable factors, or to imperfect information.

The second problem arises when deciding what to do about the information system error. The computed variance of $3,495 is not the amount that can be spent to improve information, for the $11,995 contribution was never (and never will be) achievable. Better information will be worth up to $9,000 — $8,500 = *$500*—the difference between the optimal and nonoptimal decision payoffs, computed using the error-free contribution rates.

WHEN MORE THAN ONE STATE IS POSSIBLE

Only one state may occur at the time your decision is effective. In *decisions under uncertainty* you don't know what that state will be. You know it will be one of a set of such states, and you also have (for purposes of this discussion) the *relative frequencies* with which states occur. These relative frequencies are expressed as a set of numbers between 0 and 1.0, which together add up to 1.0, and each of which relates to one state. These numbers are called the *state probability distribution*. If you allow a friend to flip a coin which cannot stand on edge, two states are possible: heads and tails. Each state is equally likely—has the same relative frequency—and so the state probability distribution is [p(heads) = 0.50; p(tails) = 0.50].

Decision Rules and Policies

A decision rule is a policy which tells you which alternative to choose to give the highest payoff when you believe a particular state is going to occur. In terms of the Popcorn King example, here are a few of the many decision rules which could have been adopted to guide you in making that decision when you do not know exactly which state might occur (Figure 15–4).

FIGURE 15–4
Popcorn King Decision Rules

If You Expect to Sell This Many Bags	Then Order This Many Bags			
	Rule 1	Rule 2	Rule 3	Rule 4
0	0	0	5	2
1	1	0	5	2
2	2	0	5	2
3	3	0	5	2
4	4	0	5	2
5	5	0	5	2

Rule 1 is the rule to use if you can tell in advance how many bags will be demanded, for it always produces the largest payoff if that demand occurs. Rule 2 is a conservative rule that will never get you into trouble, for it requires no investment and stands no chance of loss—or of profit. Rule 3 is the riskiest rule unless you are able to sell five bags. If five bags aren't sold, you suffer declining profits. You might choose rule 3 if you did not mind having leftover bags as much as you minded losing sales due to inadequate inventory. Rule 4 requires that you buy two bags of popcorn regardless of the state. Rule 4 produces the highest *average* payoff possible if the same number of bags must be bought before *every* game.

Identifying the Highest Average Payoff Alternative. To explain development of decision rule 4, you must distinguish between two kinds of decisions under uncertainty:

a) Decisions in which no information is available about the future state of nature that will occur when the decision becomes effective beyond that describing the relative frequencies of states.

b) Decisions in which, in addition to the relative frequencies of states, you know or can find out more about which state of nature will occur when the decision is effective.

Identifying the Highest Average Payoff Alternative when No Information Is Available. In Chapter 1, you relied on records of past popcorn demand at previous games. Assuming all football games are alike, the same sort of popcorn demand should occur in the future, and thus a *prior distribution* as shown in Figure 15–5 applies to possible popcorn demand levels.

When no additional information is available, you must identify the number of bags to order that will give the highest total payoff over a large number of games whose popcorn demands are distributed as in Figure 15–5. Return to the payoff table in Figure 15–1 and note

FIGURE 15–5
Prior Distribution over Popcorn Demand Levels

Number of Bags to Be Demanded	Probability of This Demand
0	0/6
1	1/6
2	3/6
3	1/6
4	1/6
5	0/6
	6/6 Total (always = 1.0)

that if you order one bag, in 0 games you will not sell this bag, in 1/6 of the games you will sell this bag exactly, and in $3/6 + 1/6 + 1/6 = 5/6$ of all games you could sell more than one bag. Your expected payoff for ordering *one* bag is then:

$$(5¢) \times (0/6) + 5¢ \times (1/6) + 5¢ \times (5/6) = 5¢$$

Your expected payoff for ordering *two* bags is:

$$(10¢)(0/6) + (0¢)(1/6) + 10¢(5/6) = 50/6¢$$

Your expected payoff for ordering *three* bags is:

$$(15¢)(0/6) + (5¢)(1/6) + 5¢(3/6) + 15¢(1/6) + 15¢(1/6) = 40/6¢$$

You should try the computation for 0, 4, and 5 bags and confirm that the expected payoffs are 0, 20/6 cents, and (10) cents respectively.

These are the average payoffs per game if the indicated number of bags is bought constantly. In no one game will the payoff be exactly that much—only the average over a large number of games will approach the expected payoff.

> Since buying two bags has the highest expected payoff for the given prior distribution, you should buy two bags before every game.

Identifying the Highest Average Payoff Alternatives when More Information Is Available. When more information is available to identify the state of nature that will occur when a decision becomes effective, it is usually possible for the decision maker to choose a different alternative for each state if he thinks that state will occur. The additional information affects the state probability distribution, making one or more states appear much more likely to occur than before. To fully realize the impact of additional information, suppose you go to the game and sell your two bags, and also have opportunities to sell two more bags. Although you bought and sold two bags for a profit of 10 cents, you wish you had known that you could have sold four bags. Ideally, you wish you had known that you could have sold *exactly* four bags so you could have realized a profit of 20 cents, just as you would have done in a decision under certainty. This is rarely possible, but progress toward this goal can often be made.

For example, when you approach a busy traffic intersection, you don't know if the intersection is clear until you are in it. As a *data-gathering process* before you reach the intersection, you glance at a traffic light, which is green. You interpret this as an indication that the intersection will remain clear until you finish crossing it. Traffic accident statistics attest to the occasional fallibility of such reasoning, but the system does work with a substantial degree of reliability.

Suppose you discover a close relationship between advance ticket sales (announced Friday before the game) and popcorn sales at the game. The data-gathering process consists of calling the ticket office and asking the quantity of tickets already sold. Figure 15–6 shows what you found out.

You can calculate the potential value of this information. Decision rule 1 in Figure 15–4 advised you to always buy the number of bags you expected to be demanded and now, through advance tickets sales,

FIGURE 15-6
Results of a Data-Gathering Process

Advance Ticket Sales	Bags of Popcorn Demanded at Game
20	0
30	1
40	2
50	3
60	4
70	5

you have knowledge in advance—perfect, unequivocal knowledge—what demand will be. In Figure 15-7 we use decision rule 1 with this

FIGURE 15-7
Calculation of Expected Value of Decision

0/6 of demand will be for 0 bags. Buy 0 bags and make 0¢. Multiply this by 0/6 and get	0/6
1/6 of demand will be for 1 bag. Buy 1 bag and make 5¢. Multiply this by 1/6 and get	5/6
3/6 of demand will be for 2 bags. Buy 2 bags and make 10¢. Multiply this by 3/6 and get	30/6
1/6 of demand will be for 3 bags. Buy 3 bags and make 15¢. Multiply this by 1/6 and get	15/6
1/6 of demand will be for 4 bags. Buy 4 bags and make 20¢. Multiply this by 1/6 and get	20/6
0/6 of demand will be for 5 bags. Buy 5 bags and make 25¢. Multiply this by 0/6 and get	0/6
6/6 = sum of weights Expected value of decision	70/6¢

perfect knowledge of the future state to compute the expected value of the decision with perfect knowledge.

The value at bottom right in Figure 15-7 is the expected contribution of the decision when you are perfectly informed about the state of the environment that will exist when the decision is effective. To compute it, you simply took the largest payoff for each state and multiplied it by the probability of that state's occurring.

Value of Information. Without the data-gathering process, the best you could expect from this decision was 50/6 cents. Having perfect information is worth an additional $(70 - 50)/6 = 20/6$ *cents*. For perfect information you would pay up to 20/6 cents per game.

448   An Introduction to Accounting for Decision Making and Control

Less than Perfect Information. Most data-gathering processes, such as those operated as accounting information systems, deliver less-than-perfect information. Imperfect information's benefits have to be reckoned against its cost so you know whether to acquire it. The marginal return on resources employed to obtain information should be the same as the marginal returns on resources employed otherwise. Assume decreasing marginal returns to scale; then if the marginal return from information is *less* than the marginal return from other resource uses, the resources dedicated to information gathering should be *reduced;* if the marginal return is greater, the resources dedicated to information gathering should be *increased*.

Imperfect information will change the prior probability distribution so that fewer states are favored. As an example of imperfect information, let popcorn demand be determined by advance ticket sales *plus* other factors about which you have no knowledge. The relations in Figure 15–8 are observed.

Here is an explanation of Figure 15–8. You are interested in the significance of advance sales = 40. Out of the last 18 games, advance

FIGURE 15–8
Example of Imperfect Information

Game	Advance Ticket Sales	Popcorn Demand	Total Times Advance Ticket Sales = 40	Total Times Advance Ticket Sales = 40 Followed by Popcorn Demand = 2	or 3
1........	30	1			
2........	40	3	1		3(1)
3........	40	2	2	2(1)	
4........	40	2	3	2(2)	
5........	50	2			
6........	60	4			
7........	40	3	4		3(2)
8........	30	1			
9........	40	2	5	2(3)	
10........	50	2			
11........	60	4			
12........	50	2			
13........	30	1			
14........	40	2	6	2(4)	
15........	60	4			
16........	40	2	7	2(5)	
17........	40	3	8		3(3)
18........	40	2	9	2(6)	

ticket sales were 40 nine times. Six of those times, popcorn demand was two bags; three times, three bags. Thus it appears that when advance ticket sales are 40, the probably of two bags being demanded is 6/9; the probability of three bags being demanded, 3/9. Figure 15–9 states the new state probability distribution.

FIGURE 15–9
Change of State Probabilities Resulting from Imperfect Information

Before Data Gathering	After Data Gathering	
$p(0 = \text{demand}) = 0/6$	0/6	
$p(1 = \text{demand}) = 1/6$	0/6	
$p(2 = \text{demand}) = 3/6$	4/6	Unique to advance
$p(3 = \text{demand}) = 1/6$	2/6	ticket sales = 40
$p(4 = \text{demand}) = 1/6$	0/6	
$p(5 = \text{demand}) = 0/6$	0/6	

What is the value of the information in Figure 15–9? The analytical process is too detailed to recount in an introductory chapter, but the essence of it is this: Each particular output of the data-gathering process (in this case, values of advance ticket sales) implies a different state probability distribution (the distribution for sales = 40 is contained in Figure 15–9). Using each probability distribution, some particular alternative has the highest expected payoff (computed just as was the expected payoff of each alternative using the probability distribution in Figure 15–5). These alternatives with the highest expected payoffs may be linked to corresponding data-gathering process outputs and form the highest payoff decision rule to use with that data-gathering process.

The best decision rule (that produces the highest payoff when used with advance ticket sales as a predictor of demand) is:

If advance sales are 30	buy 1 bag
If advance sales are 40	buy 2 bags (you can verify this one)
If advance sales are 50	buy 2 bags
If advance sales are 60	buy 4 bags

The expected value of this decision rule is *65/6 cents.* Thus, the rule based on imperfect information cannot perform as well as the rule based on perfect information (expected value = 70/6 cents), but it does much better than the rule based on lack of any additional information whatever, which had an expected value, you recall, of 50/6 cents.

Investing in Information. If you had to pay 9/6 cents in direct costs for the imperfect information in Figure 15–8 each time you decided how much to order, your additional profit would be $(15 - 9)/6 = 1\ cent.$

As with other investments, the fact that marginal gain exceeds marginal cost doesn't necessarily mean that you should incur the cost. The return must be equal to or greater than any return you receive from alternative investments. If your 9/6 cents would return you 20/6 cents in a comparable alternative investment, and you have only the 9/6 cents to spend, you should keep your ignorance, use decision rule 4 from Figure 15–4 for the popcorn ordering decision and put your money into the alternative investment.

Competing information systems should be judged not so much on how closely their output approaches perfect information but on how much net return they can produce for you. Figure 15–10 shows three

FIGURE 15–10
Criteria for Evaluating Data-Gathering Processes

	Process 1	*Process 2*	*Process 3*
Expected value per decision	68/6	65/6	60/6
Less: Expected value of decision *without* more information	(50/6)	(50/6)	(50/6)
Expected cost of more information	(10/6)	(9/6)	(1/6)
Expected contribution of information	(8/6)	(6/6)	(9/6)

data-gathering processes for the popcorn decision; it happens that the best of these is also the one which gives the least-perfect information. The reason is that its extreme economy enables it to show the highest net contribution.

DECISION MODELS FOR UNCERTAINTY

All of the decision models you have studied in this section have adaptations intended for use when environmental uncertainty exists.

These adaptations are more complex than the models intended for decisions under certainty.

Capital Allocation

Uncertainty is introduced into capital budgeting models in several ways. Perhaps the easiest to visualize is that several different economic conditions are possible, each implying a different set of net cash flows. The fact that alternative cash flows are possible does not alone make an investment proposal *"risky"* in the sense of Chapter 11; for if all economic conditions led to essentially equal cash flows, there would be little risk in the proposal. Thus, risk stems from alternative cash flows which differ in magnitude—and the greater the differences, the greater the investment risk. A decision model format which takes this approach is shown in Figure 15–11.

FIGURE 15–11
Capital Allocation Decision Model under Uncertainty

States.	State 1	State 2	etc.
State probabilities.	p(state 1)	p(state 2)	etc.
Alternatives:			
Proposal A.	Current equivalent of proposal A if state 1 occurs	Current equivalent of proposal A if state 2 occurs	
Proposal B	Current equivalent of proposal B if state 1 occurs	Current equivalent of proposal B if state 2 occurs	
etc., for all alternative investments			

To use this model, you need to know all alternative investment proposals (or investment programs) and the effect on net cash flow of all such proposals by each possible state.

Inventory Management

To simulate uncertainty in an inventory situation, one usually assumes that all costs are known, but that demand may occur at any one of several possible rates. Optimal policies (or, several alternative policies which are each *nearly* optimal) are known for each demand pattern, and the cost of implementing each one may be computed for all possible demand rates. The decision model for uncertainty for inventory management appears as Figure 15–12.

FIGURE 15–12
Inventory Management Decision Model under Uncertainty

	State 1 (demand level 1)	State 2 (demand level 2)	
States....................			
State probabilities.........	p(state 1)	p(state 2)	etc. etc.
Alternatives:			
Policy A	Cost of policy A for state 1	Cost of policy A for state 2	
Policy B	Cost of policy B for state 1	Cost of policy B for state 2	
etc., for all inventory policies			

In the inventory management decision, the choice of policy is on the basis of lowest expected cost rather than highest expected contribution. Additional methods, not based on economic order quantity analysis, exist to provide least-cost inventory policies where the EOQ assumptions are not valid.

Product Mix Analysis

Use of project planning and control and linear programming are both immensely complicated by introducing uncertainty into these decision models. A variety of approaches exist, none of them "intuitively obvious" and most of them requiring considerably analytical skill to set up and computing power to solve.

However, let us illustrate using a simple product mix analysis under uncertainty decision. Uncertainty may occur with respect to any part of the problem; let us assume that different economic conditions may occur and that to each possible economic decision there corresponds a different set of unit contribution margins. Then, assuming these margins differed significantly, you would have a different optimal solution to the problem for each set of economic conditions. Figure 15–13 shows this illustrative model.

FIGURE 15–13
Product Mix Decision Model under Uncertainty

States............	State 1 (contribution margin set 1)	State 2 (contribution margin set 2)	etc.
State probabilities.....	p(state 1)	p(state 2)	etc.
Alternatives:			
Production mix A.....	Value of objective function for product mix A in state 1	Value of objective function for product mix A in state 2	
Production mix B.....	Value of objective function for product mix B in state 1	Value of objective function for product mix B in state 2	
etc.			

The expected value of each optimal solution is determined and, subject to the results of a selected data gathering process, used as the basis for selecting a production mix.

SOME PROBLEMS IN PROVIDING INFORMATION FOR DECISIONS UNDER UNCERTAINTY

When Information Isn't Information

This problem should occur to you almost immediately. Something may be presented as a fact which isn't. Information may change your mind about which state will occur, whether it is true or false. You may receive an experimental result that indicates the sale of five bags of popcorn, yet sell only one.

Information is not information in another case—when it has no *surprise value*. If a data-gathering process leaves the prior distribution unchanged, it provides no information. This might mean the process was worthless, or it might mean you were well informed before the experiment. As a general rule, a data-gathering process should tend to indicate that a specific state will actually occur. A good information system will occasionally surprise you with an unexpected prediction. This is better than having the real world surprise you with an unexpected state of nature.

Understanding Uncertainty

Few persons share a common understanding of a single decision. What appears to be certainty to one person is uncertainty to another; a decision with two alternatives to one has six to another. When an information system serves many decision makers, it is impossible for it to satisfy all their information needs in a single, simple reporting format. An information system can do this for a single decision maker whose decision rules and values are known; great economies and compression of information can be achieved then. But for a crowd of decision makers, the best rule is for the information system to supply uncondensed, unsummarized information, in order that everyone can find therein what they require in their decisions.

Specifically, accounting systems present information as if the world and all its decisions were devoid of uncertainty, or even errors in information processing. Yet such information is used (not without complaints as to its inadequacies) to make decisions which are replete with uncertainty. Various attempts to remove the appearance of certainty from accounting information have so far not been conclusively successful; they fail against the formidable barrier of the heterogeneity of decision-making styles.

Perhaps the best attitude for the accountant is that the world would be a fully deterministic place, ideal for making decisions under certainty, if only we knew *enough* about how it works. Meanwhile, it is necessary to learn as much as possible about decisions under uncertainty.

SUMMARY

There are two basic decision types with respect to information availability—those in which only one state of nature may occur, and about which all factors and variables are determined; and those in which any one of a set of states of nature may occur when the decision is effective. The former are called decisions under certainty; the latter, decisions under uncertainty. In the former, the major recognized problem is the possibility of measurement error, which may mislead a decision maker even when the underlying events occurring are known. In decisions under uncertainty, the major problem is anticipating the unknown future state.

Quantitative decision models exist for many situations. To make these models operate at fullest efficiency, information system managers (most of whom are accountants) need to know their information requirements. Decision models do not differentiate between valid and invalid information; it is the accountant who does that.

QUESTIONS

1. Define these terms:
   a) Set of alternatives.
   b) Payoffs.
   c) Set of states.
   d) Prior distribution.

2. In which of the following situations is uncertainty present?
   a) You are going to see the play "Love Is a Color Photo" tonight and have a choice of $2, $3, or $4 tickets.
   b) You are trying to determine an admission price for municipal parks that will keep out idlers without deterring families.
   c) You must get home quickly, but don't know whether the traffic is heavier on the North Loop or the South Bypass.
   d) It is time to place an inventory order again, and you must determine how much to order (your order size will depend on future demand, which you do not know).
   e) You must decide whether to attempt to satisfy your North Atlantic oil-shipping contract with three large tankers or eight smaller ones.

3. What variables define the state of nature in—
   a) Capital allocation decisions?
   b) Inventory management decisions?
   c) Project planning and control?
   d) Product mix analysis?

4. What are the decision variables in the four decisions listed in Question 3 above?

5. Are information systems always completely accurate in describing the real world? If not, are their inaccuracies always significant in decisions made under certainty?

6. What are two problems an inaccurate information system may cause in a decision under certainty? May these problems also occur in a decision under uncertainty?

7. What is a "data-gathering process"? How can such a process add value to making a decision?

8. Recall or reread the "Rule of Information" and the "Rule of Control" from Chapter 6; then answer these questions:
   a) Is an information system adequate that gives four separate signals, corresponding to four separate possible states, for a decision in which six states in all are possible?
   b) Is a decision maker adequately equipped to cope with a decision in which one of nine possible states may occur, if he has only two alternatives from which to choose?

9. What is a decision rule? Let there be two possible states, $S1$ and $S2$, and two possible alternatives, $A1$ and $A2$. Give all possible decision rules and tell how you would choose the "best" one.

10. Here is a small decision model:

States	$S1$	$S2$	$S3$
State probabilities	0.5	0.3	0.2
Alternatives:			
$A1$	50	30	20
$A2$	30	50	20
$A3$	20	30	50

    a) What is the best single alternative (highest expected value)?
    b) What is the best decision rule if you have perfect information?
    c) Suppose a data-gathering process indicates that the state probabilities should be $p(S1) = 0.4$, $p(S2) = 0$, $p(S3) = 0.6$. What is the best single alternative? Is this consistent with the "perfect information" decision rule?

11. A new information gathering process will cost $10,000 to install and $1,000 per year. The decisions it will be used in will continue

to be made for three years, and will show an increase in expected value of $5,000 per year if the process is adopted. This entity's ITRR is 16 percent. Should the information gathering process be adopted?

12. Explain the difference between perfect information and imperfect information, and between certainty and uncertainty.

13. What is the criterion for investing in information?

14. If the cause of all uncertainty is taken to be lack of complete information, is there any difference between our uncertainty about what George Washington did on his 12th birthday and what the income of General Motors will be in fiscal 1978? Does the fact that one event is in the past and the other is in the future make any difference?

15. A company reports profits of $50,000,000. "That's good," says Sam, "because their profits were only $30,000,000 last year." "That's bad," says Sonny, "because analysts expected their profits to be $80,000,000 this year. "Well," says Sam, "since they raised their profits by $20,000,000 from last year to this, I think they will do it again and earn $70,000,000 next year." "No, no," says Sonny. "We know they fell $30 million short of their expected profit this year. Next year the management expects to make $80,000,000, so if they fall short by the same amount they'll only make $50 million again." What is going on here?

16. The Hoedown Company management decided it had to have some "hard numbers" in order to appraise the uncertainty surrounding the forecast of its income. The company identified three possible future economic situations. The expected income and likelihood of each are:

Economic Situation	Expected Income	Likelihood of Situation Occurring
Favorable	$1,000,000	0.2
Indifferent	800,000	0.3
Hostile	300,000	0.5

Explain what these numbers mean. To you, do they signify a high or low level of risk associated with this income forecast? What does management *expect* income to be? How likely is that value of income to occur?

17. The Siwel Company issued financial statements which read, in part:

Revenue	$13,000,000
Cost of sales	10,000,000
Administrative, interest, taxes	2,000,000
Net income (see note)	$ 1,000,000

(33 lines of print and 2 color pictures)

Note. The company is contingently liable in a lawsuit charging that one of the company's products when used as directed caused 17 heat exchangers in a Consolidated Dalton Power Company plant to be destroyed. The lawsuit seeks $300,000,000. The company's legal counsel assure us that the chances of our being held liable for any amount at all are very slight and that in any event a settlement would not be more than 20 percent of the amount sought, and probably much less.

How uncertain are you that Siwel earned $1,000,000 in that year?

18. When is information *not* information? To avoid the "play on words" in this question, attempt a definition of *relevant information* in decisions under uncertainty. Is your definition consistent with the accounting definition of relevant information?

EXERCISES

19. Agravaine Company is developing estimates of the markets available to it in other nations. The company is prepared to invest in these markets if it can expect to earn $100,000 or more per year in profits in a market. Here are the estimates, along with the real potential as historically observed at later dates:

Market	Estimated Potential	Observed Potential
Goronia	$450,000	$300,000
Abania	30,000	60,000
Irwinia	99,000	50,000

Is the estimation system good enough for Agravaine's purposes? How do you know?

20. Lester Company is analyzing a capital budgeting decision. The company's capital budget this year is $50,000. The company uses the current equivalent of investment proposals as a basis for these decisions. All proposals have the same lifetime, and the company is confident that economic conditions will develop exactly as it expects. The proposals and their costs and current equivalents are:

Proposal	Cost	Current Equivalent
A	$10,000	$15,000
B	30,000	42,000
C	5,000	10,000
D	10,000	8,000
E	20,000	32,000

Select the proposals which offer the highest current equivalent for an investment totaling $50,000 or less.

21. Spazz Company has reviewed its inventory functions and developed three alternative inventory policies. These policies would be effective under three different future economic environments, only one of which may occur. Here are the essential data:

	Environment 1	Environment 2	Environment 3
Probabilities.......	0.5	0.4	0.1
Policy costs:			
Policy 1	$450,000	$500,000	$650,000
Policy 2	600,000	620,000	640,000
Policy 3	550,000	450,000	700,000

Which policy has the lowest expected cost? What is the decision rule to use if perfect information is available? If the cost of policy 2 has been *overstated* above by $100,000, will using this information penalize Spazz Company?

22. Fell Company has a product mix decision which looks like this:

	State 1	State 2
Product mix 1.........	$50,000	$20,000
Product mix 2.........	20,000	60,000

The company has an imperfect information system which produces one of two results, $R1$ and $R2$. If $R1$ occurs, the state probability distribution is: $p(\text{state } 1) = 0.8$, $p(\text{state } 2) = 0.2$. If $R2$ occurs, the state probability distribution is: $p(\text{state } 1) = 0.1$, $p(\text{state } 2) = 0.9$. What is the best decision rule to use under these conditions?

23. Fell Company (see Exercise 22 above) has observed that state 1 occurs 30 percent of the time and state 2 occurs 70 percent of the time. What is the decision rule that would be used if perfect information were available? What is the expected value of the product mix that would be chosen if *no* information system were operating? What is the expected value of the decision if perfect information were available?

24. Fell Company (see Exercises 22 and 23 above) wants to know if its imperfect information system is producing a positive contribution, on the average. It determines that the result $R1$ is given

28.5 percent of the time and the result $R2$ is given 71.5 percent of the time. What is the expected value of $R1$ and $R2$ over and above the value of the decision without additional information? (*Hint*: Find the expected value of the decision when the decision rule related to $R1$ is used. Find the expected value of the decision when the decision rule related to $R2$ is used. Since $R1$ is obtained 28.5 percent of the time, the expected value of its corresponding decision rule is obtained 28.5 percent of the time. A similar statement applies to $R2$. The decision's total expected value can then be computed. From this, to obtain the net expected value of $R1$ and $R2$, you subtract the expected value of the decision without additional information.) If the information system costs $1,000 to operate for each decision, is its contribution positive?

PROBLEMS

25. Vendo, Inc. operates the concession stands at the football stadium. The university has had successful teams and sellout crowds as long as anyone can remember; the stadium is and always will be full. Oklayoming, the state in which the university is located, is very dry and of a constant temperature. From time to time, Vendo has found itself short of hot dogs to sell at games and at other times has had many left over, which it gives to a local orphanage without charge. The company reviews its records for the last 10 years and finds the following frequency of hot dogs sold:

	Total Games
10,000 hot dogs.	5
20,000 hot dogs.	10
30,000 hot dogs.	20
40,000 hot dogs.	15
Total games	50

Hot dogs sell for 50 cents and cost Vendo 30 cents each.

Required:

a) Assuming that only the four quantities listed were ever sold and that the occurrences were random events, prepare a payoff table (ignore income taxes) to represent the four possible strategies of ordering 10,000; 20,000; 30,000; and 40,000 hot dogs.

b) Using the expected value decision rule, determine the best strategy.

c) What is the dollar value of perfect information?

(Adapted from December 1972 CMA Examination)

26. The Midville city council is sitting to determine the outcome of an application by Midville Power Company for changes in the rates it charges for electricity in Midville and the surrounding area. Mr. Brownout, company president, is having an exchange with Mrs. Short, a councilwoman:

BROWNOUT: . . . to summarize, our new capacity will require debt service of $700,000 per year for 20 years, and added to our present costs of $900,000 per year related to debt repayment, we must cover $1,600,000 per year cash payments which are beyond our ability to control.

SHORT: That's clear enough.

BROWNOUT: Our total contribution will grow to $4 million.

SHORT: I know that.

BROWNOUT: Out of that $4 million would come the debt repayments, general and administrative expenses, dividends, and other costs.

SHORT: That is what I mean. Why are you coming in here asking for a 25 percent rate increase when you already are paying your obligations as they come due and will have $4.0 — $1.6 = $2.4 million left over? I don't understand.

BROWNOUT: I am coming to that, Mrs. Short. All of those expenses I mentioned add up to a cash drain per year of $2.0 million if our optimistic forecasts come true. We think that is about 50 percent likely to happen. But if these forecasts don't come true, which is equally likely, we will have an annual $2.5 million cash drain. Obviously something will have to give. To avoid that, we are seeking the rate increase. It will give us financial stability and assurance. Without the rate hike, we have a 50 percent chance of operating at a cash deficit. We are unable to take that risk. We would not build the additional capacity I referred to earlier.

SHORT: The rate hike would give you $700,000 in additional revenues?

BROWNOUT: Yes.

SHORT: Why can't you take your chances like any other business? It seems to me the only uncertainty you face is whether this council will gilt-edge guarantee your profits!

BROWNOUT: Not true! Our generating capacity, Mrs. Short, is

oil-fired, and there is a worldwide shortage of fuel oil right now. Its price could double or triple over a period of a few months. We have to have protection against such uncertainty. Also, we don't really know what the demand for electricity will be in four or five years; our predictions have failed before.

SHORT: Oh, but—

BROWNOUT: If demand is less than we expect, we have a lot of unusable capacity. If demand is more than we expect, we have to buy power from the pool at three times our cost to produce it.

SHORT: I just don't see why you have to have rates that are higher than you need right now.

Required:

a) Compute the decision model under uncertainty that faces Mrs. Short and the rest of the council.
b) Evaluate the arguments and positions of Mrs. Short and Mr. Brownout—particularly, other decision alternatives which might be more satisfactory than those two presented here.

27. The Midville Power Company allows its customers to pay by mail. Once each month it sends a bill and normally receives payment within 30 days. This month there was difficulty in getting out the statements; many were misaddressed and others did not go out until several weeks after the normal date. As a result the company is uncertain what its collections this quarter will be from billings. The company has developed, based on a sample of customers queried to determine their repayment plans, three forecasts of repayments:

	Forecast 1	*Forecast 2*	*Forecast 3*
Forecast probability	0.3	0.5	0.2
Quarterly cash collections	$500,000	$700,000	$900,000

Total billings were $1,000,000. Any *not* collected this quarter will be collected, of course, in the following quarter. Cash expenses for the quarter will be $970,000. The utility keeps a negligible bank account balance and will consequently have to borrow money to pay its cash obligations. Cash can be borrowed, but because there is a general shortage of short-term loanable funds, the utility must borrow for the *full* three months in advance and must borrow in multiples of $100,000. The interest rate is 1 percent per month on funds borrowed; cash obligations left unpaid incur a flat 10 percent penalty expense.

Required:

a) Prepare a decision model showing the utility's decision how much money to borrow and the interest expense associated with each state of nature–decision alternative combination.

b) Show the optimal strategy if the company could know exactly what its cash collections would be.

c) Show the alternative with the lowest expected interest cost if no further information is available. How much would this utility spend to obtain perfect information?

28. Blocher Oil Company has, during its 12-year existence as a drilling and exploration company, drilled 168 wells of which 21 have been successfully productive. The cost of drilling a well is variable; 30 percent of the time it is $1,000,000, and 70 percent of the time it is $2,000,000. This cost depends on factors not known before drilling is underway. If a well is successful, it produces $2,000,000 per year in oil revenues for five years, after which time it becomes dormant. There are no significant costs of pumping oil. The ITRR applied to investments in exploratory wells is 20 percent.

Required:

a) What is the current cash equivalent of the oil revenues of a successful well?

b) If no additional information is available, give the net present value of the four kinds of well that may result from drilling and the expected value of the average well drilled. Are drilling operations profitable?

c) Imagine that perfect information is available. Compute the expected value of the average well that would be drilled (no dry holes would be drilled). What is the value of perfect information?

d) Additional information is available for $100,000 per well drilled that will increase the probability of a successful well to 25 percent. Should this information be acquired?

29. Expello Company manufactures inexpensive voting machines that use a specially designed punch card to record the voter's choices. Preliminary tests of the machine show that the "stylus," an impor-

tant part of the machine, is breakage-prone. The reason for breakage is almost always the misuse of the stylus by a voter. Expello has developed an ad campaign which is intended to be released upon a community using its voting machines one to two weeks before an election, and which will educate the electorate on the proper use of its machines.

The campaign can be continued, with decreasing returns, over any desired length of time. Expello wants to know the "best" time period to run the campaign because it must provide instant on-the-spot repair of its machines.

One man can repair 50 machines per day. The out-of-pocket costs to hire, train, and provide one repairman for one election is $1,200.

A city with one million voters requires 1,000 machines. The ad campaign costs $3,000 per day in a city of this size. The relationship between percentage of machines that will break and duration (in days) of the ad campaign is:

Duration	Percent Broken
1	60
2	40
3	25
4	15
5	10
6	7
7	5
8	4
9	3

Expello does not pay for the ad campaign, but most cities will put it on to some extent.

Required:

a) Determine a decision rule for the number of repairmen (one for each 50 or fraction thereof of broken machines) to send to a city as a function of the ad campaign it puts on.

b) If Expello has to pay for the ad campaign, what campaign would minimize the sum of maintenance and ad expenses?

c) Suppose 30,000,000 voters will be using Expello machines in the next election. Twenty percent of these will experience a two-day campaign, 50 percent will experience a four-day campaign, and 30 percent will experience a seven-day campaign. How many maintenance men should Expello provide?

30. Trump Corporation stocks parts for large hydroelectric generators. Such generators rarely need other than routine maintenance, but when parts are needed (perhaps years after the original generator was installed) they are needed badly indeed. One item is the rotor of a very large generator. These rotors are available to Trump now for $100,000 apiece. In 10 years all generators using these rotors will be retired. The cost of keeping a rotor in stock is $10,000 per year. Trump would sell a rotor now for $120,000; its selling cost will rise by $5,000 per year. Any number of generator rotors may be ordered now; but none at all hereafter.

The reliability of these rotors is not established. Below are expected demand patterns:

	Number Rotors Demanded	
Years Held Before Sale	Relatively Reliable (20% Probability)	Relatively Unreliable (80% Probability)
0 (now)	0	0
1	2	3
2	0	1
3	0	2
4	2	3
5	0	2
6	0	2
7	0	2
8	0	1
9	0	0

Required:

a) Compute the ideal number of rotors to order in each case above.

b) Treating the rotor ordering decision as a decision under uncertainty, compute the best alternative of the two in (a) from a profit standpoint. Assume that unsold rotors are a total loss, and sold after the fourth year.

c) A study by engineers indicates a 60 percent probability the rotors are relatively reliable. Would this change your answer in (b)? If the study cost $20,000, did it pay for itself?

31. Keller Refining Company uses linear programming to determine the optimal output of refinery products. Each month a new problem is formulated, based on the plant capacities and feed streams coming in and contractual obligations to sell minimum amounts of various products. The company attempts to maximize total contribution margin. At present there are four products. The company has a policy of not changing the production mix unless the contribution margin increase will be at least three times the $10,000 cost of readjusting the refinery to the new mix.

In two recent months, the linear programming analysis gave these optimal production mixes and contributions:

Month	Thousands of Barrels to Be Produced				Estimated Contribution per Barrel			
	A	B	C	D	A	B	C	D
1........	5	6	7	8	$10	$8	$12	$6
2........	8	2	9	5	12	3	14	6

The mix in month 1 was actually produced. The management now must decide whether to switch from the month 1 mix to the mix which is optimal for month 2.

Required:

a) Compute the total contribution (1) if the month 1 mix is produced in month 2, using month 2 estimated contributions per barrel, and (2) if the month 2 mix is produced in month 2, using the same estimated contributions per barrel.

b) Decide which mix should be produced in month 2.

c) Suppose that the contribution per barrel on product D is actually $9. Is your choice in (b) then an incorrect decision? Should Keller Company be willing to spend any money to get correct information on this margin? If so, how much?

32. Bower Company's inventories are managed using EOQ models. The utensil inventory order point is always zero, but the order quantity is computed afresh each month using formula (11–2A) from Chapter 11. Ordering cost is $50 per order; carrying cost is $2 per unit per month. Demand varies from month to month. There is no delay between placing and receiving an order. Demand varies from month to month; any number of orders can be placed to satisfy demand. Here is a typical demand pattern:

January	February	March	April	May
60	90	30	30	90

The utensil supplier ships in only two quantities: 100 and 50 units.

Required:

a) Compute the actual cost of the 50-unit and 100-unit order quantity policies, assuming zero inventory at the beginning of the period above.
b) Compute the total cost of an EOQ policy for each month above, then the total cost for all five months.
c) Indicate the additional cost over this period that Bower Company would be willing to pay to order in EOQ lot sizes rather than in standard lot sizes.

33. Knothole Construction Company has successfully bid on an office building project and will build a major part of it. The "critical path" analysis of this project showed, after cost optimization, that there were two critical paths: A and B. The company plans to finish them both in 90 days. However, it knows there will be some variation around this figure; the statisticians and accountants have developed this information:

Path	Shortest Time	Expected Time	Longest Time	Cost per Day to Shorten
A	80	90	100	$50
B	80	90	105	50

The probabilities are, for each path:

        Shortest time 20%
        Expected time. 60
        Longest time 20

These probabilities are independent in respect to paths; that is, path A may be completed in its shortest time while path B is completed in some other time. Thus, $P(A = 100$ and $B = 105) = P(A = 100) \times P(B = 105)$, etc. There is a $300 per day penalty if the company takes more than 90 days to complete its part of the work.

Required:

a) What are the possible completion times for this project, and what is the probability of each?
b) Let there be two alternatives. The first is to simply let things stand as they do now. The second is to decrease the expected completion time for A by 10 days and the expected completion time for B by 5 days; that is, to make the maximum completion times for these paths (which are reduced by a corresponding

amount) equal to 90 days. Find the expected cost of each alternative.

c) Select the alternative with the lowest expected cost above. Do you see any basis here for a generalization about projects in which path completion times are numerically close and not perfectly controllable? How much would you be willing to pay for the information describing uncertainty in this problem?

34. Green Triangle Insurance Company offers health insurance policies to lower-middle income families who belong to groups based on churches, community organizations, etc. Each policy is especially designed for that group. Records are kept to discover how well expectations and actual results compare. Here are such records for the past ten proposals made for groups seeking policies (the company does not offer a policy if its analysis shows that the margin in the first two years will be at least 20 percent):

Proposed Policy	Estimated Income	Estimated Expenses	Policy Written?	Actual Income	Actual Expenses
1	$ 50,000	$40,000	Yes	$60,000	$47,000
2	100,000	90,000	No		
3	70,000	40,000	Yes	70,000	50,000
4	80,000	60,000	Yes	70,000	55,000
5	30,000	20,000	Yes	40,000	20,000
6	60,000	30,000	Yes	40,000	30,000
7	90,000	80,000	No		
8	20,000	10,000	Yes	20,000	15,000
9	50,000	35,000	Yes	45,000	35,000
10	40,000	40,000	No		

Required:

a) Were any proposed policies accepted that should not have been? Were any rejected that should not have been? Base your answers only on the *estimated* data.

b) Were any policies accepted that later did not perform with margin greater than 20 percent?

c) The planning director of Green Triangle wants to redesign the estimating processes, because he is unhappy at the discrepancies between estimated and actual results. Such a redesign will cost $2,000. Based on these 10 policies, and your answers to (*a*) and (*b*), would such a redesign be worthwhile economically?

d) Can you think of grounds other than accuracy in planning for changing the estimating processes?

DECISION CASE 15–1: INDIOS HANDICRAFT MARKETS, INC.

The Indios Handicrafts Markets, Inc. was originally formed as a cooperative to market handmade objects produced by various cultures. The concept was successful, and the cooperative was eventually replaced by a corporation which consolidated its operations in a large warehouse-type building in a major East Coast city. The company appears to be outgrowing this facility and wants to either improve it substantially or build a completely new one. Complicating this decision is uncertainty whether the recent rapid growth of business will continue. Here are data collected by consultants to the company to help it make a decision:

	Renovate Existing Structure	Design and Build New Structure
Original cost	$300,000	$600,000
Market value in 5 years	100,000	300,000
Revenues:		
A. Rapid growth		
Year 1	500,000	550,000
Year 2	550,000	610,000
Year 3	600,000	660,000
Year 4	660,000	750,000
Year 5	700,000	850,000
B. Slow growth		
Year 1	500,000	530,000
Year 2	520,000	570,000
Year 3	550,000	590,000
Year 4	570,000	610,000
Year 5	600,000	650,000
Fixed cash costs per year	200,000	160,000
Variable cash costs per year	40% of revenues	38% of revenues

Required:

a) Let the ITRR if rapid growth occurs be 10 percent; if slow growth occurs, 16 percent. Prepare a decision model showing states, alternatives, and payoffs. Neglect tax effects.
b) If the firm knows rapid growth will occur, which facilities improvement plan should it select? Is this the same plan it will select if it knows slow growth will occur?
c) Let the probability of slow growth be determined to be 40 percent. What is the expected value of the decision (1) with and (2) without perfect information?
d) How much (if anything) should Indios pay to receive perfect information about its future rate of growth (relative just to this decision)?

BIBLIOGRAPHY

Books

Aigner, Dennis J. *Principles of Statistical Decision Making*. New York: The Macmillan Co., 1968.

Bower, James B.; Schlosser, Robert E.; and Zlatkovich, Charles T. *Financial Information Systems*. Boston: Allyn & Bacon, Inc., 1969.

Chernoff, Herman, and Moses, Lincoln E. *Elementary Decision Theory*. New York: John Wiley & Sons, Inc., 1959.

Cohen, Burton J. *Cost-Effective Information Systems*. New York: American Management Association, 1971.

Hare, Van Court. *Systems Analysis: A Diagnostic Approach*. New York: Harcourt, Brace & World, Inc., 1967.

Luce, R. Duncan, and Raiffa, Howard. *Games and Decisions*. New York: John Wiley & Sons, Inc., 1957.

Raiffa, Howard. *Decision Analysis: Introductory Lectures on Choices under Uncertainty*. Reading, Mass.: Addison-Wesley Publishing Co., Inc., 1968.

Savage, Leonard J. *The Foundations of Statistics*. New York: John Wiley & Sons, Inc., 1954.

Articles

Dearden, John. "How to Organize Information Systems," *Harvard Business Review*, March–April 1965.

Feltham, Gerald. "The Value of Information," *The Accounting Review*, October 1968.

Mason, Richard. "Management Information Systems: What They Are, What They Ought to Be," *Innovation*, No. 13, 1970.

Mastromano, Frank M. "A Data Base Concept," *Management Accounting*, October 1970.

Rothery, Brian. "The World of Systems," *Data Processing*, April 1967.

Strassman, Paul A. "Forecasting Considerations in Design of Management Information Systems," *Management Accounting*, February 1965.

Part IV

Accounting in a Responsible Society

16

Managerial Decisions and Price Changes

IT'S HARD to find anyone today who has not heard of or been affected by price changes. A "price change" is, in precise terms, any movement (between two points in time) in the ratio of exchange (price) between any two resources. Because most exchange ratios are expressed in terms of currency, an increase in the number of dollars that must be given in order to obtain a pound of meat is an increase in the price of meat. Less obviously, it is also a *decrease* in the price of money, measured in terms of meat. If meat decreases in price, it is the same thing as money increasing in price (since you have to give more meat to get the same amount of money, or give the same amount of meat for less money).

Relative supply and demand for a scarce resource such as meat is summarized and reflected in its exchange ratio, which is usually expressed in terms of money. One would not expect all prices to increase or decrease together, since normally some commodities are becoming relatively more abundant, causing their prices to decline; others are becoming relatively less abundant, causing their prices to increase. Ideally from the standpoint of judging trends in the relative scarceness of resources, money should always be neither more nor less scarce at different points in time—money's average price should be constant.

In this chapter you learn what happens when money is relatively more or less valuable at some points in time than others—from the managerial decision-making point of view. In particular, you learn how accountants inform decision makers that money's relative scarceness is changing and should be taken into account in decision making.

THE MONEY SUPPLY

Long ago most money was in the form of some durable and useful commodity—so that if money could not be spent it could be worn, eaten, drunk, lived in, etc. As populations increased, skill specialization arose, commerce became more necessary and sophisticated, and the need developed to use a nonperishable, scarce, essentially *useless* substance for money. Gradually the civilized world turned to metals—iron, bronze, silver, and gold. The use of metals as money persists into the present time, although many nations have all but abandoned it. In the United States, the principal money is Federal Reserve Notes, which are in theory IOUs issued by the federal government (get one out and read what is written on it). The government issues or retires these in order to adjust the quantity of money in circulation (the amount of money in circulation is called the "money supply"). The proper concept of money is as something moving from one party to another, enabling each to participate in economic activity by exchanging it for goods and services at appropriate times.

Now think in aggregate terms. Imagine a country with 100,000 units of a multiuse scarce resource in circulation in its economy. This is such a versatile resource that it can be eaten, worn, made into autos, homes, planes—everything that any society or person could desire. When the resource is "used up" it is easily recycled and thus replenished. This country also has a money supply consisting of 1,000,000 "dollars." Thus on the average, each resource unit is matched by 10 dollars in circulation.

Suddenly all the citizens want as many units of the resource as they can obtain. They crowd into the resource stores, buying anything made of the resource or containing it in any form. Storekeepers, finding so much demand, raise the price of the resource and the products it appears in. These price increases serve to balance the increasing demand against the resource supply. The same amount of money is still present in the economy, but the sudden desire of everyone to have more resource when this is not possible makes the resource price go up.

Here are some other causes of such price increases:

1. An increase in the money supply, giving everyone more money with which to pursue the same number of units of the resource.
2. A decrease in the *per capita* number of units of resource available, so that each person will have to settle eventually for fewer units of resource, but has the same money as before with which to buy them.

Cause 1 is known as *inflation*. More money is available but the quantity of goods to buy is the same. Even though inflation is a specific *decrease* in the price of money, its effect is referred to as a "general price level increase." Cause 2 is more complex and usually does not affect all prices at once. In the simple economy above, suppose that autos made from the single resource are suddenly in great demand. Then everyone wants a car. Until car production can be increased, there will be a scarcity of cars, and the imbalance between supply and demand will be reflected in a high price for autos. At the same time, people will have less money to spend on the radios, houses, and the like, and will demand fewer of these items. As a result, the prices of items in less demand may decline to correct the imbalance between supply and demand. No. 2 above is most often responsible for *specific* price changes, which are different from inflation.

We mention but do not elaborate on the principal cause of increases in the money supply—increases in government borrowing. Government borrowing results in issuance of new currency. This is because the government borrows in order to pay for goods and services it receives, in effect printing the additional money it needs to pay for the goods and services. *Welfare economics* and *public finance* are two important branches of economics which deal with the problems of an adequate money supply; if you study them you will find that there are many reasons why a "constant" supply of money cannot be maintained, and why the central government debt is by no means all a bad thing.

SPECIFIC AND GENERAL PRICE LEVEL INCREASES

Let us extend our analysis of inflation. (The other side of inflation is *deflation,* a general decline in resource prices; it is unlikely to be encountered over any but the shortest time intervals.)

Specific Price Increases

First you should think for a moment about what a specific price increase is *telling* a decision maker when the money supply is constant. A price increase would be a signal that the supply of that item was decreasing relative to demand for it. There is a possibility for additional profit if your business can provide additional supply to help meet the additional demand. A price decrease would be telling you that the supply of an item is increasing relative to the demand for it. This situation may be a signal to withdraw from a market in which supply overbalances demand. Thus, specific prices changes are signals for the *reallocation* of resources, including currency, in a properly functioning market economy.

For example, suppose you make water purifiers which sell for about $100 each. Your plant has a capacity of 10,000 filters annually, and actually makes about 7,000 filters. Your profit per unit is about $20.

This year, your sales and production rise to 7,500 units. You raise your price to $110 per unit. Unit sales do not level off but climb to 8,000 units the following year. You raise the price to $120 and sales increase to 9,000 units.

You know now that you are faced with a genuine upsurge in demand but can't participate in it much longer. Your plant capacity is only 10,000 units; another year and you will be unable to further increase production. Your competitors will get the additional business. You must expand your plant. It costs $100,000, but the next year you add capacity to make an additional 1,000 units per year. The demand for water purifiers triggered an increase in supply through higher profit you expected from the expansion.

General Price Increases

Inflation Types. If inflation occurs, all prices rise more or less together, destroying the normal meanings of price changes. Businesses which can't maintain broad contact with the economic situation may be deceived into interpreting the price increases they experience as specific price increases and react to them as such. But in fact inflation does not carry the same signal as a specific price increase.

Inflation is sometimes perceived by businessmen as "cost-push" inflation; that is, their costs rise and in order to remain profitable they must raise the selling prices of their outputs. "Demand-pull" inflation is what businessmen call price increases which occur when demand generally for all commodities rises. Both types of inflation are different perceptions of the same animal. Both must be distinguished from specific price increases.

INFLATION AND BUSINESS PLANNING

The company fortunate enough to sell a product which enjoys an increase in price while product costs are constant is not uncommon. A less fortunate company may find itself selling a product at constant price when the cost of the product components is increasing, thus cutting down the profit margin and return on investment. This invites the business to become more productive, stop that particular operation, or raise its price. How can you determine what is happening in order to make correct decisions?

> The essential information will tell you which accounting costs, asset values, prices, and revenues would have occurred if there were no price changes and compare these with corresponding elements under the actual situation (which includes price changes). This information will let you judge the effect of price changes on all operations.

Two concepts of gain and loss from transactions past and future have been developed about which to organize such information. *Realized* gain or loss arises from operations and transactions which have already occurred. *Realizable* gain or loss is expected to arise from operations or transactions which are currently possible (but not necessary). For example, you buy a car for $3,000. You keep the car one year, using up one fourth of the services the car is capable of rendering in the course of its march to the junk heap. At that time you could purchase a used car exactly identical to yours for $2,000. Since the cost basis of the car is $3,000 − 1/4($3,000) = $2,250, you have a realizable loss of $2,250 − $2,000 = $250. (It is a loss because the market now values three fourths of the car's original services as it valued two thirds of them one year ago; your loss is the value in exchange of one twelfth of the original services.) Had you known of this loss in advance, you would have bought a used car one year ago with one fourth of its service potential intact (for $750), used it one year, then purchased a used car for $2,000 with three fourths of its service potential intact. In any event, your loss is not realized unless you sell your car now.

Effect of Inflation on a Business

Inflation may produce a steady, difficult-to-spot decline of a business' ability to conduct operations. This is because sale of commodities takes place after acquisition of factors of production from which to make them. To give an extreme example, assume that there is a 20 percent per period inflation rate in the prices of all goods, that you buy and pay for the inputs to your product two periods before you sell it, and that you start business with $1,000 in period 0, enough to make 10 units in that period.

Figure 16–1 assumes that the firm seeks to maintain constant levels

FIGURE 16–1
Production Declines, Profit Constant when Inflation Occurs

Period	Manufacturing Costs Cash	Units Made	Units Sold	Unit Selling Price of Product	Total Revenue	Accounting Gross Profit
0	$1,000	10	...	$120	...	...
1	1,000	8.3	...	144	...	...
2	1,000	7	10	173	$1,730	$730
3	1,000	5.8	8.3	207	1,730	730
4	1,000	4.8	7	249	1,730	730

of profit as measured in dollars. Production then declines and profit remains constant—a situation not unlike that evident in the United States in 1970 and 1971.

It is an illusion that gross profit in Figure 16–1 remains constant. Your business is using the proceeds of sales to replace its stock in trade. But by period 4, the business would require 20 percent as much currency as it did in period 0 to make the same number of units—or conversely, can only make 4.8 units with the $1,000 which made 10 units in period 0. The price of money in terms of goods is going down.

The business requires more currency to maintain the same physical levels of operation. In terms of ability to sustain these levels of physical operations, the business' real income and economic power is declining.

Maintaining Economic Power

How could such a decline be prevented? Let us imagine that the firm wishes to maintain a constant *physical* (as opposed to dollar) level of operation. Then Figure 16–1 would be revised to look like Figure 16–2.

FIGURE 16–2
Production Level Steady, Profit Rises when Inflation Occurs

Period	Manufacturing Costs Cash	Units Made	Units Sold	Unit Selling Price of Product	Total Revenue	Accounting Gross Profit	Profit Not Required by Production
0	$1,000	10	...	$120	...	...	...
1	1,200	10	...	144	...	...	...
2	1,440	10	10	173	$1,730	$ 730	$290
3	1,730	10	10	207	2,070	870	340
4	2,070	10	10	249	2,490	1,050	420

It would appear that the business is earning an upward-trending accounting gross profit. However, since increasing amounts of currency must be devoted to maintaining a constant level of production, many accountants and economists would argue that the real profit is NOT current revenue minus the cost of production. The difference between current and historical cost of production (example: period 3, $1,730 − $1,200 = $530) is an unrealized expense, one that normally is not reported on the accounting performance statements until sale of the goods produced this period. If we subtract this unrealized expense from accounting gross profit, we obtain the amount of accounting profit not required to sustain production. This is a smaller figure—$290, $340, $420—but at least it seems to be increasing!

Indices

But profit is really not increasing, and to show why we introduce the concept of a *price index*. A price index is simply the ratio of the price of a single commodity at one point in time to the price of the same commodity at some other "base" point in time. For example, the ratio of commodity "WF" price in 1974 to "WF" price in 1972 would be computed as

$$I_{wf74} = \frac{P_{wf1974}}{P_{wf1972}} = \frac{\$36}{\$30} = 1.2 \text{ (usually expressed as } 120\text{)} \quad (16\text{–}1)$$

Rather than a single commodity, we may define a "market basket" of commodities in the economy as a whole and simply add up their prices at different points in time, taking the ratio of these price sums as a measure of the change in the general value of currency.[1] For example, assume an economy with only two commodities, A and B. We define a market basket as one unit of A and one unit of B and we add their prices together at different points in time. To determine an index showing changes in the general value of currency, we take the ratio of each of these sums to the sum in a period called the *base period*. Let 1972 be the base period. Figure 16–3 shows the calculations.

FIGURE 16–3
Computation of a Series of Indices

Year	Price of A	Price of B	Total Price	Ratio	Inflation Index
1971	$16.5	$25	$41.50	41.5/50	0.83
1972 (base)	25	25	50.00	50/50	1.00
1973	31	29	60.00	60/50	1.20
1974	32	40	72.00	72/50	1.44
1975	30	56.5	86.50	86.5/50	1.73

A further refinement to the indices computed in Figure 16–3 is to multiply the ratios by 100 so that they are expressed as percentages. The index percentage for a particular year is denoted by I_x where "x" is a subscript giving the year for which the index was computed. Different kinds of indices may be denoted by different letters. Notice that at times the prices of both A and B move in a direction opposite to the index. This illustrates that inflation may exist at the same time

---

[1] This is only one of many ways to construct an index. You may, as one typical alternative, compute a weighted price sum instead of a simple price sum, choosing the weights as you see fit.

as specific price changes—a very confusing situation we shall deal with as simply as possible later in this chapter.

Real Income

We previously defined real income as the difference between current costs and current revenue. Now let us *deflate* this difference by expressing all elements leading to its calculation in dollars which have the same value in exchange as those in the first period—period 0. Of course, such dollars no longer exist after the first period, but dollars of different periods are really not comparable if their value in exchange differs significantly.

We perform the deflation by dividing each figure in the right-most column of Figure 16–2 by the inflation index for that period. We define the necessary inflation indices and perform the calculations in Figure 16–4.

FIGURE 16–4
Deflating Profit Using Inflation Indices

Period	(From Figure 16-2) Profit Not Required by Production	Inflation Index	Calculation	Deflated Profit
0 (base)	...	100		
1	...	120		
2	$290	144	290/1.44	$200
3	340	173	340/1.73	200
4	420	207	420/2.07	200

Each of the figures in the right-most column is equal to $200, the number of 1972-value dollars earned and not required to sustain production. Thus what at first appeared to be an income of $1,050 in period 4 turns out to be, after sustaining production and adjusting for inflation, only $200! These two effects were:

1. The increase in the number of dollars required to sustain the current physical volume of activity.
2. The decline in the value in exchange of currency as time progressed.

The $200 is the same profit the company would have expected if there had been no inflation and its volume had remained steady.

To Beat Inflation

You now see why an inflation should be brought at once to the attention of decision makers. The impression created by the original performance reports was that profits could be sustained through decreased levels of operation, or increased through the same level of operation, which might lead to adoption of one of these alternatives as a goal. In fact, the declining level of operations reduced profits, and the constant operations only held profits constant.

A management unaware an inflation was in progress might mistake its "larger" profits for efficiency improvements and increase its dividends, or stop making the expenditures essential for real efficiency improvements. Such a management would be caught short of capital and resources eventually as the inflation continued.

To illustrate the shortage of capital, remember that prices of new long-lived assets are rising during the inflation. An asset that could have been bought for two years' income in period 2 will, if the company holds income constant in unadjusted terms, have to be bought for $2 \times (207/144) = 2.875$ years' income in period 4.

The only real way to contend with inflation is to recognize it as a signal that the supply of money is outrunning the supply of things to spend money on. No one will want to hold money, a commodity whose value is declining. Thus, a business should look for ways to acquire real-profit-producing assets and activities in exchange for money, or debt. In other words the only way to "get ahead" in real, deflated terms is to provide services and commodities for which increased real demand can be expected.

ACCOUNTING STATEMENTS AND PRICE CHANGES

The balance sheet and the statement of income present the historical dollar equivalents of the assets owned by an entity at a point in time, the dollar claims against those assets by various parties, and a summary of activities, again expressed in historical dollars, which have affected assets and equities during a specified period. Because these statements are prepared as if the price levels of all commodities and resources were not changing, they exclude information about price level changes; they do not show the historical effect of price changes on the business' position or income.

Balance Sheet

Accounting methodologies have been developed to provide such indications. They make use of the tools we have presented in the preceding section—specifically, price indices. Let us first imagine the balance sheet of Dollar Company, as shown in Figure 16–5.

FIGURE 16–5
DOLLAR COMPANY
Unadjusted Balance Sheet
At 12-31-73

Assets		Equities	
Cash	$1,000	Accounts payable	$2,000
Inventory	2,000	Owners' equity	4,000
Fixed assets	3,000	Total Equities	$6,000
Total Assets	$6,000		

We wish to adjust this balance sheet so that it is in terms of dollars at the end of 1973. All the inventory was manufactured at the beginning of 1973. All the fixed assets were acquired at the beginning of 1970. The applicable price level indices are:

```
12-31-69 . . . . . . . . . 100
12-31-70 . . . . . . . . . 110
12-31-71 . . . . . . . . . 120
12-31-72 . . . . . . . . . 115
12-31-73 . . . . . . . . . 130
```

Cash and Cash Equivalents. Since cash is currency, no adjustment of end-of-current-period cash balance is ever necessary. The same is true of accounts receivable and accounts payable. These items are always directly convertible into units of the currency of the present moment. However, note that if we were showing (for comparative purposes) a balance sheet of one year ago, the cash balance at that point in time would have to be multipled by $(I_{\text{present moment}}/I_{\text{one year ago}})$ in order to express cash in current dollars for comparison with the current cash balance. Above, 1,000 dollars held at 12-31-72 would be equal to 1,000 (130/115) equals 1,130 dollars (of 12-31-72) held at 12-31-73. However, the 12-31-73 cash balance shown requires no adjustment.

Inventory. Assume that the inventory was made and paid for with the dollars available one year ago. To show how many dollars would presently be equivalent to that original number of dollars (which was 2,000) we must multiply the original number of dollars by the 12-31-73 value of the index and divide it by the 12-31-72 value of the index. The result is $2,000 \times 130 \div 115 = \$2,260$.

Fixed Assets. The fixed assets were acquired with the dollars available at the end of 1969. In order to show how many 12-31-73 dollars these are equivalent to, it is necessary to multiply the original number of dollars by the 12-31-73 value of the index and divide it by the 12-31-69 value of the index. The result is $3,000 \times 130 \div 100 = \$3,900$.

Often we have assets acquired at different points in time. In that case, compute the equivalent number of current dollars for each asset acquisition separately and add together all the equivalents.

The depreciation provision, if one is shown, is more difficult to compute, and we choose to omit it from this elementary presentation. Succinctly, depreciation taken in each past year must be deflated to its current dollar equivalent.

Owners' Equity. Typically, specific amounts within owners' equity can be identified, and there is a residual called "retained earnings" or some similar title. Any amounts which are specifically identifiable as to source and date can be adjusted to their present dollar equivalent. Assume that the Dollar Company was formed on 12-31-69 and that capital stock was sold for $1,000. Then the current dollar equivalent of this original investment in the firm is $1,000 \times 130 \div 100 = \$1,300$.

Since owners' equity as a whole is a residual, determine retained earnings by applying the balance sheet equation: assets minus liabilities equals owners' equity. This equality translated into current dollars is:

$$\$1,000 + \$2,260 + \$3,900 - \$2,000 = \$5,160$$

Of this $\$5,160 - \$1,300 = \$3,860$ consists of retained earnings. The adjusted balance sheet is shown in Figure 16–6.

FIGURE 16-6
DOLLAR COMPANY
Adjusted Balance Sheet
In Dollars of 12-31-73
At 12-31-73

Assets		Liabilities	
Cash	$1,000	Accounts payable	$2,000
Inventory	2,260	Owners equity:	
Fixed assets	3,900	Capital stock	1,300
Total Assets	$7,160	Retained earnings	3,860
		Total Liabilities	$7,160

You should observe that—

1. Under inflation, the number of current dollars required to represent any durable asset increases.
2. Monetary amounts do not change so long as the obligations are satisfiable in cash. In many nations, "inflation factors" are written into debt instruments to keep the amount of the debt constant in terms of the time at which the instrument is dated, rather than constant in terms of the time the instrument is due, thus protecting the creditor.
3. Comparative adjusted balance sheets would show a *dollar loss* from holding cash and cash equivalents such as accounts receivable during an inflation, and a *dollar gain* from owing money during an inflation. For example, suppose that Dollar Company owes money regularly through the year as accounts payable. The 12-31-72 $2,000 balance would be represented at 12-31-73 for comparison with the 12-31-73 statements as $2,000 × 130 ÷ 115 = $2,260, a gain through being in debt of $2,260 − $2,000 = $260—for inflation reduced the purchasing power (as measured in 12-31-73 dollars) required to pay off that much of the debt for Dollar Company!
4. It is wrong to think of the increase in owners' equity as hidden profit for the company. It is not. It is an adjustment of earnings of previous years, as stated in the dollars in existence in those years, *restated* into their equivalent amounts of 12-31-73 dollars.

You might also observe how 2 and 3 above reinforce another phenomenon that occurs during inflation: rising interest rates. A firm is best advised, within the limits of good business judgment, to avoid investment in monetary items and to borrow as much money as possible, since the price of money will be lower in the future when the debt is due.

As all businesses attempt to follow this strategy, bank deposits and short-term securities holdings drop. These are the basis for extending credit by lending institutions, and so just as loan demand is rising, the wherewithal to finance lending is disappearing. The demand for credit expands, and its supply shrivels. The result is a rise in interest rates.

The Income Statement

The traditional (unadjusted) income statement of Dollar Company is presented in Figure 16-7. Adjustment of this statement is not as

FIGURE 16-7
DOLLAR COMPANY
Income Statement
Year Ended 12-31-72

Sales revenue	$10,000
Less: Cost of sales	5,000
Gross contribution margin	$ 5,000
Less: Selling and administrative expenses	4,000
Net profit	$ 1,000

easy as balance sheet adjustment; therefore this discussion will only "hit the highlights."

Sales Revenue. Assume that sales occurred at a level rate throughout the year, and further that the change in the price index also occurred at a level rate. Then the average index at which sales were made is $(130 + 115)/2 = 122.5$. We can assume then that the sales made during the year, at times when the index ranged in value from 115 to 130, are equivalent to having all the sales made at one point in time when the price index has the value 122.5. Accordingly, we can compute the current dollar equivalent of these sales as $10,000 \times 130/122.5 = \$10,612.24$.

Cost of Sales. Let us assume that inventory one year ago was $3,000, and further that Dollar Company uses the Lifo flow of costs assumption, permitting us to compute that $5,000 - $1,000 = $4,000 are a result of production activities this year.

The part of cost of sales which was made and placed in inventory one year ago must have a current dollar equivalent of $1,000 × 130/115 = $1,130.44. Now, the $4,000 remaining represents work done all year long at a uniform rate; hence it can be assumed equivalent to work done at a time when the price index was 122.5. Therefore the current dollar equivalent of outlays for cost of goods produced and sold is $4,000 × 130/122.5 = $4,244.90. By adding together these amounts we find that the cost of sales is $1,130.44 + $4,244.90 = *$5,375.34.*

Selling and Administrative. These expenses were also incurred uniformly throughout the year, and applying similar reasoning to them produces a dollar equivalent of $4,000 × 130/122.5 = *$4,244.90.*

Monetary Gains and Losses

Earlier we hinted at the existence of gains and losses through holding money or money equivalents and owing money to be paid in the future. Now we explain how these gains and losses are computed—and they must be computed in order to preserve the traditional debit-credit equality of the accounting process and statements.

Assume that one year ago the monetary accounts were:

Cash . . . . $1,000   Accounts Payable. $4,000

Thus the amounts held through the year are the same as shown on the ending balance sheet down in Figure 16–6. Further assume that the $2,000 reduction in Accounts Payable was all paid on 1-2-73, or immediately after the current period began. We shall accordingly not be concerned with it in this analysis.

The loss through holding cash is

$$($1{,}000 \times 130/115) - $1{,}000 = \$130.43$$

The gain through holding liabilities is

$$(\$2{,}000) \times (130/115) - \$2{,}000 = \$260.86$$

All these figures go together into an adjusted income statement as in Figure 16–8. This income statement informs us that, expressed in current dollar terms, items of income and expense are about as they were in terms of their relative relationships to one another. The origi-

FIGURE 16-8
DOLLAR COMPANY
Adjusted Income Statement
In Dollars of 12-31-73
Year Ended 12-31-73

Sales revenue	$10,612.24
Less: Cost of sales	5,375.34
Gross contribution margin	$ 5,236.90
Less: Selling and administrative expense	4,244.90
Profit before monetary items	$ 992.00
Add: Net monetary gains	130.43
Net profit	$ 1,122.43

nally reported profits of $1,000, if earned uniformly throughout the year, would have an end-of-year dollar equivalent of $1,122.43; the difference is due to the decrease in inventory, and to the monetary gains and losses. The effects of inflation are most evident when a firm uses up the inputs of prior periods to make current product and sales, and/or has substantial assets and liabilities. However, business welfare during times of changing prices is difficult to properly analyze, and adequate discussion of the practical problems of describing the effects on a specific business of changing prices must be deferred to an advanced accounting course; nor for that matter have satisfactory descriptors for these effects been found in accounting practice.

SUMMARY

Price changes are of two types: specific and general. Specific price changes are signals for reallocations to meet emerging needs and demands profitably. General price changes are called *inflation* or *deflation* and in most modern economies may be attributed to conscious or unconscious government policy.

Modern financial reporting does not recognize the effects on reporting entities of price changes, since all transactions are accounted for in unadjusted historical dollars. However, the accounting profession is committed to the principle of reporting price changes and is devoting considerable resources to research and study of the price level reporting problem. Managers in turn are considering ways to be informed of the effects of price changes and their significance in business decisions.

The most likely proposals for adoption are those which call for all costs and revenues in accounting statements to be restated in terms of dollars with a common purchasing power. Such statements would still be historically based, but would no longer report historical transactions in dollars of many different purchasing powers, arising from the different points in time at which the individual transactions occurred.

Managerial information reports include some general information about price changes—but such information has yet to be integrated into managerial accounting performance reports, contribution analysis statements, and other decision-related applications. The need is there; perhaps persons who understand the need will see that price change descriptors receive proper attention.

QUESTIONS

1. How are prices determined? Why do prices change? What, by the way, *is* a price exactly?

2. The price of automobiles rises 14.3 percent during an interval in which other prices rise 5.5 percent. Approximately how large is the specific price level change in the price of automobiles?

3. The price of food goes down 0.5 percent during a period in which other prices rise 5.0 percent. Your friend claims that this proves there was no "general" price level increase in that period. Is he right or wrong? In general, do *all* prices *have to* move the same way during a general price level increase period?

4. During an interval in which the general price level rises 10 percent, the cost of food rises 5 percent and the cost of medical care rises 15 percent. Farmers and others in agribusiness claim that the cost of food actually declined. Could this be true? What is the real increase in the cost of medical care?

5. What is an *index?* For what is an index a surrogate?

6. In 1973 a commercial fishing vessel is bought for $150,000. Its estimated lifetime is 10 years, with no salvage value. Two years later, during which there was no movement in the general price level, the vessel is appraised at $130,000. Was there a holding gain or a holding loss during these two years? Was this gain or loss

realized or unrealized? (Assume straight-line depreciation in this problem.)

7. In 1973 a commercial photography laboratory buys an automatic enlarger for $2,000. The enlarger has an estimated lifetime of five years. The following year the enlarger is sold for $1,900. During this year there was a general price level increase of 20 percent. The laboratory president says, "I am very pleased that this enlarger only cost us $100 to use for an entire year." (*a*) Comment on the truth implicity accepted by the president. Is he correct? (*b*) Estimate the cost of a new enlarger at the time the old one is sold. (*c*) Assuming straight-line depreciation, what was the realized gain or loss on the enlarger when it was sold?

8. What is "cost-push" inflation? What is "demand-pull" inflation? What causes each?

9. Why do you suppose deflation would only persist a short period of time, if it were ever to occur?

10. What are the economic strategies which people and businesses attempt to follow when inflation is present? Do these strategies produce results which are in the public interest?

11. Your company has assets of: cash, $100,000; and fixed assets at cost, $100,000. Equities are: debt, $150,000; owners equities, $50,000. If your company has no activities during 1974 and the general price level index increases 10 percent that year, is your company better or worse off at the end of the year than it was at the beginning of the year?

12. What is a "monetary gain (or loss)"? From what types of assets does a monetary gain/loss arise? Does a company which on balance has more debt than liquidity gain or lose when prices generally are declining?

13. A company is asked to pay $1,000 now in exchange for a five-year noninterest-bearing note in the amount of $2,000. During this five-year period, the inflation rate is expected to be 7 percent. If the company accepts the offer, will it gain or lose in terms of the exchange power represented by currency?

14. Grimes Company issues constant-dollar (price adjusted) financial statements. The statements show "Profit before monetary items" of

$120,000 and "Net monetary losses" of $60,000. In a letter accompanying the statements, the company president advises readers to ignore the monetary losses, ". . . on the grounds that no transactions occurred and therefore the $60,000 loss does not represent any real decrement in company assets." Appraise the president's statement and give a counterargument.

15. The accountant at Onarga Manufacturing Company has read about the importance of reporting price level information. He has proposed that all performance reports to production managers be restated to reflect the effects of price changes in materials, machinery, plant, and equipment. The Onarga Company already has a flexible budget and standard cost system. What do you think of this proposal? Ideally, to whom should price change information be reported? Why?

16. Hyloe Company has accumulated inventory as follows

Date	Amount	Price Level Index
2-1-73	$10,000	100
4-1-73	10,000	120
8-1-73	20,000	80
9-12-73	30,000	150

At the end of 1973, the price index is again 100. If you are expressing inventory in dollars of 12-31-73, what is the inventory valuation?

EXERCISES

17. Wanton Company purchased a machine lathe for $40,000 in 1965. Since then, the purchasing power of money has declined; the price level index which stood at 100 in 1965 now stands at 140. In 1965, the lathe's lifetime was estimated at 36 years, with salvage value of $4,000. A uniform amount of depreciation expense is recognized each year. What would be depreciation expense this year to recognize the deterioration in money's purchasing power?

18. In 1964 the standard cost for making Euron was set up as follows:

3 units of material 1 @ $4 each
2 hours of labor @ $3 each

Prices have increased; today material 1's price level index stands at 120 versus 100 in 1964; labor rates have increased 50 percent. Find the new standard cost of a unit of Euron.

19. Imagine all the information in Exercise 18; in addition, there have been technology improvements such that only 2.5 units of material 1 and 1.1 hours of labor are required per unit of Euron. Find the new standard cost.

20. Fifteen years ago, you purchased a corporate bond paying 4 percent interest for $1,000. The interest earned was reinvested every year. The inflation rate from then until now is reflected by an increase in the price level index from 120 to 200 in the most recent month. How much purchasing power have you gained through your investment, *if any* (the value of $1 at 4 percent for 15 years is 1.800)?

21. As a jeweler, you bought gold in 1968 for $35 per ounce. You specialize in a fitting that contains one ounce of gold. Your normal procedure is to sell your fittings at triple the cost of their gold content. In 1973, you convert this gold into fittings and offer them for sale at your usual price. You are then horrified to learn that gold is selling at $95 on the free market. If you are offering 200 fittings, what is your accounting profit? Your profit calculated as current revenue—cost of sales at current prices?

22. An adjusted balance sheet shows net monetary losses of $3,000 and increases over cost in nonmonetary assets of $6,000. If the company's unadjusted operating profit is $8,000, what is its adjusted addition to retained earnings?

23. Glenn Company sold goods (proceeds: $200,000) on December 31, 1974 which it made (for direct costs of $100,000) on December 31, 1973. Its financial statements were dated June 30, 1975. The price level index was 100 at December 31, 1973; 120 at December 31, 1974; and 150 at June 30, 1975. Compute adjusted and unadjusted contribution margin statements.

PROBLEMS

24. On March 30, 1969, you borrowed $1,000 from the Midville National Bank. The rate of interest on this loan is 8 percent each year, which is payable on the anniversary of the loan date each year. On March 30, 1972, you still owe the money.

Inflation has run at the following average rates since you obtained the loan:

>March 30, 1969–March 30, 1970 . . . . . . 3%
>March 30, 1970–March 30, 1971 5
>March 30, 1971–March 30, 1972 6

Required:
a) Compute the equivalent in March 30, 1972 dollars of the loan principal on March 30, 1969. Is this amount more or less than $1,000?
b) Suppose you anticipated on March 30, 1972, that the inflation rate for the coming year would be 9 percent. Should you (if you have the cash) repay the loan on March 30, 1972, or on March 30, 1973?
c) Considering only the three years ending March 30, 1972, what has been approximately the real rate of interest in each of the three years, taking into account the effect of inflation?

25. On April 15, 1970, your firm purchased a plastic molding machine from a West German firm. The machine cost $10,000. During the year ended April 15, 1971, the molding machine produced products with a contribution margin totaling $4,000. On April 15, 1971, the value of the molding machine on the books of your company was $9,000; however, a comparable used machine could be purchased in the market for $7,000.

Assume there were no operating costs other than $1,000 in depreciation (based on straight-line depreciation over a 10-year lifetime).

Required:
a) Prepare a conventional accounting analysis of the profitability of this machine neglecting price changes.
Prepare a profitability analysis of this machine including any unrealized holding gains or losses.
c) A change in depreciation method by the controller of the firm revises depreciation for that first year to $4,000. "Well," says the vice president of finance, "that means we really just broke even on this machine this year." Comment.

26. Same facts as Problem 25 above, except that a new plastic molding machine costs $8,000 on April 15, 1971. Of course, you are not

buying a new machine, but you are wondering whether you were smart to buy the same machine one year ago for $10,000.

Required:

a) Assuming the machine could only be had through purchase, decide whether the purchase in 1970 has proven to be wise or unwise.

b) Assuming the machine could have been secured by lease for $2,500 per year on April 15, 1970, decide whether you should have bought or leased the machine for that year alone. Support your decision.

27. The Bryan Development Company has issued comparative balance sheets which are shown below:

	This Year	Last Year
Assets		
Cash	$ 30,000	$ 20,000
Accounts receivable	60,000	60,000
Inventories	100,000	110,000
Depreciable assets (net)	550,000	450,000
Land	40,000	40,000
Total Assets	$780,000	$680,000
Equities		
Accounts payable	$100,000	$ 60,000
Long-term debt	300,000	300,000
Common stock	100,000	100,000
Earnings retained for use in business	280,000	220,000
Total Equities	$780,000	$680,000

Price level index values of note are:

End of this year	130
End of last year	116
Beginning of last year	100
When depreciable assets were acquired	110
When long-term debt was acquired	80

Cash, accounts receivable, inventories, and accounts payable were all acquired uniformly throughout the preceding year and may be presumed to have all been acquired at the midpoint of the preceding year for calculation purposes. The Bryan Company was founded five years ago when the price level index was 105, and received the land as payment for some common stock at that time. The price level changes smoothly within years.

The Bryan Company took these statements to the Midville State Bank and presented them as support for its application for a $100,000 loan. The bank's response was that money was tight, but that if the company could show that, on a price-change-adjusted basis, it did no worse than break even last year, the loan would receive favorable consideration.

Required:

a) You are the new deputy controller for Bryan Development Company and are responsible for getting the loan. Prepare adjusted comparative balance sheets for this year and last year, expressing both in terms of end-of-this-year dollars.

b) Appraise the effect of price changes on Bryan Development's affairs as reflected in these two balance sheets.

c) Submit a brief statement in favor of the loan application to accompany the revised balance sheets to the bank's loan officer. Did Bryan meet his condition?

28. Herman Distributing Company is a wholesaler, buying various products from manufacturers and reselling them at a small markup to retailers. The company has been in business a number of years, during which time the price level on items carried by it was steady. In February, however, the price level began to climb, going up about one-half percent per month. On the average, inventory will be resold three months after it is acquired. The normal markup on cost is 4 percent. Here is a summary of activity during the year just ended:

Index	Month	Bought	Cost of Goods Sold
100.0	January	$ 70,000	$ 80,000 (Acquired in Oct.)
100.5	February	60,000	50,000 (Acquired in Nov.)
101.0	March	110,000	80,000 etc.
101.5	April	130,000	70,000
102.0	May	90,000	60,000
102.5	June	80,000	110,000
103.0	July	110,000	130,000
103.5	August	170,000	90,000
104.0	September	200,000	80,000
104.5	October	84,800	110,000
105.0	November	53,000	170,000
105.5	December	84,800	200,000

Normal expenses are 1 percent of cost of sales in any particular month.

Required:

a) Compute the sales revenue of Herman Company each month in December dollars.

b) Compute the adjusted and unadjusted gross margin in each month, using December dollars as the measuring unit.

c) Assume that the market value of Herman Company average assets during the year was $400,000. In terms of adjusted dollars, what rate of return did Herman earn before taxes? If the company's goal was to earn a 9 percent return, was that goal achieved on an unadjusted basis? On an adjusted basis?

29. Caleb Hayes is a New England commercial fisherman who is considering the purchase of a new fishing boat. The year is 197x, and the price of the boat Hayes is considering is $50,000. Caleb's old boat has no market value but could be used one more year before retirement from service becomes mandatory.

Inflation in the general economy is expected to run 4 percent per year. The fishing boat yard has advised Caleb that next year the price of the same model boat should be $55,000. Caleb normally keeps his surplus cash (over $100,000) invested in a mutual fund that he expects this year will return about 7 percent.

Caleb would earn the same income from fishing regardless of which boat he uses. If he buys now, his used boat will be worth $51,000 on the market in 197x + 1.

Required:

Determine whether Caleb should buy a new boat this year and justify your determination. Neglect taxes and book depreciation.

30. At Marshall Construction Company, the standard cost of a particular item, established in 1972, is $500. Now, in 1975, 1,500 items with a total cost of $800,000 have been purchased, and an unfavorable price purchase variance of $50,000 has been attributed to the purchasing agent.

The agent is unhappy about this and says, "I got those units under the market price. You fellows aren't taking into account the 18 percent increase in prices since 1972 on this item."

Required:

a) Compute the normal market price for this item if the agent is correct about the 18 percent increase in prices.

b) Compute the actual variance if the standard were revised to the price computed in (a).

c) What do you think about the agent's claim that he bought this item at a discount? Could it be true?

31. The Catskinner Construction Company, an established highway contractor, made a decision three months ago to also contract for construction of standardized utility buildings. The cost estimates developed as standards for these operations are, per square foot:

Labor.	$1.75
Materials (exterior)	2.50
Materials (interior)	0.80
Materials (foundation).	1.00
Electrical and plumbing	0.35
Total.	$6.40

A crew was hired and trained, and last month the first such job, for a 4,000-square-foot enclosed warehouse, was undertaken. The costs as accumulated are:

Labor.	$ 7,500
Materials (exterior)	12,000
Materials (interior)	3,100
Materials (foundation)	4,500
Electrical and plumbing	1,800
Total.	$28,900

Earl Brown, Catskinner controller, was distressed by the differences between these figures and those he had projected as a basis for the bid. "They cut the margin we'd counted on almost in half," he said. "Yet I know those job foremen really wasted nothing out there." "The trouble," an established building contractor told him at lunch a few days later, "was that you picked up costs that were a year old on which to base your estimates. Why, labor has gone up 15 percent since you got those figures." Brown was intrigued and discovered, with a little research, the following index numbers applying to cost categories:

Category	Index (Year Ago)	Index (Month Ago)
Labor.	100	120
Materials (exterior)	75	90
Materials (interior)	105	105
Materials (foundation)	130	145
Electrical and plumbing	120	160

Mr. Brown realized he could separate the effect of price increases from the efficiency-inefficiency effect by recomputing his standards.

Required:

Recompute the standards for Mr. Brown; then prepare an analysis report showing separately the effects of efficiency and price changes on his first job.

32. During 1973, a composite price level index for the inputs to Anthony Corporation's product lines had an average value of 105. In 1973, production greatly exceeded sales, so that the company built up inventories at year-end with a cost valuation of $4,000,000 as opposed to $500,000 at beginning of the year. Cost of sales in 1973 was $3,500,000 (counting only standard direct variable costs). Business declined dramatically in 1974, so that production operations were suspended entirely in January 1974 and only resumed in October 1974. At the time production was resumed and for the remainder of 1974, the composite inputs price level index stood at 115.

The standard direct variable unit cost of Anthony's product was $35. In 1973, there had been no purchase price variances but there had been an average $3 per unit average efficiency variance.

Required:

a) Indicate the average purchase price variance related to production, if any, during the 1974 production.

b) The average efficiency variance during 1974 production was $5 per unit. Indicate whether or not this is related to the price level change while production was suspended, and why.

c) Anthony Company sold its product for an average 30 percent markup over standard direct variable costs. If the company sells the oldest units in inventory first, and sells 100,000 units in 1974, what is its contribution on sales in 1974? Is this the same contribution on sales earned in 1973?

d) Although technically not realistic, assume that the entire contribution from sales is available to acquire inputs for future production. For how many units could inputs be purchased with the 1973 contribution from sales (use 1973 prices)? With the 1974 contribution (1974 prices)? Why is there a difference? (In making this calculation, consider only the unit standard cost and purchase variances; ignore efficiency variances.)

DECISION CASE 16–1: ANTENNA CONSTRUCTION COMPANY

Antenna Construction Company was founded in 1959 by Mr. Ken Cooper to build custom antennas to meet the communications needs of industry and government. The company was extremely successful, and Mr. Cooper was fortunate in assembling a talented management team to operate the company. As years passed and the company prospered, the managers pressed Mr. Cooper to establish a profit sharing or stock option plan, but he durably resisted their pressure. Finally, as one key man after another left the firm for other opportunities, Mr. Cooper agreed in principle to sell a group of the managers a controlling interest in one part of the business—called the Midville operation.

"I will sell you this operation for a sum in cash, to be paid *now*, equal to the estimate of earnings over the next five years that the Midville operation will produce," said Mr. Cooper.

The earnings estimates, prepared by the accounting firm selected jointly by Mr. Cooper and the managers, were:

1974	$100,000
1975	120,000
1976	150,000
1977	200,000
1978	260,000

The total of these figures was $830,000—more than the managers had expected. The accountants explained, "In forecasting these earnings we not only took into account the growth in business for the Midville operation and its increasing efficiency as volume increases, but also the substantial effect of the inflation we expect in years ahead." The price level indices provided by the accountants were

NOW	100
1974	110
1975	120
1976	140
1977	160
1978	200

"Well now," said the spokesman for the managers, "We do not think we should pay in valuable dollars now for future dollars that are going to be less valuable."

Required:

a) Evaluate the spokesman's argument qualitatively. Is his position reasonable to you?

b) Compute the purchase price the managers should designate as a counteroffer to Mr. Cooper if they wish to discount the effect of inflation, yet offer the equivalent of five years' profits.

c) Of course, Mr. Cooper's "five years of earnings" is an arbitrary way of expressing price. Recalling some of the material in Chapter 11, can you suggest a way of developing a purchase price that will compensate for expected inflation and other factors as well? Don't do any calculations.

BIBLIOGRAPHY

Books

Accounting Research Division. *Reporting the Financial Effects of Price-Level Changes*. Accounting Research Study No. 6. New York: American Institute of Certified Public Accountants, 1963.

Dyckman, T. R. *Investment Analysis and General Price Level Adjustments*. Studies in Accounting Research No. 1. Evanston, Ill.: American Accounting Association, 1969.

Edwards, Edgar O., and Bell, Philip W. *The Theory and Measurement of Business Income*. Berkeley, Calif.: University of California Press, 1961.

Rosen, L. S. *Current Value Accounting and Price-Level Restatements*. Toronto, Canada: The Canadian Institute of Chartered Accountants, 1972.

Articles

Furlong, William H., and Robertson, Leon H. "Matching Management Decisions and Results," *Management Accounting,* August 1968.

Garner, Don E. "The Need for Price-Level and Replacement Value Data," *Journal of Accountancy,* September 1972.

Petersen, Russell J. "Price-Level Changes and Company Wealth," *Management Accounting,* February 1973.

Rosenfield, Paul "The Confusion between General Price-Level Restatement and Current Value Accounting," *Journal of Accountancy,* October 1972.

Ross, Dean "Is It Better to Be Precisely Wrong than Vaguely Right?" *Financial Executive,* June 1971.

17

Taxes and Decision Making

THE INCOME tax and other tax laws have not developed systematically or to accomplish coordinated purposes. The result, in most civilized countries, is a jumble of governmental levys upon many of the things we do that have economic or pleasurable significance. Compliance with these levys and the bureaucracies which collect them is good in the United States—not so good in other Western nations. Consider the number of jurisdictions which may tax you:

    Federal
    State
    County
    City
    School district
    Water or other utility district
    Other districts (e.g., flood or mosquito control)

Taxes may have these purposes:

    To raise money
    To selectively encourage or discourage specific activities such as capital investment
    To discourage imports
    To redistribute wealth

Here are some of the activities which give rise to taxes:

Owning property
Earning money
Gambling
Dying
Giving gifts
Smoking, eating, drinking
Driving
Traveling
Sleeping away from home
Sleeping at home
Acquiring goods made in foreign countries

This chapter reviews taxes and their effect on economic activity. If the U.S. economy operated perfectly, taxes would be devised not to interfere with the competitive processes of resource allocation. This ideal is not achievable, so from time to time tax policy is amended to pursue well-stated goals and *otherwise* interfere as little as possible with resource allocation processes.

TAX SPECIALISTS, PROCESSES, AND INSTITUTIONS

Managers are not so much interested in the computation of taxes as in the relationships between the nature and timing of business activities and tax liabilities. A major example of such a relationship that affects capital asset acquisition decisions was given in Chapter 13. Tax specialists who have expert knowledge of such relationships are found primarily in the legal and accounting professions.

Tax processes and institutions are part of the framework of public finance and monetary system management that pays for government services, keeps currency circulating, and prices stable. At the federal level, Congress enacts tax laws. With the help of tax specialists and industries affected by tax policy, the basic income tax law (first passed in 1913 and recodified in 1939 and 1954) undergoes adjustment by each Congress. The Internal Revenue Service, a part of the Treasury Department, is responsible for taxpayer relations and revenue collection. The IRS maintains a nationwide seven-region computer system to keep track of the tax status of all income-producing persons and businesses. To help administer the tax law, the IRS has prepared its own regulations which interpret the law and have official status within the IRS.

To submit a tax return in compliance with law, regulations, and applicable precedents is easy for many taxpayers to do alone, using IRS forms and self-help booklets. Most businesses, however, require tax specialist services to prepare a proper tax return and compute an appropriate tax liability. The tax specialist is an important part of the voluntary tax collection system; his function is to take the facts as given to him by the taxpayer and compute the lowest possible tax liability consistent with these facts and the tax laws and regulations. The taxpayer is responsible for the facts; the tax adviser is responsible for applying his expert knowledge of taxation to these facts.

Naturally, there are disputes about the meaning of the law and the IRS regulations, and the IRS has a process whereby disputes over a taxpayer's liability can be arbitrated. If this internal arbitration does not satisfy either party, the dispute can be taken to a federal court. The U.S. Tax Court and the federal courts give decisions which result in a continuing interpretation of the basic tax law, making it (like other bodies of law) adaptive to changing business phenomena.

TAX POLICIES OF LOCAL GOVERNMENTS

Local governments rely heavily on taxes on property and sales as sources of revenue, and to date the federal government has respected this reliance by not introducing its own property or sales taxes. Local governments also tax income, but not so heavily or successfully as does the federal government.

The extreme differences in taxation between localities has virtually disappeared. Most states now have a sales tax of 5 to 7 percent. Taxes on property are high in all urban areas, ranging from about 2 to 4 percent of market value. Even so, property and sales taxes at these levels don't supply the total revenue needs of local governments, and the federal government is experimenting with "revenue-sharing" of its own tax receipts with the states.

Sales taxes are not favored by authorities because they are regressive;

that is, they tend to fall more heavily on those who have lower incomes. Property taxes are theoretically more acceptable since they tax wealth. In practice, property taxes are deficient for four reasons: (1) They are extremely high, out of all proportion to benefits received in return. (2) They are a tax on the value of one's property rather than on one's *equity* in property, putting those who borrow money to buy property at a tax disadvantage. (3) Property of equivalent value is taxed at different amounts by different taxing entities. (4) Land speculation is encouraged when undeveloped property is taxed at lower amounts than developed property. Speculation withholds property from development in order to drive its price up. Land speculation is further encouraged by taxation of gains from most land sales at low long-term capital gains rates. There is very little risk in land speculation since property values tend to increase as a result of population and economic growth. Theory advocates, and practice is turning to, taxing land at its value in its *most productive use* regardless of the current application. This encourages landowners to put land to its best use in order to pay the taxes—or sell it to someone who will. However, bear in mind that land development, while desirable from the viewpoint of a taxing authority, may be undesirable from an aesthetic, ecological, environmental, or other viewpoint.

IMPROVING THE TAX SYSTEM

Even if no new tax laws are passed, the changing nature of economic activity assures that tax systems' effect on the individual's tax liability will not remain the same. As an example, monetary inflation and rising productivity combine to give most persons higher incomes in successive periods, subjecting them to ever-higher taxation rates. The tax system, if purchasing power before taxes is constant, leaves the individual with steadily less purchasing power *after* taxes during inflation.

The tax systems' effect on business also changes. The IRS, for example, makes rules which determine the amount of depreciation a business may deduct from revenues to determine taxable income. When a business invests in depreciable buildings and equipment, its depreciation deduction rises, protecting income from taxation and saving cash for the business to use internally or distribute as dividends. The IRS has latitude in determining depreciation rules, and can use them to encourage investment during times of economic slack or discourage investment during a time of economic expansion and potential inflation.

There is discussion and argument over changes more far-reaching than these evolutionary or "fine-tuning" changes. Improvements in the tax system are proposed to advance two goals:

1. Reduce interference of taxes with normal allocation of resources, and
2. Broaden the tax base to reduce alleged inequities.

In this section we discuss some of the current changes proposed or taking place in the tax system to further these goals.

Taxing Nonprofit Entities

Foundations, churches, charities, some hospitals, leagues, fraternal orders, and similar groups are given the special status under the tax law of being exempt from some taxes so long as they pursue humanitarian purposes. These organizations may be exempt from taxes on income, property, and/or their sales or purchases. Since these tax-exempt organizations control a large percentage of the wealth in the United States, and account for much of its total commerce, governments forego a considerable sum of revenue by extending tax-exempt status to so many organizations. Considering foundations only, the Ford Foundation, Johnson Foundation, Rockefeller Foundation, Carnegie Foundation, Kresge Foundation, Moody Foundation, Richardson Foundation, Mellon Foundation, and 20,000 others may distribute all their income or about 5 percent of their assets, whichever is greater, for charitable purposes instead of paying taxes. Congressional critics have raised the question whether the provisions of the tax law permitting tax-exempt status and thus excluding such organizations from the tax base are actually in the public interest.

Those who say tax-exempt status may be indefensible point to the growing share of the national wealth and income beyond taxation (for foundations only, presently about $25 billion in total assets at book value) at a time when tax revenues are increasingly harder to come by. They argue that taxation of at least some of the income of these entities would reduce this accumulation, providing necessary tax revenues and a more equitable distribution of the tax "burden." Should, for example, a church be exempt from taxes on the land under its parking lot, or on the income from its business investments?

Those who argue for the tax-exempt status of such entities say that their accumulation of property is a national response to the greater demands being placed on them by an urban society, and that such private-sector entities are much more efficient in providing "risk resources" for meeting social needs than government would be if government got the tax revenues and the responsibilities the foundations now have.

The following restrictions, in addition to the minimum payout requirement already given, have been placed on foundations:[1]

1. No foundation may own more than 20 percent of the stock of any one company.
2. Each foundation must pay a federal tax of 4 percent of its investment income.

Such restrictions have the general effect of limiting foundation growth, diversifying foundation holdings, and broadening the tax base.

Value-Added Tax

This would be a kind of national sales tax, levied against any increase in value given to produced or processed goods. Thus, if a businessman buys materials and labor for $40 and sells them for $60 (in some different form), he would pay taxes on $60 — $40 = $20 of value added—regardless whether he made a profit on the exchange! (The $20 could be eaten up by overhead, selling, and administrative costs.) The value added would not penalize profitable businesses (which pay the taxes now), nor would it penalize very efficient firms with higher than normal profits. Companies with losses would pay tax since the tax is on "value-added" through operations and is not an income tax.

The value-added tax is used in Europe. There, the tax is rebated to exporters on sales abroad. The effect is to make the manufacturer's cost of foreign sales equal to the cost of economic inputs only. Interna-

---

[1] "New Ball Game for the Foundations," *Forbes,* June 15, 1972, pp. 65–66.

tional agreements prevent subsidies for exports; the rebate of the value-added tax is not a subsidy. On the other hand, the profits tax in the United States does not attach directly to foreign or domestic sales and any refund of or exemption from this tax would be interpreted by other nations as a subsidy of export sales.

Those who oppose the value-added tax argue that it is regressive, resembling a national sales tax and paid by individuals to the extent they are consumers rather than to the extent they receive income. The counter argument is that the tax could be rebated to individuals or families with incomes below some arbitrary level.

The value-added tax has been proposed as a source of revenue to fund operation of local governments should the *ad valorem*[2] tax prove inadequate for that purpose (see discussion of tax policies of local governments). The tax would be collected by the federal government and paid to local governments.

Federal-State Revenue Sharing

States and municipalities depend on property and sales taxes for most of their revenues, with lesser amounts deriving from the income tax. The former two sources are being used to the fullest extent possible; the latter source has been essentially preempted by the federal government. While the federal government is not in especially sound financial condition, it does have the advantage over state and local governments that it can print money it needs to spend in excess of its tax revenues. State and local governments almost without exception are badly in need of financial help, which can only come from the federal government.

Revenue sharing is the name coined to apply to proposals under which federal revenues would be channeled to local governments. These revenues, deriving primarily from the federal income tax, would be used by local governments to meet local needs. Those who favor revenue sharing feel that it will restore the vitality of local government, giving it resources to deal with such problems as welfare and unemployment, public health care, public education, law enforcement, and re-

---

[2] A Latin phrase meaning "based on value."

gional public transportation. Those who oppose revenue sharing feel that local governments will lose control of their finances to the central government, that government as a whole will become more centralized and unresponsive, and that federal finances will further deteriorate, with attendant inflation and higher taxes.

The 1972 modest revenue-sharing plan to distribute $5 billion over a five-year period is certain to be changed and expanded. Accountants can be expected to contribute to this process through financial controls development and interpretation of the law to determine the proper disbursement of federal funds to each eligible government entity.

Negative Income Tax

Millions of citizens receive payments from the federal government. These payments are for social security, medicare, various degrees of disability, and other causes. Millions more receive payments from local governments for the causes above as well as payments to mothers with small children, unemployed men and women, and others. These are called "transfer payments" by economists because they transfer income from some segments of the population to others. The money to provide these payments comes from tax collections and deficit financing. Although it is perhaps unfair to do so, most persons lump these payments together in their minds and think of them as "welfare" and regard the total as "too high." The total is very high, high enough to stimulate a lively debate over a national income distribution policy. There are proposals in the Executive and the Congress for reforming the entire system of government payments to persons to make it more efficient, equitable, and economical.

Let us consider one kind of payment—that to unemployed persons. This payment is made largely by states, supplementing their own funds with money received from the federal government. At present, the payment usually stops if an unemployed person secures a job, even though the job pays little more than does the "welfare" program. There is little incentive under this kind of system, from a purely monetary point of view, for the individual to actually seek employment if he is only substituting one kind of payment for another of similar amount, and sacrificing his leisure time to boot. The result is that second and third generations in the same family are becoming adults knowing nothing about job markets or learning a skill, depending entirely on government payments for survival and unable to participate in the economy.

One way to slow down this phenomenon would be to continue all or part of the government payments after a job is obtained. For example, let "welfare" payments be $250 per month. The head of the household secures employment paying $250 per month. Instead of stopping entirely, the government payment drops to $200 per month, making a total income of $450 per month. In a few months the head of the household receives an increase to $350 per month; the government payment drops to $150 per month and total income is $500.

These graduated family subsidies have been called the negative income tax. It is a *negative* tax because it contemplates a payment by the government to taxpayers instead of the conventional arrangement under which taxpayers pay money to the government. As you can see, at some point the head of the household will no longer receive government payments but will start paying a positive income tax to the government. He is never penalized for seeking employment, as he is under the present system.

The cost of a negative income tax would be very large—some put it as high as $100 billion per year. This payment would be partly offset by the $10 billion savings achieved by eliminating the present government-payments bureaucracy which administers the existing system, and by eliminating $30–$60 billion of the payments made by it. In place of many different payments for different purposes and under different conditions (one person may collect under more than one program), there would be only the income test for eligibility and amount of payment.

Many persons object to such a system, arguing that it is immoral to pay money to working Americans. The issue is before Congress as well as before the public. The next few years should tell whether a beginning will be made toward the negative income tax in the United States, or whether the present system will be reviewed, reformed, and retained.

ACCOUNTING FOR TAXES

There are enough differences between the way income is calculated for financial reporting and managerial purposes, and the way it is calculated for tax computation purposes, that often the tax will not bear a logical relationship to financially reported income. An example of this situation is the use of straight-line depreciation for financial reporting (to increase the income figure by deducting as little depreciation as possible) and simultaneous use of accelerated depreciation for determining income subject to tax (to decrease the taxable income figure and therefore the tax). To dramatize the possible difference, imagine a business earning revenues of $150,000 per year and with expenses other than depreciation of $50,000 per year. The company's only asset is a depreciable one costing $200,000 and obtained at the beginning of this year. The asset has a five-year life and no salvage value. Straight-line depreciation is $200,000/5 = $40,000 per year. Accelerated depreciation this year is $200,000(5/5 + 4 + 3 + 2 + 1) = $67,000. The latter is deducted from revenue to calculate taxable income:

Financial income:
$150,000 − $50,000 − $40,000 = $60,000
Taxable income:
$150,000 − $50,000 − $67,000 = $33,000

Difference = $27,000

The $27,000 difference in income is taxed at the rate of 48 percent, so that income tax payments in that year are $27,000 × 0.48 = $12,960 *less* than if taxable and financial income were the same.

Now, you should see that over a five-year period the *method* of depreciation does not matter; the same amount of depreciation will be taken ($200,000), and therefore income will be the same, and taxes will be the same. This is illustrated in Figure 17–1. Accounting authorities argue that it is misleading to report tax expenses *lower* than what is apparently due on reported income at some times, yet at other times report tax expenses which are *higher* than what is apparently due on reported income (for example, in the fifth year of the asset's life above, accelerated depreciation would only be $13,000, leading to a tax $11,000 higher than that apparently due on reported income).

The accounting solution is to report the difference between actual tax liability (paid to the government) and what the tax liability would be if figured on reported income. This difference is positive early in the life of an asset and negative later when actual tax liability exceeds

FIGURE 17-1
Comparison of Depreciation Methods

Cost of asset: $200,000
Lifetime: 5 years
Salvage value: $0
Income before taxes and depreciation: $100,000 per year

	1. Depreciation		2. Taxable Income (Income Less Depreciation)	
Year	Straight Line	Accelerated	Straight Line	Accelerated
1	$ 40,000	$ 67,000	$ 60,000	$ 33,000
2	40,000	53,000	60,000	47,000
3	40,000	40,000	60,000	60,000
4	40,000	27,000	60,000	73,000
5	40,000	13,000	60,000	87,000
	$200,000	$200,000	$300,000	$300,000

	3. Tax Liability		4. After Taxes Cash Flow	
Year	Straight Line	Accelerated	Straight Line	Accelerated
1	$ 22,300	$ 9,340	$ 37,700	$ 23,660
2	22,300	16,060	37,700	30,940
3	22,300	22,300	37,700	37,700
4	22,300	28,540	37,700	44,460
5	22,300	35,260	37,700	51,740
	$111,500	$111,500	$188,500	$188,500

apparent tax liability. The difference is called "Provision for Tax Expense Incurred but Not Paid." For an example of its computation, consider the facts in Figure 17-1. In year 1 the business, using straight-line depreciation to compute financial income, would have taxable income of $60,000 and tax expense of $22,300.[3] In the same year, tax liability computed using accelerated depreciation is $9,340, computed from taxable income of $33,000. Year 1's addition to the provision for tax expense incurred but not paid would be $22,300 − $9,340 = $12,960. Here are the entries for all five years:

Year	1	2	3	4	5
Change in provision	$+12,960	$+6,240	$0	$−6,240	$−12,960

[3] Refer to Appendix 17A for an explanation of how to compute business tax liabilities.

Thus, reported income tax expense is kept in proper relation with reported income, recognizing that over the long run reported income and taxable income will total to the same figure and that differences between them are only due to differences in the timing of income and income tax expense recognition.

ACCOUNTANTS AND TAX POLICY

During the early decades of their history accountants limited themselves to tax return preparation and tax planning for individuals and businesses. The former has become highly routinized and is often done using computers. The latter consists essentially of (*a*) putting as much income as possible into the capital gains category, where tax rates are lower, (*b*) spreading taxable income over as many entities as possible (to avoid the progressive tax rates on income concentrated on a single entity), (*c*) selecting transactions and timing them to take maximum advantage of deductions and exemptions in the tax law, and (*d*) minimizing total estate and gift taxes paid by an individual and his estate.

Accountants' long experience in these areas has left them the most informed profession in the United States about the ways tax laws affect economic behavior of individuals and businesses. As such, accountants have acquired a responsibility to participate in the process of developing tax laws and policies. This process is much more than one of closing loopholes and eliminating tax inequities. The problems of stability and efficiency in a tax system as large as ours, in a society as decentralized as ours, are extremely complex; it is unavoidable that accountants will be expected to use their knowledge of taxation and its consequences in the public interest.

SUMMARY

The system whereby government entities raise money to finance their own activities affects virtually all economic activity. The great and the small pay taxes, whose amounts are determined according to laws and regulations so complex that professional specialists are often required to interpret them. Tax effects are not all predictable in advance; tax effects also change as the nature of economic activity changes. Consequently the tax system is always under scrutiny and subject to revision. Accountants, because they help individuals conform to the tax laws, know better than any other professional class what are the effects of taxes on individuals. Accountants thus should be involved in criticizing and changing the tax system. Four probable areas of future tax change where accounting expertise is needed are: (1) taxation of nonprofit entities, (2) new sources of revenue such as the proposed value-added tax, (3) revenue sharing between federal and state governments, and (4) reform of the welfare system.

The rules which determine income tax *liability* don't always agree with the accounting principles which determine income tax *expense*. One result has been difficulty, in financial reporting and even in managerial decision making, in describing the effects of taxes on economic decision making through the accounting system.

APPENDIX 17A: COMPUTING THE CORPORATE INCOME TAX

This tax is levied primarily by the federal government. There are state income taxes as well, but they follow the form of the federal tax and are for much smaller amounts. The computation of the federal corporate income tax liability is:

Liability = 0.22 (corporate taxable income up to $25,000)
+0.48 (corporate taxable income in excess of $25,000)
+0.30 (capital gains during year)[4]

Each term in this equation has a special meaning. We are not concerned with these meanings as would be a professional tax consultant, so our definitions are somewhat looser and intended to convey conceptual meaning. "Corporate taxable income" is virtually the same as the accounting income reported in the annual financial statements. The tax is levied on income *before* deduction of dividends. "Capital gains" are the profits made through sale of investments in such assets as land and securities, You can see that the rates in the equation above favor

---

[4] This is the alternate capital gains tax rate; a corporation with taxable income less than $25,000 would use 0.22.

smaller corporations and favor income earned from capital investments. Since individual income tax rates progress up to 70 percent, the law also favors corporations over individuals.[5]

Effect of Corporate Income Tax

The 48 percent rate on income in excess of $25,000 means that the government is a partner to that extent in a business' activities. Thus, profits may be only 52 percent of their pretax amounts and expenses only 52 percent of their apparent magnitude. You saw this in Chapter 13 when you studied the effect of taxes on capital investment decisions. As another example, suppose interest rates are 8 percent. Interest is deductible from revenue to determine profit and therefore deductible from revenue to determine taxable income. Thus, a dollar spent on interest reduces taxable income but also reduces the tax liability. The net extra cash outflow as a result of the interest payment is not $1 but only 52 cents. The real rate of interest is not 8 percent but $0.52 \times 8 = 4.16$ percent.

This "sharing" by the government of business profits and expenses tends to make the government interested in the efficiency of business management and the profitability of the business establishment. This interest is more than academic. The government does not undertake any major programs, budget reallocations, or even spending reductions until it has evaluated their effect on its major source of operating revenue. On a more positive side, the government has established many agencies (as the Small Business Administration) which seek to develop the profitability of various types of businesses, incidentally strengthening them as sources of tax revenues. The result is an ever-closer mutually dependent relationship between government and business. The eventual equilibrium of this relationship is not yet clear.

Operating Income and Capital Gains

There is a fundamental bias in the federal tax law in favor of income earned from capital investment appreciation. Such income is called

---

[5] However, the maximum tax on wage-earned individual income is 50 percent.

"capital gains" and is taxed at a much lower rate—30 percent for corporations—than operating income. This lower rate causes businessmen to seek out capital appreciation opportunities. The effect may be to cause businesses to forego investments in operations which will not result in capital gains. To see this, consider two alternatives, one a noncapital expenditure and the other a capital expenditure. Assume the company insists on a 10 percent return after taxes. The pretax return on the noncapital investment (an example would be depreciable equipment) would have to be enough to pay the taxes and still leave the 10 percent return, or $10/(1 - 0.48) = 19.25$ percent. Similarly, the pretax return on a capital investment (as in land held for appreciation) would also have to be enough to pay the capital gains tax and leave a 10 percent return. In this case the lower capital gains tax rate would require only a $10/(1 - 0.30) = 14.29$ percent return. It appears reasonable to suggest that all other things equal, the tax laws do create a bias toward investment in capital items.

Capital Losses

Long-term capital losses are first offset against long-term capital gains in the year of recognition.[6] If there is a *net* capital loss, the business may carry this loss back three years and forward five years to reduce the amount of any capital gains which occur in that nine-year period. Any capital loss remaining after five years is "down the tubes." No capital loss may offset any ordinary income for a corporation.

To illustrate, Figure 17–2 is a schedule of capital gains and losses for the Yippee Corporation from 1964 to 1970.

Spreading Gains and Losses over Several Periods

The tax law recognizes that businesses have good and bad years; there are tax law provisions whereby a business can offset the income

---

[6] Long-term capital gains or losses are those occurring as a result of selling a capital asset held for more than six months. This chapter does not discuss short-term capital losses.

FIGURE 17-2
Illustrative Schedule of Capital Gains and Losses

Year	Net Capital Gains (Loss)	Gain Offset by Loss and Year of Loss	Taxable Capital Gain	Loss Carried Forward	Loss Expiring
1964	$(500,000)	$ 0	$ 0	$500,000	$ 0
1965	0	0	0	500,000	0
1966	300,000	300,000 (1964)	0	200,000	0
1967	(100,000)	0	0	300,000	0
1968	0	0	0	300,000	0
1969	0	0	0	100,000	200,000 (1964)
1970	200,000	100,000 (1967)	100,000	0	0

of good years against some or all of the losses of bad years and thereby pay taxes only on the excess of income over losses for a period of years. Such provisions produce what are called "carrybacks" when a loss is carried back to offset income of subsequent periods. A loss may be used to offset income earned up to three years before the loss occurs, and up to five years after. The provisions as to the treatment of capital losses and operating losses provide for the same periods of carryback and carryforward but must be applied to each type of loss independently.

As soon as a net operating loss occurs, the unfortunate business would file refund claims for the preceding three years (assuming it had profits in any of those years!), saying in effect to the Treasury: "Look, we have made less money over the past four years than we thought we would, and we have overpaid our tax. Please refund $xxxx to us." Such tax refunds are important sources of cash to businesses which are losing money. If there is still an excess of loss over the past three years' income, this excess may be used to offset operating income during the five subsequent years.

In 1968 the Yippee Corporations's operating loss was $2,000,000. Income for the previous three years was $1,200,000, on which the company had paid taxes of $306,000. Upon filing amended returns, the Yippee Corporation receives this entire amount as a tax refund. In 1969, there is a loss of $200,000. In 1970, the firm's operating income is $900,000. The remaining $800,000 of the 1968 loss and $100,000 of the 1969 loss offset this profit, and there is no tax liability in 1970.

The company breaks exactly even in 1971, 1972, and 1973; in 1974, there is an operating profit of $50,000; this is offset by $50,000 of the 1969 loss. At the end of 1974, the last $50,000 of the 1969 loss expires and cannot be used as a tax deduction any longer.

The effect of these rules is generally equitable. In business planning, operating losses produce cash because of their deductibility from past income; capital gains produce cash because of the lower tax on them. If a loss has to be suffered, it should be an operating loss; gains should be capital gains.

Tax Deductions

The government accepts as deductions from revenue (to find taxable income) most of the expenditures which accountants allow as expenses. The principal difference is that whereas an expense to an accountant is the dollar amount associated with *any* resource sacrifice related to a period or to income-producing activities occurring during the period, a tax deduction to the government is only ordinary and necessary expenses (plus uncontrollable losses, as to hurricane or earthquake). The government will not allow excessive, extraordinary, unnecessary expense of any kind as a tax deduction—be it entertainment, salary, production, or whatever. Businesses keep extensive records to justify the expenses they incur as ordinary and necessary.

QUESTIONS

1. Are the following statements true or false?
    a) T F The accountant's job is to help his client to find as many tax loopholes as possible.
    b) T F The Supreme Court initiates tax laws and rules at the federal level.
    c) T F All tax collections are supervised by the Internal Revenue Service.
    d) T F The taxpayer has no choice but to pay the tax liability assessed against him by the IRS.
    e) T F Foundations do not have to pay any federal taxes at all.

f) T F It is preferable that accountants report as "tax expense" for a period the amount of tax liability actually paid that year.

2. How does the federal tax law appear to favor corporations over individuals? Capital gains over ordinary income?

3. What is a negative income tax? Do you personally favor such a proposal?

4. At the present time the social security system of benefits is fully financed from taxes deducted from payrolls. A person earning $15,000 per year paid $468 in social security taxes in 1972. In that year, the average retired couple received benefits of $224 per month.[7] By increasing the tax, higher benefits can be paid; or by decreasing the tax, benefits can be lowered. What is the purpose of the social security system? Is it an insurance system? How do you think social security benefits ought to be determined? Do you think politics and inflation ought to have an influence on social security taxes and benefits? As the birth rate drops and the number of older persons relative to the number of wage earners rises, what do you think will happen to social security taxes?

5. Businessmen prize their capital assets and argue that even depreciable asset gains and losses ought to be taxed at the lower capital gains rates rather than ordinary income rates. Can you think of any reasons to tax capital gains and losses at lower rates? Some persons do not think capital gains and losses should receive preferential treatment. Can you think of any reasons to eliminate the differential between capital gains and ordinary income in taxation? Why do you think depreciable assets are not given capital asset status? Would you change that?

6. A common proposal by economists and special interest group representatives is that if some particular industry or activity is in the public interest, it ought to receive special tax treatment. Thus, export sales profits need not be taxed at the full rate until the cash to pay them has been brought back to the United States. There is a 7 percent tax *credit* on the purchase of most depreciable assets. The former encourages exports, the latter encourages investment.

---

[7] *Time,* July 17, 1972, p. 61.

Do you think the tax system ought to serve such functions? Can you think of more efficient ways to perform them?

7. I. Noe Plenty, an economist of repute, proposes that a tax be placed on all discharges from industrial sites—such as smoke, noxious or poisonous chemicals, etc., to increase the cost of business activities which befoul the environment. Inoe Moore, another economist, responds that most businesses would simply pay the taxes and continue operating as before. Attempt to develop this idea briefly and think of two or three simple situations in which it might be tried.

8. Gargantuan Oil Company receives a 22.5 percent exemption of its gross revenues derived from oil production from any taxation whatever. It justified this exemption, saying: "When our oil is gone it can't be replaced. We have to spend money looking for more. That's why we are allowed this exemption. Besides, if it is removed and we have to pay the extra tax, that tax will just be passed on to motorists and other energy users in the form of higher prices." Take a counter position and make your argument.

9. In the chapter it is stated that the federal government cannot really take an antibusiness stand if that would impair its revenue base. Develop a few of the implications of this statement if—
    a) A large and general depression appeared about to develop.
    b) It appeared that driving automobiles caused "seat cancer" and would have to be abolished.
    c) A sudden prospect appeared for a hugely profitable major industry which, due to a technicality, was presently illegal.
    d) Fifteen hundred very wealthy individuals paid no taxes at all, year in and year out.

10. The Beaver Corporation earns $25,000 before taxes. It declares a dividend of $10,000. What is its tax liability?

11. Mr. Curtis Hanley derives all of his $80,000 income before taxes from a business which he operates and of which he is sole owner. His tax is $22,000. Would his taxes be lower if he incorporated his business? Disregard personal deductions.

12. Chen Corporation bought a piece of land for $60,000 in 1970. In 1974 the land was sold for $95,000. The expenses of the sale were $5,000. What was the tax liability arising from this transaction? Was this an ordinary gain or a capital gain?

13. In the 1960s Bray Company had this schedule of capital gains and losses:

Year	Gain	Loss
1960	$1,000	
1961		
1962		$(1,000)
1963	2,000	
1964	3,000	
1965		
1966		
1967		(4,000)
1968		(4,000)
1969	1,000	

    Considering only these years, what was the net amount of tax paid by Bray Company on its capital gains and losses? (Or, if applicable, what was the net amount of capital loss carryforward?)

14. Zeal Foundation has assets of $1,000,000. In 1974, it received income of $45,000. In that year, the tax on receipts is 4 percent and the minimum payout is 5.5 percent. The foundation made gifts of $46,000 in 1974.
    a) How much tax does the foundation have to pay?
    b) Is the foundation in compliance with all applicable laws?

15. Go-Go Company is located in a country which has both an income and a value-added tax. The value-added tax is 20 percent of the difference between the cost of direct production inputs and sales revenue; the income tax is 40 percent of corporate income after deducting the value-added tax. The company's sales in 1975 are $31,000,000. Company records show that direct costs of inputs was $11,000,000. Other costs are: indirect production costs, $3,000,000; administrative costs, $7,000,000; miscellaneous, $1,000,000. Compute Go-Go's tax liability.

16. Which of the following do you think are taxes? What might the nontax items be, if not taxes?
    a) Postage stamp fee.
    b) Charge for registering a machine gun.
    c) Charge for a gambling license.
    d) Charge for a liquor license.
    e) Charge for electricity purchased from a city-owned power plant.
    f) Charge for garbage collection.
    g) Import duties.
    h) Charge for drivers' license.

EXERCISES

17. The Traeger Company earns income from two sources. One source is heavily protected, and so the company only pays about 5 percent tax on it. This source accounts for 30 percent of the company's income before taxes The other source is taxed at regular rates. If the company earns $100,000 before taxes, what is its tax?

18. Adam Smith is an unemployed head of household. He has no source of income other than "welfare" payments from local, state, and federal government amounting to $200 per month. Mr. Smith pays about $100 per year in income taxes on these payments. Mr. Smith is willing to work, and in fact has been offered a job paying $300 per month; however, his welfare would be cut $1 for every $1 he earned as salary. His taxes at the $3,600 level would be about $250 per year. Finally, he has a chance to join an experimental program in which his welfare payments would be cut 50 cents for every dollar he earns. His taxes at the point of maximum earnings would be $300. Compute Smith's income if he joins the experimental program and takes the job.

19. The "velocity of money" is the number of times a dollar trades hands, on the average, after it is earned. Assume that this "velocity" is 8; that is, if you earn $1, then you spend part of it, and those with whom you spend it also spend part of it, until it has circulated fully eight times. The government may collect taxes on the dollar as income every time it circulates. Imagine that the average tax rate is 20 percent; how much in taxes can the government expect to have from a dollar entering the economy as wages earned?

20. Refer to Exercises 18 and 19 above. Let the government be considering a "negative income tax" plan that would cost an extra $15 billion in welfare payments. Those receiving payments under this plan would have net income of $8 billion from jobs, which they otherwise would not hold. Is it possible that this plan could result in enough tax revenues to offset its cost?

21. Hillis Company is a corporation with revenues of $500,000; direct cost of sales of $200,000; depreciation allocable to sales of $50,000; selling, administrative, and general costs of $100,000; dividends of $40,000; interest expense of $20,000; and contributions to politi-

cal candidates' campaigns of $10,000. In addition, the company had a capital loss of $40,000 and a capital gain of $50,000—both long term. Compute the tax liability.

22. Skint Company has just bought an automatic welder for $110,000 with salvage value of $10,000 and lifetime of five years. The company is not profitable now but expects to be very profitable in the third, fourth, and fifth years it holds this asset. Suggest a depreciation method for the welder and calculate the savings assuming a 48 percent tax rate over a method you would use if there were to be income in all five years.

PROBLEMS

23. The Eralsa Company has been in operation for six years. In its first year it incurred a $200,000 operating loss; the second year, a $100,000 operating loss. In the third, fourth, and fifth years, modest profits of $25,000 each were earned. This year, the company had a $300,000 operating profit. In addition to the operating losses, the company in its first year bought a depreciable asset for $50,000; it sold the asset later (in the fourth year) for $30,000 (including depreciation).

In the second year, the company bought a piece of property which it thought would be needed for future expansion. In the fourth year, company plans changed and the property was sold. The net buying and selling prices were $60,000 and $40,000, respectively. Later in the fourth year, the company bought some bonds for $50,000 as an alternative investment to the land. This year, in need of cash, the bonds were sold for $68,000, net.

Required:

Compute the tax liability of Eralsa Company for the current year, taking into account all carrybacks and carryforwards of capital and operating gains and losses. Consider only years and events described.

24. Creel Fishbait Company makes artificial lures and mass-produced angling equipment ranging from the lures to electric trolling motors. Much of the plant is old, and the directors have discussed replacing it with newer, more automated equipment. A study showed that the necessary equipment would have a lifetime of 12 years (for tax purposes the lifetime of depreciable equipment is different from its lifetime for economic purposes; the tax lifetime is 8 years in

this case), would cost $2,500,000, and have a salvage value of about $100,000.

The company is not graced by a strong credit rating. The vice president of finance is scraping at every source for funds to pay for the new equipment. "What sort of depreciation are you using?" asked the bank loan officer. "Straight line," says the VP. "No, I mean for your tax return," returns the loan officer. "That's it," says the VP. "Well, if I were you I'd look into sum-of-years' digits for my tax return," says the loan officer. "You might pick up a little extra cash there. We'll loan you 50 percent of the purchase price, you can get 40 percent internally as you've already shown me, and it could be the rest would come from reduced tax payments." "But I thought you paid the same tax whatever method of depreciation you use!" cried the VP. "Aha, when you get your figures done and can explain why even though that's true everyone prefers accelerated depreciation for tax purposes when they can get it, *then* we'll talk some more about a loan," concluded the loan officer.

Required:

a) Prepare a table similar to Figure 17–1 showing aftertax income in years 1–12 of the new asset acquisition using sum-of-years'-digits and straight-line depreciation. Pre-tax annual income is $1,000,000; tax rate = 40 percent.

b) Add a column to this table showing the amount saved (or lost) by using sum-of-years'-digits depreciation.

c) If you consider the taxes deferred by using sum-of-years'-digits depreciation during years 1 and 2 as a loan towards purchase of the machinery, will the Creel Company be able to finance its purchase? Assume a 40 percent tax rate.

d) Provide the explanation requested by the loan officer.

25. Midville School District has been told, as a result of a taxpayer's lawsuit, that it can no longer collect property taxes to pay the cost of operating the district's schools. The assessed valuation in the district is $385,000,000. The assessed tax rate was about $2.50 per $100 valuation. Apparently now none of this can be collected and the district is looking for other alternatives. Here are some other facts about the district:

Population	130,000
Per capita income	$2,200
Number of households	37,000
Retail sales	$0.4 billion

There is a regional airport in the district, as well as a number of manufacturing plants accounting for about 20 percent of the work force. Unemployment is about 4 percent.

Required:

Identify and develop as many sources of local revenue as you can for the school district. You may assume that there is a 3 percent state sales tax and a small state property tax. There is a state income tax of 5 percent of the federal tax. Divide your answer into two sections: (*a*) sources you can document from the information given, and (*b*) other sources.

26. Graham Browning operates a variety-store chain. Recently he came into a $250,000 inheritance which he intends to invest in his business, which has not been doing well lately. Last year, his chain showed a $400,000 operating loss. In previous years, profits were very small, and only $50,000 of the loss was carried back.

At present, Browning intends to acquire one or more profitable stores. He would prefer to acquire profitable stores in order to have income against which to carry forward last year's loss. Browning expects his present operation's income pattern to be:

Year	Income
1	$30,000
2	50,000
3	50,000
4	60,000
5	70,000

A small chain's owner recently died and the estate executor wishes to sell it. The chain's projected income would be:

Year	Income
1	$80,000
2	80,000
3	80,000
4	80,000
5	80,000

Required:

a) Produce a schedule showing how much of the previous year's loss could be offset by income from the small chain if it were purchased. Arrange the schedule by years.

b) To the above schedule, add a column showing the amount of taxes that could be offset by income from the proposed acquisition.

c) Do these tax savings make the proposed acquisition more valuable? Using net-present-equivalent analysis as explained in

Chapter 13, compute the present equivalent of these tax savings if Browning's ITRR is 10 percent.

27. Dynamic Gimmick Corporation is looking for an unusual way to raise capital. "I have," said the treasurer, "A good idea. We shall issue a new kind of note. The note will bear interest at 1 percent per year and have a 10-year life." "But," said the president, "those notes will only sell at $680 per $1,000 face value. And when they mature, we have to pay $1,000. What's the advantage?"

"Simple. We'll sell them for even less: $600 per $1,000 face value. We can deduct the interest expense plus one tenth of the $400 discount from our income, which is taxed at a 50 percent rate. The buyer will have to pay income tax on the cash interest he receives, but when the note is due, he will pay only a 25 percent tax on the $1,000 − $600 = $400 capital gain he will report. We get the capital with low interest payments, and he gets income partially sheltered from taxes."

"Well, it sounds nutty, but calculate the cash flows and present equivalents and let's see."

Required:

a) Look at the investor's side first. Let the going interest rate be 7 percent. Compute the investor's cash flows after taxes for the proposed note and for an ordinary note with 7 percent interest, each with a 10-year life. Let the investment in each be $600.

b) Discount the cash flows in (a) using ITRR = 3.5 percent (after tax interest rate). On the basis of the resulting current equivalents, which note should an investor prefer?

c) Now look at Dynamic Gimmick's side. Compute their cash flows after taxes for both types of note; don't forget the $40 per year tax deduction for discount—it adds $30 per year to cash flow. Discount both cash flow streams at 3.5 percent. Which note should Dynamic Gimmick issue?

Note: The current equivalent of 10 payments each spaced a year apart discounted at 3.5 percent is 8.3165; and the current equivalent of $1 paid in 10 years discounted at 3.5 percent is $0.7089.

DECISION CASE 17–1: THE ENERGY SHORTAGE

The United States recently experienced indications that its economy may not be able to produce all the energy it would like to consume.

Although reserves of coal, petroleum, natural gas, and uranium are adequate for many more decades of consumption, energy from these sources is in short supply and becoming shorter.

Factors which may be wholly or partly responsible for the energy shortage are:

(1) Lack of coal, gas, and oil extractive capacity.
(2) Lack of energy transportation capacity.
(3) Lack of sufficient means to convert energy into more convenient forms—oil to gasoline, coal to gas, oil to electricity.
(4) Lack of foreign exchange reserves to pay for energy imports.
(5) Waste of existing energy through auto travel, air conditioning, heating, outdoor lighting, etc.
(6) Lack of profit incentive to provide energy.
(7) Regulations intended to accomplish other purposes such as conservation or removal of pollution which also reduce energy supply or increase energy consumption.

A government task force to study ways to bring energy supply and demand into balance has been formed, and you have been invited to join it.

Required:

Suggest ways to accomplish the task force's objective. Include ways to use governmental tax policy at the national and local levels to bring energy supply and demand into balance.

BIBLIOGRAPHY

Books

Bierman, Jr., Harold, and Drebin, Allan R. *Managerial Accounting: An Introduction.* 2d ed. New York: The Macmillan Co.: 1972.

Bittker, Boris I., and Eustice, James S. *Federal Income Taxation of Corporations and Shareholders.* 3d ed. Boston: Warren, Gorham, & Lamont, 1971.

McCarthy, Clarence F. *Federal Income Tax.* Englewood Cliffs, N.J.: Prentice-Hall, Inc., 1972.

Raby, William L. *The Income Tax and Business Decisions.* 2d ed. Englewood Cliffs, N.J.: Prentice-Hall, Inc., 1972.

Sommerfeld, Ray M.; Anderson, Hershel M.; and Brock, Horace R. *An Introduction to Taxation*. 2d ed. New York: Harcourt Brace Jovanovich, Inc., 1972.

Articles

Baylis, A. W. "A Concise Statement on Income Tax Allocation," *Accountants' Journal,* April 1971.

18

The Public Interest and Contemporary Accounting

THE MODERN accounting profession is aware of responsibilities beyond its traditional field of private enterprise. Accounting shares this awareness with segments of society which are entitled to an objective description and appraisal of their programs, interests, and claims.

As one indicator of this interest *The Journal of Accountancy,* the publication of the American Institute of Certified Public Accountants, has published an impressive number of articles dealing with the actual or potential contribution of accountants to the management of various social-type problems. Here are a few recent ones, their dates, and authors:

"Socio-Economic Accounting" (November 1968) by David F. Linowes, pp. 37–42.

"The Modern Management Approach to a Program of Social Improvement" (March 1969) by Robert Beyer, pp. 37–46.

"The Role of Accounting in Emerging Nations" (January 1969) by David F. Linowes, p. 18.

"Macroeconomics and Accounting Practice" (June 1969) by Henry R. Jaenicke, pp. 35–39.

"The Black Minority in the CPA Profession" (October 1969) by Bert N. Mitchell, pp. 41–48.

"The Accountant's Social Responsibility" (January 1970) by Ralph W. Estes, pp. 31–39.

"Social Responsibility of the Profession" (January 1971) by David F. Linowes, pp. 66–69.

"Integration in Fact—A Test of the Professional Accountant as a Citizen" (April 1971) by Edwin R. Lang and John Ashworth, pp. 41–46.

"The New Generation and the Accounting Profession" (May 1971) by George S. Odiorne, pp. 39–43.

"Accounting: A Bridge Across the Generation Gap" (May 1971) by John Lawler, pp. 44–48.

"Accounting and Ecology: A Perspective" (October 1971) by James E. Parker, pp. 41–46.

"Pollution Control through Social Cost Conversion" (November 1971) by Floyd A. Beams and Paul E. Fertig, pp. 37–42.

You may observe that these articles are general in nature and conceptual in title; scanning a few of them will confirm that this is also true of the substance. However, the *Journal of Accountancy* does not publish reports of specific applications; it reports trends and philosophies. The trend these articles report is the accountant's increasing involvement in detailed applications of interpretive accounting to pollution, integration, regional development, economic planning, tax reform, and international economic development.

FACTORS TENDING TO INVOLVE ACCOUNTING IN SOCIAL PROBLEMS

First of all, accounting is a major (though young) established and responsible profession. It is natural and proper that when problems arise, people turn to accountants just as they turn to lawyers, doctors, architects, civil engineers, and other professions with a tradition of service. When large groups of people experience the same problem—such as racial or economic discrimination, environmental pollution, or regional stagnation—then these groups turn to both practicing accountants and to accounting as a discipline and institution for help in managing their difficulties.

Aside from this natural exposure to problems, the nature of the accounting discipline itself places accounting squarely on the front line in public interest resource allocation decisions.

Accounting Is a Measurement Discipline

Accounting assigns numbers to objects. Accountants measure costs, income, revenue, and expenses. Anyone who wants to know the money benefits of a program, the money sacrifice of a problem solution, the money equivalent of a resource—must rely on the discipline of accounting and the analytical powers of accountants. And because proposed solutions to problems involve the reallocation of resources, it is unavoidable that questions arise concerning the costs and benefits of resource reallocation. The designation of such costs and benefits again involves accounting skills.

Accounting Is Entity Oriented

This point was first brought to your attention in Chapter 1. All accounting statements are identified with an entity of some sort. The first accounting entities were individual proprietors. With increasing degrees of abstraction, accounting entities came to include partnerships, corporations, foundations, governments, and entire nations. Entity orientation is essential in accounting because it affords the focus of attention. In preparing accounting statements you measure the transactions of an entity, the net effect of a set of transactions on an entity, the assets of an entity, and the equities (claims upon, or interests) of other entities in this particular entity.

Entities and Goals. The 1960s were characterized by recognition of many interest groups as entities, where a decade before such an identification would not have been accepted as reasonable. Consumer groups are entities. Racial minorities are entities. City dwellers are an entity. Those who wish to stabilize the planet's ecology are an entity. Those who favor population control are an entity. Recipients of welfare payments are an entity. We may agree or disagree about the purposes and representations of such *social entities,* but we no longer deny that they exist with respect to the particular set of problems or goals they advocate and which are peculiar to them.

Accounting may be used to describe the assets and equities, revenues and expenses of the programs advocated by social entities. In fact, the entity orientation of accounting makes it inevitable that social entity spokesmen and analysts will use the language and methods of accounting as a medium of expression and persuasion. For example, those favoring medicare in the early 1960s stated that this federally sponsored health-insurance program would, if adopted, save billions of dollars for the children of persons covered by the program. Irregardless of the truth of the statement, note that the speaker was describing two social entities (one is older persons and the other is their children) and the benefits each would receive from an aggregate transaction consisting of the medicare program, and in so doing was using the jargon and structure of accounting.

If social entities can be identified with respect to a set of goals and/or problems, it follows that such entities may overlap each other—that some of us have membership in many entities at once and may change our memberships frequently. This means that in order for a social entity to be heard, it must be represented by a special interest group or organization which acts as a semipermanent "guardian" for that social entity. For example, the AFL–CIO is one organization representing the social entity *labor,* the AAUP represents college professors, the Sierra Club represents environmentalists, Consumers Union represents consumers, and so on. These special interest organizations are, however, *not* the social entity they represent; and one cannot subrogate such an organization for the entity itself in any policy formulation or application, except at considerable risk.

The Attest Function

Whether in public or private accounting, the name and reputation of the individual accountant is regarded by nonaccountants as a guarantee that information the accountant produces is supportable by reasonable evidence. The most dramatic example is the auditor, an accountant in public practice who specializes in the examination of financial statements which a business (usually a corporation) proposes to publish (see Chapter 1). The auditor's examination is conducted to gather information and evidence which will allow him to express an opinion as to whether the proposed financial statements present fairly the financial position and results of operations for the company they relate to, and on a basis consistent with that of the preceding year's financial statements. A favorable auditor's opinion on published financial statements is accepted by most entities affected by the business' operations as conclusive evidence that the statements are reliable. When an auditor is found to be violating this essential trust (whether accidentally or purposefully), sanctions including lawsuits and expulsion from the auditing and accounting professions may be visited upon him.

Extending the Attest Function. Recent thought has suggested the auditor's attest function might profitably be extended to other forms of information. Thus, independent auditors might gather evidence to support an opinion that an engineering study of a proposed freeway was properly executed and that its conclusions are supportable, reasonable, and stated fully and clearly. It is up to others then to decide if those conclusions are acceptable. Such an opinion would serve to focus attention on the issues raised by the freeway proposal and engineering study and eliminate the "my engineers are better than your engineers" sort of controversy that makes the source of information rather than the direction it points the overriding (and wrong) issue.

One may imagine accountants someday expressing public opinions on proposed bond issues, regional development plans, government budgets and performance reports, and other activities which involve social entities and resource allocation. These opinions would *not* be for or against the proposals. They would cover instead the basic set of facts laid out for the public to use in deciding the issue. The opinion would state whether these facts were complete, fully stated, supported by evidence, and otherwise adequate as a basis for decision, all with respect to a set of generally accepted principles governing the formulation of such opinions. A deterrent to such opinions is the cost of gathering the evidence to support them and the lack of resources by special interest groups to defray these costs. It is possible (but not especially probable) that governments and foundations may compensate accountants for these expenses, should extension of the attest function actually materialize.

ACCOUNTANTS' SPECIAL ANALYTICAL TOOLS

Aside from the logical and institutional structure of accounting which causes social entities to turn to accountants for assistance, accountants possess a number of skills that are useful in defining problems and selecting solutions to problems.

Performance Reports

You have already seen that the accountant in management prepares reports depicting actual versus expected performance—reports which are necessary if managers are to infer causes for unexpected operating results. Such reports may also be prepared for activities in the public sector and for relations between social entities. A performance report may be prepared showing, for example, a timetable for industrial pollution control alongside actual progress in achieving such control, measured in terms such as tons per day of major pollutants released into water bodies and the atmosphere.

Marginal Analysis

Marginal analysis reveals the differences between alternative courses of action. In the private sector, you use marginal analysis to decide whether to make or buy a required input, whether to invest in a capital project, whether to acquire a new product line, and countless other decisions. Your decision is always based on the marginal addition each alternative will make to some particular measure of your welfare (or the welfare of the entity you represent).

Marginal analysis also has its place in the analysis of social goals and policies. A government decision whether to impose a surtax on imports (and whether to discontinue the surtax) is made because of the *differences* such a surtax is expected to make in a whole series of areas in which the national welfare is affected: international balance of payments, foreign relations, domestic inflation, the federal budget deficit. A consumer organization's decision to sue the government to release the results of government consumer appliance testing comes because of the difference such information may make to consumers who must choose between these appliances. Since accountants through experience, practice, and training are skilled in providing information for marginal analysis, their contribution to the soundness and validity of public decisions relative to social goal budgeting should be especially important.

Forecasting

Large-scale computer based forecasting models can be produced for any entity. One particularly useful class of forecasting model used especially in economic development is the "input-output" model. This model's theory is related to linear programming (Chapter 14) and critical path analysis (Chapter 13). It is used to study the effects on all segments of a regional or national economy when an investment or extra demand is applied to any one segment of the economy.

In the state of Oklayoming, to offer a conjectural example, there was a large minority of underemployed skilled workers. Everyone recognized that the problem confronting this state was to create an economic development program which would generate a maximum demand for the skills these workers possessed. Accountants worked on a team to develop an input-output model of the state's economy and used the model to determine where new investment should be encouraged to achieve the greatest demand increase for skilled labor. Once the type of investments needed were identified, the state began a nationwide campaign to attract industries of that type. The result was a series of selective investments which reduced Oklayoming's structural unemployment problems.

Data Banks

Accountants in business organizations maintain large quantities of up-to-date information, organized and classified so it can be quickly scanned and, if relevant to any particular decision or problem, presented to a decision maker. Such data "banks" prove extremely useful to managers who are pursuing a line of thought and need information to complete their work quickly.

In the public sector, especially when governments are involved, there is a tendency to resist centralized information systems whenever the information is about individuals. Although the technology exists, there is no sensible reason (other than economy) why there should be a file on any individual accessible by all branches of the government—there is too much "Big Brother" about it. The result is that the position of "government information manager" has emerged overnight as one of the most sensitive and important responsibilities in the public sector.

Data banks containing purely economic information pertaining to a region, a nation, or the global economy can be helpful to private sector investors determining whether they should invest in the area and if so in what ways. A regional data bank would provide instant answers to questions businessmen ask when scouting for investment opportunities.

> For example, suppose a business is looking in the Ozark region for a place to locate a heavy-equipment overhauling and repair facility. The business wants local financing, so it needs to know what banks are large enough to handle the capital requirements of the facility's construction. Another requirement is a labor force of 200 for the plant, which the company wishes to be drawn from a total local labor force of at least 10,000 persons. Finally, the company has placed an upper limit on the taxes it will pay. All of these requirements can be phrased as questions to a computer programmed to operate a data bank. A list of all locations potentially satisfying these initial screening criteria is prepared and printed out by the computer. After examining the list, the company searchers pinpoint three locations for detailed investigation. This process has required less than half a day and cost practically nothing to collect information which would otherwise have required weeks and cost thousands of dollars, and the Ozarks have 200 jobs and a new plant that otherwise would have passed them by.

In preparation of data banks, you would make use of the accounting double-entry system of classification and its ability to accommodate measurements made in more than one dimension. Unfortunately the design of such data banks is beyond the scope of an introductory text.

Systems Studies

The "systems" approach is a current notion which deserves considerable attention. At its best, a systems approach is a straightforward detailed study of *all* the operations of an economic or other entity. In this context, systems work is widely done, and the principles of systems analysis are a unifying factor within and between such disciplines as medicine, biology, economics, and marketing as well as accounting.

Some persons have held out that a system approach could solve any problem; that problems exist only because problem solvers are too narrow and confined. In practice, responsible systems analysts have learned that any broadening of the definition of a system increases by many orders of magnitude the complexity of the model required to represent that system—in many cases, to the point of making it impossible to develop models and therefore impossible to study and resolve problems. Most systems are too complex for even a team of analysts to full perceive. Responsible systems work at this time is limited in scope but promising and high in potential.

In accounting, application of systems study is limited to analysis, design, and appraisal of information systems. Within this limit, systems analysis has been developed into an important accounting tool, its value proven by the performance of thousands of business information systems. However, information systems have not been developed to serve public sector entities. As a result, social entities and individuals receive unreliable and "managed" information from special interest organization publicists and thus have difficulty seeing their problems and potential solutions as clearly or objectively as private sector managers and investors see theirs.

To illustrate a typical problem here, consider the social entity which is defined by the transportation function in the United States. Transportation is available by airplane, truck, bus, car, pipeline, and other media, each of which is organized as an industry to present and promote its own advantages over competing modes. All depend to some degree on government subsidy, regulation, and protection. To sustain this government support, all transportation industries produce a flow of information directed at the public and intended to generate pressure on the government to support that industry. Airlines and airline support industries want more and "better" airports; highway contractors want bigger, "safer" highway systems; railroads want an end to "excessive" taxation and subsidies to rivals. In that situation it is difficult to generate support for an integrated transportation policy, especially one which might introduce a new service such as public municipal transportation systems for metropolitan areas.

Conceivably accountants, acting on behalf of those affected by transportation services, could develop information systems which would indicate where and when transportation service deficiencies exist and how they should best be treated. The only difficulty with this kind of proposal is identifying an appropriate entity to sponsor such work; accountants have to be paid salaries like everyone else and neither private sector businesses nor public accounting firms have in the past shown inclination to undertake such projects. Perhaps this will change.

On a broader front, accountants could participate in systems studies of nonbusiness functions in society. A state-sponsored program to train men and women in industrial skills to help them find work was revised, based on a systems study, to provide training for service-type jobs such as home appliance repair, tree surgery, and security guard—for the system study showed that service-type jobs were plentiful whereas industry-type jobs were actually declining in the state. Accounting knowledge of business trends contributed to the success of this study. Another state, studying its system of criminal corrections, concluded that a major cause of recidivism among "graduates" of the correctional system was that the job training offered was out of date—experience in the prison laundry, making license plates, and primitive farming—and of little real value to any employer considering such a person for employment. Although the proposals for advanced vocational training would require increased spending on the correctional system, they were at last word receiving serious consideration. Again, the technical knowledge of business possessed by accountants influenced the study's recommendations.

ACCOUNTING AND ECONOMIC POLICY

Accounting is involved now in formulation or evaluation of national and local economic policies. An "economic policy" is some policy of government whose effects are measurable in economic terms. This section is organized to illustrate accounting participation in economic policy formation in several problem areas—taxation, inflation, and public sector economic growth.

Taxation

Approximately 30 percent of the income of Americans and American businesses is paid in taxes. There is every reason to believe taxes will go up not down in the future. Accountants do not control tax policy at any government level. Nevertheless, accountants are a part of the system which is responsible for tax law. Accountants have an intimate knowledge of tax effects on all sectors of society. As taxes increase, accountants will share the responsibility for assuring the equity of new taxes. Although many persons do not believe that tax policy should be subordinated to achievement of national goals, others hold that tax policy can encourage some goals, discourage others, and still raise government revenue equitably. As one example, consider the often-heard statement, "The government ought to put a tax on pollution-producing processes, to raise their cost and make them uneconomical compared with 'cleaner' processes."[1]

Another possibility would be tax credits for activities judged favorable to the public interest. A mining company strip-mining coal in West Virginia would receive tax credits for restoring the landscape to a semblance of its former contours. The extra expense of doing this would be wholly or partially offset by lower taxes.

Although the primary responsibility for working out such tax policies rests with public finance and other economic specialists, the accountant is the only man who is really in a position to estimate their effect on specific individual businesses. Many of the industrial pollution situations in the United States can be controlled through a relatively small number of firms whose responses may, through study, be objectively anticipated for specific tax proposals. Accountants can conduct these studies.

Special tax provisions might offer credits for hiring and training members of minority groups, for maintenance of mechanical antipollution devices on motor vehicles, for urban or industrial development in the older parts of large cities, for managerial compensation to serve with community development corporations, for promoting export sales,

---

[1] Attractive and simple as this sounds, it would not work just that way. It is likely that the polluting processes would be shut down here and relocated in foreign countries with less-restrictive pollution regulations. Even if this didn't happen, the extra costs to U.S. manufacturers would be passed on to consumers and tend to price U.S. goods out of international markets, upsetting international trade and the balance of payments. Thus, control of industrial pollution will require close international cooperation.

and for other programs judged to be in the public interest. In all cases, the effects of proposed tax policies should be worked out and verified by accounting consultants.

Subsidies

Many of the effects discussed above might also be accomplished through simple selective direct subsidies. One proposal at this writing is to replace many welfare programs with a "negative income tax" (see Chapter 20 for a fuller discussion) or direct subsidy to anyone earning less than some minimum salary. Accountants can and do contribute to cost-effectiveness studies comparing this proposal with existing welfare structures.

However, subsidies have important effects on the behavior of those receiving them, as to a lesser extent do tax penalties and credits. The lack of a tax on the "income" of nonprofit organizations has produced an explosive increase in the total assets controlled by such organizations and serious questions about their efficiency of asset utilization. Persons receiving welfare or other payments (such as farmers) sometimes organize into special interest groups which seek extension and perpetuation of subsidies for their own sake and not for whatever contribution may be made to the national welfare. The depletion allowance given to extractive industries is an example of a tax benefit and the protective attitude towards it of those who benefit therefrom. The national highway building program has been criticised as a subsidy to those using highways (and those building them!) and as a penalty to other modes of transportation, and a considerable amount of influence is exercised to continue the federal and state highway construction programs. There are few industries which could anticipate indifferently the withdrawal of their government business patronage.

CERTIFICATION OF FINANCIAL STATEMENTS

Certified Public Accountants have performed the important function of attesting to the fairness and consistency of corporate financial reports since about 1900. The practice may have arisen as a result of the substantial British investments in U.S. business after the Civil War and the desire of British investors for accurate information about the condition of those investments. There is a general feeling among investors that a favorable opinion on financial statements by a CPA lessens the probability that the financial statements do not accurately present financial position and results of operations. Investors are more willing to act on the basis of information they are reasonably certain is true than on the basis of information they doubt is accurate.

The single major issue that complicates financial reporting, for both the reporting entity and the auditing CPA, is this: The business continues throughout several reporting periods, earning its profits as a result of all its operations, yet it must report its income and expenses for arbitrary intervals which have no relation to the profit generation process. Here are two examples of this problem:

1. An expensive plant is purchased. The plant will last 25 years and will be operated throughout that interval. Then, a final determination can be made whether the plant contributed to business profits. However, at annual intervals business financial statements must be prepared, and these statements must declare whether the plant is profitable during the year preceding the financial statement date.
2. A construction company undertakes a three-year construction project. Profit will be earned only on the entire contract, yet annual financial statements will be issued and these statements will include an estimate of profit or loss on the partially completed project.

In order that financial statements be issued, the business must make judgments as to the portion of cost of such assets or projects which has produced a benefit in the current year reported upon. The dollar figure used, whatever it is, is a surrogate for the benefits received or expired in this reporting period. When that figure appears in financial statements, others will use it to make investment decisions. If these decisions turn out to be wrong because the costs or benefits allocated to a particular reporting period are obviously wrong, users of the financial statements in which they appeared will be justifiably looking for some entity to take the blame and responsibility.

Certified Public Accountants have taken the responsibility of examining the evidence underlying financial statements—the paid and canceled checks, the invoices, the approved requisitions, payroll vouchers, minutes of board meetings, tax returns, depreciation calculations, inventories, assets, and all other things which may tend to support the complex representations in a business' financial statements. The result of this examintion is a standard "short form" opinion that the financial statements—

> ... present fairly the financial position of the------------Company at (balance sheet date) and the results of its operations for the year then ended, in conformity with generally accepted accounting principles applied on a basis consistent with that of the preceding year.
>
> E. L. Summers, CPA

This is a most interesting statement, and the phrases in it deserve attention, laden as they are with legal and traditional significance. However, we will only discuss that phrase, "generally accepted accounting principles" which is unique in that these principles *have never been defined.* Lack of definition is not for lack of trying; the American Institute of Certified Public Accountants, the major organization of professional accountants and the acknowledged spokesman of the profession, has recognized such definition as its major challenge almost since the date of its organization.

The present approach to the problem of defining generally accepted accounting principles is an independent Financial Accounting Standards Board. This board is, roughly speaking, responsible for authoritative definitions of accounting principles which all AICPA members are obliged to generally accept as a basis to which financial statements must conform. The board issues these definitions as a series of Opinions, additional numbers of which appear irregularly. The Opinions are "committee" efforts and usually represent reasoned compromises among alternative positions advocated by various members of the FASB (who are distinguished accountants appointed for three-year terms). As such the Opinions are extremely detailed and carefully spelled out; they do serve as a practical guide to accountants preparing opinion on financial statements.

The FASB's predecessor, the Accounting Principles Board, was criticised because its members were practicing auditors, corporate accountants, or security analysts and were therefore not obviously objective in their deliberations. A 1972 study by the AICPA's "Wheat Committee" (named for its chairman, Francis Wheat) proposed the seven-person FASB, financially independent of the AICPA, unassociated with any business, paid to do full-time work an accounting principles definition. This proposal has been approved by the AICPA. The sponsoring Financial Accounting Foundation has been established and, in 1973, the Financial Accounting Standards Board became operational.

Why is the CPA's opinion on published financial statements important? We have already stated that this opinion seems to satisfy investors that the statements do not contain deliberate major falsehoods or distortions. This is important because it moves financial statements closer to the concept of "perfect information" discussed in Chapter 15. The better informed the investor, the more efficient will be his resource allocation decisions. They will be more efficient because he is not paying part of the cost of uncertainty and ignorance regarding his investments. To illustrate this point, let us imagine two companies exactly alike in all respects and with exactly similar prospects (never mind if the prospects are good, bad, or indifferent—that is unimportant). You must buy the equally priced securities of only one of these two companies. You know about Company A; you know *nothing* about Company B. Chances are, you will prefer the securities of Company A because you know more about the risk you're taking.

Now suppose you must buy the securities of *both* companies. You will pay a higher price for Company A securities than for Company B securities. The lower price on B securities gives you a margin of safety for unforeseen events which may occur and affect the value of B securities. On the other hand, since you know everything about A securities, you know exactly what you are willing to pay for them and there is no need for a margin of safety. You are always ready to act with respect to A securities; you are always reluctant to act on B securities. Information improves your efficiency as an allocator of resources and makes your investment decisions more timely, more productive, safer, and more profitable. To the extent that audit opinions contribute to better information, they are contributing to faster, wiser resource allocation. If the CPA's audit opinion is compromised, published financial information becomes less reliable, investment decisions use it less, and the cost of capital allocation to profitable opportunities becomes higher.

ACCOUNTING AND SOCIAL INDICATORS

The service of accountants to social entities presupposes that indicators of the goals, objectives, and welfare of such entities can be found and measured. The argument is heard that accounting should be defined simply (and very broadly) as "communication of information necessary for the attainment of goals."[2] This definition goes well beyond the communication of purely financial information and the self-assumed role of the AICPA as discussed in the previous section.

The future acceptability of this definition may depend on acceptance of the notion that an economy, in order to see where it is going and plan its activities, must be able to compare past performance with expectations for the same period. This is the basic principle of control in businesses—but businesses are tightly controlled by their managers, and the national economy is, despite some efforts to mitigate its more pronounced excesses, at this writing a glorious and frightening Bedlam.

However, if we accept the notion of social entities, the need for indicators of social achievement and well-being surely exists for these entities whether or not they have the degree of internal organization which characterizes business entities. What sort of indicators might these be?

A paper by Nestor E. Terleckyj[3] suggests 22 possible indicators arranged in six groups:

I. *Freedom, Justice, and Harmony*
   (The author did not in his paper suggest any indicators of these goals)
II. *Health and Safety*
   A. Mean life expectancy at birth

---

[2] Robert K. Elliot, "Accounting in the Technological Age," *World* (Publication of Peat Marwick Mitchell & Co., CPAs), Winter 1972, pp. 23–27.

[3] Nestor E. Terleckyj, "Measuring Progress Towards Social Goals: Some Possibilities at National and Social Levels," *Management Science,* August 1970, pp. B-765 to B-778.

B. Number of persons with chronic disability conditions
C. Violent crime rate
III. *Education, Skills, and Income*
   A. Index of average achievement in language
   B. Percent of age group completing college
   C. Average earnings
   D. Number of persons outside mainstream of labor force
   E. Number of persons below present poverty standard
   F. Number of persons in near-poverty conditions
   G. Number of persons with permanent losses in levels of living over 30 percent
IV. *Human Habitat*
   A. Proportion of persons living in inadequate housing
   B. Proportion of persons living in satisfactory neighborhoods
   C. Index of cost of travel and transportation
   D. Percent of persons exposed to bothersome pollution
   E. Percent of persons regularly taking part in recreation
V. *Finer Things*
   A. Number areas for preservation of beauty
   B. Number of scientists active in basic science
   C. Number of active artists
   D. Average time free from work and chores
VI. *Economic Base*
   A. Gross National Product

Terleckyj did not pretend that this was a complete or final set of indicators; and, indeed, it appears that some of them (such as IV-B) despair of objective measurement. Terleckyj concluded his presentation with these points (pp. 775–77):

1. Articulation of social goals is important for ascertaining whether they are being reached.
2. Existing statistical systems are not geared to articulating and reporting social goals.
3. Development of simple systems to reflect progress toward some of the generally acceptable goals is feasible.
4. If such systems are to serve as vehicles of information to the general public, they have to be simple and clear-cut.

5. Development of larger systems (to measure more complex social indicators of progress) depends on progress in basic work that is yet to be done.

If indeed public policy is being made in a knowledge vacuum in this country, it is a serious situation that all of us, readers and textbook writers alike, need to correct. As members of accounting or another business profession you should be prepared to participate, both in collecting information for public decision making and in such decision making itself.

SUMMARY

The policy of the accounting profession is to extend its unique analytical skills and institutional structure into the public service as often and as effectively as possible. Those logical aspects of accounting which are most useful in public service are its measurement and entity orientation and its ability to mark progress toward goals. The independence of accountants and their traditional exercise of the attest function are similarly useful. The tools accountants use most effectively in public communication are the same ones that serve them best in the managerial function: performance reports, marginal analysis, forecasting, data banks, and system studies. The major issues which accountants have already engaged are domestic economic policy and financial statement certification. In the future, accountants are expected to extend their attest function to the information presented for public decisions and to participate in the development of social indicators. Because of their involvement with information processing, accountants cannot avoid contributing to the public interest and are determined to do so in the wisest possible ways.

QUESTIONS

1. A large lake near your hometown may be drained to make room for a subdivision. It is one of four large lakes and is known for its wildlife, including snakes, alligators, ducks, geese, and so on. Your town is growing fast due to new industry, and developers are urging

haste in providing new homes for these people. The hometown ecology group wants to preserve the lake. The city council can make the decision since the lake is in the city limits. Discuss the roles accountants will have with the city council, ecology group, and developers. Do you see anything wrong with accountants working with each of these entities?

2. What is the attest function? How would the attest function be exercised if it were extended beyond the auditor's opinion on financial statements?

3. Why is accountants' independence important to their exercise of the attest function? What is independence, as accountants use the word?

4. "Accounting is a measurement discipline," the chapter says. This conveys only part of the story, just as the term, "law is an advocacy discipline" is not a comprehensive description of that profession. What other dimensions of accounting can you think of to round out your picture of that discipline?

5. What is a social entity? What is a special interest organization? How do these two serve each other? How can they *not* serve each other?

6. By and large accountants are good citizens—they pay all of their taxes, do not engage in illegal acts, and contribute to charities. Why should there be any addiitonal public service aspect to their lives and work than, say, there is to the lives and work of house painters or computer programmers? What is unique about accounting as an institution that suits it for public service?

7. In 1971 the U.S. Congress passed a law which will prohibit the discharge of all pollutants into navigable American waterways by 1985. Indicate how accountants may be expected to participate in helping industry and government comply with this law.

8. A large city has these problems:
    (1) Garbage disposal.
    (2) Drinking water.
    (3) Industrial water.
    (4) Recreational areas.

(5) Additional residential areas.
(6) Electrical power.
(7) Fuels.

An engineering study has suggested that a systems approach be taken to find complementary solutions to all these problems. Explain what a systems study is and how accountants might participate in a systems study concerning these particular problems.

9. In the country of Hungalia, disposable packaging materials have become a major problem. These are made by a monopoly company at an average price of $0.02 and sold to various packagers for $0.04. Last year the monopoly company made and sold 400,000,000 packages. These packages were mostly put into garbage containers, making up 10 percent of the country's total garbage volume. Disposing of garbage in Hungalia costs $80,000,000 per year. About 20 percent of the used packaging was strewn about the countryside, creating a litter problem and necessitating a $40,000,000 per year litter-cleanup operation, about 30 percent of which was due to the packaging litter. The government is thinking of putting a tax on disposable packaging. (*a*) What should be the size of the tax (if it is to cover the complete disposal of all packaging)? (*b*) At what level should the tax be levied—consumer, packager, or monopoly company?

10. What is a data bank? Why is it very important that rapid-access information be up-to-date?

11. A major industry in the United States is in deep economic difficulty—unable to sell its product or pay its bills. It asks Congress for a $100,000,000 per year annual subsidy—and states that its only alternative is to relocate in a foreign country with lower labor and material costs and import its product into the United States. The company points out that it has an annual payroll alone of over $200,000,000 and other contributions to the economy in excess of the subsidy sought, whereas if located abroad it would drain $400,000,000 out of the United States and aggravate the balance of payments. Make the case against the subsidy.

12. The Commission of the European Economic Community is preparing supranational European restrictions on industrial pollution. What do you think should be the role of accountants in developing these restrictions?

13. Refer to Question 12 above. How could accountants help insure compliance with these restrictions?

14. "It seems to me that all this environmental control talk just means more restrictions on businessmen trying to make a buck," says your friend the company president. Explain to him what governments are going to have to do, and how accountants can help with the task of allocating some parts of the environmental control function to business, and some parts to government. What should be the criterion for deciding how the splitup should be made?

15. The Midville city council is meeting, and it is upset. As a result of a series of community self-appraisal meetings held over the past nine months, the council has before it a city master plan calling for urgent capital and operating expenditures totaling $750,000,000. The council, after an exhaustive study of all present and conceivable future sources of revenue, can only see $410,000,000 of funds in sight to pay for the master plan. Obviously, something has to go. Your firm of CPAs is engaged to suggest criteria for dropping some projects from the master plan. The criteria are not to include any political considerations. Make a brief summary of some possible criteria.

BIBLIOGRAPHY[4]

Books

Fertig, Paul E.; Istvan, Donald F.; and Mottice, Homer J. *Using Accounting Information: An Introduction.* 2d ed. New York: Harcourt Brace Jovanovich, Inc., 1971.

Vatter, William J. *Accounting Measurements for Financial Reports.* Homewood, Ill.: Richard D. Irwin, Inc., 1971.

Articles

Beams, Floyd A. "Income Reporting: Continuity with Change," *Management Accounting,* August 1972.

---

[4] Items cited in chapter introduction not repeated.

Bergwerk, Rudolph J. "Effective Communication of Financial Data," *Journal of Accountancy,* February 1970.

Beyer, Robert. "Pilots of Social Progress," *Management Accounting,* July 1972.

Buckley, John W. "Accounting Principles and the Social Ethic," *Financial Executive,* October 1971.

Caplan, Edwin H. "Behavioral Assumptions of Management Accounting—Report of a Field Study." *The Accounting Review,* April 1968.

Capon, Frank S. "The Totality of Accounting for the Future," *Financial Executive,* July 1972.

Dembowski, Sig. "The Management Accountant," *Management Accounting,* April 1973.

Enthoven, Adolph J. H. "The Changing Role of Accountancy," *Finance and Development,* June 1969.

Gilbert, Lewis D. "What Stockholders Expect from CPA's in Financial Reporting," *The Ohio CPA,* Spring 1971.

Hagerman, Robert L.; Keller, Thomas F.; and Petersen, Russell J. "Accounting Research and Accounting Principles," *Journal of Accountancy,* March 1973.

Kell, Walter G. "The Auditor's Responsibilities in Financial Reporting," *Michigan Business Review,* March 1967.

Linowes, David F. "Accounting for Social Progress," *New York Times,* March 14, 1971, sec. 3, p. 14.

Mosich, A. N., and Hamilton, Robert E. "The Decline or Rise of Accounting," *Journal of Accountancy,* July 1972.

vonBert, William G. "Accounting for Responsibility," *Journal of Accountancy,* November 1972.

Index

Index

A

Accountants
  and attest function, 531, 540
  and auditing, 531
  and decision model analysis, 249
  and decisions, 3
  as government information managers, 535
  and information validity, 455
  and tax policies, 512
  as tax specialists, 502
Accounting, defined, 3
  analytical tools, 532
  applications in activity analysis, 68
  approximation to fixed costs, 63
  and behavior, 291
  for business activity, 34
  and economic policy, 537
  entity orientation, 530
  evolution and history, 32
  financial, 19
  information functions, 280
  and linear programming, 420
  managerial, 3, 18
  as a measurement discipline, 530
  measurement of profit, 8
  potential for use in economic decision making, 39

Acounting, defined—*Cont.*
  principles, 541
  principles board, 541
  profession, 17
  profit calculation, 41
  profit and inflation, 479
  and the public interest, 528
  in the public sector, 18, 90
  records of economic activities, 89
  and social indicators, 543
  and social problem involvement, 529
  specializations and careers, 17
  statements
    expressed in dollars, 37
    multidimensional, 36
    and price changes, 482
  for taxes, 509
  and uncertainty, 454
Acquisition cost components for capital investment, 326
Activities subject to learning effect, 179
Activity analysis
  and linear programming, 402
  and semifixed costs, 289
  two or more products, 73
  using percentages, 73

553

554   Index

Activity base
  choice of, 197
  definition, 198
  standard value of, 199
Activity level
  analysis and profit maximization, 74
  analysis purposes, 59
  effect of change, 71
  and inflation, 479
  physical, 479
Activity mix and profit, 402
Activity standard
  defined, 163
  and standard costs, 162
Activity statement, 35, 41
Ad valorem tax, 507
Alternatives, set of, in decisions, 435
American Institute of Certified Public Accountants, 18, 528, 541
Analysis of performance, 284
Attest function, 531
Attest function extensions, 532, 540, 545
Auditing, 17, 531, 540
Average cost
  behavior, 67
  defined, 63
Average revenue, 64

B

Balance sheet
  adjusted for inflation, 483
  characteristics when adjusted for inflation, 485
  defined, 43
Base period, 480
Basic profit and Investor's Target Rate of Return (ITRR), 316-17
Bedlam, 543
Behavior
  and accounting reports, 291
  and planning, 292
  and pressure, 292
  and pressure reduction, 296
Breakeven point
  computation formula, 69

Breakeven point—*Cont.*
  defined, 68
  and semifixed costs, 289
Budget
  administrative, 125, 143
  advisers, 117
  capital, 126, 144, 315
  cash flow schedule, 127
  committee of board of directors, 117
  committee of president, 117
  components, 120
  cost of goods manufactured statement, illustrated, 139
  cost of goods sold statement, illustrated, 140
  defined, 116
  detail level, 122
  estimation using standard costs, 164
  first draft, 119
  flexible, 125
  and control
  as formal planning and communication system, 130
  main ideas, 281
  and planning, 281
  formula defined, 284
  indirect manufacturing costs, illustrated, 138
  installation steps, 129
  intermediate range, 121
  labor requirements, illustrated,
  long range, 120
  manufacturing, 124, 134
  operating
    defined, 121
    preparation, 128
  participation and pressure, 295
  policies, 117
  and pressure, 296
  process
    management questions, 281
    organization, 117
    and profitability, 117
  product line performance statement, illustrated, 142
  purchases, 124, 136
  reasons for having, 116

Budget—*Cont.*
  regional sales performance statement, illustrated, 141
  research and development, 126
  revising expense estimates, 283
  sales, 123, 133
  systems study prior to installation, 130
  used to identify problems, 117
Bumppo, Natty, 293
Business, typical activities, 34

C

Capacity
  changes to improve total contribution, 417
  and fixed annual costs, 201
  increments and profit, 290
Capital
  expenditures or investments, 315
  factor in production, 91
  gains and losses as carryforwards and carrybacks, 515
  long and short term gains and losses, 515
  taxation of gains and losses, 514
Capital investments
  factors to consider, 320, 330, 437
  and information, 320, 440, 451
Carrying cost; *see* Storage cost
Cash
  adjusted for inflation, 483
  basis for accounting statements, 42
  basis for capital investment analysis, 316
  flow and taxes, 324
Causal network, 253
Certified Public Accountant, 19, 539
Chief budget officer and responsibilities, 117
Computers
  and budgeting process, 132
  and capital investment decisions, 331
  and inventory management, 358
  and performance analysis, 286

Computers—*Cont.*
  and project planning and control, 386
  and standard cost estimation, 175
  and time sharing, 175
  used to revise cost standards, 176
Congress and tax laws, 502
Constraints
  arising from productive activity, 404
  defined, 406
  inequalities, 404
  in linear programming, 403
  system, as a graph, 406
  technological, 408
Contribution
  of additional information in decisions, 450
  analysis
    and joint products, 255, 262
    of planning decisions, 248
    and production level, 263
    and sunk costs, 251
  per unit
    defined, 68
    and objective function in linear programming, 407
Control
  and accounting representation, 280
  of activities showing a learning effect, 179
  defined, 166
  and flexible budgeting, 282
  and indirect costs, 196
  of inventories through a management system, 358
  of large scale projects, 373
  limits, 170
  and management knowledge, 298
  of manufacturing processes, 220
  of projects based on completion time and cost estimates, 379, 387
  at responsibility centers, 93
  rule of, 167, 250
  and standard cost variances, 165
  and standard costs, 161
  using accumulated costs, 97

Control—*Cont.*
  using linear programming, 417
  out of, defined, 166
Controllership, 18
Cooper, J. F., 293
Corporate income tax, 513
Corporate taxable income calculation, 513
Cost
  allocation and decision making, 205, 251, 252, 264
  analysis for project planning and control, 373
  assignment reports, 227
  assignment reports and documentary support, 229
  assumptions permitting historical cost use in accounting, 38
  average, defined, 63
  basis for classification, 60
  basis for valuation of resources, 38
  of capital expenditures, 326
  classifications, 94
  controllable, 94
  controllable, effect of time period, 101
  detail at responsibility centers, 99
  direct, 95
    in linear programming problem formulations, 417
  discretionary, 95
  fixed, defined, 60
    effect of change on breakeven point, 70
    effect on product cost, 100
    in investment decisions, 323
    operating, per unit of capacity increment, 290
    planning of, 288
  flow in job costing, 224
  flow at service centers, 195
  indirect, defined, 96
    accumulation, 96
    allocation basis, 99
    prediction, 96
  inflation adjustment need, 489
  of information, 34, 439

Cost—*Cont.*
  of information errors, 438
  and inventory management, 347
  of inventory policy, 350–51
  of inventory shortage, 347
  and joint products, 255
  marginal, 62
  of ordering inventory, 347
  overhead, 194
  per equivalent unit, 231
  project, 374
  relevant, 95
  semifixed, 289
  standard, 159
  standard, establishing, 170
  step, 373
  of storing inventory, 347
  sunk, 251
  total or average in decision making, 250
  total cost curve, 62
  unit
    defined, 220
    does not affect inventory management decisions, 348
  variable
    defined, 60
    effect of change in, 71
  variances, defined, 160
  and volume behavior, defined, 61
  of wrong inventory policy, 357
Cost of sales adjusted for inflation, 486
Costing
  direct, 202
  full absorption, 202
  job
    defined, 220
    flow of costs, 222
    and process costing compared, 230
  of joint products, 255
  methods effect on income, 204
  process, 220, 230
Critical path—defined
  analysis history, 386
  defined, 379–80
  multiple, 386

Index   557

Critical path—defined—*Cont.*
  shortening, 384
Currency
  units of account in accounting reports, 37
  value of, 474

D

Data banks, 534
Data gathering process
  defined, 446
  evaluation of, 450
Decision making
  and asset replacement analysis, 327
  and capacity changes, 417
  and certainty, 436
  and contribution analysis, 248
  and control, 165
  and data gathering processes, 446
  and decision models, 249
  and expected value of decision, 447
  and further processing of joint products, 259, 262
  and inflation, 482
  and information, 250
  and information aggregation, 454
  and information system performance, 435, 438
  and inventory management, 346
  and investments, 320, 330
  and joint products, 253
  and linear programming, 410
  and long- and short-run, 68
  make or buy decision, 250
  more information available, 446
  no more information available, 445
  and overhead allocation, 205
  and planning, 116
  and price changes, 477, 482
  and process continuation, 265
  on product continuation, 256
  on production levels, 59, 262
  in production mix decisions when unit contribution margins change, 413
  and profit maximization, 75
  at responsibility centers, 92

Decision making—*Cont.*
  rules, 249
  and sunk costs, 251–52
  and taxes, 501, 514
  and uncertainty, 436, 443, 450
  value of information, 447
  whether to acquire information, 450
Decision model
  defined, 249
  for inventory management, 349
  sensitivity to information, 439
  for uncertainty, 450
Decision models terminology, 435
Decision rule
  best, 444
  defined, 444
  linked to additional information, 449
  selection, 444
Decisions, economic, 9, 250
Demand
  for inventory, 348, 350
  for money and commodities, 474
  rate for inventory, determining factors, 348
Depreciation
  and investment decisions, 324
  methods compared, 511
  tax effect, 324, 510
Direct cost and standard cost, 164
Direct costing, 202
Direct production inputs schedule, illustrated, 135
Documents supporting manufacturing cost allocation, 228

E

Economic activity, defined, 89
Economic development and accounting, 529
Economic order quantity models
  computations illustrated, 351
  for inventory management, 349
  without shortages, 352
Economic planning and accounting, 529

Economic theory
  and cost-volume behavior, 61
  success in application, 60
Economy
  definition, 13
  private sector, 13
  problems with, 17
  public sector, 16
Efficiency
  experts, 162
  of production center use of service center indirect services, 196
  of service center, measured, 196
  variance, 168
Entities, social, 530
Environment
  in decision making, 6
  uncertainty in, 8
Equivalent units
  computation, 231–32
  defined, 230
  and physical units, 232
Expectations and reality in decision making, 437
Expected step time completion, 377
"Eyeball" estimate of standard costs, 171

F

Factors of production, 91
Feed-forward, 42
Financial Accounting Standards Board, 19, 128, 541
Financial Executives Institute, 19
Financial reporting rules effect on planning and business activities, 128
Financial statements certification, 540
Fixed assets adjusted for inflation, 484
Fixed cost
  and costing methods, 204
  defined, 60
  in investment decisions, 323
  planning, 288
  semifixed, 289
Fixed overhead spending variance, 201

Flexible budgeting principles, 281
Forecasting
  accuracy required, 437
  as analytical tool, 534
  role in decision making, 437
Full absorption costing, 202
Future sums, 320

G

gain, realized and unrealized, 477
generally accepted accounting principles, 541
goals
  articulation and reporting, 544
  conflict, 5
  metamorphasis, 5
  orientation, 4
  priority, 5
  of social entities, 530
  and standard costs, 162
  unfulfilled, 5

H

High-low method to estimate standard costs, 171
Historical cost; see Cost
"How" and budgets, 281

I

Income
  and capacity, 290
  and deflating, 481
  effect of direct and full absorption costing, 202–4
  measurement and inflation, 478
  taxable, 514
Income statement
  adjusted for inflation, 486
Income tax on corporations, 513
Independence of accountants, 532
Index numbers
  base period, 480
  construction, 480
  defined, 479

Indirect cost
  allocation and decision making, 205
  defined, 96
  and modern business, 194
  as overhead, 194
  product allocated, 200
  production-allocated, 198
  and standard cost, 164
Inequalities as constraints, 404
Inflation
  and accounting statements, 482
  cost-push, 477
  defined, 475
  demand-pull, 477
  effect on a business, 478
  and interest rates, 485
  and ITRR, 317
  and money supply, 482
  and progressive taxation, 504
  and real income, 479
  and sustaining production, 491
Information
  and capital investments, 320, 322
  and control, 280
  cost, 34
  data gathering processes in decision making, 446
  in decisions, 248, 250
  describing expected payoffs, 437
  from linear programming problem solutions, 410
  perfect and imperfect, 448
  and planning, 292
  from price changes, 477
  for project planning and control, 373
  reduces risk, 542
  rule of, 250
  surprise value, 453
  system
    error and decisions, 438
    evaluation, 450
    formal, 295
    informal, 295
  technology, 18
  and uncertainty, 8
  value, 447

Institute of Management Accounting, 19
Integration and accounting, 529
Interest rate and inflation, 485
Internal Revenue Service, 502
Inventory
  adjusted for inflation, 484
  demand or withdrawal rate, 348
  function, 345
  and job planning, 221
  level, as a function of time, 346
Inventory management
  computations illustrated, 351
  comment on EOQ cost formulas, 353
  cost savings with EOQ policies, 354
  delay in restocking, 354
  and EOQ models, 349
  and information error, 440
  and irregular deliveries, 356
  parameters affecting, 347, 437
  and policy, 345
  and safety stock, 355
  and sensitivity analysis, 357
  without shortages, 353
  simple and sophisticated models, 349
  systems, 358
  typical "bin" method, 348
  and uncertainty, 451
Inventory parameters effect on order quantity and replenishment point, 350
Inventory policy
  based on models, 346
  in budget, 123, 134
  cost, 350–51
  and desired level of service, 346
  optimal, 351
Inventory shortage and safety stock, 355
Investment decisions
  criterion, 330
  under uncertainty, 451
Investment security, 16
Investors
  function in private sector, 15

560 Index

Investors—*Cont.*
  target rate of return
    defined, 316
    factors affecting, 316
    illustrated, 319

J

Job
  control report, 223
  costing
    appraisal, 230
    comparison with process costing, 230
    defined, 220
    documentation, 224
    information flow, 223
    similarities with process costing, 220, 230
    and standard costs, 226
  specification sheet, 220
  transfer ticket, 223
Joint products
  cost allocation, 264
  and decision making, 253
  defined, 254
  and pricing decisions, 256
  and production level, 262
Journal of Accountancy, 528

L

Labor assignment report, 223
Labor as factor of production, 91
Labor report, 222, 226
Learning effect
  computations, 179
  defined, 177
  plotted on linear scale graph paper, 178
  plotted on log-log paper, 180
  and resource inputs, 177
  and variances, 178
Least squares regression analysis
  to estimate standard costs, 173
  underlying assumptions, 174
Lifetime of investments, 323

Linear aggregation vector, 40
Linear cost changes in projects, 387
Linear programming
  activity substitution, 414
  additional information outputs, 410
  applications, 331, 402
  assumptions, 403
  and capacity changes, 417
  and companywide control, 419
  conditions for optimum solution, 408
  constraints, 404
  constraints satisfied by optimal solution, 409
  and cost volume profit analysis, 402
  graphical solution, 408
  and indirect costs, 407–8
  and information error, 442
  minimization of costs, 410
  nonnegativity, 405
  objective function, 407
  and performance reporting, 418
  and production mix, 402
  resource shadow prices, 416
  resource values, 415
  satisfying constraint system, 407
  sensitivity analysis
    defined, 410
    lower limit, 413
    upper limit, 411
  shadow prices, 415
  similarity to accounting, 420
  total contribution, 407
  and uncertainty, 452
Linearity and linear programming, 403
Long range planning and capital investments, 315
Long run decisions, 68
Loss carryforwards and carrybacks, 515

M

Management
  by exception, 162
  of corporations, 14
  as factor of production, 91
  and tax effect on decisions, 502

Managerial advisory services, 18
Marginal analysis, 533
Marginal cost, 62
Marginal revenue, 64
Materials
  assignment report, 223
  as factor of production, 91
  requisition, 225
  and supplies report, 222
Measurement, defined, 7
Monetary gains and losses, 487
Money
  defined, 474
  supply, 474, 482
  time value, 316
Motivation
  through budget committees, 129
  and pressure, a general model, 295
  and pressure, illustration, 292
  and standard costs, 162, 297

N

National Association of Accountants, 19
Negative income tax, 508
Net cash revenue in investment decisions, 322
Network
  and critical path, 380
  expected completion time and costs, 383
  of a project, 377
  showing step relationships, 378
Nonnegativity in linear programming, 405
Nonprofit entities, 505
Nonprofit entities restrictions, 506

O

Objective function in linear programming, 403, 407
Opportunity cost of wrong inventory policy, 357
Order cost of inventory, 347, 350
Order point, 354, 360

Order quantity, 346, 350
Order quantity, optimal, 351
Organization
  formal, 295
  informal, and pressure, 295
Overhead
  allocable from service to production centers, 198
  allocation and decision making, 205
  allocation report, 222, 227
  cost flow, 195, 196
  costs categories, 194
  defined, 194
  fixed, 195, 201
  fixed spending variance, 201
  and performance reporting, 202
  product-allocated, 200
  reconciliation of product-allocated and incurred overhead, 202
  at service and production centers, 195
  variable
    allocation rate, 198
    defined, 484
Owners' equity adjusted for inflation, 484

P

Paciolo, Luca, 33
payoff
  in decisions, 436
  highest average, 444
Perfect information
Performance
  analysis, 284
  measurement at production centers based on use of indirect services, 199
  measurement at service centers, 197
  and pressure, illustrated, 297
  report
    administrative, 287
    defined, 42, 533
    of overhead and indirect costs, 202
    and sales, 286

Performance—*Cont.*
  report—*Cont.*
    and uncertainty, 454
    using linear programming, 417
Physical units
  conversion to currency equivalents, 37–38
  and equivalent units in process costing, 232
Planning
  and accounting profit, 60
  and behavior, 292
  capacity increments, 290
  capital investments, 315
  fixed costs, 288
  and inflation, 477
  and learning effect, 177
  long range, 119, 315
  production jobs, 221
  projects, 373
  semifixed costs, 289
  and standard costs, 163
  using linear programming, 410
Planning Executives Institute, 19
Pollution control and accounting, 529
Present equivalent, 320, 327–28
  calculation illustrated, 328
  factors, 321
  and ITRR, 329·
Present value; *see* Present equivalent
Pressure
  and employee hostility, 297
  model defined, 292
  and productivity, 297
  reduction, 296
  responses by individuals, 295
Price changes
  and accounting statements, 482
  general, 475
  and resource reallocation, 476
  specific, 475
Price
  defined, 10
  effect of change, 71
  of money, 474
  variance, 167
Prior distribution, 445

Pro forma financial statements, 116, 127, 145
Probability of states of nature, 443
Process costing, 220
  comparison with job costing, 230
  cost relationship formula, 233
  and equivalent units, 230
  and physical units, 232
  steps, 232
  and valuation of units completed, 231
  and valuation of end of period work in process, 231
Product mix
  and information error, 442
  and information requirements, 407, 437
  and profit, 402
  and uncertainty, 452
Production
  center and measurement of efficiency, 196, 199
  center, defined, 92
  efficiency variance, 201
  factor of, 91
  job planning, 221
Productivity and pressure, 297
Profit
  and activity, 41
  affected by inflation, 478
  and capacity increments, 290
  condition for a maximum, 76
  control using linear programming, 419
  estimation, 64
  expressed in currency only, 37
  expressed in physical units, 36
  and inflation, 478
  maximized, 74, 402
  measure of satisfaction, 7
  motivation for economic activity, 8
  performance—factors affecting, 59
  planning; *see* Budgeting
  point, defined, 70
  and processes involving joint products, 262

Project
   completion time, 374
   cost behavior, 376
   cost savings, 381–86
   costs, 375, 381
   critical path, 379
   description network, 377–78
   network representation, 383, 385–86
   planning and control, 373, 437
   planning and control and information error, 441
   total cost formula, 376
   total cost illustrative graph, 382
Public finance, 475
Public interest and accounting, 528
Purposive behavior, 4

R

Rate of growth and ITRR, 318
Rate of return
   defined, 329
   for investors, 316
Real estate development and taxes, 504
Reconciliation of actual and standard costs with variances, 169
Regional development and accounting, 529
Relative frequency of states of nature, 443
Relevant cost
   in decisions, 250
   defined, 95
   and inventory management, 348
Reorder point; see Order point
Reorder quantity; see Order quantity
Replenishment point, 346, 350, 354
   optimal, 351
Resource allocation
   efficiency and information, 542
   and taxes, 505
Resources
   contribution to product value, 415
   control over, 10
   conversion, 12
   distribution, 12
   exchanges, 10

Resources—*Cont.*
   "market basket," 480
   prices, 10
   scarce, as constraints, 404
   scarcity, 10
   scarcity and price changes, 473
   substitution, 12
   transformation same as conversion, 12
   value, 11
   value computed using linear programming, 415
Responsibility center
   defined, 92
   production, 193
   service, 195
Restocking; see Replenishment
Revenue
   and prices, 63
   relevant, 95
   sharing, 507
Risk
   categories, 319
   and compensation, 319
   defined in investment decisions, 318
   and ITRR, 319
   reduced by information, 542
Rule of control, 167, 250
Rule of information, 167, 250

S

Safety stock
Sales forecast
Sales revenue adjusted for inflation, 486
Sales variances, 283
Satisfaction
   defined, 4
   measurement, 6
   and purposive behavior, 4
Selling and administrative expense adjusted for inflation, 487
Semifixed costs, 289
Sensitivity analysis
   of EOQ policies, 357
   of linear programming problem solutions, 411

Service center
  defined, 93
  efficiency measurement, 196
  performance measure, 197
Service efficiency variance, 198
Setup costs; *see* Order cost
Shadow prices, 416
Shadow prices calculations, 421
Short run decisions, 68
Shortage
  cost effect when very high, 352
  cost of inventory, 347, 350
  of inventory, 346
Signals from price increases, 476
Simplex algorithm, 420
Social entities, 530
Social goals articulation and measurement, 544
Social indicators and accounting, 543
Span of control and standard costs, 159, 161
Square roots computation using table, 360
Standard costs
  and activity standards, 163
  and actual costs, 169
  advantages, 159
  behavioral effects, 176
  defined, 160
  establishing, 170
    comparison of methods, 174
    and computers, 175
    estimation equation, 164
  and expectations, 298
  and goals, 162
  and income and asset measurement, 163
  and job cost accumulation, 226
  and learning effect, 178
  maintenance of, 175
  and management span of control, 161
  and motivation, 298
  of output, 163
  and planning, 163
  uses, 160
  and variances, 165

State
  probabilities change due to information, 449
  probability distribution, 443
  of nature in decisions, 436
  and prior probability distribution, 436
  variables definition in different decisions, 437
Step
  completion time, 378
  completion time estimation, 378
  cost change per unit time, 380
  cost estimation, 376
  cost formula, 381
  cost illustrative graph, 382
  costs and time, 374, 380
  dummy, 377
  identification, 374
  network designation, 377
  shortening, 384
  stretching, 384
Stockout cost; *see* Shortage cost
Storage cost of inventory, 347, 350
Subsidies, 539
Sunk costs in decision making, 252
Sunk costs do not include recoverable costs, 253
Supply of money and commodities, 474
Surprise value of information, 453
Systems studies, 535
Systems study in budgeting, 130

T

Target rate of return, investors', 316
Tax advisory services, 18
Taxes
  allocation between periods, 510
  base, 505
  carryforwards and carrybacks, 516
  on corporate income, 513
  deductions from revenue, 517
  and depreciation, 505
  and economic policy, 537
  effect and investment decisions, 324

Taxes—*Cont.*
  estate and gift, 512
  exemptions from, 505
  improvements, 504
  liability versus expense, 513
  of local governments, 503
  and nonprofit entities, 505
  property, 504
  and public policy, 538
  reform and accounting, 529, 538
  resemblance to subsidies, 539
  sales, 503
  on specific activities, 502
  types and purposes, 501
  value-added, 506
Technology effect on cost standards, 176
Terleckyj, Nestor E., 543
Time period effect on cost classification, 101
Time sharing, 175
Time value of money, 316
Transfer payments and taxes, 508

U–W

Uncertainty
  and decisions, 436, 450
  and environment, 8
  and information, 8
  and inventory management, 356, 360
  and ITRR, 318

Uncertainty—*Cont.*
  nature of, 454
  and planning, 280
Unit costs, 220
Valuation using accumulated costs, 97
Value-added tax, 506
Value of information, 447
Variable overhead rate, 198, 200
Variances
  from budget, 286
  definition, 160
  efficiency, 168
  fixed overhead spending, 201
  and learning effect, 178
  and managerial control, 165
  price, 167
  production efficiency, 201
  sales, 283
  service efficiency, 198
  significance in performance reports based on linear programming, 419
  significant action taken, 170
  significant, defined, 169
  and span of control, 161
  of step completion times distribution, 441
Welfare and taxes, 508
Welfare economics, 475
"What if" and budgets, 281
Wheat Committee, 542

This book has been set in 12 and 11 point Garamond, leaded 2 points. Part and chapter numbers are in 24 point Craw Modern, part titles are in 24 point Helvetica and chapter titles are in 18 point Helvetica. The size of the type page is 27 × 45 picas.